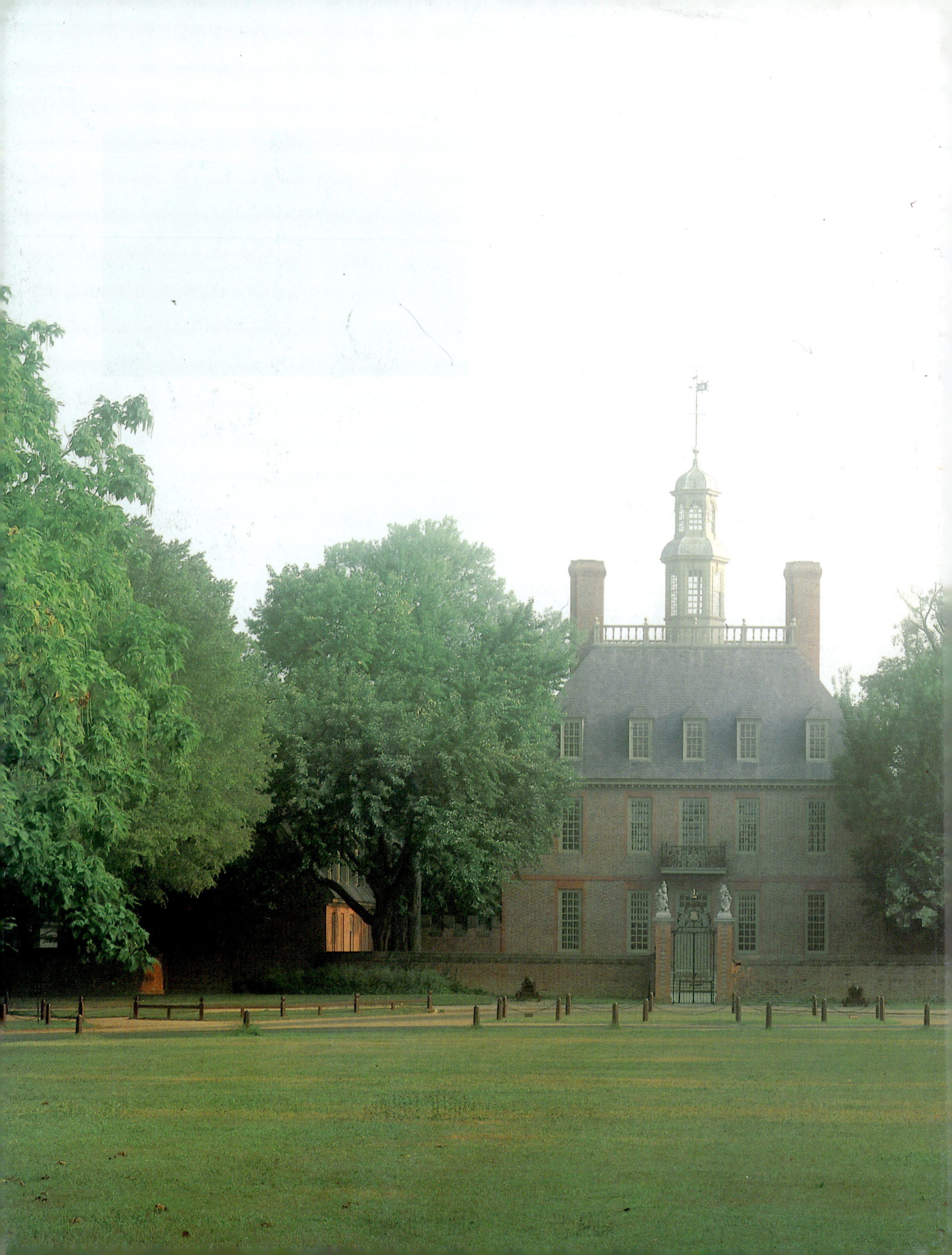

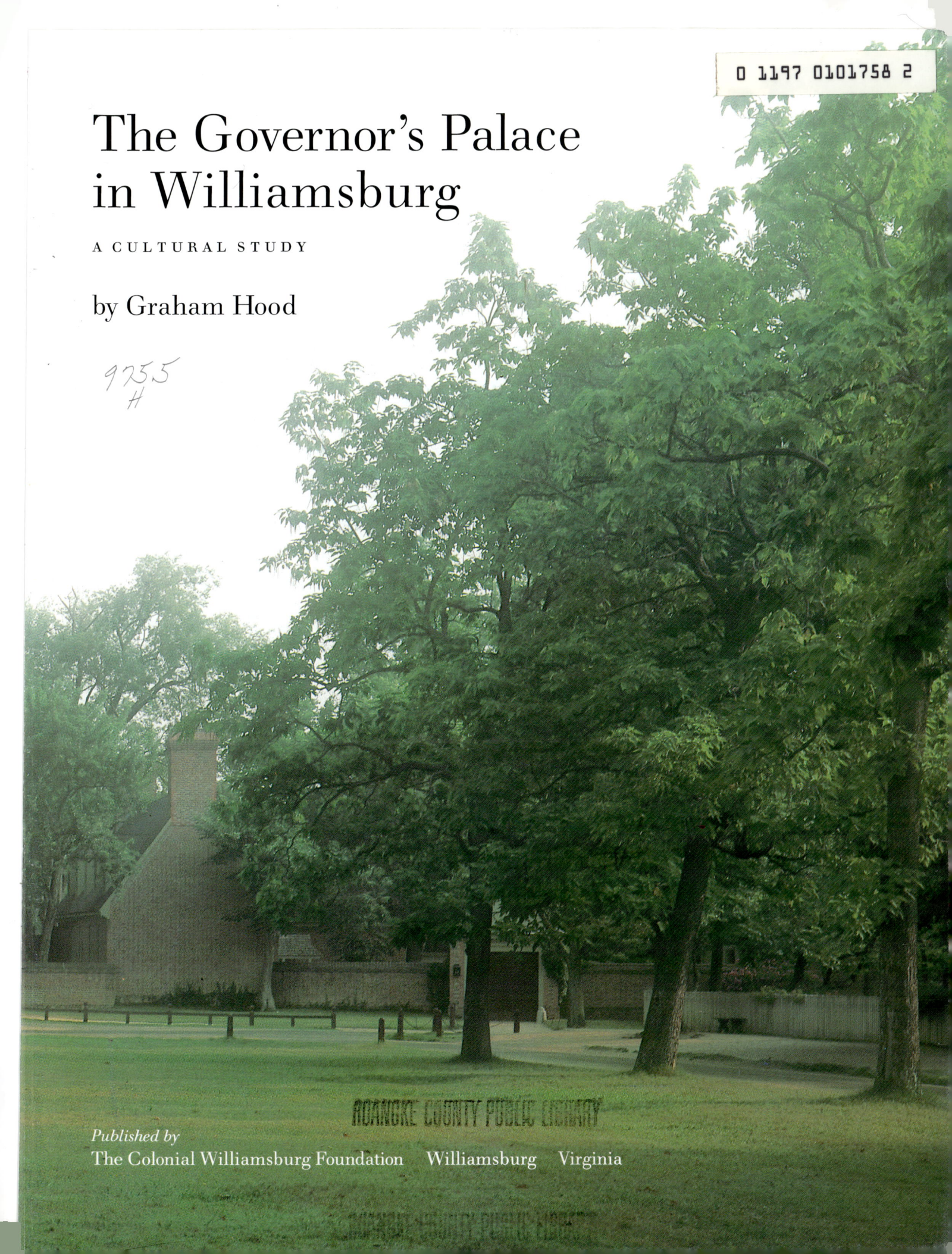

The Governor's Palace in Williamsburg

A CULTURAL STUDY

by Graham Hood

Published by
The Colonial Williamsburg Foundation   Williamsburg   Virginia

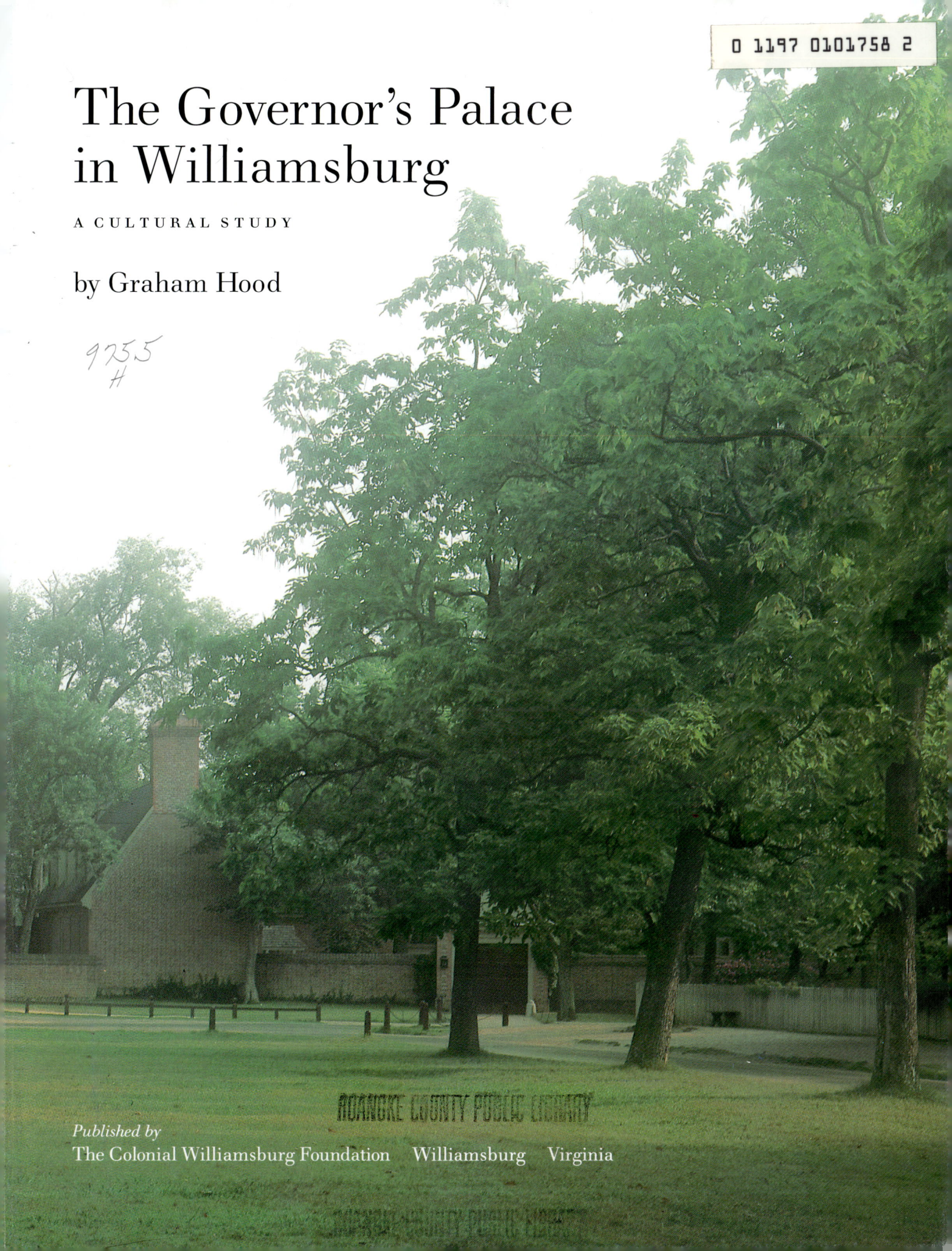

The Governor's Palace in Williamsburg

A CULTURAL STUDY

by Graham Hood

Published by
The Colonial Williamsburg Foundation   Williamsburg   Virginia

WILLIAMSBURG DECORATIVE ARTS SERIES
Graham Hood, *Editor*

Chelsea Porcelain at Williamsburg
  by John C. Austin

English and Oriental Carpets at Williamsburg
  by Mildred B. Lanier

English Silver at Williamsburg
  by John D. Davis

The Governor's Palace in Williamsburg: A Cultural Study
  by Graham Hood

New England Furniture at Williamsburg
  by Barry A. Greenlaw

*Rebellion and Reconciliation: Satirical Prints on
  the Revolution at Williamsburg*
  by Joan D. Dolmetsch

The Williamsburg Collection of Antique Furnishings

Wallace Gallery Decorative Arts Publications

Eighteenth-Century Clothing at Williamsburg
  by Linda Baumgarten

Worcester Porcelain in the Colonial Williamsburg Collection
  by Samuel M. Clarke

© 1991 by The Colonial Williamsburg Foundation

All rights reserved,
including the right to reproduce this book
or portions thereof in any form.

Library of Congress Cataloging-in-Publication Data

Hood, Graham, 1936–
   The Governor's Palace in Williamsburg:
a cultural study / by Graham Hood.
      p.   cm. — (Williamsburg decorative arts series)
   Includes bibliographical references and index.
   ISBN 0-87935-082-2
     1. Material culture—Virginia—Williamsburg.   2. House furnishings—
Virginia—Williamsburg.   3. Governor's Palace (Williamsburg, Va.)
4. Williamsburg (Va.)—Buildings, structures, etc.   I. Title.   II. Series.
F234.W7H66   1991
975.5′4252—dc20   91-15951
                                                              CIP

ISBN 0–87935–082–2

Distributed by
The University of North Carolina Press   Chapel Hill, North Carolina
Book design by Greer Allen
Printed in Hong Kong

FOR MY DAUGHTER
Sarah

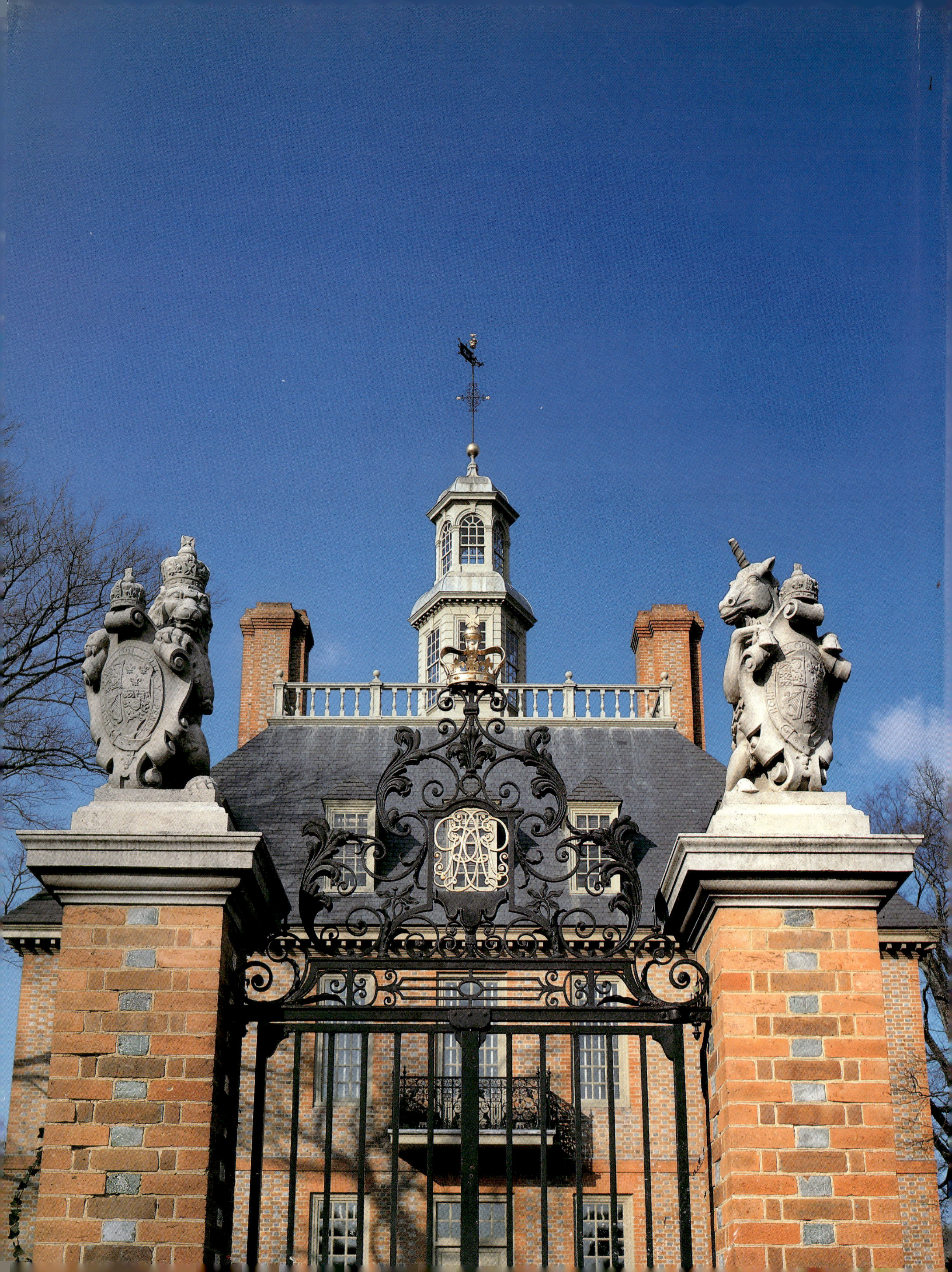

Contents

12 Prologue
26 *The Inventory*
38 *The Setting*

74 Ceremony
80 *The Hall: The Power of the Crown*
98 *The Middle Room Upstairs: The Presence of the Governor*

118 Public Life
122 *The Dining Room and Parlor: Apartments of Conversation*
168 *The Ballroom and Supper Room: Fashionable Gatherings*

196 Private Life
202 *The Bedchambers and Study: The Person of the Governor*
228 *The Family*

269 Epilogue

287 Appendix 1:   *Botetourt Inventory*
296 Appendix 2:   *Fauquier Inventory*
298 Appendix 3:   *Dunmore Schedule of Losses*
298 Appendix 4:   *1710 Furnishings Proposal*
299 Appendix 5:   *Eden Schedule of Losses*
303 Appendix 6:   *Tryon Schedule of Losses*
307 Appendix 7:   *Campbell Inventory*

314 Notes
332 Acknowledgments
335 Index

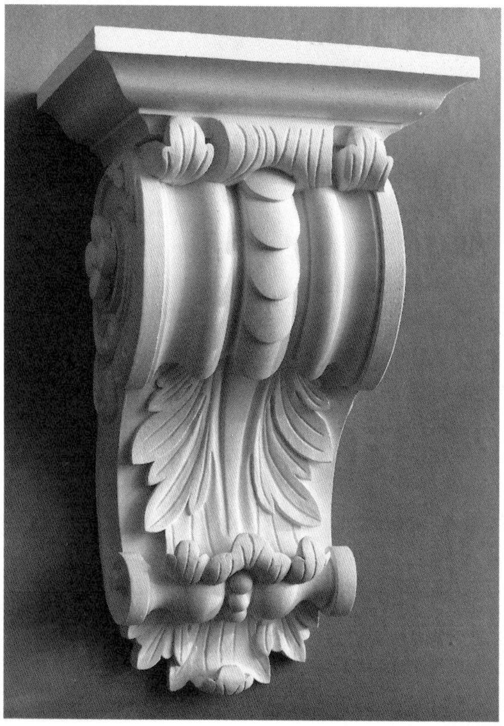
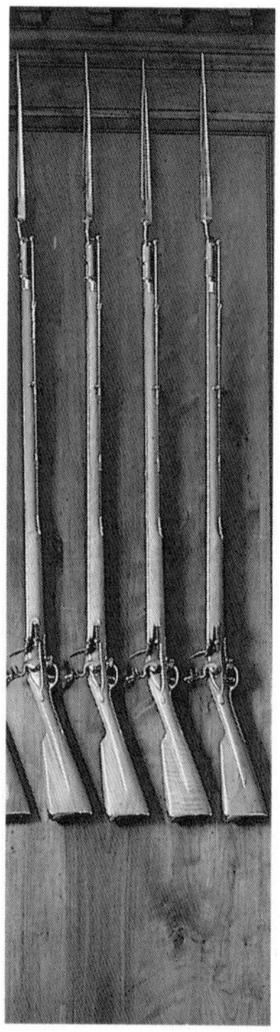
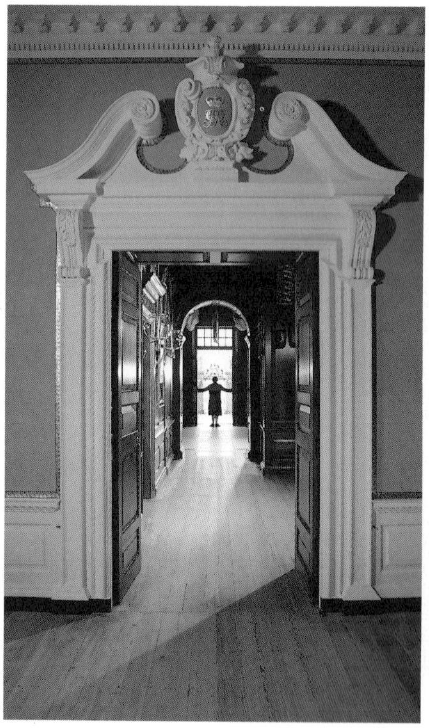
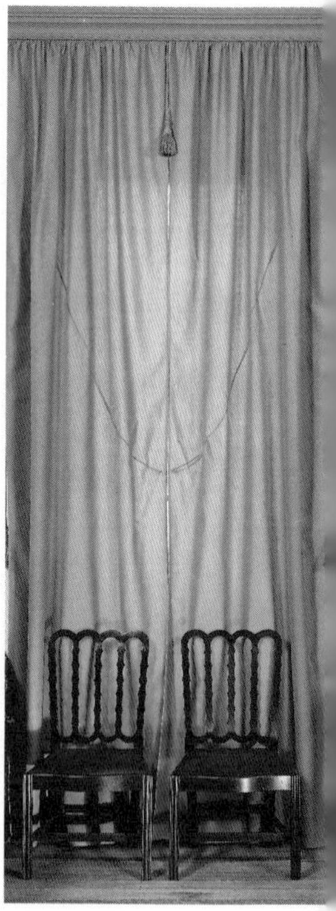

"When a house is said to be furnished, it conveys the idea of its being fitted up with every necessary, both useful and ornamental. In furnishing a good house for a person of rank, it requires some taste and judgment, that each apartment may have such pieces as is most agreeable to the appropriate use of the room.

There is certainly something of sentiment expressed in the manner of furnishing a house, as well as in personal dress and equipage.

The kitchen, the hall, the dining parlour, the anti-room, the drawing room, the library, the breakfast room, the music room, the gallery of paintings, the bed room and dressing apartments, ought to have their proper suits of furniture, and to be finished in a style, that will at once shew, to a competent judge, the place they are destined for."

—Thomas Sheraton, *Cabinet Dictionary*

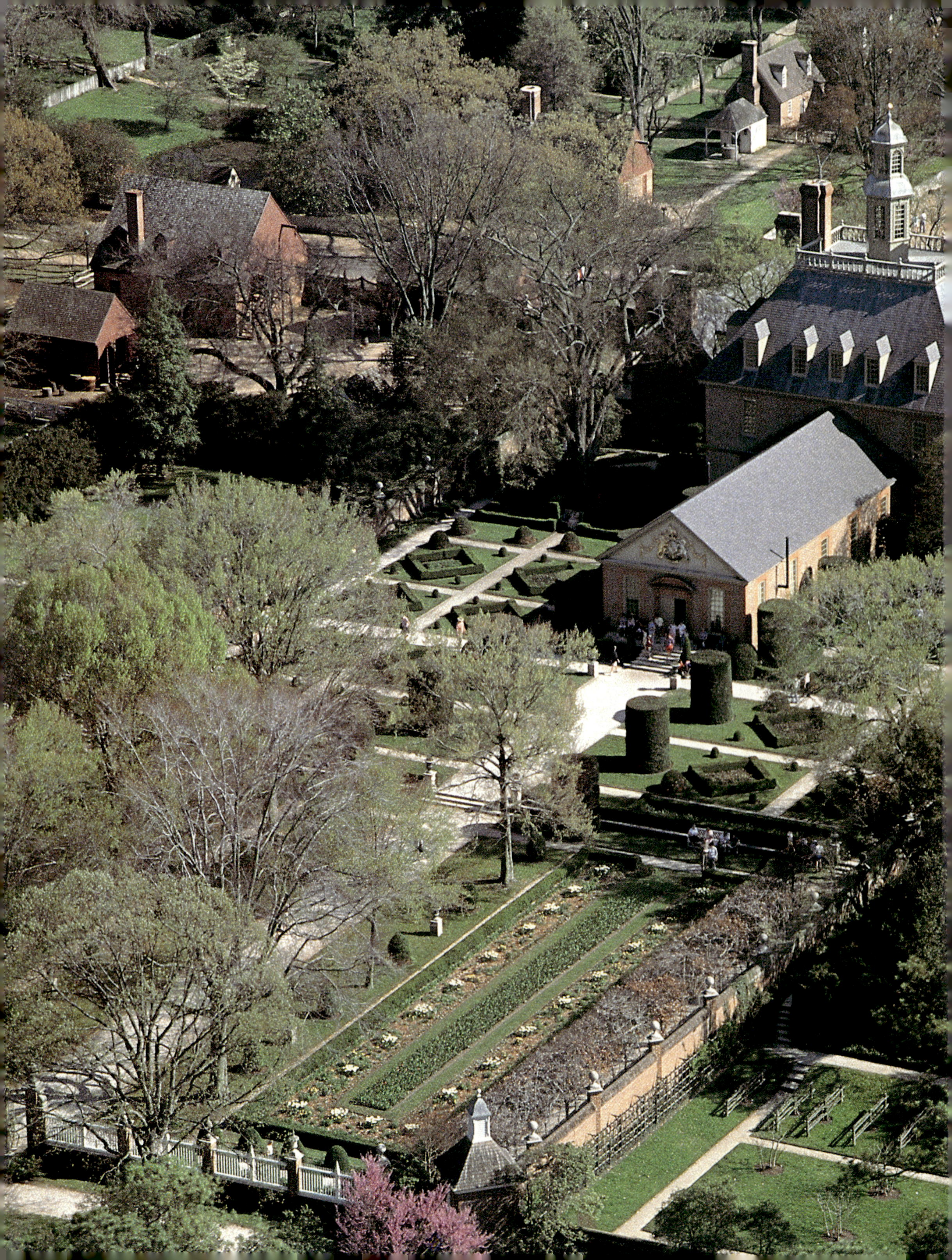

Prologue

Prologue

On Monday, October 15, 1770, a little after one o'clock in the morning, Norborne Berkeley, Baron de Botetourt, died at the Governor's Palace in Williamsburg, having been in residence for two years as "his Majesty's Lieutenant, Governor-General, and Commander-in-Chief of the Colony and Dominion of Virginia, and Vice-Admiral of the same." His death had seemed imminent for two or three days, so a search had been made of his private papers for a will covering his personal estate in Virginia. All that was found was a testament written in England four years previously. The General Court of the colony was currently in session in Williamsburg and later that same day appointed as trustees of the late governor's Virginia estate a most distinguished group of men—William Nelson, president of his Majesty's Council; John Randolph, attorney general of the colony; Robert Carter Nicholas, treasurer of the colony; John Blair, Jr., clerk of the Council; and George Wythe, clerk of the House of Burgesses. Theirs was the responsibility to carry out the known wishes of the testator and the principal legatee and the authority to settle Lord Botetourt's outstanding debts in the colony.[1]

Botetourt had been the first governor to reside in Williamsburg in more than sixty years, in contrast to his six predecessors who had held the lesser title of lieutenant governor. Because of his rank and the great respect that Virginians had developed for him, and because his principal legatee was in England and a duke, no less, the trustees turned to their task with a certain punctiliousness. Attorney General Randolph wrote immediately to the duke of Beaufort, Botetourt's nephew, to inform him of the "melancholly" event. He described the discovery of the English will and the appointment by "our Supreme Court" of trustees to "collect and secure [the] property" of the late governor, his "most esteem'd Friend." He broached the question of whether the duke would allow Botetourt's successor in the governor's post to "take the Estate as it stands," noting that the new official would "find every thing very handsome and fit for his Reception." Randolph pointed out some of the more notable items in

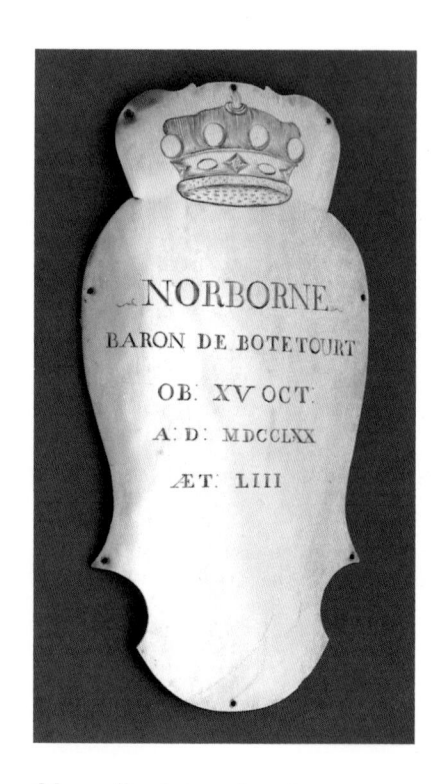

Silver coffin plate made and engraved between October 15 and 19, 1770, by William Waddill, goldsmith and engraver who was located on the Duke of Gloucester Street in Williamsburg. H: 10"; W: 5³⁄₈". Courtesy, College Archives, Swem Library, College of William and Mary.

Botetourt's estate, the elegant carriages, several "remarkable handsome" horses, a good stock of claret and Madeira, and some Negroes trained as gardeners. He also listed the large quantity of stationery, a "small tho a very useful Collection of Books, a good Deal of Furniture proper for the office of a Governor," a great amount of linen—"in short every thing proper for the Residence of a Governor."[2]

Great planter and councillor Robert Carter, Botetourt's neighbor, had written to the duke several days earlier warning him of the onset of the illness of his "noble, most worthy, and near Neighbor, who has effectually obtained the Love and affection of every Person residing in his Government." Carter then wrote to the duke on the morning of Botetourt's death, apprising him of the sad event and of the search for a will made by an appointed committee of the General Court headed by the "Treasurer of this Province."[3]

Continuity of government was secured on October 15 by Nelson's election by the Council to the position of acting governor, the proclamation of which was issued the same day. The Council and the gentlemen of the General Court went "into deep mourning" for "the great and good Lord Botetourt," joined evidently by "most of the Principal Gentlemen in the colony . . . in such general esteem was his Lordship and so universally lamented."[4] The trustees then turned to the matter of the funeral. The late governor's rank and noble title clearly warranted a formal ceremony; indeed, it called for the provincial equivalent of a state funeral. "Managers" were appointed to "conduct" it. They sent invitations, heavily outlined in black, to gentlemen and ladies of the community the following day.

Williamsburg, October 16, 1770

The Gentlemen appointed to conduct the Funeral of his Excellency Lord BOTETOURT, present their Compliments to all Gentlemen and Ladies, and beg the Favour of their Attendance at the Palace at Two o'clock on Friday next.

The procession to begin precisely at Three, and move to the Church, where the usual Service will be performed; after which the Corps will be conducted to the College Chapel, and there interred.[5]

In the meantime, the trustees moved to address the legal requirements of the estate, including an inventory of his lordship's personal effects and the payment of outstanding debts. Nicholas appears to have been given the primary responsibility for this task. He in turn retained Peter Pelham, the governor's clerk, to assist in compiling the inventory, and then advised William Marshman, Botetourt's butler and chief household officer at the Palace in Williamsburg, and his under butler, Thomas Fuller, to stay on to protect the contents of the Palace, to assist with the inventory, and to contribute their intimate knowledge of the household operations to the complex matter of debt

The Right Hon.ble NORBORNE BERKELEY, BARON de BOTTETOURT, late Governor of Virginia.

Done from a Medallion of the same size in the Possession of John Norton Esq.

To the General Assembly of Virginia, this Plate is most humbly Inscrib'd by their Obliged humble Servant

H. Ashby.

LONDON, Publish'd as the Act directs 21.st March 1774, by H. Ashby Russel Court Covent Garden.

settlement. Marshman was by repute a "most valuable and faithful Servant" who had shown unusually "tender care, . . . vigilance, and constant assiduity" during Botetourt's last illness. Fuller was likewise judged to be a reliable assistant. The two servants' tasks proved to be sufficiently onerous and complicated that they were detained for a year before they were able to leave their posts and return to England.[6]

News of the governor's death traveled quickly throughout the tidewater region. At Sabine Hall in the northern neck of Virginia, great planter and former burgess Landon Carter noted it in his diary for Monday 15 but had the governor dying prematurely: "Yesterday came a letter endorsed from Colo. Tayloe with the death of Ld. Bottetourt, our Governour, who left us the 13th in the morning. A melancholly piece of News." Even in the normally querulous confidence of his diary, Carter expressed strong praise for the man:

A fine Gentleman is dead and truely Noble in his Public character. He, as anecdote says, was pitcht upon to be the Agent of a dirty tyrannic Ministry; but his virtues resisted such an employment and he became the instrument of a dawning happiness; and had he lived we should have been so: for through his active and exemplary virtue, order everywhere revived out of that confusion that our own dissipative indolence had thrown us into.[7]

By Wednesday, October 17, Scottish merchant William Aitchison of Norfolk had written to his fellow countryman, Charles Steuart, with genuine sadness and foreboding:

[Botetourt] is greatly and justly lamented indeed this Country could not have suffered a severer loss and where will his Majestie find one so well qualified in every Respect to succeed him for my part I never expect to see his equal here.[8]

On the same day, Robert Beverley, from his vast plantation on the Rappahannock River, sent the news to his London agent, Samuel Athawes, commenting on the loss of the governor whose "Conduct during his Residence amongst us has with great Propriety endear'd him to all ranks of People."[9] And from the Palace, a "very Afflicted" William Marshman wrote to a steward of the duke of Beaufort of his "utmost Grief and consternation" at the loss of his "Dear kind Master." He continued in a more intimate and touching vein to his brother in a later letter:

My Loss is very great, and I deeply Lament it; for, in Lord Botetourt, I always experienced more of the Friend and Father, than of the Master: I believe no Servant had ever heaped upon him such continual proofs of kindness from any Master, as I receiv'd from that Generous and Good Man . . . I never knew him guilty of a Vice, but had daily and hourly proofs of his Humanity and Benevolence of all Mankind.[10]

Norborne Berkeley, baron de Botetourt, stipple engraving in sepia red. Engraved in London in 1773 by H. Ashby from the profile wax portrait taken from life by Isaac Gossett in the mid-1760s. H: 7"; W: 4¾". CWF 1954-130.

PROLOGUE 15

These private expressions of grief from "all Ranks of People"—great planters, merchant, and servant—are inevitably more genuine than the formal obsequy that appeared in the *Virginia Gazette* on Thursday, October 18, extolling the "many great Virtues and amiable Qualities" of this "best of Governors, and . . . best of Men."[11] As *private* sentiments, they clearly evoke Botetourt's personal warmth and the gentility of which his noble title was a reflection—"the grace of polished life," as Edmund Randolph later so felicitously phrased it. They reveal the great respect that Botetourt had inspired by his careful execution of public duties and leave no doubt that the colonists genuinely cared for and admired him. It was his unusual combination of admirable qualities and high rank that prompted colonial officials to proceed to organize the most elaborate funeral ever recorded in Williamsburg. Though Botetourt had gently expressed his preference for an informal funeral in his will of 1766—"I desire that I may be . . . carried to my Grave in the most private manner by my own Servants"—William Nelson later explained to the duke that "the Managers, and we believe the whole Country, thought themselves call'd upon by every Sentiment of Gratitude and Affection to pay the most respectful Regard to his Lordship's memory."[12]

Planning the orchestration of such an ambitious ceremony and gathering the necessary materials probably started the day Botetourt died. Joseph Kidd, local upholsterer and former servant in Botetourt's "family," assisted the "Managers." He accumulated more than seven hundred yards of black cloth and crepe to make coverings for the governor's seat, pulpit, altar, communion table, and reading desk at Bruton Parish Church. He bought carpets, suits of mourning for the governor's servants, streamers for the horses pulling the hearse and accompanying the procession, and tied white hatbands and scarves for the official participants in the cortege. Three coffins were assembled, an "inside" one, probably of pine, lined with "fully ornamented" Persian [silk]; a lead one; and an outer one of black walnut covered with crimson velvet, then neatly ornamented "in the best manner," studded in a decorative fashion with white nails. The outer coffin was furnished with escutcheons, with silver handles and a silver plate engraved with the deceased's name, age, and date of death. Joshua Kendall, a Williamsburg carpenter who had also been a member of Botetourt's "family," supplied two of the coffins, certain other materials, cloaks, and black staffs, while local silversmith William Waddill provided handles and trimming for the exterior coffin; these were preferred to the japanned set sent by another undertaker, cabinetmaker Benjamin Bucktrout. A pall to be carried over the coffin was lined with Persian (more than two hundred and twenty yards of this material were purchased) and edged with lustring. The hearse was trimmed with black cloth and decorated with escutcheons coated with silver leaf. Escutcheons were placed in the church and in the

"An English funeral" drawn and engraved by T. V. Schley in *1735*. H: *5¾"*; W: *16"*. Private collection.

CONVOI Funebre des ANGLOIS.

college chapel. Staffs for mutes accompanying the hearse were blackened, while cloaks, velvet capes, scarves, hats, gloves, handkerchiefs, shoes, buckles, buttons, and stockings were purchased for members of the household and the principal mourners. Altogether three hundred and fifty yards of ribbon were acquired. A huge number of "Funeral cakes" and other food was prepared in the Palace kitchen and wine decanted for the company, which was expected to be "very numerous." Men were employed to lay out the corpse, shave it, and place it inside a white lustring shroud on the mattress and pillows in the inner coffin. Others were hired to write to "the company" and assist the mayor and city council, while others were engaged to act as bearers. Kendall took up the floor of the college chapel and prepared the vault—a highly traditional and honorific resting place for the governor, particularly appropriate in view of his affection for the institution and his regular attendance at the chapel.[13]

The cost of supplies and labor for the funeral was £550, in excess of one-quarter of the governor's annual salary—a sum that would have paid the wages of the entire household staff for several years. Such elaborate preparations inevitably led to a complex, intricately sequenced ceremony, fully commensurate with the colonial officials' esteem of the office and person of the governor and of their own standing relative to him. It is undoubtedly the most completely documented instance of the formal panoply of colonial Virginia society, in serried ranks from social-political, religious, and educational leaders down to servants and perhaps even slaves.[14]

The description of the event, heavily bordered with black, appeared in the supplement to Purdie and Dixon's *Virginia Gazette* of October 18, 1770.

Friday, October 19

This being the day appointed for interring the remains of our late beloved Governour, at one o'clock the Church, College, and Capitol bells, began tolling; and the company repaired to the Palace, according to invitation, precisely at two. At three, the corpse being placed on the hearse, the procession began to move, in the following order, to the church, both sides of Palace street being lined with the city militia, and those of York and James city counties.

The HEARSE
Preceded by two mutes, and three on each side the hearse,
Outward of whom walked the pall bearers,
Composed of six of his Majesty's Council,
And the Hon. the Speaker, and Richard Bland, Esq;
of the House of Burgesses.
His Excellency's servants, in deep mourning.
The Gentlemen of the Clergy, and
Professors of the College.
Clerk of the church, and Organist.
Immediately followed the hearse the Chief Mourners
Gentlemen of the Faculty.
Mayor, Recorder, Aldermen, and
Common Council, of the city,
With the mace born before them.
Gentlemen of the Law, and Clerk of the General Court
Ushers, Students, and Scholars, of
William and Mary college,
All having white hatbands and gloves.
And then the company, which was very numerous,
Two and two.

At the western gate the corpse was removed from the hearse, and, carried by eight bearers, the Gentlemen appointed supporting the pall, placed in the centre of the church, on a carpet of black. The altar, pulpit, and his Excellency's seat, were likewise hung with black. Then the service began; and an anthem, accompanied by the organ, was sung, conducted Mr. Woolls. The Rev. and Hon. the Commissary then delivered a discourse, from Psalm xlii. part of the 7th verse, *Put thy trust in God*; which, joined to the deep affliction felt by the whole audience for the loss of such an excellent man, and so good a Governour, drew tears from many. Sermon being ended, the corpse was again placed on the hearse, and the company moved in the same order to the College, entering at the front gate, and so proceeding through the College to the chapel, where the corpse was deposited in a vault, the militia firing three vollies at the interrment. The coffin was of lead, with a cover of crimson velvet, adorned with silver handles, and a large silver plate, on which was this inscription:

NORBORNE Baron de BOTETOURT.
Ob. xv Oct. MDCCLXX.
AEtat. LIII.

Even the manner in which the notice of the funeral was typeset in the *Virginia Gazette* indicates the formal hierarchy of the ceremony. It unmistakably conveys the colonists' seriousness of purpose—the complex deference that they felt they owed this representative of the sovereign, this nobleman of polish and virtue. The tiered ranks of Virginia society in attendance personified the hierarchy. Mutes in the vanguard exhorted, by their example, respectful silence. Then came the councillors, who were nearest the office and person of the governor and had clear precedence over the rest of the assembled company and who held the protective pall over the body. Equal in rank with them were the Speaker of the lower house of the Virginia Assembly and the senior burgess, personifying the larger body of the province of which the governor had been both leader and member. Immediately following—the smaller social unit succeeding the larger—came the governor's servants as representatives of the body of the household or "family" over which he had also presided. Professors and clerics symbolized the passage of the body, to be received into the earth at the college, and the passage of the soul through the channels of faith, of which the clergy were the officers. Professors also embodied the respected realm of higher learning. The mayor and city fathers represented the city within which the action took place. Gentlemen of the law and representatives of the General Court personified the order holding the fabric of provincial society together. The presence of students and scholars of the college acknowledged the special affection that Botetourt had felt for the institution. Finally, the "very numerous" company drawn from the capital city and its surrounding area were contained within the boundaries secured by the militia.[15]

The funeral was very elaborate, but no more than was called for in the minds of the trustees and other gentry involved in the decision. It was incumbent on them to recognize and pay deference to official rank and noble title; they were also obliged, in deciding on the form that their "respectful Regard" should take, to keep in mind the colony's own honor and self-esteem. The "Managers" clearly believed that the ceremony should formally acknowledge the relationship that had existed between governor and governed and sensed that the community endorsed their decision. Since Botetourt's was a life in which the "whole Colony" had "considered herself so exceedingly interested," it was fit and proper that the final ceremony should be an appropriate cultural expression of the interaction that had taken place between the governor and all those "residing in his Government." The funeral was thus a metaphor for the governor's life, and the gentry's choice of its complex form a key to their perception of how that life had affected and interacted with their own. That the event was so precisely articulated, without the benefit of any formal "Rules of Precedency," and made known to a wider public in that form reinforces this interpretation.[16]

As the funeral was a ceremonial expression of the kind of life the governor lived in Williamsburg, so the inventory is a material expression—much more copious in detail if less compelling in the narration—of the same life. The funeral therefore conveys the tone and quality of the "Residence amongst us" that the inventory, with its extraordinary detail and its convincing association with certain functions of living in dedicated spaces, expands upon greatly.

The funeral was very expensive. William Nelson adopted a highly deferential tone with the duke on this subject lest he object to the cost. But Nelson also sought reassurance that the duke and his circle of friends in England would regard the ceremony as worthy of the departed nobleman and his much more noble heir: "It will afford . . . no small satisfaction, if the manner, in which it was conducted, shall meet with the approbation of your Grace." The duke's response was condescending and generous—"so very handsome a funeral . . . so much Order and Decency." If Nelson was worried that the funeral might have had a somewhat provincial quality to it in the minds of English aristocrats, his fears were needless. In virtually every respect it was similar to a well-documented, elegant English ceremony of 1772 for a member of the conspicuously rich and fashionable Heathcote family of Rutland, directed by one of the leading London upholsterers and cabinetmakers, Thomas Chippendale.[17]

Five days after Botetourt's funeral "an exact and perfect Inventory" began to be taken of all his possessions. In the following six days the sixty-one living and working spaces in the residence that contained more than sixteen thousand objects were inspected and tallied. Indeed, Nelson enclosed a copy of the inventory in his letter to the duke of October 30, pointing out that "many pieces of the Furniture are in the best Taste," that most of the "Liquors are good in kind," that the "Slaves are reckon'd orderly and valuable" (adding a brief explanation of why Botetourt had found it necessary to purchase slaves at all), and that the considerable expense of maintaining the horses had been allayed by arranging their sale to a local gentleman. Nelson asked for decisions from the duke on the disposition of the effects and the settling of the estate, begging him "to be as particular and explicit as possible in every respect, that we may be able with the greater certainty and precision to answer your Grace's expectations and wishes."[18]

The duke responded to Nelson on the day following his receipt of the acting governor's letter, conveying fulsome thanks and compliments to the Council, the trustees, and all who had been involved in the funeral and in the legal processes. He proceeded to present to the colony his late uncle's portraits of the king and queen, then hanging in the Palace ballroom, and the state coach (so conspicuous a feature of Botetourt's courtliness). He offered to erect a monument to his uncle in the college chapel. Of the effects, he requested the return of the private and public papers, personal accessories and jewelry, three

First page of the working copy of the inventory of the effects of Lord Botetourt, taken at the Governor's Palace in Williamsburg between October 24 and October 30, 1770. Folio size. This copy of the inventory survived with the state papers in the Virginia State Archives, Richmond. A fair copy, neatly transcribed by Botetourt's clerk, Peter Pelham, was sent to the fifth duke of Beaufort and has survived at Badminton House, Gloucestershire.

An Inventory of the Personal Estate of his Excellency
Lord Botetourt ~~as left at his death~~ began to be taken the 24th of Octor 1770.

His Landskip Watch & walking
cane (Mr Attorney)
Cash found in the house — £57.2.1½

In the front parlour
2 Leather Smoking chairs
2 Card Tables, mahogany
1 Walnut Writing Table
1 Couch Mahogany frame
  covered with checks
1 small looking Glass
Jefferson's Map of Virga
Bowen's & Mitchell's Map of
  N. America
1 pr Tongs, shovel, poker and Fender
1 hearth Broom
11 Chelsea china figures, 2 Venitian blinds

In the Closet
1 old fireas'd Beauvreau
1 Mahogy Card Table
1 large black Ink stand
1 small Japan'd do
1 Queenswa Supper Stand
1 Venitian blind
1 Glass Lanthorn
6 Med. Vases

In the Hall & Passage below
2 Mahog'd Damask Elbow chairs covered
  with checks
8 Chairs of the same
10 large globe lamps

Dining Room
2 leather smokg chairs
12 mahy chairs hair bottoms
1 large mahg dining table
1 smaller do
~~1 marble sideboard table~~
1 walnut writg table
1 mahogy plate warmer & 12 bottle stands
1 mahogy wine cooler
1 mahogy library table containg papers
  publick & private
1 mahogy Desk, containg sundry papers
  private & public, one embroid'd pocket book
  a miniature drawing, 1 diam. mourng ring &
  a pair of gold sleve buttons, pruning knife & a
  steel pencil.
1 white wax taper & stand.

Dining Room
1 black Ink stand
13 wax portraits
1 Shovel, pair Tongs, poker & Fender & hearth
  broom
1 mahy fire Screen
11 Chelsea china figures
Henry's Map of Virga
1 Oval lookg Glass
3 Venitian blinds
1 East India fire lock
1 small readg desk, 1 large oyl Cloth at Mr Kidd's

In the Bowfat
2 large enam. china bowls
2 lessr blue & white do
2 pr English china candlesticks
56 pieces ornamental china
12 large cut water Glasses
12 Small do
4 large cut glass tumblers
5 small do
28 cut wine glasses
4 Strong beer glasses
1 Hock glass

1 full Box raisins
Box & 9 pieces
of English Sweet
meats — part of
a Box of Bar-
bados Sweet
meats — part
of a Box rock
Sugar — part
of a candie
Lemon Peel
part of a Box
of English
Sweet meat
4 dozn
Oranges

Ball Room
3 large mahogy dining tables
1 large round walnut do
12 mahogy chairs hair bottoms
1 large Dutch stove
3 glass lustres with 6 branches each
6 gauze covers
2 large printings of the King & Queen gauze covers
2 Venitian blinds

Supper Room
1 large Dutch stove

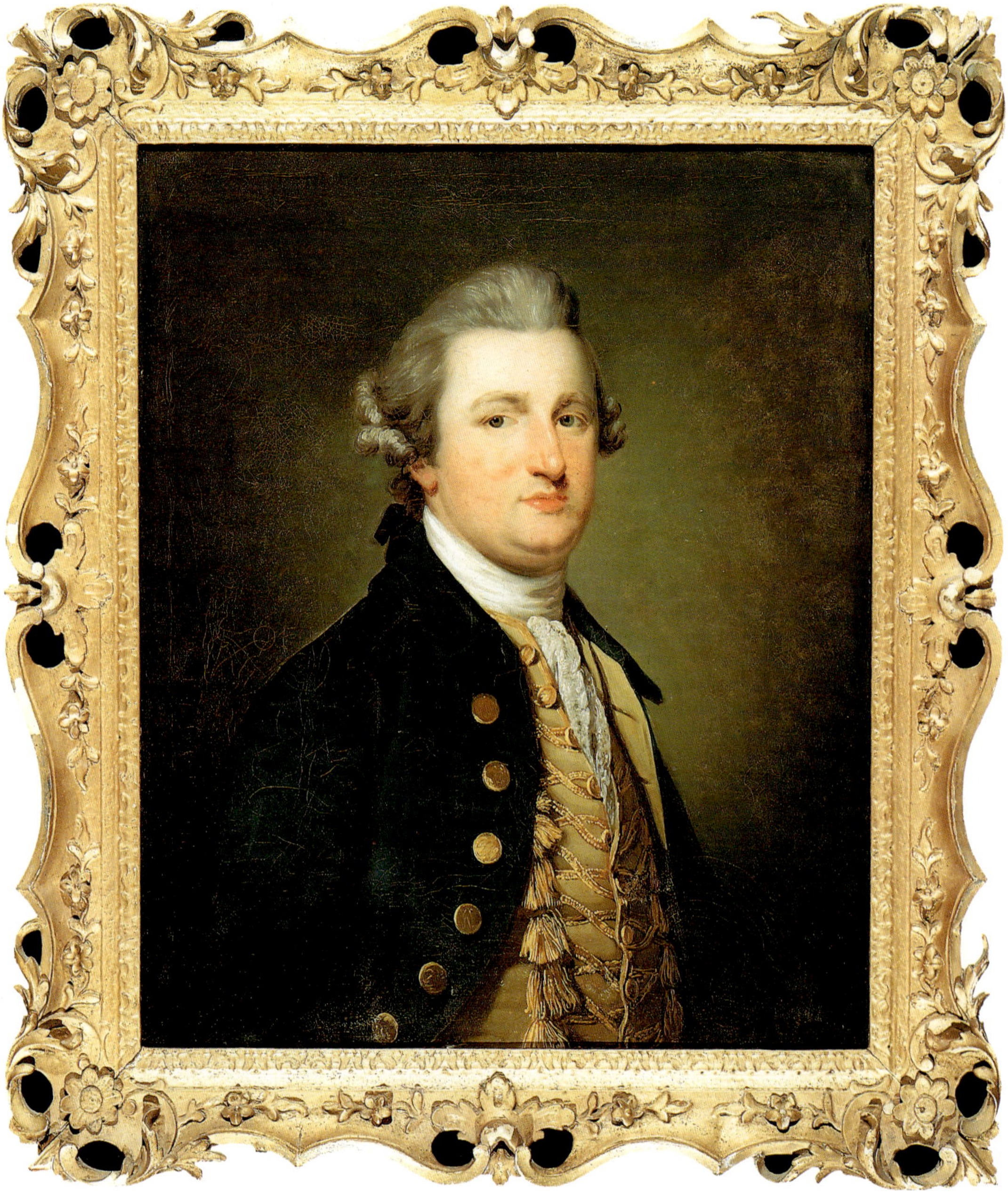

Henry Somerset, duke of Beaufort, painted 1769–1770 by Francis Cotes, probably in London. This portrait shows the twenty-five-year-old son of his sister as Botetourt would have remembered him, his only nephew and longtime ward. H: 30″; W: 25″. CWF 1990-74.

pipes of Madeira, and all books, maps, plate, china, and linen. As for the remainder, "I desire [it] may be disposed of to the best advantage either by public or private sale."[19]

When the succeeding governor, John Murray, fourth earl of Dunmore, wrote from New York declining to purchase Botetourt's estate, the trustees planned a public auction, which was held over several days in mid-May 1771. Purchased "for the Country" and presumably left at the Palace were more than three hundred pounds worth of goods. The rest of Botetourt's possessions were sold to a cross section of colonists—gentry, merchants, tradesmen. Only the purchasers and the amounts spent were specified in the surviving accounts, not the items themselves (except for the horses). Because of the uncertain economic climate, the trustees decided to allow notes of payment, collectable over several months. It was therefore not until May 5, 1772, that the General Court was able to examine the trustees' accounts. It declared itself satisfied and promptly remitted the balance of the cash from the estate to the duke of Beaufort.[20]

The remarkable documentation concerning this chain of events—the death of Lord Botetourt, the personal assessments and recollections of the governor, the elaborate funeral ceremony, and the meticulous identification of his material possessions—provides an unusual opportunity to examine precisely what was proper and fit for a governor living and working in the colonial Palace, to discern exactly what he did need to perform his duties so acceptably and to live such an agreeably polished life. Since he was a thoughtful and businesslike man, we can presume that he had acquired virtually all of his possessions for specific reasons and purposes. What those purposes were and how they clustered and cohered to form such a compellingly successful and attractive whole to his contemporaries is the subject of this book. Successful and attractive Botetourt had been, at least to the majority of colonists who spoke out on the subject. If they owed the governor such a carefully elaborated parting ceremony, what cultural contributions had he made to them? And what, if anything, had he received from them in return?

The complex codes of eighteenth-century behavior—the condescension of superiors consciously accommodating themselves to those of lesser authority, rank, and wealth; the deference of subordinates yielding to the real or implicit power or experience of those in authority; the subtle but clear distinctions of social rank or hierarchy; the formal gestures and responses; the genuine feelings—all of which are so apparent in the circumstances surrounding the Botetourt funeral and in the event itself, set the tone for this book and for the ensuing analysis of cultural patterns, statements, and exchanges at the Palace that become evident as we probe the Botetourt inventory for its inherent layers of meaning.[21] Though the inventory is subdivided into the

FIRST FLOOR

SECOND FLOOR

Floor plans of the first and second floors of the Governor's Palace in Williamsburg, as reconstructed in 1931–1933. They were derived in 1929–1930 from archaeological evidence, the Jefferson sketch of the first floor dating from the early 1770s, the Botetourt inventory list of rooms, and the architectural evidence provided by the Bodleian Plate. Drawing by James F. Waite, 1991.

sixty-one living and working spaces that the residence comprised, the possessions enumerated in it were all intertwined in one life. Thus it is with subject divisions in this book—distinctions are made but they are in a sense artificial: ceremony and hierarchy, public, social, and private life, state room and servant's chamber, and the distinctive patterns of living that they represent were still all part of one life in one residence.

Having set the tone in the prologue, the time, the place, and the method are established in the remaining two chapters of section one. The chapter on the inventory describes in greater detail the articulation of that extensive document and how I have tried to interpret it in order to understand further the patterns of Botetourt's life and culture that made him appear to be "the instrument of a dawning happiness" in the colony. The chapter on the setting explains the Palace, its articulation of spaces, its functions, and its history—more precisely, the cultural history of its occupants—prior to Botetourt's residence in it.

As the most ceremonial spaces in the building (though by no means the only ones), the hall and middle room upstairs have been grouped into the second section. The dining room/parlor and ballroom/supper room combinations were also scenes for ceremonies, but even more they were the setting for the governor as public official and leader of Williamsburg society. This becomes section three. The bedchamber and office "apartment" help to reveal the private side of the governor, as much as any high public official in the eighteenth century had a private life. Botetourt's fully documented "family" of servants provided the support he needed in order to run such a complex and busy establishment. This constitutes section four. Finally, the Epilogue details the cultural effect on the colony of Botetourt's death and the failure of his successor to maintain the cultural hegemony and heritage that had seemed so secure during his brief tenure in office.

PROLOGUE 25

The Inventory

The "Inventory of the Personal Estate of his Excellency Lord Botetourt began to be taken the 24th of October 1770." Three men were mainly responsible for the massive task of inspecting and inventorying the sixty-one spaces in which more than twenty persons lived and worked—Robert Carter Nicholas, treasurer of the colony; Peter Pelham, the governor's clerk; and William Marshman, chief household officer to the unmarried nobleman. Presumably other members of the "family," notably Silas Blandford, the "land steward," and under butler Thomas Fuller, contributed significantly to the undertaking. Though Marshman was thoroughly familiar with every aspect of the operations of the residence, including the kitchen, stables, and park, and probably played the key role in the process, Nicholas was the trustee responsible. His hand is evident—adding, correcting, clarifying—in many sections of the twelve folio pages that constitute the working copy of the inventory. Nicholas also compiled a much shorter list, probably concurrently, of "Standing Furniture" at the Palace: items purchased for the residence by the colony, bequeathed by former governors, or acquired from their estates for the use of succeeding officials in the building (Appendix 1).[1]

The Governor's Palace was divided into the three traditional functional areas: house, stables, and kitchen. In the center, connected with the flanking areas only by a wall or perhaps a covered way, stood the main house, comprising the state rooms and the apartment(s) of the governor (and his immediate family, if they had accompanied him from England).[2] Forward of the main house on the east were the stables, coach house, and associated buildings, while the kitchen complex stood correspondingly on the west. The men taking the inventory began in the main house, starting in the southeast corner with the front parlor and its closet. From there they proceeded to the hall and then the passage that led to the dining room. Moving to the newer part of the house and still proceeding toward the rear, they then inventoried the ballroom and supper room. Returning to the front of the building, they concentrated on the service rooms on the west side of the house: the powder room, the "Little Middle Room" with its capacious closet, and the pantry and adjoining closet.[3]

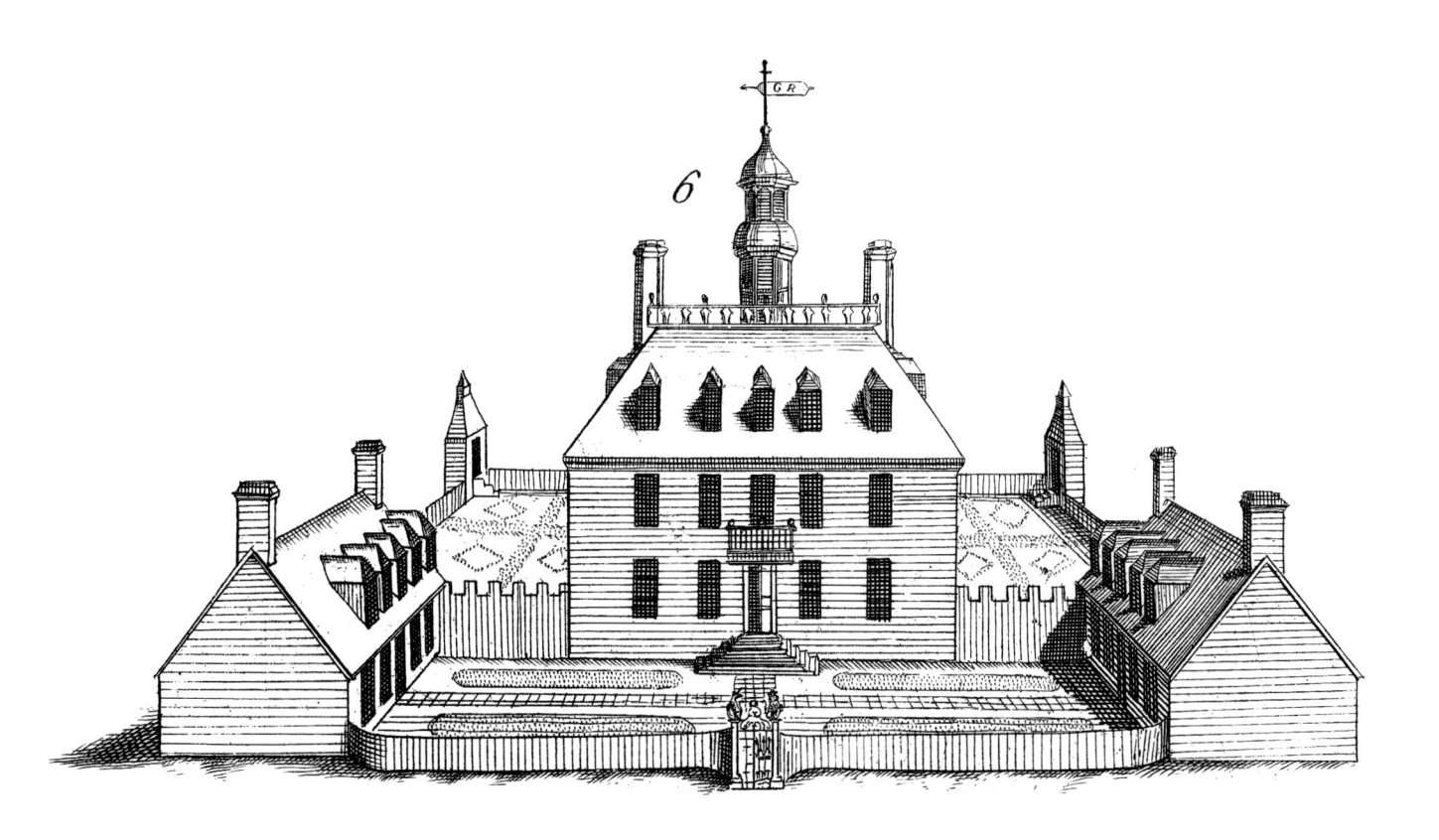

Moving to the second floor, the men inventoried the passage at the head of the main stairs, the library on the west side, a closet (probably above the ballroom), and the large bedchamber "over the Dining Room" on the east side of the passage. Proceeding in a clockwise direction, they tallied the contents of the adjoining closet and the chamber over the front parlor, the "Middle Room," "His Lordship's Bed Chamber" in the southwest corner, the adjoining closet, and the library. The books in the library and all the clothing in the bedchambers were listed separately from the remainder of the "effects."

From that point the myriad contents of the four storerooms were itemized. These rooms stood either on the second floor, between the ceiling and roof of the ballroom and supper room wing, or on the third, garret floor of the main block of the house. Several servants' living spaces also on the garret floor were then inventoried. Moving perhaps via the servants' staircase, the men then inventoried the cellars, comprising nine distinct and probably lockable spaces plus a passage. That completed the main house.

Of the "Out-Houses," the men dealt with the stable and coach house first, perhaps because their contents were of such high value, then the livestock, grain, Negroes, poultry, and the garden and park implements. The

The elevation of the Governor's Palace from the engraved copperplate discovered in the Bodleian Library, Oxford, in 1929 and subsequently known as the "Bodleian Plate." Engraved in London from a drawing made in Williamsburg between 1732 at the earliest and 1747 at the latest. It is the only known elevation of the original building.

coachman's and groom's rooms and closets, the laundry, dairy, gardener's room, and servants' hall were inventoried. Perhaps this particular group of spaces or that on the opposite side of the south courtyard contained the room or rooms for the governor's secretarial staff.[4] Items in those spaces were the property of the crown and were not included in the Botetourt inventory. Moving to the group of "Out Houses belonging to the Kitchen," the men inventoried the larder, smokehouse, coal house, salt house, charcoal house, scullery, servants' hall, and finally the kitchen. The latter contained several large storage spaces, probably the servants' hall, its own cellar, and the cook's handsomely furnished bedchamber. This concluded the compendious list of "every thing proper for the Residence of a Governor."

In compiling the inventory without attaching values to the individual items, a most unusual occurrence in eighteenth-century Virginia documents, the trustees may have been guided by the same scruples that prevented them from listing the late governor's clothing—"thinking it rather indelicate to particularize his Lordship's wearing Apparel in the Inventory" (though they did attach a separate list of it all subsequently). They may also have received assurance from the court that the late governor's personal wealth was substantial and secure enough to cover any foreseeable debts in the colony.[5] From the documentation it is possible to estimate that the value of the items in the inventory amounted to about six thousand pounds sterling, three times the governor's annual salary, and a huge sum considering that the estate contained no land (which was all in England, of course) and only seven slaves. Such an estate set the governor far above all but a tiny handful of Virginia gentry.[6]

Supplementing the expansive detail of the inventory are the accounts submitted to the estate by local merchants and tradesmen. As these were bills for goods provided and services rendered, they include monetary values for certain items that appear in the inventory; they thus provide further information on aspects of the inventory that would otherwise remain enigmatic. In addition, Botetourt's English papers include financial records for the years prior to his departure for Virginia to assume the governorship in 1768. Bank passbooks, tradesmen's bills, and vouchers specify items he ordered in London for his new post and residence in the colony, both prior to his departure and while he was abroad. The Palace records also include account books kept by his staff, petty cash books that constitute a daily record for various expenses connected with the household and the governor personally, a kitchen account book, a "park" account book, a record of the servants' salaries, as well as sundry letters and receipts.[7]

What is so persuasive about the inventory and its related documents is the great particularity of detail, the internal consistency, the frequent corroboration of the same items from different sources, the clear proof that the men took pains to amend and correct the working copy of the inventory in many places in

Page from an account book kept by London cabinetmaker William Fenton detailing a standing account with Lord Botetourt. On this page are descriptions of the elaborate library table Botetourt used in the Palace dining room, a strong box kept in the pantry, a wine cooler or cellar for the dining room, three fire screens decorated with maps, one of which stood in the dining room, and three desks. From the Badminton Papers, courtesy, the Duke of Beaufort.

				12
1769	William Fenton		607	10 11½
Apr. 15	For 23 foot 6 Inch desks & one 3 foot	21 - -		
	For a large & very neat mohogainy lybery table of very fine wood Covered with leather the moulding Richly Carved on 83 wheel Castors	24 - -		
	For a small Iron Chest to be put in one of the Cuberts of the table	3 - 8 -		
	For a mohogainy Cellor lined with lead	4 - 4 -		
	For 3 fire Screens with maps on both Sides	3 - 10 -		
	For large packing Cases & matts	2 - 2 -		
	For Expences putting on board	- 12 -		
	Fentons Bill Total		58	16
	Car.d Over		666	6 11½

order to make it as "exact and perfect" as they could. An old box with a little whiting in it, "thread and pins etc. in library table draw," one broken paper of pearl barley, two remnants of rush matting, a small quantity of tar in the cellar adjoining the laundry—these were items of such inconsequential value that it is almost incongruous to see them alongside the great array of silver, the large stock of smart linens, the "5 Grey Coach Horses and 1 Mare," the pipes of Madeira that all represented a legacy of considerable value to the duke. The methodical care and the detail are very convincing. But for the diligence and thoroughness of these men, how else would it have been possible to gauge the extent and quality of the most portable and commonly visible index of the governor's social status and cultural ambition—his clothing? Its lengthy itemization from the complete suit of pale crimson cut velvet down to socks and underwear in assorted colors and materials is a rare survival. Each individual volume in the library was noted by title and location. The instances of corroboration between the inventory and other elements of the documentation are numerous and certainly sufficient to endorse William Nelson's claim that the inventory was an exact and perfect catalog of *all* Botetourt's effects.

In its meticulous detail and clear spatial organization, the inventory re-creates for us the varied landscape of the Palace and those who made it all work. Moving through the sequence of diverse spaces, sixty-one of them in all, resembled passing through a small English village or substantial manor house complex except for the presence at the Palace of Negro slaves. With that proviso, the Palace compound must have seemed a microcosm of English life. It encompassed a great range of spaces, from the most ceremonial, which were furnished with brilliant symbols of the crown—coats of arms, weapons, flags—to the least ceremonious, such as the "Small Room Adjoyning to Poultry House," containing only one old mattress and two old blankets for the slave assigned guard duty over the livestock and poultry. The spaces functioned for a wide range of occupants, from the governor, who was most evident in his office and in his private apartment on the second floor, through butler, steward, cook, coachman, gardener, and so on down to the most menial hirelings. To Nicholas, the only Virginia-born member of the group taking the inventory, the resemblance to a great plantation would have been obvious despite the physical compression that characterized the urban setting of the Palace. Its congeries of brick and wooden buildings, each group of which "formed a little handsome street," its gardens, terraces, rows of trees signifying formal approach—all these elements were noted in great Virginia plantations of the period. Conspicuous by their absence from the Palace setting, however, were the distant huts or clusters of buildings (quarters) for huge numbers of black laborers and field hands.[8]

Enumerated in the inventory of the Palace and specified in the accompanying documents are more than sixteen thousand things "proper for the office . . . [and] . . . Residence of a Governor." Each one of those things was a part of the "every thing" that the urbane John Randolph believed was sufficient for the office and residence of the governor to function. Each one of those things played some kind of role—however small or occasional—in the way the governor's office and house worked and operated. Thus the inventory clearly articulates what Botetourt believed he needed to execute the public and social roles he was assigned.

This great quantity of things is segregated in the inventory into subgroups corresponding to designated spaces within the Palace complex, which were all described by function—dining room, kitchen, and so on. The majority of the things were in the individual spaces by design (according to function) rather than by accident or merely to assist the inventory takers in their task. This makes it possible to determine how segregated subgroups of this huge array of things assisted in the performance of specific and varied functions at the Palace, all of which were associated with the wishes and needs of the governor. Social spaces and the objects in them denote social activities and functions. Thus the accumulated and diverse functions of living are revealed and our understanding of them is greatly expanded by the accumulated lists of things and the ways they are segregated or grouped. Patterns of activities emerge from this kind of examination of spaces and things, patterns of functioning, patterns of living, patterns of attitudes and beliefs.[9]

Since the mere presence of these dedicated groups of things, each one of which had something to do with the business of the governor's life and work in the Palace, is not always sufficient proof that the activities denoted by the things were actually carried on in the spaces in which the inventory listed them, I use corroborative evidence whenever possible. Sometimes this comes from other documents in the governor's papers, sometimes from other governors' documented practices. Much of it is from contemporary English sources—architectural writers or social commentators offering their prescriptions or observations on how certain spaces should be or were being used. In view of the fact that the governors were of recent English origin, Botetourt particularly, I believe this source of evidence is logical and appropriate. I also use contemporary Virginia sources, of course, and they often illuminate the patterns of activity that are only implied by the other documentation.

Implicit in patterns of activities are patterns of beliefs. Responsible and well-regarded men such as Botetourt did not act or behave capriciously. They had reasons and motivations for doing what they did at certain times in certain places. In public and social situations their actions were for the most part what they believed they had to or should do. These patterns of beliefs are often connoted by the word "culture." I use this word in the development of the theses in this book in two ways. "Culture" means first "the . . . refinement of mind, tastes, and manners; the condition of being thus . . . refined." It also connotes "an idealized pattern of meanings, values, and ideas differentially shared by members of a society, which can be inferred from the non-instructive behavior of the group and from the products of their actions, including material artifacts, language, and social institutions."[10]

In reference to the "refinement of mind, tastes, and manners," the word "culture" generally conveys something more demonstrative and more elevated than can usually be found in the terse, enumerated facts of an estate inventory. But the facts actually represent objects or things mostly acquired or used by choice or preference to perform designated functions, assist in specific activities, or play a role in certain settings. Historically these things *were* demonstrative and active, not merely passive numbers. They were inextricably connected with tastes and manners and *were* seriously considered and evaluated, intellectually, socially, economically, even morally. For example, precisely defined hierarchies of subject types for paintings were formulated in the French academies in the seventeenth century and still held sway throughout Europe by the fourth quarter of the eighteenth century. Carefully articulated programs of exterior and interior architecture, fittings, and furnishings were drawn up by intellectual architects and clients throughout the eighteenth century, Lord Burlington being a highly influential advocate of this important element of living. Socially, objects played a vital role in differentiation, in distinctions implied by different types of materials (ranging from precious to base) as well as by quantity and degree of elaboration. Codes were formulated for furnishing various parts of the house with distinguishing types of objects of graded qualities. Socially, objects also played a vital role in cohesion, in the rituals of dining or dancing, for example. Economically, objects were a fundamental component of trade and commerce, locally, nationally, and internationally. Because of the vital place they occupied in national and international economies, objects (or consumer goods, as they are sometimes called) were politicized in this period and played roles in political trends and conflicts.[11]

The proliferation of these goods in the eighteenth century caused moralists much anguish: Would luxury—as epitomized by the dramatic rise in the quantity and quality of material possessions—lead to surfeit, excess, and inevitable decay? Some lamented that "pernicious . . . Luxury . . . vitiates the Morals of the People" and "poisons a whole Nation." Despite their jeremiads, the flow of goods continued unabated. Rather than deprive themselves of the benison of material abundance, thoughtful consumers suggested that profusion and elaboration were not automatically luxurious and therefore reprehensible but instead indicated choice, preference, and *refinement*. Practitioners of energetic consumerism were, they concluded, exercising "the refinement of mind, tastes, and manners."[12] The

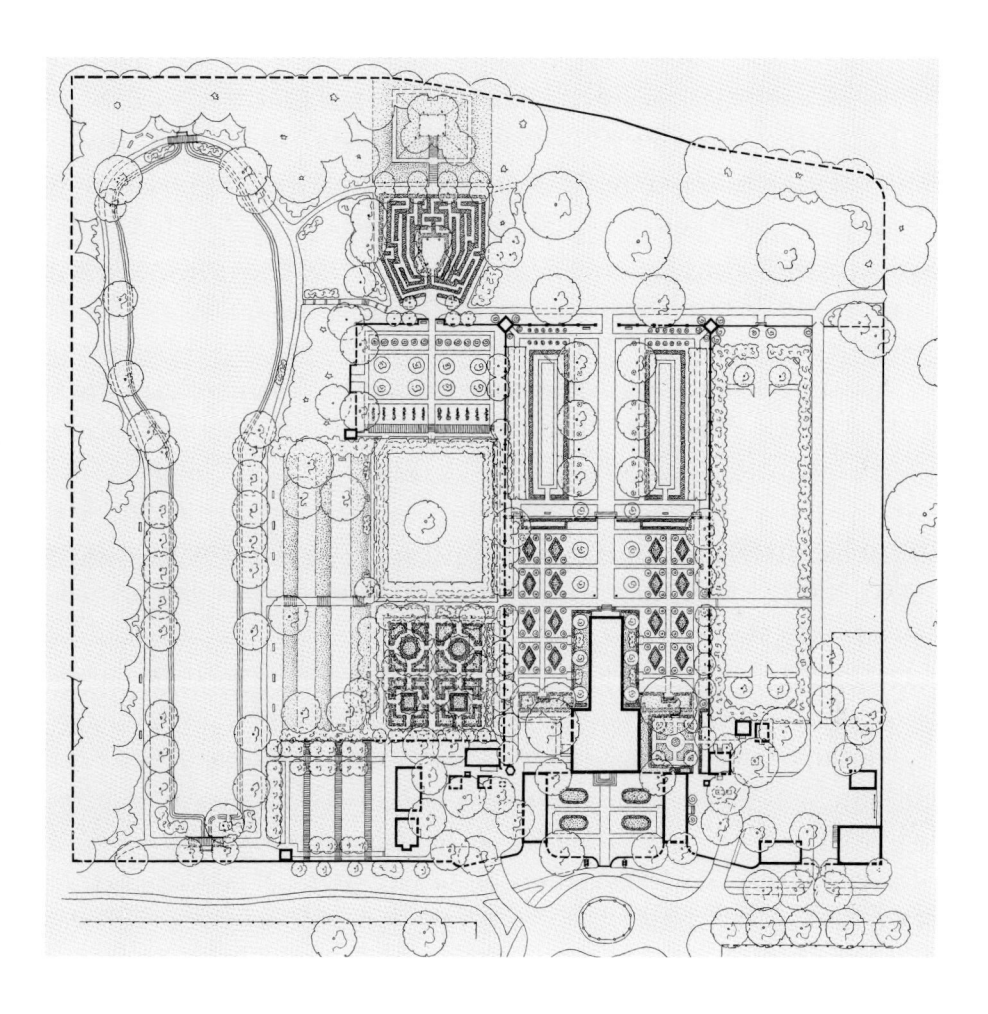

Architects' 1931 plan of the Palace.
CWF

Botetourt inventory, in its remarkable amplitude and detail, provides an unusually complete index to the governor's refinement, to his "grace" or polish—that aspect of his life that the colonists clearly found of considerable interest.

The inventory and the supplementary documents also reveal an "idealized pattern of meanings, values, and ideas, differentially shared by members of a society," for which anthropologists often use the word "culture." Objects reflect such a pattern in that they reveal activities and choices, they convey beliefs and preferences, values and ideas, all of which were shared at the Governor's Palace among a wide variety of social types. Activities were carried out there and choices purposefully made for a colonial society that was as diverse as the microcosm of English society at the Palace. Culture is something inherent and something expressed, something normative and something conspicuous, something acquired and something transmitted. Culture is inherent and expressed in the sum of the individual lives at the Palace that were all devoted to sustaining the figurehead of the governor. It is also inherent and expressed in those colonists who interacted with him with "Gratitude and Affection" and who found him admirable and praiseworthy. Culture is the way of life that Botetourt brought with him from an English county via London and adjusted in the encounter with the colony of Virginia and its inhabitants. Culture is the Virginians' mode of living and those aspects of the governor's life—ideas, words, deeds, comportment, possessions—that they found worthy of attention, absorption, and emulation. Culture is a phenomenon that emanates from the top of the social hierarchy down through the various levels, and ripples outward from the elite center to the edges of society, from the capital to the distant provinces: "The People of fortune . . . are the pattern of all behaviour here," commented one close observer of the Virginia scene in the early 1770s, succinctly expressing this view of cultural transmittal.[13] Culture is also inherent and transmitted generationally, being distinctive to various social, religious, or ethnic groups, for example. For the Virginia society with which Botetourt interacted there were clearly different cultures, the most conspicuous (other than that of the gentry) being, of course, that characteristic of the black race. On the interaction between this governor and this group the inventory and its related documents also sheds light.

What was happening in England, culturally as well as politically, was the paradigm for most (white) colonists. In the first decades of the eighteenth century, as affluent Virginians endeavored to stamp the countryside with the marks of their English civility by constructing large public and private buildings and creating a gentry life-style, it was quite appropriate for visiting professor Hugh Jones to observe that "the habits, life, customs, computations, etc., of the Virginians are much the same as about London, which they esteem their home." Edmund Randolph, born in the mid-eighteenth century into one of Virginia's most prominent families, later stated that "every political sentiment, every fashion in Virginia appeared to be imperfect unless it bore a resemblance to some precedent in England." He also noted "an almost idolotrous deference to the mother country."[14] Those colonists who most often came into contact with the royal governors were "trying to be country gentlemen in the English manner." They even wrote instructions on conduct for their children that might have graced the later pages of Chesterfield.[15]

This general pattern of social emulation was articulated clearly, albeit in an official context, by Robert Carter, president of the Council and acting governor after the death of Lieutenant Governor Hugh Drysdale in 1726. Probably the richest man in the colony, Carter wrote from his plantation on the Rappahannock to the clerk of the Council, William Robertson, in Williamsburg, instructing him on the preparations for the king's birthday ball at "The Governors house[,] to be Sure . . . the fittest place" for the ceremony. "I resolve to have the Birthday kept with as much Show as it was by Coll Drysdale," Carter wrote. "You may very well conclude when I laid in that wine at Town I had this day in my thoughts in case a Governor should not Arrive. What ever Sorts of drink Coll Drysdale had I would have the Same and in all respects keep pace with him. My Salary is as large and I thank God I have as little reason to be Sparing of it."[16]

The colonists' cultural absorption from the mother country and those of its polished representatives with whom they interacted has been well noted by historians. Indeed, some have pushed it to the point where they have perceived in the colonies a "sense of inferiority that expressed itself in imitation of English ways, and a sense of guilt regarding local mannerisms."[17] Such a viewpoint, however, discounts the necessity for the colonists to adapt to local conditions, downplays the impulse of some of them to rebel against the values of the mother country they no longer lived in, and devalues the strength and ingenuity of the vernacular culture that resulted. Certain historians have begun to redress the balance between culture as a phenomenon that is readily discerned and tracked through time and space from the most articulate, thoughtful, and affluent elements of society down to the least articulate, the uneducated, the poor, and culture as a protean and flexible expression, of merit when it evinces individual or group variation from the elite model.[18]

Nevertheless, it is undeniable that the improvements in the material standard of living evident throughout the social hierarchy in England and the colonies in the second half of the eighteenth century had the effect of making virtually all colonists more dependent for their cultural well-being on approved English-made or English exported goods than ever before. The phrase "recently from London" became synonymous with the cutting edge of approved modishness and smart acceptability, signifying both taste *and* quality in merchandisers' and tradesmen's promotions. Consumer goods were widely recognizable symbols of social identity and social advancement in this period, inextricably bound up with perceptions of status or social standing. Increasingly mass-produced, they were imported in huge numbers and were as recognizable in Williamsburg, Charleston, and Annapolis as they were in London, Bristol, Edinburgh, and Dublin. Manufacturers and retailers fomented notions of fashion to justify the production and sale of ever-increasing varieties of consumer goods—fashion meant novelty and change and implied the necessity for constant awareness of what was current and socially approved in order to maintain one's own social status. Exuberant consumerism became as evident in Virginia and the other colonies as in England. (Wedgwood, for example, claimed in the 1760s that the islands and continent of North America constituted one of his major markets.) One Virginia great planter, Robert Beverley, writing to England about furniture and fittings for his new house shortly after Botetourt's death, admitted "I would willingly consult the present Fashion, for you [see] that foolish Passion has made its Way, even into this remote Region." For many colonists the royal governor was the exemplar of fashion or a conduit of socially approved information about such things, as close to the center of the cultural matrix as most of them would ever get. He had seen what was happening "at home," he had brought with him examples of what was *au fait* in the right circles, he was an exceptional agent whose word and deed could help them maintain as much of an awareness of their cultural status as of their political standing, a matter of which they were growing increasingly self-conscious.[19]

The interaction between governor and governed during Botetourt's administration occurred at a time of abnormal political intensity between mother country and the American colonies. The very appointment of a full governor and nobleman had been brought about by the colonies' concerted response to the Stamp Act and the upheavals that ensued. While Virginians saw the appointment as a compliment to them, a recognition by the ministry of a new level of maturity on their part, they were clearly alert for signs from him that their maturity was suspect, perhaps even intolerable. Botetourt, noted in England for both tact and firmness, was instructed to be particularly vigilant for signs of ingratitude or defiance. In such an environment cultural sensibilities were undoubtedly heightened, and the interaction that occurred did so in an unusually sensitive atmosphere.[20]

Careful analysis of the inventory and its related documents within the clearly defined historical and physical context of Lord Botetourt's administration and residence in the Governor's Palace discloses patterns of living within the established spaces, articulates the cultural life of the governor as it was evidenced in the building, and reveals the nature of his cultural interaction with those around him. From this emerges a broader pattern of cultural life. Lest it be said, however, that the brief two-year tenure for the first full governor of the colony to reside in the Palace in Williamsburg presents too atypical a picture, I link and compare Botetourt with the six other men who directly represented the monarch in the colonial capital. What better link to choose than the very place where their office took visible form, where their culture found its most frequent expression, and upon which the inventory casts so much light—the Governor's Palace itself? Two governors and five lieutenant governors resided in the building, performing many identical functions, occupying the same set of rooms (although the two largest rooms were only added at mid-century and therefore were available only to the four later officials), and using in common a small number of objects that were purchased early on by the colony for their use there (included in the "standing furniture"). While the material evidence for the occupancies of the other officials is distinctly limited in comparison with that for Lord Botetourt, enough survives to demonstrate the existence of certain unifying patterns and particular themes that run through the sixty-one years the building served as the viceregal residence.

Comparisons with the life-styles and residences of governors in adjacent colonies are also illuminating. Did they manifest similar cultural values, or did Virginia, and more particularly Williamsburg itself, exert powerful influences on the Palace and its occupants in the way it can be seen to have spawned certain characteristic features of architecture or cabinetmaking? Fortunately, three southern governors left records of their possessions in the form of schedules of losses—Governor Robert Eden of Maryland who fled from Annapolis in 1776, William Tryon, governor of North Carolina from 1765–1771, whose effects were burned in his New York house in 1773 shortly after his removal there, and Lord William Campbell, governor of South Carolina from 1773 to 1776 and resident in Charleston for one year with his family before his abrupt departure. Governors Eden and Tryon stayed in the Palace in Williamsburg for short periods, while the former also entertained in Annapolis the Virginia governor as well as prominent planters who were acquainted with the Williamsburg residence. The governors and colonists with whom they interacted undoubtedly made comparisons at the time.[21]

Compiled so methodically and supplemented as it is by the related documents, the Botetourt inventory is an index and directory of life at the Governor's Palace within a given period of time. It is revelatory of the architectural spaces in the residence, most of which still served the purposes they were designed for sixty years after they were built. It identifies and helps us further understand elements of the life that occurred in those spaces, multiple functions sometimes happening in the same space. Vital ingredients of eighteenth-century life are pinpointed in certain rooms—ceremony and hierarchy, public and social intercourse, private life and interaction with the support staff. As the inventory was "exact and perfect," this study is not subject to the vagaries or fecklessness of survival of actual artifacts for its interpretation of the governor's cultural life. Indeed, as a study it is considerably reinforced with actual objects, many of them identical to those listed in the inventory and in some cases the same ones. Thus the inventory, or at least sections of it relevant to those spaces now publicly viewed in the reconstructed Governor's Palace in Williamsburg, is reinforced by the presence of the actual or closely comparable three-dimensional objects as such inventories rarely are.[22]

This analysis should add to our understanding of the social adoption of fixed architectural spaces in a specific Virginia context in the mid- to late eighteenth century, though it deliberately refrains from an analysis of the architectural detailing within those given spaces since they are all now reconstructed. Much current material culture or architectural history scholarship focuses on trends in the spatialization of functions within given social groups. In using the portable objects, the accessories of living, to explain what the patterns of living at the Palace were, I am pursuing the same goal of exploring social and artifactual experience in late colonial Virginia, but from a somewhat different direction.[23]

The Setting

The Governor's Palace was the first and one of the largest of the series of "Georgian" brick mansions that characterized and have come to epitomize the emergence and flowering of the Virginia gentry style in the first half of the eighteenth century. Built at a carefully selected point in the axial symmetry of Governor Francis Nicholson's baroque town plan, the Palace was erected and roofed by 1710, was ready for occupation by 1715, and had been embellished with ornamental gardens and a park by about 1720. Apart from the mid-century addition of the ballroom and supper room wing on the back of the house, the possible conversion of the front courtyard and garden to a carriage turnaround about the same time, and apparent changes to the service areas, the residence remained relatively stable in exterior appearance and interior functions from its initial occupancy by Lieutenant Governor Alexander Spotswood about 1715 until its destruction by fire in 1781. While it is possible that the manner in which some of the rooms were used did change as the century progressed, particularly after the addition of the north wing, the early plan set a pattern of "Georgianization" that later governors such as Fauquier and Botetourt accepted and used with success. They surely perceived that the Palace had been one of two or three key buildings in the planning and development of the new capital city at the beginning of the century and learned that in form and internal organization it had influenced the Virginia gentry's choices for their own mansions, their own visible centers of authority throughout the colony.[1]

By the end of the first century of settlement certain Virginians were painfully conscious of the still undeveloped nature of the colony—"The first and eldest of the English Plantations in America . . . looks all like a wild Desart," wrote Henry Hartwell, James Blair, and Edward Chilton in their report to the Board of Trade in 1697. What the colony lacked were civilizing amenities: "As to all the Natural Advantages of a Country, it is one of the best, but as to the Improved Ones, one of the worst of all the *English* Plantations."[2]

The city of Williamsburg, Virginia, drawn ca. 1781. The manuscript map is undated and unsigned but has survived among the Simcoe Papers, CWF. Despite the schematic quality of the rendering, the trees on Palace green are clearly visible. This view also shows the grass oval, to which Jefferson refers in his sketch of the first floor of the Palace, situated between the offices flanking the main building. The geometry of the town plan as depicted here is stricter than in the so-called Frenchman's Map of Williamsburg of 1782. Overall size, H: 8"; W: 30".

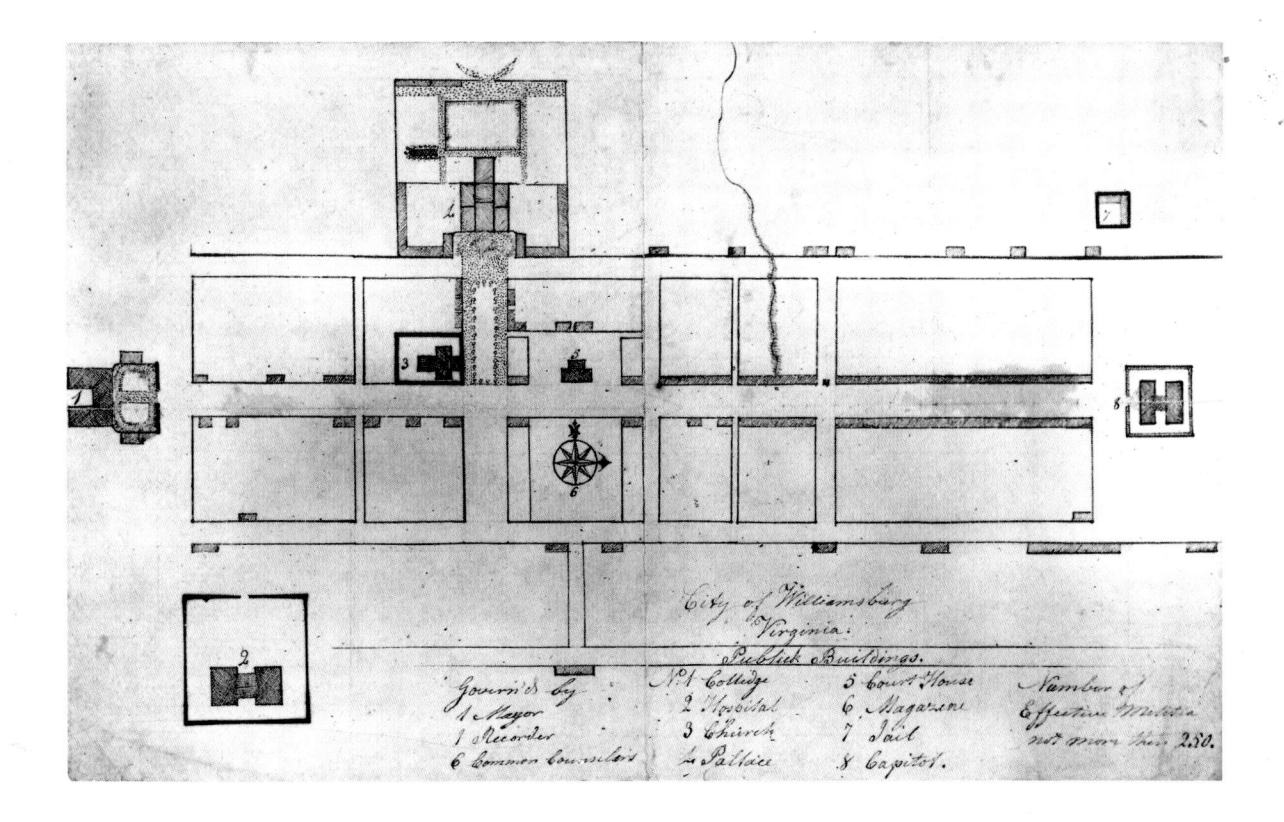

Whether the three men were unduly misanthropic or cleverly calculating is arguable—the upshot was that within three years incoming governor Francis Nicholson had developed a striking plan for a new capital city, and the Lords of Trade had begun forcefully to urge the colony to provide "a good house" for the governor as part of the complex of new government buildings there. Nicholson received orders to send a design for the house to London, which, in light of his known creative energy and talents, it is difficult to imagine he did not do. Land for the residence was purchased in 1701 but the colonial government, still paying for the construction of the statehouse (or "Capitol," as Nicholson christened it), delayed appropriations for the structure until 1706. Possibly to mollify Nicholson's successor, Lieutenant Governor Edward Nott, who arrived in Williamsburg in 1705, and certainly to forestall further criticism from London, the assembly finally passed in 1706 an act "directing the building an house for the Governour of this Colony and dominion." The assembly asked Nott to provide a "draught" for the house but he demurred—"I Leave it wholy to you to give such directions therein, as You think proper."[3] Thereupon the assembly appropriated three thousand pounds to erect "with all convenient expedition" on a sixty-three-acre lot on the north side of the town a two-story house of brick, fifty-four feet wide by forty-eight feet deep, with cellars, vault, sash windows, slate roof, and a kitchen and stables. They

THE SETTING 39

further directed that the house be built and furnished according to the discretion of a local overseer, Henry Cary.[4]

What slowly emerged under Cary's direction, with certain prominent Virginia gentry undoubtedly contributing their suggestions, was a tripartite arrangement of centrally placed house flanked by pavilions or "offices detacht," the kitchen group on one side and the stables group on the other, both separated from the "Dwelling-House" in order to keep the latter "more cool and Sweet" in the characteristic Virginia pattern. The main block consisted of a two-story, double-pile, central passage plan (the "Georgian" plan) set on a high basement in a cubical mass with repetitive, ordered facade and steeply pitched roof punctuated with dormer windows and surmounted by a platform and tall cupola. Perpendicular to the facade of the main house stood the pavilions, one story, single pile, central passage in plan, their roofs also with dormers. One end of each oblong pavilion lined up with the facade of the main house. Together they formed three sides of the front courtyard, the fourth side consisting of a wall and gate. The house stood at the terminus of Palace Street, which was perpendicular to the main axis of town, called Duke of Gloucester Street, running between the college and the Capitol, approximately two-thirds of its length toward the college. As the executive center of the colony the Palace joined newly constructed buildings that served as the legislative and educational centers of the colony and an older church that was the religious center of the town.[5]

The elevation of the Palace was engraved about 1740 in London, presumably copied from a drawing made earlier in Williamsburg. Measurements of the first floor rooms were included in a sketch by Thomas Jefferson probably dating from the 1770s and were verified by archaeological investigations of the Palace site 1930–1932. The house we see today, meticulously reconstructed on its original foundations in the early 1930s, was dramatically different from any residence erected in the colony prior to that time. For the most part, architecture in Virginia during the first century of settlement was "impermanent," built almost wholly of wood in the "post" or "earthfast" construction types, comparatively small in scale and intended for a limited lifespan. By the turn of the century, however, large brick "public" buildings began to appear in the new capital city—the College of William and Mary in the 1690s, and the Capitol, completed in 1705. The latter evolved as a variation and enlargement of the previous statehouse at Jamestown, and consisted of a doubling of the customary courthouse plan. Though the Palace was built with public money and was a government building, it was a dwelling house for the governor, and it was the private house form that it took.[6] Conspicuously larger and grander than any previous residence in the colony, it was a cause of great pride—"The best house that I have heard of in america," wrote Councillor Philip Ludwell to William

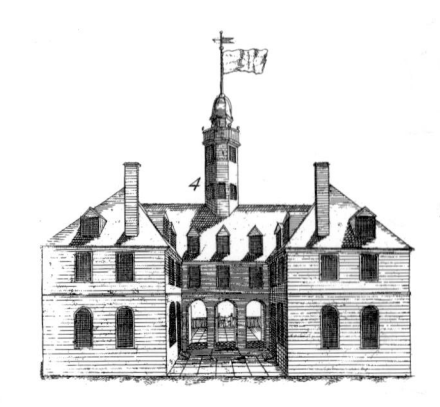

Above, north elevation of the Capitol from the Bodleian Plate showing the building after the installation of the chimneys (and fireplaces), ca. 1722.

Above right, College of William and Mary from the Bodleian Plate, the so-called Wren Building in the center, flanked by the Brafferton School (for Indian boys) on the left, completed in 1723, and the President's House on the right, constructed by 1732.

Right, measured sketch of the first floor of the Governor's Palace drawn by Thomas Jefferson probably in the early 1770s. Dimensions of interior spaces, height of roof, and certain external measurements and details are given. Shaded areas refer to possible architectural changes or additions to the original fabric. L: 7½". Courtesy, Coolidge Papers, Massachusetts Historical Society.

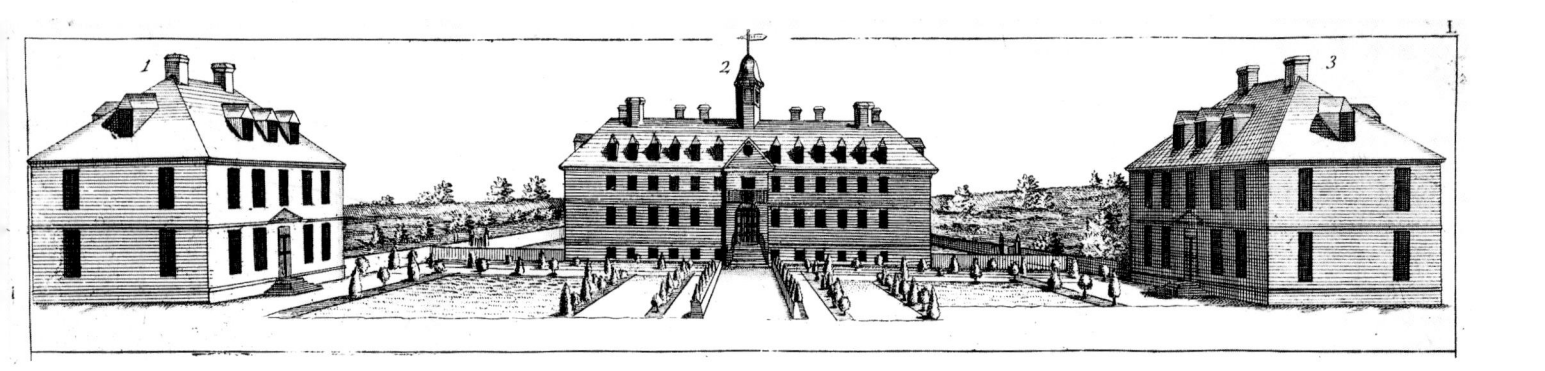

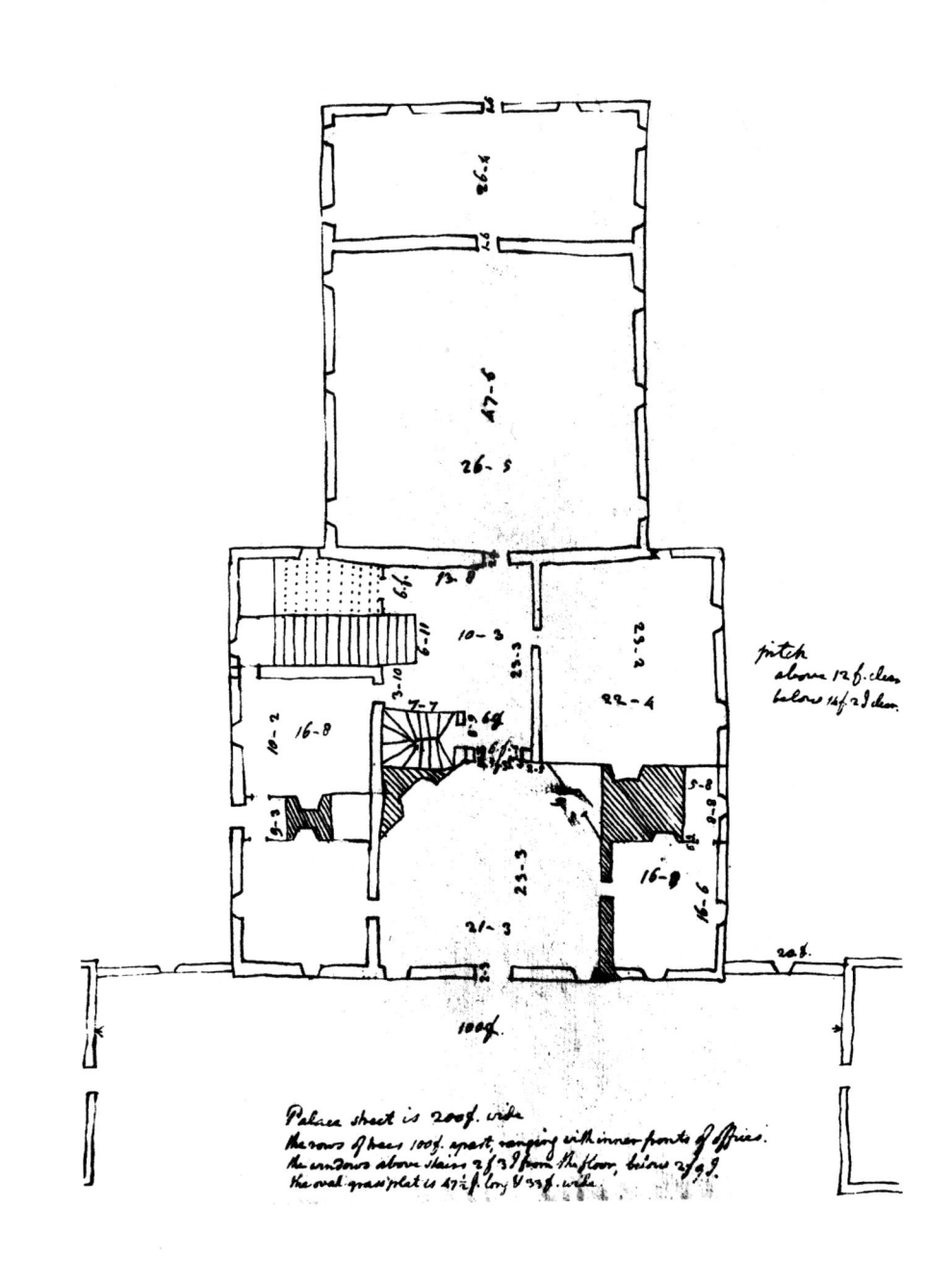

Palace street is 200 f. wide
the rows of trees 100 f. apart, ranging with inner fronts of offices.
the windows above stairs 2 f. 9 I from the floor, below 2 f. 9 I
the oval grass plat is 47½ f. long & 33 f. wide.

Blathwayt in England. Former acting governor Edmund Jenings, writing to the same official, elaborated: "The Governors house regular and neatly furnished, the Colledge . . . Capitol . . . Ornaments [of society] not to bee equalled in America." In his revised *The History and Present State of Virginia*, Robert Beverley compared the Palace to the other public buildings and judged it to be "not the largest, but by far the most beautiful." Visiting Oxford clergyman Hugh Jones, in his evaluation of *The Present State of Virginia* of 1724, went even further: "A magnificent structure . . . finished and beautified with gates, fine gardens, offices, walks, a fine canal, orchards, etc. . . . the ornamental addition of a good cupola or lanthorn." He concluded that the suite of public buildings was "justly reputed the best in all the English America."[7] What these opinions all affirm is that the Governor's Palace was the crowning glory of a group of brick buildings that marked the beginning of permanence for gentry society in Virginia. They were a highly visible sign of the stabilization of society after the impermanence of the previous century. In the following decades came county courthouses, Anglican churches, and private mansions solidifying the power structure of the ruling elite in the colony.[8]

Whether the design of this extraordinary new building derived from European academic sources or from a local synthesis of evolving architectural ideas (but on a larger scale than any house previously erected in Virginia) is unclear. It was undoubtedly the product of local builder Henry Cary with advice, in all likelihood, from local gentlemen who believed themselves possessed of certain talents in the design sphere. Externally *and* internally the building was of a type built for rural gentry and urban merchants in late seventeenth- and early eighteenth-century England. Dutch architectural pattern books of the second half of the seventeenth century perpetuating the classical Italian ("Palladian") tradition of the sixteenth century may also have been consulted. No obvious local antecedent for the main house has survived, though the design for the pavilions was probably developed from a local form that then became by the mid-eighteenth century one of the most popular Virginia house types. An exceptional example of domestic architecture, the Palace was clearly the result of the governor interacting with the local gentry; the governor was, in effect, the patron—in Nicholson, perhaps the inspiration of the scheme, and in Spotswood, the one who brought it to completion and added the embellishments. The local gentry participated in the design of the building and passed resolutions and appropriations to make its construction possible. This conjunction of visions and resources produced a residence of stylish English derivation, the first in a line of remarkable examples of domestic architecture in colonial Virginia that were closely related in spirit if not precisely in delineation. With them the gentry visually stamped their own social order and political authority on the colony in the succeeding sixty years.[9]

Internally, the almost square block of the main house was divided into a series of repeated squares resulting in a strong axial symmetry and a clear sense of order and control—the essence, in formal terms, of the "Georgian" plan. Bisected equally between the front and the back and between each side, the house contained a strong central axis in the hall that extended back into a narrower passage. Virtually square, the hall was almost identical in size to the two squares at the rear flanking the passage, one of which was evidently designated as the dining room, the other being divided into the main staircase and three small service spaces. Two smaller squares, approximately two-thirds the size of the larger unit, flanked the hall at the front of the house. The second floor duplicated the first almost exactly. Placing the hall (the all-purpose room that constituted the main area of activity in the house) and extending it into a passage (a place of transit into the more private parts of the house) in the exact center was both traditional and innovative in Virginia. As the primary point of access and interaction with life outside the residence, the hall or main room was well established. But its central placement and extension back into the inner spaces of the house in the form of a passage foreshadowed the "central passage plan" that changed the entire spatial hierarchy of the Virginia house in the eighteenth century. Furthermore, the Palace hall was more purposeful in clarifying the social hierarchy than the conventional Virginia hall of the time. Since there was a large social space beyond the hall—the dining room, in which a major part of the occupants' public life was to be carried out—the hall was clearly designed as a space to impress and then segregate visitors according to their rank and mission. It was also designed as a space of occasional public assembly. In this it was emphatically English in character rather than Virginian.[10]

The hall was the main arrival point of the house and the focus of the approach from the town up the long allée of Palace Street. Visitors had to pass through a sequence of progressively condensed spaces to get to it, which lent the experience a certain intensity. From Palace Street, which was two hundred feet wide, the visitor proceeded to the courtyard, which was one hundred feet wide, through the main facade that occupied half the width of the courtyard, to enter the hall that was half the width of the facade. This was a purposeful progression. From the wide open public space of Palace Street, over whose considerable length the structure commanded public attention and admiration, the visitor was clearly directed to the hall that was the vital meeting place of the outside and the inside world, the most important room in the Virginia house, "the heart of the planter's order . . . the center of [his] world." It was conventionally the space where life outside the house encountered and interacted with the occupants' inner, more private existence. It could assist or impede further contact as the occupants desired or as the status of the visitor warranted—at the Palace, as we have seen, of primary importance. For social commingling it was a space of periodic entertainment and assembly, at the Palace for the official hosting of the larger world beyond. Undoubtedly, it was the Palace occupant's rank and dignity that justified the sequence of staged spaces, each one of which was designed to heighten the visitor's sense of preparation for and anticipation of encounter.[11]

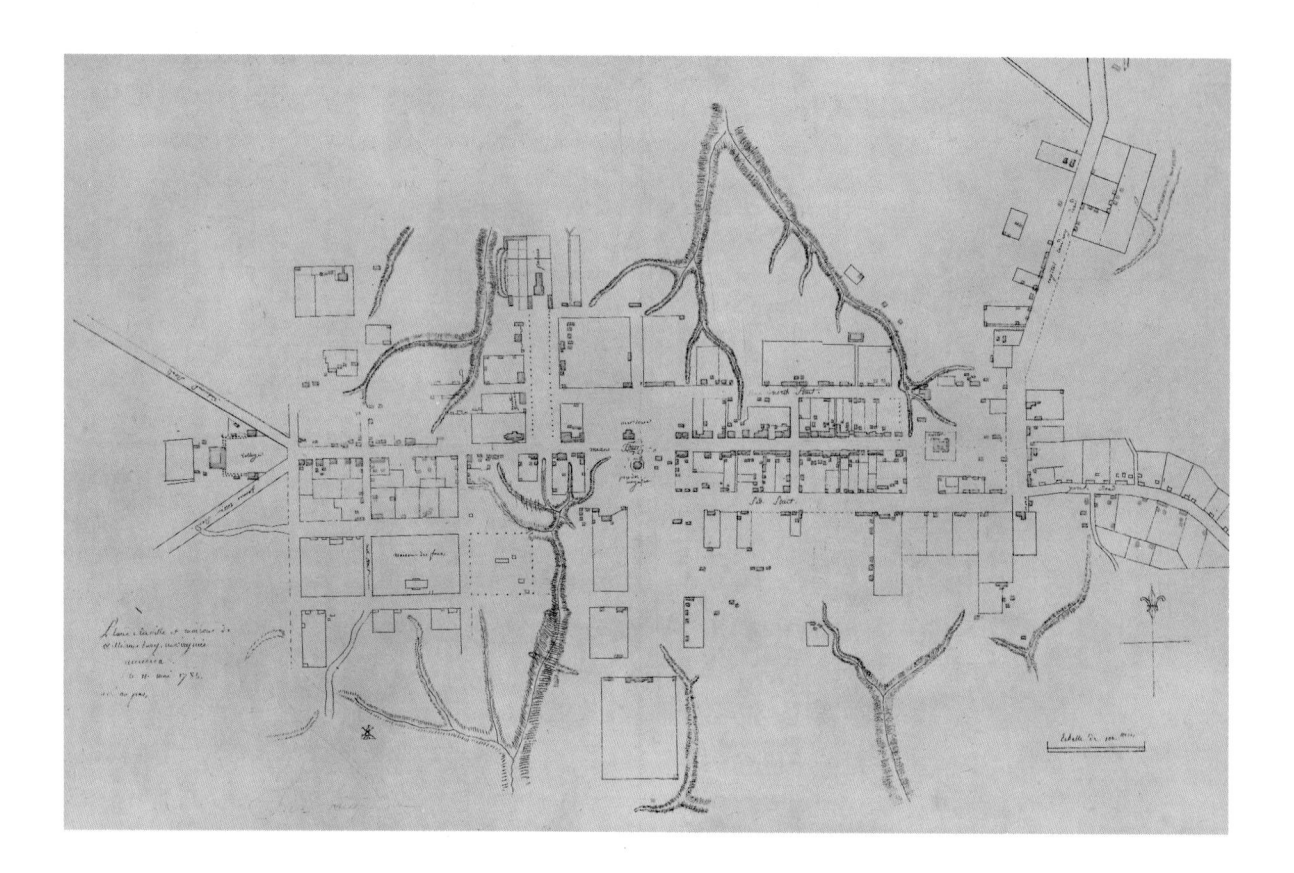

This same pattern of progression, with innumerable variations, became characteristic of later great planters' houses in Virginia. But for the residence of the chief executive of the colony, the designers added a further element—a major space on the second floor. Whether the ceremonial potential of this was fully realized by the local gentlemen in the initial plan is not clear. However, the new Lieutenant Governor, Alexander Spotswood, certainly seized on it when he arrived in Williamsburg in 1710. Finding the structure far from complete, Spotswood urged the assembly to proceed with "The finishing of it and as you Designed it for an honourable Reception, so I hope you no Less Intend to Make it a Comodious one." This the assembly almost immediately did with a formal legislative act and appropriation of money.[12] Their specifications included a proposal for acquiring a nucleus of "convenient and ornamental" furnishings for the building (Appendix 4) that gave much more attention to the space on the second floor, directly above the hall and identical to it in size, than to the lower room. Designated the "great Room in the second Story," the upper room was the proposed repository of the majority of

The "Frenchman's Map" of Williamsburg, drawn in 1782 probably by a French military officer, shows the small capital city in considerable detail. It gives an excellent depiction of the long allée of Palace green, the line of dots presumably representing the catalpas planted by Lieutenant Governor Gooch in 1737. The walls of the forecourt shown in the Bodleian Plate are absent from this rendering. Clearly conveyed here is the spaciousness of the approach to the Palace and the implied connections with the city, yet the openness of the area beyond the compound to the north. H: 16½"; W: 25⅛". Courtesy, College of William and Mary.

the furnishings, which were quite elaborate. The great room was clearly the ceremonial apex of the house, reached after progressing through the hall, the passage beyond, up the grand staircase, and along the passage at the head of that. Its position in the center of the front of the house on the superior level and at the terminus of a parade of rooms that began with the otherwise major space of the hall signaled its appointment as a room of state reception. This was confirmed by the inclusion among its furnishings of "two large looking glasses with the Arms of the Colony on them according to the new Mode"—extremely costly, difficult to obtain, and symbolic of "honourable Reception."[13]

Further evidence of the unusual ambition of the Palace plan was the inclusion of three social spaces on the first floor *in addition* to the hall. Though these rooms were generically included in the term "lower Apartments" in the 1710 proposal, each of the four main rooms on the first floor was of sufficient social importance to merit a chimney glass. The large square room in the rear corner, similar in size to the hall and connected through the passage, was an "intermediate" space, not fully private but certainly more so than the hall. Next to it on the same side of the house was one of the smaller rooms flanking and opening into the hall. It is likely that these were "the great dining room and parlor thereto adjoining" referred to in 1727—the spaces were so identified in the Botetourt inventory. If the large room at the rear served as the dining room initially, and the specification of a typical dining room "Marble Buffette or sideboard with a Cistern and fountain" for the lower apartments in the 1710 proposal supports this notion, it was one of the earliest rooms so designated in a Virginia residence and a major social innovation for its time. With its appointment the act of dining was recognized as having a profoundly important social role, conspicuous as a key element of gentry civility, of display, and of cohesion.[14]

Of the space on the west side of the hall opposite the parlor, no record has survived until its use in 1770 as a butler's pantry. As it was considered worthy of a chimney glass in the 1710 proposal, it is likely that it initially served a more formal, social use, perhaps as a bedchamber, perhaps as a semiprivate room for the governor and his family. The rooms on the second floor except for the great room are similarly unrecorded until their identification in the Botetourt inventory as bedchambers and a library. They probably served these purposes throughout the building's occupancy. Botetourt chose the bedchamber in the southwest corner of the house for his own use and the room on the same west side, connected to the bedchamber through a closet, as a library or study. This constituted a small apartment that allowed him a certain privacy more than any other space in the complex. The garret floor contained sufficient spaces for children's and servants' bedrooms, perhaps as many as eight or ten persons sleeping there when the occasion demanded.

Initially, most service functions were probably contained in the two pavilions that took shape between 1710 and 1715. Kitchen-related activities were conventionally delegated to one, and stables, coach house, and garden functions to the other. This arrangement was still acceptable in the mid-1760s, since Tryon's Palace was designed thus. Three surviving sets of floor plans for the North Carolina residence show slight modifications and variations that the design allowed within the general scheme indicated above. In Williamsburg by 1770, as the Botetourt inventory proves, additional units had been added to the outbuildings as the need had arisen—coal house, charcoal house, salt house, and so on. Unfortunately, it is impossible now to be precise about their locations, archaeological investigation in the 1930s providing few clues and revealing substantial disturbance to the site after 1781.[15]

Surrounding the house were gardens and open spaces of which more will be said later in this chapter. Between 1715 and 1722 Spotswood developed the assembly's original plan of a "Garden . . . adjoining to the said house," two hundred and fifty-four feet by one hundred and forty-four feet, "levelled and enclosed with a brick wall, four foot high, with ballustrades of wood upon the said wall, and . . . handsome gates." An "orchard and pasture ground . . . enclosed with a good ditch and fence" were also specified in the 1710 act.[16]

The remaining rooms that constituted an important part of the inventory's contents and that played a vital role in Botetourt's plans for the social use of the Palace were the ballroom and supper room. They were added at mid-century in a single-story wing seventy-five feet long by thirty-one feet wide, both a physical and a functional continuation of the hall and passage. The ballroom was one-quarter again as wide as the hall and almost a double-square in size, while the supper room was a single square. Clearly, the social functions that the governor was obliged to host at the Palace as part of his official duties had, after three decades, outgrown the spaces available. The new rooms—"assembly rooms" in the parlance of the period—were exceptionally commodious by the standards of the gentlemen who had designed the building originally.[17]

An exceptional product of the cultural interaction of governor and gentlemen at the beginning of a period of real growth and maturity in colonial society, the Governor's Palace established an architectural precedent and provided a cultural tone for Virginia's mansion builders for the rest of the century. It was the earliest appearance in the colony of the Georgian plan with a central hall or passage, a scheme of spatial organization that was adopted by and tailored to the individual needs and preferences of most subsequent patrons of substance and ambition during the century. Although the ceremonial great room on the second floor was inappropriate for many domestic situations, it was incorporated into certain well-known houses, while the combination of dining room and parlor came into widespread use after mid-century. Even the later rooms of assembly, the

Tryon's Palace, New Bern, North Carolina, elevation and floor plan of main house and pavilions, 1766–1767. Functional relationships to the older Governor's Palace in Williamsburg are clear even if the elevation of the main house and its disposition of rooms are more stylish to the decade of the 1760s than the older building would have appeared. Courtesy, Public Record Office, London. Photograph courtesy, North Carolina Archives, Raleigh.

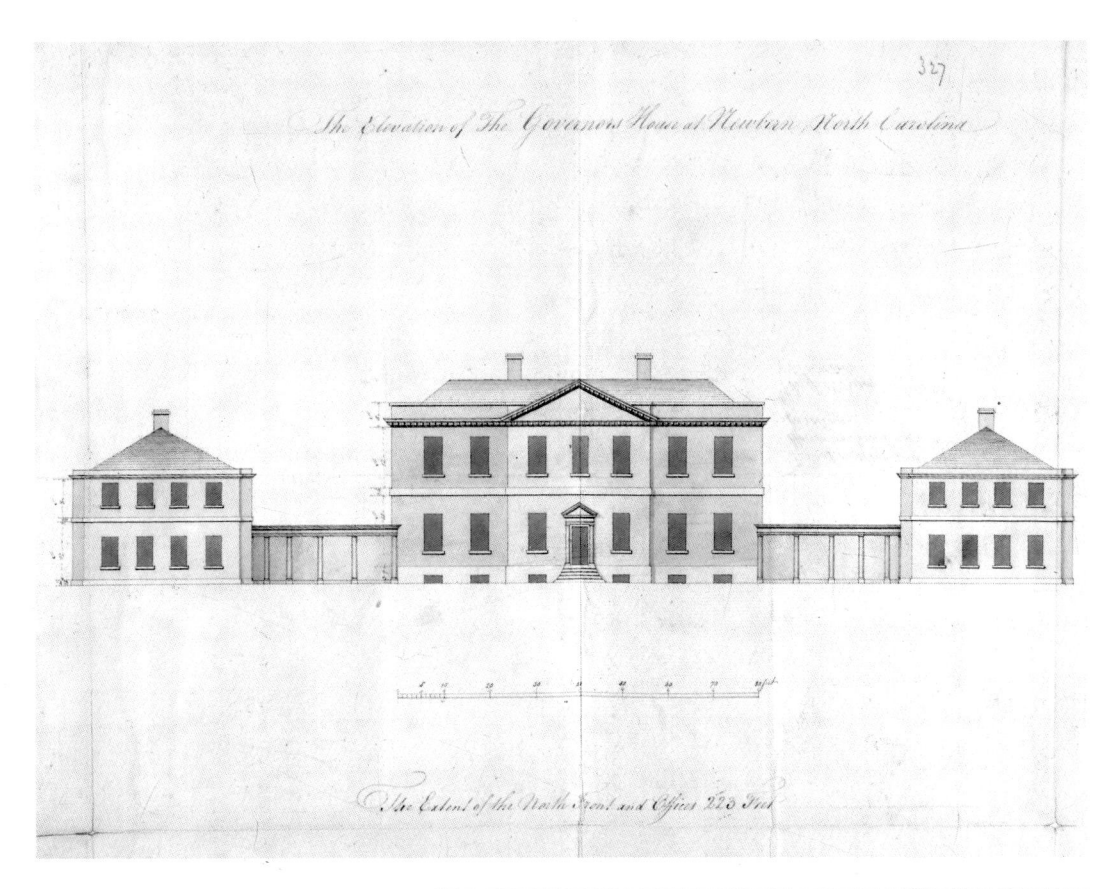

The Elevation of The Governors House at Newbern, North Carolina

The Extent of the North Front and Offices 223 Feet

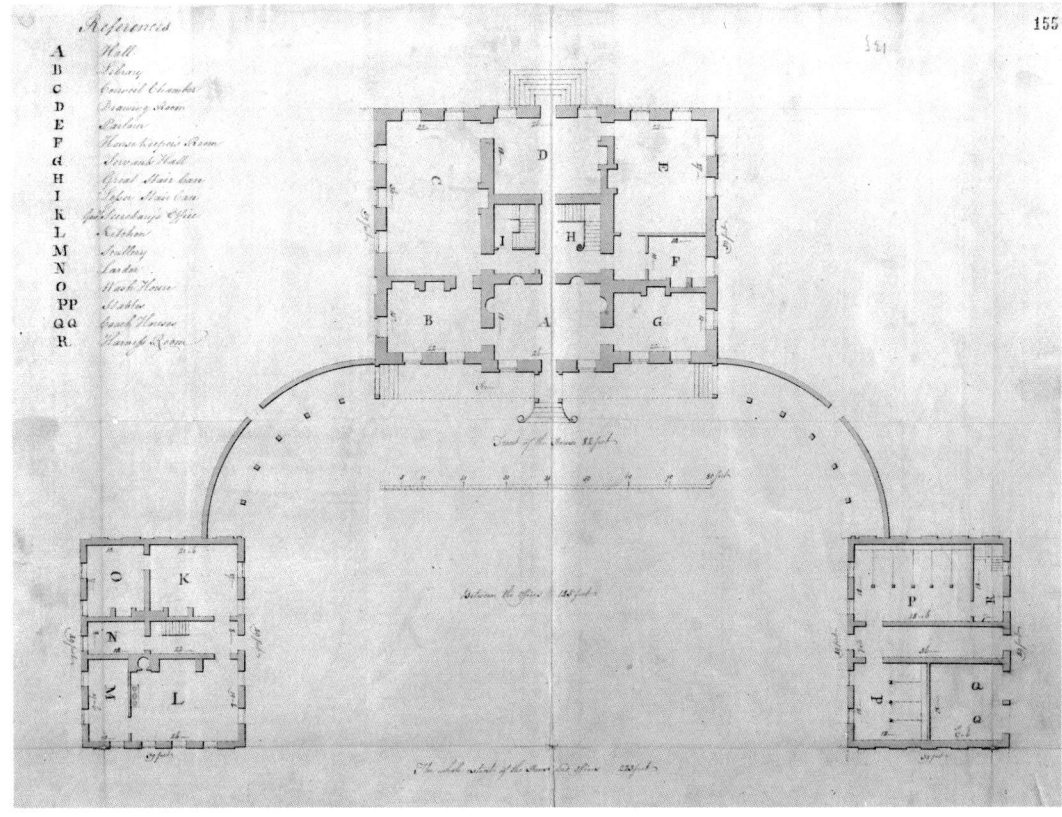

References

A. Hall
B. Library
C. Council Chamber
D. Drawing Room
E. Parlour
F. Housekeeper's Room
G. Servants Hall
H. Great Stair Case
I. Back Stair Case
K. Secretary's Office
L. Kitchen
M. Scullery
N. Larder
O. Wash House
P. Stables
Q. Coach House
R. Harness Room

ballroom and supper room, were at the forefront of a strong regional demand for such spaces. The Palace's distinctive elevation inspired and influenced two closely related buildings, the Brafferton School and the President's House that completed the college forecourt by 1735, as well as a host of dependents outside Williamsburg, adapted and varied in many individual ways generally in the direction of greater restraint and plainness. The tripartite arrangement of main building and dependencies became common in Virginia, with the floor plan of the latter being widely repeated almost verbatim.[18]

At the instigation of the English authorities to whom they paid deference, therefore, the Virginia gentry undertook the construction of a brick mansion for their chief executive in the first decade of the century that became an ornament to their society and a visible sign or symbol of their determination and success. It provided a compelling architectural presence and striking spatial arrangements (and thus a role model) for social practices associated with gentry authority and gentry civility. Visually and symbolically it was effective and influenced in turn those who had played a part in its appearance in the colony. In the two or three decades after its completion, brick mansions in the Georgian style, expressive of the economic power, social superiority, and cultural ambition of gentry society, were as conspicuous by their presence in the Virginia countryside as they had been by their absence earlier.[19]

In the carefully articulated spaces of this ambitious residence, precisely sited in the landscape and society of early eighteenth-century Virginia, the governor had defined duties to perform and responsibilities to fulfill. He was both an office and a person, a bureaucrat and a social leader of society. For these diverse functions the primary spaces of the Governor's Palace were planned, the same spaces that the Botetourt inventory and related documents show to have been full of official and personal life. The governor also needed the support of a retinue or large "family" to perform his duties successfully; their manifold work spaces lay in the main house and in the ancillary structures that bordered it.

The governor was the nexus in the system of receipt and disbursement of information to and from the government in England and the chief executive in the daily operation of the processes of government in the colony. He served as the personal representative for and the symbol of the crown. A great deal of official and certain confidential correspondence to the Board of Trade and the Secretary of State for the Southern Department originated with the governor, almost all of which was copied and dispatched in triplicate (by separate vessels) to guard against loss at sea. In the colony the governor functioned as the final authority in civil, judicial, and fiscal matters, in many military and naval details, and in occasional religious issues, yet all of his decisions were subject to being overruled by the authorities in England, often for practical reasons that were more apparent

President's House, College of William and Mary, completed by 1732. This building mirrors the Brafferton School on the opposite side of the college forecourt, which was built a decade earlier. It shows obvious stylistic dependence on the Governor's Palace, built a decade before that, in the high basement, the articulation of the facade, the steep pitch of the roof, and the central passage, Georgian plan. The house and the school form the forward arms of the tripartite plan, the expansive college building in the center being the equivalent of the main house.

there than in the colony. He adopted ceremony to reiterate the authority of the crown and set a personal standard and example in his role as cultural ambassador from the mother country. He was a link—and since Virginia was the oldest of the crown's North American colonies and by the eve of the Revolution the richest and most populous, he was a key link—in a complex bureaucratic chain that stretched throughout the Caribbean and the continent of North America. His office entailed vital political, military, and revenue responsibilities but his actual power was limited and he periodically found himself a shuttlecock between the authorities in England and the increasingly assertive colonial legislature.[20]

The governor received his commission or instructions from the ministry in London. Though details of government evolved and the balance of powers subtly shifted, at the time the Palace was built the governor acted on behalf of the king in granting land and in naming officers to places of trust in the colonial government. He ordered elections for the lower house of assembly—the House of Burgesses—and convened, prorogued, or dissolved the house. He presided over the appointive Council ("his Majesty's Council in Virginia"), the colonial equivalent of the upper house of assembly, and managed its executive business. He recommended to the crown new appointments to the Council. He also presided over the General Court, serving as supreme justice of its courts of chancery and appeals. He could exercise his power in criminal proceedings and issue special conclusions of oyer and terminer to county courts to try slaves. In addition to certain authority in naval affairs, the governor bore responsibility for commissioning officers for the land forces and the militia, the latter increasingly delegated to

THE SETTING 49

county lieutenants or regional "colonels." He was commander in chief of any standing army except when the crown had appointed a career officer to serve on the continent. His was the ultimate responsibility for the payment of public money in the colony, to present ministers for induction into their parishes and to discipline them, and to issue certificates of naturalization and licenses for marriage and ordinaries.[21]

Twelve members of the Council were appointed by the crown to assist the governor, to advise and consent to his role in Virginia. Drawn from the colony's social and political elite, the Council became a progressively coequal body with the governor as the century advanced, involved with him in nearly every area of his responsibility, often against his wish. The Council convened on the governor's authority but appointed interim or acting governors from its membership to assure continuity of government between the departure or death of a chief executive and his return or the arrival of his successor. It met in its own richly appointed chamber in the Capitol, had its own clerk, and accumulated its own increasingly important law library. It also met from time to time at the Palace, presumably in the great room in the second story. Though the relationship and interaction of the governor and the Council was frequently colored by vigorous dissent, opposition, even strife, councillors were closest to the governor in authority, responsibility, and experience as well as in culture and attainment.[22]

Members of the lower house of assembly and its officials such as the Speaker and the clerk frequently consulted with the governor at the Palace on matters of state or local concern and mingled socially in its assembly rooms at festive times or in the dining room on more personal occasions. Councillors also came to the Palace frequently, as individuals or as a group. So did lawyers on legal and judicial business, clergymen on religious matters or career prospects, officers on military or militia details, Indian agents, sea captains for Mediterranean passes, foreigners seeking to change their nationality, and a multitude of petitioners for the governor's favor or influence. Visiting British government officials and dignitaries came to visit and stay. Men with a range of letters of reference and introduction presented themselves. Indian chieftains or their emissaries came on vital matters of security or local matters of discontent to pay their own equivalents of state visits.

Symbolically the head of the extended family of the entire colony, the governor was also the head of a household "family" of some twenty to thirty persons whose sole task was to sustain him in person and in office. This group of people included his wife, who was expected to share the responsibilities of hosting official visitors to the residence, a secretary and clerks, white servants both free and indentured, and slaves. In addition, the governor occasionally had a private secretary, full governors were entitled to a chaplain, and some governors' wives had children with attendant nurses and/or governesses as well as a companion (often a female relative).[23]

The governor's secretary or clerk maintained an official space either in the main house or in a room in one of the dependencies and shared it with clerks who transcribed letters and filed documents. This individual was generally a Virginian or someone who had lived in and been accepted by the community, undoubtedly providing periodically a local point of view or information that was valuable to the governor. The clerk may have acted as de facto private secretary to some of the governors. He presumably executed certain of the governor's routine tasks such as the signing of licenses and the issuance of Mediterranean passes. In Botetourt's time the latter were kept in the large closet off the front parlor, which suggests that the room was a primary or subsidiary work station for this official. In the 1760s and 1770s the clerk was subsequently appointed to the minor but still relatively lucrative government post of keeper of the Public Gaol as a reward for meritorious service to the governor.[24]

For single or unaccompanied governors the steward or butler (or housekeeper in lesser establishments) assumed responsibility for the household service activities. Included in his or her duties was supervision of the maintenance and daily cleaning of the house and contents by a variety of staff ranging from the "groom of the chambers" to housemaids and chambermaids. The steward or butler supervised the footmen when they were standing guard in the hall, on call, carrying messages and running errands into town, or, at the most demanding time of the regular day—midday dinner—doubling as waiters. The dining table and other aspects of the dinner ritual required expert supervision by the butler in its extensive preparation and in the gathering of a varied assortment of equipment

Topcoat and waistcoat of a suit of livery for Lord Botetourt's male servants, reproduced from an eighteenth-century example in Colonial Williamsburg's collections. The colors are documented as Botetourt's, while the large, conspicuous brass buttons are embossed with the crest from his coat of arms. CWF.

including plate and glass from the pantry, china from the little middle room and its closet under the main stairs and the kitchen supply area, and wine, beer, and other liquors from the cellars. Wine had to be most carefully handled and decanted. The housekeeper supervised the cleaning and constant airing of the bedchambers, the changing and periodic delousing of the beds, the sanitary procedures, and seasonal changes of curtains, carpets, and linens. In Marshman's case the butler was also the bookkeeper, eventually for the entire establishment. He kept the petty cash and other valuables in the strong box in his office (the pantry) and maintained very careful watch over the large quantity of valuable silver or plate stored there when not in use.

Supervising the varied operations and staff of the kitchen complex was the province of the cook, who sometimes also acted as housekeeper. Under cooks and specialists such as pastry cooks worked in the kitchen with the help of kitchen maids and with supplies brought in by the larder maid and the dairy maid. The scullery maid kept the china and other utensils of food preparation and service clean in her work area, while the laundry maid washed and ironed the table linen as well as bedding and personal clothing in hers. Lengthy food preparation and careful cooking, fastidious handling and inventorying of valuable dinner, breakfast, and tea china, glass, and linen, and maintaining the varied and complex equipment used to perform or assist in all of the above tasks required constant vigil. The importance of this area of the household's operations, together with the value of the supplies and equipment involved, accounted for the high ranking that a cook merited in the family hierarchy. Much thought and skillful planning were involved in the main meal of the day at which the governor frequently entertained numerous guests. Supper, too, constituted a meal in which visitors to the Palace were involved. On ceremonial occasions the quality of the food offerings and the way they were displayed in the supper room were critical to the success of the "brilliant" events. Every day a minimum of twenty persons in the household had to be fed. The kitchen was a functional area in which plentiful resources and much trust were invested, and the governor took care to see that the trust was not abused and his resources dissipated.

The third functional area of the household contained the indispensable components of livestock and wheeled vehicles, the foodstuffs production for the kitchen, and the visual and cultural enhancement of the environs of the house (the gardens and park). In more ambitious households these functions were supervised by the land steward. To him fell the responsibility for the numerous vehicles ranging from the prestigious and valuable coach, ornate carriages, and chairs to the humble but indispensable cart (for everyday delivery). These items were kept in the coach house under the direction of a coachman who might also double as the carter. Extremely valuable and highly prestigious when a matched set, the horses were the shared responsibility of coachman and groom. In their living quarters in

"Cuisinier, Patissier, Traiteur, Rotisseur," an engraving from Diderot's Encyclopédie *of 1771, shows a remarkably well-equipped and well-staffed kitchen in operation. The extensive array of intricate equipment for the kitchen in the Botetourt inventory, the number of specialists known to have been employed, particularly for special occasions, and the possibility that Lord Dunmore employed a French cook make this a not unreasonable illustration for the operation of the Palace kitchen.* H: 9½"; W: 6½". CWF 1953-46.

The horses and wheeled vehicles, the great quantity of highly specialized equipment associated with them, and the number of staff required to operate and maintain it all meant that this aspect of Palace life required a massive investment and spacious quarters. This English print of the 1750s, drawn by J. Seymour and engraved by T. Burford, shows a section of a well-appointed stables. H: 11⅜"; W: 15½". CWF 1956-123.

coach house and stables, these two servants kept and maintained the varied and extensive equipment used with the horses and vehicles. Maintenance or repair work on a larger scale required the services of the resident blacksmith and carpenter, both of whom needed special facilities. Stable boys might double as gardeners and, under the supervision of the head gardener, help with the livestock and poultry and with the foodstuffs production areas, the Palace park or farm, and the kitchen garden. Maintaining and constantly improving the formal gardens was the head gardener's task. It was necessary for him to keep abreast of current fashion and taste in that sphere.

Senior servants were assigned single or shared chambers in the garret of the main house, the kitchen, or the stables complex. The size and quality of their furnishings depended on their rank. Lower servants might share a room with upper servants or be assigned a space to share with their work-related equipment. The lowest servants and the slaves slept in attics or were relegated to spaces that served a guard function near valuable items like the horses. All these servants and slaves and the functions they performed contributed to the pyramidal support system at the peak of which stood the governor.

The Botetourt inventory and its related documents form the primary evidence from which this cultural study of life at the Governor's Palace derives. Since Lord Botetourt purchased a large number of items sight unseen from the estate of his predecessor, Francis Fauquier, then discovered on his arrival that he could employ many of them in similar spaces and situations, periodic reference is made in this study to Fauquier's cultural ambitions and attainments as well as to Botetourt's. Fauquier was closer in temper and in culture to the nobleman than any of the other officials who resided in the building. But analysis of the building and its spaces is incomplete without repeated references back in time to the earlier occupants as well as occasional excursions forward in time to the brief and unsettled administration of the last royal representative to hold office in the Palace, Lord Dunmore. With the physical nature of the setting established—the construction of the building, the disposition of its spaces, the official and personal responsibilities of the incumbent and the staff needed to sustain him—it is necessary to review the earlier occupants' contributions to the composite tradition of culture that Botetourt and Fauquier inherited when they assumed office.

Alexander Spotswood was the first executive to reside in the Governor's Palace, but in defining the nature of the cultural tradition in Williamsburg it is impossible to overlook the governor who envisioned the building, who may even have helped to design it, Governor Francis Nicholson. The latter's legacy in Williamsburg and its effect on future generations was enormous even though he left the colony before construction of the Palace started. Nicholson's achievements both literally and figuratively set the stage for cultural growth in the capital city in the succeeding seven decades. Lieutenant governor of Virginia from 1690 to 1692, Nicholson resided in Williamsburg as full governor from 1698 to 1705. In between these tours of duty he served as lieutenant governor of Maryland and was instrumental in—probably chiefly responsible for—the design of its new capital, Annapolis, with its intriguing variation on the baroque town plan and the establishment there of certain public buildings including the statehouse and King William School (to which he made important donations). During his first short incumbency in Virginia Nicholson was heavily involved as donor and sponsor in the establishment of the College of William and Mary at the old Middle Plantation (soon to be renamed Williamsburg). An active trustee of the college, he probably helped to procure a design for the building while he was in England from 1692 to 1694. It was natural for this former army officer turned civil servant to seek assistance through the conventional channels of the Office of the King's Works, the surveyor general of which was Christopher Wren. Within a generation it had become Williamsburg lore that the first college building was constructed to a design by Wren (more probably one of his assistants in the office) but adapted to local conditions by responsible authorities in the colony.[25]

Nicholson's second incumbency saw no less than his design of the new Virginia capital and the establishment of colonial government there in the most ambitious statehouse—or Capitol as he symbolically named it—built up to that time in the American colonies. Little more than an embryo community in the late 1690s, Middle Plantation possessed an Anglican church and, more importantly, a fledgling college and grammar school. It thus seemed an auspicious location, away from the unhealthy environment of Jamestown, for the new center of government and the new assembly building made necessary by the destruction of the previous one by fire in 1698. Nicholson's primary role in the geometric layout of the town, its axial main street stretching between the college and the Capitol, is beyond dispute; his influence on the form of the new statehouse was probably

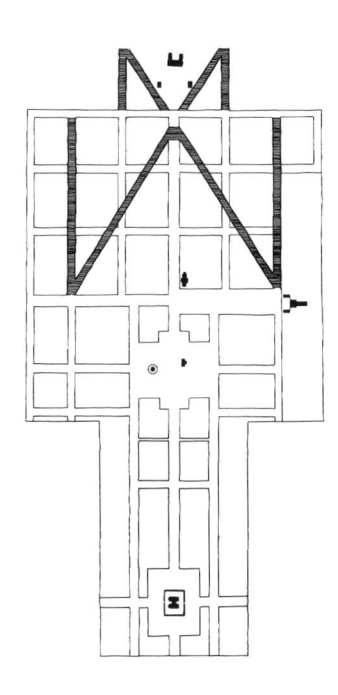

The Capitol as reconstructed 1930–1932 from the south showing the apsidal ends (revealed by archaeology) of the General Court room on the left and the lower house of assembly, the House of Burgesses, on the right.

The town plan of Williamsburg "as it might have been developed by Francis Nicholson" early in the eighteenth century. Conjectural drawing by John W. Reps.

equally decisive. It is instructive to see the building through the eyes of an Oxford graduate, Hugh Jones, who held the chair of natural philosophy and mathematics at the College of William and Mary, 1717–1721. Jones visited the Capitol when it had been in use for several years and the small town was beginning to take shape. In glowing terms he portrayed the building as "a noble, beautiful, and commodious pile . . . built . . . by the direction of the Governor." He called attention to the ways in which the building's form followed function—"The Secretary's office with all the courts of justice and law, held in the same form, and near the same manner, as in England," with one side of the H-shaped building being devoted largely to the House of Burgesses, "not unlike the House of Commons," and the upper floor on the other side containing the Council Chamber, "where the Governor and Council sit in very great state, in imitation of the King and Council, or the Lord Chancellor and House of Lords."[26]

The prototypes that Jones cited were obviously crucial to Nicholson's grand design. The new city was given a momentous name that linked it directly to the king. The center for higher learning had already been granted the names of the joint monarchs. An English prototype had already given its name to the church. The title of the young prince, the duke of Gloucester, in whom was vested the royal succession, was conferred on the main street. The new center for government, endowed with a grand but potent lineage by its Roman title, was based on the quintessential British symbols of Commons and Lords and the laws ensuing from them. All of these elements were carefully contrived within the discipline or

THE SETTING 55

"civilized order" of a baroque town plan, the type that was much favored in Restoration England after the great fire of London.[27]

Nicholson played a pivotal role in setting down in the wilderness in bricks and mortar the great symbols of civilized British society. All of the subsequent colonial governors lived with them. The only element not in place by the time of his departure was the executive, administrative center, separated from the legislative. Since the site for it was carefully planned and he had been instructed to send a design for it to London, and since money was appropriated for it by the assembly and construction began only a year after his departure, the suspicion that Nicholson had already addressed his considerable talents to the matter of the Palace's design is inescapable. Nicholson was by nature a builder, fascinated not only with the grand design but also in the details of planning and architecture sufficiently to become in later years a subscriber to Colen Campbell's immensely influential pattern book, *Vitruvius Britannicus*.[28]

Though Nicholson appears to have been denied a formal education and had, indeed, come to maturity in the army, as a boy he had served in the household of Lady St. John (later the Marchioness Winchester), which probably gave him a cultural education he could not otherwise have received. Through this post he came into contact with the Yorkshire gentry. Proof of his intellectual curiosity and attainment is evident in his later election as fellow of the Royal Society. William Byrd II of Virginia also became a member of that august body in 1697. Nicholson's preoccupation with symbols of culture is illustrated by such diverse actions as the presentation of a silver mace to the House of Burgesses, a large contribution toward the cost of installing the portrait of the monarch in the Council chamber of the Capitol, the placement of a carved relief in "cutt bricks" on the Capitol with emblems of the sun, moon, and Jupiter above the queen's name, and the institution of annual "Olympick Games" modeled on the ancient ritual for young men in Virginia. His widespread patronage of the Anglican church in America and its support organization, the Society for the Propagation of the Gospel in Foreign Parts, has been estimated to total over two thousand pounds, a huge sum for a man without inherited wealth. His beneficence reached Bruton Parish Church in Williamsburg and the chapel of the College of William and Mary, of course. He gave both cash and tangible objects to the cause of education in the New World, scholarships, buildings, and endowments. Many years before his death he decided that his personal library should form the basis for the library of the College of William and Mary. The catalog of his books that he drew up in 1695 reveals his deep and abiding interest in theology as well as in history, philosophy, and the natural world. He was a patron of naturalists and cartographers. John Banister, author of a "Treatise on the Flora and Fauna of Virginia," and Mark Catesby, who lived for several years in Williamsburg before returning to England to produce his massive *Natural History of Carolina, Florida and the Bahama Islands*, benefitted

Signature of Francis Nicholson from a letter of 1698. Blathwayt Papers, CWF.

Modern rendering of the Palace compound. CWF.

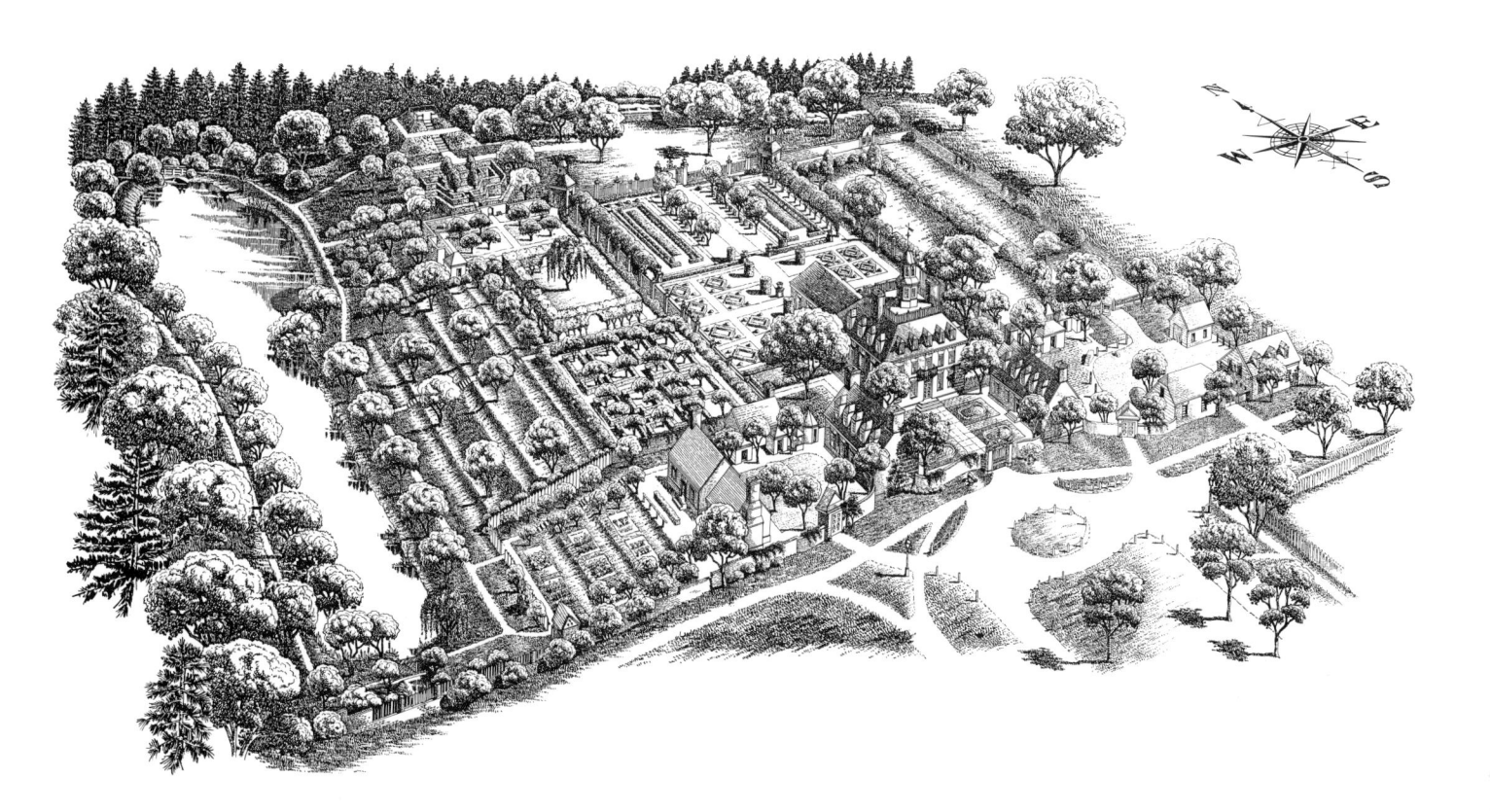

from his support and encouragement. He personally financed what was perhaps the most lavish and ambitiously orchestrated ceremony ever held in Williamsburg to commemorate the death of William III and the accession of Queen Anne in 1702.[29]

Unquestionably a man with a grand vision, imperious and obsessed according to some Virginia oligarchs, "born drunk" in the opinion of a native American onlooker, Nicholson put the precise and clearly demarcated stamp of the English heritage on the Chesapeake landscape with dramatic success.[30] His great accomplishment and enduring legacy, in the short span of seven years and in what was still essentially a rude and untamed land, was no less than to give form, substance, and almost instant visibility to the heritage and to articulate it so deftly that no one could be under any misapprehension. With it came the full panoply of state, royalty, ancient tradition, civil liberties, and splendid civilities. Culturally as well as politically this heritage was potent and highly visible; the great *crises de conscience* that many suffered in the years immediately preceding the Revolution attest to its efficacy. This was the accomplishment of a man of action certainly, but a thoughtful, sensitive, cultured one—no brusque soldier-administrator.

Nicholson was succeeded (after the brief incumbency of Edward Nott) by another unusual ex-soldier, Lieutenant Governor Alexander Spotswood. On his arrival in Williamsburg in 1710, Spotswood found the Governor's Palace far from complete. With the style and brio that seemed imperious to some colonists, Spotswood set to, goading the assembly to appropriate additional funds for the building and assuming control of the project himself. He completed the pavilions and outbuildings and lingered affectionately over the interior appointments of the main house, conspicuous among which was an ornamental display of weapons in the front hall. His supporters found the contrivances he introduced "ingenious" and "accomplished" while his detractors found them spendthrift. He took such pains over the details that adversaries accused him of misusing public funds, an easy front for more deep-seated political opposition. When he turned his ambitions to the immediate environs of the Palace he alienated other powerful Virginians. His plans to enhance the long approach to the Palace from town, for example, brought him into conflict with John Custis. "I think he called it a visto," wrote the native-born garden enthusiast with a note of chagrin that he had not known the fashionable terminology or of scorn for Spotswood's pretentiousness.[31] Behind the walls and fences of the Palace compound the lieutenant governor shaped terraces or "Falling Gardens," dammed a stream to create an ornamental canal and fishpond, and established "fine gardens . . . walks . . . orchards," and "a very large Park . . . [for] Deer," all appropriate gentry embellishments for this first mansion in the capital. Whether or not his plans for the gardens were influenced by the 1715 edition of Piganiol de la Force's *Description des Chateaux et Parcs de Versailles* that he later presented to the college is unknown. But his ownership of the volume is indicative of the scope of his interest in this subject. It was during his administration that the building came to be called the Governor's "Palace" rather than "House." Some historians have interpreted this as a derisory term and have attributed it to Spotswood's opponents, but it was surely commensurate with the lieutenant governor's well-developed and well-known sense of official decorum that the residence should assume an established title for the executive center of a large governmental district. The term was appropriate, without evident derision, when Tryon built his residence in New Bern, North Carolina, some fifty years later.[32]

Spotswood also played a key role between 1710 and 1716 in the rebuilding of the college (devastated by the 1705 fire) in the form in which it was subsequently known, depicted on the "Bodleian plate" of about 1740 and in the portrait of the first president, James Blair, about 1735–1740. He designed a new brick building for Bruton Church and contributed one-third of its construction cost. He also built a brick powder magazine located in the middle of the town. In his mind the cultural heritage that he saw around him in Williamsburg needed the bulwark of such a military presence with its reassuring prospect of military success (in one of the most glorious phases of which he himself had participated, with the armies of John Churchill, duke of Marlborough, in the Low Countries). Spotswood's embellishments of Nicholson's design for the new capital city were thus considerable—he

Alexander Spotswood, oil on canvas, attributed to Charles Bridges, Virginia, ca. 1735. H: 52"; W: 39½". This somewhat damaged painting has long been attributed as a likeness of the forceful soldier-administrator. The distant view may represent the garrison of Tangier, his birthplace. When this portrait was painted, Spotswood had been out of power for thirteen years and had assumed his role of a Virginia colonel and entrepreneur. CWF 1940-359.

THE SETTING 59

completed the axial part of the town plan that terminated in the executive center of government, resuscitated the main building of the college, helped to create a modern brick structure for the established church, and perpetuated the military presence in the capital by the construction of the magazine.[33]

Though he expended much of his formidable energy on securing the frontiers of the colony against the threat of the Indians, French, and Spanish, Spotswood was still a cultural force. "It is difficult to be determined in which respect he chiefly excelled," observed Hugh Jones, who admired the governor's accomplishments, "Either in being a compleat gentleman, a polite scholar, a good governor, or a true churchman." Behind the banalities of Jones's prose is the substance of Spotswood's considerable achievement. The lieutenant governor maintained the patterns of patronage that his predecessor had established, though without the earlier official's unusual personal generosity. His sponsorship and participation in a major building program for the capital were fundamental. His layout of the Palace gardens contributed significantly to the tradition of Williamsburg becoming a garden city, a characteristic that attracted much comment by the end of the colonial period. To balls or "assemblies" in the city he brought new vigor and a constant patronage, and he was influential, perhaps responsible, for the appearance of the theater on Palace green by 1716, the first theater on an established site in all the American colonies. Less noteworthy a patron of education than his predecessor, Spotswood still provided a school for Indians at Fort Christanna and paid its expenses himself. Constantly aspiring to a courtly style, he left an enduring legacy at the Palace in the arrangement of weapons in the hall; the display was expanded and preserved by successive occupants until the building was vacated by the last representative of royal government. His early friendships with a number of the richest and most powerful of the Virginia gentry and his subsequent adoption of the role of Virginia gentleman on vast estates in Spotsylvania County in the second quarter of the century as the Virginia gentry enjoyed their first cultural flowering reveal the strength of the bond between the British heritage and the colonial gentry to which Nicholson had given such cogent visible expression.[34]

Following the very brief administration of Lieutenant Governor Hugh Drysdale, Lieutenant Governor William Gooch arrived to find the Palace "an excellent one indeed, all manner of conveniences that you can imagine, an handsome Garden, an orchard ful of Fruit, and a very large Park."[35] His incumbency (1727–1749) spanned the second quarter of the century and paralleled the entrenchment and enrichment of polite society in Virginia, the manifest increase in gentility and civility, the cultural advancement conjoined with material expansion. Many proud brick mansions stimulated and inspired in part by the Governor's Palace were erected during Gooch's administration by one or more members of Virginia's great families—the Burwells, Byrds, Carters, Lees,

View of the "Wren Building" taken from the portrait of James Blair, first president of the college, attributed to Charles Bridges, 1735–1740. This view shows the building seen from Brafferton School. The phoenix is, of course, a reference to Blair's successful efforts to raise endowment for the fledgling institution.

Westover, the Byrd family seat, built on the banks of the James River by William Byrd II or his son and perhaps the most famous of all Virginia's colonial mansions. It is certainly the one most frequently used as the symbol of English gentrification of the colony.

Harrisons, Pages, Randolphs, and Wormeleys, to cite the more conspicuous. The first academic portraitist arrived in the colony with letters of introduction to Gooch and proceeded to memorialize this generation of colonists in oil on canvas, including the first (and only) colonial Virginian ever knighted, Sir John Randolph. A nobleman, Lord Fairfax, arrived to take possession of ancestral lands—a suitable adornment for the increasingly self-conscious gentry society. William Parks established himself in the still small capital, published a weekly newspaper, and printed official works for the governor and legislature. He also issued pamphlets and books on such eminently gentry topics as fencing, an exercise in which Gooch was eager for his son to distinguish himself. Parks established at his printing office a retail outlet for books imported from London that was still operated by his successors when Thomas Jefferson was governor, 1778–1780.[36]

The college forecourt was completed during Gooch's administration by the addition of the President's House, and John Custis developed at the terminus of the Palace vista what was reputedly the finest garden in colonial America. Peter Scott, the first cabinetmaker in Virginia known by name, established himself in the city and remained for almost forty years, playing a prominent role in the creation of a distinct regional school of furniture making. When the Capitol burned in 1747, the same year that Gooch received a baronetcy, the governor took a decisive part in resisting determined factional efforts to move the capital of the colony farther inland. Too great an investment had already been made, in the minds of Gooch and cooler-headed Virginians, in making visible in Williamsburg all the symbols and appurtenances of civilized British society. The Capitol was accordingly rebuilt and equipped with a separate structure for the storage of records that stretched back almost one hundred and fifty years, the oldest English records on the American continent.[37]

During Gooch's governorship came large prints from England of the natural life of the colony drawn and engraved by Mark Catesby, who had spent some years in Virginia on two earlier visits, befriended and encouraged by Francis Nicholson and such gentry as William Byrd II, John Custis, and John Clayton. Catesby perpetuated the tradition of scientific curiosity that was at least a century old—John Tradescant had journeyed to Virginia in 1637. The great Popple map of North America was completed at this time, and work began on the map that eventually became known as the Fry–Jefferson map of Virginia, the most complete and successful depiction of the colony in the colonial period. Thus the boundaries, settlements, and topography of the colony and important elements of its flora and fauna were clearly and scientifically delineated and circulated.[38]

The powder magazine and guardhouse located in the center of the town represented imperial strength in defense against potential threats, both European and native American. Spotswood saw a line of such military buildings, including wooden forts and outposts, as a vital necessity for the protection of British gains on the continent.

62 PROLOGUE

Bruton Parish Church took its present cruciform from its rebuilding by Spotswood during his tenure as lieutenant governor. The tower and steeple at the west end were added during the residency of Lord Botetourt. The brick structure provided further visible proof of the entrenchment of government in the colonial capital and of the cultural attainment of society there.

Robert Dinwiddie (lieutenant governor from 1751 to 1758) is a shadowy figure in the cultural history of Williamsburg. Inspecting the Palace after Gooch's departure in 1749, members of the Council found it "in ruinous condition," a marked contrast to the lieutenant governor's satisfied declaration of twenty years before. Extensive refurbishment and the addition of a large wing containing the ballroom and the supper room prepared the Palace for Dinwiddie's occupancy by 1752. During the 1750s the major preoccupation of governor and gentry became the defense of what had been attained and established by imperial Britain on the American continent against the threat of imperial France. The "years of defeat" from 1754–1757 engrossed Britons who had settled on the American continent—how could they best organize themselves against incursion and how much could they persuade the ministry to contribute?—as much as it engaged the authorities in London, who were determined to repel the French and were desperate for as much local assistance (men, money, matériel) as they could

THE SETTING 63

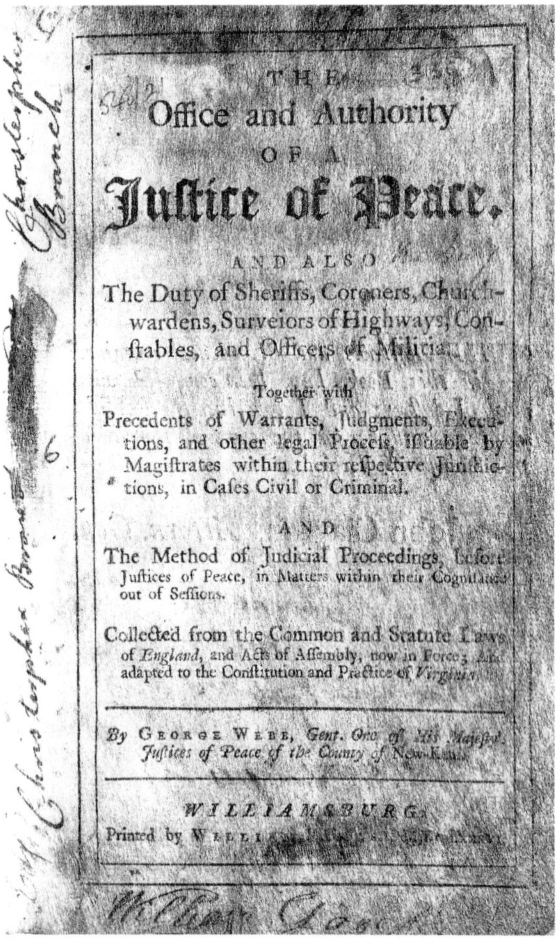

THE

Office and Authority

OF A

Justice of Peace.

AND ALSO

The Duty of Sheriffs, Coroners, Church-wardens, Surveiors of Highways, Constables, and Officers of Militia.

Together with

Precedents of Warrants, Judgments, Executions, and other legal Process, issuable by Magistrates within their respective Jurisdictions, in Cases Civil or Criminal.

AND

The Method of Judicial Proceedings, before Justices of Peace, in Matters within their Cognizance out of Sessions.

Collected from the Common and Statute Laws of *England*, and Acts of Assembly, now in Force; and adapted to the Constitution and Practice of *Virginia*.

By GEORGE WEBB, *Gent. One of His Majesty's Justices of Peace of the County of New-Kent.*

WILLIAMSBURG:

Printed by WILLIAM [illegible]

Right, Henry Popple's grand, eight-feet-high map of the British Empire in America, with "The French and Spanish Settlements adjacent thereto," published in London in 1733. Compiled for government purposes, this was the first map of North America in the eighteenth century to attempt great inclusiveness and complete accuracy. While failing in both these aspects, it was nevertheless dispatched to the official centers of each of the colonies and remained the official reference as well as a monument of mapmaking for many years. CWF 1955-408.

Left, blue jay, engraved and colored by Mark Catesby in London, 1731–1745, from drawings he made during his residence in Virginia earlier in the century. His was the first published natural history of the southern colonies, a monumental achievement. H: 13¾"; W: 20¼". CWF 1984-147, 68.

Mann Page II by Charles Bridges, painted in the Williamsburg area, 1740–1745. This portrait is a superb realization of the generation of colonial gentry who stamped authority and culture on the otherwise untamed wilderness of Virginia. H: 46½"; W: 36½". *Courtesy, Joseph and Margaret Muscarelle Museum of Art, College of William and Mary.*

Lieutenant Governor William Gooch's copy of George Webb's Office and Authority of a Justice of the Peace, *printed in Williamsburg in 1736 by William Parks.* CWF.

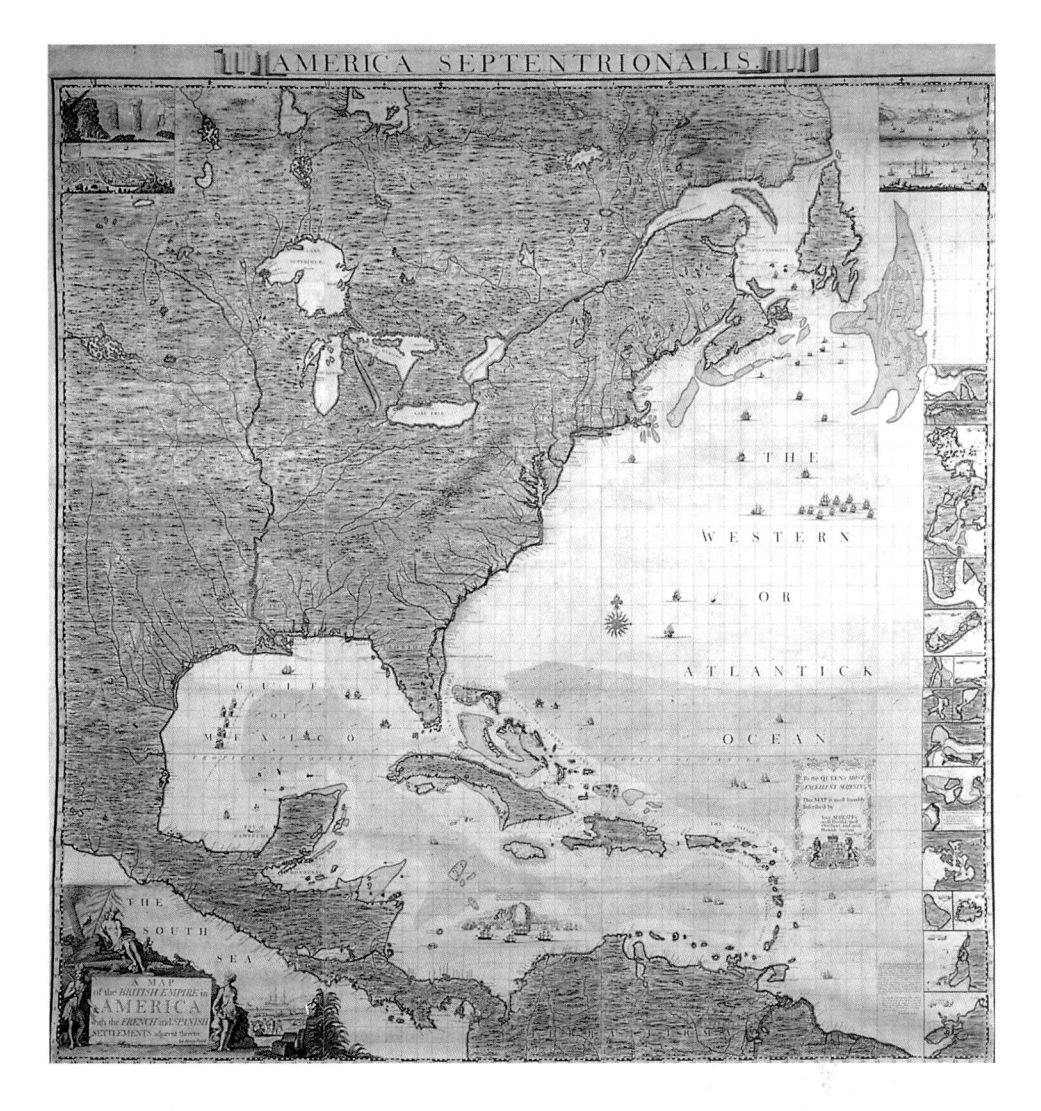

possibly get. Too much was at stake. In these years polarization began to develop between British-Americans, who were determined to avail themselves of all elements of their British heritage, and British authorities, who failed to understand that their distant progeny were fast coming of age.[39]

Setting a pattern that was repeated for each of the succeeding governors, Virginians engaged in the disbursement and acquisition of the more conspicuous of Dinwiddie's personal effects when he left the colony after his short administration. His coach was acquired by a member of the Braxton family; his chariot and beds were bought by Peter Randolph; his tea table and the plate, especially the fashionable epergne, were purchased by the Tayloe family; and his silver table was acquired by a Page family member. This presaged a period of unparalleled material consumption in the following fifteen years. English exports to North America rose 120 percent in the period 1750–1773. The "consumer revolution"

To be SOLD *at* John Greenhow's *Store, near the Church, in* WILLIAMSBURG, *for ready Money, on reasonable Terms,*

BROADCLOTHS, Stuffs, Shags, Flannels, Negro Cotton, Rolls, Ofnabrugs, *Irish* Linens, Sheeting, Linen, Cambricks, Lawns, Muslins, *India* Damasks, white Calicoes, Humhums, *India* Dimity, printed Linens, Cottons and Calicoes, Cloaks and Cardinals, genuine Drugs and Medicines, Wholesale or Retail, at an unusual low Price, particularly the best picked Bark, Crucibles, Silversmiths casting Sand, Anvils, small and large Shears, and most Sorts of Tools for that Business, Watchmakers Tools, and a Variety of Materials for the Trade, Sets of Blacksmiths Tools, complete or separate, Surveyors Instruments, and Books for their Instruction, a large Assortment of Carpenters and Cabinet Makers Tools and Materials, Tools and Materials for almost every Business, various Sorts of Instruments for drawing Teeth, Pocket Cases of Surgeons Instruments, genteel Dressing Boxes for Travellers, Pinking Irons, Sheet Iron, Iron Pots from one Quart to twenty five Gallons, Iron Dogs and Backs, Iron and Copper Tea Kettles, Mortars, Skillets, Salamanders, Bread Hoes, a great Variety of Mill Saws, Pit and Crosscut Saws, Saws of all Sorts, with both Steel and Iron Plates, very neat Fowling Pieces with false Breeches, Bridle Locks, Water Pans, Rasps and Files of almost all Sorts and Sizes, Steel of all Sorts, Spinet Keys and Wire, wove Brass Wire for Wheat Fans and Riddles, Ditto for *Indian* Meal and Flower, Closestool, Bed, and Warming Pans, polishing Powders of most Sorts, Borax, crude Sal Ammoniac and Argol, Logwood, Redwood, Fustick, Madder, Galls, Alum, Copperas, Indigo, Old Spirits, best and common Arrack, *Madeira, Lisbon,* red Port, Claret, *Canary,* and *Renish* Wines, mixed Sweetmeats, preserved Ginger, Orange Chips, candied Angelica, Barley Sugar, white and brown Sugar Candy, Anchovies, Olives, Capers, Vinegar, best and common Olive Oil, Groats, Split Peas, Rice, Sago, Salop, all Sorts of Spices, Currants, single and best double Bed Blankets, early Garden Peas, and various Sorts of fresh Garden Seeds, Canary, Rape, Lucern, Timothy, Sainfoin, Clover, Flax, and *French* Furze Seeds, Ounce Threads of most Prices, Cambrick Thread, Cotton, coloured, and Marking Threads, Chalk, Whiting, Garden Spades and Rakes, Ditching Spades, Iron Fenders, Cinder and Dust Shovels, Trevets, Pothooks, flat and Box Irons and Stands, Scythes and Scythe Stones of all Sorts, a Variety of Toys, Jack Chains, Well Chains, Chain Traces and Back Bands, large and small Fryingpans and Drippingpans, Half Gallon Case Bottles, Bottle Corks, Sheet Cork for Seines, Tar, Rosin, Salt, Coffee, Chocolate, Bohea, Green, Congo, and best Hyson Teas, imported before the Association, Candlesticks, a great Variety of Money Scales and Weights, Brass Scales and Weights from one Pound to fifty six, Bed Screws and Bunts, Staymakers Knives, Whalebone, Tabby, Ticking, and every other Material for the Trade, Working Canvas, and Worsteds of all Shades, Tailors Shears and Needles of all Sorts, Hand Reading Glasses and Spectacles, Concave and Convex Ditto, green Preservers and Visuals, Watchmakers Magnifyers, most Sizes of Anchors and Tongues for Silver Buckles, Locks of almost all Sorts, both curious and common, particularly large Iron Case Locks for Doors, and large Padlocks for Prisons, most Sorts of Nails, Hinges, and Materials for Building, Window Glass, Linseed and Train Oil, Paints of most Sorts, Hunting Horns, Dog Collars large and small House Bells, Key and Curtain Rings, Stone Buttons set in Silver, Stone Hair Pins, Tortoiseshell and Horn Poll Combs, Horn, Ivory, and Box Combs, Crystals for Sleeve Buttons, Earrings and Lockets, Foil of various Colours for Jewellers, Hour Glasses, large and small rich China Bowls, China, Glass, Tin, and Delf Ware of most Sorts, Cart and Chair Wheel Boxes of most Sizes, Block Tin, Tin Sheets, Spelter, Pewter Ware, Glass Mortars, Bedticks, Pewter Measures, Ivory Memorandum Books and Pencils, Silk Purses, coarse and fine Hats, Brushes and Pencils of most Sorts, Lamps, Vermin and Beaver Traps, Fiddles and *Roman* Strings, *German* Flutes and Fifes, Shoe Lasts, Wooden Heels, Machine, Shoe, and polishing Blacking, Spinel, Breeches Ball, Buckskin Breeches, Looking Glasses of most Sizes, Flax Hackles, Wool, Cotton, and Stock Cards, Hoes, Axes, Adzes, Trowels, Currying Knives, *Ward*'s Ether for the Headach, Ringworm Earth, Glue, *Mezzotinto* Prints, *Pyrmont* Water, Sifter and Search Bottoms, Coffee Mills, curled Hair, Barbers Pipes, Silk, Thread, and Riband, Candle Moulds, Cock Gaffs, neat Horse and Womens Scissors, Necklaces, Beads and Bugles, most fashionable Sorts of Trimmings for Hat Makers, white, Worsted, and Cotton Stockings of all Sorts, a Variety of Stationary and Books, such as Family Bibles, Dictionaries, Dispensatories, *Tissot* and *Fothergill* on Health, *Bracken's* Farriery, &c. and many Hundreds of other Articles.

66 PROLOGUE

Left above, Francis Fauquier, oil on canvas, attributed to Benjamin Wilson, London, ca. 1757. H: 36"; W: 28". This somewhat dark image shows the future colonial official in his role as philanthropist and humanitarian, for it was painted for the Foundling Hospital of London, where it has remained to this day. Courtesy, Thomas Coram Foundation for Children, London.

Robert Dinwiddie, miniature on ivory, signed C. D., probably by C. Dixon, London, ca. 1749–1751. This shows the experienced bureaucrat probably on the eve of his departure for Virginia, where he was lieutenant governor from late 1751 until early 1758. CWF 1938-177.

List of goods advertised by John Greenhow at his store on Duke of Gloucester Street, adjacent to the Palace vista, in 1771. An amazing variety of goods was offered to the inhabitants of the now burgeoning colonial capital, indicative of the explosion of consumer goods made available to an ever-widening market throughout the empire.

began to occupy men's minds as much as the political one. The deleterious effects of this were noted by the succeeding governor, Francis Fauquier, in a report to the Lords of Trade in 1762 on the subject of the colonial issuance of paper money and the ensuing imbalance in exchange rates with the English sterling standard:

> The great Rise of Exchange is altogether attributed by some Men to the Emissions of [colonial] Paper Currency, but I am entirely of Opinion there is a much more fundamental Cause for this Rise, to wit, the Increase of the Imports, to such a Height that the Crops of Tobacco will not pay for them, so that the Colony is so far from having Money to draw for in England; that they are greatly in Debt already to the Mother Country, which Debt is daily encreasing; as the Merchants of great Brittain too sensibly know.[40]

Lieutenant Governor Francis Fauquier, who succeeded Robert Dinwiddie in 1758, lacked his predecessor's lengthy experience in the colonial bureaucracy but shone as a man of culture and intellect. A former director of the South Sea Company and a cosmopolitan London gentleman, he developed a warm cultural relationship with Virginians that survived the later phases of the Seven Years' War, the vexing problems with the Cherokee Indians, the acrimony of the clerical dissension following the Twopenny Act, the traumas of the Speaker Robinson imbroglio, and the shocking reactions in Virginia to the Stamp Act, the Declaratory Act, and the Townshend Duties. That, in ten years, was no small accomplishment. Humanitarian and enlightened, competent and resolute in office, Fauquier was a "most punctually diligent Man" in the opinion of president of the Council John Blair and "the ablest man who ever filled the chair of government here" in the mature judgment of Thomas Jefferson. He was extraordinarily effective as the embodiment of the urbane and enlightened contemporary British culture.[41]

Fauquier came to Virginia as a fellow of the Royal Society and a corresponding secretary of the Society for the Encouragement of Arts, Manufactures, and Commerce—the latter as apposite a metaphor for his perceived role in Virginia society as could be found. He was the exemplar of the man of culture who used his office to support learning and patronage and his influence to improve the lot of those around him. Young men of good family and intellectual promise profited from his keen interest, while at the opposite end of the social scale the desperately disturbed, the insane, and the enslaved benefitted from his humanitarian beliefs. He did not hesitate to impart his views on the plight of the indigent and native peoples to his superior, General Amherst, whose opinions on such matters were far from admirable. Questioning the wisdom and some of the doctrinal beliefs of the established church was a natural extension of his rational intellect, and he incurred much official displeasure on this account. He left a potent legacy of fearless intellectual investigation and of heterodoxy in that generation of Virginians who played such a prominent part in the creation of a new society and an independent nation.[42]

THE SETTING 67

During his administration, Fauquier witnessed soaring material consumption, the quest by a large cross section of society for the luxury and consumer goods they believed would enhance their modes as well as their standards of living. A commentator in the *British Magazine* in 1763 noted that "the present vogue for imitating the manners of high life hath spread itself so far among the gentle folks of lower life that in a few years we shall probably have no common people at all." Material goods were an increasingly desirable constituent of these "manners," and contemporary obsession with them was as conspicuous in the colonies as in England. In 1762 Fauquier wrote of the growing debt this caused in Virginia. In noting the significance to the English merchants of the consumer trend, he touched a nerve—when political events interrupted or diverted people's minds from the flow of goods, the effect was dramatically evident. Three years later, for example, the colonists' responses to the Stamp Act produced a reaction in manufacturing areas in England as well as in Whitehall:

Of late there has been a total stagnation of all business; thousands of poor manufacturers at Birmingham, Sheffield, Yorkshire, etc. etc. have been turned off, and are now starving for want of employ; and what the consequences will be, unless the Stamp Act is repealed, God only knows, as all the orders for goods to be sent to North America are conditional, and not to be sent until the act is repealed.[43]

Escalating material consumption in the colonies in the third quarter of the eighteenth century highlights the subject of colonial cultural growth. Cultural development in America was as significant for the colonists as their increasing political self-esteem in the period of the Seven Years' War. From the 1740s on, in fact, the colonies grew progressively conscious of their place in the system of English culture that was ever more buoyant and self-confident. They recognized it and exploited it. As luxuries and other consumer goods became more conspicuously an element of taste and culture, and as fashion impelled the constant update and replacement of these goods, so the colonists became more eager consumers and America a more vital market for producers and retailers. Growing increasingly populous and self-confident, the colonies also perceived more clearly their place in a system of perceptions, preferences, and ambitions that had a distinctive national (English) character, even if their physical distance from the cultural capital meant that they nurtured provincial variants of national norms (in the way that English, Scottish, and Irish provinces did). Though some historians have regarded this colonial interdependence as servitude to the superior taste of the mother country while others have heralded American self-assertion and independence in small and inconsequential details, it is clear that the colonies looked on themselves inherently as provinces of the English nation, integral elements in an imperial cultural system which, in fact, constituted their patrimony.[44]

The irony of this development was that their greater maturity and self-confidence did not automatically lead to greater freedom of cultural expression. As

Norborne Berkeley, the future baron de Botetourt, as a young man, ca. 1745–1755, oil on canvas, artist unknown. Courtesy, the Duke of Beaufort.

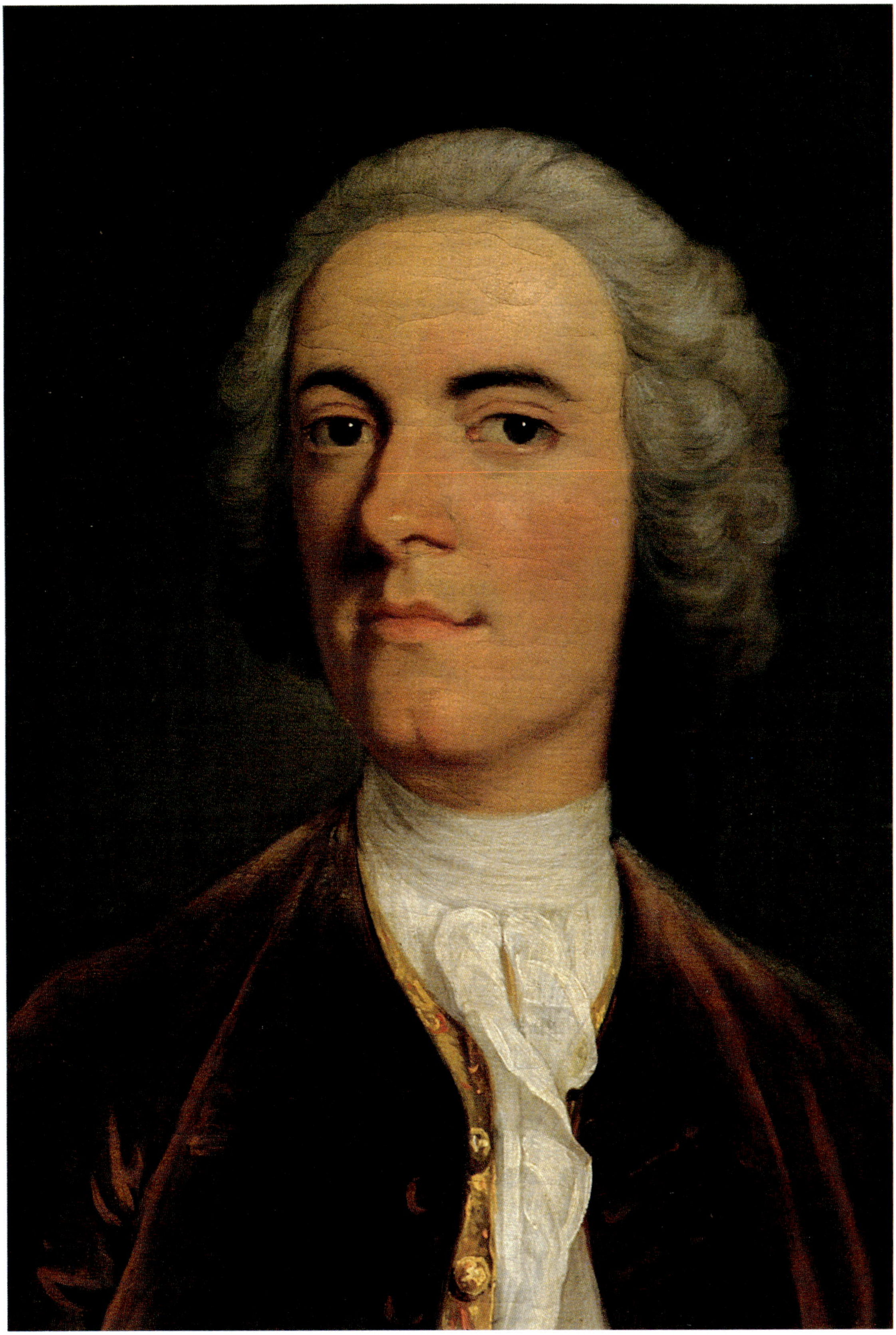

taste became progressively more prescribed and sanctioned by fashion and manufactured goods with their approved standards of modishness became increasingly accessible and desired, as printed and published patterns for buildings, interiors, furnishings, and dress were more widely distributed, so consumers grew more sensitive to approved models and more dependent on them. They became more self-conscious of correct form. This was as true for colonial societies as it was for high-style and gentry levels in England. Though heightened awareness of correct form did not always induce certainty in cultural matters, it did raise the level of consciousness to standards that had passed rigorous inspection by refined minds. This new threshold of awareness, this new level of cultural maturity in colonial society was a notable element of the "setting" into which Fauquier and Botetourt came to pursue their official and personal roles and, importantly, to become for some of their acquaintances role models. It was for their gentlemanly qualities of refinement and virtue that they were elevated in most Virginians' minds above the increasingly strident squabble of politics and were venerated.

How significant events in Virginia in the later years of Fauquier's administration were to the English authorities can be gauged by the decisiveness with which they responded to the lieutenant governor's death. The news reached London in mid-April 1768, shortly before intelligence was received of the circular letters and petitions from American legislatures protesting the Townshend Duties. To a ministry acutely sensitized by colonial reactions to the Stamp Act the new colonial unrest was deeply disturbing. A successor was clearly needed with the forcefulness and authority to impose the ministry's and the king's will on colonial subjects without inflaming them further, a paternal disciplinarian of the right political persuasion. Despite the inconvenient fact that there was a current governor of Virginia—Jeffrey Amherst, who had no intention of taking up his office in the colony—difficult decisions were made, Amherst was removed, and by the end of October Lord Botetourt was in Virginia, the first full governor to step ashore in sixty years.

A member of an ancient West Country family, Norborne Berkeley had been a Tory member of Parliament for Gloucestershire for more than twenty years. He had moved in comfortable gentry circles, developing his inherited coal fields and improving his estates, until his sister, by virtue of her marriage to the younger son of the second duke of Beaufort, became the fourth duchess upon her brother-in-law's death in 1746. Berkeley's political and social standing in the county was thus greatly strengthened. He became a prominent figure in commercial and industrial circles in the prospering port of Bristol. His brother-in-law's death in 1756 resulted in his appointment as one of two trustees for his nephew, the fifth duke, in his minority, a position of great local influence and prestige. On the accession of George III in 1760 and the departure of the Whigs from power, Berkeley became a groom of the bedchamber to the king. He subsequently

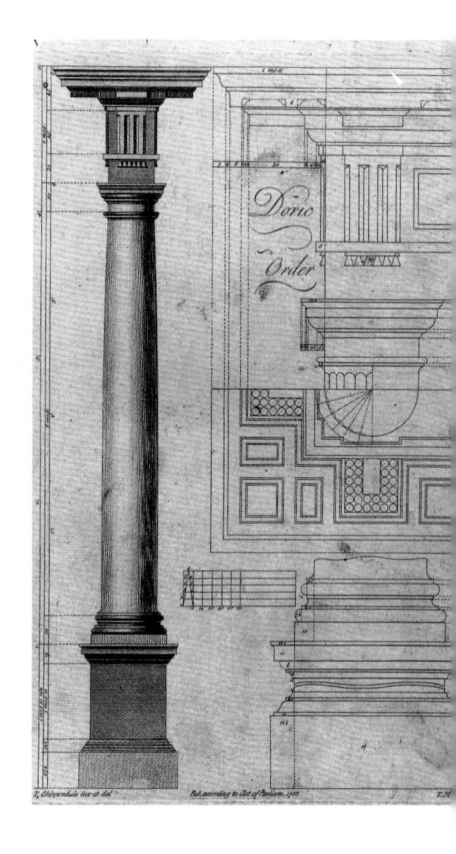

Plate 2 of Thomas Chippendale's Gentleman and Cabinet-maker's Director, *published in London in 1754, a copy of which was subsequently owned in Williamsburg at Anthony Hay's Cabinetmaking Shop on Nicholson Street. Botetourt's brother-in-law was a charter subscriber. The first seven plates of this most famous of all eighteenth-century English pattern books emphasizes the founding of the craft in the classical tradition and the necessity for classical correctness—"The very soul and basis of [the] art."*

Badminton House, Gloucestershire, the main facade to the north. William Kent added the cupolas and pediment in 1746–1747 and remodeled James Gibbs's earlier pavilions. Kent's work took place during the first years of Botetourt's sister being duchess.

petitioned for and was granted the ancient barony of Botetourt, a title that had been connected with the Berkeley family centuries before. Thus in 1764 he moved to the House of Lords and became a lord of the bedchamber at court. In 1768 he was fifty-one years old, lord lieutenant of the county of Gloucester and of the cities of Gloucester and Bristol, politically experienced and reliable, successful and well connected, urbane and sensitive, generous but laconic, a man known for his tactful firmness—"his *douceur* is enamelled on iron," observed Horace Walpole. He left London in August and arrived in Williamsburg on October 26, 1768. Of his new residence he wrote in a letter to his superior, the earl of Hillsborough, Secretary of State: "My house is in admirable order, the ground behind it much broke, well-planted, and water'd by beautiful Rills; and the whole in every respect just as I could wish."[45]

Ceremony

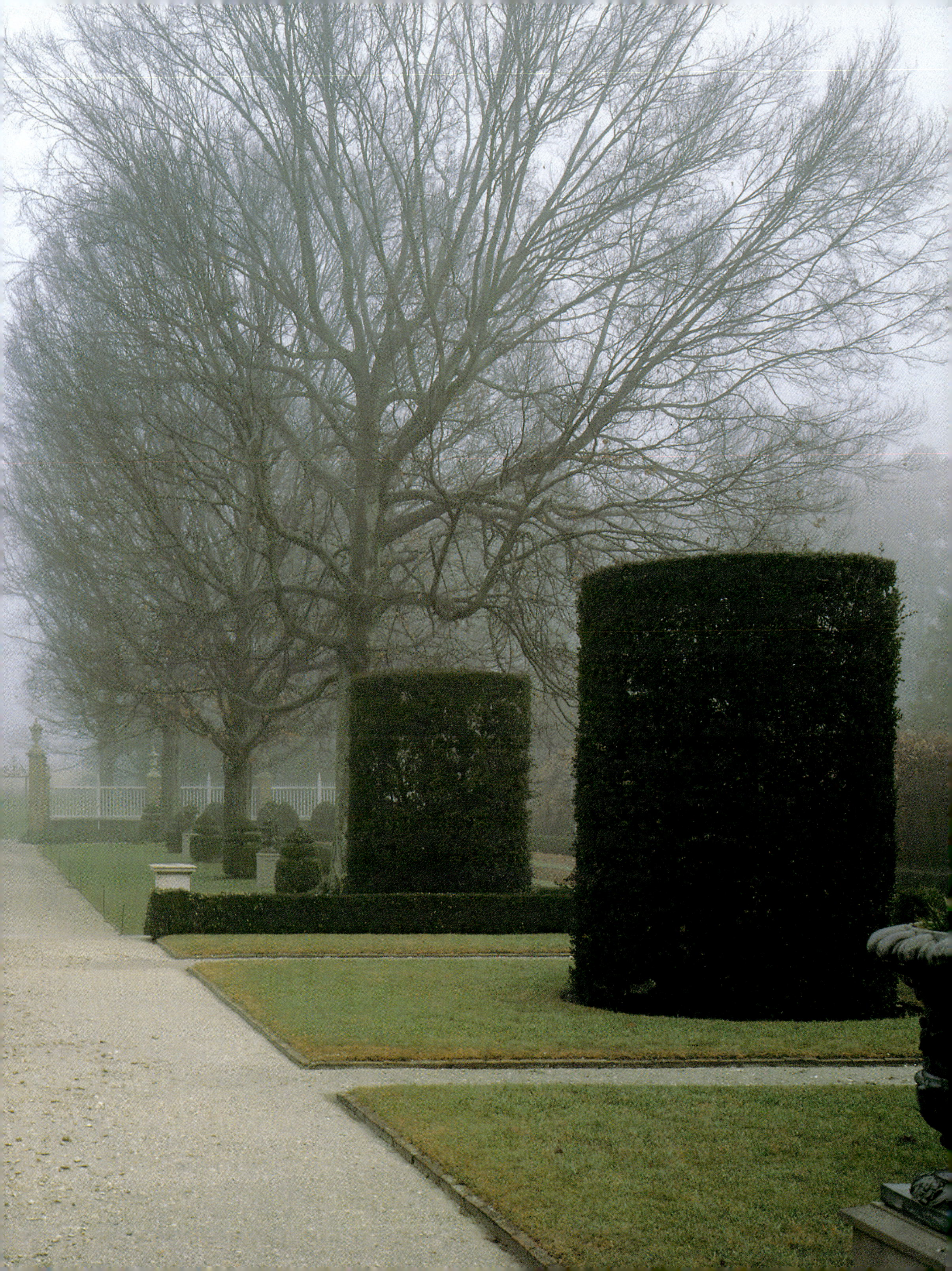

Ceremony

In the buildings used to formulate and administer government, and in the courthouses and the churches that enforced order and generated harmony in eighteenth-century Virginia, ceremony was an essential constituent. The Governor's Palace was one of those buildings. Ceremony reinforced authority by stressing hierarchy—the clearly graded social levels that indicated different degrees of attainment, resources, and responsibility. Ceremony buttressed authority by its reliance on tradition, its adherence to form, and its frequent display of actual or symbolic representations of power. It constantly reaffirmed, in one or more of its component parts, the essential framework of society and helped to focus attention on the power that organized and ordered it. That power was often present at ceremony in symbolic form—the most widespread symbol in colonial Virginia being the royal coat of arms, prominently displayed in buildings used for administrative, legislative, legal, and religious purposes. The royal arms represented, of course, the monarch, not a person but a concept, a symbol itself for Virginians of the protection that the powerful leader of society provided for the people.[1]

Symbolism was an essential part of ceremony. It was evident both in things and in actions. At the Governor's Palace symbols and symbolic actions were most conspicuous in the two most formal rooms in the residence, the hall and the great room in the second story. These were the rooms of parade, of frequent ceremony, and they were filled with symbolic things—the royal coat of arms, the seal of the colony that indicated the governor's power of royal proxy when he attached the seal to important documents, the livery of footmen, and, most distinctive of all because it was most impressive, the great quantity of weapons arranged in formal patterns. The path of parade encompassed the hall, the passage beyond, the great staircase, the upper passage, and the terminus in the great room on the second floor. It was symbolic of the visitor's status or the importance of his mission how far along this path and into the inner core of the residence he would be allowed to proceed. The governor's retainers, his symbolic bodyguard, would screen incomers and allow them to go so far according to their rank. These proceedings would be accompanied by symbolic gestures such as the clear acknowledgment of precedency, the bow, and so on.

At the Palace (a symbolic term) the governor organized and led ceremonies that commemorated special occasions, pertaining most notably to royalty. The anniversary of the monarch's accession, the king's and queen's birthdays, the birth of a successor to the throne, the death or coronation of a monarch—all called for ceremonies that were generally festive in nature. Great military victories for the sovereign state and successful peace treaties were celebrated. State visitors such as neighboring governors and Indian emissaries required different, more formal ceremonies. The Council periodically met at the Palace attended by some ceremony and provided formal celebrations for incoming governors. The governor rode in ceremony in his coach from the Palace to the Capitol to convene or prorogue the lower house of assembly or to take his place as justice in the General Court.

Before mid-century most of the ceremonies enumerated above took place in the hall and extended into the middle room upstairs, two of the three most spacious public rooms in the building. Yet the events outgrew these spaces. It is a measure of the perceived importance of these occasions that the colonial authorities appropriated a substantial sum of money for extra spaces at the Palace for ceremonial assemblies and other large functions. After mid-century most festive occasions would have been concentrated in the new ballroom and supper room while the older spaces were preserved and retained for primarily honorific state occasions. On these an extra measure of dignity was bestowed by the traditional placement of the spaces and by their pointedly symbolic contents.

Certain daily activities were infused with less portentous ceremony. They are often termed rituals and are most visible in the colonial period, because most often recorded, in the lives of the gentry and upper classes. The acts of rising from sleep, for example, often from an ornate bed that was the symbolic descendant of the "bed of state" and of dressing assumed certain ceremonial aspects and were dignified by the term *levee*. Ceremony was evident at mealtimes, particularly the main meal at midday with its distinctive drawing together of host and guests in one space, the intricately sequenced and varied activities of the central part of the ceremony in the main space, then the important withdrawal to yet another space. The richer the household the more carefully planned and lavishly equipped with foodstuffs and accoutrements the event was. The serving and drinking of the novel beverage tea had a ceremony and specialized accoutrements all its own.[2]

One of the earliest ceremonies recorded in Williamsburg was also one of the most flamboyant spectacles ever organized by a colonial governor of

Virginia. The occasion was the accession of Queen Anne in 1702, and behind its expansive scale lay the brilliant energy of Governor Francis Nicholson. First the governor and Council ordered all county militia units to muster at their respective courthouses and proclaim the accession with drums, trumpets, and gunfire. Then the governor, the Council, burgesses, clergy, trustees, officers, masters and students of the college, neighboring militia, and representatives of Indian tribes all assembled in Williamsburg, June 18–19, 1702. Approximately two thousand troops, forty Indians, and an unspecified number of citizens gathered for the ceremonies. Foot soldiers and cavalry trooped in front of the college in varied formations. Buglers, oboists, and violinists stood at three different levels, including on the balcony of the college building, and at the start of the ceremony, when the death of William III was proclaimed, played a dirge in unison. Proceedings were directed by a "constable with scepter" who, after an oration on the late king had been read by a "bishop" in a specially erected tent, transformed the occasion into a joyous ceremony proclaiming the new monarch. Nicholson, the highest ranking official present, was clad in mourning for the first part of the ceremony, then in a blue uniform trimmed with braid for the second. Rounds of gunfire from small arms and cannon accompanied the proclamation of the queen. An elaborate dinner followed and liquor was distributed to the populace. The troops then led a parade to the Capitol, which was still under construction, where the queen was again proclaimed. The governor entertained bountifully in the evening, distributing largesse to the sound of bugles and gunfire as a sign of his loyalty to a gracious sovereign. A remarkably complex fireworks display brought the evening to a close.

The following morning the troops reassembled, maneuvered, and proclaimed their oaths of allegiance. Another dinner marked by "pomp and sumptuousness" was held, after which a tournament was devised by the governor, a "rifle match" followed by Indians exhibiting their skills in archery. In the evening a dance or assembly was arranged for the gathered gentlemen. At a certain point in the festivities an Indian queen was brought in, to whom all the gentlemen present doffed their hats. The queen bowed in return and was invited by the governor to dance to the music played by the instruments previously mentioned. The queen, however, danced an Indian dance that caused such astonishment in the eyes of the company and so confounded their notions of the proper forms of ceremony that all they could do was laugh.[3]

Despite the introduction into this ceremony of surprising elements of the native American culture, Nicholson succeeded by sheer force of imagination and splendid energy in setting the ceremonial pattern in Williamsburg that endured for almost a century. On this occasion of the accession of Queen Anne and the affirmation of the Protestant succession, much of the symbolism

Coat of arms of George III, carved and polychromed about 1760–1770. H: 35"; W: 43". CWF 1974-177.

CEREMONY 77

represented the power of arms and of empire, the strength and resources needed and available to face possible enemies within as well as certain ones without. This imagery was later incorporated into the Governor's Palace and is most visible in the two rooms that have been grouped and isolated in this section—artificially so, since at the time they were used they constantly interacted with and were dependent on other spaces within the building. Yet like most spaces in the Palace, they served multiple purposes and the congruence of the public official and the man who held the office is nowhere seen so clearly as in the most ceremonial "great room in the second story."

By the end of the colonial period formal ceremony was on the decline in Virginia for all but a few of its inhabitants—the most elite or conservative ones.

An Indian Queen or Chieftain's wife—Herotoans, wife of Pomeoc—with her daughter, who holds an English doll dressed in Elizabethan clothes. The queen appears as she presumably did every day, rather than for formal occasions. Drawn by John White in 1585.
H: 10⅜"; W: 5⅞". *Courtesy, British Museum.*

Jonathan Tyres and his family at the tea ceremony, oil on canvas, painted in 1740 in England by Francis Hayman. The tea accoutrements, the elegant clothing, and the formal setting all point to the seriousness of this activity in eighteenth-century life. H: 29½"; W: 40½". *Courtesy, National Portrait Gallery, London.*

This development makes the highly elaborate nature of the Botetourt funeral even more remarkable. Governors like Tryon and Dunmore who did not appreciate this trend and who stood on ceremony in the traditional English mode provoked strong reactions. Typical of the move away from rigid codes of ceremonial behavior in the colony were the removal of such archetypal ceremonies marking human rites of passage—baptism, marriage, burial—from the church to the private (often gentry) house. The new generation of republican Americans grew cautious of ceremony that echoed too resonantly of monarchical practices.[4]

The Hall
THE POWER OF THE CROWN

The entrance or hall of any well built house ought always to be expressive of the dignity of its possessor . . . the furniture ought also be designed in a manner adapted to inform the stranger or visitor where they are, and what they may expect on a more general survey of every apartment.[1]

First in the parade of formal rooms at the Governor's Palace, the hall vividly expressed the dignity of *its* possessor. Its awesome display of weapons—consisting at full complement of more than eight hundred muskets, carbines, pistols, and swords—was designed to provoke in most visitors a dramatic realization of the power of the imperial presence in the New World. All who beheld this symbol of Old World authority, except perhaps representatives of Indian tribes wavering in their loyalty to the English king or rebellious colonists from about 1773 to 1775, must have drawn reassurance, encouragement, and strength from it. That the weapons were arranged in ornamental patterns was an important element of the artifice, for it implied that power judiciously disposed led to civilizing order. This public/domestic armory, this ceremonial display was planned as an integral part of the Palace by the man who completed the building about 1715, Lieutenant Governor Alexander Spotswood. Yet from mid-century onward there was a clear perception on the part of the colonists that the arms had become theirs—"for the Use of the Country." Sixty years after their installation, the removal of the weapons was one of the most conspicuous acts of the colonial authorities immediately following the flight of the last royal governor, Lord Dunmore, in 1775. Significantly, the display of weapons is the most fully documented item or group of items in the entire building throughout its long occupancy by the royal officials. It was a compelling symbol of political power and social order.[2]

At least four years before he considered the building ready for occupancy, Spotswood was engaged in planning and installing the arrangement of arms in the Palace. On October 29, 1711, William Byrd "went to wait on the Governor but he was not at home and I walked after him to the new house and found him

Imperial strength was immediately visible in the first formal space in the Governor's Palace. This powerful symbol greeted visitors to the official building from the time of its first occupancy by the royal deputies until the eve of the Revolution, when the arms were seized by the colonial militia. The weapons were initially installed, of course, and were maintained over the ensuing sixty years for the colonists' protection.

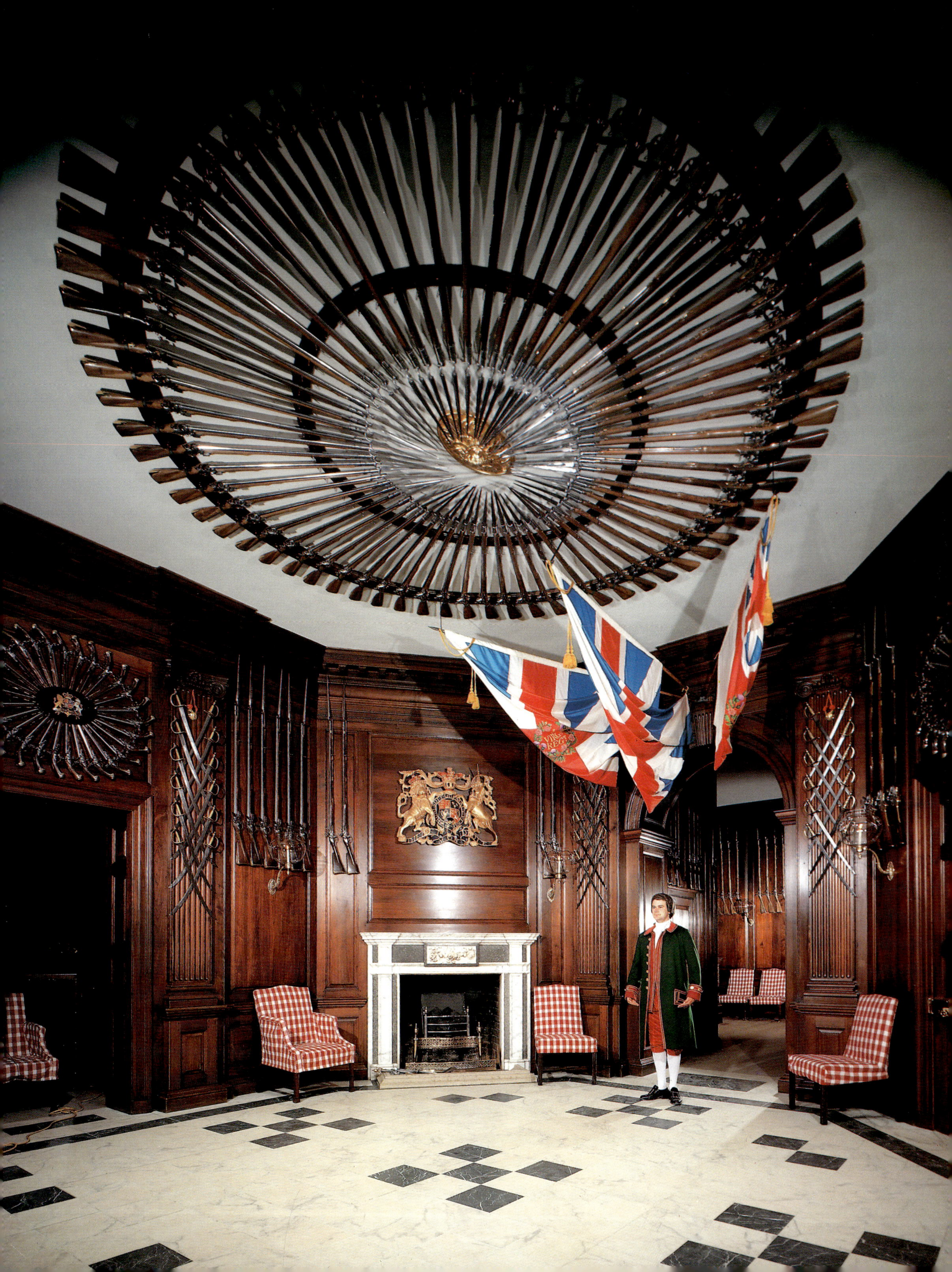

there and saw several of the Governor's contrivances, and particularly that for hanging the arms." The following month Spotswood was actually "putting up the arms," which he later wrote were "so fine a sett . . . I must confess they are far beyond any usually deliver'd out of the Tower while I serv'd in the Army." Their unusual quality may have prompted him to take special care with the arrangement or go to extraordinary lengths in the elaboration of it. With his characteristic flair for the dramatic gesture, Spotswood devised a symbol of the imperial presence on the threshold of the wilderness that was far more effective than heraldic arms or flags and was as impressive as the great brick buildings that his predecessor had instigated. The numerous complaints later filed by colonists resentful of his arrogant and spendthrift methods contained no hint of dissatisfaction with this expense.³

Noted by the Reverend Hugh Jones in 1722 as a distinguishing feature of the Governor's Palace—"a great number of the best arms nicely posited, by the ingenious contrivance of the most accomplished Colonel Spotswood"—the arrangement grew from 160 muskets in 1715 to 276 muskets, 100 carbines, 193 pistols, and 264 swords by mid-century. The display thus outgrew the hall and must have occupied wall space along the path of parade from the hall to the passage beyond and up the great staircase to the passage and "great room" on the second floor. A similar enrichment of ceremonial spaces designed for the reception of state visitors was planned in Annapolis soon after Spotswood had completed his installation in Williamsburg. In 1716 the Maryland Assembly proposed that "an handsome House be built for the Lodging and Securing the publick Magazine of Arms in this City . . . So contrived that It may Serve likewise for a Council Room and to receive the Country and Strangers that may resort to his Excellency the Governour on any publick occasions." The Maryland plan condensed into three rooms the functions that spread through three buildings in Williamsburg—the powder magazine that Spotswood was currently building, the Council chamber in the Capitol, and the ceremonial rooms in the Palace. While the Annapolis Council chamber contained furnishings that were similar in character to those installed in the middle room upstairs in the Williamsburg Palace, there is no further mention of the display of weapons in the Maryland capital in contrast to the numerous references throughout the century to the Williamsburg arrangement.⁴

Virginia's governor was not the first colonial official to use this symbolic device. In 1697 the governor of New York, Benjamin Fletcher, showed his arrangement in Fort St. George to Benjamin Bullivant, who later commented:

> His Exc . . . was pleased to show me his dineing roome, a Large and goodly hall, wainscoated and Cornished throughout, and upon the wainscoat round the Roome were handsomely placed about 300 Choice firearmes, and on the mantle piece over the chimney, 8 or 10 Large and well cleaned Blunderbusses, all of Brasse. His Exc. was

The arms extended, by reason of their sheer quantity, into the "passage below," the space that connected the hall with the dining room, staircase, and rear of the house.

pleased also to shew me his study, which was a goodly parlour, Lined on one part with pistolls sett in Rondellos after the manner of ye guard chamber at Whitehall or Windsor (but not so numerous) also sundry Indian weapons, an Indian stone hatchette, or ax, a Buckler, a poleax, some Scimatars very pretty to behold and sett in good order.[5]

Bullivant's description suggests that the space in Fort St. George in which the arms hung must have been similar to the hall in the Williamsburg Palace, "Large and goodly" in size and serviceable as a dining room. The arms were ornamentally arranged or "handsomely placed" on the walls above the paneled wainscoting and contrasted sharply with the white plaster, the muskets varied with brass blunderbusses. A smaller display in the governor's study of wheels of pistols invited comparison with the well-known arrangements of arms in royal buildings in England, a resemblance that was also noted in the Williamsburg context later.

The arrangement of arms in the Williamsburg Palace was unquestionably ornamental in form. Byrd's notation of the "Governor's contrivances" and Jones's choice of such phrases as "ingenious contrivance" and "nicely posited" are endorsed by a 1758 reference to the arms "adorning the Govrs House." The display was most graphically described and placed in context in a later comment by St. George Tucker, Williamsburg resident, jurist and antiquarian, and observer of many of the stirring events in the vicinity during the Revolution—"a considerable number of muskets etc. was always to be seen in the Entrance of the palace, where they were arranged upon the walls in an ornamental Manner, as in the Tower of London."[6]

Important evidence for the precise form of early eighteenth-century arms arrangements in royal contexts has survived in a series of drawings for a display

THE HALL 83

Left, wheels of guns often centered around a japanned plaque embellished with the coat of arms of the owner—in this instance, the king—introduced artistry and a civilizing quality into the symbol of power. The crossed swords form a highly decorative pilaster.

Right, the arms extended along the path of parade, up the main staircase, to the ceremonial room on the upper floor at the center of the house. The "passage up stairs" was a waiting space dignified by a grand lantern, looking glass, and three "large Roman Catholic pictures" for perusal.

(probably at Hampton Court Palace or Windsor Castle) by the "furbisher" who designed the installation at the Tower of London, John Harris of Eaton. Circles and half-circles, ovals, and diamonds of muskets, carbines, and pistols form the predominant patterns, interspersed with drums, cartouche boxes, halberds, pikes, furled flags, and half-suits of armor. Visually compelling and aesthetically pleasing, the designs were extremely efficient for accommodating large quantities of weapons within relatively restricted spaces. Missing items were quickly noticed, moreover, since they detracted from the strict symmetry of the displays—an excellent inventory keeping device.[7]

Evidence for a contemporary arrangement of arms in a residence is provided by the exceptionally rare, unchanged installation at Chevening House, Kent, a house that by unusual coincidence embodies architectural features similar to the Palace and that was owned by the man who became Secretary of State for the

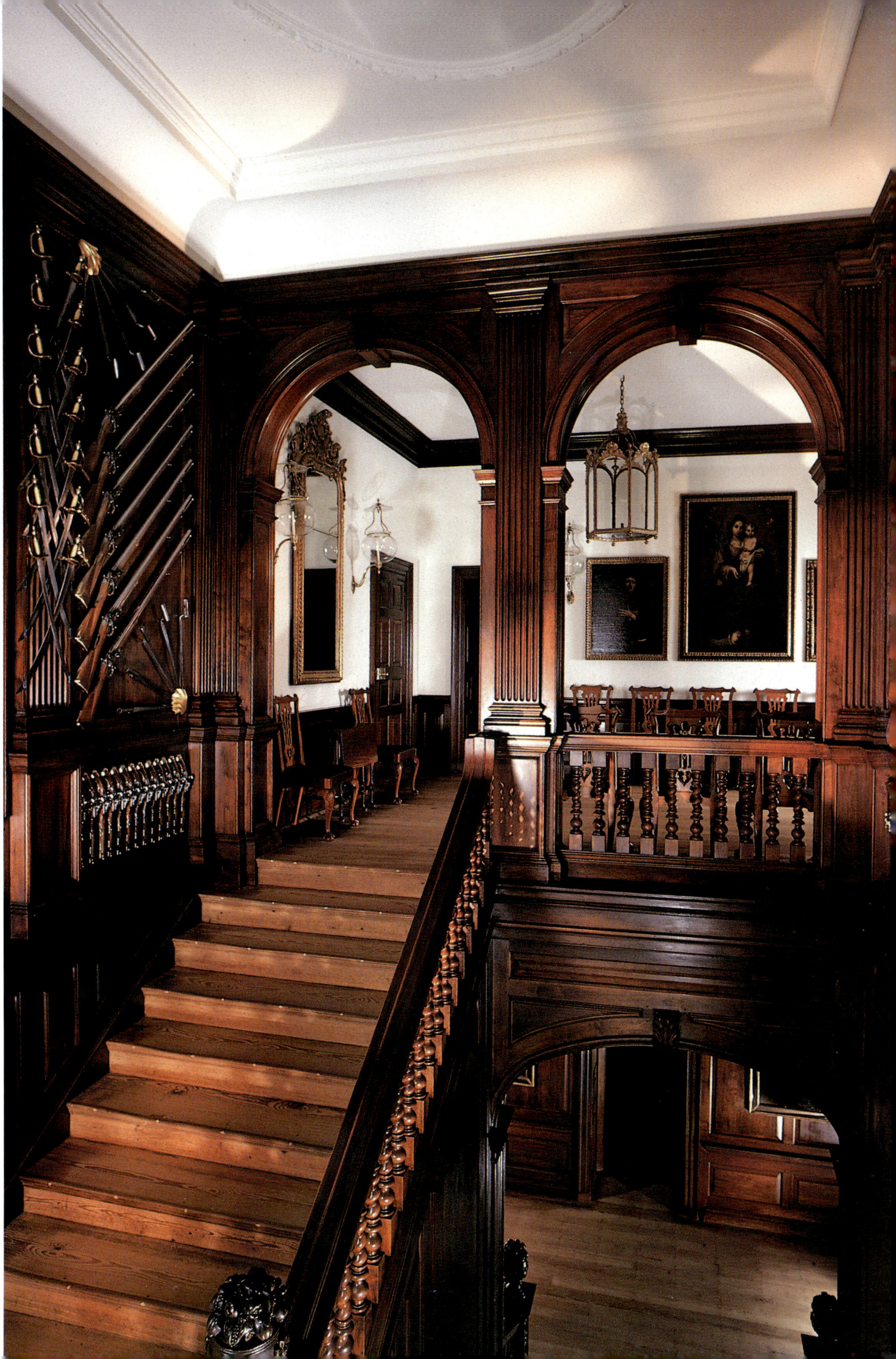

Southern Department in 1714, thus Spotswood's immediate superior, James Stanhope. The installation resembles the royal displays in many ways. At Chevening the arrangement also includes swords and plugged bayonets and extends into the stairwell as it must have done at the Palace in Williamsburg in order to accommodate the large quantity of weapons known to have been kept there.[8]

The arrangement of arms was an intrinsically powerful symbol, and it needed careful supervision. Periodic requests or reminders that the weapons be kept in good working order were made by governors and colonists—the display was more than mere ornamentation. Indeed, to those on the frontier engaged in defending his Majesty's territories against the French or the Indians, the weapons were a valuable, even vital resource. But by the 1750s the display had become such a traditional fixture of the Palace that dismantling it was not lightly undertaken. Sir John St. Clair wrote from the frontier in 1758, "I have this instant received a Letter from Mr President Blair acquainting me that he will not dismantle the Governors house at Williamsbourg of the Kings Arms . . . Surely when the Ministry sent these Arms over they never were intended for adorning the Governors House." As late as 1774, when Dunmore made his flamboyant gesture of marching to the frontier to impose the imperial will on the Shawnee and when weapons were taken from the arrangement for his use, the governor ordered that they be "soon after replaced out of the Magazine." As symbol or ornament, the display was clearly of importance in Dunmore's mind.[9]

In 1775 the symbol was tugged between forces that were more bitterly opposed than they had been in 1758. Dunmore probably put some of the weapons into the hands of the marines whom he brought into the capital to help maintain

Late seventeenth-century drawings for an arms arrangement at a royal palace, probably Hampton Court or Windsor, by the "furbisher" of the Tower of London, John Harris of Eaton. Length of drawing above, 42½". Courtesy, Tower of London, Department of the Environment. Similar, contemporary arrangement in its original format at Chevening House, Kent, seat of Lord Stanhope. Photographs, courtesy, the Administrative Trustees of the Chevening Estate.

86 CEREMONY

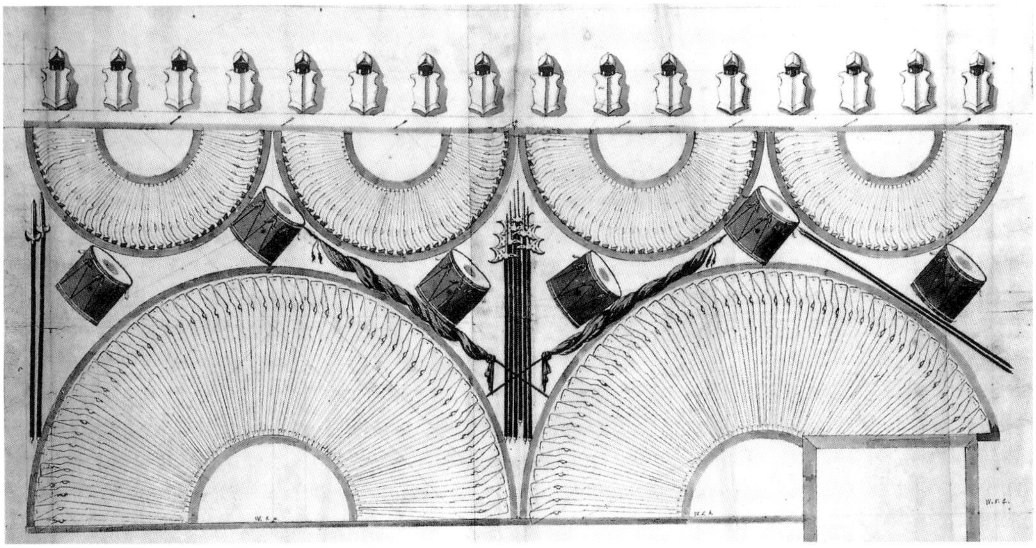

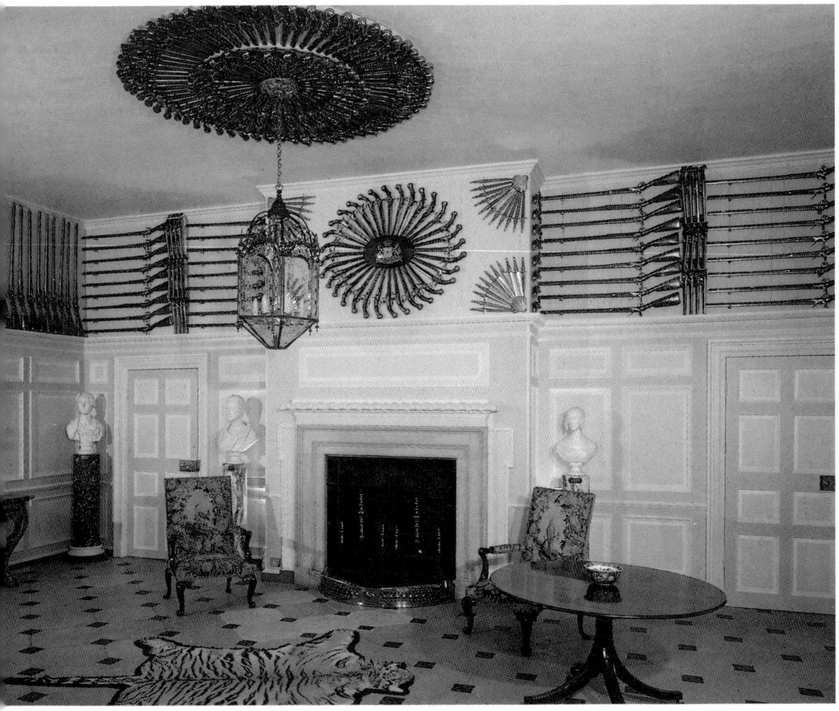

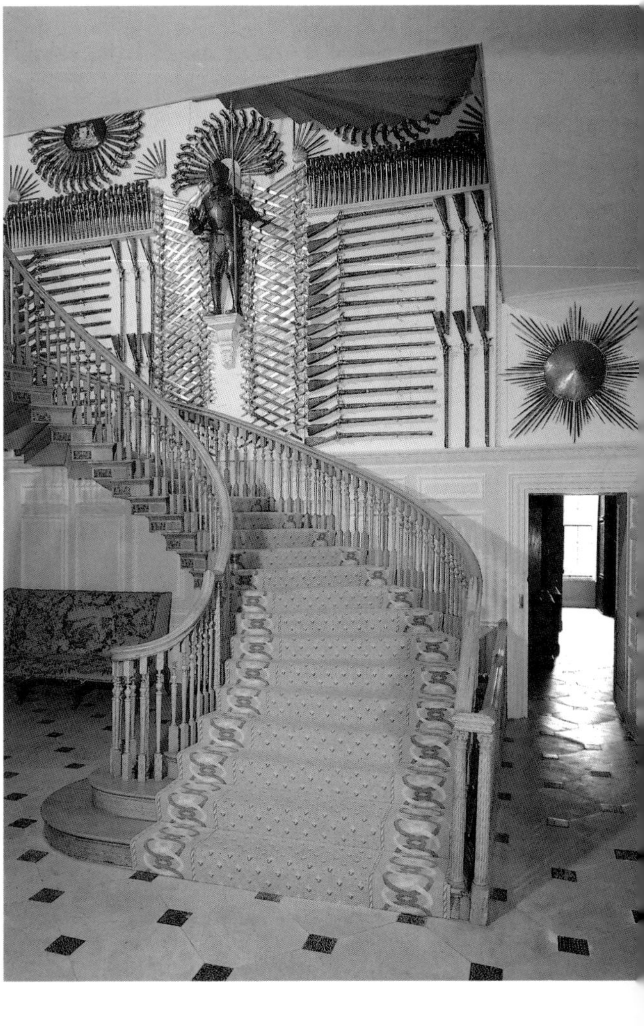

order. His tactics failed and he fled. From his vantage point on a warship in the York River he refused to accept the polite requests and avowals of the assembly "that the Arms belonging to the King, which have for so many Years been lodged, may still remain, in the Palace." The day after the colonists received Dunmore's response they carefully dismantled the arrangement, transferring under their own guard the 230 guns and 292 broad and small swords from the royal arsenal to the magazine that they controlled, which was symbolically located in the center of the city.[10]

Among the items inventoried in the hall in 1770 were "arms and colours." These were undoubtedly the royal coat of arms, either carved in relief then gilded and painted or painted on a flat board (or canvas). "Colours," flags, or banners hung en suite with the arms. The most obvious location for such regalia was the overmantel above the fireplace, visible immediately to those entering and surrounded by the weapons. Obligatory symbols for government buildings, courthouses, and churches, royal coats of arms reminded all present that the king was the keeper of order and defender of the faith, the foremost civil, legal, and spiritual authority in the realm, *"next and immediately under God* supream governor over al persons and cases as well Ecclesiasticall and Temporall."[11]

The coat of arms and the arrangement of weapons were symbols of imperial sovereignty so forceful in combination that they cannot have been overlooked in this first, commanding space in the Governor's Palace to which all genteel members of the "country" were periodically bidden for purposes of celebration or business. In this space the artifacts were shared symbols of patriarchy, of rank and civility, mutually understood and accepted. In the imperial society of which these genteel persons were all members, the monarch was the supreme patriarch, the viceregal governor was the provincial patriarch, and the Virginia gentry were local patriarchs. The symbols with which the first large formal space in the Palace were arrayed cannot have spelled out the hierarchy more clearly.[12]

By the middle of the eighteenth century, however, most colonial governors probably deemed an arrangement of arms in their residences somewhat old-fashioned. In the hall of his palace at New Bern, North Carolina, for example, William Tryon planned niches for statues (though the figures never arrived). The somewhat gentler nature of his symbolic statement—the civilized familial order rather than the stern authoritative system—was apparently endorsed in May 1770 by a visiting English dignitary who promptly composed a Latin inscription to be placed over the rear doorway of the hall; the inscription ended "May the house and its master be examples to future ages so that they may cultivate in this place the arts, morals, justice, and law." In Annapolis by that date the magazine/Council chamber structure was in disrepair, the arms in disorder and scattered round the city.[13] By the third quarter of the eighteenth century, it was more common to find in the halls of great English houses trophies of arms modeled in stucco, still

Hall of Tryon's Palace, New Bern, North Carolina. The niches were intended for statues that never arrived. Those seen above are modern installations. The inscription was placed over the door to the left, leading to the dining room and main staircase.

symbolic of rank but merely a token gesture to the tradition of force and regional authority. Botetourt's display of weapons at his country seat in Gloucestershire in 1770, for example, consisted of fewer than thirty weapons and was discreetly maintained in the servants' hall. But in Williamsburg Fauquier and Botetourt chose to retain the display of arms even though they were not career military men like most of their predecessors. Their decisions were probably more in deference to tradition and to imperial power than to considerations of potential use, a crucial indication of the value that these two unmilitary governors placed on the symbol itself. The display of weapons in the Palace at Williamsburg was the only arrangement in the residence of a governor in North America (known to us today) with such a long tradition—a fitting symbol for the oldest and largest of the English colonies.[14]

Between 1715 and 1750 the hall was the logical and indispensable space in the building for the large public receptions that the governor by virtue of his office was required to host. At such times the room clearly played the traditional seventeenth-century role of meeting place between the outside world and the inside lives of the occupants. Yet it differed from most contemporary Virginia halls in that it did not also function as the dining room and general multipurpose room for the family. Apart from its practical uses for service and transit to other parts of the residence, it was mainly a space for *public* reception, most notably the "large companies at public feasts," the ceremonies and balls that became increasingly a feature of gubernatorial life in Williamsburg.

The most frequent ceremony held at the Palace for which the hall was the logical and appropriate setting because of its size and its accoutrements was the annual commemoration of the king's birthday. It was incumbent on the governor to celebrate this event with style and it was a mark of loyalty, indeed it was expected, that all of the local gentry should attend. In 1718 Spotswood noted that he "had 200 Persons to Entertain" at his house for the king's birthday, a ceremony that included a "Play w'ch was Acted on that Occasion"; unless he exaggerated the numbers present—not inconceivable since the details of the event were included in his defense against charges of misusing official property—that was a very large gathering to accommodate at the Palace, even by using all the public spaces available.[15] The birthdays of other members of the royal family were also celebrated, as were incoming governors, peace treaties, and other memorable events. A particularly notable ceremony was organized on the accession of George II: "We went and proclaimed the King at the Capitol, in the Market place, on the Colledg green. Pack the Herald on horseback, Governor [Gooch] and myself [Robert Carter] in first coach. The guns fired 3 times. Invited to dinner at the Pallace. After drank all the roial healths. Guns fired at every health. 3 tables. Rack punch at each table. Governor drank all the healths at the table. We took our leaves at 12 clock." When William Gooch was sworn in as governor shortly before the proclamation of the king, he was entertained by colonial officials at the Capitol, after which he repaired to the Palace and "according to the custom . . . entertain[ed] the town and all the neighbours around us." Spotswood initiated subscription balls on a regular basis in the colonial capital and some of those were presumably held at the Palace as well as the Capitol. These various ceremonies grew in number and size during Gooch's administration to the point where it was desirable or necessary by mid-century to add the ballroom and supper room wing to the Palace in order to relieve the pressure in the hall.[16]

By mid-century the social usages of the Palace hall must have been similar to those described by Isaac Ware in England in 1752:

> In more magnificent houses [the hall] should always be made as large as the rule of proportion to the entire building, and to the other rooms, will allow. . . . In town a hall is a place of reception for servants . . . in the country, where there are other ways into the house, the hall may be an elegant room, and it is there we propose its being made large and noble. . . . It serves as a summer-room for dining; it is an anti-chamber in which people of business, or of the second rank, wait and amuse themselves; and it is a good apartment for the reception of large companies at public feasts.[17]

The room was certainly large and noble and its embellishments made it elegant. Undoubtedly it was the primary room of reception for large companies, and it may also have served as the space for summer dining in the characteristic Virginia

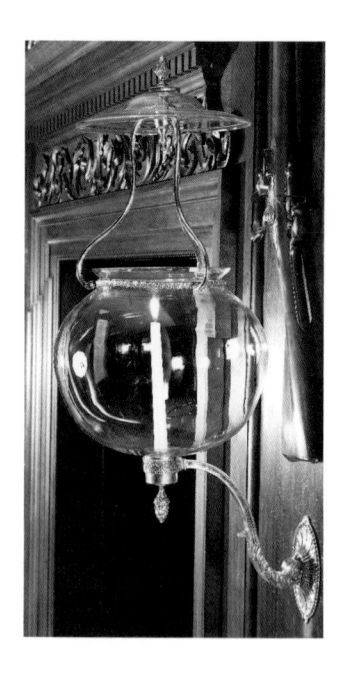

Reproduction globe lamp and shade of brass and glass. Grand in size (their overall height is 36"), there were sixteen of these imposing lighting devices along the path of parade from the hall to the middle room upstairs. Nothing resembling this conspicuous display of wealth and sophistication existed anywhere else in the colony.

manner (described later in this chapter). It was also essential for business purposes, for the servants who made the residence work, and as a reception area for those who came to the Palace to wait on the governor. After the addition of the ballroom and supper room and the transfer of the celebratory events to those new spaces, the hall might be presumed to have taken on a primarily business role. Ware's analysis of the functions of such a room, for example, was incorporated into the 1774 *Builders Dictionary* and supplemented with this statement: "In the Houses of Ministers of State, Magistrates, etc., it is the place when they dispatch Business and give Audience."[18]

The primary evidence, however, for the actual uses of the hall at the Palace in the third quarter of the eighteenth century lies in the Botetourt inventory. In the late 1760s the hall and the passage beyond contained two mahogany red damask elbow chairs complete with check covers and eight backstools with the same upholstery and covers. On the walls hung ten large globe lamps. Supplementing these elegant items were the colony owned "Arms and Colours," two looking glasses, six fine leather buckets, and two stepladders. The damask chairs were among the most expensive items Botetourt had purchased from the estate of his predecessor, Francis Fauquier (it is not possible to determine where they were kept during his administration), and were a conspicuous expression of wealth and status. Rarely found in the colonies, they were certainly not intended for use by "people of business, or of the second rank." Even with the protective case covers, the damask upholstery was too expensive and too sensitive to be subjected to the rigors of daily use. Typical hall chairs of the time were chosen for durability, generally having wooden seats or leather upholstery. Inexpensive Windsor chairs were even coming into vogue for hall use in this period. Botetourt's decision to install some of his most expensive seating furniture in the hall proves that he had a design ulterior to daily business and common reception. Business was essential, certainly, but for this the check case covers were serviceable, smart, and modish enough. Ceremony was more important; for these occasions the portable case covers were easily removed and the damask revealed to contribute its formality to the proceedings. Botetourt obviously intended to augment the effect that the weapons created in the room by introducing elegant appurtenances that evoked dignity and nobility and perhaps even produced echoes of the regal ceremony that he had observed during his years at court.[19]

The large glass globe lamps sustained the eloquent effect. They were imposing in themselves and when lighted for the ceremonial occasions that occurred chiefly at night, their lights flickering on all the polished steel of the weapons above them on the walls and glowing on the red damask of the chairs below as well as on the livery of footmen in attendance, they created an ambience at the beginning of the formal parade of rooms at the Palace that could not be matched in any other building in the colony. The importance of

Red damask back stool, one of a set of ten, including two with arms, or "elbows," that stood in the hall and passage. Distinguished by their sophisticated form and very expensive upholstery, such chairs were rarely seen in the colony. For daily use they were covered with the smart check cases seen on p. 81. Mahogany, English, ca. 1760.
H: 37¾"; W: 23". CWF 1978-181.

Left, leather-seated furniture in the parlor and its adjacent closet, which was also furnished with work items, and the plentiful prints for contemplation and maps for reference suggest the function (at least some of the time) as a waiting room and place of business.

Right, reproduction leather fire bucket for sand or water, an essential preventative device in a large building. That the buckets were listed as "standing furniture" suggests that they were painted with the arms of the colony rather than with those of the crown.

brilliant lighting for state ceremonies was a well-established tradition and its appearance in this location in the Palace was symbolic—there was a much higher level of artificial lighting in situ in the hall than in any other room in the building except for the ballroom, a space in which the presence of the crown was also emphasized.[20]

However grand the setting was on ceremonial occasions, people still needed to come to the Palace during the day on business and had to be accommodated. For this purpose leather seated chairs were more serviceable and more appropriate. A set of such chairs stood in the parlor, the space directly adjoining the hall; being standing furniture they were older and probably less stylish and so were suitable for common reception. This placement of furniture strongly suggests that Botetourt had removed the function of "anti-chamber for persons of business" from the hall to the adjacent parlor, thus retaining the hall for primarily ceremonial purposes, keeping it as a room redolent with authority and expressive of viceregal dignity.

Governors Tryon and Campbell both owned sets of damask chairs but reserved them for their richest social rather than ceremonial rooms. Tryon kept his set of twelve, upholstered in blue damask and complete with check covers, in his "Chints Room," while Campbell's extremely elegant set of twelve crimson *silk* damask chairs, including elbow chairs en suite with a settee, the entire group furnished with linen covers, stood in his richly appointed drawing room. Botetourt owned a second set of damask chairs, however, placed in the room directly above the hall, the middle room upstairs, that served both ceremonial *and* social purposes.[21]

Among the remaining items grouped in the hall according to the inventory were two stepladders. They were essential to reach and service the arms, customarily hung high on the walls beyond normal reach, and were undoubtedly kept in the closet of the hall, shown in Jefferson's drawing. They were probably also used to replenish the candles in the globe lamps on a regular basis. Leather buckets were also listed, necessary containers for sand or water and precaution against fire; they were almost certainly decorated with the royal arms or with those of the colony. The looking glasses listed dated perhaps from the original order for the Palace furnishings placed by the colony about 1710 and probably hung on either side of the door leading into the dining room where they would reflect light from the stairwell into an otherwise dark passage and add a measure of elegance to the impression that people using the stairs would receive.

"The hall . . . is [also] a spacious apartment, intended as the room of access where servants in livery attend," wrote Robert Adam, one of the foremost architect-designers of the 1760s and 1770s in England. Certainly Lord Botetourt kept footmen in livery in the hall. As a "man of parade" he brought with him to Virginia the formal lineaments of an aristocratic life-style, heavily dependent on ritual and protocol. An essential element of this artifice was the retinue, a carefully structured hierarchy of retainers employed to convey outwardly their master's power and prestige and to maintain a proper distance between him and those who were not his equal. Thus the petitioner for the governor's favor, having been confronted with the authority of the sovereign in the form of the coat of arms and the display of weapons, was obliged to submit to the scrutiny of liveried footmen in the hall before being admitted to the presence of the chief executive himself. This may have been the practice followed by all the governors. Perhaps Botetourt's popularity was in part due to the fact that, more than his predecessors, he was to the manner born and could bring it off with disarming grace. Dunmore tried it, with less success.[22]

Fauquier also kept footmen in the hall. In June 1760 as the final insult in an acrimonious relationship, the Reverend John Camm delivered to the lieutenant governor a letter from the Privy Council that had been opened. Camm's insouciance sent Fauquier into a rage: " 'Westmore' (speaking to one of his white Servants) call my Negroes, call all my Negroes!' Two Negro men appeared, then he called for a Negro Boy who, likewise came. 'Here' (says he), look at him, look at him (pointing at Mr. Camm); that you may know him again. If ever he should come to ask for me suffer him not to enter my doors.' "[23]

Footmen in the hall—"the room of access"—clearly had the authority to grant or refuse admission to visitors who came to the Palace without a specific appointment. Although only two men and a boy could be summoned in the incident with Camm, Fauquier's stress on "all" his Negroes suggests that there were more. Furthermore, the fact that Fauquier's steward was on call outside the room in which the governor and Camm met implies that the visitor also had to pass by him in order to be admitted to the lieutenant governor's presence. If Fauquier observed this ritual, we may be sure that the aristocratic Botetourt did, and with greater ceremony. He kept at least four footmen, perhaps more, white as well as black. Evidently they were not only ornamental but also necessary, for the custom of visitors coming to the Palace without appointments seems to have been well established. Gooch noted of an unwelcome visitor in 1746 that "when he wants money he comes in an afternoon when he is sure to find me alone." Dunmore later endeavored to smooth some local feathers ruffled by his initial hauteur by naming "office hours, when every Person concerned might attend on Business."[24]

Because of the scattered, fragmentary nature of the evidence, it is difficult to draw comparisons between ceremonial and business functions in the hall at the Palace with those in the other southern governors' residences. Certainly there seems to have been no comparable effort made to create the eloquent and forceful mise-en-scène found in the Palace in Williamsburg. Tryon's intentions at his palace in North Carolina were evidently to cultivate "the arts, morals, justice, and the law" (in that order). Niches for statues were installed, but no evidence for other furnishings has survived. The furnishings he lost in the fire at his New York residence in 1773 included only lanterns and leather buckets in the hall. An incomplete reference to a passage between the parlors in Eden's residence in Annapolis mentioned merely a lantern and a green Windsor chair.

With the Virginia gentry, however, a practice of usage of this primary space comparable to that described by Isaac Ware in 1756 is apparent. An English visitor in 1732 noted the characteristic "passage thro the house in the middle which is the Summer hall and Draws the air." Inventory evidence shows tables and sets of chairs to accommodate dinners for large groups of people, particularly in the oppressive Virginia summer when cross ventilation was necessary for relief.[25] The hall also provided a formal place of assembly: "After the ceremony of

Detail from The Honey-Moon, *one of a series of four paintings on "Modern Love" by John Collet, painted in England ca. 1760–1764. This shows the liveried footman with a letter, doubling as a waiter carrying a plate of toast, unfortunately snared by a family pet.* H: 27". CWF 1969-48, 3.

The "passage" or entrance hall at Westover, Charles City County, Virginia. This mid-eighteenth-century building shows the developed wide central space for access, gathering, and, during the "dog days" of summer, essential ventilation.

Introduction, and our Congees were over, we took our seats in a cool passage where the Company were sitting," Fithian wrote in 1774, implying a degree of traditional formality mingled with the more fashionable custom of relaxed sociable assembly that appears to typify the transition to the last quarter of the eighteenth century. Another entry from his diary, however, describing an incident at Nomini Hall the preceding day, suggests that a traditional space where the owner could "dispatch business and give audience" was also an important consideration: "An old Negro Man came with a complaint to Mr Carter of the Overseer . . . the humble posture in which the old Fellow placed himself before he began moved me. We were sitting in the passage, he sat himself down on the Floor clasp'd his Hands together, with his face directly to Mr *Carter*, and then began his Narration."[26] Given the autocratic nature of plantation society, Carter had as much power to dispense justice or influence the course of events as many a "magistrate or minister of state." In such situations, and in view of the degree of authority with which the planter was invested, it is tempting to see in the frequent mention of a couch in the hall or passage of plantation houses a vestigial reference to that powerful symbol of authority, the "chair of state," of which some examples were still in situ in English country houses in the early eighteenth century. Numerous references to livery in Virginia gentry inventories of the second and third quarters of the eighteenth century suggest that the great planters also used the hall or passage as "the room of access where servants in livery attend," investing the space with a degree of formality that would be particularly notable on the frequent ceremonial occasions in which they engaged.[27]

Among the references to the contents of the hall of the Palace in the eighteenth century, the Tower of London was invoked on two separate occasions. To the English mind the Tower was an archetype, synonymous with power and the use of force. The association may not have been entirely coincidental, for the imposing size of the Palace and its deliberate setting at the end of a long allée, sheltered behind walls at the edge of the community, could readily convey the impression of a small fortress. Spotswood certainly summoned up such imagery when he wrote of his predecessor, Francis Nicholson, who envisioned the building: He "was a COMMANDER IN CHIEF without a *single Centinel to defend [him] in this Dominion.*"[28] That the early governors were selected because of their professional military background only serves to reinforce this view. Dunmore, likewise a professional soldier, quickly adopted siege tactics and mentality when confronted by irate colonists in 1775. The essential military ingredient of imperial power is surely symbolized and made more explicit by a fuller understanding of the arsenal at the Governor's Palace, installed within recent memory of civil disorder in Virginia and at a time of international stress for the empire. That it was maintained through generations of increasing order and harmony is a testimony to its efficacy and powers of communication.[29]

Yet this extraordinary assemblage of artifacts, far more remarkable (and remarked) in its totality than in its individual parts, is a prime example of a symbol that also changed over time and played subtly different roles in different social and political circumstances. Spotswood may, indeed, have felt at times besieged by internal and external forces. The power of the weaponry would then have given him some reassurance. Yet even by the end of his administration it was noted that the arms were "nicely" hung and emphasis was placed on the ingenuity and sophistication of the arrangement—terms of deference to an accomplishment that speaks more of civility and ceremony than of military strategy. By the middle of the eighteenth century there was a greater feeling of internal security despite certain anxieties over the French threat in the early years of the Seven Years' War. In an intriguing parallel, the 1753 guide to the Tower stressed that the predominant responses to the displays in the Small Armoury were astonishment and gratification of a taste for the "Admirable Combinations of Art." Thus the step after conquest was civilization—force was not displayed nakedly but was refined by ornamentation. Astonishment at the degree of power was succeeded by association and, therefore, gratification. This surely was the paramount consideration for the later governors in Williamsburg, and was enhanced by Botetourt with expensive damask in regal colors, brilliant lighting effects, and the trappings of a retinue to heighten the impressive ceremonial elements inherent in the space. Although the arms could still be put to use when necessary, the ensemble was employed by such popular governors as Fauquier and Botetourt more as an expression of an elevated social situation. The hall seems then to have been at least as much a space for social statement as it was a space for social use. As much as any other formal room in the Palace it would seem to have been informed by "sentiment"—namely "the feelings excited in our minds by means of the senses"—the quality that Sheraton declared was certainly "expressed in the manner of furnishing a house."[30]

At the end of Dunmore's short tenure the arms again briefly invoked and threatened force. But over a span of sixty years the colonists had come increasingly to assume that the weapons were theirs by right and, aided by Dunmore's prudence (or weakness), quickly secured them. On Thursday, June 24, 1775, sixteen days after Dunmore had fled the Palace under cover of night, the arrangement of arms was quietly and soberly dismantled by "a party of twenty-four gentlemen" of the town and in open daylight trundled on three carts to the public magazine. Thus did the substance of the most frequently noted symbol of majesty and empire at the Governor's Palace pass into the possession of the local populace.[31]

The Middle Room Upstairs

THE PRESENCE
OF THE GOVERNOR

That the great Room in the second Story [of the Governor's Palace] be furnished with gilt Leather hangings[,] 16 chairs of the same, two large looking glasses with the Arms of the Colony on them according to the new Mode, two small Tables to stand under the Looking Glasses and two Marable Tables[,] Eight Glass Sconces.[1]

A great room intended for state . . . Its place is in the middle of a house, or at the head of a gallery, and it is a kind of magnificent hall . . . the purpose . . . was the reception of great visitors.[2]

A key ceremonial role was envisioned for the middle room on the upper floor of the south front of the Palace. Its central location, its elevation above ground level, and its grand size proclaimed its importance, and, when most elegant and formal furnishings were proposed for its embellishment about 1710, it was described as the "great Room in the second Story." Linked in parade to the hall, above which it stood and to which it was identical in size, the great room also commanded the vista of Palace green southward toward the center of the town. When surveyed from the long advance of this vista, the room's importance was evident in the full-length central window, wider and longer than the others in the facade, with a wrought-iron balcony appended to it. Sixty years after its initial design, even after the ballroom and supper room had been added to the Palace, the room still fulfilled a vital ceremonial purpose to judge by the quality of the items it contained. Its prominent placement was complemented by rich furnishings of crimson damask and large looking glasses with carved and gilded frames, some of them emblazoned with the arms of the colony. According to the Botetourt inventory, the seal of the colony was also kept in this room, being the formal symbol of the governor's power of proxy for his royal master. All these elements enhanced the role of ceremony, the dignity of the space, and the power of the governor ensconced in it—the chief executive and the foremost figure of authority in the colony.[3]

Initially, the room was to be outfitted, perhaps at Spotswood's urging, with the impressive furnishings included in the proposal for "rendering the

The middle room upstairs, looking south toward the center of the capital city. One of the most formal and lavishly furnished rooms in the colony, the carved, gilt frames combined with large areas of silvered glass, the plentiful crimson damask, the leather wall hangings, and the chandelier all spelled wealth and privilege.

98 CEREMONY

new House Convenient as well as Ornamental." No other room in the residence commanded such attention in 1710, nor was it appropriate that it should, for the great room was intended to occupy a place of eminence. It was the successor to the late medieval "great chamber," which in grand English houses was a room for the immediate family of the noble owner, placed on the second floor off one end of the great hall, to which most of the important ceremonial functions of the household had ascended from the earlier great hall. The great chamber was more private and more dignified than the hall, adjacent to sumptuous bedchambers, and reached by a staircase that in itself became progressively more elaborate and impressive. In the seventeenth century, however, the dining functions gradually disappeared from the great chamber and separate parlors for family use were introduced so that what activities remained in the great chamber were largely formal and ceremonial.[4]

Placing this great room at the center of the house in the second story at the head of the stairs was a calculated study in superiority in the late seventeenth and early eighteenth centuries. Its appearance in Williamsburg so early in the century was commensurate with the importance of ceremony in proclaiming the power of the crown through the presence of the vice-regent. The room's height above the surrounding terrain suggested the governor's appropriate "condescension" to the town. Internally, its gilt leather wall hangings—a refinement of the seventeenth-century taste for tapestry-hung reception rooms that had already made an appearance in Virginia—created an opulent, even ostentatious, effect. Sixteen chairs upholstered with the same gilt leather occupied most of the unbroken wall space in the room, forming a parade of their own and leading visitors' eyes to the large looking glasses with the arms of the colony on their crests that probably hung on the piers of the south wall between the three windows, facing the main door into the room. That the glasses were specified as large, with crests enriched by coats of arms, would have made them very expensive. The "new Mode" prescribed for them may have been the colorful *"verre églomisé"* or the Huguenot-inspired, shallow relief-carved and gilt type. Pier tables under the glasses, formal marble tables, and expensive glass sconces to light the room brilliantly at night completed the eloquent effect—"ornamental" indeed, in the language of the officials responsible for it. The conjunction of carefully sited space and rich appointments that were symbolic of high position and great means thus produced a setting at the climax of the ceremonial parade that was fully consistent with the presence and dignity of the governor in office. The progression past the imperial weapons, the royal coat of arms, and the banners to the elevated station of the middle or great room attuned the visitor for reception in a sumptuously furnished chamber by the resident head of state.[5]

A close parallel between the middle room, its siting, its stated furnishings, and its intended purpose and the most ceremonial room in the "Council House" proposed in Annapolis six years later is strikingly evident. That building was designed "that It may Serve likewise for a Council Room and to receive the Country and Strangers that may resort to his Excellency the Gouvernor on any publick occasions." The "fashionable" leather chairs and the numerous lighting devices in its Council room represented a striving for richness of effect and grandness of occasion. There is no mistaking the ceremonial intention, in the fully developed, seventeenth-century ceremonial tradition, of these similar and carefully contrived settings.[6]

Between the 1710 proposal and the Botetourt inventory of 1770 no primary evidence for this room survives. By the latter date the function of corresponding rooms in English country houses had changed slightly. No longer called "great chambers," such rooms had generally become known by mid-century as "saloons." The "great room intended for state" described by Isaac Ware was labeled a saloon or salon.[7] Later in the century Sheraton portrayed "a state saloon-room, in which are entertained ambassadors, courtiers, and other personages of the highest stations." That grand room was distinguished by large looking glasses on the piers and over the mantels, pier tables, and walls covered with paper or other material, very similar to the Williamsburg room's furnishing scheme. Here was "concentrate[d] the elegance of the whole house, and . . . the highest display of richness of furniture." Obviously, such a room was designed to impress, although the nicety of eighteenth-century manners required that "the grandeur . . . is not to be considered, as the ostentatious parade of its proprietor, but the respect he pays to the rank of his visitants."[8]

The Botetourt inventory enumerates furnishings for this room that correspond explicitly, in material terms, to the codes articulated above. Ambassadors, courtiers, and other great visitors *were* a consideration in the small colonial capital of Williamsburg. Moreover, it is possible to isolate a comparable group of objects in Fauquier's inventory (in which locations were not given) and conclude that his earlier use of the room probably resembled Botetourt's in important respects. To postulate that the room had a perceived role over and above the preferences of individual governors, much like the hall directly below, is therefore reasonable.

In the middle room in 1770, in addition to the looking glasses adorned with the arms of the colony that were described in the list of standing furniture as "2 long looking glasses with red gilded frames," the Botetourt inventory listed "1 large Glass on the Side of the Room with carved gilt frame" and a large chimney glass with a carved gilt frame. Thus a total of four "large" looking glasses hung in the room, supplemented, furthermore, by a "Glass Lustre [chandelier] with six Branches," the property of the colony and a rare artifact of the most conspicuous elegance. The looking glasses created the illusion of space and light, their glittering richness combining with the glass chandelier to proclaim unusual wealth and high rank. Further enhancing their rich effect was the crimson damask selected for the three suites of window curtains and valances as well as for the eight backstools and two armchairs. That it was specified as crimson and was different from the *red* damask in the hall is an important distinction for crimson was more expensive than red. It was the color prescribed by custom for state rooms in England, where even the throne or chair of state and its accompanying canopy were conventionally covered with crimson damask or velvet. This color distinction was designed to heighten the dignity of the setting and to emphasize the regal associations with the ceremonial activities for which the room was designed.[9]

Reproduction silver matrix for the seal of the colony of Virginia during the reign of George III. Maximum diameter 5". The large quantity of silver in these matrixes—over seventy ounces—symbolizes the importance attached to the wax seal that it created and the ceremony of attaching that seal to a formal document.

102 CEREMONY

Multiple views of the middle room upstairs showing the lavish quality of its accoutrements. The large, gilt-framed looking glass on the side of the room and the gilt-framed chimney glass, plus the gilt brackets for ornamental pieces such as porcelain, all accentuate the formality of the experience provided in this space. Silver accessories, including the seal, stood in the desk drawer compartment of a case piece of furniture that also contained the governor's formal, outer clothes.

THE MIDDLE ROOM UPSTAIRS 103

The gilt leather hangings, ordered about 1710, may have survived until 1770 if they were ever installed. No evidence has appeared. Careful handling would have ensured their survival, and they were sufficiently expensive and prestigious when new to warrant such treatment. Robert Eden maintained a "gilt leather parlour" in his gubernatorial residence in Annapolis, thus providing a documentary parallel for the survival of the rich hangings in Williamsburg. Gilt leather, gilt carved frames, gilt brackets, crimson damask curtains, cornices, and upholstery, silvered looking glasses, a large mahogany table, the two rounded ends of which served as pier tables under the pair of glasses, a carpet—all this was surely the colonial equivalent of "the highest display of richness of furniture" and an apt setting for the governor in his ceremonial office. Such rich surroundings were also commensurate with the dignity of his Majesty's Council when it met at the Palace, as it periodically did. That the seal of the colony was listed in the middle room in the inventory is further proof that the room was designed and used for state purposes; the heavy solid silver matrix was used to make the wax seals customarily attached to government documents, thereby bestowing on them the authority of the king. The seal was used for such a purpose by Lord Botetourt at a Council meeting, almost certainly in the middle room, two months before his death. The seal was patently an object of symbolic importance.[10]

In all probability, this room was the setting for the reception in Williamsburg of "ambassadors, courtiers, and other personages of the highest stations." Their periodic visits to the capital were attended with considerable ceremony. That they were native Americans did not preclude the customary ceremonies. Indeed, their potential military might caused officials to treat the Indians with respectful and traditional protocol. The governors spent huge amounts of their official time attending to Indian matters. Dinwiddie received the emperor and empress of the Cherokee nation with an entourage including "the young Prince . . . several . . . Warriors and great Men" in 1752 at the newly refurbished Palace, an event fully reported by the newspaper.[11] Fauquier met with Chief Little Carpenter of the Cherokee nation in 1765 for a "Conference at my own house." And on August 17, 1770, Botetourt and the Council received at the Palace the Indian chief Salloue, who addressed the gathering and delivered a letter from the Cherokee chief, Oconostota. After strings of white wampum were exchanged, Lord Botetourt, on behalf of the king, delivered an address and presented Salloue with a copy in letter form, "the Seal of the Colony being first appended thereto."[12]

Whether or not the Indian chieftains and ambassadors appreciated the stylistic niceties of the middle room's appointments, they were hardly impervious to the sumptuous effect of patterned crimson material, shining gold, and silvered glass, proclaiming that this was the governor's inner core of power and

Print of three Cherokee chieftains who made formal "state" visits to Williamsburg and then to London in 1762. They were received by colonial officials and then by George III and caused a stir in contemporary London by their splendid appearance and the transcultural purpose of their mission. Published by George Bickham, ca. 1765. H: 9³⁄₈"; W: 11¹⁄₄". CWF 1958-484.

The family of John Offley Crewe, portrayed in their country house parlor or drawing room by Arthur Devis about 1744. An idealized setting, undoubtedly, but a perfect realization of three generations of a formal, ambitious family seen "at ease" for the tea ceremony in spacious surroundings that spelled achievement and station. H: 33"; W: 40⁵⁄₈". Present whereabouts unknown.

prestige. Indeed, it is possible that the ceremonial effect of the formal parade, from the martial display in the hall ascending to the richly appointed middle room, impressed itself more strongly on potential adversaries than on allies —and the Indians were the only potential adversaries to be received here until the imminent hostilities between imperial Britain and her colonial subjects in the early 1770s. Until that time, Virginians obviously regarded the symbols of prestige and the apparatus of power as a bulwark to their sense of security and self-esteem rather than a threat to it, a clear link to the traditions of the crown and great nobility in England.[13]

Neighboring Governors William Tryon and Robert Eden, also "personages of the highest stations," paid official visits to Lord Botetourt at the Palace in 1769 and 1770. Tryon, in particular, completing the construction of his own palace in New Bern, probably took note of the long continuity of governance manifested in the room by the mingling of older and newer furnishings.[14] The naval hero Sir William Draper (famous for his role in capturing Manila from the Spanish in 1762) visited his former neighbor from Bristol here in 1770 en route to New Bern where he penned the epithet for the hall of Tryon's Palace. And in January 1770 Lord Botetourt received at his Palace an official delegation consisting of the mayor, corporation, and citizens of Williamsburg who presented him with a petition protesting the proposed removal of the customs house from Williamsburg to nearby Bermuda Hundred. The middle room was the most appropriate setting for such dignitaries to be received by the governor in the formal panoply of his office.[15]

Though ceremony in the middle room may have been at its most contrived and elaborate during the reception of state visitors, it was also evident and implicit in other, more frequent activities for which the room was utilized, according to the

THE MIDDLE ROOM UPSTAIRS 105

fashion of the time, the time of day, and the occasion. After mid-century saloons began to decline in importance in English houses, especially those in which the state function was not paramount, while drawing rooms became more popular and more frequently used. The drawing room—"the chief apartment of a noble, or genteel house, to which it is usual for company to draw to after dinner" (in Sheraton's words)—came to be used on quite relaxed and informal occasions as well as on very formal ones. It warranted the most elegant furniture since it was "for the reception of persons of the highest rank," but it was also the place in which to sit and relax and converse. It thus was the setting for ceremony on several levels.[16]

The drawing room often took on a more feminine appearance than other rooms of reception in English houses (particularly the dining room) because of the custom of ladies withdrawing from dinner first, leaving the men to their political or other male-oriented conversation over the dinner table. Sofas and paintings were introduced, being symptomatic of an increasingly tolerant attitude toward comfort and informality. Sofas were a soft, relaxing form of seating, while paintings might include views and even genre scenes as well as the more formal portraits of royalty and family. At the Palace the group of furniture in Fauquier's inventory that corresponds so closely to that which Botetourt used in the middle room actually included a settee and ten pictures in gilt frames as well as two card tables. Perhaps it was the wish of Catherine Fauquier to treat the middle room as a convenient and attractive drawing room when it was not serving as a state saloon room. The presence of paintings, which might inspire contemplation or provoke discussion, and the availability of the card tables for games and pleasantries in small groups evoke an atmosphere of relaxed sociability.[17]

Botetourt, however, changed the scheme, perhaps because of his bachelor status or possibly on account of his superior rank and more conscious formality. He moved the card tables to the front parlor, where there were pictures (thirty-four scripture prints) and a large upholstered piece of seating furniture (a couch). He perceived the middle room as a space, to use Sheraton's words, in which "to concentrate the elegance of the whole house . . . nothing of a scientific nature should be introduced to take up the attention of any individual, from the general conversation that takes place on such occasions. Hence, the walls should be free of pictures, the tables not lined with books . . . as the design of such meetings are not that each visitant should turn to his favourite study, but to contribute his part towards the amusement of the whole company."[18] These words invoke the ceremony of the "circle"—the device of placing chairs in a circle within the room to initiate and facilitate group discussion rather than allowing splinter groups to indulge in their own talk or activities. Some observers in the third quarter of the century felt that this

The middle room, used for the reception of company after dinner, might well have been the scene of a group conversation in which the arrangement of the (admittedly formal) furniture played an important role in facilitating the function.

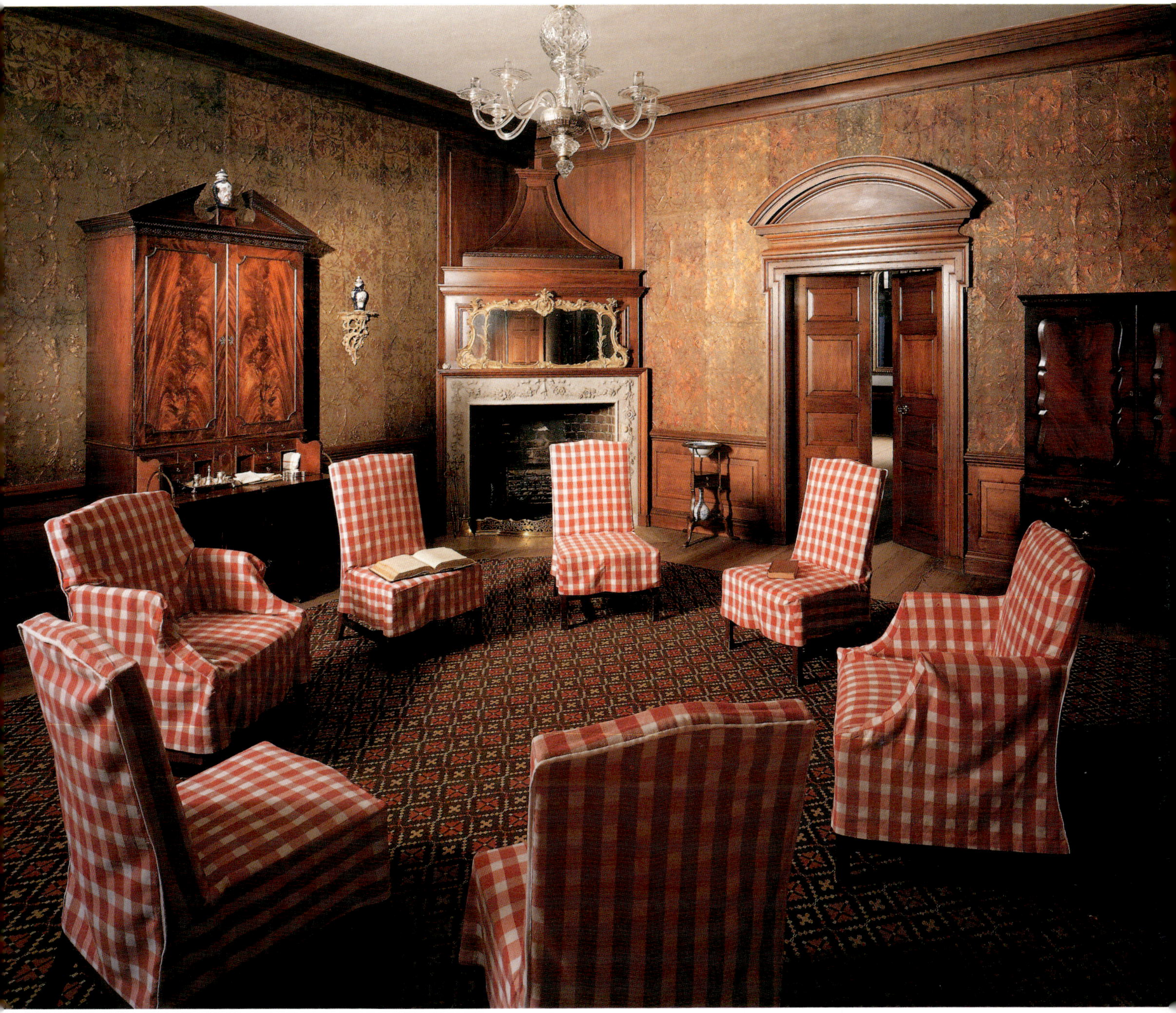

custom was fading from upper levels of society after several generations of popularity, but its appearance in Sheraton's work toward the end of the century illustrates the strength of the tradition. Botetourt was nothing if not sincere, almost earnest, in his pursuit of cultural interests, and it is in character for him to have espoused a formal structured device for coordinating conversation. Through his experience at court for almost a decade before his arrival in Virginia he would have been familiar with such formal social customs. His conscious employment of ceremony, furthermore, and his awareness of the heightened degree of condescension and deference implicit in his superior rank were probably motivating factors in his adopting the more formal approach to the furnishing and use of one of the most ceremonial rooms in the residence. That is not to say that he eschewed relaxed forms of sociability, however. He may indeed have offered his less formal guests a choice after dinner—withdrawing to the parlor for cards (of which there were 144 packs listed in his inventory!) or withdrawing upstairs to the middle room for genteel, but organized, group conversation in the ritual circle or, in winter, semicircle in front of the fire.

Early in the day, well before the dinner ceremony occurred, the middle room served the governor in the private capacity of a dressing room. In this room stood two clothespresses, each well stocked with elegant clothes. Suits of crimson cut velvet with gold buttons, scarlet, blue, and white wool suits trimmed with gold and silver, silk waistcoats edged with gold lace, scarlet frocks—Botetourt stored virtually all his outer clothes in the middle room, though he had such an abundance that they overflowed into the clothespress in the large bedchamber, normally assigned to guests. Botetourt also kept a "Wash Bason Mahog. stand compleat" in the middle room, an intimate item in the midst of so much grandeur. A similar piece was assigned to each bedchamber. The washstand and the clothes together with the location of this room next to his bedchamber all point to its functioning as a dressing room. Fauquier used the middle room in a similar way since the group of items in his inventory that closely resembles the group Botetourt selected for the room included a pine dressing table, almost certainly covered with a fine white linen "toilette" or cloth, and "12 Neck Cloths."[19]

In addition to its formal and social uses, therefore, the middle room served the governor in a private capacity as a dressing room and anteroom to his own bedchamber. But how private was it? The official associations of the room and its rich furnishings suggest that Botetourt may have used it for the typical eighteenth-century gentleman's ceremony of the levee. While there is no firm reference that the levee was a customary practice in Williamsburg, it was a social convention throughout the century and the governors would unquestionably have been familiar with it. The levee was as informal as routinely putting the finishing

The Levée from William Hogarth's series The Rake's Progress. *In satirical manner, it shows the gentleman in skullcap and informal dress surrounded by a motley assortment of petitioners for his attention, while others wait in the background. The variegated group indicates the nature of the occupations and pursuits in which a gentleman was expected to engage.* H: 12 3/8"; W: 15 1/4". CWF 1967-566, 2.

touches to the dress and wig while dispatching mundane business matters with retainers, close associates, or the inevitable petitioners for a multitude of favors, or as formal as being "at home" to the local populace. George III practiced the latter regularly, on a grand scale of course. Twice a week he "showed himself to his loyal subjects." After a ritual dressing in the state bedchamber at St. James's Palace with a lord of the bedchamber in waiting, in which capacity Botetourt had served for several years, the king would appear in the adjoining privy chamber to the high officials of his court and government, and then to the populace in the presence chamber. Those who were not of high rank needed an introduction to attend the levee, but the king tried to speak to everyone. It was very formal, but it worked—"I find it does a man good to be talked to by his sovereign," said Dr. Johnson.[20] Botetourt's familiarity with this ritual, his instinct for "parade," and his innate ability to ingratiate himself with people are persuasive reasons to suggest that he carried this ceremony to the colonial capital, albeit on a more domestic scale. He referred in a letter to his nephew to "d[o]ing Companies" at the Palace, but it is not clear whether these occurred in the morning, as a levee would, or the evening.[21]

"A dressing-room in the house of a person of fashion," commented Isaac Ware in 1756, "is a room of consequence, not only for its natural use in being the place of dressing, but for the several persons who are seen there. The morning is a

THE MIDDLE ROOM UPSTAIRS 109

time many chuse for dispatching business; and as persons of this rank are not to be supposed to wait for people of that kind, they naturally give them orders to come about a certain hour, and admit them while they are dressing."[22] So many of Ware's observations and comments on social customs correspond to the perceived social uses of the spaces in the Governor's Palace that it is not unreasonable to assume that the levee occurred in Williamsburg also, in one form or another, despite the lack of firm documentary reference. The governors clearly had demanding schedules. When one of them, Lord Dunmore, neglected to make himself as available as his predecessors, there was a storm of local protest. It was characteristic for the eighteenth-century gentleman with wide responsibilities to conduct certain business in his dressing room in the morning. It was also customary for men in public office to make themselves visible to "their subjects." Washington was very conscious of the need for this during his first presidency and in 1789 instituted a weekly event that he termed "visits of Compliment" but that his close advisors called "levees." Jefferson and others felt that these events turned into "unrepublican, aristocratic affairs," and in 1801 he noted, "Levees are done away."[23] For the governor in the Palace in Williamsburg, the middle room provided a setting in which his authority was explicit and in which the regalia of his status were fully visible.

Understanding the multiple uses of the middle room is impossible without reference to the adjoining "Passage up Stairs," the space between the head of the stairs and the middle room. It was, as its name suggests, a place of transit. It was also in 1770 a waiting room or antechamber to the middle room. Botetourt furnished it with twelve chairs, a small table, a large looking glass, and "3 large Roman Catholick Pictures." He also kept it lighted with six globe lamps and a lantern since it was part of the path of parade from the hall to the middle room. It mirrored both Sheraton's description of an antechamber: "A room that leads to the principal apartment . . . where servants wait, or strangers, till they may be spoken to by those on whom they attend," and Isaac Ware's: "This use of the dressing-room shews also the necessity of a [adjoining] waiting-room. . . . Though these persons [petitioners] are expected at a certain hour, they cannot always be admitted the moment they come, therefore they must have some place where to stay. When they are not there, [the space] is convenient for the principal servants, who should have a room where they may be near their master, and in call." The proximity of the passage to Botetourt's bedchamber and study made it ideally "convenient for the principal servants" to be stationed there on call when it was not being used for more pressing business.[24]

The functions of the waiting room in a similar place of business were vividly described in 1750 by William Gooch, who had returned to London from Virginia and was seeking improvement in his financial situation. Petitioning "Mr. P." for assistance in his efforts, Gooch was advised by a secretary to "go to the antichamber, which I did, and sat there for above two Hours, seeing others call'd for that came in after me, until my Patience was quite subdued." He finally left word "with the Master of the Ceremonies, that if Mr. P. should ask for me, he should lett him know, I would pay my Duty to him another time."[25] At the Governor's Palace petitioners and others on official business were undoubtedly segregated likewise according to their social or professional standing by the governor's secretary or butler. Lesser ones were presumably accommodated by the secretary in the first floor parlor, the closet to which probably served as his office.

On the walls of the passage, for the edification of waiting petitioners, were hung pictures of a scriptural nature similar to those in the front parlor, which also served as a waiting room, during Botetourt's administration at least. The passage contained three "large Roman Catholick Pictures," the parlor thirty-four scripture prints, all belonging to the colony. In such an Anglican stronghold Roman Catholic pictures might have seemed out of place. However, comparable items could be seen in several Protestant churches along the eastern seaboard—seized by the authorities from pirate ships which, in turn, had captured them from Spanish vessels destined for the New World. Lacking great intrinsic value, they were consigned to public buildings to decorate otherwise bare walls. Churches in Boston, Maryland, and Wilmington, North Carolina, contained similar objects.[26]

The passage upstairs was both the principal place of transit on the second floor, leading from the two staircases to all the chambers on that floor and also to the garret level, as well as a waiting space for those who attended the governor in his library or in the middle room. Like the parlor, which also served as a waiting space, the passage was furnished with scriptural pictures.

The social uses of the middle room in the venerable Palace at Williamsburg were paralleled in the residences of other southern governors. Tryon actually named a room in his new palace in New Bern the "Council chamber." It was where the Council met, occasionally in joint session with the assembly. Its furnishings included full-length portraits of King George III and Queen Charlotte supplied by the crown. Tryon's personal collection of royal portraits of William III, Queen Anne, George I, George III, and Queen Caroline probably adorned the walls of this chamber also. They later figured in the more complete list of his furnishings in the New York residence in 1773, comprising a selective group of royal portraits most unusual in the colonies. The New Bern Council chamber also contained two large mahogany dining tables with green broadcloth covers, thirteen elbow chairs upholstered with horsehair (probably black), three large gilt pier glasses and two gilt sconces, a carpet, and window curtains of green moreen, fringed and tasseled. Other than the difference in the color of the textiles—green and black in contrast to the crimson featured in Williamsburg—the quality and type of furnishings closely resembled those that Botetourt used in the middle room.

Though the Council chamber stood on the first floor of Tryon's Palace, its relationship to nearby rooms was similar to the middle room in Williamsburg. It adjoined the library and the drawing room (called the dining room in an alternate set of plans). But it does not appear to have served as a drawing room itself, for it was clearly a separate state room; moreover, the bedchambers and dressing rooms were all on the second floor as was customary in England at the time the residence was built. Balls and other assemblies probably took place in the new Council room, the largest and most convenient space in the residence for such events. Prior to the completion of Tryon's Palace the Council had held a ball for the governor in the "Great Ball Room" of the courthouse in New Bern, adjourning to supper afterward in the "Long Room" on the upper floor. The Council had also used one of these two rooms for its meetings before it moved to its elegant new location in the Palace.[27]

Eden's Annapolis residence did not include a designated Council chamber, but in view of the dilapidated condition of the earlier magazine and Council room and the incomplete state of the new "Stadt House" it is likely that his "Long Room" or the "Gilt Leather Parlour" served the state function. Into the latter Eden had introduced crimson damask window curtains and a pier glass with a carved and gilt frame, items of a patently ceremonial nature. But the presence of paintings and card tables in the gilt leather parlor resembles Fauquier's furnishing scheme for the Williamsburg middle room more than Botetourt's. The "Long Room" or saloon on the first floor of the Annapolis residence was also sufficiently elegant for the Council, with its numerous chairs, large mahogany tables, and fifteen highly valued "elegant peices of painting." Yet the dining and tea equipment and gaming table inventoried in the room evoke an atmosphere that was more relaxed than formal.[28]

Lord William Campbell's house in Charleston, South Carolina, was richly furnished though he lived there so briefly. In his schedule of losses the first room listed was labeled the "dining room" though it contained none of the items conventionally used in such a room. It probably served rather as a drawing room, for the schedule included both a breakfast parlor and a dining parlor with the appropriate dining accoutrements. The "dining room" was distinguished by rich materials and a crimson color scheme; indeed, *silk* damask, an expensive material rarely found on seating furniture in the colonies, covered the settee and twelve chairs while crimson silk damask curtains were listed in storage. Three pieces of "red velvet paper hangings" were also listed in storage, probably left over from a recent installation. If the "red velvet paper," an expensive and formal wall covering, was installed in the "dining room"—and it was the only room in the schedule in which a prevailing color scheme was noted—the combination of textured wall covering with patterned silk upholstery and curtains was certainly commensurate with "the chief apartment of a noble, or genteel, house . . . for the reception of persons of the highest rank."[29]

However, neither the New Bern palace, the Annapolis residence, nor the Campbell townhouse featured the architectural artifice that lent such drama to the approach to the inner presence of the middle room upstairs in the

The previous view of the fireplace (p. 103) shows the summer installation of chimney board, deemed more attractive than the smoked interior of the opening. Winter fireplace accessories, however, had an important decorative quality of their own, aided by the colorful pattern of the carpet (taken up in the summer), which was possibly of the "Scotch" type.

Williamsburg Palace. Despite Tryon's predilection for formal ceremony and ritual, to which the North Carolinians did not take kindly, his newer residence appears to have embodied the more relaxed attitude to these codes that is characteristic of the later eighteenth century. By contrast, the Williamsburg Palace was architecturally the offspring of the highly ceremonial seventeenth century, and a strain of this seems to have lingered on in the way Botetourt used the room. There are evident similarities between the latter and Lord William Campbell's most formal room, though Campbell's house was not an official residence provided by the crown or the colony, while his marriage into the South Carolina patriarchy might have predisposed him to settle for a less formal ambience than obtained in Williamsburg under the courtly Botetourt. Neither Botetourt nor Campbell hung pictures in their drawing rooms, following Sheraton's dicta, in marked contrast to Tryon, Eden, and Fauquier. The two aristocrats probably shared the perception that the formal codes for such situations, so clearly delineated by contemporary English observers, were natural and appropriate to transplant to the colonial context.[30]

Elsewhere in Virginia, the only parallels to the state occasions in the middle room of the Palace occurred in the Council chamber at the Capitol. Since the middle room also served as a drawing room, it may have provided a prototype for the "drawing room" at Tazewell Hall, the handsomely appointed Williamsburg house of the attorney general, John Randolph. The similarities are remarkable, befitting a high official of the colony—a large pier glass and a chimney glass, both with gilt frames, crimson curtains, "handsome ornamental china branches" (lighting devices), a large Turkey carpet, ten "handsome" mahogany chairs, and prints of the king and queen. Yet the added presence of card tables, tea tables, teakettle stand and "Nanquin" tea china, mahogany settees, china figures on the chimneypiece, and two "Dutch pieces of painting" implies a more relaxed and informal atmosphere—akin to Fauquier's use of the middle room—than the formal, unmarried Botetourt seems to have thought fit for "the character and ordinance of a state saloon-room" in his official residence.[31]

In his innovative designs for Coleshill (Berkshire) of about 1650 the brilliant architect Sir Roger Pratt moved the location of the great chamber away from its traditional placement on one side of the house to a position of increased prominence and heightened ceremonial significance in the center. It was one of the important precedents for locating the "great room" in the middle of the second story of the Governor's Palace two generations later. "Let the fairest room above be placed in the very midst of the house," Pratt declared, "as the bulk of a man is between his members."[32] His vivid analogy invokes the image of a man in a firm, formal posture, the kind of stance, figuratively, that was required of the governor at the Palace on ceremonial occasions. The analogy also conjures up an image of strength and breadth either appropriate or delusory for the person to whom this "fairest room above" was a public, official arena. It further evokes the physical characteristics of a man, more private perhaps, but unmistakable nonetheless. Here, too, it is significant in view of the numerous uses to which the room was put. No other space in the Palace juxtaposed to quite the extent that the middle room did the public persona and the private person of the governor and the artifacts he needed to sustain them. No other room encompassed such a wide range of ceremonial activities from state occasions to daily dressing ritual and after-dinner conversations. The room clearly provided a stage—symbolically located and sumptuously appointed—for the interaction of the representative of the crown with a wide range of people on a variety of different levels.

Ceremonies and symbolic forms that served to reinforce authority and generate harmony in eighteenth-century society, that served the purposes of intimidation and accommodation in state and church, had to be widely recognizable. They became relatively standardized, with few variations. Virtually all of them implied hierarchy, gradations of physical and social power that were articulated yet inextricably related. To a Virginia society that was so imbued with the physical and social forms and values of the militia, that was so organized by the scattered courthouses and churches, the symbolism of the weapons at the Governor's Palace was as unmistakable as was the progression to a sumptuously appointed inner sanctum that conveyed superiority. Like the spaces within the other public buildings and the ceremonies and symbols used in them, the spaces and the symbolic accoutrements of the Palace were designed to express ideals of order and harmony, of mediating conflict and maintaining authority.[33]

Courthouses and churches were the largest structures most Virginians ever saw and entered. Only a few private plantation houses and the Governor's Palace were on a similar grand scale. Their size was meant to arouse awe and respect for the functions they housed and to symbolize the idea that the order and harmony they represented was grander than the individuals within it. In eighteenth-century Virginia this order was in reality imposed by elite male dominance. ceremonially exhibited in the procession of the justices, the belated group entry of the gentry into church services, and the progression of governor and Council or those they received in state through the hall to the great room on the upper level of the Palace. These ceremonies were accompanied by special effects such as the justices' wigs and hats and their raised bench, the gentlemen's conspicuous clothing and their private pews, the Palace's appointments and its parade of rooms.

Dominance or intimidation produced order, but accommodation was necessary for harmony. In the sequence of spaces at the Governor's Palace that the parade from the hall to the upper middle room represented, intimidation was readily apparent in the symbols of the crown and its power, especially to subjects whose loyalty needed to be reaffirmed or to those of a different nation. Accommodation was evident in the utilization of the upper room as a space for civilized and peaceful intercourse, the art of conversation, the communication of ideas, and the conducting of daily affairs. The enduring images of the effects achieved by these ceremonies and symbols are of success and of failure. Cultural ideals emanating from England were successfully assimilated by a provincial people despite their eventual claim that they were of a different national character and should therefore be independent. The symbols of power, however, failed to encourage accommodation and sustain assimilation; after years of increasingly proprietorial instincts the local gentry firmly assumed their own control of the weapons. More poignantly, the native Americans received the brunt of much of the force that the weapons represented, suffered, and never became assimilated.

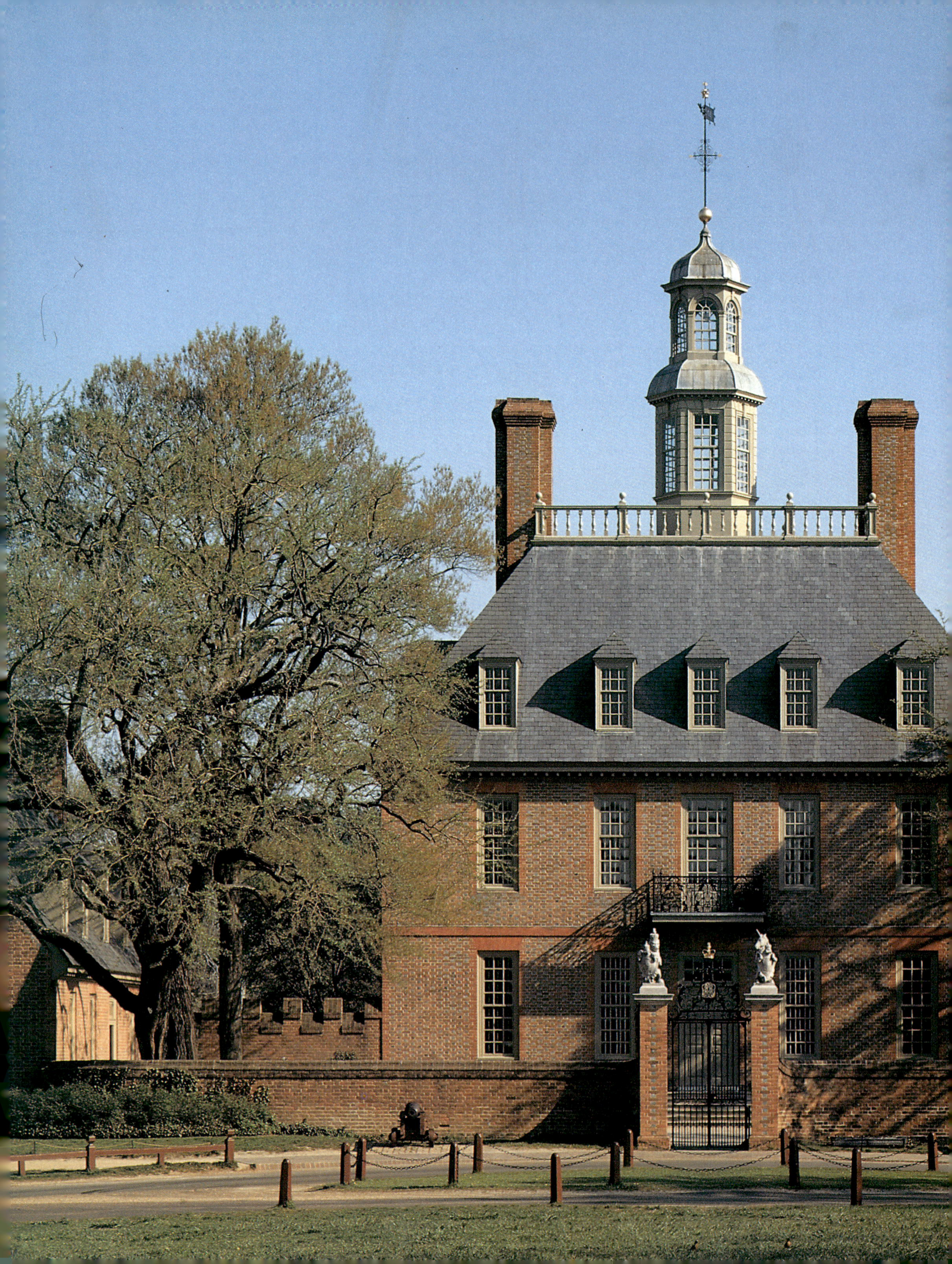

Public Life

Public Life

The very words used in the eighteenth century as names for the four rooms in this section are words that describe or imply social action—dining, parlor (derived from the verb to talk), ball, and supper. They are terms for prominent social activities at the core of such concepts as hospitality, sociability, fashion, and dance that illuminate the public articulation of society and the deployment of public spaces in Virginia in the late colonial period. The words are resonant and allusive and restore energy and animation to social groups and social spaces that were once filled with life.

The rooms were designed primarily to work as pairs. In an early reference to the Palace interior the dining room was linked to the smaller parlor adjoining it, and the two rooms appear to have been used in tandem whether the main activity was the important midday meal or whether it was mundane official business.[1] At midday the parlor provided a useful gathering space for the host and his guests while the dining room was being prepared and certain foods brought in. After the meal the parlor could serve as a withdrawing room if the middle room upstairs was not selected. During the governor's business hours the parlor probably fulfilled a waiting room function for those visitors expecting to see the governor in his office. Ballroom and supper room worked in tandem when a large company or assembly was gathered for a festive or ceremonial event, music and dancing taking place in the larger ballroom and refreshments being elegantly laid out in the supper room. In the terse listings and enumerations of the inventory are grouped objects that were essential for the proper functioning of the above activities in the style appropriate to the rank of the governor. Through these concise notations the spaces once again become dynamic, the activities real and urgent, the cultural interactions between different minds and mindsets apparent and satisfying.

Hospitality was a fundamental ingredient of gentry life. An insufficiency of it was one of the charges filed against Governor Francis Nicholson by certain Virginia gentry early in the century. His opponents claimed that his hospitality

Portrait of William Byrd II of Virginia, oil on canvas, painted in London perhaps about 1705. This is a likeness of a typical English country gentleman of the period, the model on which the successful Virginia planters and tradesmen endeavored to fashion themselves and their sons. H: *49½"*; W: *39¾"*. CWF *1956-561.*

was "most scandalously penurious, no way suiting the dignity of her Ma'ties Governour, having but one Dish of meat at his table." Such a complaint would have seemed merely ludicrous to the authorities in England were the governor not, in fact, expected to maintain an appropriate social presence. That presence, that "dignity," was symbolized by the dining table and the abundance and quality of its contents and offerings. By deploring this deficiency in Nicholson's performance, his opponents drew attention to the slight to the colonists' self-esteem. Dignity commensurate with high status involved both host and hosted, and the act of feeding in the middle of the day occupied a central, crucial part in the display and maintenance of official and social decorum.[2]

William Byrd II, the Virginia-born contemporary of Nicholson, who spent most of his impressionable years in England, has been described as leading a life of "supercharged sociability," "relentless" hospitality, and "incessant visiting." "At home and abroad an utterly public man," Byrd expected as much of himself in this social role as his peers evidently did of the English governor. The leading Virginia planters had a crucial investment in keeping the social fabric together and making it work; the governor likewise had a commitment to making the system of social cohesion work. Fervent social activity was the Virginians' response to the inherent thinness of colonial society. The system they created was a construct, an artifice that was essential to their claims to gentility and sophistication. Without such men and their social ambitions, Virginia "polite" society might not exist.[3]

Hospitality has also been equated with "good neighborhood" and the ceremony of dining with recurrent acts of social cohesion. This "relentless" activity was not only for purposes of sociability. Byrd and his peers were continually at work, making contacts, striking deals, developing friends, gathering information. "Good fellowship" and finances were never far apart. If it was an "American style," the governors did not comment on its distinctive provincial nature, though their reactions varied. Spotswood declared that life in the tiny colonial capital at the beginning of his administration was "Neither in a Crowd of Company, nor in a Throng of Business, but rather after a quiet Country manner." Gooch, however, was constantly worried about the endless round of company and the attendant costs.[4] Neither Fauquier nor Botetourt expressed his opinion on the subject. They entertained. Both had experienced the active life of London, while Botetourt had for many years held provincial office in Gloucestershire. The social environment in Virginia apparently did not strike them as being sufficiently different to comment.

"American style" or not, active sociability was an established eighteenth-century custom that was as conspicuous in the third quarter of the century as it had been earlier. Hospitality was deeply gratifying to Virginians, even compulsive, as Rhys Isaac has pointed out. Certain colonists constantly put their sophisticated life-styles on parade—they had been created only through massive effort, which the ostentation served, in turn, to justify. Various acts of hospitality and plentiful offerings of food and libation were intimately related to the inner core of self-esteem in Virginia gentry society. It was widely expected that the governor would participate in this ritual pattern, extending hospitality as befitted the representative of majesty, and it was assumed that the gentry would be involved and partake on a recurrent basis.[5]

From the need for hospitality and sociability sprang the urge to assemble in groups to eat, to drink, to talk, and also to dance. Dances, balls, or "assemblies" were widely approved occasions for social and sexual encounter and offered unusual opportunities for social advancement. To know how to dance was a necessary qualification for admission and membership in the gentry class. It was a mark of ambition, a badge of gentility, de rigueur for gentry women. Balls frequently marked important occasions and anniversaries. The king's birthday ball at the Palace was the height of the Williamsburg social year. Balls and assemblies also celebrated rites of passag were approved outlets for high spirits, and accepted venues for matchmaking. To some, their appeal may have been the opportunity on a miniature scale and without harmful consequence to dissolve order and formulate it again. The motion of the dance is an evocative image to summon up the ceaseless action of society, its disciplined rules as much as its freedom of movement. It incorporated definite hierarchy and precedence, yet in Virginia it was also the scene of the extraordinary transsocial phenomenon of men and women in stylish apparel dancing the slave-derived African "jig."[6]

Fashion, that "bauble," that "foolish passion," unprecedentedly dynamic, even mercurial in this period was closely associated with the material objects that were called into action in these spaces. Items for the dining ceremony and clothing donned to make a distinctive appearance at a sociable assembly were prime among the fashionable requisites of the day. The accoutrements of the table, as well as the foodstuffs, were indicators of social position or social ambition as surely as were the kind of clothes worn, the materials, and the styles. These consumer goods were closely linked to the barometer of fashion, and Virginians were as active as any group within the British empire in the "revolution" that saw ever-greater quantities of goods in ever-increasing variety becoming affordable to an ever-expanding range of purchasers. Fashion called for constant update and it entailed continual comparison and competition. While novelty may have been fashion's main contribution to decorative styles, it undoubtedly stimulated genuine innovation in the major arts of the time.[7]

In the fifteen years preceding the outbreak of the American Revolution, fashion and the material objects with which it was inextricably entwined became politicized. During the years of the Nonimportation Agreements certain kinds of goods became distinctly controversial. These goods may or may not have served to unify otherwise disparate elements of American society—to give them at least some points of mutual identification and interest—as Breen has argued. Nonetheless, the kinds of possessions that denoted affluence, she items associated with social prestige and superior discernment preoccupied Anglo-American society of the 1760s and 1770s. American taste in consumer goods undoubtedly became thoroughly anglicized in this period. For many who came to the Palace the governor was as close—both in time and space—as they would ever get to what was really happening in influential circles "at home."[8]

PUBLIC LIFE 121

The Dining Room and Parlor
APARTMENTS OF CONVERSATION

"To understand thoroughly the art of living, it is necessary, perhaps, to have passed some time amongst the French, and to have studied the customs of that social and conversible people," declared the prominent architect-designer Robert Adam in 1773. Hardly a novel observation, it was nonetheless effective as a foil to introduce his explanation of a peculiarly English custom—the extended use of the dining room and its vital place in the sequence of primary rooms. He continued, "Their [the French] eating rooms seldom or never constitute a piece in their great apartments, but lie out of the suite, and in fitting them up, little attention is paid to beauty or decoration. The reason of this is obvious; the French meet there only at meals, when they trust to the display of the table for show and magnificence, not to the decoration of the apartment; and as soon as the entertainment is over, they immediately retire to the rooms of company. It is not so with us."[1]

In contrast to the Frenchmen's love of female company and consequent disinclination to spend long periods of social time segregated from them, Englishmen had forged for themselves a more male-oriented society. "Accustomed by habit, or induced by the nature of our climate," Adam explained, "we indulge more largely in the enjoyment of the bottle. Every person of rank here is either a member of the legislation, or entitled by his condition to take part in the political arrangements of his country, and to enter with ardour into those discussions to which they give rise; these circumstances lead men to live more with one another, and more detached from the society of the ladies. The eating rooms are considered as the apartments of conversation, in which we are to pass a great part of our time."[2]

What Adam had in mind in describing men's detachment from ladies was the English custom of the ladies withdrawing from the dinner table after the dessert course to a separate place, leaving the men to their primarily political, certainly male-oriented conversation and as much wine and tobacco as they could consume. The dining room, in his parlance, thus became the

The conversation function of the dining room could well occur around the fireplace in cold weather, in the "semi-circle" mentioned in contemporary accounts. The fire screen, which served to radiate the heat, is in this instance the only item in the building with a good history of having belonged to Lord Botetourt.

apartment of conversation for men and the nearby room to which the ladies retired, the parlor or drawing room, was the location for their segregated activities and talk. These rooms were therefore "a piece in the great apartments" and were treated accordingly, architecturally as well as in the choice of their furnishings.

In the seventeenth century, the eating ceremony or "entertainment" in grand English houses was gradually removed from the "great chamber," the splendid room in the center of the house on the second floor. (It had ascended to that location a hundred years or so before, from the vestiges of the medieval great hall.) It was moved first to a parlor, sometimes called the dining parlor, then to the dining room. In the grandest houses there was a great or state dining room *and* a lesser dining parlor nearby. The latter room could also serve as the withdrawing room. Eventually a separate drawing room was introduced but the rooms were still designed in pairs. The pattern was generally copied, even in less pretentious houses and in the colonies. In 1727, for example, in the terse language of the executive journals of the Council of Virginia specifying repairs

The trappings of gentility pressed into the service of fellowship, civilized intercourse, and wide-ranging communication. Dozens of varied artifacts made from many different materials brought from around the world performed integral roles, along with the equally diverse foods and wines, in the playing out of the dinner ceremony. Into this arena also came news from around the world to be disseminated to the governor's Virginia guests. Likewise, news from around the colony was communicated at this table, some of it undoubtedly transmitted to and found to be useful at Whitehall.

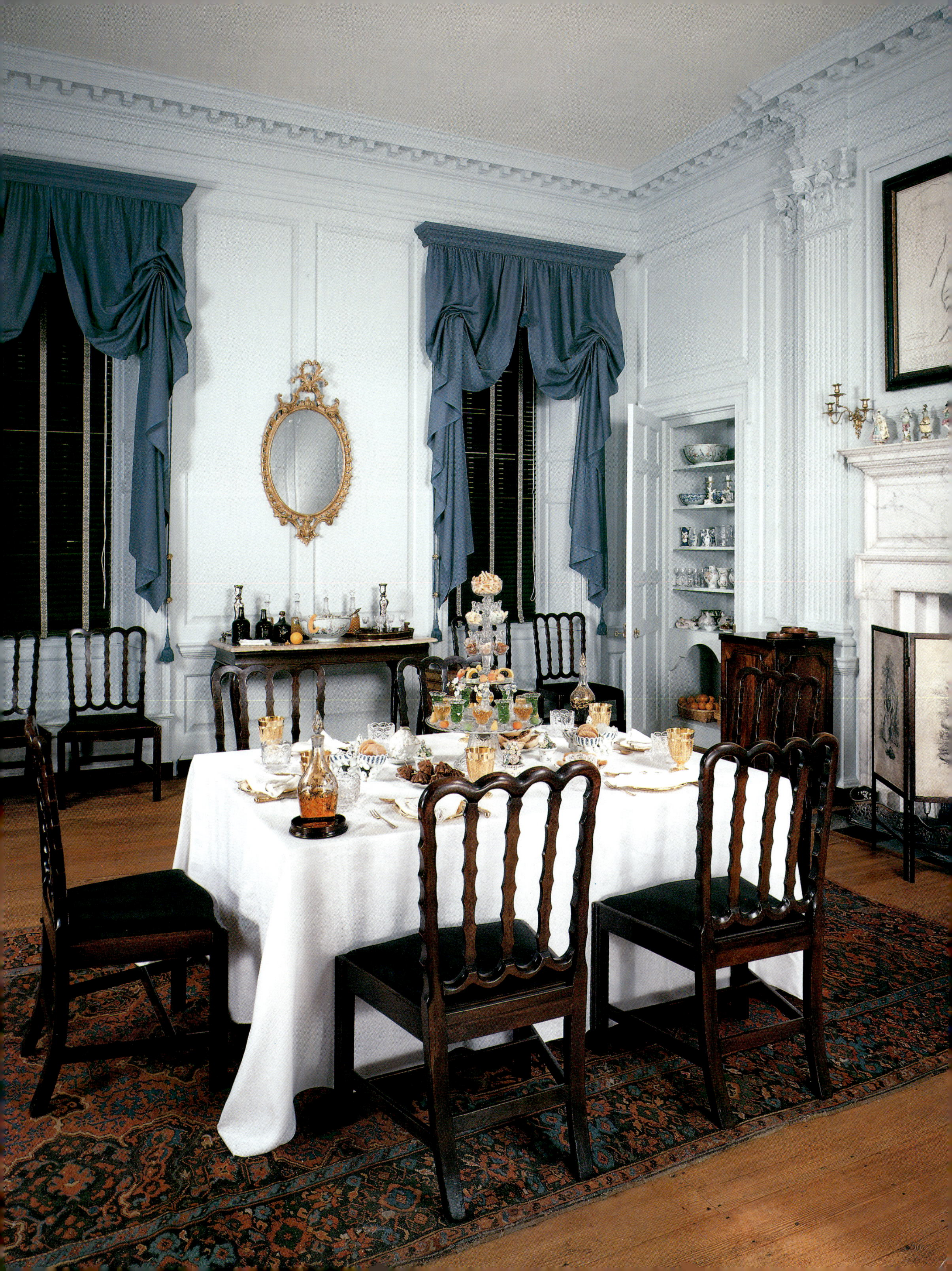

necessary for the Palace, there appeared a notation for painting "the great Dining Room and Parlour thereto adjoining."[3]

Dining rooms and parlors worked in tandem, though they were always subject to individual choice and variation on the part of the owner or occupant, especially in an official residence where the parlor might be invaded by business functions and therefore be too public for ladies to retire to in comfort after dinner. Unfortunately, people with business to conduct with the governor could not always be relied on to come *before* dinner. While it was the general rule for ladies to remain in the dining room until the dessert course was finished and then move to an adjoining drawing room for tea and their own inimitable forms of conversation, sometimes their desire to separate themselves from the clamor of male conversation led to a drawing room being placed some distance from the dining room. To confuse the issue, in the colonies in the 1760s dining room and drawing room were synonymous terms for some people. Benjamin Franklin added "a Drawing Room or Dining Room" to his house in Philadelphia in the 1760s, for example, and proudly told his sister that in the "new Room we can dine a Company of 24 Persons." At Tryon's Palace, the two terms were certainly used for the same room, though in that residence there was also an adjoining parlor. On formal occasions, therefore, the ladies probably withdrew to the parlor where they could be joined later by the gentlemen; when the dining room was vacated the servants could clear the dishes, collapse the tables, and push them back to the walls, transforming the room into a drawing room to which all the company could return if they wished.[4]

Fithian's diary provides valuable insights into social customs and room usages in gentry society in Virginia in the early 1770s. Though Nomini Hall was full of children and to a certain extent was organized around them, the rooms retained clearly specified functions—all the chambers on the second floor were devoted to sleeping, while on the first floor stood a ballroom, a study, a dining room for children, and a dining room "where we usually sit" for company. The Carters' dining room doubled as the drawing room—"So soon as we rose from supper, the Company form'd into a semicircle round the fire." In other words, in this domestic environment the family and guests merely withdrew to another part of the room, organizing themselves in the ritual circle (or, in this instance during winter, semicircle) for the ensuing conversation. Only once in Fithian's experience—and it was in another household—did the ladies retire early from the table leaving the men to their wine and conversation. Fithian's lack of surprise on noting this occurrence suggests that it was a not unusual custom.[5]

In addition to a room in tandem with the dining room for use after dinner, custom also prescribed (when possible) a room in which company assembled *before* the meal. Robert Adam briefly mentioned in his discourse a

Winter and summer arrangements for the dining room feature, above, a fire screen and a carpet that was often covered with broadcloth to absorb stains from spilled food and, below, a painted canvas floorcloth and a chimney board. The chairs are of an uncommon type and have a connection with both Lords Botetourt and Dunmore. One example, almost identical in detail to those shown here, with a history of having been in the Palace, has survived in a Virginia family.

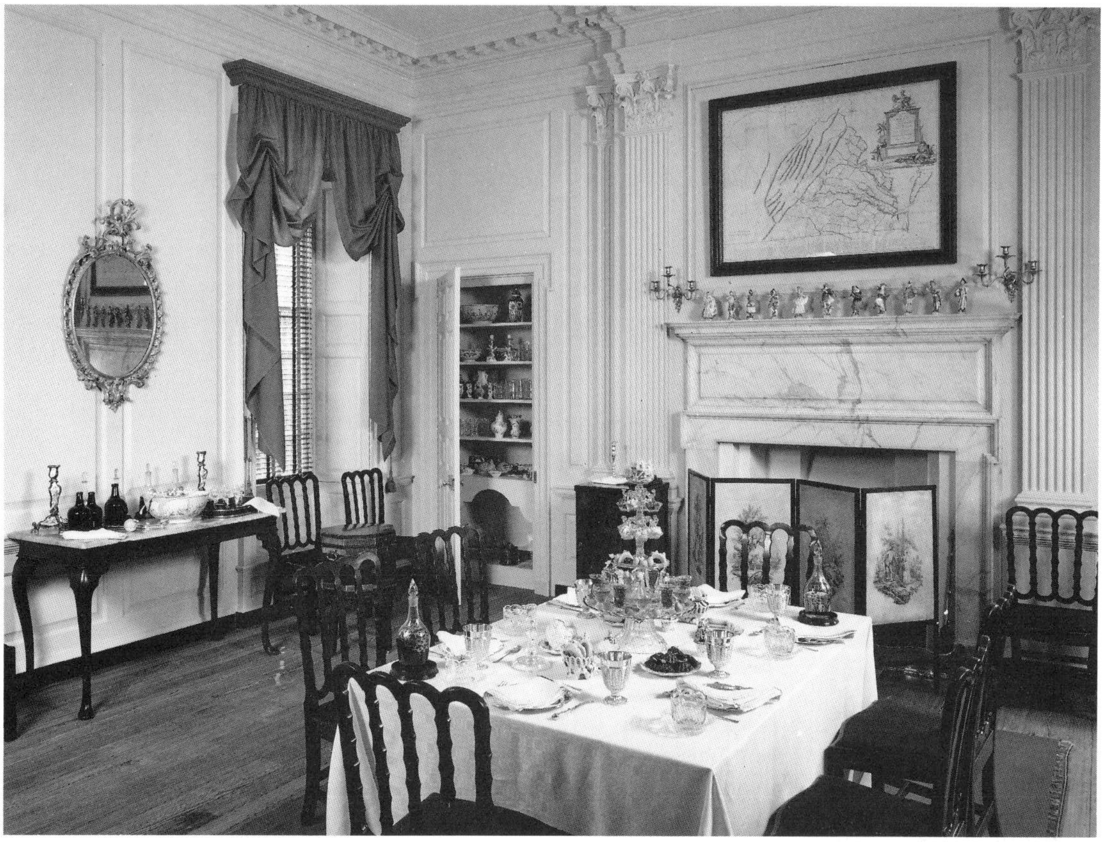

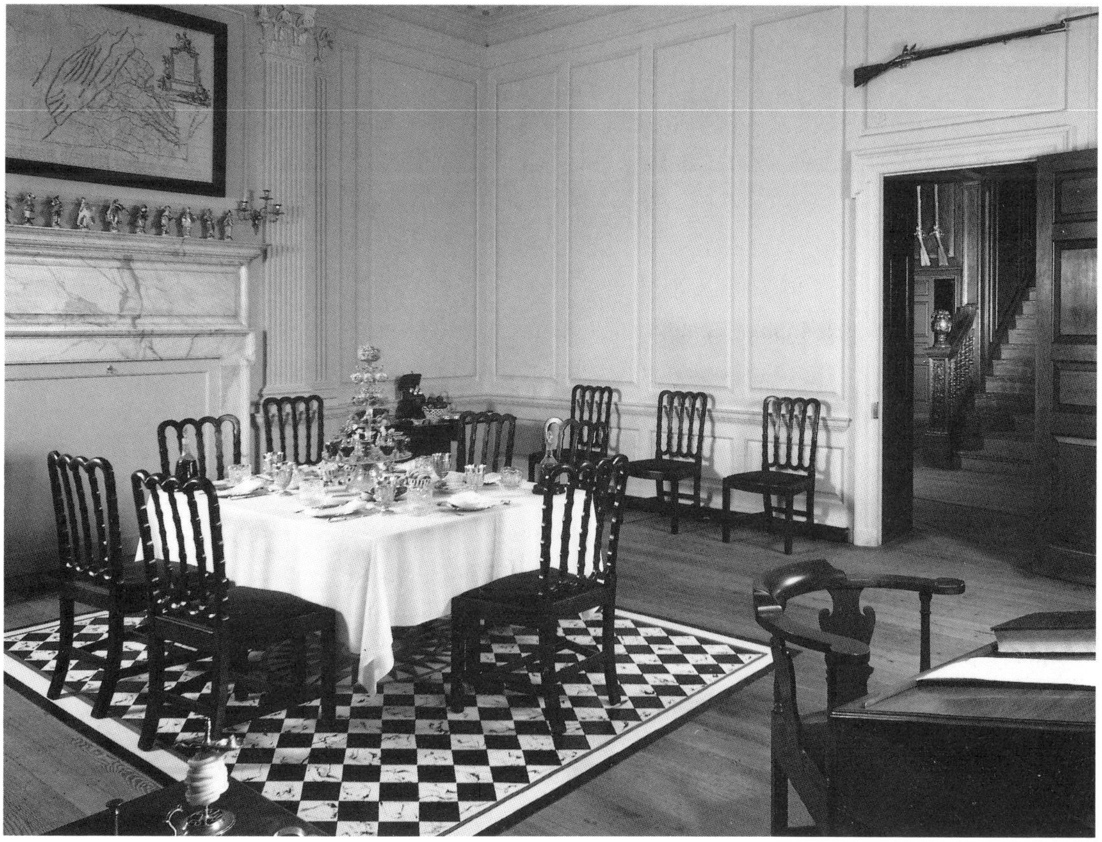

space leading off the drawing room "for the reception of company before dinner." A short aside from Gooch confirms that, while he was in residence at the Palace in Williamsburg, the initial part of the dinner ceremony required a separate space—"when things were upon the Table . . . [we] . . . were call'd to Dinner and came into the Room."[6] This gathering space was most probably the parlor or on grand occasions perhaps the middle room upstairs. After dinner the ladies probably retired for cards, tea, and conversation to the parlor when it was not needed for business functions or upstairs to the middle room where they might eventually be joined by the gentlemen. On many occasions, however, there were no ladies present. Botetourt was unmarried, and other governors' wives were absent in England for long stretches of time. Many dinner guests at the Palace were men in town on business or travelers from afar and they were rarely accompanied by their wives. At such times, and they were probably frequent, ladies' sensibilities did not have to be spared and politics could dominate the dinner conversation from beginning to end.

While it was customarily "fitted up with elegance and splendor," the dining room was appointed in a different manner from the other principal rooms. Wall coverings such as damask and tapestry were avoided for they tended to "retain the smell of the victuals." The 1727 reference to the Palace "great Dining Room" quoted above shows that its walls were painted, in

At those times the governor had declared as "Office Hours," the front parlor, immediately adjacent to the hall, almost certainly served as a space in which the clerk could conduct business while visitors waited. The room was also furnished with elegant items such as the modish Chelsea china figures and card tables, useful when the room provided a leisure function.

128 PUBLIC LIFE

contrast to the gilt leather hangings recommended for the great room on the second floor. By the 1770s, according to tastemaker Robert Adam, appropriate decoration for dining rooms included statues and paintings together with a looking glass that hung en suite with the sideboard.[7] Earlier, Fauquier appears to have hung his "8 pieces of painting" (appraised at forty pounds and twice as valuable as his library) in the dining room along with an oval looking glass. Botetourt brought few paintings with him other than the royal portraits, so he decorated the walls of the dining room with a group of wax portraits, retained the oval looking glass that Fauquier had used, and introduced a large, newly engraved map of Virginia.[8]

Early in the century the tables on which dinner was served were round and could not be butted together. If the company was too numerous for the main table, smaller tables were introduced and separate conversations ensued. William Byrd II recorded such an instance in 1711 when he "waited on the Governor home to dinner where we found Mrs. Churchill and several other ladies and my wife among them. The table was so full that the Doctor and Mrs. Graeme and I had a little table to ourselves and were more merry than the rest of the company."[9] By the third quarter of the eighteenth century, however, dining tables were made with squared ends so that they could be joined together and the company unified. Botetourt's large mahogany dining table and "1 smaller ditto," when placed together, would certainly have accommodated twelve diners using the chairs that were kept in the room.

Dinner was served in the early afternoon, at which time footmen turned into waiters "well instructed" on the fine points of the ceremony. They had prepared the dining room and embellished the table from the staging area across the passage—the "little middle room" and its large storage closet under the stairs are shown by the inventory to have served this function. Footmen brought in the dishes filled with food directly from the kitchen outside; the inventory listed virtually all the serving dishes (fashionable Staffordshire creamware) in the servants' hall adjoining the kitchen rather than in the main house. After they had placed the dishes on the table, the footmen took guests' plates, which had been kept warm in the mahogany plate warmer in the dining room, to the dishes as requested. The governor carved the main meat dish or perhaps delegated the honor to his wife as William Gooch periodically did to his wife during his administration. Drinks were provided by the butler, probably assisted by the under butler, from the marble-topped sideboard—the same piece of furniture had served this indispensable function in the room since the earliest days of its use.[10] Glasses normally stored in the "bowfat" or cupboard in the dining room as well as in the butler's pantry were filled on request from the table—"calling for drink"—certain wines being kept chilled in the mahogany wine cooler near the sideboard while others were kept in glass decanters identified with silver bottle labels. Beer was also served. A change of wine between courses obliged the butler to rinse the glasses at the sideboard rather than change them, then carry them back to the table on one of the numerous silver salvers the governor owned. On special occasions the dessert course required a complete redressing of the table with multitiered glass pyramids ornamented with little glass pails full of candied fruit or similar sweets and adorned with flowers, with "ornamental china" probably including exotic little figures from the bowfat, perhaps even with a miniature Chinese temple set with shells. Dessert knives, forks, and spoons with silver gilt or porcelain handles added an extra flourish. Botetourt had a much more extensive choice of silver or gilt accoutrements for this elaborate aspect of the "entertainment" than the previous governors, particularly the six gold cups which must have struck most of his guests as being quite grand.[11]

Dinner concluded with the habitual ceremony of toasts. By proposing the health of the king (or the king and queen together) the governor initiated the final stage of the ceremony and retained control of it. Other individuals subsequently proposed toasts to which all the guests or merely another individual could respond. For those not initiated in the ways of the table, the various rituals could be complicated. Philip Fithian at Nomini Hall confessed that they took time to master. One day in the absence of both Mr. and Mrs.

Carter he was called on to share with one of their sons the duties of "Director of the Ceremonies at Table." He passed the test. "I have them at last all by heart," he wrote; it had taken him three months. Another incident at Nomini Hall shows that maladroit performance of this particular aspect of the ceremony was taken as a sign of social inferiority. One guest struck the tutor as "unacquainted with company for when he would, at Table, drink our Health, he held the glass of Porter fast with both his Hands, and then gave an insignificant nod to each one at the Table, in Hast[e], and with fear, and then drank like an Ox."[12]

Toasts proclaimed political affinities or personal loyalties and could be used as a diplomatic way to mend fences. Gooch found himself in the unfortunate position in 1747 of calling for an apology at the dinner table from a visitor who had been recommended to him by his brother, the bishop of Norwich. This man had the previous day, Gooch wrote, "at my own Table . . . in a most insolent manner . . . affront[ed] my wife and Sister." To Gooch's considerable dismay, the visitor, "like a Statue, as stiff and immoveable" failed to respond in the desired manner; "at last calling for Drink, 'tis true he drank my health, [but] took no notice" of the ladies whose code he had previously transgressed. Fauquier also chose the dinner table as the scenario for an expected apology from a more eminent guest, the Reverend William Robinson, commissary to the bishop of London in Virginia, in 1760. This, too, never materialized. During the early 1770s toasts to "the Sons of America," the "Northern Sons of Liberty," and "Success to American Trade" were heard throughout Virginia, though not at the Palace. Less provocative ones were drunk to absent friends, charming young ladies, or "a good price for our commodities!"[13]

A cut-glass pyramid hung with little baskets for fruit or candies and embellished with tiny vases for silk (or fresh) flowers was the centerpiece of the dessert table. An exceptional arrangement for this course might feature the expressive little porcelain figures that otherwise adorned the mantelshelf. The figures were specified as "Chelsea," having been produced at the small factory outside London in the 1750–1770 period when it enjoyed certain royal patronage.

The elaborately orchestrated social ritual of dinner was carried out with the aid of an extraordinary range and number of imaginative, highly decorative accoutrements. It engaged many members of the governor's household. Liveried footmen conveyed a wide range of foods from the production center in the kitchen and an extensive choice of wines from the cellars to the carefully prepared dining room and then became a part of the ceremony itself. Through the various stages of the ceremony a great array of fashionable goods was brought into service, drawn from a huge stock of such items. Botetourt could choose, for example, from fifty-three damask tablecloths and three hundred and eighty matching napkins normally stored in the linen closet. He owned a further forty-eight tablecloths that were designated either for breakfast or servants' use, and an additional sixty napkins specifically for the tea ceremony. These fine patterned linens were very costly. At dinner he could utilize a variety of ceramic tablewares including the novel and ultra-fashionable queensware made by Josiah Wedgwood, promoted by its royal patronage, and soon in demand in vast quantities by American consumers. Chelsea porcelain also boasted royal patronage, and Botetourt's twenty-two intriguing little figures in this novel soft paste could be the focus of a dessert display for the dinner or supper table. When not used thus the figures were sufficiently distinctive to adorn the mantelpieces of the dining room and the parlor.[14]

Chinese blue and white porcelain accompanied silver salts, cruets, butter boats, a soup tureen, a bread basket, and knives, forks, and spoons in graded sizes, along with various types of cut and engraved drinking glasses, decanters, cruets, salts, and almost four dozen cut-glass "wash hand glasses" and saucers. These were a refinement that few overlooked. With such a variety of types and forms some guests were probably awed and some bewildered, for fashions (and forms) changed rapidly. An instance of the sometimes dubious effects of novelty is found in a letter from William Nelson to Francis Fauquier, Jr., in London, in 1768: "Mrs. Nelson is obliged for your present of the Necessaries for a Dessert: tho' I Fancy she will be puzeled to bring them into use." While the Nelsons were members of an older generation (born in the first quarter of the century), they were certainly among the gentry elite. Their bemusement at the precise function of these new "baubles" shows how quickly fashionable items succeeded each other in this period of exceptional consumerism.[15]

Botetourt entertained Virginians in the dining room during the period affected by the Townshend Duties when colonists "began to speak of consumer goods in highly charged moral language." He was in office when the Nonimportation Agreement of 1769 came into effect. The governor evidently disagreed in private with the ministry's policy, possibly defusing local resentment against himself as the figurehead for that policy. Virginia ladies made their gesture, however, by appearing at a ball at the Capitol in December 1769 in Virginia cloth dresses in contrast to their customary silks, satins, and brocades. Botetourt put a good face on it. No hint of hostility to the governor's egregious display of elegant consumerism has survived in the letters of the period. Perhaps his gestures were all conciliatory—he later bought a Virginia cloth counterpane, for example, and installed it in a guest bedchamber—or perhaps his great politeness was unexceptionable. In any event, no Virginian who sat through dinner or witnessed the supper table when it was set up with refreshments during balls and assemblies at the Palace during Botetourt's administration can have failed to take note of the sheer abundance of elegant artifacts of public and social display.[16]

Beyond the contributions that the dining room undoubtedly makes to the history of manners and fashion in colonial Virginia, it is apparent that the dinner ceremony also provided the occasion at the Palace for intellectual exchanges, some of them wide-ranging and momentous. In essence, the dining

Above, Colonel (and burgess) George Washington as he appeared to portraitist Charles Willson Peale during the period when the sitter was a frequent dinner guest at the Palace. Oil on canvas, 1772. H: 50½"; W: 40½". *Courtesy, Washington and Lee University.*

Right, John Murray, Earl of Dunmore, oil on canvas, painted by Sir Joshua Reynolds in 1765 in the "grand manner," which, in different context, was the British attitude calculated to put most leading colonists in a distinctly irritated frame of mind. Dunmore's attempts to improve his finances and support a large family through speculation in American land did nothing to assuage the matter of his Scottish ancestry. Virginians especially bridled at the propensity of Scottish merchants and traders to drive particularly hard bargains. H: 93"; W: 57½". *Lent to the National Gallery of Scotland by Mrs. E. Murray.*

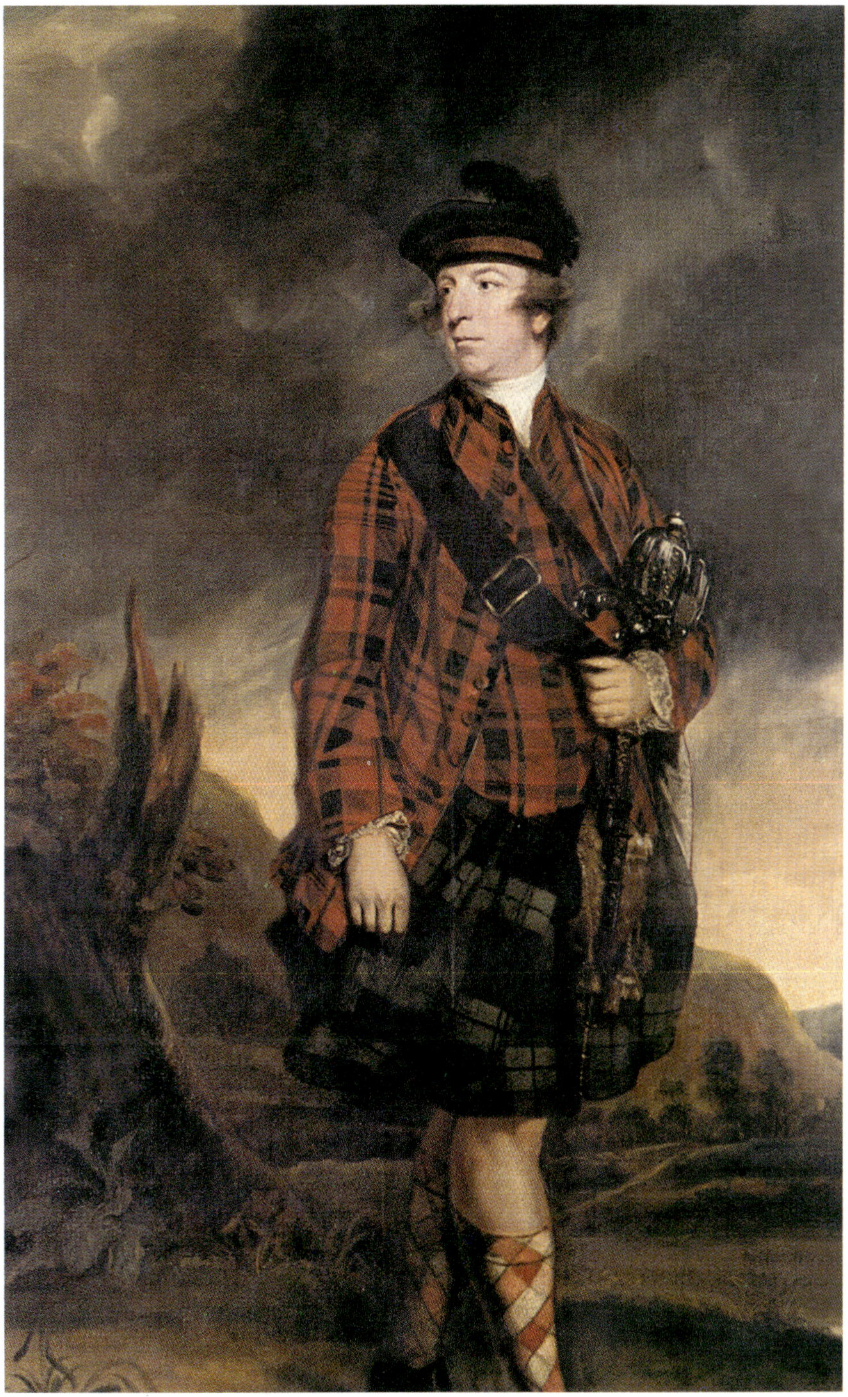

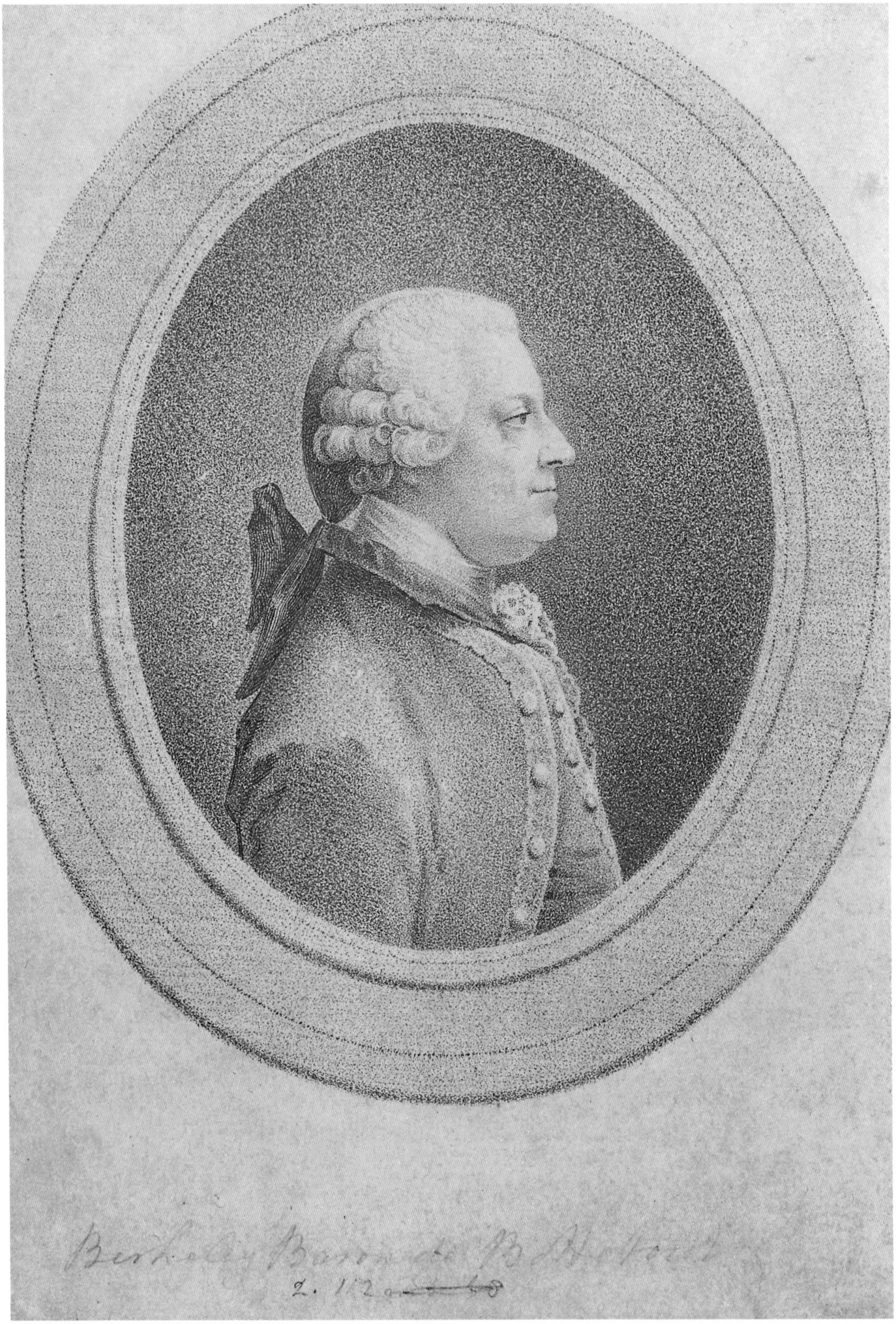

An earlier state of the print of Lord Botetourt shown on p. 14, without inscription or other identification. An unusual example, perhaps, of an artist's proof in the printmaking process. CWF 1960-883.

room and the dinner table constituted a central forum for the gathering and dissemination of information, advice, and opinions. Here important townsmen interacted most frequently with the governor and could perhaps be less guarded with him in his social role than they were in a more official setting such as the Capitol. Here influential Virginians from diverse parts of the largest of his Majesty's North American colonies could communicate with the governor when they came to the capital for sessions of the assembly or the courts. Visitors from other colonies and other countries, students, and friends also came to dine, to learn, and doubtless to be learned from. In this network the governor occupied a key role. He enriched his guests' minds from his own store of knowledge and culture, dispensed information (highly selective on occasion) about events and opinions in London, and in turn gathered all he could for his own purposes or to send back overseas. When the colony was still so sparsely served by newspapers and periodicals, the communication that took place at the Palace—and specifically in this room—was a crucial factor in the "political arrangements of [the] country" as well as in the elevation of mind and soul through the genteel art of conversation.[17]

Evidence to support this social pattern emerges from the pages of the exceptionally laconic diary of burgess George Washington. As Washington's reputation grew, so did the number of his visits to the Palace. In the spring and fall he traveled to Williamsburg from his plantation to attend sessions at the Capitol and within a few days of his arrival he had usually dined with the governor and with other key figures such as the Speaker of the House and the attorney general. There was a clear pattern of social interaction, no doubt traditional but obviously effective. Within five days of Botetourt's arrival in the colony in October 1768, for example, Washington had "dined at the Mayors" and was "Entertained at the Govs." Two days later he dined at the attorney general's with the governor. On his next visit to Williamsburg he dined at the Palace twice and attended a ball there, all within a two-week period. Later that year he dined with Botetourt and Governor Eden of Maryland and had dinner at the Palace three times within five weeks. On one of those visits he also took his stepchildren with him. His relationship with Lord Dunmore seems to have been quite convivial (ironically, in view of later conflicts), for the tempo of his visits to the Palace increased. One day, for example (November 3, 1772), he breakfasted, dined, *and* supped at the Palace.[18]

The location of Washington's estates made it prudent for him to maintain a connection with the Maryland colonial government also. In addition to dining with Eden in Annapolis several times from September 1771 to October 1773, he stayed with the governor periodically, often for several days at a time. In return, Eden stayed at Mount Vernon for a total of fourteen days between December 1771 and September 1773. Washington and Eden also visited

Philadelphia together in May 1773, dining with Governor Penn a number of times during their twelve-day visit.[19]

In pursuing this repeated round of social engagements, Washington's purpose was less to seek the stimulation of intellectual or culturally wide-ranging conversation than it was to glean information. The pattern in Williamsburg is unmistakable—he made the rounds as soon as he arrived in town and briefed himself on the current state of affairs. Several generations earlier an English visitor had observed that Virginians "read men by business and conversation," and Washington was squarely in that tradition. Other prominent or aspiring men in the colony undoubtedly did the same thing, though contemporary letters and diaries describing the practice are few.[20]

The mingling of the social act of dining with public politics and business was characteristic of an official residence. It became particularly intense in troubled times. A lengthy narrative of a visit to Williamsburg by Dr. Philip Mazzei, best known for his later friendship with Jefferson, details how quickly politics could introduce conflict into an otherwise pleasant atmosphere of sociability. Italian-born Mazzei had come to Virginia in 1774 after eighteen years as a merchant in London. On his arrival, he established business contacts and then "went to see Lord Dunmore, Governor of Virginia, to be naturalized. I had already visited him when I was formerly in Williamsburg, and he had extended me an invitation to dinner, which I was unable to accept. That day, I accepted and promised to return early." Despite the presence at dinner of Lady Dunmore and three of the children the conversation soon turned to politics, on which subject Mazzei's lengthy residence in London had given him a decided viewpoint. He argued that "the unnatural policy pursued by the Cabinet of Saint

Statue of Lord Botetourt, carved in marble by Richard Hayward in London 1772–1773. Commissioned by the colonial assembly, it stood on the Capitol piazza in Williamsburg from 1773–1801. Such was the popularity of the late governor that the Virginia state government even paid for an annual cleaning of the statue during the Revolutionary War. Overall height 11'6". Courtesy, College of William and Mary.

James in subjugating the Colonies, was that of 'Divide et impera,' and to attack them separately." Committees of correspondence had sprung up in response. Dunmore, according to Mazzei, had reacted to these events indecisively and, being admonished by the ministry, became more militant. "Believing that he could make a convert of me," Mazzei concluded, "he became so intimate that I easily saw the weakness of his mind and the meanness of his heart."[21]

Lord Botetourt had the prescience to turn a similar occasion—likewise an application for naturalization—into a diplomatic bounty for himself and a commercial success for his visitor. Though the governor may have been disturbed at the time by the colonies' Nonimportation Agreement, the businessman in him responded vigorously to an opportunity: "Youll please know that Lord Botetourt who is always doeing Good," wrote James Parker from Norfolk in August 1770, "is the father of that Scheme . . . for the Incouragement of Making Wine." The governor was petitioned by a French baker named d'Estave for naturalization. Botetourt, "who is Constantly enquiring into Matters in General," soon discovered that the man had grown up on a vineyard in the Bordeaux region and knew how to "Cultivate the Grape." Having experimented with local varieties of wild grapes d'Estave believed he could make a tolerable Burgundy from them, an occupation that had tantalized Virginians since Robert Beverley's well-known wager early in the century that he could produce seven hundred gallons of wine on his estate in one year. In the 1760s Charles Carter had even been awarded a gold medal by the Society for the Encouragement of Arts, Commerce, and Manufactures of London, in part for his vineyards at Cleve, but he died before he could develop them. After further enquiries by Botetourt revealed that d'Estave was not a fraud, the governor helped to sponsor a bill in the assembly that resulted in £450 for land, labor, and supplies being allotted to d'Estave for a vineyard on a hundred-acre tract about one mile from Williamsburg. D'Estave was given six years to try the experiment on condition that "he will instruct and show his Vineyard and Works" to every freeholder who visited him in that time.[22]

The advocacy and lobbying endemic to politics and business were the perpetual concomitant of the governor's dinner table conversation. They intensified in the troubled times of the late 1760s and early 1770s, particularly in this setting where the governor was not ceremonially set off from the other citizens by virtue of his office, as he was at the Capitol for instance. The dining room was thus the scene for petitioning and patronage, for opportunism and encouragement, for insinuation and retribution, in sum for all of the diverse characteristics normally encountered in the "political arrangements of [the] country."

What layers of experience, what intellectual traits did Botetourt bring to these encounters? As the first man to reside in the Palace with the elevated rank of governor was he somewhat above the hurly-burly of daily place-grubbing? After all, previous full governors had avoided any possibility of conference or confrontation in the colonial capital by staying away from the continent altogether and hiring deputies in their stead. Botetourt, however, gave every indication of enjoying his tour of duty in Williamsburg. His background as a Member of Parliament for Gloucestershire, a successful businessman, and an avid colonel of the county militia gave him much in common with many of the Virginians with whom he interacted at the Palace. Although not a career military officer like the majority of governors, like the Virginia colonels he was keenly involved with his local militia. As a Tory and a provincial squire he had spent most of his twenty years in Parliament in opposition. Along with Virginians, he knew what it was to be far from the centers of ministerial power.[23]

Botetourt had established himself as a successful figure in the rapidly expanding port city of Bristol, which had many ties with the colonies. While he had enjoyed the benefit of a comfortable inheritance (as had Fauquier and most of the Virginia grandees), he sought to augment it with acumen, skill, and energy. Fauquier's professional experience appears to have been limited to a directorship in the South Sea Company; in contrast, Botetourt had aggressively developed his inherited coalfields and had also invested successfully in local brass and copper industries. One of these enterprises, the Warmley Company, prospered to the point that it employed over two thousand people by 1767 and was one of the largest businesses in England. (Botetourt's investments in the metals industries paralleled former governors' initiatives in Virginia —Spotswood with iron foundries, Gooch with iron mines, and Fauquier with lead mines).[24]

His attainments and his affable character helped Botetourt forge a position of respect, even trust, in the colonists' eyes, though only those Virginians most loyal to the crown would have been completely frank or unguarded with him on all political matters. After all, some could still look upon him as "the Agent of a dirty tyrannic Ministry" (in Landon Carter's words). Yet even when he "expressed his disapprobation . . . in very angry terms . . . and exercised his most extreme authority" by dissolving the assembly in May 1769 because of its Townshend Act resolves, the colonists recognized that Botetourt could hardly avoid performing the unpleasant duty. A clear assessment of that incident was provided by John Page, Jr., in May 1769: "The Assembly . . . were so provoked at the Resolves of the Lords and Commons that they enter'd the Resolves, for which his Lordship thought proper to dissolve them. This has not lessen'd him in their Esteem, for they suppose he was obliged to do so; he is universally esteemed here, for his great Assiduity in his Office, Condescension, good Nature and true Politeness."[25]

Page from William Marshman's petty cash account book that reveals Botetourt's auditing of the monthly disbursements and his signature of approval in the lower left. Courtesy, the Duke of Beaufort.

Virginians discovered with pleasure that Botetourt had trained himself as a man of business. (His systematic nature is evident in such small ways as his routine auditing of the servants' account books.) It was his punctiliousness, or "assiduousness" as the colonists described it, allied with perfect gentility that ultimately drew their greatest plaudits. He quelled any initial misgivings they might have had—would he turn out to be an effete aristocrat, a court sycophant, a corrupt milord?—by proving himself a model of business deportment against which they judged others and found them wanting. "We are very happy in our Governor Lord Botetourt," commented Thomas Everard, former mayor of Williamsburg. "His affabillity and great Attention to the due administration of every part of his Duty has gained him the affection and confidence of the whole Colony [;] if some other Governors on the Continent were as well disposed to serve the People they preside over Harmony would in a great Measure soon be restored among them."[26] In his attention to the daily demands of the bureaucracy Botetourt maintained and even exceeded the standards set by earlier governors and career civil servants, Gooch and

THE DINING ROOM AND PARLOR 139

Fauquier, who were remembered with esteem and affection by Virginians. One observer of contemporary Virginia mores, however, thought that this was a recently elevated virtue among the gentry: "For he seems now to be best esteemed and most applauded who attends to his business, whatever it be, with the greatest diligence." The same observer later advised a friend: "Be diligent, in a proper course of business, and you will be great." Botetourt's sense of responsibility, his assiduousness, was another token, if the colonists needed one, of the seriousness with which he regarded them, their demands and requirements, their amour propre. His successor, Dunmore, on the other hand, aroused their ire because he made it appear as if he looked on them as unruly and irresponsible, as if he disdained them and considered them unworthy of his attention.[27]

Far left, Francis and Catherine Fauquier portrayed by William Hogarth in 1730. This detail from Hogarth's ambitious group portrait of the Woolaston family gives an unusually sympathetic glimpse of the affluent and well-connected young man-about-town. Courtesy, Leicester City Museum and Art Gallery.

Near left, detail of the figure of Thomas Jefferson taken from The Declaration of Independence *painted by John Trumbull between 1787 and 1797. Trumbull painted Jefferson from life several times and is presumed to have created the most reliable likeness of the young statesman at this stage in his remarkable career. The Jefferson for whom Lieutenant Governor Fauquier was so seminal a figure, however, presumably evinced rather more of the bloom of youth than the serious, somewhat gaunt Virginian depicted in Trumbull's famous history painting. Courtesy, Yale University Art Gallery.*

Active political arena as it undoubtedly was, the dining room was also the scene of momentous events that had implications, perhaps, beyond even weighty matters of state. These events were dinners and concerts, and they included intellectual exchanges on philosophy, religion, and the arts that altered the lives of attentive young colonists such as Thomas Jefferson, John Page, and Robert Carter. In brief but portentous passages of his autobiography, Jefferson referred to events that occurred in this room during the governorship of Francis Fauquier more than a decade before his own occupancy of the building as chief executive. Jefferson's phrases are so allusive and open up so extensively vistas of cultural influence and dissemination that they merit lengthy analysis. His recollections stretched back to his arrival in Williamsburg in 1760 to enroll as a student at the College of William and Mary shortly after Fauquier had assumed office. Jefferson soon had the "great good fortune" to meet at the college William Small, professor of mathematics (and later of rhetoric and moral philosophy), who had come from London the same year as Fauquier. Both teacher and administrator were men of the Enlightenment, intelligent, well read, urbane, humane, insatiably curious. A man "profound in most of the useful branches of science," Small had a "happy talent of communication, correct and gentlemanly manners, and an enlarged and liberal mind." This teacher of breadth and polish challenged and expanded his student's mind and also "introduced me to the acquaintance and familiar table of Governor Fauquier, the ablest man who had ever filled that office. With him, and at his table, Dr. Small and Mr. Wythe, his *amici omnium horarum*, and myself, formed a *partie quarrée*, and to the habitual conversations on these occasions I owed much instruction."[28]

That Jefferson specified "table" twice in two sentences seems too obvious to ignore—the influential conversations that opened up new intellectual worlds for the eager young man from the hinterland clearly took place for the most part in the dining room at the Palace. While it must be acknowledged that some scholars have questioned the fidelity of the elderly statesman's memory, it should be stressed that several years before he wrote the above autobiographical sketches he had confided to a friend that "at these dinners I . . . heard more good sense, more rational and philosophical conversations, than in all my life besides. They were truly Attic societies."[29]

Jefferson's musings reveal in clear focus the paradigm of the conjunction of English governor and the local gentry. Fauquier was a representative of the intense, sophisticated, urban culture of London; his company in this instance included two members of the colonial gentry, one, George Wythe, a little younger than he, urban, and local; the other, Jefferson, much younger, rural, and from a far distant location. With this group a fellow Briton, William Small, also interacted. The effect was seminal and profound, as the distinguished

THE DINING ROOM AND PARLOR

George Wythe drawn from life on April 25, 1791, in Williamsburg by John Trumbull. This is the view of Wythe that Trumbull placed in his Declaration of Independence. *Pencil on paper.* H: 3"; W: 3". *Courtesy, Free Library of Philadelphia, Rosenthal Collection.*

statesman acknowledged decades later. Though it is not uncommon for young men to be deeply influenced by their tutors, in colonial society the governor was capable of exercising at least as much influence as the professor and, in many instances, perhaps, on a more urbane level.

What kind of man was Fauquier that he affected the brilliant young man so? Unfortunately, much about him remains elusive. That his knowledge and experience were as attractive and provocative as Small's "regular lectures in Ethics, Rhetoric and Belles Lettres," we have Jefferson's testimony. Fauquier presumably imparted his interest in natural philosophy and natural history to the student—he kept the first records on the weather known in Virginia and submitted a paper on the subject to the Royal Society, of which he was a fellow. Jefferson remained interested in this phenomenon all his life. He probably taught Jefferson to use the scientific instruments he owned (an interest that Wythe shared) and perhaps the rudiments of medical science. Characteristic of a product of the Enlightenment, he specified in his will that his body be autopsied and the ensuing report circulated so that he might "become more useful to my fellow Creatures by my Death than I have been in my Life." His humanity manifested itself in his concern for the slaves he owned, a circumstance he regretted but could not circumvent. His will provided that his slave mothers and children be kept together after his death even if it resulted in a much lower sale price. He was also concerned about the wretched plight of the mentally ill in Virginia and drew up proposals for the establishment of an institution to deal with the problem—within five years of his death it had materialized, the first hospital in America devoted specifically to the treatment of the insane.[30]

Fauquier's earlier contacts in London with a wide range of cultural organizations and artistic acquaintances probably dazzled the attentive young man who had grown up in a distant rural society bereft of such opportunities. His familiarity with belles lettres was probably more extensive than Small's. If, about this time, Jefferson could include William Hogarth's *Analysis of Beauty* in a short list of only seven titles on "Criticism on the Fine Arts" for his prototypical library, it is probably no coincidence that Fauquier had known Hogarth well. In addition to being depicted in one of Hogarth's ambitious group portraits (the Woollaston Family) Fauquier had been as active as the artist in the affairs of the Foundling Hospital in London. He may well have shown Jefferson some of Hogarth's moralizing print series—they became popular in Virginia from mid-century onward. The second title in Jefferson's prototypical library was Webb's essay on painting; Fauquier had known painters other than Hogarth in London, including Benjamin Wilson who had also painted his portrait. Fauquier's brother William was a prominent member of the Society of the Dilettanti and had assembled a notable collection of old master and

William Small drawn by an unknown artist in the 1770s. Even this relatively unaccomplished draftsman has captured an unusual alertness in the influential teacher's character. Courtesy, City of Birmingham Assay Office. Photograph, courtesy, Professor John McKnight.

The reconstructed Public Hospital for the Insane, originally completed in Williamsburg in 1773. Fauquier proposed and Botetourt was an important contributor to this humanitarian institution.

contemporary paintings. Governor and student shared a passion for music—Fauquier had known the great composer George Frideric Handel and probably other lesser composers and musicians of the day. Jefferson, we know, developed a consuming passion for architecture; Fauquier had known James Gibbs, one of the greatest architects of his day in England, and had been a beneficiary in his will. Again, it may be no coincidence that Jefferson's first book

Badminton House painted by the famous Venetian artist Antonio Canaletto on his only visit to England, in 1748–1749. Kent's additions and remodeling were less than two years old when the great artist, so well known for his vedute of Venice to English aristocrats who had been on the Grand Tour, painted this scene and another of the view of the park from the house. Botetourt's sister was already ensconced as mistress of this grand estate when this remarkable view was painted. Courtesy, the Duke of Beaufort.

on architecture (in his old age he recalled the excitement of its acquisition from an elderly cabinetmaker in Williamsburg about 1768) was Gibbs's *A Book of Architecture*.[31]

Though Jefferson failed to elaborate on any intellectual acquaintance he may have had with Lord Botetourt, it is evident that the same system of patronage prevailed under that governor and that he too was a person of culture. Less distinctively a man of the Enlightenment than Fauquier, Botetourt still evinced "the grace of polished life," to cite Edmund Randolph's felicitous phrase. He attracted many in the colony by his "fascinating manners." While his mind probably moved more easily in pragmatic ways than it did in philosophical, he had still been acquainted with many cultured, influential, and intelligent men in London for thirty years. He knew Fauquier's brother William through his long membership in the Society of the Dilettanti and perhaps Francis Fauquier himself. He certainly knew James Gibbs, who had worked for Botetourt's sister at Badminton. The two men received honorary degrees from Oxford University on the same day at the same ceremony inaugurating Gibbs's great Radcliffe Camera there. Furthermore, Botetourt had spent much time at the recently built Ditchley, near Oxford, the seat of his friend the earl of Litchfield (co-guardian with Botetourt of the fifth duke of Beaufort in his minority). Ditchley was one of Gibbs's greatest domestic works.[32]

It was through his sister's marriage into the ducal family of Beaufort, and her subsequent (and unexpected) assumption of the title of duchess, that Botetourt had met and intermingled with a circle of artists and craftsmen and their work to which even his own fairly affluent background would not normally have given him an entrée. His sister was his only sibling and they were particularly close, a relationship that intensified when her husband, the fourth duke, died in 1756 leaving his son and heir a minor of twelve years. Named an executor for the estate and one of two trustees for the young fifth duke, Botetourt closely supervised the affairs of the family and the education of the young man during the following decade. Prominent architects such as William Kent, James Gibbs, Henry Flitcroft, Francis and William Smith; painters of the renown of Antonio Canaletto (on his sole visit to England in the late 1740s he painted views of Badminton) or the more conventional Thomas Hudson; leading London cabinetmakers such as Thomas Chippendale and William and John Linnell; sculptors such as John Michael Rysbrack; goldsmiths such as the incomparable Germain family of Paris; and a host of lesser but still highly talented artists and craftsmen were associated with the Beaufort family, and therefore with Botetourt. In the mid-1760s, after he came of age, the fifth duke began to make improvements to his London townhouse and employed the leading firm of Robert and James Adam, the tastemakers of the new classical style. Botetourt undoubtedly kept an avuncular eye on that work since his own townhouse was located nearby. At the same time, the duke's sister and her husband, Sir Watkin Williams Wynn, were contracting with Adam for their new townhouse in London, which eventually contained some of his finest work.33

Botetourt also brought to the "habitual conversations" of the dinner table a cultural dimension that no other governor residing in the Palace had provided—he had been on the Grand Tour. While his father's death may have cut his stay short, he had been to Italy, the artistic mecca of the cultured English upper classes. Furthermore, his appointment in the 1760s to a post at court and consequent exposure to an even wider range of artistic endeavor can only have enlarged his experience—however little Buckingham House resembled Versailles. His contact with the work of the Adam brothers, his familiarity with the Ramsay state portraits of the king and queen, copies of which he purchased and had shipped to Williamsburg, and his undoubted knowledge of the work of Johann Zoffany for the royal family in the 1760s must have given him a knowledge of at least the rudiments of the changing tastes of that decade. As a member of the Society of the Dilettanti he had served on a subcommittee with Stuart and Revett, planning an expedition to Asia Minor in order to investigate its antiquities. The two architects' previous publication, *The Antiquities of Athens*, had appeared in 1762 and had become one of the cornerstones of the

Left, Johann Zoffany's charming and highly detailed view of the sons of George III at Buckingham House, about 1760. Oil on canvas. H: 44"; W: 50¼. Courtesy, Her Majesty the Queen.

Center, mezzotint of James Gibbs, architect, published by McArdell about 1750. A view of his famous Radcliffe Library (or Camera) at Oxford is shown in the lower right. H: 15¼"; W: 11¼". CWF 1967-343.

Right, Peale's portrait of William Pitt that has been in Virginia since 1769. Oil on canvas. H: 95¾"; W: 61¼". Courtesy, Westmoreland County Historical Society.

146 PUBLIC LIFE

Elizabeth Berkeley, fourth Duchess of Beaufort, after a portrait by Sir Joshua Reynolds. The closeness of the bond between Elizabeth and her brother Norborne is sympathetically revealed by an unknown painter in this view of the young Berkeley children aged about ten years. Both paintings are at Badminton. Courtesy, the Duke of Beaufort.

new appreciation for classical antiquity. Botetourt's interest in classicism was well expressed in the garden he devised at his country house, Stoke Park, in the 1750s and 1760s, which included obelisks, tombs, and a model of the "Monument of ye Horatii at Albano."[34]

In view of his exposure to such artists, architects, and craftsmen and his long involvement with the Dilettanti, it is difficult to imagine that Botetourt was oblivious to the current art scene in London in the mid- to late 1760s in which the rapidly developing career of American-born Benjamin West was especially noteworthy. West's extraordinary history paintings of classical and contemporary subjects attracted much attention and brought him the approval of George III, who appointed him to the post of History Painter to the King. West's rising fame was of great interest to the colonists and notices of new paintings were heralded as proof of colonial genius—*The Return of Regulus* (1769) and the masterly *Death of General Wolfe* (1770) were announced in the *Virginia Gazette* as his most recent and much acclaimed works.[35] While Botetourt resided in Williamsburg, one of West's numerous American pupils, Charles Willson Peale, completed and shipped a large portrait of the statesman William Pitt to Virginia as a presentation piece for a group of gentlemen in Westmoreland County. It caused a stir locally as, of course, had the occasion for its commission originally—Pitt's speaking out in Parliament against the

THE DINING ROOM AND PARLOR

Stamp Act and for the colonies, for the cause of "Liberty." In Peale's portrait Pitt was shown garbed in classical Roman toga with symbols of liberty in the foreground. The painting was extensively discussed and its classical iconography fully explained in separate editions of the *Virginia Gazette*, with the disclaimer that the resemblance was "quite unlike the prints we have hitherto had of his Lordship." Botetourt must have joined in the discussions provoked by the prints and the portrait, for he would undoubtedly have known Pitt in Parliament and have been familiar with West's work through the king's interest. It is more than likely that he would also have been aware of the work in progress by London sculptor Joseph Wilton on two full-length statues of Pitt in comparable classical attire commissioned by the assemblies of New York and South Carolina and delivered in 1770. Peale's portrait was probably derived from Wilton's format. As discussions at the Palace moved from the subject of the portraits to the style of representation, Botetourt drew on his unusual qualifications and experience of the style's origins and early development in London. In all likelihood he played a critical role in furthering the local understanding of this new classical style through the ranks of the local population.[36]

In all these interactions between older and younger men and between patrons and artists and craftsmen, the element of patronage was ubiquitous. Patronage consisted of reaching and encouraging by instruction, example, and precept; it was also commissioning, purchasing, and recommending. Patronage was a governor's prerogative and obligation, an ingredient of the complex actions and beliefs that composed condescension. Jefferson acknowledged that he "owed much instruction" to Fauquier. Benjamin Franklin acknowledged the encouragement he had received as a young man from Sir William Keith, lieutenant governor of Pennsylvania.[37] Both Benjamin West and Charles Willson Peale owed similar debts to the governors of their respective provinces. Indeed, both gifted young colonials had been actively patronized by the governors, whose largesse combined with that of local gentry enabled them to undertake the obligatory pilgrimage to Italy to study the great masters. West, whose talent was such that the gentry sponsored him in the hope that he would return and become an "ornament to his country," decided to stay in London, but he acknowledged his debt to Lieutenant Governor James Hamilton of Pennsylvania and others and repaid it by his unfailing kindness to young colonials seeking assistance or tuition in the English capital. Peale never reached Italy, deciding that study with West was his first priority. In London he became homesick for Maryland, whose governor, Horatio Sharpe, was his major sponsor. When Peale's portrait of Pitt arrived in Virginia, public interest was so high that it would seem to have created a propitious atmosphere for commissions, and soon Peale was on his way south, stopping first at Mount Vernon. Colonel George Washington, in a gesture that precisely paralleled the

Charles Willson Peale as portrayed by West in 1768–1769. Oil on canvas. H: 28¼"; W: 23". *Courtesy, New-York Historical Society.*

Right, a copy of the great Bolognese artist Guido Reni's Zeus and Europa. *Oil on canvas.* H: 45"; W: 34". *Courtesy, William Cameron. This was painted about 1766 by Matthew Pratt and exhibited in Williamsburg in 1773.*

patterns of patronage already discussed, assured an Annapolis friend that he had "no doubt of Mr. Peale's meeting with very good Incouragement in a Tour to Williamsburg, for having mentioned him to some Gentlemen at our Court, they seem desirous of employing him in his way down."[38] Another Hamilton protégé, Matthew Pratt, having studied with West, visited Williamsburg soon after his return to America and organized the first commercial exhibition of paintings there ever recorded in the colony. Housed in Mrs. Vobe's tavern on Duke of Gloucester Street near the Capitol in 1773, it included examples of Pratt's work and copies of West's paintings and of old masters, the latter being the first examples in oil that most of the colonists would have ever seen.[39]

    Patronage was something the governor should dispense. It was an integral part of his cultural equipage to patronize gifted young men. It was de rigueur, if only at token levels, to patronize local tradesmen. But unusual talent must be recognized and encouraged. A finely documented example of such patronage in Virginia occurred at the Palace in the 1730s. William Gooch received, entertained, and supported an immigrant painter named Charles Bridges. Trained in England, Bridges sought commissions in the affluent colony where the competition might be reckoned sparse. Unlike the painters mentioned above, however, he was not on the threshold of his career but was sixty-five years old when he came to Williamsburg in 1735. He had the prescience to obtain letters of recommendation to Gooch from the bishop of Norwich, Gooch's brother, and to James Blair, commissary and president of the college. Gooch's response to his brother speaks clearly for itself: "Mr. Bridges I have already loaded with my civilities, tho' it looks a little odd for a Governour to show so much favour to a Painter, as to lend him Coach to fetch his Daughters and Son, and his waggon for two days to bring up his Goods, and to entertain him at Dinner and Supper several times since his arrival, and to promise him as soon as he's settled that he shall begin to show the country his Art, by drawing my picture, but all this I have done, and upon yr. recommendation shall continue to do him all the Service in my power." Soon after his arrival Bridges had met Attorney General Sir John Randolph, William Byrd II, and former Lieutenant Governor Alexander Spotswood and had secured commissions to take their portraits as well as those of their wives and children. Bridges remained in Virginia for a decade painting the gentry's likenesses, the first documented painter of quality in the colony. Byrd declared that "had he lived so long ago as when places were given to the most Deserving, he might have pretended to be the Sergeant-Painter of Virginia." Even so, Bridges received hospitality and patronage from the lieutenant governor—as exemplar—and then from the gentry that were equivalent to recognition by such an office.[40]

Cultural dissemination through patronage is the most directly documentable form of influence and cultural interaction, particularly the support given to younger, more impressionable men. Jefferson was probably one of many to benefit from the older men's tutelage and hospitality. John Page and Robert Carter, scions of two of Virginia's wealthiest families, were among others who came into Fauquier's orbit. On his return from two years in England Carter was described by his cousin and contemporary John Page as "inconceivably illiterate, and also corrupted and vicious." The significant meliorating factor in Carter's subsequent development, Page believed, was that he "conversed a great deal with our highly enlightened Governor Fauquier ... from whom he derived great advantages." They traveled to New York together in 1762 and the following year visited Charleston, South Carolina. Robert Carter occupied the house next to the Palace, was passionately interested in music like Fauquier and Jefferson, like the latter amassed an important library, and eventually became an executor of the lieutenant governor's estate.[41]

John Page, the future governor and lifelong friend of Jefferson, became an amateur scientist, meteorologist, and inventor, much after Fauquier's heart. He was influential in the founding and for some years served as president of the Society for the Advancement of Useful Knowledge, established in Williams-

Robert Carter, namesake and scion of a powerful father, seen in London in fancy dress about 1750. Portrait on upper left attributed to Thomas Hudson. Oil on canvas. H: 50"; W: 40". Courtesy, Virginia Historical Society. Lower left, in a more rural mode, is his longtime friend and also member of a leading family, John Page, painted by John Wollaston in Virginia, 1755–1757. Oil on canvas. H: 50¼"; W: 40¼". Courtesy, College of William and Mary. A powerful representative of an earlier generation, James Blair was the commissary of the Bishop of London in Virginia and first president of the College of William and Mary. The college's renaissance and endowment was the achievement of Blair and is alluded to in the view of the "Wren Building" through the window. Portrait attributed to Charles Bridges, 1735–1740. Oil on canvas. H: 49"; W: 39¾". Courtesy, College of William and Mary.

150 PUBLIC LIFE

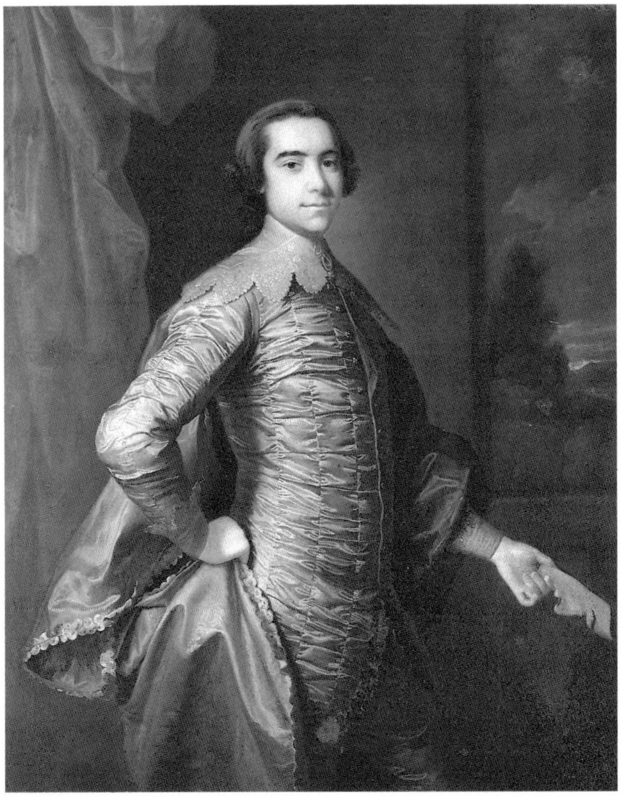

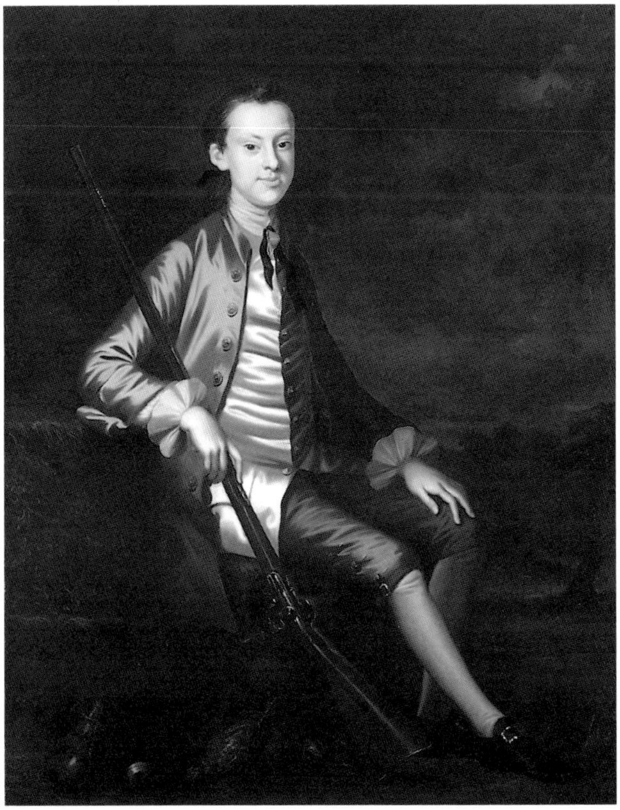

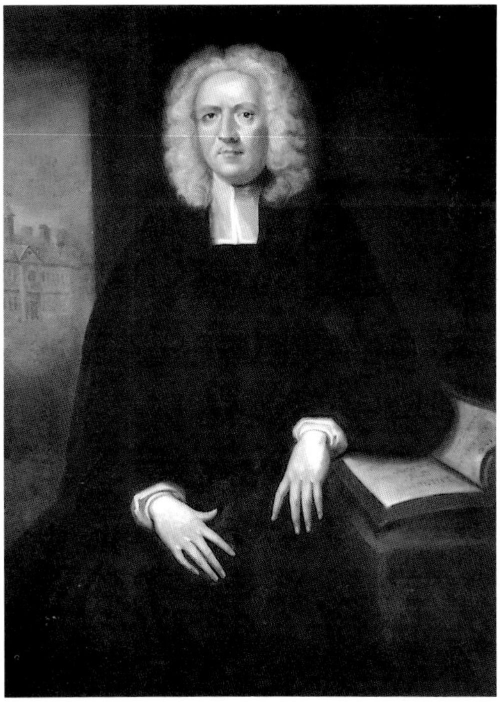

burg in 1773 on the model of the Royal Society. The seeds for this endeavor were probably planted by Fauquier and Small, both fellows of the Royal Society. While Dunmore was one of the sponsors of the new society in Williamsburg, it may have been more from deference to his position than from his inherent interest in philosophical advancement—of him Edmund Randolph wrote, "to external accomplishment he pretended not . . . his manners and sentiments did not surpass substantial barbarism." Most of the initiative for this ambitious cultural effort came from the gentry, particularly those who had absorbed the Enlightenment ideas of earlier governors.[42]

Botetourt clearly channeled his encouragement of learning into a local establishment. "The College of William and Mary is my present object," he wrote to his nephew in December 1769. "The Boys seem pleased with my attention, and promise to do their utmost to crown my Labours with success—We have many plans of reform under consideration, will send them to you when they are resolved."[43] There is little doubt that Botetourt accepted and enthusiastically cultivated the patronage role inherent in his title and his office. It was during his administration that two new professors, the Reverends Samuel Henley and Thomas Gwatkin, arrived at the college from London and Oxford respectively. Initially, they promised to breathe new life into an institution that had "sat in Darkness" until "our never to be forgotten" Lord Botetourt bestowed his "wise, noble, and truly patriotick Measures" upon it. The author of the above words, "An American," in a letter to the *Virginia Gazette* of November 21, 1771, went so far as to state that Virginia was "a poor illiterate Country" prior to Botetourt's arrival. In a somewhat more measured vein, Edmund Randolph emphasized Botetourt's "warm patronage of learning and religion."[44] The governor's plans for reform of the college have unfortunately been lost except for the annual award of two gold medals, one for excellence in "Philosophical Learning," the other for outstanding achievement in "Classical Learning." Botetourt believed in them so firmly he wrote to England that they "must go on though it was to cost double the money." Presented first in 1772, they were the first medals for scholastic excellence established in America.[45]

Among Botetourt's protégés was a young man called Richard Starke. Of uncertain background, his name appears in the Palace documentation during Botetourt's administration. Starke borrowed some volumes of plays and Molière's works from the governor's library and still held them when Botetourt died. In a letter to the duke of Beaufort, Starke portrayed the governor's benevolence as "distinguish[ing] me by a considerable degree of his countenance, and attention . . . by whose civilities I have been flattered, and by whose conversation, and example I have been greatly honoured and improved," phrases similar to those used of Fauquier by John Page. In the same letter to the duke Starke noted that Botetourt had intended to donate one hundred pounds to the construction of the Public Hospital for the Insane in Williamsburg—a characteristic act of compassion for the late governor, since he had also been a trustee of the Bristol and the Gloucestershire infirmaries. Starke later became a committee clerk of the House of Burgesses (probably a sinecure appointment by Botetourt) but died suddenly in 1772.[46]

Apparently endowed with a personable nature and a certain acumen, might Starke have become another Page or Wythe, perhaps even a minor Jefferson? That is uncertain, of course. What *is* clear is that without the paternalism of the governors and the tradition of beneficence, the history of the colonies would have to be rewritten. Beyond their sponsorship of young men of good family—appointed as upper servants, clerks, or secretaries to the governors and eventually moving on to sinecures within the government or to other profitable positions—the governors exercised a pervasive influence on colonial society that may never be fully detailed. It was an inherent element of the structure of society. Fauquier himself felt he owed such a debt to his patron, the earl of Halifax, that he left him a bequest of a diamond ring to the not inconsiderable value of one hundred guineas, while Gooch acknowledged that he owed his baronetcy to the duke of Newcastle.[47]

If patronage in its many forms and on many levels was the governors' to bestow, its bestowal was not a necessary consequence of birthright or of influential recommendations. It had to be worked for, earned, and treated with gratitude and circumspection. The young man who "affronted" Gooch's wife and sister-in-law at the dinner table came to Virginia armed with recommendations from the bishops of Salisbury and Norwich, both of whom had known his "worthy father." In normal circumstances the governor would have gone out of his way to help, but instead he went to great lengths to enumerate the young man's defects of character that precluded too much support. "Manners, so necessary to form a man, who setts out into the wide World," wrote Gooch to his brother, "he is an absolute stranger to." Insulting the host's wife and sister-in-law at the dinner table Gooch deemed unpardonable. The young man was conceited and "humoursome" or moody, "such a valetudinarian and so tender of himself," boastful of his "lewd and unnatural Lust." He regarded the company of colonial gentlemen as his due though they all despised him and only tolerated him in order to "gett some of his money at Cards." Gooch concluded that he had "nothing to give, all Places upon a Vacancy being disposed off at Home."[48]

Recalling the intellectual and cultural debts he owed Fauquier, Jefferson stressed his participation in the governor's musical gatherings: "The Governor was musical also, and a good performer, and associated me with two or three other amateurs in his weekly concerts." In Jefferson's mind, music was a natural extension of the "rational and philosophical conversations" and the

Gold medal for scholastic excellence, commissioned by Lord Botetourt in 1769–1770 and presented for the first time in 1772. This particular medal was awarded to Nathaniel Burwell of Carter's Grove in 1772. D: 1¾". CWF, gift of Charles Lee Burwell. 1982-205.

cultural milieu from which they sprang.⁴⁹ Fauquier was the embodiment of such culture. A tolerable player himself, he organized regular performances at the Palace in which he and the young student participated. Whether these musical soirées took place in the dining room or elsewhere at the Palace is unknown, but it is likely that dinner table conversation would frequently have turned to musical matters. Fauquier owned a small collection of music and instruments and employed as his last clerk Peter Pelham, who doubled as the organist at Bruton Parish Church. Botetourt also employed Pelham, but his involvement in music was less obvious than his predecessor's. An interest in or appreciation of music was an essential ingredient of "polished life," however; Botetourt indicated that at least he enjoyed it as shown in one of the few inimitable, chatty, and informative woman's letters to have survived from this period in Williamsburg.⁵⁰ Dunmore and his family were quite musical—they imported three organs (including a "very small organ for teaching birds"), a harpsichord, a forte-piano, and a sticado or xylophone. Guests at Dunmore's Palace during the year his family was in residence might be treated to after-dinner musical diversions by two of his daughters. Similar tableaux were presented at Tazewell Hall, where after dinner the two daughters of the attorney general, the "two greatest beauties in America," sang and played on the harpsichord and guitar.⁵¹

The most poignant account of the role of music in an area where there were few if any professional musicians and little opportunity to hear music other than that played by oneself or one's immediate family emerges from the pages of Fithian's diary. For his employer, Robert Carter, "music [was] his darling Amusement . . . It seems to nourish, as well as entertain his mind," Fithian mused. Carter played virtually every evening, before, after, and frequently during supper. He gave lessons to his daughters and insisted on their practicing regularly, sometimes inveigling the tutor into his musical soirées too. It was obviously a discipline and an aesthetic pleasure for him, as well as a spiritual necessity. His instruments consisted of a harpsichord, glass harmonica, forte-piano, guitar, violin, German flutes, and an organ imported from London in his Williamsburg house. He also owned numerous volumes of music.⁵²

Another of Fauquier's vital interests was natural history and its concomitant natural philosophy. It was an enthusiasm shared by other governors, whether they manifested it formally in the reorganization of the landscape by design and gardening or more scientifically in the study of botany. The reorganization of the landscape in Williamsburg and specifically around the Palace by Governors Nicholson and Spotswood was completed early in the century. The college's garden had been designed about 1695 by an assistant to William III's gardener, George London, specially brought to the colony for that purpose. That the Palace gardens themselves, envisioned and laid out on a

Chamber organ and serinette of the types that were brought to the Palace by Lord Dunmore. The chamber organ is attributed to William Holland of London and was made between ca. 1770 and 1782. H: 88½"; W: 38½". CWF 1980-187. The "very small organ for teaching birds" is, in this rare labeled example, of French origin. H: 5¾"; W: 10½". CWF 1988-19.

somewhat aristocratic scale by Spotswood, had apparently influenced a number of the Virginia gentry in their efforts to improve and articulate their own landscapes would, in all probability, have been pointed out to Fauquier and Botetourt. Gooch had beautified the vista from the Palace into town in 1737 with catalpa trees that were mature by the time of Botetourt's arrival. He too had much experience in this field. He had shown his first interest in the subject as a young man in the 1740s; his contributions to the planning and laying out of the open spaces of the spa town of Cheltenham were an important factor in its development and growing popularity. When the opportunity to remodel his own estate presented itself, he employed Thomas Wright, the leading landscape gardener in England in the period between the decline of William Kent and the advent of "Capability" Brown, and achieved there "the perfect integration of landscape and architecture . . . a remarkable Classical landscape." Wright's extensive work at Stoke Park and later, and on an even grander scale, at Badminton was among his most important. Botetourt's guests at the Palace included several gentry who at that time were occupied with their own projects of remodeling houses and gardens—Jefferson, Washington, and Robert Beverley to cite a few among many. They may well have found Botetourt's knowledge and experience in these matters to be an intriguing and useful source of information.53

Botetourt had a lively interest in natural history, to judge by the evidence of his petty cash account books. They document the frequent arrival at the Palace of local gentry's footmen carrying ornithological specimens ranging from an eagle to a "pye-Ball Wood-pecker" and hummingbirds. Occasionally it was a "large green worm" or a red snake. Botetourt subsequently dispatched one of his clerk's sons to London with an owl as a present for Queen Charlotte—a pleasant instance of reverse cultural diffusion, but one with a very long history. As early as the 1690s specimens had been sent by Daniel Parke from Williamsburg to John Evelyn, the antiquarian, in London. In the same decade, the scientist John Locke had written to the college for specimens from its botanical garden. Thus began a tradition of feverish transatlantic activity of shipping and receiving specimens, seeds, plants, books, and information. It clearly intrigued Botetourt before he ever visited the New World; a diary he kept for the year 1753–1754 (preserved among his papers at Badminton House) shows that he planted at Stoke Park about one hundred plants from America. His enthusiasm continued; listed in his inventory at the Palace were "60 flint glass Bottles for preserving Insects," while in the library was noted a copy of John Clayton's *Flora Virginia*. Like many men of latent scientific curiosity Botetourt must have been beguiled, perhaps aroused, by the teeming, sometimes exotic quality of the American landscape and its natural denizens.[54]

That the natural world was a source of genuine interest for Botetourt can be inferred from observations included in the draft of a private letter, probably to his sister, giving his first impressions of the American continent. While he dutifully followed protocol, observing the correct forms and saying the right things, it was evidently the landscape that excited him. He journeyed from Hampton Roads to Williamsburg "by a delightful road through forests of magnificent pines and tulip trees lighted up by a glorious sun." His new residence was "an excellent house," but its setting merited a more eloquent passage: "Behind it are about 150 acres of beautiful ground, finely broke, planted with tulip trees, oaks and pines, and watered by rivulets. I am told the meadows are covered with white clover in the spring." He later bought trees to plant in this "park" to improve it further.[55]

As the intellectual center of the house and the setting for frequent cultural interaction between governor and gentry, the dining room is abundantly documented. It provided the environment for the constant exchange of a host of ideas, experiences, and civilities—a place from which elements of English culture rippled out to the edges of English society. It also functioned as a kind of government communications bureau—a colonial center through which essential political and commercial information was sent to and from London. To discover that the room also served as the governor's office, which the Botetourt inventory proves, is a logical extension of the roles and functions described above. The multiple uses of the space thus clearly reveal the commingling of the public and social lives of the governors. Several major case pieces stood in it, each designed for office pur-

Watercolor of a magnolia drawn by Botetourt's niece, Lady Henrietta Somerset, in 1763. The prominent botanical artist and watercolorist Georg Ehret was brought to Badminton during the 1760s to teach the aristocratic young girls this genteel art. His bills show in detail his numerous visits and the supplies he brought with him. Ehret was earlier connected with Catesby's work and had brought into England the technique, learned from fellow German artist Barbara Regina Dietzsche, of setting the specimen on a mysterious dark brown ground, such as seen in this lovely example of the amateur's art. Watercolor on vellum. H: 9½"; W: 7¼". CWF 1989-395, 14.

A view of Stoke Park after Botetourt's death. Engraved after a drawing by Francis Nicholson, 1790–1800. Present whereabouts unknown.

The desks kept in the dining room, and their contents, show the multiple use of the room for business. Botetourt's library table was undoubtedly similar to the one shown in plate 54 of Chippendale's Director, *though to judge by cabinetmaker William Fenton's description of it in his account, somewhat more elaborate in its ornamentation.*

THE DINING ROOM AND PARLOR 157

poses—one mahogany library table "containing sundry papers public and private," one mahogany desk "containing sundry papers private and public," one walnut writing table, and a small reading desk. Four large pieces of furniture in the room associated with writing, reading, and general office work—and actively associated as will be shown below—are too many to be the result of random placement or a migration of objects after the governor's demise. They point clearly to the purposeful use of the room as an office, not unreasonable considering its attractive size, placement in the suite of rooms, and pleasant view of the gardens.

Fauquier used the dining room as an office, too, as indicated by a brief phrase from William Robinson's prolix and tedious retelling of wrongdoings, insults, and slights at the time of the Twopenny Act of 1759. In his own words, Reverend Robinson, commissary to the bishop of London in Virginia, found himself at odds with the governor because of his political activism and even opposed him on certain points of the catechism. The clergyman claimed that he waited on the governor at the Palace and offered to apologize for his behavior if he had unwittingly caused offense. Fauquier seemed conciliated and invited Robinson to dine with him the following day. However, rumors reached Robinson that evening that he was about to make a semi-public apology at dinner at the Palace the following day, which led him to believe that Fauquier had taken his offer more literally than it was meant or that he had been tricked into an impossible position. The next day, when dinner was finished, Fauquier left the room so that the clergyman could apologize to the remaining selected guests ("persons of the first distinction"). Rather than apologize, however, Robinson remonstrated, claiming that the governor should be the one to apologize for he had, during the interview the previous day, "deliberately" misled the clergyman—"in the very room" in which Robinson was then left with the other guests. Robinson's "waiting on" Fauquier in his office one day and dining the following day thus occurred in the same room.[56]

One of the largest case pieces of furniture in the room, the library table (in modern parlance, a partner's desk), Botetourt had ordered new in the summer of 1768 from London cabinetmaker William Fenton with whom he had a standing account. It was described as "a large and very neat mahogany lybery table of very fine wood covered with leather the moulding richly carved on 8 3-wheel casters." At a cost of twenty-four pounds it was equal to a half-year's salary for the governor's principal servant. Botetourt had purchased Fauquier's library table sight unseen from the estate but on his arrival had relegated it to the butler's pantry. The new governor obviously wished to make his own statement in the office with this large and imposing piece of furniture. It did not take kindly to the Virginia climate; in June 1770 it was repaired by Joshua Kendall, who had emigrated in Botetourt's retinue as a carpenter and later established himself in business in the town. Kendall charged the governor for "Easeing Drawers and fixing on Moulding to My Lord's Library Table." It contained at least fourteen lockable drawers for papers and personal objects and provided ample space for the writing equipment the governor needed (a black inkstand and a wax taper and stand).[57] At this large and very neat table, Botetourt opened and read letters from the ministry that many colonists would dearly have liked to get their own eyes on, particularly at the time of the Townshend Act resolves. In this room Botetourt, characterized in England as a "Professor of the laconic," penned letters notable for their firmness tinctured with elegance. Walpole had sensed that Botetourt's "*douceur* was enamelled on iron," after all, and certain of his letters affirm the substance of that witty aside.[58]

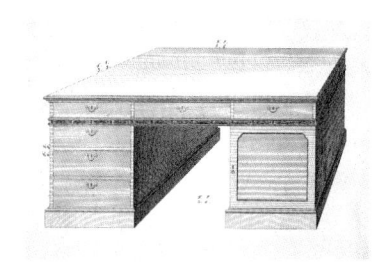

Plate 54 of Chippendale's Director, *similar to Botetourt's library table.*

Though many of his callers came from distant parts of the colony, the governor was able to pinpoint their properties and interests on John Henry's large map of Virginia that he kept in the dining room. Indeed, Botetourt was partially responsible for this newly engraved map, supporting Henry (father of Patrick Henry) in his efforts to procure a royal warrant and subscribing ten pounds toward its production. Henry had aimed to supersede Fry and Jefferson's earlier map, but he was ultimately judged to be the less accurate cartographer. Among the numerous maps in his collection, Botetourt kept two copies of the Fry and Jefferson map in the adjoining parlor while assigning pride of place in the dining room, over the fireplace on the mantel, to the newer product—its stylish, neoclassical cartouche making the rococo counterpart on the Fry and Jefferson map seem quite old-fashioned. In view of the political sentiments for which Henry's son was already notorious, Botetourt's choice and prominent siting of the map constituted a deft and graceful diplomatic touch that cannot have gone unnoticed.[59]

In this room Fauquier opened letters from London that contained stinging rebukes from the ministry; he had amended some of their directives in order to make them more palatable to the colonists. But he confessed to a friend, "I acknowledge to you freely that I have become so much a Virginian." On propitious occasions he would rise from his desk to greet a visitor and take him by the hand—"a constant token of good will in this Country," he thought it necessary to explain to an English correspondent. This response of gentry civility was what he judged it appropriate to make to the deference due him as the king's representative, a deference that also included doffing the hat when passing or meeting him in the street—"a compliment I never failed to pay the Governor . . . because custom here gave it to him from everybody."[60] The deferential removal of the hat in church, in the presence of the king's arms in court, and presumably in the Palace and Capitol as well as in the presence of gentlemen and ladies of equal or superior rank extended on ceremonial occasions even to its removal in the presence of portraits of persons of distinction.[61]

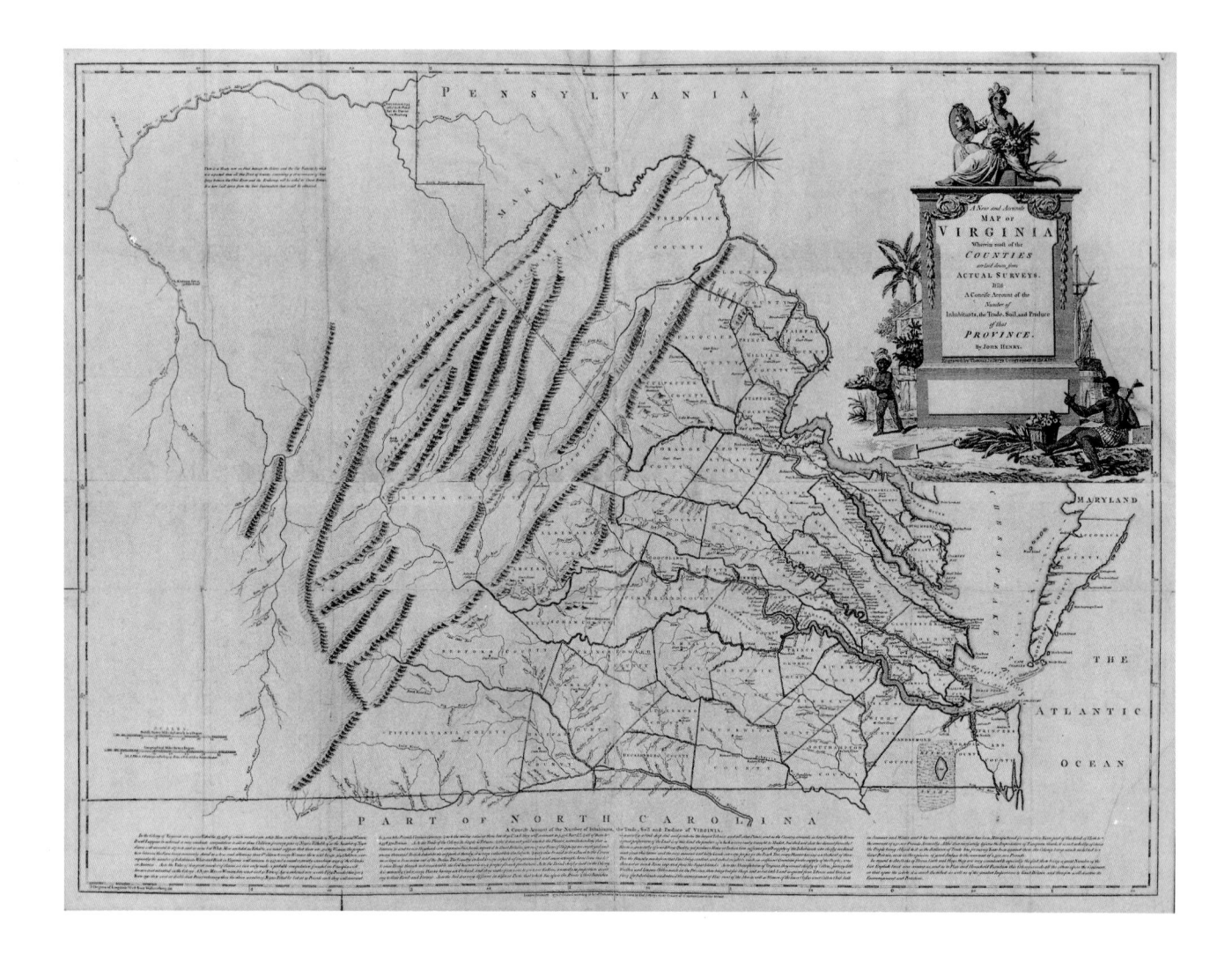

In this room Fauquier grew incensed by what he considered the truculence of the clergy. He chose it as the arena to transpose a private argument between himself and the Reverend John Camm into a public conflict that had long and bitter ramifications. In the dining room Fauquier alienated the clergyman by symbolically refusing his hospitality, and in the hall he humiliated him by giving "orders concerning him to the slaves"—"the greatest affront" that could be given to another white man in the colony.⁶²

Perhaps Gooch, too, ran his generally benign administration from this room. His private letters (something of a rarity for the Virginia governors) reveal personal concerns such as expectations of gain that were not met: "Ever since I arrived I have been in the midst of company and luxury" due to the entertaining, principally in this room, that he believed was required when the assembly or the courts were in session and for which he had to pay. "A constant great expense of Housekeeping" for birthday balls, other celebrations, and

John Henry's map of Virginia of 1770, engraved in London by the royal geographer, Thomas Jeffrys. It was Henry's ambition to supersede the Fry-Jefferson map with his own. It failed to have the critical success he hoped for because of its numerous inaccuracies and omissions. H: 45⅛"; W: 58½". CWF 1955-486.

160 PUBLIC LIFE

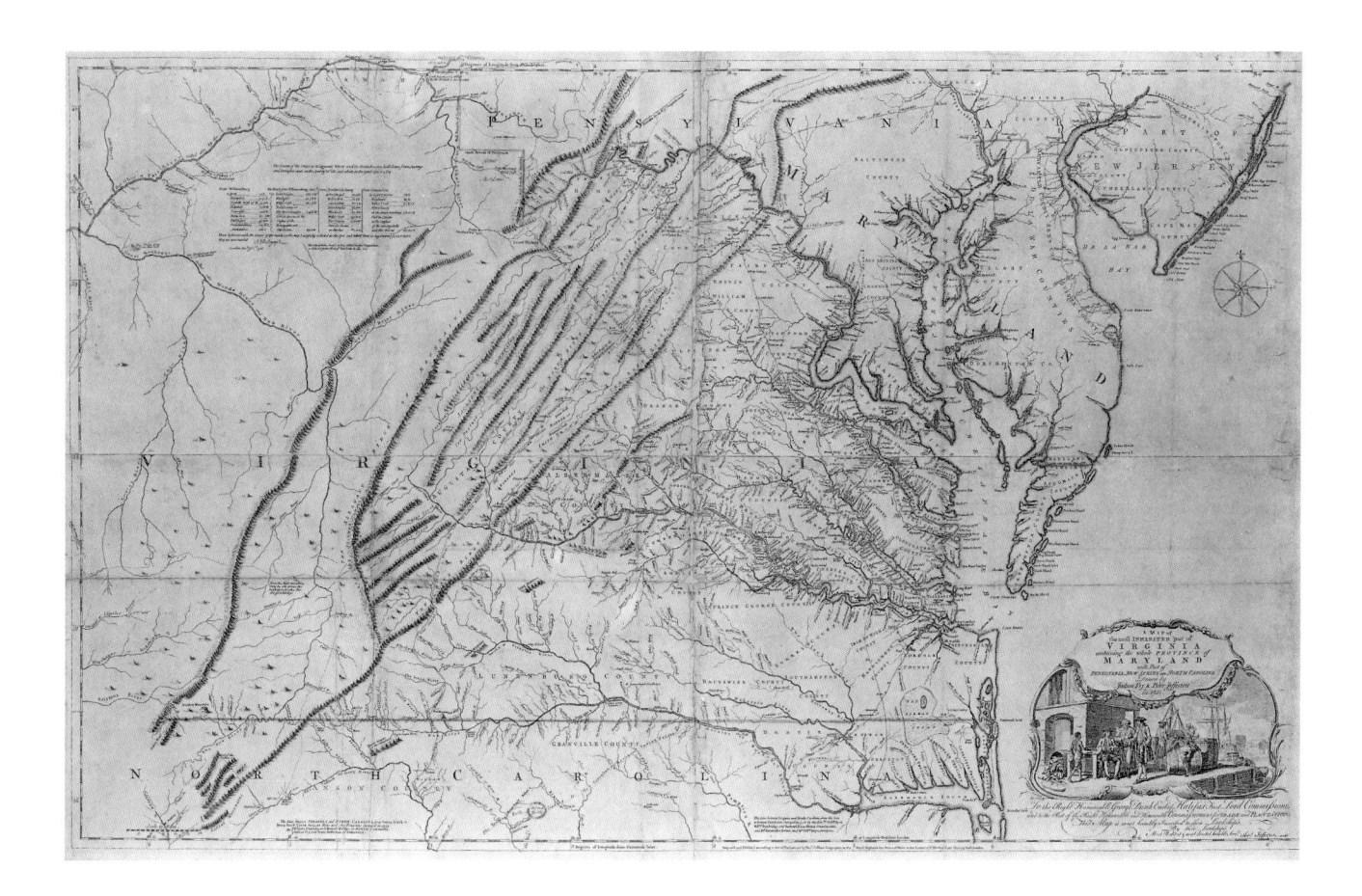

The Fry-Jefferson map of Virginia, first drafted in 1751 and engraved by Thomas Jeffrys, but not issued until 1755. It was subsequently revised three times (but issued with the same date) until the 1775 edition was so identified. The most popular map of Virginia, then and now. H: 30½"; W: 48½". CWF 1951-233.

generally maintaining his office seemed to be his lot. He also found the constant writing irksome—"Excuse my hurry for this week I have more writing than an Attorney's Clerk" . . . "I have had more writing work this Conveyance than ever I had in my Life." The climate often compounded despair: "The weather is extream hot, I can hardly write my hands are so moist."[63]

The parlor worked in tandem with the dining room at times of social and professional use. For a space in which host and guests could gather before dinner or to which diners could withdraw after the ceremony, the furniture shown in the inventory was fitting. A couch, chairs, two card tables (a third stood in the adjoining closet), and the equipage that could easily be brought from the little middle room across the passage all facilitated the usual social functions that dinner guests might engage in. That the parlor played a business role is strongly suggested by further analysis of the above furnishings. The seating furniture in the room was mostly upholstered with leather, which was chosen for durability rather than for fashion. Much of it belonged to the colony and was probably older and less stylish than that owned by the governor. Leather-covered furniture generally stood in secondary rooms such as the butler's pantry or in those spaces where hard use was expected, the passage upstairs, for example. Thus it is likely that the parlor appeared to many visitors to be more a room of service than a room of fashion. Neighboring governors did not consider leather appropriate upholstery for their "parlours." Their preferences ranged from horsehair, such as Botetourt chose for his dining room, to the considerably more expensive damask. The thirty-four scripture prints in the Williamsburg parlor provided suitably edifying matter for waiting petitioners to peruse, in the same way that the "Roman Catholick Pictures" did for those in the passage upstairs, the waiting function of which has already been shown. Whether or not those waiting in the parlor reacted to the prints with quite the

Portrait of clerk of the Council Nathaniel Walthoe, oil on canvas, attributed to William Dering about 1750. Though a stylish representation, the fact that he was shown wearing his hat apparently discomfited the sitter to the extent that when he bequeathed the portrait to William Byrd III, he expressed the hope that it could hang with the portraits of British worthies at Westover, despite the hat. A diamond ring was included with the bequest, perhaps to make his wishes more acceptable. H: 29¾"; W: 24¾". CWF 1956-562.

George Montague Dunk, Earl of Halifax, dictating to his secretaries, gouache, attributed to Daniel Gardner, after Hugh Douglas Hamilton, ca. 1765–1767. An exceptional picture in that it shows a powerful man in the act of purposeful business, with the staff and artifacts necessary for him to perform it. H: 17¾"; W: 38". *Courtesy, National Portrait Gallery, London.*

same ingenuous delight as the Presbyterian Fithian—"I spent much of this Day . . . among the works of mighty-Men; I turned over *Calmets*, Scripture prints, they are beautiful, and vastly entertaining"—is questionable, but the choice of religious material on the walls of the two spaces seems to be more than pure coincidence.[64]

That the hall held damask chairs implies that people coming to the Palace on business waited elsewhere than in that highly ceremonial space. Damask was not for the everyday petitioner, only for people of consequence. Such a spatial arrangement was not atypical, for the architect Isaac Ware had noted in 1756 that "of these two front rooms [either side of the hall] that on the right hand [as the Palace parlor was] may very conveniently be made a waiting-room for those persons who are of better rank than to be left in the hall."[65] Botetourt may have decreed that the parlor should be used instead of the hall during "business hours," those of the better rank being shown upstairs to wait

THE DINING ROOM AND PARLOR 163

in the passage. It is also possible that the strict gradations of class practiced in England (particularly in London and the major urban centers) were considered unnecessary and undesirable in colonial society.

In these matters custom was flexible and custom was changing. Robert Adam proposed in the early 1770s that "the anterooms on each side [of the hall], are for the attendance of the servants out of livery, and also for that of tradesmen."[66] At the Governor's Palace tradesmen were probably accommodated by the butler in the pantry on one side of the hall directly across from the parlor. As Botetourt's chief household officer, the butler kept the accounts and checked the bills. A room for servants out of livery would probably have been described in the inventory as a servants' hall, however—it would hardly have been labeled a parlor. In the newer palace at New Bern a room off the hall was called a servants' hall in the late 1760s. At the Palace in Williamsburg the servants' hall(s) stood outside the main building.

Whatever subtleties of protocol or refinements of genteel practice did obtain under Botetourt, it is apparent that the parlor and its adjoining closet also offered a suitably equipped work space for the governor's clerk. A writing table, two inkstands, a wax taper and stand, a bureau in the closet, and valuable Mediterranean passes were items for business use, particularly the latter.[67] Among his other duties the governor's clerk had to report details of the sale of each pass and account for the monies involved. Maps of Virginia lend further credence to this use of the space; a certain percentage of the visitors to the Palace came on business, such as procuring licenses, that was customarily dispatched by the clerk.

At New Bern the dining room in the Governor's Palace was alternately described—and presumably used—as a drawing room. Tryon probably transferred that practice to New York; indeed, the dining room there contained card tables and *two* dozen chairs (more than customary for dining rooms). The prevailing color scheme for Tryon's dining room was the same as for Botetourt's, blue being specified for window curtains and chair covers. His "Chints Room" may have been elegantly furnished for a parlor, but both terms were used for the same room. It featured blue damask window curtains and backstools fitted with blue and white check covers. It also contained card tables and an unusually elegant firescreen inset with a painted silk panel, protected by a green silk cover when not in use. Eden's "gilt leather parlour" probably functioned (like Botetourt's middle room upstairs) more as a drawing room than a parlor since the curtains were crimson damask, the walls were hung with gilt leather, and the room was embellished with a "handsome pier glass and a fine piece of [landscape] painting." His "right hand parlour" on the other side of the passage featured thirteen "pieces of painting" including

When not required for business, the parlor could be quickly set up as a place for leisure and relaxation, for tea or coffee, and for cards, as the footman is doing here.

classical ruins, "landscips, Battle peices." Later termed "the picture parlour," it may have served as conventional parlor and breakfast parlor combined since it also contained a card table and a dining table. Beyond these two parlors stood the "Long Room" equipped with the furniture necessary to make it function as a dining room. It probably accommodated large assemblies and meetings also. Campbell maintained both a breakfast parlor and a dining parlor, the former containing a couch (as did Botetourt's front parlor) as well as breakfast and dining tables; the latter was hung with blue moreen curtains like the dining rooms previously cited.[68]

In Virginia every house of pretension featured a dining room or dining parlor and a room nearby that functioned or at least doubled as a parlor or drawing room. Their lists of furnishings exhibit a remarkable consistency. Virginia grandees maintained a level of hospitality approaching, if not equal to, the governor's. This was particularly true in the political context of high officials in Williamsburg such as the Speaker, the attorney general, and the treasurer. The dining rooms of these houses formed successive stations, along with the Palace, on periodic fact-finding and opinion-seeking visits to the capital. They were presumably very active when the assembly or the court was in session. At splendid Tazewell Hall, Attorney General John Randolph maintained an elegant dining parlor and "a small ditto." The former was decorated with ornamental china branches and five pictures plus prints of the king and queen, while the latter contained a harpsichord and a writing table in addition to the dining equipment. Ornamental china and glass, including a remarkable cut-

THE DINING ROOM AND PARLOR 165

glass epergne or centerpiece with twelve branches, baskets, and ornaments etc., was stored in some quantity in a beaufet ("bowfat") for use in these rooms.[69]

The attorney general's brother, Peyton Randolph, seems to have lived at a less conspicuously elegant level, symbolic perhaps of his official role as mediator and stabilizing force. His dining room overlooking Market Square in the middle of town must have doubled as a drawing room for company of any size. Four expensive looking glasses distinguished it from the Virginia norm, however. Perhaps the family pictures, not included in the inventory, also hung here. This was the historic setting where the first draft of Jefferson's tract, "A Summary View of The Rights of British America," was read to "a large company" including the committee of correspondence in August 1774, in the absence of the ailing author.[70] In a completely different spirit, but just as characteristic of Virginia society, John Tayloe at Mount Airy—a house "ornamented with various paintings and rich pictures"—kept in his dining room "besides many other fine Pieces . . . twenty four of the most celebrated among the English Race-Horses, Drawn masterly, and set in elegant gilt Frames." Even Botetourt's selection of the dining room as office was not idiosyncratic, for numerous Virginia houses featured desks and/or desk and bookcases in the

The dining room of Mr. Speaker Randolph, one of the most important communication centers in the city. The largest, newest room of the house, overlooking the market square and middle of town, it also had traditional links to Sir John Randolph and a powerful family network.

room, including Kenmore, Berkeley, Morattico, the Ambler house, and the Nelson house.[71]

Fithian's exclamation of surprise and delight at the appearance of a Virginia gentry dining room fully prepared and awaiting the guests—"the room looked luminous and splendid; four very large candles burning on the table where we supp'd, three others in different parts of the Room; a gay, sociable Assembly, and four well instructed waiters!"—leaves no doubt about the social importance of the effect that appearances in this room were calculated to make. Beyond that, his frequent reportage of dinner and supper conversation between the Carters and their incessant guests and also between father, mother, and children clearly expresses the high value that the adults placed both on the occasion and on the setting for intellectual, cultural, and social exchange. Discussions on philosophy, music, reading, mathematics, astronomy, immortality, religion, apart from politics and slavery, all took place in this room. These were surely kin to the "habitual conversations" in the Palace dining room from which Jefferson derived such rich benefit. In this society dinner was not simply an elegant, lavishly equipped ritual designed to ornament or dignify the daily need to appease hunger. It was a central meeting place for the exchange of ideas, opinions, information, and experiences, an event or ceremony in which women and children as well as men could participate fully.[72]

In the somewhat different, more masculine ambience of the Governor's Palace no other room provided such a constant setting for the customary observance of condescension and deference, the habitual exchange of civility, and the cultural interaction of metropolitan and provincial experience. The public official and the social presence mingled there and interacted freely with a wide range of the local population, to the incalculable benefit of some of the participants in these "truly Attic societies."

The Ballroom and Supper Room
FASHIONABLE GATHERINGS

From the time Spotswood first occupied the Palace about 1715 until midcentury when the ballroom and supper room were added, the large assemblies that gathered there to celebrate coronations, royal birthdays, peace treaties, and other notable events must have placed a considerable strain on the building's resources. As the Capitol was more capacious, some festivities were held there instead. When that building burned in 1747, however, not many months after the grand ball to celebrate the Hanoverian triumph at Culloden, there was no alternative site; it was probably more than coincidence that the large addition to the Palace for the express purpose of public assemblies was built within a short time of that fire. In any event, ballrooms were the fashion and all the rage, so much so that Isaac Ware facetiously observed in 1756 that "in houses which have been some time built, and which have not an out of proportion room, the common practice is to build one to them: this always hangs from one end, or sticks to one side, of the house, and shews to the most careless eye, that, though fastened to the walls, it does not belong to the building."[1]

The new ballroom and supper room wing at the Palace did, indeed, protrude from the end of the building, but as compensation it must have made an enormous difference to the handling of large groups of people in the residence. "The custom of routs has introduced this absurd practice," Ware continued. "Our forefathers were pleased with seeing their friends as they chanced to come, and with entertaining them when they were there. The present custom is to see them all at once, and entertain none of them; this brings in the necessity of a *great room*, which is opened only on such occasions, and which loads and generally discredits the rest of the edifice."[2] Routs were fashionable assemblies, large evening parties, or receptions, a popular social custom that continued to grow in strength through the century. In Williamsburg in the third quarter of the century the term "Companys" was also used. Yet the demand for increased space for assemblies at the Palace was more than just "present custom," however absurd or regrettable to those like Ware, or attractive to others, the custom was. Ceremonies to proclaim new monarchs, to celebrate royal birthdays, marriages, births and deaths, and unusual victories or peace treaties were official necessities and inevitably required large assembly spaces in the colonial capital.

Prior to the expansion of the Palace, the hall was the principal point of assembly for these official events. At times people must have flowed from the hall to the dining room and the middle room upstairs, indeed, throughout the building. If Spotswood hosted two hundred people for the king's birthnight and Gooch "entertained the town" on the occasion of his inauguration, conditions at the Palace must have been very crowded. The cost to the governors was also burdensome. But despite the discomfort of the crowded conditions and the cost, the events continued in full spate. They were an essential part of the paternalistic system and the governors cannot seriously have envisioned ever dispensing with them.[3]

One of the most lavish official ceremonies of this kind was occasioned by the news in July 1746 of the "Glorious Victory gain'd over the Rebels" at Culloden. Because the assembly was in session when the news arrived and many important colonists were in town, the event was deemed worthy of a "Grand Entertainment," though Lieutenant Governor Gooch was ill and unable to attend. Whether it was his confinement at the Palace that prompted the decision to hold the celebration at the Capitol or whether it was the anticipated size of the gathering is unclear. But the event was so noteworthy that it merited an exceptionally full (and rare) account in the *Virginia Gazette*, that conveys in vivid detail the formal sequences and elaboration that such a gathering required:

On receiving the News, in this City, of the Glorious Victory gain'd over the Rebels, by his Royal Highness the Duke of Cumberland, an universal Joy seem'd diffus'd among all Ranks of Persons; the General Assembly being met, and much Company in Town, a Grand Entertainment was made at the Capitol, on Tuesday Night, suitable to the extraordinary Occasion, by the Honourable the President and Council, Mr. Speaker, and the rest of the House of Burgesses; to which his Honour the Governor, who continues indispos'd, was pleas'd to contribute very largely. In the Evening, a very numerous Company of Gentlemen and Ladies appear'd at the Capitol, where a Ball was open'd, and after dancing some Time, withdrew to Supper, there being a very handsome Collation spread on three Tables, in three different Rooms, consisting of near 100 Dishes, after the most delicate Taste. There was also provided a great Variety of the choicest and best Liquors, in which the Healths of the King, the Prince and Princess of Wales, the Duke, and the rest of the Royal Family, the Governor, Success to His Majesty's Arms, Prosperity to this Colony, and many other Loyal Healths were chearfully drank, and a Round of the Cannon, which were remov'd to the Capitol for this Purpose, was discharg'd at each Health, to the Number of 18 or 20 Rounds, which lasted 'til near 2 o'Clock. The whole Affair was conducted with great Decency and good Order, and an unaffected Chearfulness appeared in the Countenances of the

Company All the Houses in the City were illuminated, and a very large Bonfire was made in the Market-Place, 3 Hogsheads of Punch given to the Populace; and the whole concluded with the greatest Demonstrations of Joy and Loyalty.[4]

Perhaps traditionalists like Ware might have argued that formal rites such as kings' birthdays and military victories could be celebrated without making them an excuse for excessively large sociable gatherings which in turn created the need for additional spaces to accommodate them. But Ware and his ilk were outnumbered. Routs were in vogue and to stay, and not for official purposes only. A potent factor in their growing popularity may have been the fact that they were one of the few ceremonies outside the family and the church in which women were full and active participants. It was on the occasion of a ball

On entering the ballroom from the front of the house, the visitor was greeted with the large, imposing portraits of the reigning monarch and his consort in a setting of considerable elegance.

170 PUBLIC LIFE

Lord Botetourt intended to paper the supper room also, probably to achieve an effect comparable to the ballroom. The room "at rest" has a spartan quality that belies the elegance and gaiety of the festivities it was built to accommodate.

at the Capitol at the time of the Nonimportation Agreement in 1769, for example, that a group of Virginia ladies made one of their rare, concerted political actions by appearing in "homespun" dresses—"a lively and striking instance of their acquiescence and concurrence in whatever may be the true and essential interest of their country." For younger people, inevitably, balls provided important opportunities for rituals of courtship or merely flirtation, which one visitor thought "the principal business in Virginia" for participants and spectators alike.[5] The forces that led people to find in these gatherings or assemblies their outlets for social interaction on a complex variety of levels were accentuated in Virginia by broad, sparse patterns of settlement that spawned few towns or large communities. In the vast, otherwise "silent country" such assemblies were necessary to sustain sociability and mitigate loneliness. They were deliberately created, in face of the great uncertainties that were so distinctive a feature of life in early Virginia, to foster congeniality and promote a myriad of shared relationships. And since they invariably entailed the playing of cards, they provided a further opportunity for the colonists to indulge in that ritual and compulsive outlet for assertive sociability and competitiveness.[6]

Virginians at the beginning of the eighteenth century were no strangers to formal assemblies. As early as the 1670s four gentlemen in the Northern Neck had subscribed together for the construction of a "Banquetting House . . . to make an Honorable treatment fit to entertain the undertakers thereof, their wives, mistress and friends yearly and every year." In 1702 occurred the most ambitious and lavishly described event ever held in early Williamsburg, commemorating the death of King William III and the accession of Queen Anne—a two-day combination of public ceremony, dinners, and assembly that surely owed its scale and energy to the dynamic governor, Francis Nicholson. The attention to careful sequences, to order, and to fine apparel—for example, the young Indian queen was noted as wearing "nice clothes of a French Pattern . . . her ornaments" and a beautiful crown "set with stones . . . artistically"—became a characteristic of later balls and assemblies. With its fireworks displays, its military drills, its music, its "rifle match," and Indian archers, the ceremony, in the description of the Swiss traveler who noted it for posterity, has the fantastic quality of a scene from Shakespeare or of drawings for a masque by Inigo Jones.[7]

With his flair for the dramatic and formal gesture, Alexander Spotswood contrived to sponsor sociable gatherings on a weekly basis during spring and fall seasons in the colonial capital. Private subscription assemblies were also held at the Capitol from time to time. William Byrd II frequented both the governor's and the private assemblies, noting them in his diary. By the 1720s they became such a feature of the town that the Reverend Hugh Jones commented "at the Governor's House upon birth-nights, and at balls and assemblies, I have seen as fine an appearance, as good diversion, and as splendid entertainments in Governor Spotswood's time as I have seen any where else."[8] William Gooch later boasted that "there is not an ill dancer in my government"—a key to the social importance often associated with this recreational activity—while Fithian observed drily, "Virginians . . . will dance or die." That the legislature was willing to commit two or three thousand pounds of government money to pay for the new wing at the Governor's Palace seems evidence enough of how widely perceived the need for it was.[9]

Public rooms of assembly became a conspicuous feature of polite society in the eighteenth century. Among the first and most famous in England were the York Assembly Rooms, completed in 1731–1732 and comprising a large room for dancing and two smaller rooms for refreshments and cards. Bath had rooms that could be utilized for such purposes, and dancing assemblies appeared in the colonies, in Charleston and Philadelphia, toward mid-century.[10] The pattern spread quickly. In Williamsburg, for example, roughly contemporary with the addition of the ballroom and supper room wing to the Governor's Palace, large spaces were added to or incorporated in the houses of conspicuous local officials—John Blair, president of the Council, Peyton Randolph, appointed attorney general in 1748 and Speaker of the House of Burgesses in 1766, and John Randolph, a prominent lawyer who became attorney general in 1766 and whose house, Tazewell Hall, boasted both a saloon and a "gallery." In the third quarter of the century George Washington began construction of a ballroom at one end of his house, while his contemporary, councillor Robert Carter, designated a large space on the first floor of his new house in the Northern Neck of Virginia as a ballroom.[11] Civic ballrooms, provided by public subscription and "dedicated to the most elegant recreation," also appeared in this "age when the polite arts by general encouragement and emulation have advanced to a state of perfection unknown in any former period." Fredericksburg boasted a large assembly room and two companion rooms "for retirement and cards" in the 1770s, while Fithian mentioned ballrooms at Tappahannock (Hobbes Hole) and Marlborough, Maryland, which may have been public. Tavern keepers in Williamsburg also perceived the need to provide large, new public spaces, notably Henry Wetherburn (the "Great Room") and Alexander Finnie (the "Apollo Room" at the Raleigh Tavern). At times of political tension tavern keepers even offered their accommodations as an alternative to those "who did not choose to attend at the Palace," a precedent established in the period of disaffection between Spotswood and the burgesses, as early as 1718.[12]

The new wing at the Palace was unusual in that it contained two rooms rather than the one often built in the colonies or the three customary in England. It was probably thought that there were already enough rooms in the building for the mandatory card games and that the need was for spaces for dancing, music, and refreshments. These new spaces may have been inaugurated by a grand ball given by Lieutenant Governor Dinwiddie to commemorate the king's birthday in November 1752 at which "very elegant Entertainment, at the Palace . . . were present, the Emperor and Empress of the *Cherokee* Nation, with their Son the young Prince, and a brilliant Appearance of Ladies and Gentlemen." Presumably attended by the "Several . . . Warriors and great Men and their Ladies" who were specifically identified in the emperor's retinue at a celebration the previous evening, the Indian dignitaries would have added a spectacular quality to an already theatrical event (accentuated, surely, by a concluding fireworks display in Palace Street orchestrated by Lewis Hallam, manager of the Williamsburg theater). Indeed, the state visit had started the previous day when the governor and the Council, after receiving the Indians at the Palace (very probably in the middle room upstairs), had entertained them at the theater later with a performance of *Othello*—the presentation being so realistic that the sword fights quite alarmed the empress, who "immediately order[ed] some about her to go and prevent [the actors] killing one another!"[13]

    This particular commemoration of the king's birthday may have been the most dramatic ever held in the ballroom, though a "brilliant Appearance of Ladies and Gentlemen" occurred at many assemblies there, to judge by William Small's observations. Advising a young man about a faculty appointment at the College of William and Mary in 1765, Small noted that "one Suit of handsome full dressed Silk Cloathes to wear on the Kings birthday at the Governors [is essentially] the only time you will have occasion to appear *fine* in the whole year—but then it is expected that all English Gentlemen attend and pay their respects . . . as to the rest of your Wearing apparel you may dress as

As gentlemen and ladies danced, musicians played, and spectators gossiped and flirted, inevitably the gentlemen played cards in other rooms, just as inevitably drinking and sometimes even singing.

174 PUBLIC LIFE

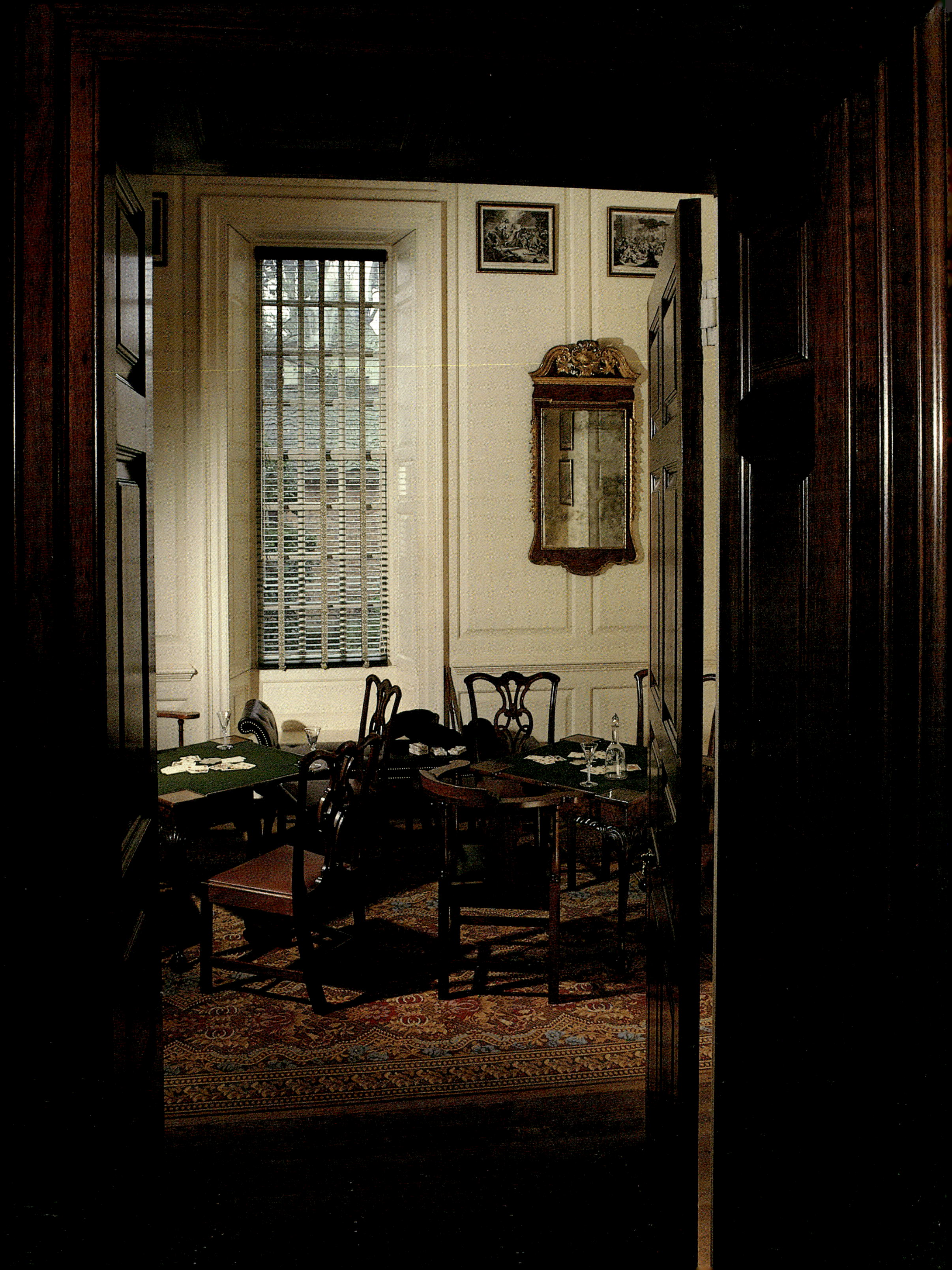

you please." With all the gentlemen attired in silk suits, brocaded, embroidered, or at least edged with lace, gold, or silver thread, and the ladies appropriately en suite, the effect of these assemblies in the Palace ballroom was surely elegant and colorful indeed.[14]

An invitation to the Palace from Lord Botetourt must have been appealing, even intriguing, to many, for his social standing gave him a cachet that his predecessors had conspicuously lacked. "[Though] I have seen his excelency . . . I have never had the honour of being introduced to his Lordship but that is an honour I did not expect," wrote a young woman of gentry family during his administration.[15] Botetourt's social attainments received much publicity when he appeared in Virginia. The *Virginia Gazette*'s report of the governor's arrival, though it smacks of a panegyric, singled out the Council's praise of "our Most Gracious Sovereign, which have determined him to make choice of a Nobleman of your Excellency's many eminent virtues and distinguished abilities to rule over and to reside among us." The newspaper published a further report on the particulars of Botetourt's lineage. Of special note to readers were his relationships at court—not only for the particular influence they implied but also for the social éclat they connoted. In a very rare contemporary report of a public appearance by Botetourt in Virginia, an observer stressed that "the Governor's deportment was dignified and his delivery was solemn. It was said by those who had heard and seen George III speak and act on the throne of England, that his Lordship on the throne of Virginia was true to his prototype. He spoke very slow, with long pauses."[16] Perhaps these accounts were prompted by a measure of self-congratulation on the part of the colonists that they now merited a full governor, though the interest in matters monarchical may not have been shared by the whole of the populace. Yet the tenor of the various reports is unambiguous.

The royal court provided the hierarchical model for the colonial "court," of course, and Virginians' interest in the niceties of protocol, in the correct hierarchy and social forms, grew to the point where it was necessary to define the "Rules of Precedency" for a colonial society, given official sanction by the College of Heralds and published in the *Virginia Gazette* in 1774. Assemblies and balls required complex procedures and spawned their own parade, their own formal rituals, quite beyond the archetypal subtleties and varieties of diplomatic encounter between male and female participants. In order to be there in the first place, it was necessary to have a certain status—to have been properly brought up for it. Small used the word "Gentlemen" to denote the social level; Fithian in Virginia succinctly characterized it thus: "Mrs *Carter* . . . is also well acquainted (for She has always been used) with the formality and Ceremony which we find commonly in high Life." How to act at a ball was an important lesson to be taught to gentry children. Dancing masters were thus

"Grown gentlemen taught to dance," and "grown ladies taught to dance," two prints satirizing the contortions that fashion seemed to demand of its adherents, enforced by those who were its minions. In the case of these prints, taken from paintings by John Collet, the satire was accentuated by the elderly subjects, male and female, pushing their torsos and their limbs into grotesque postures. Engravings dated 1767. H: 11 15/16"; W: 9½". CWF 1952-152, 153.

a desirable feature of maturing society and reinforced the canons of decorum and genteel behavior in "polite company." So seriously did they and their patrons take this responsibility that masters might reinforce their lessons with corporal punishment, even in the presence of parents. This element of behavior was so essential to gentry life, so vital to the structure of sociability that a great Virginia planter might direct in his will, without perceived contradiction, that in the event of his early demise his daughters "be maintained with great frugality and taught to dance." Fithian quickly became aware of the inadequacies of his upbringing on his arrival in Virginia. When entreated to join in a dance at Nomini Hall, he "declined it . . . and went to my Room not without Wishes that it had been a part of my Education to learn what I think is an innocent and an ornamental, and most certainly, in this province is a necessary qualification for a person to appear *even decent in Company*" (italics added).[17]

At the Palace the governor signaled the opening of a ball by dancing with a carefully chosen partner—an honor that everyone present recognized. To maintain appropriate order and decorum and to follow the correct sequence of dances, a master of ceremonies or director was desirable. Without one, "of Corse a great deal of confusion must Insue," observed Mary Spotswood, a descendant of the former lieutenant governor in Williamsburg in 1769–1770.[18] Beau Nash had established the principles of control and formal sequence at assemblies early in the century in England, and his name had become synonymous with this essential component of fashionable gatherings. One of Nash's chief aims had been to "promote society, good manners, and a coalition of parties and ranks," in other words, an elegant, organized venue where "people of every degree, condition, and occupation of life (if well dressed and well behaved) met amicably . . . together." This surely was an unexceptionable ambition of which any governor could fully approve. In a brief description of the king's birthday celebration of May 1770, Botetourt's protégé was called "Starke the Beau Nash," inferring that the governor's instruction of young men also included indoctrination in the social proprieties.[19]

Among the fluid and complex patterns of order and movement at a ball, more or less hidden currents of physical feelings were perceptible, running the gamut from the coquettish to the heartfelt. A brilliant description, brimming with innuendo, of a ball in Norfolk clearly illustrates the metaphor of the "chase":

> It so happened then, you must know, that my Lord and Lady Dunmore, and their family, came to pay a visit to Norfolk; (some time in the year 1774, I think, tho' I won't be sure) and our people turned out to receive 'em in style. Indeed you never saw such a fuss as we made. . . . we thought we couldn't do too much to honor our guests. So among other things, we made 'em a grand ball at the old Masons Hall, . . . and all the gentry of our town were there of course. And besides, we had sent off an express to Princess Anne for Col. Moseley, who was reckoned the finest gentleman we had, to come to town with his famous wig and shining buckles, to dance the minuet with my lady—for our poor Mayor, Captain Abyvon, was afraid to venture upon such a thing. And there too we had all the British navy officers, Capt. Montague, and the rest, with their heads powdered as white as they could be. What was best of all, all our pretty girls, far and near, came out to grace the scene. . . . So, by and by, the fiddles struck up; and there went my Lady Dunmore in the minuet, sailing about the room in her great, fine, hoop-petticoat, (her new fashioned air balloon as I called it) and Col Moseley after her, wig and all. Indeed he did his best to overtake her I believe; but little puss was too cunning for him this time, and kept turning and doubling upon him so often, that she flung him out several times, (at least by his looks, he was on a wrong scent more than once) and he couldn't come near her to save him. Bless her heart, how cleverly she managed her hoop—now this way, now that—every body was delighted. Indeed, we all agreed that she was a lady sure enough, and that we had never seen dancing before—After this our Lord Mayor was obliged to take out Lady Catharine for another minuet. But the poor Captain was laboring hard in a heavy sea all the time, and, I dare say, was glad enough when he got safe moored in his seat. Then Capt Montague took out Lady Susan—and I remember the little jade made a mighty pretty cheese with her hoop. Then came the reels; and here our Norfolk lads and lasses turned in with all their hearts and heels.[20]

For those with a limited span of attention on the rituals of the dance, cards were customary. Whether the tables were set up in the supper room or kept in the

"We were all extremely happy in each other's company," wrote one visitor to a Virginia ball, "the ladies being perfectly free and easy and at the same [time] elegant in their manners." Such an event was often characterized, and probably with some justification, as "a brilliant Appearance of Ladies and Gentlemen."

parlor probably depended on the occasion and the size of the group expected. At Bath and York, for example, separate rooms were set aside for them. Botetourt's twelve dozen packs of cards were far more than his three card tables could accommodate, so it is possible that card playing groups spread throughout the residence. Fithian's account of the splendid five-day ball at Lee Hall in 1774 may describe what was the general practice in Virginia: "As soon as I had handed the Ladies out [of the coach], I was saluted . . . [and] introduced into a small Room where a number of Gentlemen were playing Cards." His narrative suggests a room as close to the front door as the Palace parlor was. Fithian continued: "But all did not join in the Dance for there were parties in Rooms made up, some at Cards; some drinking for Pleasure; some toasting the Sons of america; some singing 'Liberty Songs' as they call'd them." These extra, primarily male-oriented activities imply that more ladies than gentlemen participated in the actual dancing—an occurrence that Fithian observed was not unusual.[21]

For younger participants the evening could be emotionally exciting or poignant, even wrenching. Fithian, in the confidence of his diary, occasionally overcame his scruples and recorded the personal feelings that such encounters aroused: "Soon after he danced Miss *Dolly Edmundson*—a Short pretty Stump of a Girl; She danced well, sung a Song with great applause, seemed to enter into the Spirit of the entertainment—A young Spark seemed to be fond of her; She seemed to be fond of him; they were both fond, and the Company saw it—He was Mr Ritche's Clerk, a limber, well dress'd, pretty-handsome Chap he was—The insinuating Rogue waited on her home, in close Hugg too, the Moment he left the Ball-Room."[22]

In his diary Fithian wrestled with his natural instincts, struggling to subject them to the discipline of his Presbyterian training. His continued account of the ball at Hobbes Hole reveals how quickly his training reasserted itself and the finer points of gentry civility gained the upper hand: "Miss *Aphia Fantleroy* danced next, the best Dancer of the whole absolutely—And the finest Girl—Her head tho' was powdered white as Snow, and crap'd in the newest Taste—She is the Copy of the Goddess of Modesty—Very handsome; she seemed to be loved by all her Acquaintances, and admir'd by every Stranger."[23]

Many derived a sense of emotional satisfaction and aesthetic fulfillment from the dance. "The reels, cotillions, etc., you dance with anybody you please, by which means you have an opportunity of making love to any lady you please," commented one English visitor. One of his companions at a great Virginia plantation made an admirable impression: "Her elegant figure commands attention wherever she moves." He concluded that "we were all extremely happy in each other's company, the ladies being perfectly free and easy and at the same [time] elegant in their manners. They would grace any country whatever . . . To see everything go so smooth, and such harmony prevail . . ."[24]

Throughout the evening the profoundest satisfaction may have flowed from the perception that basic and unruly human instincts could be disciplined and subsumed into a richly caparisoned order and an elevated harmony: "Several Minuets danced with great ease and propriety; after which the whole company Joined in country-dances, and it was indeed beautiful to admiration, to see such a number of young persons, set off by dress to the best Advantage, moving easily, to the sound of well performed Music, and with perfect regularity, tho' apparently in the utmost Disorder."[25]

From order there emerged harmony, out of freedom came control, fluidity led to discipline, movement to order—it was these properties of the dance that the participants took pleasure in and the spectators took note of; however, no such harmonic resolution was evident in the typical Virginia jig. "A Bacchanalian dance," in the opinion of one prim onlooker, it seemed hardly fit for "a polite assembly." "Borrowed . . . from the Negroes," the jig evinced no "method or regularity," but rather was "irregular fantastical." It was one of the paradoxes of polite society in Virginia that gentlemen and ladies in their brilliant apparel should be found on social occasions created by the artifice of gentility and decorum dancing a dance borrowed from their slaves. The union of opposite features in the jig was of a different order from the dances mentioned above—perhaps a perfect symbol of Virginia society in these years—gentry men and women with their acquired English appearance obeying the rules of

English decorum yet assimilating the rhythms of the enslaved Africans who shared their landscape. No evidence has survived to tell us whether or not the jig was danced in the ballroom of the Governor's Palace.[26]

In order for the governor and his household to stage a ball certain preparations were necessary, as the account books kept by William Marshman at the Palace reveal. Musicians were engaged, varying in number from six to eight—a considerable increase over the two fiddlers and a French horn that Fithian observed at the Lees' grand five-day ball. Extra servants were hired from neighbors for the event ranging from a "black woman helping in the house" to unspecified servants borrowed from Robert Carter and Thomas Everard on Palace green and Commissary James Horrocks at the college. Specialized help was essential—servants whose training and experience had equipped them to work at the Palace such as the attorney general's cook, under cook, pastry maid, and footman. Porters, "2 sentinels for [the] Great Door" and two for the kitchen door, and Negroes to light the candles, all were hired. Some of the governor's servants were paid extra for waiting on the guests, though they received only one-quarter the rate of each musician, for example. The governor's clerk, Peter Pelham, was paid the same rate as a musician (£1. 1. 6.) for "attendance" at Botetourt's last ball, but whether for musical services or not is unclear. When the ball celebrated the king's birthday night, a local merchant named Brammer was paid ten pounds for distributing "Bumbo" that the populace might drink the health of the monarch and his family. Thus those who were not high enough in the social hierarchy to attend at the Palace could still feel some sense of participation in the festivities in honor of the king. From the extensive preparations in the kitchen, from getting the rooms and all the glass, china, and silver ready for the event, to assisting with the crush of many coaches in front of the building during the course of the evening, and to attending to the various needs of the people present, the balls consumed great quantities of time, labor, and money.[27]

A ball had much of the theater about it. It is no accident that the first theater in America was established by a dancing master in Williamsburg, and probably no coincidence that its location was close to the Palace. A more formal connection between a state ball and the theater has already been noted in the context of the inauguration of the ballroom wing at the Palace. Most of the governors were interested in and patronized the theater, while the later ones may well have organized amateur theatricals in the ballroom. Botetourt was interested in the subject to the extent that he brought a twenty-volume set of *Select Plays* to Williamsburg with him. His clerk, Peter Pelham, is also documented to have conducted local performances of *The Beggars' Opera* in conjunction with visiting troupes of players.[28]

1769	Brought forward	£	s	d
		131	10	3
Oct. 26th	To 8 Musicians at 21/–6 each	8	12	0
	To 2 Centinels at 10/ each	1	0	0
	To Cleaning the Well	0	7	6
27	To Capt. Webb's Bill ✓	22	17	3
	To the Farrier's Bill ✓	4	16	7½
	To Mr. Holt's Bill ✓	39	13	6
	To Mr. Nelson's Bill for Peach Brandy ✓	10	10	0
28th	To Major Traverse's Bill ✓	65	5	7
	To Mr. Anderson the Smith's Bill ✓	9	11	1½
	To Mr. Sparrow on Acct. ✓	20	0	0
	To Mr. Horrocks's Order ✓	40	0	0
30th	To Mr. Calvert for Freightage of Madeira ✓	11	6	9 ✓
	To Mr. Brammer's Bill for Bumbo y. 25th 9ber ✓	10	0	0
	To Mr. Montgommerie as pr. Order ✓	48	0	0
	To Messrs. Purdie & Dixon for Newspapers ✓	1	17	6
	To a Barrel of Limes ✓	1	10	0
31st	To Mr. Sparrow on Acct.	24	0	0
Novr. 1st	To 4 Negro-Men for taking the Ship	0	7	6
	To my Lord 6 Pistrines	0	7	6
	To Mr. Bucktrout's Bill ✓	19	11	4
	To the Barber for Dressing 10 Servts. 25th Oct.	0	12	6
2	To a Barrel of Limes recd. the 21st past	1	10	0
	To 1 Do. recd. this day	1	10	0
	£	474	15	11

Balls and assemblies were inevitable and indispensable. The governor must honor his royal master and call on his loyal subjects to join him in that act of deference. And he must perform his benign paternal role in society, making himself widely available to both men and women on occasions of festivity when his authority was not the paramount consideration. On such occasions the ballroom and the adjoining social spaces, as well as the service areas necessary to support them, were the scenes of social interaction between governor and colonists on the broadest possible scale.

However "brilliant [an] Appearance" the participants in a ball at the Palace may have created in the third quarter of the eighteenth century, it is clear that by 1768 the setting itself was conspicuously in need of upgrading, in Botetourt's

Excerpt from petty cash account book kept by William Marshman, detailing some of the preparations (and consequent expenses) for a ball, including a sizable outlay for "Bumbo" for the populace. Courtesy, the Duke of Beaufort.

The plain blue paper—a royal preference—the glittering gilt border, the gilt frames of the portraits, and the quality of the setting must have all contributed to a most impressive experience for the first visitors to the ballroom after Botetourt's refurbishment.

estimation at least. The outstanding furnishings in the room between 1768 and 1770 were the ones he imported—the royal portraits, the three glass chandeliers, and the polished "Dutch Stove." What was in the room prior to his arrival is impossible to determine, except for the pieces belonging to the colony. The latter consisted of nineteen mahogany chairs with leather bottoms, eight long stools, and eight stucco brackets high on the walls to support the brass branches that provided lighting. Not only did Botetourt introduce sophisticated and expensive objects but he also completely refurbished the room. "I observed that Ld B. had hung a room with plain blue Paper, and bordered it with a narrow stripe of gilt Leather, which I thought had a pretty Effect," wrote Cambridge-educated Robert Beverley to his London agent, Samuel Athawes, a few months after the governor's death. Joseph Kidd, the governor's "groom of the chambers," probably installed it and certainly performed minor repairs on it in November 1769 and again in June 1770, the only room in the Palace for which any record of wallpaper exists.[29]

Lord Botetourt obviously deemed the refurbishing and refurnishing of this room sufficiently important to invest a considerable amount of money in it. As his bank passbooks and the accompanying vouchers prove, he made this decision and ordered the major materials and furnishings for the ballroom even before he left London to embark for Virginia. At the beginning of August 1768 he ordered chandeliers, stoves, wallpaper, paint, and gilt border. He had commissioned the royal portraits from the king's portrait painter, Allan Ramsay, several months before, and though he had yet to see them, he ordered them to be crated and sent on to Virginia where they arrived "perfectly safe" two weeks after he did. Botetourt later wrote to Hillsborough: "Mr. Ramsey never did two better. We are all delighted with them."[30]

Who apprised the governor-designate in London in the summer of 1768 that the ballroom was large enough for the full-length portraits and the chandeliers, that it would need so many yards of wallpaper, and that it lacked any source of heat? Whose taste and judgment were sufficiently persuasive for Botetourt to place the orders without waiting to see the room for himself? Perhaps it was one of Fauquier's sons, or his widow. Perhaps it was William Small, who knew the Palace well, or George Mercer, Virginia representative for the Ohio Company, who was in London in the summer of 1768 petitioning Hillsborough for a government position. Mercer confided to his brother in Virginia that Botetourt had "employed [him] as his Councillor, as to the first arrangement of his family Affairs in Virginia," and claimed that he had given Botetourt advice and information "Such as indeed it is impossible any one about him could have given." Whomever it was advising Botetourt, it was the governor himself who made the decision to spend a sum amounting to approximately one-quarter of his annual salary to outfit the ballroom. He obviously judged it to be a setting worthy of a distinct public statement, the nature of which was patently connected with the monarch. "Vert de tere Blue" paper and gold border had been the king's choice for his personal rooms at Buckingham House when he first occupied them in the mid-1760s; this combined with the royal portraits created an association or image that could hardly be overlooked.[31]

The "King's birthday at the Governors" was the primary social event of the Williamsburg season, on which occasion the royal portraits would have become a focal point of deference. Other royal anniversaries throughout the year were celebrated at the Palace with balls and assemblies, and for these also the portraits were essential symbols. The new wallpaper and gilt border recalled the royal preference. Glittering cut-glass chandeliers heightened the elegance, as they did in the prototypical York Assembly Rooms. Was it neces-

Full-length portraits of George III and Queen Charlotte, the "state portraits" painted by the king's principal painter of official likenesses, Allan Ramsey, and his assistants. These majestic icons were required for British embassies and missions and were dispatched to numerous colonial governors' residences in the 1760s. Few colonists can ever have seen, in painted form, such elaborate and emphatic statements of the sumptuousness and grandeur of the British monarchy, risen to new heights on the victories of the Seven Years' War. Yet not a single comment on them, from all those who must have seen them in the Palace, has survived.

sary for the governor so insistently to remind the assembled gentlemen and ladies to whom they owed allegiance? Fauquier evidently did not find it so. Surely the key to the appearance of these sumptuous items in the ballroom was that by the late 1760s the political circumstances had changed, requiring the presence of a governor rather than a deputy, accompanied by fashionable equipage with clear political connotations.

If, however, the ballroom and supper room were "opened only on such occasions" as royal anniversaries and accessions—even more infrequently than the occasions that Isaac Ware had described for similar rooms in English houses—then the effort and expense of the refurbishment and of all the accoutrements would have seemed disproportionate to the numbers of people reached. Indeed, the absence of any form of heating in the room prior to Botetourt's arrival suggests that it was used only in temperate seasons or when the large crowd present and the energetic movement of the dancers would have created some warmth of their own. But Botetourt did introduce heating into the ballroom, as well as four large dining tables and thirty-nine chairs, and entertained groups of people for dinner at the Palace who were far too numerous to be accommodated in the dining room. Though company at the Palace was always plentiful—"Every since I arrived I have been in the midst of company . . . at first respect brought them; in October the General Court; in November the Court of Oyer and Terminer; and for this two months past the general Assembly, and next month the General Court again"—Botetourt seems to have gone further than his predecessors. To Hillsborough he wrote in May 1769 when the General Assembly was in session: "52 dined with me Yesterday and I expect at least that number to day."[32]

The Palace dining room was clearly too small for such large gatherings. The ballroom and supper room wing, on the other hand, contained six "large" or "long" dining tables, a total of forty-seven chairs, and plenty of space for large dinners. If Botetourt's strategy was thus to entertain Virginians on an expansive scale at balls and dinners on a year-round schedule in order to convince them of his, and his Majesty's, benevolent paternalism, then the expense of outfitting the site of this exercise was undoubtedly worthwhile. For gatherings of burgesses and others from far distant places in the colony, the portraits would be particularly appropriate, if not compelling. Thus the ballroom evidently became for Botetourt not only a room of sociable assembly but also a room of official parade where the interaction that took place between him and the colonists might be on a more formal level than that which generally occurred in the dining room.[33]

Close scrutiny of the Botetourt inventory reveals that there were also plans to refurbish the adjoining supper room, though it was already equipped with a large, ambitious glass chandelier with twelve arms (in contrast to the six-armed type that the governor imported for the ballroom), sixteen chairs, and two tables, all of which were standing furniture. Botetourt did install one of the "large dutch stoves" and definitely intended to paper the room. In storage on the third floor of the Palace were the "oznabrigs intended to paste the paper on in the Supper Room" and a long box containing "Gilt bordering intended for the Supper Room." Though the supper room undoubtedly presented an elegant appearance when fully dressed, the tables laden with cut-glass pyramids, ornamental china, silver plates, dishes, and hollowware all glittering under the light of the chandelier, it is clear that Botetourt had *not* papered it but had instead devoted most of his attention to the ballroom as the principal room of assembly and focus of political cultivation.[34]

Lord Botetourt introduced a new element of luxury into the Palace with the central heating devices for the ballroom and supper room. These novel "warming machines" were designed to make the spaces in which they stood more comfortable year-round and to give the owner of the house a greater number of options in the uses of the spaces. The double chair-back settee on the left is part of a suite of furniture of local manufacture with an excellent history of having belonged to Lord Dunmore.

The effect of Botetourt's furnishing changes was apparently as dramatically successful as his revival of colonial enthusiasm for royal governance and the English paternal system. The wallpaper in the ballroom, more than all the other material objects in the Palace, was the item that the gentry can be seen to have most copied. Within a few months of its installation, Thomas Jefferson had ordered identical supplies for the house he was beginning to build at Monticello. Robert Beverley ordered plain blue paper in 1771 for the elegant house called Blandfield he was building on the Rappahannock. In 1773 Robert Carter ordered plain blue paper with a border "figured with Chinese Rail" for Nomini Hall, a marked contrast to the floral patterned paper he had imported for his large house in Williamsburg (next to the Palace) ten years earlier. George Washington planned to decorate with plain paper the ballroom that he began to add to his house in the early 1770s; his preference was for a green color, a variant of the same refiners' verditer that produced the blue.35

One reason for the apparent popularity of this decorative scheme may have been the fact that it was the king's personal choice. Another reason for many Virginians was probably that voiced by Robert Beverley in the letter referring to the plain blue paper he had seen at the Palace. He wrote: "I have been some Time Employed in building an House, and as I am desirous of fitting it up in a plain neat Manner, I wd. willingly consult the present Fashion, for you [see] that foolish Passion has made its Way, even into this remote Region." Beverley's preference for the "plain neat Manner" aligned him with the majority of the Virginia gentry in the third quarter of the century.36 It was this characteristically reserved taste that the early, anti-rococo phases of the new classical style of the 1760s reached. Like many of his affluent fellow Virginians, Beverley wished to be regarded as fashionable (or at least conversant with the newest fashion) but found the degree of ornament associated with the "modern" or rococo style in household furnishings and accoutrements of the 1750s and early 1760s to be excessive, both in appearance and cost. While there was, even at the height of the rococo movement in England, a definite reactionary strain in certain types of "useful and ornamental" wares, the preference for plain and neat in contrast to "wrought," "worked," or highly ornamented was clearly in tune with the aesthetic of the early neoclassical period and therefore deserved the approbation of being "the present Fashion." Further, there is no question that the philosophical underpinnings of the new classical style were more in accord with Enlightenment tenets than the whimsical, aristocratic, perhaps even effete character of the rococo taste.

Botetourt's conscious decision to employ this mode of decoration in the most sociable room in the Palace may be seen as an example of brilliant prescience or merely as a happy accident. Whichever it was, it worked. For sophisticated, traveled men like Beverley and Carter it was the new mode to which they had a strong attraction. For ambitious men who had not traveled, like Washington and Jefferson, it seemed innately to strike the right chords. The governor helped to usher in the new style—which then took hold. A comparable example of influence and dissemination, indeed, a dramatic instance of the adoption of the new style can be seen in an episode concerning Nathaniel Burwell, one of the first year winners of the Botetourt medal and a young member of the great planter group. When he came into his inheritance of Carter's Grove in early 1771, he appears to have planned a refurbishment of the house and asked his uncle and guardian, acting governor William Nelson, to write to his well-established contacts in London for certain supplies. Nelson

In the summer months Botetourt's staff installed gauze covers to protect the valuable portraits and chandeliers from dust, pollen, and fly specks. The room was then officially "at rest." The stoves or warming machines created in recent years for the refurnished ballroom and supper room were based on the original stove commissioned by Botetourt from Abraham Buzaglo in London for the Capitol (seen on p. 271), and on evidence supplied by the maker's well-illustrated trade card or letterhead. On the main panel of the adaptation stove, we have placed Botetourt's own coat of arms.

wrote Samuel Athawes ordering stone steps and marble chimneypieces and enclosed a drawing that the young man had prepared. The surviving marble mantels at the house show that Burwell designed and specified a somewhat restrained ornament for the mantel in the neoclassical style, incorporating classical urns of the type he may well have seen on the Buzaglo stove that Botetourt commissioned for the House of Burgesses shortly before he died and which was in situ by early 1771; or perhaps on the Buzaglo stoves that Botetourt had placed in the ballroom and supper room. The style was a little too novel for the elderly Nelson: "If you understand it [the "draught" of chimneypieces and steps], or the statuary, it's more than I do," he confessed to Athawes, but he endorsed the younger man's choice.[37]

From 1768 until the onset of war, Virginians thus came into contact with various manifestations of the "new style" or the "present fashion." Botetourt's innovations at the Palace were followed by Peale's 1769 portrait of Pitt that embodied in its classicizing treatment the novel theories of his master, Benjamin West, as well as the neoclassicism of sculptor Joseph Wilton. The "Roman" aspect of Pitt's likeness was properly noted in newspaper accounts in Virginia and attentive colonists can hardly have misunderstood the reference. The Buzaglo stove was installed in the Capitol in early 1771 and the Botetourt statue, to be discussed in the Epilogue, in 1773. In 1774 a carver and gilder in Williamsburg, George Hamilton, advertised in the local newspaper his skill at creating "Ornaments and Decorations for Gentlemen's Houses," all "after the new Palmyrian Taste"; this craftsman may well have played a role in creating the elegant stucco ceilings in the classical taste at Kenmore, Fredericksburg, which may also be related to those at Mount Vernon. Also in 1774 Washington sent an order to London for a complete silver service to mark the wedding of his stepson, Jackie Custis. The service has survived and is in the full Adamesque style.[38]

To push this ripple effect further, and perhaps to the point where evidence might be seen to be on at least equal terms with coincidence, takes us to the first Continental Congress with two of the Virginia delegates who were burgesses and familiar with the Palace. George Washington and Richard Henry Lee (who had spearheaded the movement culminating in the Peale portrait of Pitt and in whose house the portrait hung for a period of time) both attended the first Continental Congress in Philadelphia in 1774 and, at the end of the sessions, both sat on the committee to commission a presentation piece for Charles Thomson, the Congress's indispensable secretary. What resulted from that commission was the first dated piece of *American-made* silver in the new style. Whether this can be directly attributed to the influence of the Virginia governor may be doubted, but it should also be pointed out that another Virginian, Thomas Jefferson, has been credited with commissioning the first datable piece of American furniture in the new style, also in Philadelphia, in 1776.[39]

Statehouses and courthouses in the colonial capitals contained spacious rooms that often doubled for the evening reception of sociable assemblies. Balls were held in New Bern before the new palace was constructed and at Annapolis in the separate Council chamber. In 1744 William Black attended a ball in the Maryland capital in the "Council Room, where most of the Ladies of any Note

A taste for the new classical style, introduced into Virginia during Botetourt's tenure and in part by him, quickly spread through the Virginia gentry. Young men of means such as Nathaniel Burwell of Carter's Grove (who undertook some remodeling in the mansion upon coming to his majority in 1771) called for ornament in the new taste. One charming and somewhat naive example, the mantel in the "Refusal Room" at Carter's Grove, has survived. By 1774, when George Washington ordered a silver service from London for the marriage of his stepson, John Parke Custis, to Eleanor Calvert, the taste was well established. Photograph of the "Custis service" courtesy, Mount Vernon Ladies Association of the Union.

in the Town was present, and made a very Splendent Appearance." In an adjoining room wines and sweetmeats were available and also cards, dice, and backgammon for those "not Engag'd in any Dancing Match." Later in the period it obviously became desirable for such occasions to be held at the governor's house. In all likelihood, Tryon used the "Council Chamber" in his new residence, and Eden may have staged an assembly in his "Long Room." The latter room contained "1 elegant iron stove" (one of the most expensive pieces of furniture in the house) and may even have been the intended site for some of the six "Handsome Chandaliers," probably glass, that were still in packing crates and stored in the servants' hall when the inventory was taken in 1776. At £285 these items were very expensive indeed. It is conceivable that both stove and chandeliers were inspired by Eden's visit to Williamsburg.[40]

Private houses of pretension, as well as communities that prided themselves on their progressive or civic spirit, also aspired to or created large rooms of assembly in this period. Mount Vernon and Nomini Hall are among those houses in which commodious rooms were actually designated as "ballrooms," but others such as Tazewell Hall and Monticello featured larger than normal spaces that could certainly accommodate balls. Many houses utilized grand halls (or occasionally large saloon-like rooms upstairs) for this purpose — Carter's Grove, Shirley, Sabine Hall, and Tuckahoe included a room that could

THE BALLROOM AND SUPPER ROOM 191

be described, in the colonial context, as "an elegant room . . . large and noble . . . a good apartment for the reception of large companies at publick feasts."[41]

Men and women congregating periodically in the evening for a fashionable assembly, for dancing, music, cards, refreshments, conversation, flirtation, and gossip, was one of the most attractive and flourishing social rituals of the eighteenth century. When the population was affluent and plentiful, elegant rooms were expressly constructed and set aside for assemblies. When they were not available, other suitable social spaces were pressed into service. It was inevitable that one of the largest residences in Virginia, the seat of the chief executive of the colony that took seriously its preeminence in size and age among the other colonies, should be considered the most decorous setting for rooms designed specifically for balls and assemblies. It is certainly characteristic that the man who served as the first full governor in the building, who paid real attention to deference and to parade, should view the same rooms as the most fitting space for regal embellishments, interior appointments that both tacitly and explicitly acknowledged the royal leader of society to whom he and the other users were subject.[42]

Few fashionable assemblies were without their element of politics. Indeed, some were overtly for that purpose. For gatherings at the Palace of large groups of men who had convened in Williamsburg primarily for political reasons, the ballroom was a most auspicious setting. The king himself, the head of the extended family and a civilizing force, was present in life-size, icon form to remind those gathered there of where their loyalties lay. The ballroom was a principal point of social exchange—the king and his government depended on provincial gentry to help them govern, in return for which they distributed protection and largesse in many forms. It was a primary space where the "expectation of a mutual exchange of services" between governor and governed was apparent.[43] It was also a space of cultural exchange, for the introduction and display of new fashion as an important component of gentility. That this was clearly perceived and absorbed we have seen above. For some the entire artifice was unquestionably effective. For others only partially so. Yet even those subjects assembled in that room who were soon decisively to reject the king's claims for political allegiance, Washington and Jefferson most conspicuously, were content to absorb and take with them elements of his culture that they might subsequently adopt for their own purposes.

Elegant houses and possessions, bountiful hospitality, and energetic sociability were at the very heart of the endeavor by eighteenth-century Virginians to make their society more permanent and graceful than it had been in the first hundred years of settlement. The governor was widely expected to be a leader in these activities and, indeed, in the paired public and social spaces of the Palace he can be seen to have met those expectations. He generously extended hospitality at the dinner and supper tables, provided convivial occasions in the ballroom, and set or communicated standards of modishness with interior decoration and a wide range of accoutrements. Daily ceremonies presented opportunities for unusual and far-reaching intellectual exchange, social events provided occasions for personal interaction and advancement, and gay assemblies produced intellectual harmony, sensual satisfaction, and emotional enrichment. And because the governor was the foremost representative of the monarch in this provincial society, politics was a constant undercurrent, becoming particularly noticeable in the decade before the Revolution.

The relentless sociability that characterized late colonial Virginia society became only a memory after the Revolution, its passing noted with nostalgia or with a smart satisfaction in the newer modish attitudes. The Enlightenment legacy of Fauquier and Botetourt also became a memory, though it was surely more influential in its effects. The intellectual benefits that Jefferson and others derived from their interaction with Fauquier were richly acknowledged. Botetourt's influence was perhaps less direct, but by his introduction into the colony of neoclassical modes and ideas he helped to expose members of the Virginia intelligentsia to the world of Enlightenment thought of which neoclassicism was an important cultural ingredient. The governors thus served as the conduit for the introduction of seminal ideas to the colonial gentry, who were ready to seize them and put them to use.[44]

Silver tea urn made by Richard Humphreys of Philadelphia in 1774 as a gift from the Continental Congress to its secretary, Charles Thomson. H: 21½". Gift of the Barra Foundation to the Philadelphia Museum of Art.

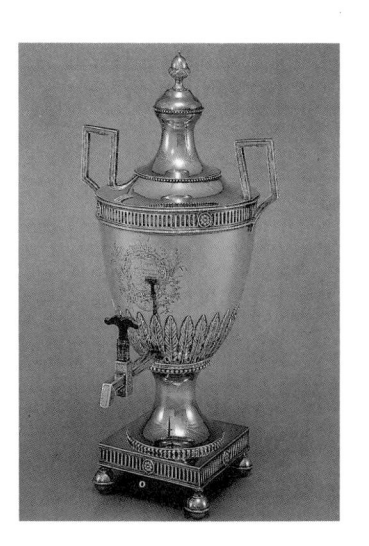

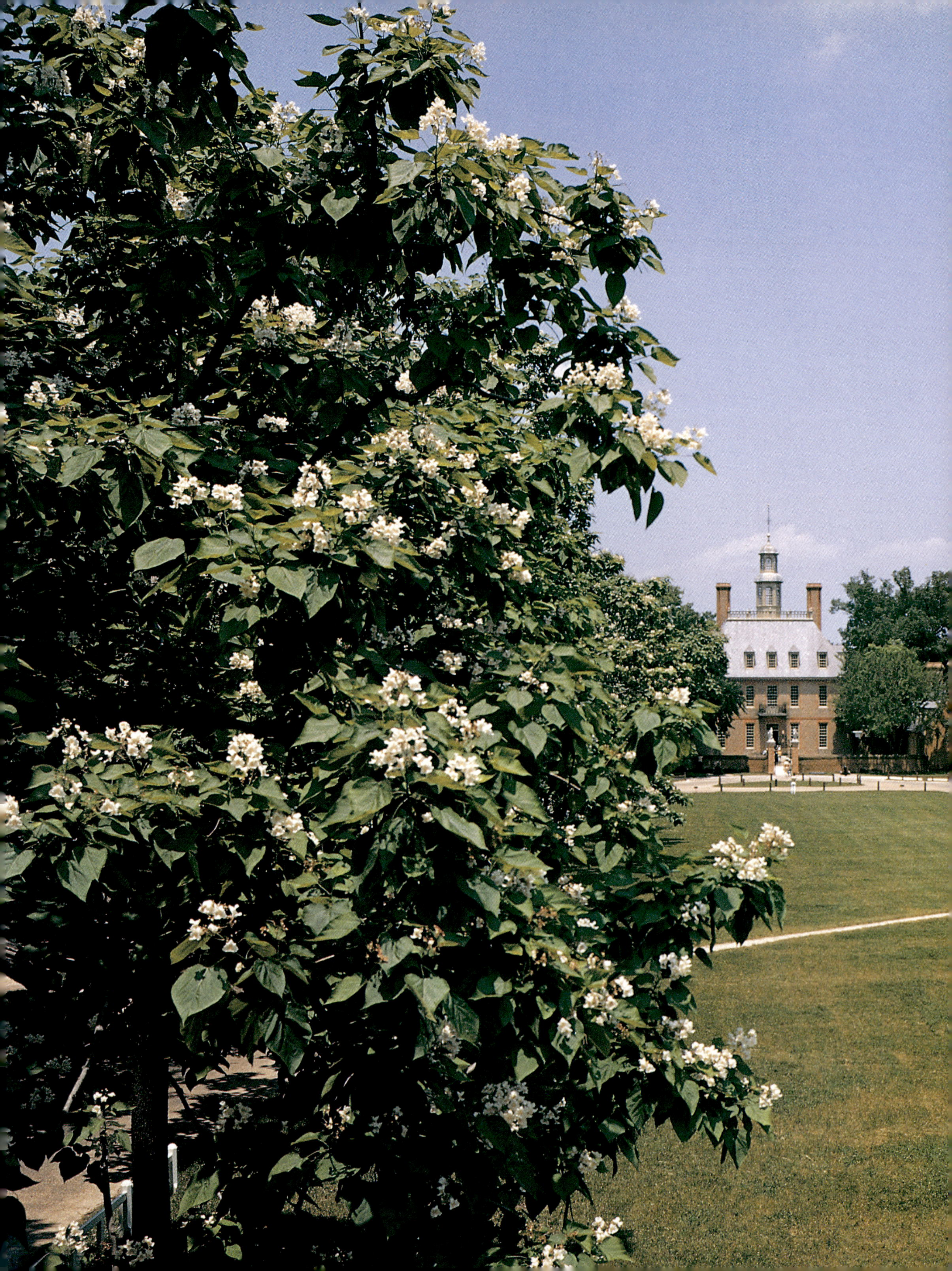

Private Life

Private Life

In a public building or official residence the private life of the occupants and their patterns of domesticity were often confined to non-public areas such as the bedchamber apartments. This was particularly true in the Governor's Palace, which was too small to contain non-public spaces on the main floor not required by the service staff. The patterns of living normally associated with bedchambers are of the most private and intimate kind, including the basic human rites of procreation, birthing, and death. Certainly each of the occupants of the Palace had private and intimate moments in their busy lives, sexual union must have occurred, at least one child (officially) was born in the building, and three of the governors died there. Yet the great paradox of the eighteenth-century officials is that, though much of their time was spent on written communication, little of a truly private or personal nature has survived in written form.

While the general development of internal spatial arrangements in domestic buildings from the early seventeenth century had been toward the creation of zones of privacy for the principal occupants, any analysis of life in an official residence raises a fundamental question: even by the mid- to late eighteenth century, how much was it possible for people in the midst of the extended family of clerks, servants, and slaves to be truly private? In the context of Virginia plantation life—the elite white patterns of living that are, perforce, most comparable to the life-styles of the Palace's occupants—a "public" mode also seems to have obtained, which prompts a further question: how much did elite whites and their immediate kin *wish* to be truly private? The innermost worlds of private feelings, self-examination, and secret urges in this colonial society are most difficult of access. They are further obscured by the conventions of written expression, of formulaic language and (by modern standards) facile phraseology that seem to veil true emotion and private thought.

Inferences can still be drawn and assumptions made. Surely the occupants experienced and expressed the full range of emotions in the more private spaces of the Palace—perhaps Spotswood's egotistic pride in the completion of

A kin family group of English country gentry stock, oil on canvas, painted by Thomas Bardwell in 1736. Gathered for the group memento, three generations of the Brewster family sit with a few possessions in a spacious interior—all of which could easily have been in Virginia. The first academically trained portrait artist had arrived in the colony the year before this group portrait was painted in East Anglia. H: 48½"; W: 57⅜". CWF 1971-3374.

PRIVATE LIFE 197

the building; his illicit passion for his "neice," Mrs. Russell, whom he brought with him to Williamsburg ostensibly to share his social role; his rages of jealousy and envy over the depredations of the Council on his official powers; the widow's sorrow of Mrs. Drysdale; the paternal pride of William Gooch that turned to grief when his son, Billy, died within a year of his marriage; the frequent torpor or debilitation that the hostile climate could induce; the inner pain and despair of Francis Fauquier over his long illness; the precarious pride of Botetourt in the prowess of his natural son and his deep familial satisfaction in the close relationship with his sister and her children; the (widely rumored) clandestine urges of Dunmore for sexual exploits and excessive drinking, or his pleasure in his gracious and most popular consort who joined him for the last festive but ill-fated year of his administration, and perhaps his pride in the child she bore him at the Palace; the inadequacies or inner doubts that official demeanor could mask; the insecurities that an amorphous, overextended bureaucracy or the proximity of frontier conditions might engender; the failures of nerve . . . and so on. All these can be supposed, presumed, or extrapolated from the most minimal of references or from our own imagination. In fact, what these most private spaces tell about the private worlds of the men and women who occupied them is severely limited. This is especially regrettable in that they are the only spaces in the Palace containing a room or rooms that the wife of the governor, when she was in residence, might call her own, where she might be encountered as an individual rather than the male official's social adornment.

"Kin" family relationships were most uncommon at the Palace in comparison to the frequency with which they are encountered in Virginia gentry society in the eighteenth century. By "kin" is meant the large group of husband, wife, several or many children, parents, siblings, and their families. Only Dunmore, of all the governors, brought several children with him, and then for only one year. Gooch had one son who matured, married, and died in Williamsburg, while Fauquier had two grown sons, only one of whom spent much time in Virginia. Botetourt and Spotswood were not married. It was not uncommon for governors to send their wives back to England for their health (while writing their own requests to the ministry for permission to do the same thing). Certainly in the period for which most of the evidence survives, the ten years or so preceding the Revolution, the governor resided in the Palace separated from his kin family. Yet his extended family of clerks, servants, and slaves was always in evidence. Almost all of the surviving information points to life at the Palace as a series of relationships, gestures, and interactions that extended outward through the circle of servants and slaves to the world beyond, rather than inward to his closest kin. It is definitely on these more social aspects of the governor's personal life that the inventory, as it relates to these particular spaces, casts most illumination.

An unknown English family at tea, oil on canvas, ca. 1730–1735. The daughters serve while the gentleman on the left (father or grandfather) is interrupted by the butler or steward for business. In this rendition each of the characters seems to occupy a private space. There is visible none of the pleasant, personal interaction that becomes so apparent in paintings later in the century. H: 36"; W: 48". CWF 1936-686.

Recent studies of the evolution of familial relationships in Chesapeake gentry society in the eighteenth and early nineteenth centuries by Daniel Blake Smith, Rhys Isaac, and Jan Lewis have traced the slow emergence of the "affectionate sentimental family." Men and women became increasingly comfortable in expressing warm, positive emotions toward each other, their parents, siblings, children, and others with whom they came into frequent close contact. Scholars have disagreed, however, on the intensity and speed with which this progress from rigidified, seemingly unfeeling codes of relationships toward more modern, open, and spontaneous emotional expression occurred in the eighteenth century. Smith argues that the range of affectionate emotional expression (and, therefore, feeling) opens up substantially in this century, whereas Lewis considers that ideals of order, harmony, and tranquillity were still preeminent in the typical Chesapeake gentry family and that they tended to supersede or suppress other, more spontaneous emotions. Isaac acknowledges that the written evidence shows increasing freedom of expression in the realm of domestic virtue and happiness, though he doubts it is quite so pervasive or so liberating of emotional restraint as Smith maintains. Important questions of the modern interpretation of changing social systems and modes of expression are also raised. How can we be sure that the same familiar expressions used by different people refer to the same range or intensity of feelings? How often are apparently reassuring phrases—the approved vocabulary of sensibility and gentility—used as a cover for insecurity, a substitute for loneliness, an alternative to lack of feelings? The answers to these questions are as evasive as the indications of the governor's inner, emotional life at the Palace.[1]

The Grymes children of Virginia, oil on canvas, painted about 1750 by John Hesselius. Despite the convention that children should appear to be miniature adults, the artist has introduced a note of revelry in the figure of the youngest child on the right, his gaiety seeming to alleviate the attempts at seriousness by the others. H: 56"; W: 66¼". Courtesy, Virginia Historical Society.

200 PRIVATE LIFE

It is particularly unfortunate that this is so. Into what was unquestionably the slowly evolving emotional freedom of the American family, what insights and advice might not the fraternal Fauquier and the paternal Botetourt have provided—or gained? If Fauquier could remonstrate with his superior, Amherst—to whom Indians were "pernicious vermin" to be "hunted down with dogs" and exterminated by any means, fair or foul, including the presentation of blankets infected with smallpox spores—that "White, Red, or Black; polished or unpolished Men are Men," what beneficial counsel might he not have dispensed within his circle of Virginia gentry friends? If Botetourt could create such warm relationships within his extended family that his butler, in a personal letter to his own brother several weeks after the governor's death, confided that "in Lord Botetourt, I always experienced more of the Friend and Father, than of the Master," what assistance and personal example might he not have provided to those Virginians with whom he came into contact? Unfortunately the record, other than those instances mostly cited in the chapter "The Dining Room and Parlor," is silent.[2]

Because the governors at the Palace were temporarily transplanted from their other homes, and because the evidence for domestic relations with their kin families is so scarce, I have not considered it appropriate to compare their experiences with those of the Virginians with whom they interacted. On the subject of the extended family, however, there is more evidence and comparisons with the colonial attitudes and activities are more valid. Here the most conspicuous difference between the English background and the Virginia experience was, of course, the presence of slavery, a phenomenon that the governor could not personally stand apart from any more than he could publicly overlook, however conscious he might be of the rising opposition to the institution within the empire by the closing years of the colonial period.

The Bedchambers and Study
THE PERSON
OF THE GOVERNOR

When the interior spaces of the Palace were initially laid out, the arrangement of rooms on the second floor was characteristic of traditional, medium-sized English houses of the period. The middle room or great chamber for ceremonial activities occupied pride of place in the center of the front of the house and was approached by an open staircase and a passage. To each side of the central room lay a bedchamber with accompanying closet—one for the governor, the other for his lady. Beyond these chambers was another room, on the east side a large room identical in size to the dining room directly below it, and on the west a small room near the backstairs. The latter was termed the "library" in the Botetourt inventory and "study" in the list of standing furniture. Each suite of rooms, on the east side and the west, formed an individual "apartment" in which some of the most intimate, private moments in the governor's life took place and where his "kin" family was expected to relate most closely with him.

Because the first floor rooms were so frequently taken over by business or by the activities necessary to keep the establishment functioning, it was important for the governor and his wife to have rooms to which they could withdraw. In late seventeenth-century parlance, each of the rooms beyond the main bedchamber (and its closet) would have been called a withdrawing room. If the early governors occupied the west bedchamber as Botetourt later did, their wives would have had the use of a large withdrawing room on the east side in which to entertain close friends or be with their family. Since the middle room could double as the governor's withdrawing room, it is likely that the small room in his "apartment" on the west side served as a dressing room, or as a "closet" in the seventeenth-century sense—that is, a cabinet or inner office, the precursor of the study or small library of later decades.[1]

How the early governors used this arrangement of spaces is unknown. Spotswood's "niece," Mrs. Russell (who, as may be expected, precipitated a host of scurrilous rumors in town), was probably assigned one apartment, using it in the manner described by William Byrd II when he visited the governor's

The chintz bed, bed round carpet, and night table in the chamber over the dining room. Dressing table and green bamboo chair stand in the background.

Williamsburg residence prior to his occupancy of the Palace: "After dinner I went to make a visit to Mrs. Russell in her chamber and drank some tea with her. Then we went down and played at piquet." This incident clearly occurred on the upper floor since the two "went down" subsequently to play cards. Whether or not Byrd was entertained to the still novel tea ritual in the lady's bedchamber or in the adjoining antechamber or withdrawing room is not clear. Either would have been acceptable since Byrd was at this time a close friend of the lieutenant governor and was probably regarded as sufficiently intimate to be received in the lady's personal quarters.[2]

THE BEDCHAMBERS AND STUDY 203

For Gooch the extra spaces were convenient since he brought his wife and her sister to the Palace. The two ladies probably occupied the two rooms and connecting closet on the east side, for the social status of his sister-in-law was similar to that of his wife and she would have expected comparable accommodations. Since most of the governors were men of mature years and were periodically ill, the division of sleeping spaces was acutely important. By midcentury, written and visual sources illustrate the activities that naturally occurred in withdrawing rooms, or dressing rooms as they came to be called—tête-à-têtes between women, children at play or being near their mother, and so on: "This afternoon I saw company in my dressing room for the first time since it being finished," wrote Mrs. Boscawen in London in 1748. Such activities were still informal, however, for friends or members of the family. As the century progressed, ladies' apartments, especially in town, became more private: "It would be an act of the greatest possible indecorum to go into it [the lady's dressing room-bedchamber suite], unless the visitor were upon a very familiar footing with the family." There are references to dressing rooms on the second floor of the Palace for both Fauquier and his wife in the 1760s. Whether the small closet adjoining the west bedchamber or that between the two east bedchambers was so designated is not known.[3]

Discourses on bedchambers or the apartments of which they formed a central component are conspicuously absent from the works of architectural writers such as Isaac Ware. Mid-century pattern books are similarly mute. By the 1770s the private apartments on the upper floor of a grand house were typically arranged thus: "On one hand is the Dutchess's bed-chamber, an antiroom for the attendance of her maids, her toilet or dressing-room, her powdering-room, water closet, and outer anti-room, with a back stair leading to intersols for the maid's bed-room and wardrobes, etc. On the other hand is a dressing-room for the Duke, a powdering-room, writing-room, water-closet and stairs to intersols for His Grace's valet-de-chambre, and wardrobe, etc."[4] There was actually little difference between this grand scheme and the layout at the Palace, which resembled earlier spatial arrangements, except for the scale and the number of separate rooms devoted to different functions. By the 1770s the major change in great English houses was that the principal bedchambers were mostly on the upper floor, rather than on the main floor as they had been earlier. In Virginia the gentry tended to retain the earlier custom.

As Botetourt was unmarried, he needed but one apartment. He occupied the southwest bedchamber and used the adjacent room as his library or study. He would thus have been able to offer the apartment on the east side as a guest suite to important visitors such as neighboring governors Robert Eden and William Tryon. Eden visited Botetourt shortly before his death, while Tryon spent a week at the Palace in 1769 accompanied by his wife and infant

The dressing room of a lady of fashion in England in the 1760s. Shown is the dressing table covered with "toilette" and toilet service and complete with dressing glass. It stands in front of the window for maximum light. The easy chair is a characteristic bedchamber or dressing room item. The painting is of the actress, Mrs. Abington, by Zoffany, dated 1768. H: 39"; W: 44½". *Courtesy, National Trust (Egremont Collection, Petworth).*

daughter. Tryon's newly completed palace at New Bern provided seven bedchambers plus two dressing rooms on the second floor, a substantial improvement over the older arrangement at the Palace in Williamsburg. When Gooch entertained Lord and Lady Baltimore and their entourage for a week in July 1733, it probably caused considerable inconvenience in the residence, but the lieutenant governor was satisfied that his guests "parted from me well pleased with the Entertainment I gave them."[5]

In comparison with the ducal apartment described above, Botetourt lacked only a powdering room, though there was a small room so designated immediately below on the first floor, and a water closet. Instead of the latter he kept in his bedchamber a silver chamber pot, a decorous accoutrement, as well as a mahogany night table with close stool pan and chamber pot. His writing room or study was immediately adjacent, as were the back stairs to the servants' rooms on the third or garret floor. The inventory shows that four of Botetourt's servants slept on the garret floor where they were near at hand.

For most of Dunmore's short tenure he was alone in Williamsburg while his wife and children waited in England to join him. His use of the second floor was presumably similar to Botetourt's. When Lady Dunmore arrived with six children in 1774, the resources of the second floor of the Palace were probably strained.[6] Some of the children were presumably bundled up to the third floor where there were three bedchambers, occupied in Botetourt's time by some of the principal servants.

The bedchamber/dressing room apartments of Botetourt in Williamsburg, Eden in Annapolis, and Tryon in New Bern were all on the second floor according to the fashion in England at the time. When Tryon moved to the older residence in New York, however, this group of rooms appears to have been on the first floor together with the Council chamber, parlor, and dining room. It was still the convention in Virginia for the principal bedchamber to be on the first floor, perhaps because of the climate, perhaps for tradition. Yet it was obviously

The bedchamber over the front parlor featured a Virginia cloth bed, numerous prints, and several of the green bamboo chairs.

206 PRIVATE LIFE

The governor's bedchamber, the bed hung with the summer mosquito curtains, the chest of drawers full of intimate clothing. The closet beyond, complete with dressing table, served as the most personal space in the governor's apartment.

subject to individual adjustment; at fashionable Nomini Hall, for example, the main bedchamber was on the second floor near the room where the Carters' five daughters slept (concern for their physical security probably dictated the location). The first floor spaces were dedicated to dining room, a dining room for the children, Carter's study (also called the library), and "ballroom." There were no designated dressing rooms for either the planter or his wife, but that may have reflected the necessities of a large family and the decision to devote two rooms on the second floor to "occasional company" (which, given the nature of Virginia society, was quite the opposite to occasional).[7] Dressing

THE BEDCHAMBERS AND STUDY 207

rooms rarely appear in Virginia inventories, and the activities normally carried out in such a space were more often confined to the bedchamber and/or its accompanying closet.

The Palace bedchambers were the scenes of birth, illness, and death. Precisely nine months after her arrival in Williamsburg, the very popular Lady Dunmore was "delivered of a baby daughter" at the Palace—the only child born to a governor in the building during the sixty-five years it served as the chief executive's residence. Dunmore diplomatically christened his daughter Virginia, a charming touch that did him little good politically. Drysdale was the earliest governor to die in the Palace, in 1726. Some of his effects—"divers pieces of furniture belonging to the late Governor which are not only convenient but ornamental to the Gov's House"—were purchased by the colony from his widow and may still have been in use in Botetourt's time.[8] Gooch constantly suffered from the Virginia climate and was frequently ill. On one occasion official business was sufficiently important that a committee of burgesses waited on him in his bedchamber at the Palace. In his later years Fauquier endured "numerous infirmities" even to the point where he was forced to "employ the hand of another" to deal with his personal correspondence. Thus he was often confined to the second floor in later life. After much suffering he died at the Palace in 1768.[9]

Botetourt, too, died at the Palace, as previously noted. A hitherto unpublished letter gives an account of his last hours with intimate knowledge and vivid detail that are forcible reminders of how tiny are the fragments of recorded daily life at the Palace that have survived. Because it is so rare, the letter is quoted extensively:

The Irrepairable loss this Colony has Sustained by the death of Lord Botetourt will be long lamented by all who loved Order and Justice, Indeed the whole Continent Suffers, he was a pattern for all Governors, he was taken with a Slight fever the 23[d] of September which he had got the better of, it returned in a week after, he would attend to business as long as he could and I believe did not consider himself in a dangerous Situation till the friday before he died, it Seems he had Desired Seccari to inform him if his Case was even Doubtfull, but I do not understand it was ever done, or indeed till after he had three fitts on friday, in which he was Greatly Convulsed. that the Doctor thought him so, when he gave it as his opinion that there was no hopes of his Recovery after the third fit he Slept a little, and when he waked he Called to Mr. Starke, who was then waiting upon him (with some of his Ldshs Servants) and from whom I had this information, Said he wishd the Speaker was there, he Could Convince him now, Starke offered to go for him, but he would not allow him Saying he understood Mr. Randolph was not very well and he would not disturb him, but if he was there he was Sure he could Convince him, for he now knew he was dying and he would not wish to put it off. It seems the Speaker and him some little time before that, had, had an argument, the Sp.[r] insisted, however Virtuous a man might live yet when he Saw

Corner of his Lordship's bedchamber showing fireplace and night table with its sanitary devices. A deathbed scene of 1787 shows the ill man, his family in attendance, making his final will and testament. Engraving. H: 9⅞"; W: 15⅝". CWF 1959-83, 11.

death approaching he would Still wish to live a little longer, the Governour was of a very different opinion. that Same night after a little dose of Sleep he Called his Servant (Marshman) and told him no man ever had a more faithfull or better Servant than he was, You must Says he go home to the Duke of Beaufort he will provide for You, the Man burst into tears, and his Ldshp chid him fy Marshman why do you unman yrSelf, do You envy me the happiness Im goeing to enjoy, what have I lived for. Stark told me he heard him Say Sometime before day 'tis a little unluckie, had I stayd a little longer the people in America would have been Convinced, that I had their good at heart, but tis Right what ever is is Right, this he repeated twice or thrice; after this he never had his Senses, on Saturday he had a very Violent hiccap, on Sunday being given over by the Doctor, the treasurer Some others who were there gave him a dose of Jameses powders, which Mr. Nicholas told me he thought relieved him a little, he Died about one oclock on Monday morning 15th Oct. I Sett of[f] for the City that morning but had the melancholy news at the ferry, I stayd till he was buried on friday following, his Body was put into a Deal Coffin, and one of lead covered with Crimson velvet, with a plain plate upon it of Silver, bearing his name age and death, he lys in a vault under his own pew in the Colledge Chappel, and So far as I am Capable of judging a mansion in Heaven cannot be better employd, then being inhabitated by the immortal Soul of the Great Lord Botetourt, Every action of his life here, has had the trewism on the face of it, in the words of Parson Wilkie, the lowly Shrub might as well attempt to Vie with the lofty Oak, as me to attempt the Character of So great a man.[10]

The different kinds of filial relationships that Starke and Marshman experienced with Botetourt have already been cited. Clearly there was reciprocated affection, and some of the dying man's last words were of concern for his

THE BEDCHAMBERS AND STUDY 209

faithful servant's future. In recounting the governor's final days, Marshman later noted in his letter to his brother that "Myself and the Under Buttler were his Only Nurses Day and Night during his illness; I was not my self half an hour from him the whole time. . . . His Expressions to me, at several times, were tender and Affectionate beyond my power at present to describe. He meant to do something for me, but it pleased God to order it otherwise . . . my Loss is very great, and I deeply Lament it . . . no Servant had ever heaped upon him such continual proofs of kindness from any Master, as I receiv'd from that Generous and Good Man." Starke himself, in a letter to the duke of Beaufort the week following the funeral, observed the "tender care, the vigilance, and constant assiduity of Marshman Ld. Botetourt's Butler during the illness of his kind Master." Starke also communicated to the duke, with the most particular deference, what he believed was the close relationship between the late governor and himself: "May it please your Grace: Your late noble and affectionate Uncle Ld. Botetourt having been pleased to distinguish me by a considerable degree of his countenance, and attention. . . . There are few, very few who better knew the excellence of his disposition, or were more perfectly convinced of the justice, the honour and impartiality of his Conduct through a short but happy Administration, than myself."[11] Though the tenor of these letters and accounts is undeniably moving, the language in which the sentiments are conveyed is to modern eyes stilted and formulaic and offers little insight into the inner worlds of those involved. Even the dying man's final words, reportedly conveying his concern that "people in America" might never perceive that he had had their best interests at heart, instinctively arouse a mild skepticism.

What the above accounts do reveal more clearly is how the network of spaces was used interconnectedly on such occasions. As the governor lay dying in his bedchamber, Starke, "who was then waiting upon him (with some of his Ldshs Servants)," undoubtedly sat in the bedchamber, the adjoining closet, or the study connected to it, with easy access to the passage beyond, to the main stairs, and to the private stairs that connected with the servants' bedchambers on the third floor (in the manner of the "intersols" noted earlier in the ducal residence). Furthermore, Marshman's center of operations, his office or pantry, stood directly below the governor's bedchamber, with access by the private stairs. Guard had to be maintained at all times over the silver and other valuables in the pantry, so the two principal servants probably took turns there, sleeping when necessary on the couch in that room (complete, as the inventory shows, with mattress, blankets, quilt, and bolster). Such utilization of governor's bedchamber, study, and service spaces would have left the passage and the middle room upstairs free for the visitors who undoubtedly came to call on the governor during his illness.

The writing table in the library was probably where Botetourt wrote personal letters to his sister and her children and confidential communications to the Ministry.

The functions of the study or library were always personal and private, even though they may have changed slightly in character in the years since the Palace was built. An indispensable element of the main bedchamber apartment in European great houses since the early seventeenth century, the closet or cabinet (later termed study or writing room) was considered the innermost, personal sanctum of the great man. It was a setting for private indulgence as well as unofficial consultation. The French word *cabinet*, subsequently anglicized, came to be used in a formal manner to describe the group who gave close counsel in it. A back stairway near the cabinet was essential so that those needed for advice or amusement could enter out of sight of people waiting formally in the main concourse for an audience. Though the study at the Palace was architecturally similar to the private closet or study of European houses, the configuration of the private stairs, apparently opening into the passage upstairs near the door to the middle room, would seem to contradict such clandestine practices. It is not known if the room was used in this secretive way. If it was, contemporary residents of Williamsburg—given the nature of their surviving sentiments—would have been inclined to believe that Botetourt's close advisors were necessary for him to maintain political equilibrium between opposing forces, while Dunmore's were agents of political iniquity or personal vice.[12]

Retaining the old-fashioned term *cabinet*, the *Builders Dictionary* of 1774 defined the space and its functions in a way that aptly describes Botetourt's study: "The most retired place in the finest apartment of a building, set apart for writing, studying, or preserving anything that is curious or valuable."[13] It was probably to this room that Botetourt retired from the bustle in the rest of the residence—for example, when he hastily penned a note to Hillsborough that "52 dined with me Yesterday and I expect at least that number to-day—most of whom are already arrived and waiting for me. 3 o'clock just returned from the Council." In a similar vein, he wrote his beloved sister, "The Assembly being now sitting and my house full of Company I have only time to give You a very few lines."[14]

On the functions of the bedchamber apartments and the patterns of living that occurred in them, the inventory casts further light, though it is mainly of a social rather than an intimate nature. Bedsteads and fashionable "beds" (the eighteenth-century word for the curtains, quilts, coverlets, sheets, pillows, bolsters, etc. that went with the wooden components), containers of different types and sizes for clothes, certain equipment for sanitation, washing, and shaving, "toilet" or dressing tables, the ubiquitous seating furniture and the equally ubiquitous writing equipment—these were spread throughout the rooms in appropriate groupings. Botetourt presumably slept and died in "His Lordship's Bed Chamber" in the most elaborate bed in the residence—indeed, it would have been one of the costliest items in his possession, one of the most elaborate and ostentatious.

The primary bedchamber in houses of fashion and ambition was invariably dominated by a large and grandiloquent bed. In the seventeenth and eighteenth centuries beds of grand men reached heroic proportions. They were among the most expensive pieces of furniture in the house. Bedchambers in palaces and in houses that royalty might visit were lavishly furnished. State beds could stand sixteen feet or more high, be extensively gilded, and require so many yards of precious material—cut velvet or oriental silk, lace, and gold or silver fringe—that the cost was staggering. Some of them were so exceptional that they have been perennially preserved, now standing "magnificently dreary" (in Horace Walpole's words) as fragile monuments of a very different

The books were minutely specified in the inventory, as were the blue curtains that protected them from dust and light, blue venetian blind, check curtain, and carpet. The clock has a history of ownership at the Palace by Lord Dunmore.

culture. By the third quarter of the eighteenth century, though state beds were still commissioned periodically, the custom had declined. Even so, they could still be elaborately carved or decorated and hung with many yards of exorbitantly expensive material. They continued to be symbols or extensions of the social and political importance of their owner for another century.[15]

Botetourt's bed was minimally described in the inventory as "1 Mahog. Bedst^d 2 Matrasses, 1 Bolster 2 pillows 2 blankets 1 white quilt/Chintz and green satten furniture and 1 bed carpet." It was probably the one he had acquired from the estate of Fauquier for twenty-five pounds, the most expensive single item in Fauquier's entire inventory after the slaves, pipes of wine, coach, and gold watch. Listed in Fauquier's inventory in concert with the suite of eight chairs, two stools, and the large and small chests of drawers (that later also stood

The governor's chintz and green satin bed, complete with the "double drapery" curtains called for by the original tester frame of this ca. 1770 Virginia bed, and prescribed as stylish in contemporary pattern books.

in Botetourt's bedchamber), it was probably used personally by the elderly lieutenant governor. Whether Botetourt supplied new furniture (curtains, valances, and cornice) for the bed is unknown, but the terse language of the inventory does not suggest a contrivance sufficiently elaborate for a man of "parade." However, the price he paid Fauquier's estate for the bed is close (in sterling equivalent) to the amount that governor Eden later claimed for the principal bed left in his Annapolis residence in 1776. In his schedule of losses Eden cataloged the item as "1 Mahogany 4 Post bedstead with white Dimothy furniture, ornamented Cornice with Vases compleat," together with the appropriate feather bed, mattress, pillows, and counterpane. The greater detail in this description (characteristic of a claim for replacement or reimbursement, as opposed to the cryptic language of an estate inventory) gives the impression of a greater elaboration. An ornamented superstructure added to the bed, complete with "vases" or large finials at each corner, would have certainly created a striking effect befitting a man of substance and pretension. Tryon's bed, for which he also claimed compensation, was similarly elaborate: "1 Mahogany Bedstead, Venetian Cornishes, fluted and turned posts, India Chints hangings, lined throughout with Calico Muslin." A "Chintz Pillimpon" (palampore or coverlet) also came with it. Tryon's bed was hung with chintz as was Botetourt's, but being lined with muslin instead of satin may have conveyed a slightly less elegant appearance. But the "Venetian Cornishes" were certainly modish, requiring curtains that pulled *up* in the "drapery" style (rather than sliding sideways on a rod) in the elegant fashion of the day. It is safe to assume that Botetourt's bed was similar in type and value to the expensive, fashionable, and carefully described beds that neighboring governors owned. It undoubtedly occupied a dominant position in his principal bedchamber and was regarded there as the traditional, sumptuous symbol of his "estate."[16]

Two stools were among the appurtenances of the governor's bedchamber at the Palace—another gesture to tradition, considering that eight chairs with yellow upholstery also stood in the room. Stools were frequently supplied with grand beds in eighteenth-century England, were upholstered en suite, and stood at the foot of the bed. More portable than chairs, stools were used for retainers or simply as multipurpose seating forms for the room's occupant(s).[17] A washstand equipped with looking glass, a night table, and two chests of drawers for the storage of the governor's intimate clothing ("his Lodp's Linnen, Gloves, Stockgs . . . and caps etc."), plus jewelry and related personal items of value, complete the list of primary furniture in the governor's bedchamber.

Among the remaining furnishings of the bedchambers, one group of objects conspicuous for their modishness were the twelve "green bamboo chairs with check cushions." Divided between the two east bedchambers, they were undoubtedly the same as the "12 Bamboo chears Blew and Gold with lutestring

In his Lordship's bedchamber stood the smart and highly portable washstand that contained space for the swing glass and a chamber pot. The stools are also shown here at the foot of the bed.

quishons" and check cases that Botetourt had ordered from London cabinetmaker William Fenton in 1768. Their cost, £24.5.0, was close to that of the expensive bed. Confusion between blue and green is not uncommon in the period, though there is the unlikely possibility that Botetourt had had them repainted in Williamsburg. Almost certainly made of beech turned to simulate bamboo and equipped with woven cane seats, the chairs were in the forefront of fashion for the time. No earlier examples than these in the colonies are known at present, and few in England.[18]

In the study or library chairs were conspicuous not so much by their unusual attention to fashion but rather by their absence. When they were needed, however, they could easily have been brought in from the adjoining passage, where there were twelve, or from the governor's bedchamber, which held eight. That this room lacked comfortable seating furniture for extended reading might be considered surprising, but it was also a simple matter to remove books to nearby spaces for that purpose. At Nomini Hall, for example, Mrs. Carter eschewed the privacy of her husband's sanctum and took books to the more public ballroom, where she read them lying on a couch. The children's tutor, however, was not allowed such a privilege, even though Carter had otherwise given him free use of his "overgrown" collection.[19]

References in other Virginia documents to such sophisticated beds and bedchamber seating furniture as that the governor owned are most uncommon. However, the Washington correspondence includes a particularly revealing account. Shortly after his marriage to one of the richest women in the colony, Washington ordered from London a bedstead with "fashionable blue or blue and white" chintz curtains, the carved cornice to be covered with the same material, as were chairs, window cornices, and window curtains in the same room, "in order to make the whole furniture of the room uniformly handsome and genteel." The cost of labor and material for these items in 1759 corresponded to the price Botetourt paid for his bed from the Fauquier estate a few years later. Washington's purchase—carefully thought out and precisely described—perfectly demonstrates the kind of action taken by a Virginia gentleman to display his social and economic ambition and improvement through the careful choice of symbolic objects.[20]

Botetourt's groom of the chambers, Joseph Kidd, brass nailed twenty prints to the walls of the governor's library in 1769, as well as hanging maps here—the latter were a notable feature throughout the residence. The desk in the large bedchamber belonged to Lord Dunmore. Beautifully made of the finest mahogany, in Williamsburg, it is an exemplar of the "neat and plain" taste of many British gentry in the third quarter of the eighteenth century.

Portrait of an unidentified man in a plain elbow chair, interrupted while reading in front of the fire. Oil on canvas. Perhaps painted by Henry Walton, English, ca. 1770. The artist caught a charming look of expectancy on the young man's face as he seemingly awaits a comment from his interrupter. H: 30"; W: 26¼". CWF 1936-688.

For the typical library, custom prescribed pictures or sculpture of inspiring, thought-provoking subjects. At the Palace, in addition to a map of North and South America, there were twenty prints that had been "brass nailed" to the walls in 1769 by Joseph Kidd. This reference implies a formal arrangement with large brass or iron rings fixed to the tops of the frames and hooked over bright, large-headed brass nails to produce a decorative effect. The subject matter of these particular prints is unknown, but Sheraton later emphasized that "such prints as are hung in the walls [of the library] ought to be memorials of learning and portraits of men of science and erudition." One hundred years earlier the practice of ornamenting such a room had been essentially the same—Pepys had boggled at the king's closet in Whitehall with "such a variety of pictures and other things of value and rarity."[21]

Among the remaining contents of the second floor chambers there were two distinct groups of items that provide unusual insights into the governor's cultural attitudes and ambitions. Both groups were itemized separately from the inventory, though both lengthy lists—of his clothing and his books—were promptly dispatched to the duke. The governor's clothing was stored in four separate containers in three rooms—his bedchamber, the middle room, the chamber over the dining room—with additional items arriving as the list was being compiled. Cursory references to "apparel . . . linnen . . . stockgs" and so on would normally be as detailed a description as we could expect of that important indicator of the governor's personal and official presence—his "personal dress," to cite Sheraton's revealing statement that I have used as the frontispiece to this book—were it not for the unusual diligence of Botetourt's trustees. "Thinking it rather indelicate to particularize his Lordship's wearing Apparel in the Inventory," wrote William Nelson to the duke of Beaufort on October 30, 1770, "we have there omitted it, but, for your satisfaction, we send you a distinct Account of every Article." This they dutifully did, itemizing every piece in the large and small chests of drawers in his Lordship's bedchamber and in the clothespresses that Botetourt had brought new from London in 1768 and had placed in the middle room and the adjoining bedchambers.[22] A gentleman's apparel was the most commonly visible and widely understood indication of his status and wealth. It was the outer man; so the trustees' delicacy in this matter is puzzling unless it was the intimate clothing that seemed to them to be a little too private to itemize and describe. But they did. Their list runs the gamut from a rich suit of pale crimson cut velvet with gold buttons to flannel drawers and one hundred and fifty-two pairs of stockings (Appendix 1). This "distinct Account" of Botetourt's clothing is most uncommon and affords a vivid, detailed picture of the kind of personal appearance a governor thought it appropriate to make in the southern colonies.

Tryon and Eden both demurred at listing theirs and their wives' lost clothing, despite the copiousness and intricacy of detail elsewhere in their claims.

Ten suits, twelve frocks, twenty waistcoats, thirteen pairs of breeches, and sundry other coats, waistcoats, greatcoats, and capes; hats, gloves, and thirty-two pairs of shoes; six wigs, sixty-two shirts, handkerchiefs, stocks, and so on constitute a formidable wardrobe. To complement his formal attire he could choose any one of five small swords he owned as an emblem of his status. It is telling that Botetourt had brought with him all his clothes from his Gloucestershire country house "except the Regimentals." He obviously envisioned making the same appearance in Williamsburg that, as the uncle and former guardian of one of the most powerful dukes in the West Country, he did in England. His best clothes had been worn at St. James's Palace. Yet no one in Virginia, to judge by the surviving records, thought them out of place in the colony. In an age when it was generally the breach of manners and custom rather than the observance of them that aroused comment, no one gossiped or confided to paper any misgivings about the tone of Botetourt's dress. Since he had been briefed about the conditions in Virginia before he left London, he had without doubt determined that his wardrobe would be suitable to local conditions. (Only his extravagantly gilded state coach, acquired secondhand from an uncle of the king, seemed to some observers in Williamsburg to be in danger of going a little far.)[23]

Velvet and silk in scarlet, crimson, blue, white, and black, "laced" or trimmed with gold and silver—these were the materials of which his suits were fashioned, expensive and generally considered elegant. Yet it appears that his clothes were conservatively styled, according to a unique eyewitness account of Botetourt's deportment at a formal event in Williamsburg. In his description of the governor opening "his first and only Assembly" at the Capitol, David Meade recalled that Botetourt's "costume was of the ordinary fashion of the day, but handsome and rich; the coat of a light red color, of gold thread tissue."[24] This must be the same as the complete suit of gold tissue (silk woven with gold threads) and "1 do. of a larger pattern" that were included among the clothes stored in the middle room upstairs. Such precious materials would have given the governor a most distinctive appearance at assemblies in town, in the eyes of many observers, yet obviously they were not so extravagantly fashioned as to set him apart.

Botetourt's social obligations in England had undoubtedly required him to pay considerable attention to his dress. His wardrobe was extensive and, as the inventory shows, the materials were rich. Since he was not oblivious to fashion, it would be safe to presume that his clothes were stylish. Yet Meade, who had left England as a boy of sixteen, some years before he wrote the above account, described them as being of "the ordinary fashion of the day," that is,

One of the sliding trays of the clothespress contained several of Botetourt's small swords, his formal insignia of gentlemanly status. Comparable to suits in his extensive list of apparel are, at left, a suit of silver gray satin brocaded in light blue and yellow. CWF *1953-838. Shown on the right is a lightweight broadcloth suit embroidered with silver thread, in a fashionable cut of the 1760–1770 period.* CWF *1964-32.*

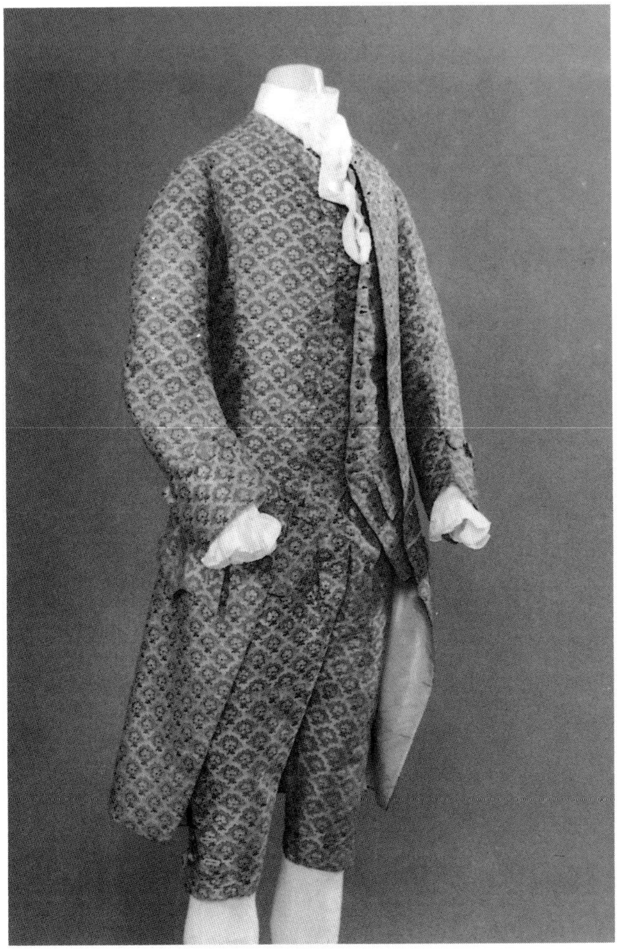

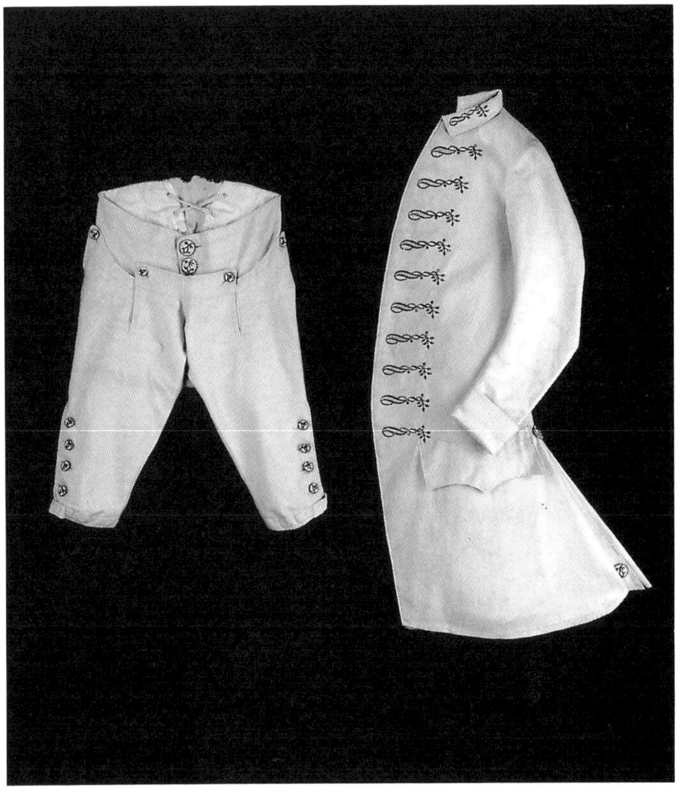

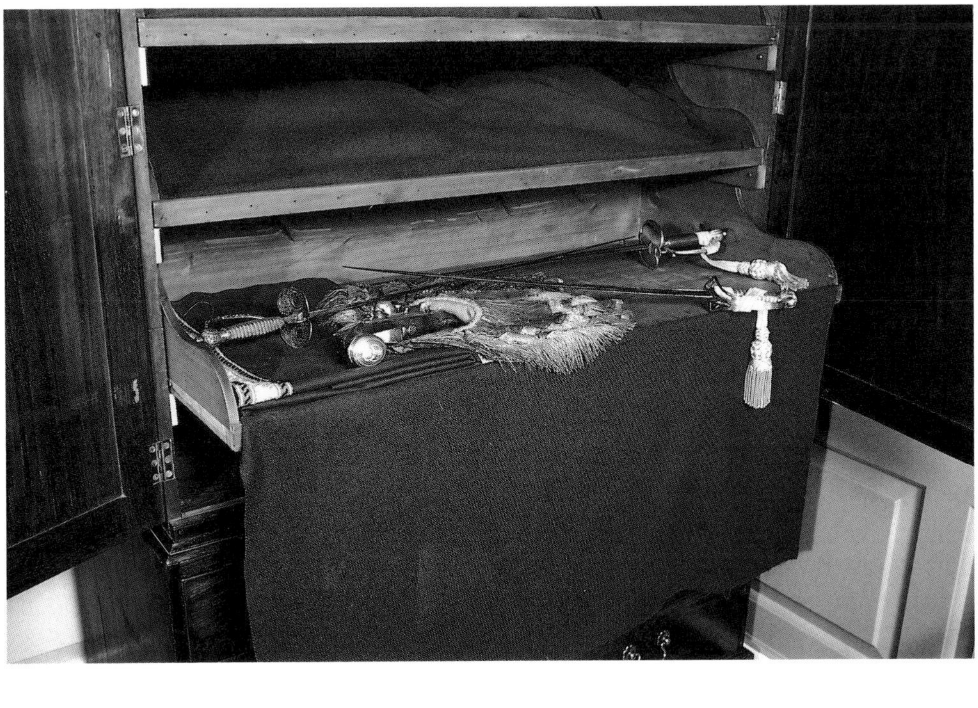

comparable to what could be seen in Virginia at the time. His judgment endorses other contemporary comments on the richness of Virginians' attire. Even in the first quarter of the century, Hugh Jones had observed that "very good families . . . dress after the same modes, and behave themselves exactly as the gentry in London." Peter Collinson, a London merchant with worldwide contacts among the fraternity of naturalists and the friend of a number of prominent men in Virginia (though he had never been to Virginia himself), advised John Bartram on a visit from his native Pennsylvania to eminent Virginians in 1737 that he should purchase new clothes: "These Virginians are a very gentle, well dressed people—and look, perhaps, more at a man's outside than his inside."[25] More exotic language was employed by the Reverend Jonathan Boucher writing to an old friend in England in 1759: "Solomon in all

A Virginia gentry lady, Mrs. Gavin Lawson, oil on canvas, painted by John Hesselius in 1770. Her dress is of pale blue satin with a white stomacher and plentiful lace at the sleeves. H: 49¾"; W: 39". CWF 1954-262.

220 PRIVATE LIFE

his Glory was not array'd like one of These [Virginians]. I assure you, Mrs. James, [even] the common Planter's Daughters here go every Day in finer Cloaths than I have seen content you for a Summer's Sunday. You thought . . . my Sattin Wastecoat was a fine best . . . I'm noth'g amongst the Lace and Lac'd fellows that are here." Boucher concluded with a comparison that he knew his correspondent would understand: "So much does their Taste run after dress that they tell me I may see in Virginia more brilliant Assemblies than I ever c'd in the North of Engl'd, and except Royal Ones P'rhaps in any Part of it."[26]

Boucher had extensive acquaintance with the Chesapeake gentry, but his observations are somewhat at odds with the more phlegmatic remark by William Small that a member of the college faculty in Williamsburg in the

Lucy Burwell painted at leisure, probably by Matthew Pratt, in the environs of Williamsburg, ca. 1773–1774. Oil on canvas. Her pose and occupation were the epitome of gentility for a daughter and wife of the great planter class. H: 36"; W: 29". Courtesy, Virginia Historical Society.

1760s needed only one handsome suit of "full dressed silk cloaths" for the king's birthday ball once a year—otherwise he could dress as he pleased. Even the most impressively wealthy man in the colony in the first half of the century, Robert Carter, had downgraded excessive finery ("a fine gay cloke"), asserting that it might have been apropos in London but not on a plantation in Virginia: "I love plainess," he declared.[27] Obviously, fashion was a matter of personal choice as much as a reflection of social pressure and competition. Certainly there were no Macaronis in Virginia, taking fashion to what many contemporaries considered absurd extremes. Yet the exotic, elevated hair styles and extravagant hats associated with the Macaronis (providing rich fare for lampoons) are evoked in a comment by Landon Carter in 1772, grumbling about the wife of one of his plantation managers (emphatically not gentry level) who acted "the part of a fine Lady in all her towering aparell with at least two maids" to wait on her. Competitiveness there undoubtedly was; Gooch ruefully confessed that his son's fiancée was "unwilling to come into my Family" from Maryland in 1740 "and be seen in Virginia with the same Cloaths she had the last summer."[28] The effects of consumerism, nowhere more powerful than in the field of fashionable attire, were felt in Virginia as extensively—some thought insidiously—as they were in provincial England. Botetourt's abundant quantity of clothing was a symptom of it; the reaction it produced in David Meade is an important yardstick by which to measure the Virginia context.

The contents of Botetourt's library were neatly listed title by title, shelf by shelf. The resulting compilation might be thought to offer an unusual insight into the private world of the governor, in contrast to most of the items inventoried in the second floor chambers and the scarce evidence about these spaces that does survive. The library, however, was small and appears to have been used mainly as a working reference library. John Randolph actually described it as "a small tho a very useful Collection of Books" in his letter to the duke of Beaufort. Titles in law, politics, trade, commerce, and history predominate over the fine arts. The governor was obviously a generous lender, for numerous volumes were missing—"lent out and not returned . . . at Mr. Carter's . . . Mr. Stark [has]"—and also a periodic borrower, as the "books doubtful to whom they belong" implies. Whether Botetourt had left part of his library in his London townhouse is unclear; only a few "old books" were included in the inventory of his country house, Stoke Park, from which sixty-three volumes were sent to Virginia in 1768, most of the titles appearing in the Palace inventory later.[29]

It says much for Botetourt's seriousness of purpose that his bookshelves should contain so many volumes on statutes, laws, and commentaries. Politics and trade were reasonably well represented, though Bolingbroke's works were conspicuous by their absence. Ancient and modern history formed almost one-fifth of the library with a notable emphasis on titles pertaining to the American continent—"Pounal on the Colonies," Stith's *History of Virginia*, *The History of the Five Indian Nations*, and so on. Reflecting Botetourt's cast of mind and perhaps indicative of the primary purpose of the library is the total of thirteen different dictionaries, unusually large in such a small group of books. Religion was carefully, if somewhat conventionally, treated. Natural history was an obvious interest, though not deep or extensive if his books are an accurate guide. The "Fine Arts" or literature tallied in this library does not suggest a man of pretension to wide culture, though the twenty-one volumes of plays surely disclose an enthusiasm for the theater. "The entertainments of fiction . . . useful as well as pleasant" consisted mainly of Pope, Shakespeare, Molière, Swift, and a few titles by Milton, Richardson, Fielding, and Smollett. Eight volumes of Voltaire's works and fifteen of Madame de Maintenon's letters and memoirs stand out, however, in addition to an unidentified "parcel of pamphlets and old Magazines" and three books of prints and drawings bound in pasteboard.[30]

Botetourt may have achieved his reputation for assiduous attention to business at the expense of a more cultivated mind on the subject of the "Fine Arts." His library in Williamsburg was light in comparison to Tryon's, for example, on the topics of literature, poetry, novels, fables, architecture, and the classics—and Tryon does not convey the impression of a man of broad culture. In purely numerical terms, Botetourt's library was little more than a third the size of Tryon's. Eden's books were not listed. Campbell's library consisted of about the same number of titles as Botetourt owned, although his music books and magazines boosted the number of volumes to twice that in Botetourt's possession. A much wider representation of literature and works of the imagination appeared in Campbell's library than in Botetourt's. None of these governors, however, owned anything like the thirteen hundred volumes that Dunmore claimed to have lost when his possessions were seized in Williamsburg. As none of the many descriptions of that governor hint even remotely that he was a lettered man, his claim to such a notable library must remain open to question.

Tryon had planned his fairly spacious library to adjoin the Council chamber in his palace at New Bern and to be immediately accessible to the hall. He probably used the room as his office and study, for no other room in the residence was designated as such. When he moved to the older residence in New York, however, he did have a "study" located between the bedchamber and his dressing room—obviously a more intimate space resembling that used by Botetourt. A large mahogany bookcase with glazed doors was listed among the furnishings there. It is questionable if that piece of furniture was sufficient to hold the approximately four hundred and fifty volumes he claimed were consumed by the fire, but there is no indication of where else he might have kept them. Eden's bookcases also stood in his study, which was located formally on the main floor near the two parlors. Probably the most ambitious piece of furniture for a library among this group of royal governors was owned by Lord William Campbell and kept apparently on the ground floor of his Charleston residence. Among portraits and musical instruments in the room was a "large mahogany library" with glazed doors, seventeen feet long.

It is a prejudice of those who love books to believe it unlikely for a man to achieve the kind of demeanor portrayed by a sophisticated contemporary as "the grace of polished life" without more frequent incursions into "the spacious field of the imagination" than is suggested by the list of books Botetourt had with him in Williamsburg. Yet Jefferson's later experience as a resident of this building may provide a clue to understanding his predecessors' attitudes to their libraries at the Palace. Though his career is outside the scope of this book, Jefferson was the bibliophile par excellence to occupy the Palace. About the time Botetourt's library was inventoried, Jefferson lost "almost every book" he owned in the fire that gutted his mother's house at Shadwell. Within three years he had amassed a new library of twelve hundred and fifty volumes (four times the size of Botetourt's), excluding music and his books in Williamsburg. How many of these he saw fit to move to the Palace in 1778 is unknown, but it is doubtful if it was more than a small nucleus for only one box of books was listed among his possessions transported from Williamsburg to Richmond on the removal of the capital there in 1779. It is likely that Randolph's description of Botetourt's library as "small tho . . . very useful" was equally true for most of the governors, who saw life in this official residence as being too hectic or of too limited duration to allow them the leisure to do justice to a large library.[31]

Botetourt's library fell far short of the *basic* library that Jefferson recommended about this time to his kinsman, Robert Skipwith—and Jefferson was rather disparaging about the learning of his Virginia compatriots. Whether Botetourt impressed the intellectually precocious future president to the extent that Fauquier did is uncertain, but it is doubtful if Jefferson thought much of his library. Yet Fauquier's library, it must be stressed, was also remarkably small, to judge by his inventory at least. Perhaps his sons carried some of his books back to England with them, for Fauquier's inventory includes only "1 small collection of books" at the modest sum of twenty pounds plus "Ditto of music and instruments" at ten pounds. Compared to important libraries in the colony, such as Robert Carter's fifteen hundred volumes at Nomini Hall, and even more to William Byrd's approximately four thousand volumes shelved in twenty-three double-sized bookpresses at Westover plantation, Botetourt's library in the Palace was modest indeed. Small as it was, however, it can be shown to have played its part in cultural dissemination. A number of the books were lent out to others in the community, while the set of Shakespeare had apparently been

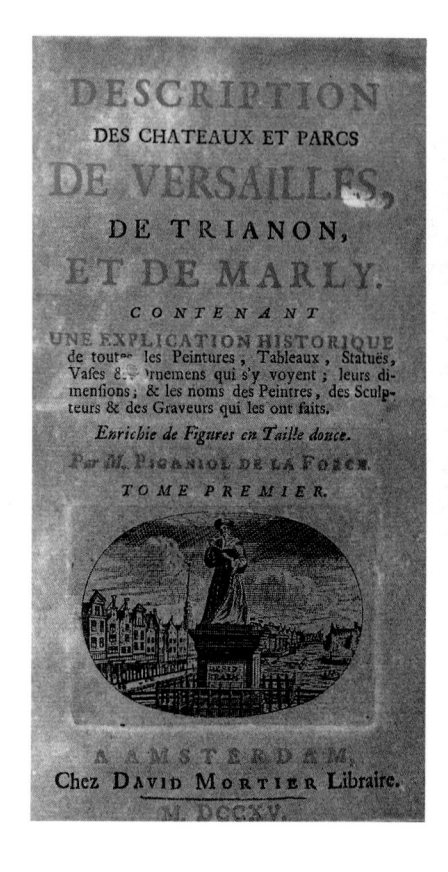

Alexander Spotswood's book on the mansion and gardens of Versailles, which he gave to the College of William and Mary in 1740. This book may have provided him with many provocative thoughts for his own palace building and landscaping. Courtesy, Special Collections, Swem Library, College of William and Mary.

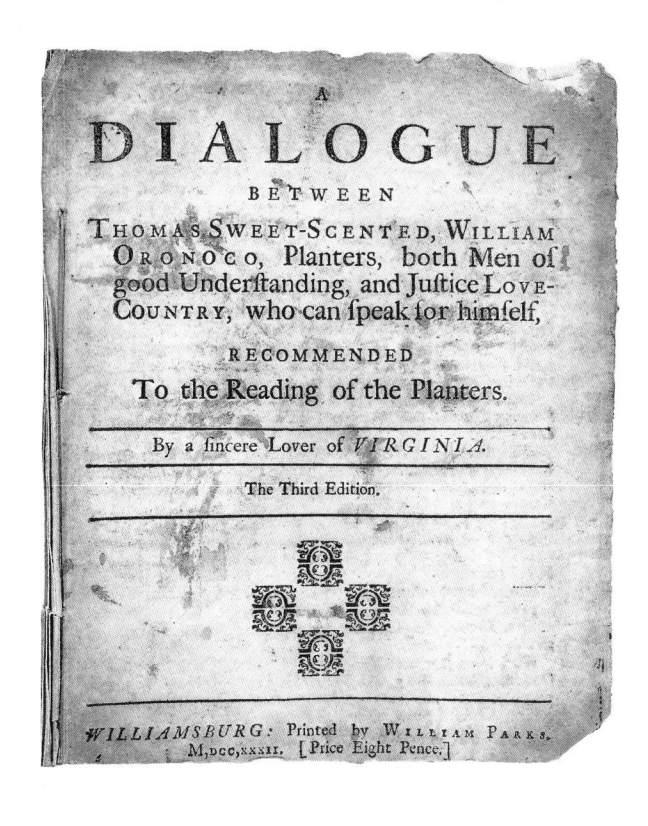

The books in Botetourt's inventory were listed precisely by title and shelf. Identical volumes, acquired in recent years, provided evidence for the required amount of built-in shelving. At left is Gooch's political pamphlet, printed in Williamsburg in octavo size in 1732. CWF.

promised to Botetourt's protégé, Richard Starke (according to the latter's letter to the duke of Beaufort). Starke may be the same man who wrote his own book shortly thereafter on aspects of Virginia's legal system.[32]

The Palace library was one of a number of reference libraries in town probably available to borrowers on a selective basis. The oldest of these was at the college, inaugurated with a significant benefaction from the personal collection of then Lieutenant Governor Francis Nicholson (cataloged in 1695). Unfortunately, many of those actual volumes were lost in subsequent fires. At the Capitol, the Council library was an invaluable resource from the beginning of the century onward. By the 1730s, an important library was located in the

THE BEDCHAMBERS AND STUDY 225

Randolph House on Market Square, compiled by Sir John Randolph and later expanded by his son, Peyton. After the latter's death, the library and the presses housing it were purchased by Jefferson and eventually became part of the first Library of Congress. George Wythe on Palace green can also be assumed to have owned a significant library.33

A number of books formerly owned by the governors have survived. Among these the most evocative is Jean Aimar Piganiol de la Force's *Description des Chateaux et Parcs de Versailles*, published in Amsterdam in 1715 and presented by Spotswood to the college at his death. What this volume might have added to the experience the lieutenant governor had gained in the Low Countries and what it meant to his plans to complete the Governor's Palace and its gardens can only be surmised. Both Fauquier and Dunmore owned copies of *Quintus Horatius Flaccus*, the latter's including the bookplate of the Prince of Wales and the date 1757. Fauquier's copy of Matthew Prior's *Poems* of 1754 and Dunmore's six-volume set of Pope's edition of Shakespeare's plays have also survived. Stephen Hales's *A Treatise on Ventilators* merited a place in both Fauquier's and Botetourt's libraries, the latter's copy having inexplicably survived.

It was during Gooch's administration that the first printer, William Parks, moved to Williamsburg from Annapolis and in 1731 produced an imprint of John Markland's *Typographical Ode on Printing* dedicated to Gooch. Parks also printed in 1732 Gooch's own pamphlet, *A Dialogue Between Thomas Sweet-Scented, William Oronoco, Planters, Both Men of Good Understanding, and Justice Love-Country*, in which Gooch defended the Tobacco Inspection Act of 1730. Parks and his successors established a book sales operation at their printing office from which Jefferson, for example, was still insatiably buying books at the time of his governorship in the late 1770s. In December 1778 he acquired copies of "Gibb's designs" and "Inigo Jones's do," each for the not inconsiderable sum of ten pounds—an indication of his engrossing interest in the subject even in that distracting period.34

Lord Botetourt's personal apartment consisting of his bedchamber and study with a closet connecting them undoubtedly provided him with his most private spaces in the Palace. Yet life for a public official in an official residence was relentlessly public. Despite the extraordinary wealth of detail concerning the daily life of this governor in this particular building, little of substance has survived to describe or suggest the inner man behind the successful public persona. One of the few intimate shelters a man or woman in such a position sought at the time was the diary or private daily memorial. Notable diaries kept by public men in Virginia include those of great planters William Byrd II and Landon Carter, who lived comparably open lives in the midst of their extended families. Their diaries illuminate life in communal situations in Virginia both at the beginning of the eighteenth century and at the end of the colonial period. Yet they are more illuminating of relationships than they are of inner growth, turmoil, creativity, or exploration. It is the outside world that these diaries reflect through the particular prisms of the planters' writings, rather than the inner world. From Lord Botetourt's stay in Virginia there are no diaries and few personal letters. What remains is the public man, the man of fashion whose clothes were spread throughout the chambers on the same floor, the man of business whose library was dedicated mainly to usefulness.[35]

Botetourt's use of the second floor apartments and the objects with which he furnished them reveal an attention to fashion deeply rooted in tradition that was characteristic of the landed gentry. The sense of spaciousness at the Palace evoked by the list of dedicated rooms for sleeping, dressing, withdrawing, and studying is at odds with the actual size of the physical space, yet it must have set him apart (unencumbered with children as he was) from the typical Virginia gentleman. This, in the eyes of his Virginia guests, may have augmented the particular English flavor of the establishment. His newly acquired furnishings for these chambers were stylish. Though it is doubtful if he would ever have gone to the lengths that his late brother-in-law, the fourth duke, did in the great Chinese bedchamber at Badminton House, outfitting it with salmon pink, handpainted Chinese wallpaper and painted chinoiserie furniture by the modish London firm of Linnell, Botetourt's blue and gold bamboo chairs were typical of that general level of patronage, in a slightly later style. Their presence in the guest bedchambers at the Palace must have invited the same kind of scrutiny as the governor's silk suits laced with gold. Colorful chintzes and checks, Wilton carpeting, and the gold of chairs and looking glass frames mingled with the traditional crimson of parade. Botetourt's library suggests that he was primarily a man of business—the assessment, indeed, of most of those with whom he interacted in Virginia. Yet it is possible that he had read a wider range of books in England, as he had availed himself of a wider range of cultural opportunities. On the iron core of business there was, after all, enameled a *douceur* (to invert Walpole's phrase) or a "grace" (to use Randolph's) that must have been more than mere artifice.[36]

The Family

I desire that I may be . . . carried to my Grave in the most private manner by my own Servants . . .

—*Will of Lord Botetourt, 1766*

It is now expedient that I should dispose of my Slaves, a part of my Estate in its nature disagreeable to me but which my Situation made necessary for me; the disposal of which has constantly given me uneasiness whenever the Thought has occurred to me. I hope I shall be found to have been a merciful Master to them and that no one of them will rise up in Judgment against me in that great Day when all my Actions will be exposed to public View. For with what face can I expect mercy from an offended God, if I have not myself shewn mercy to those Dependent on me. But it is not sufficient that I have been their master in my life. I must provide for them at my Death by using my utmost Endeavors that they Experience as little misery during their Lives as their very unhappy and pitiable Condition will allow. Therefore I will that they shall have Liberty to choose their own masters, and that the women and their Children shall not be parted; that they shall have six months allowed to make such Choice, during which time they shall be maintained out of my Estate . . . I request it as my last dying Wish, that any person who shall retain a favorable Opinion of me, would become purchasers of such Slaves . . . always remembering that they once belonged to me, and had been accustomed to kind Treatment which for my sake I hope they will continue to shew to them.

—*Will of Francis Fauquier, 1768*[1]

Thoughtful householders acknowledged that servants, while liberating their masters from menial drudgery, entailed a social, financial, and moral obligation. The slaves that many colonists found necessary for their livelihood were valuable, though frequently troublesome and always demanding. The complex nature of these resources and responsibilities produced many bonds of different kinds, resembling the man/woman/children relationship in numerous ways. It was quite natural, therefore, to use the word *family* to describe the group of people engaged in the business of making the household *work* on a daily basis. (The word actually derived from the Latin word *famulus*, meaning servant.)

The pantry was the center of the household operations in Botetourt's time. It served Marshman as an office, and at the library table here he kept the accounts that have been discovered in recent years. It also served as the storage room for the large quantity of plate and the numerous decanters and wineglasses. Sleeping facilities were provided by the couch.

THE FAMILY 229

The family was more than just a service unit. Servants lived on the premises, sometimes spent all their working lives with one master, were often indebted to him, and took their places in a series of complex relationships that frequently engendered loyalty and affection. To both masters and servants these relationships could be meaningful. That they were deeply significant to the governors is shown by the statements cited above, the context of which is surely a portent of their gravity and sincerity. In the finality of the last rite, the paternal Botetourt sought only the intimacy of his servants. In his last testament Fauquier, characteristically more fraternal, turned yet again to the less fortunate or privileged, seeking to help those he was in a position to help, even to a degree that set him apart from the majority of his contemporaries.

Signature of Lieutenant Governor Francis Fauquier.

The larger the house and estate and the more diverse and onerous the responsibilities of its leader, the larger, more varied, and more internally specialized was the family necessary to maintain it. In the colonies an unusual opportunity existed for a broad cultural exchange between the leader of the household, the white servants, and the slaves. In the governor's establishment this could be something of a novelty, for most of the servants had come with him from England or had been brought over subsequently and thus had little or no familiarity with slaves and their customs. The picture of the governor's family that the inventory and its related evidence produces is quite clear. Initially an English paradigm on a reduced scale, it changed in form as it adapted to the new environment and to different circumstances. Upper and lower white servants, both free and indentured, male and female, mingled with male and female slaves, hired as well as owned, in the pyramidal support system that enabled the governor to fulfill his responsibilities and effectively carry out his duties. Evident in this infrastructure are "patterns of meanings, values, and ideas," which are the focus of this analysis more than a description of the duties of each servant and slave; these are typically given in (mainly English) letters, diaries, and servants' directories of the eighteenth century.[2]

William Nelson's revelatory letter of October 30, 1770, to the duke of Beaufort stated what was probably the practice for most governors in planning the establishment of their colonial households: "His Lordship brought over with him a good many white Servants, and, after a short Trial, found it convenient and necessary to purchase and hire Negroes to assist in the business of his Family, and do the Drudgery without Doors." Botetourt brought with him twelve white male servants; two years later at least two of the servants had died at the Palace, two had returned to England, and three had left the governor's employment to go into business in Williamsburg on their own. The governor purchased and rented slaves to assist, supplement, and replace whites and hired other white servants from establishments in town for special events that placed an undue burden on the regular household. It is a commentary on

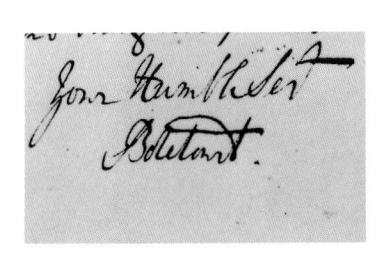

Signature of Lord Botetourt.

colonial practices that the number of servants Nelson regarded as "a good many" would undoubtedly have been considered in a normally affluent English context a small complement. That he also considered it necessary to include in his letter the phrase "after a short Trial" as a justification for the governor's use of slavery is a further insight. After all, before he even left London Botetourt had bought one of Fauquier's slaves sight unseen. Furthermore, he had obtained a great deal of information there about his future position that can hardly have overlooked the subject of his family and the prospective use of slaves.[3]

At the Palace the minimum complement of servants and slaves was about twenty persons, a number that increased to approximately thirty under some governors or on special occasions. White servants constituted half to one-third of the labor force. Gooch's family was listed (in the smallpox epidemic of 1748) as thirty-two, larger by ten persons than Botetourt's, though this figure did include his kin. It is not known how many slaves Gooch possessed. Dunmore claimed to have owned in Williamsburg in 1775 twelve "indented servants mostly tradesmen," who had about four years left to serve, together with an unspecified number of slaves. Fauquier kept three white servants and owned twelve slaves, six male and six female, with five children belonging to the latter. Botetourt owned seven slaves, three male and four female with one child. The governors periodically hired slaves with special skills; one of the Burwell slaves from Carter's Grove, a gardener named James, served Fauquier, Botetourt, and Dunmore consecutively, being rented by them fairly consistently on a yearly basis for an annual charge of approximately 15 percent of his purchase price.[4]

In addition to household staff and slaves, the governor hired a secretary or principal clerk and probably several assistant clerks or scribes for the business of copying official documents and correspondence. At least three clerks were employed by Fauquier, the first two being young men of good Virginia families who, having proved themselves with the governor in this position, procured through his patronage permanent posts in the colonial administration. His last clerk, Peter Pelham, was retained in the position by Botetourt.[5] Dunmore employed James Minzies as his clerk but also brought with him a private secretary or gentleman-in-waiting who proved to be unpopular with the colonists, being characterized as arrogant, cynical, and a sinister influence. Botetourt and Dunmore as full governors were also entitled to a chaplain. They appointed young clergymen to their households, but little is known of them.[6]

The head of the family was patriarchal to his slaves and at least paternal to his white servants. On him rested the responsibility for the organization of the family as well as its moral and physical well-being. "I must take care to keep all my people to their Duty, to set all the Springs in motion and to make every one draw his equal Share to carry the Machine forward," wrote William Byrd II

THE FAMILY 231

of his plantation family early in the century. Such paternalism was frequently noted in the later diaries of Landon Carter at Sabine Hall and of Philip Fithian, observing the behavior of Robert Carter at Nomini Hall. Indeed, the bondage between master and members of the family (especially blacks) in Virginia was so close that certain planters could not help but see their own traits reflected in the behavior around them—"these poor people suffer for my sins," Byrd confided to his diary.[7] Servants and slaves necessitated properly condescending behavior on the part of the head and his kin family (an ideal that was not always possible to live up to). Children were taught this behavior at an early age: "Be Calm and Obligeing to all the servants, and when you speak doe it mildly, Even to the poorest slave; if any of the Servants committ small faults that are of no consequence, doe you hide them. If you understand of any great faults they commit, acquaint y'r mother, but do not aggravate the fault," wrote Daniel Parke from England to his daughter in Virginia about 1699. "Be kind and good-natured to all of your servants. It is much better to have them love you than fear you," he noted on a later occasion. Botetourt was mindful of his faithful servant's future welfare even on his deathbed—"you must go home to the Duke of Beaufort, he will provide for you." The family was an intimate assemblage of individuals, intricately entwined in a community that was a microcosm of the larger world, each member deriving (at best) some sense of self-worth from their contribution to the unit and expecting leadership and protection from the head of the household.[8]

The functional groupings of Botetourt's family are clearly underscored by the inventory—first the main house; second the kitchen and its dependent activities; and third the stables, coach house, garden, and park. This division was constantly noted in the Palace documents from its initial concept to Dunmore's schedule of losses approximately eighty years later. Only the Botetourt inventory, however, clearly listed each component of the three groups— the main house and cellars; the "Out Houses belonging to the Kitchen," comprising larder, smokehouse, coal house, salt house, charcoal house, scullery, kitchen, cook's chamber, and servants' hall (as well as a specially designated "cook's cellar," probably beneath the main house); and stables, coach house, granary, areas for farm vehicles, equipment, and assorted livestock, poultry, and slaves, garden sheds and gardener's room, coachman's room and groom's room with adjoining storage closets, laundry, dairy, and another servants' hall.[9]

This arrangement resembled the division of functional areas of the palace at New Bern. There, the two dependencies were linked to the main house by a covered way and contained the kitchen, scullery, and laundry (with servants' chambers above) to the left of the main house, and stables, coach house, and harness room (with granary above) to the right. Except for the

The splendidly gentrified young Charles Calvert of Maryland, accompanied by his personal servant in appropriate apparel. Painted in 1761 by John Hesselius. Oil on canvas. H: *50¼"*; W: *37⅞"*. *Courtesy, Baltimore Museum of Art.*

location of the laundry, the exact siting of the New Bern plan was probably similar to that at the Palace in Williamsburg, for there was only one service door in the latter according to Jefferson's sketch—and that was on the left side for the more necessary access from the kitchen; it opened into the service rooms comprising pantry and storage/meal preparation areas.[10]

At Tryon's Palace a space was included for the secretary's office in the kitchen dependency. Early drafts of the architect's plans show this room paired with the laundry. Indeed, one plan suggests that the only entrance into the secretary's office was through the laundry, an unceremonious arrangement that later got modified. The Virginia governor's secretary presumably had an office; unspecific references to "the Office" do exist, but no shred of eighteenth-century evidence for its location survives except for the inventory, which implies that a space in the main building was used as such.[11]

The tripartite format was common to Virginia mansions, albeit modified to suit particular conditions. Kingsmill and Carter's Grove, both located near Williamsburg, were similar to the Palace model. A variation on the plan could

THE FAMILY 233

References

A	Hall
B	Library
C	Council Chamber
D	Drawing Room
E	Parlour
F	Housekeeper's Room
G	Servants Hall
H	Great Stair Case
I	Lesser Stair Case
K	Gov.'s Secretary's Office
L	Kitchen
M	Scullery
N	Larder
O	Wash House
PP	Stables
QQ	Coach Houses
R	Harness Room

Floor plans of the dependencies of Tryon's Palace. Above the kitchen were servants' accommodations while over the stables and coach house was a granary. Courtesy, Public Record Office, London. Photograph, courtesy, North Carolina Archives, Raleigh.

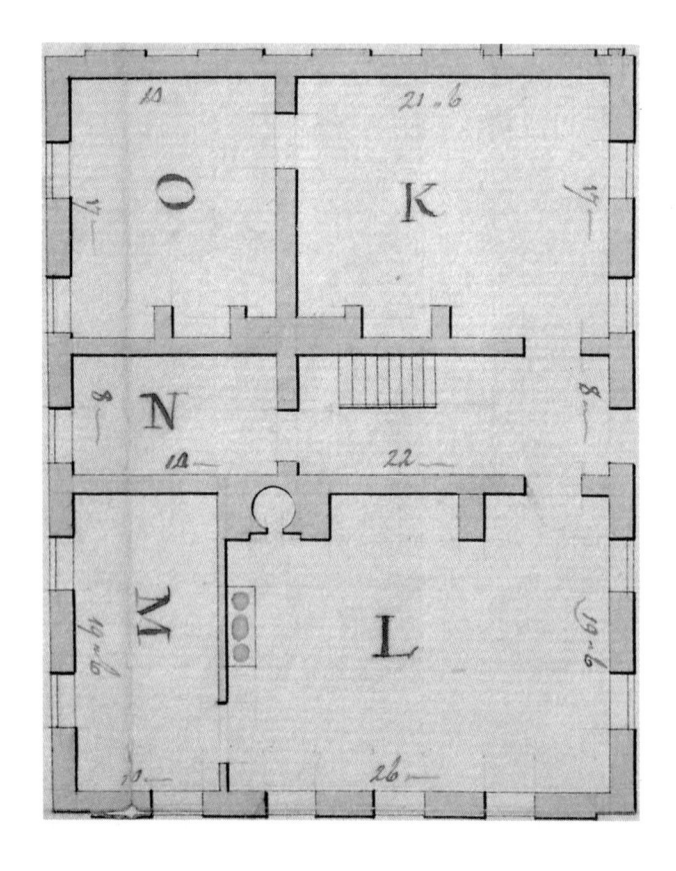

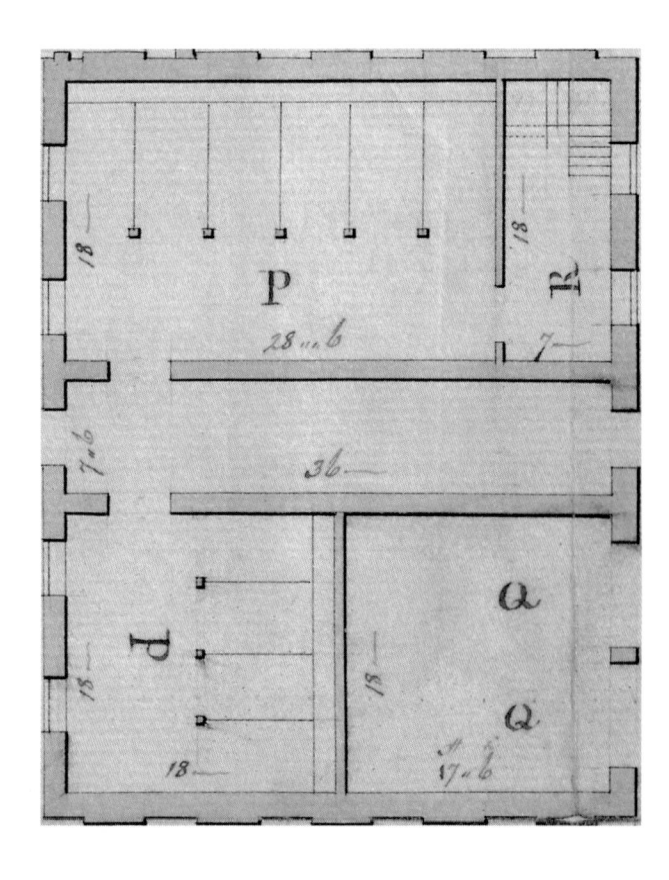

Conjectural drawing of Nomini Hall and its major "offices," drawn at the direction of Thomas Tileston Waterman.

be seen at Nomini Hall, built about the same time as Tryon's Palace. Nomini had four main dependencies set in pairs at an unusual distance from the main house (one hundred yards). Stable and coach house stood on one side, while "school-house and workhouse" (or wash house) stood on the other. In conjunction with the latter were a kitchen, bake house, dairy, storehouse, and "several other small Houses; all which . . . form a little handsome Street." Characteristic of most plantations was an abundance of small buildings for slaves and equipment, creating the appearance of villages or small rural communities.[12]

Botetourt was well acquainted with the hierarchy of an elaborate retinue, for he was intimately connected with a ducal household and was fresh from a formal post at court. The Badminton archives, for example, into which his abundant records were assimilated divulge such details as the precise seating arrangement for servants at dinner on one of the ancillary estates, while innumerable vouchers, daybooks, and account books kept by the servants at his three English estates specify in great detail the activities necessary for the estates to prosper and the system of rewards and remunerations involved. At Stoke Gifford, his principal estate which he occupied with less frequency after his appointment at court, Botetourt kept approximately thirty-four servants. He brought only twelve servants to Virginia, of whom at least seven were previously in his employment. Some regarded their service in Virginia as a temporary tour of duty and left their wives in England, sending back a portion of their wages as support. Some had served Botetourt for many years and were deeply loyal. One was a second generation servant training to become a steward, as his father had been for many years at Stoke. Three of them later set up in business in Williamsburg, apparently with Botetourt's blessing (one of them with a loan). Whether they had come to Virginia with this intention is unknown—there is no reference to an indenture, though Dunmore's statement quoted earlier shows that this was not exceptional.[13]

The names and occupations of the twelve servants were recorded on the muster list drawn up by the purser of the naval vessel *Rippon*, which brought Botetourt and his family to Virginia. Their duties are confirmed by an analysis of the Williamsburg records. The only servant not precisely designated on the list was William Marshman, described as "gentleman" probably in deference to his senior status in the household. This was an unusual appellation for one who had not held such responsibilities for long, and no one in Virginia referred to him thus. To the Virginia gentry, Marshman was the governor's butler or steward. Perhaps it was the rank of his master, a lord and only one step from ambassadorial status, that earned Marshman this title from the naval official. Accompanying Marshman in the retinue were the usual functionaries: cook, under cook, and under butler; an "assistant" whose responsibilities are shown by the accounts to have resembled a land steward's; a "groom," described elsewhere as "groom of the chambers"—a house servant rather than a stable hand; coachman, groom, and postilion for horses and rolling stock; and gardener, carpenter, and (black)smith. Conspicuously absent from the muster list was the increasingly important member of large English households in this period, the auditor or accountant. Marshman, and subsequently the land steward, Silas Blandford, Jr., fulfilled this role for Botetourt in Williamsburg, though the governor regularly appended his initials to the monthly accounts, judging them to be "allowed" or correcting them. Also absent from the retinue were females such as housekeeper, chambermaid, housemaid, laundry maid, dairy maid, scullery maid, all of whose duties would have been confined to the house and kitchen complex and not solely devoted to the assistance of the lady of the household, had one accompanied Botetourt. However, female servants were later brought into the Palace service roster and were probably mostly slaves.[14]

William Marshman was the key functionary in Botetourt's Virginia family. Indeed, he later noted that "I had always everything under my care since we have been here." He assumed at least four vital functions in the household that on a large English estate were normally assigned to different individuals— house steward (including auditor), butler-valet, housekeeper, and secretary.

The Palace cellars contain original walls and floors. There is evidence for two vaults. In this well-controlled environment were kept thousands of bottles in brick bins and the hugely expensive pipes of imported wines.

THE FAMILY 237

Previously he had occupied a position in Botetourt's London house, though there is no doubt of his presence at Stoke also, for one of the bedchambers in the 1768 inventory of that house was assigned to him. It is unlikely that his was a senior position there, however, for his annual salary and allowance (excluding militia pay) was only £12.5.0 (sterling), compared to the annual £63 for William Sparrow, later the cook at the Palace. Marshman's salary subsequently increased to £40 in Williamsburg, reflecting his increased responsibilities.[15]

Marshman's loyalty, indeed his sincere affection for his master, was fully articulated in a long letter to his brother after the governor's death. His devotion was clearly appreciated by Botetourt and reciprocated: "His expressions to me, at several times [during his final illness]," Marshman noted, "were tender and affectionate beyond my power at present to describe." Recognizing Marshman's faithful service, the duke later presented him with the perquisite of Botetourt's large wardrobe—perhaps befitting a man whom others of similar social status could perceive as a gentleman. Marshman may well have considered the richer clothes as above his rank and sold them. The perquisite probably did not equal the hundred pounds sterling that Botetourt bequeathed his longtime steward, Silas Blandford, Sr. (the only servant so specified in his will), but as compensation Marshman was kept on for a year at full salary to assist the executors and received an extra year's wages from the estate to boot (two years' salary constituted approximately 60 percent of Blandford's bequest).[16]

Marshman's principal work area at the Palace was strategically (and symbolically) located adjacent to the hall and next to the service entrance. Here he could keep track, if he needed to, of visitors entering both front and side doors, the latter being tradesmen and servants. Here he coordinated the accounts from both sides of the Palace compound, the kitchen to the west and the stables, garden, and park to the east. In his office, or pantry as it was termed, at the library table relegated from the previous governor's office, he supervised not only personnel but also the valuable contents—the large inventory of silver consisting of over six hundred pieces including gold, gold plate, and elaborate cutlery listed en suite (a major asset and, of course, highly susceptible to pilferage); cut and "flowered" glass, primarily decanters and drinking vessels; the "physic closet," kept under lock and key, also subject to theft; the indispensable iron chest or safe for petty cash and valuables; certain wines, liquors, and, more important, the keys to the well-stocked cellars; four pocket pistols; a chest of tools; and, by no means unimportant, two hundred fifty molded, dipped, and spermaceti candles and lamps.[17] In all, over one thousand six hundred items were listed in the pantry in the Botetourt inventory, excluding the large quantities of china and accessories for food and beverage service in the adjoining service/storage areas. That Marshman or his designate periodically slept in this room is implied by the presence of a ticken couch with bedding, a wash-

Botetourt and his English servants listed as supernumeraries on the naval vessel that brought them to Virginia in the fall of 1768. Admiralty Muster Books, courtesy, Public Record Office, London.

The fastidiously neat signature of William Marshman, from a page of his daily accounts. Courtesy, the Duke of Beaufort.

Supernumeraries Borne for Victuals only by Adm.ty Order

N° Entry	Year	Appearance	Whence and whether Prest or not	Place and County where Born	Age at Time of Entry in this Ship	N° and Letter of Tickets	MENS NAMES	Qualities	D.D. or R.	Time of Discharge	Year	Whither or for what -on	Straggling	Neglect	Slop-Cloaths supplied by Navy
12 Sept	12 Sept		Lord Botetourt's Victualer				Tho.s Towse	Ad	D						
"	"	"	"				Will Marshman	Smith	D	26 Oct.r	1768	Virginia			
"	"	"	"				Jn.o Kidd	Groom	D						
"	"	"	"				Jn.o Cook	Cook	D						
"	"	"	"				Silas Blandford	Assistant	D						
"	"	"	"				Will Knight	Groom	D						
"	"	"	"				Tho.s Gale	Postilion	D						
"	"	"	"				Tho.s Fowler	Under Butler	D	29 Oct.r	1768	Virginia			
"	"	"	"				Ja.s Simpson	Gardner	D						
"	"	"	"				Ja.s Kindle	Carpenter	D						
"	"	"	"				Sam.l King	Postilion	D						
"	"	"	"				Jn.o Draper	Smith	D						
22	" 22						The Right Hon.ble L.d Botetourt		D	26 Oct.r	68	Virginia			

		£	s	d
	To Mary Jaques D.o	0	7	0
	To Mary Marshman D.o	0	7	0
	To House Bill	1	0	0
	To Washing Bill	0	4	5½
	To the Duke's Maid	0	10	6
p.d June 24	Rec.d the full Contents W Marshman	18	17	4

stand and razors, and a chest of drawers for clothes. Security, both for the numerous valuables in the room and for the adjacent front and side doors, was obviously a prime consideration for this space and those who used it.

Marshman probably had another, more private sleeping space assigned to his use. His status merited it. A bill for "cutting and altering Mr. Marshman bedstead" of May 1770 probably referred to a bed that stood in the room on the garret floor at the front of the main house, directly over the governor's bedchamber. The only other front bedchamber on this floor was occupied by Silas Blandford, accorded a roughly comparable status in the household. Two mahogany field beds equipped with the red check curtains that appeared in most of the servants' bedchambers stood in this garret room, together with an oak chest of drawers, an old painted table, washstand, and a map of Bristol—serviceable, inconspicuous furniture, neither too rich nor too mean. If Marshman did use this room, he obviously shared it with another servant, probably his under butler, Thomas Fuller. Like Marshman, Fuller had been a member of the Gloucestershire militia—receiving from that source income that Botetourt made up out of his own funds—and was hired at the same salary.[18]

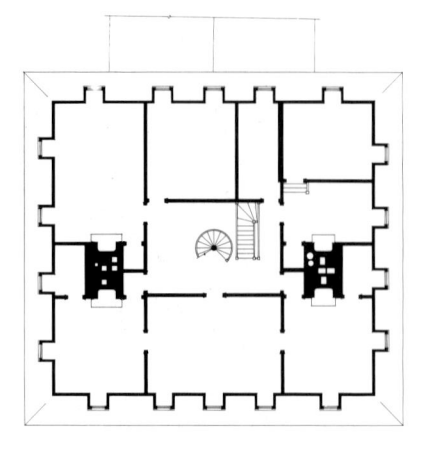

Floor plan of the garret floor of the Governor's Palace as reconstructed in 1930–1932. The staircase leads to the commanding cupola and the balustraded roof, which affords a magnificent view of the capital city. Drawing by James F. Waite.

Marshman may have interacted with a wider range of Virginians than the governor himself. As butler he would have been at least partially (and unofficially) privy to many of the conversations in the dining room while providing the important ingredients of wine, beer, and liquor to the diners and supervising the service that the waiters or footmen provided in the room. Undoubtedly he was a presence at balls and assemblies in the building, coordinating both regular and temporary servants. In the meticulously written pages of the daybooks he recorded manifold encounters that required at least his knowledge and often his approval, tacit or otherwise. His many contacts not only included members of the governor's own family, from steward to slave, but he presumably dealt freely with many of the local gentry's servants, as well as with visiting dignitaries, with their secretaries or gentlemen-in-waiting (Governor Tryon's Mr. Edwards and possibly Sir William Draper's man) and stewards (those serving Sir Thomas Adams and probably Governor Eden). Local slave owners and their slaves, tradesmen, beggars, and Indians completed the array—a rich diversity of people up and down the social scale. With all of these people at all times Marshman's conduct, as his master would have been at pains to point out, had to be fitting for the senior representative of a man who was a senior representative of the monarch himself.[19]

Through Marshman's hands were channeled funds controlling the temporary addition to the staff of servants belonging to such local dignitaries as Speaker Randolph, Attorney General Randolph, Treasurer Nicholas, Secretary Nelson, Commissary Horrocks, and the following gentlemen—Messrs. Carter, Everard, Burwell, Wythe, Dawson, Tazewell, and Byrd. He presumably

orchestrated the periodic use of specialists such as cook, under cook, pastry maid, and musicians hired from affluent neighborhood establishments or from within the community. Frequent payments to the local gentry for their "servants for waiting" came under his direct supervision. Carters and postilions (white and black, presumably) from the community supplemented the more frequently hired gardeners for necessary work outside the house. Footmen bringing messages and presents of fruit, vegetables, or birds or other biological specimens for the governor were all tipped and the accounts recorded. Christmas boxes (not always handed out the day after Christmas, but recorded for weeks afterward) he ordered to be made up and distributed to the sexton, the woodman, the carter's men, the newspaper delivery boys, the tailor's boys, and the Negro servants as well as to groups of servants belonging to the aforementioned gentlemen. They varied in value according to the importance or contribution of recipient(s) or master. Marshman hired musicians, sentinels, porters, boys to light candles, and extra waiters for ball nights and called in doctors for servants, nurse and midwife for the laundry maid, and hairdressers for the servants. Indians (occasionally specified as Pamunkeys and one as "belonging to the Colledge") received payment from him for earthenware (pans), wildfowl, or simply for charity. Hardly a week went by without a visit from at least one beggar, less often a male than a female ("a poor woman"). In two years Marshman disbursed over twenty-one pounds to beggars, a sum equal, for instance, to a year and a half's salary for the coachman. Marshman also presumably gathered and distributed among the staff the tips or "vails"

The plate cupboard in the pantry, lined with green "baize," and containing a quantity of silver that would have caused most colonists to stop and look again. Marshman's account book records payments for Christmas boxes, for newspaper subscriptions, and to beggars.

242 PRIVATE LIFE

that visitors to the Palace left as a token of their appreciation. Vails were divided among the servants according to their responsibility and were a standard part of their remuneration.[20]

Among Marshman's daybook entries early in his stay in Williamsburg were payments and gratuities to the "black servants," a "black woman," and so on. Within six months his terminology had changed. Henceforth they were "Negroes"; he never wrote the word "slaves." Negroes for work in the garden were the most numerous, but a "black waiting man" was obviously for house duty. Marshman's interaction with Negroes was not confined to work; four unnamed Negro men were rewarded for "taking the thief." Later, five Negro men listed by name were paid considerably more for "aiding to catch the racoon." Negro women were assigned work probably in the kitchen and house. One female slave, Hannah Crew, was purchased from Fauquier's estate, while another was bought locally within a month of the governor's arrival. Susan, a

The "Little Middle Room" was one of the service/storage suite of rooms on the west side of the first floor. It was a staging and preparation area for food and beverage service in the dining room and parlor.

THE FAMILY 243

Negress, was later hired for a year and paid wages of six pounds, approximately 40 percent of Marshman's basic pay (without militia allowance). To Susan fell the supervision of "a Negro wench" hired from a local slave owner. An ominous entry in January 1770 to "flogging of Matt" signaled the appearance at the Palace under Botetourt of harsh discipline. Thereafter, both male and female slaves were flogged, a local individual named Lavie seemingly specializing in the flogging of women. Six instances were recorded in the daybook in the remaining nine months of Botetourt's tenure, including Matt again and female slaves Sarah, Doll, and Phillis. How Hannah Crew, the slave Botetourt had purchased from Fauquier's estate who was reputedly "accustomed to kind treatment," looked on this practice at the Palace can only be surmised. Flogging was a widespread punishment for breach of discipline at the time, notably in schools, in the military, and on plantations. At the latter, even white indentured servants might be severely punished by whipping, which was regarded not only as punishment but a necessary corrective for aberrant behavior or failure to complete assigned tasks. That flogging of Negroes did not appear in the Botetourt records until fourteen months after he and his family arrived in Virginia may suggest an unfortunate aspect of the reverse process of acculturation.[21]

Marshman undoubtedly exercised direct, daily supervision over the house servants. They included the under butler, the groom of the chambers, footmen, and probably various housemaids. Thomas Fuller, the under butler, performed duties similar in many respects to Marshman's. His salary was also similar (except for a smaller militia allowance), but it remained at that level. He, too, sent money back to his wife in England. On Botetourt's death he was granted the perquisite of "a parcel of old glass" in the powder room—a seemingly modest legacy. Following the under butler in the conventional English hierarchy came Joseph Kidd, groom of the chambers. However, his salary in 1768 was at a higher level than both Marshman and Fuller's. Within sixteen months of signing on for Virginia, Kidd had left the governor's employment and became "a very honest" tradesman in Williamsburg, where he stayed until the outbreak of war, specializing in his acquired skills of upholstery, paperhanging, and painting. Kidd's long bill for work performed for the governor after he left his service indicates that the parting was amicable.[22]

At least five men answered to Marshman in the regular capacity of footmen, doubling not only as waiters but also, at least three of them, as postilions. William Knight, Samuel King, and John Rodgers were definitely white and Cesar and Matt were black. The suits of livery they wore in the house proclaimed their status. Some of them also received striped waistcoats and breeches, the conventional uniform of grooms and postilions. For service outdoors in inclement weather they wore green Newmarket coats with deep

From drawings made on the site at the time of the surrender of Yorktown in October 1781, the French artist Louis-Nicholas van Blarenberghe produced in 1785 a panoramic painting of the great event. It included views of the some local people, slaves as well as gentry. Courtesy, Musée de Versailles, France.

collars of crimson velvet. Crimson velvet waistcoats were also worn by certain men. Footmen Knight and King both received wages and vails at the same rate as Fuller, though they were not allowed the extra modest stipend "for washing" that Marshman, Fuller, and Gale the coachman received. Their private quarters were unspecified in the inventory, though the number of beds in subordinate chambers (including the couch in the pantry) corresponded to the white servants in residence at the time of Botetourt's death. Where the black footmen and the other slaves slept is uncertain. Only one old mattress and two old blankets for probable slaves' use were recorded in the "Small Room adjoyning the poultry house" for a man to guard against the pilfering of that valuable commodity. Where the other slaves slept is not even hinted at amid the great mass of detail in the inventory.[23]

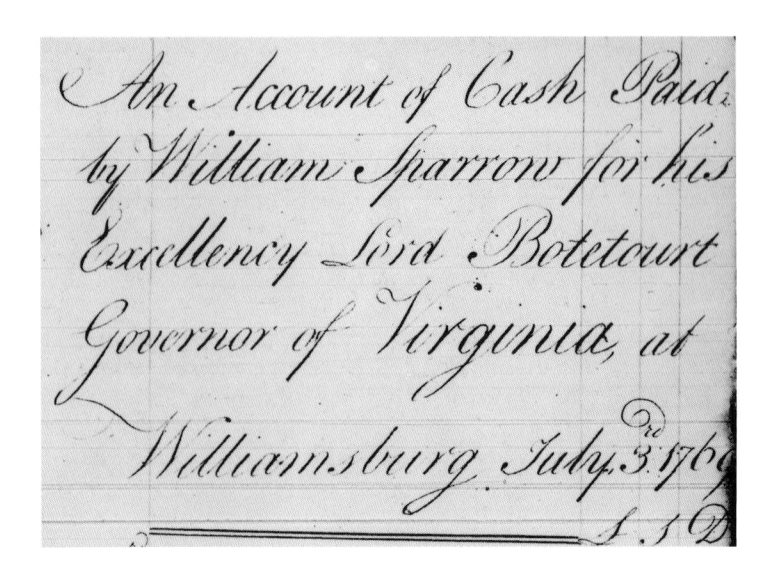

Among the prospective pitfalls in the supervision of a combined white and black work force was the delicate balance in status and rank that had to be maintained. "It is the greatest affront that can be put upon a free man here to give orders concerning him to the slaves, it is what a white servant would not endure with any patience," wrote William Robinson in Williamsburg in 1763.[24] Fine distinctions of social status were no new thing to English servants in the eighteenth century, but the variety of distinctions based on racial origin rather than on (even minute) differences of rank doubtless had to be learned.

Marshman stayed in Williamsburg for a year after the grievous loss of his master, assisting with the myriad details of the estate, ingratiating himself with the trustees and others with whom he came into contact. To Nelson he was "a most valuable and faithful servant," and to Nicholas "a person of great merit." It is clear that he was conscientious, loyal, scrupulous, obsequious, fastidious with details, and meticulous with appearances, precisely the kind of person that a prosperous, active householder needed to organize and supervise "the business of his family."[25]

Botetourt was evidently a man of sensitivity who cared for people below his rank, especially those who had served him faithfully in responsible positions. He took note of the faithful service of his steward, Silas Blandford, Sr., in his will and recommended that his "Successors . . . employ and trust him." Fauquier also described in his will the devoted service of his housekeeper and cook, Anne Ayscough, whose husband worked for him as the gardener. He bequeathed to "my cook . . . Two hundred and fifty pounds sterling in

First page of the kitchen account book kept by William Sparrow when he was cook to the governor. Though full of useful information, it does not provide the same remarkable insights into life at the Palace as Marshman's petty cash accounts.

JOSEPH KIDD,

Upholsterer, in Williamsburg,

HANGS rooms with paper or damask, stuffs sophas, couches, and chairs, in the neatest manner, makes all sorts of bed furniture, window curtains, and mattrasses, and fits carpets to any room with the greatest exactness.—N. B. He will go to Gentlemens houses in the country to perform any of the above articles.

At his LEAD MANUFACTORY, behind the church, may be had all sorts of sheet lead, pipes for conveying water from the tops of houses, cisterns, milk pans (which will keep milk sweet and cool in the height of summer) still worms made and mended, and every other article in the plumbing business.

He also undertakes all sorts of HOUSE PAINTING, GILDING, and GLAZING; and paints floor cloths, chimney boards, and signs, according to directions.

On the death of a FOOTMAN.

IN service sweet had gentle *Knight* grown old,
 Beneath belov'd command, when he was told,
Your master, *Knight*, alas! will quickly die.
Will he alas! says *Knight*, then so shall I;
I cannot live if he must life resign;
When'er he goes his summons must be mine.
This moment, *Knight*, has born away you Lord;
I follow straight, says *Knight*, and kept his word.
How good that master! how divinely kind!
Such love who kindled in his footman's mind!
How soft that footman's heart, in whom the love
Of such a master could so fatal prove!
Blush eastern slaves; for you, seduc'd by pride,
To share a master's fate have madly dy'd.
You found yourselves of towering hope bereft,
Or spurn'd a dwindled world your Lord had left;
But true affection, without noise or strife,
Untwists, a gentle *Knight*, the cords of life.
He needed not the poniard's boastful stroke,
By silent gratitude whose heart was broke.

Botetourt's groom of the chambers, Joseph Kidd, went into business for himself in Williamsburg after a relatively short period of service to the governor. He continued to work at the Palace as well as make bed curtains and floor cloths, hang wallpaper, paint houses, and manufacture lead articles. A large payment from Botetourt to Kidd may have been an initial loan to help him get started. William Knight had served Botetourt as a footman for many years. His death occurred at the same time as that of his master and merited this ode in the Virginia Gazette.

recompence of her great fidelity and attention to me in all my Illnesses, and of the great Oeconomy with which she conducted the Expenses of my kitchen during my residence at Williamsburg as his Majesty's Lieutenant Governor, when it was in her power to have defrauded me of several hundred pounds."[26] Fauquier's lengthy illnesses and consequent inability to audit the household accounts may have been unusual; clearly he kept no intermediary (such as Marshman, the butler and accountant) between the cook and himself, though he did employ a butler. Fauquier's statement highlights the responsibility and relative independence of senior members of the household staff.

In the hierarchy of the eighteenth-century household it was a short step from butler to cook. Thomas Towse was Botetourt's first cook at the Palace, assigned first place on the purser's muster list above Marshman. Indeed, on the eve of their departure for Virginia Towse's salary was one and three-quarter times that of Marshman, a sign of his importance in the household and of the sphere of his authority. Within two months of his arrival in Virginia, however, Towse died and his place was filled by the under cook, John Cooke. This was probably a temporary arrangement, for Cooke's salary did not increase from the thirty pounds he received as assistant, which was still somewhat more than Marshman was paid. By July Cooke had returned to England and the position of cook was taken by William Sparrow, who had come out for the post at a salary of sixty-three pounds, one-fifth more than Towse was paid and half again as much as Marshman's new rate. Sparrow stayed for approximately a year before he returned to England, his place being taken by a Mrs. Wilson, a local woman whose son had become the gardener.[27] The cook's sphere of authority encompassed supply and storage areas—larder, coal house, charcoal house, the glass and linen cupboards or closets, and cook's cellar; preparation areas such as the kitchen itself, the salt house, and the smokehouse; service area in the scullery; and off-duty areas in servants' hall and cook's bedchamber. The cook supervised the under cook, pastry cook, baker, kitchen maids, scullery maid, and laundry maid. Additional, mostly temporary, help also came under the cook's aegis. The account books show that John Randolph, the attorney general, frequently rented his cook, under cook, pastry maid, man, and girl to the governor at times of special need, as did William Byrd and probably others.

A daybook kept by Sparrow in conjunction with Marshman's accounts illustrates what was ordered and consumed at the Palace, both routinely and on special occasions. Foodstuffs and local produce were typical of the period, but the expense of the "Governor's table" was very considerable, even without taking into account the cost of equipment, wages, and sundries other than provisions. Under Cooke the monthly bill posted by Marshman averaged between thirty and forty pounds. Sparrow provided more prodigal fare. For the first five months of his tenure the average monthly cost for the kitchen rose to almost seventy pounds, which at an annual rate constituted 40 percent of the governor's basic salary. After an exceptionally expensive December (1769) in which basic costs (not including Christmas boxes) amounted to almost one hundred pounds, references to Sparrow decrease. His name disappeared entirely from the Williamsburg records after payment of six months' salary to him in February 1770. Thereafter, Blandford evidently took over the finances of the kitchen operation, being the only name in the accounts on a regular basis. If so, and payments recorded by Marshman were for kitchen provisions only, the monthly average expenditure returned to the rate it had been under Cooke, still about a quarter of the governor's salary and patently a major factor in his budget.[28]

Preparing sophisticated refreshments for ball nights and dinners for groups numbering more than fifty, over and above the constant round of visitors, called for considerable skill and planning. A certain adroitness was also required to work harmoniously with neighboring gentry's servants and to supervise a resident staff of white and black men and women. This important staff member shared in, and was to a degree responsible for, a key component of the governor's cultural image. The quality of the governor's table was the special province of this man or woman, and all the factors listed above—the high salary scale, the significant cost of supplies, the wide range of supervision exercised, and above all the number and type of people the product reached and affected—prove the significance of it.

The cook traditionally enjoyed one of the best appointed private living areas among the household staff. "Cook's bed chamber" at the Palace certainly

A supper table at the governor's ball was as much a visual spectacle as were the dancers. Intricately shaped cakes, jellies, and ices from tin molds; little china figures sparkling amidst candies and fruit; modish Staffordshire wares, transfer-printed; glass pyramids; cut and flowered glasses for wines; a small gazebo or temple set on a large mirrored plate and arrayed with accessories to represent a winter scene; these were all part of the cook's art that had to equal the master's ambitions in this sphere.

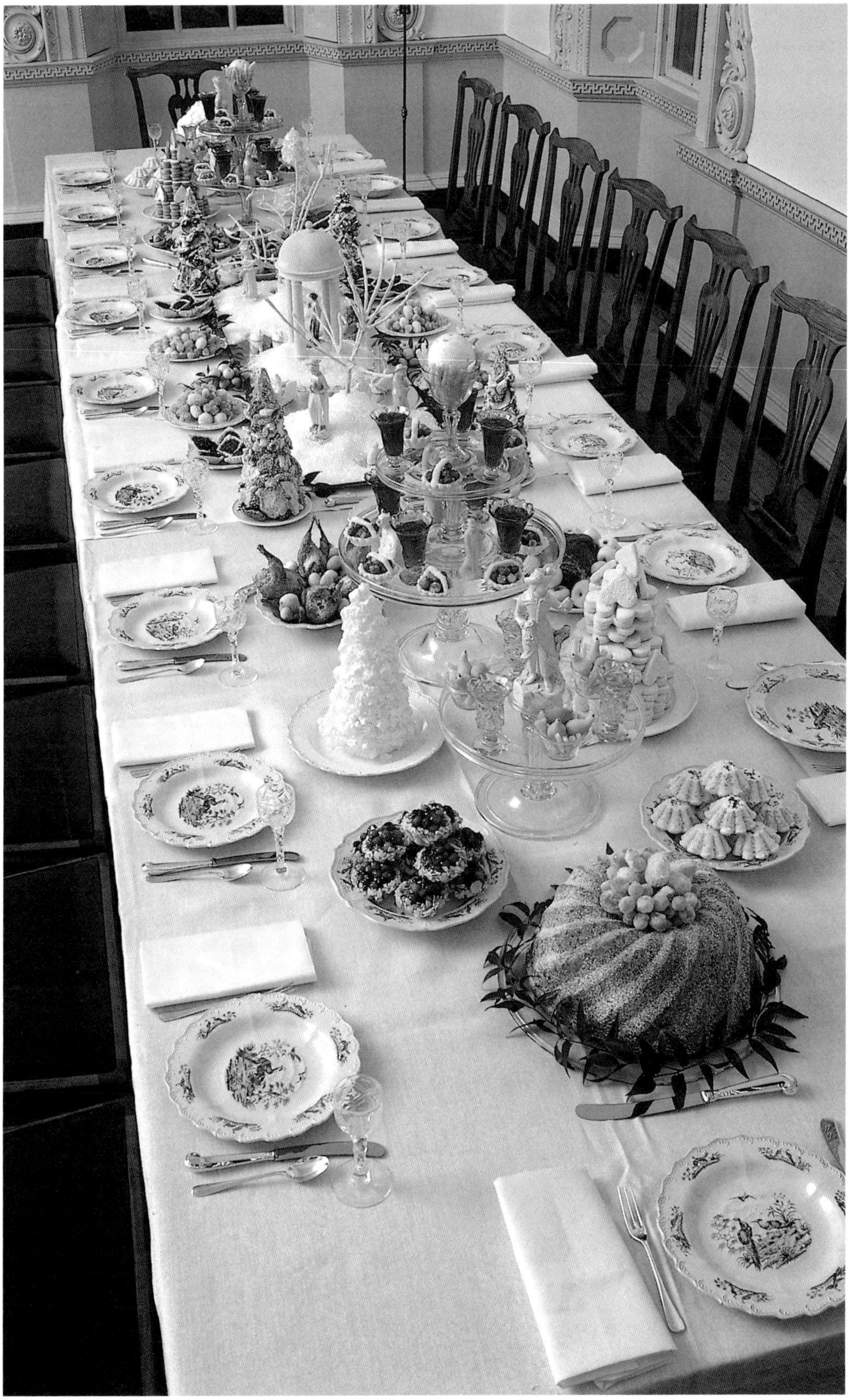

stood out by virtue of the superior quality of its furnishings—it was the only servant's bedchamber with window curtains, for example. Though the field bed with red check curtains was similar to that of the other senior servants, eight chairs plus two tables of mahogany set a distinctive tone. A green easy chair, an armchair, and a mahogany tea table were tokens of a special status, as were a walnut desk, fifteen prints, and a tea service. The briefly noted "6 Artificial flowers. l glass tumbler" convey a charming decorative touch. Only the pantry, the principal work/storage space in the entire household, featured such superior furnishings. Presumably Mrs. Ayscough during Fauquier's administration and Mrs. Scott and M. Lefebure during Dunmore's occupied the same room and maintained order in the nearby servants' hall.[29]

Centered around the stables, the third functional service area at the Palace was the responsibility of the land steward or clerk of the stables. It comprised, in graphically revealing sequence, state coach, chaise and chair, cart, horses, cows, pigs, sheep, Negroes, poultry, tools for garden and farm, coachman's work center, groom's work center, laundry, dairy, gardener's room, and servants' hall. Permanent staff, probably under the direction of Silas Blandford, included the coachman and carter, Thomas Gale; the gardener, James Simpson first, succeeded by James Wilson, with numerous black assistants, permanent and temporary; the smith, John Draper; the carpenter, Joshua Kendall; the groom, Samuel King, and other postilions as needed; and blacks to help in the laundry and dairy. It was obviously the main foodstuffs supply center of the household and, equally as important, the vital center for transport of both a ceremonial as well as a functional, mundane kind.

Conspicuous among Blandford's responsibilities, indeed, the first item listed in the inventory for this area, was the state coach. Freshly refurbished, carved and gilded even to the edges of its wheels, it probably made most people in Williamsburg look again. "When his Lordship went down to meet the Assembly it was in much greater state than any Governor of Virginia had ever before displayed. The chariot he rode in was a superbly finished one, presented to him by William, Duke of Cumberland, uncle to George Third, and was intended for his state carriage, the Virginia arms being substituted for the royal English."[30] This reminiscence by David Meade of Botetourt's ceremonial progression from the Palace to the Capitol has in the past seemed awestruck if not hyperbolic. Yet English tradesmen's accounts included in the Botetourt papers prove in minute and sustained detail that Meade was essentially accurate. Whether Botetourt purchased or received as largess the "Second hand State Berlin that was the Late Duke of Cumberland's" in September 1768 is still unknown. Yet in every other detail this extraordinary element of Botetourt's "parade" is described in the accounts. For a total cost of well over

Botetourt's state coach must have resembled this remarkable example in numerous ways, though it was undoubtedly less richly ornamented with carving. This grand coach was designed for the Lord Mayor of London in 1757 at the height of the rococo period. It is decorated with allegorical paintings attributed to G. B. Cipriani, and was first used in 1762. Courtesy, Museum of London.

two hundred pounds the state coach was refurbished for the governor, the panels gilt with pale gold and painted with the arms of Virginia, all within a rich border of ornament. The carriage body with its carved work as well as the wheels were gilt. The mechanisms were renewed. The upper sides were japanned black and the roof was covered with leather. New upholstery of crimson flowered velvet edged with silk lace and silk fringe was installed. All the brasswork was polished and lacquered with gold varnish. New reins of crimson worsted were supplied. And the body was "garnished with 1000 new large gold varnished brass nails" in decorative trim. Added to the expense of this elaborate work was the cost of packing and shipping—not inconsiderable in view of its bulk—and the even greater expense of a matched team of six horses to pull the coach. Altogether, Botetourt's ceremonial gesture of the state coach

THE FAMILY 251

was as expensive an artifice as the ballroom. Indeed, it was probably as carefully considered and contrived an artifice as the ballroom. When colonists came to the Palace, many were made aware of the royal presence through the careful choice of furnishings in the ballroom. When Botetourt went to the colonists, they were made aware of the royal presence through the choice of an equally ornate artifact with clear ties to the king and court.[31]

The accompanying matched set of six gray horses was hardly less courtly and must have appealed to affluent Virginians whose love of horses was well known. They were of great value, being comparable to two years' salary for the entire white staff of the stable complex. A true mark of distinction, particularly among rural gentry, the horses struck even the suave attorney general as "remarkable handsome." He described them thus in his letter to the duke immediately following the governor's death, one of Botetourt's few possessions he specified. Other Virginia gentlemen concurred with the estimate. William Nelson bought them first, with the proviso that he would offer them at the same price to the incoming governor; he was conscientious enough to retain Botetourt's coachman to look after them. William Byrd III bought them nine months later at the sale, a surprising purchase in view of his straitened circumstances at the time. But he soon sold four of them to George Washington. The latter's ledger confirmed that they were gray and that they were the "late Lord Bottetourt's." Their association with the state coach cannot have been forgotten by the successive purchasers of these choice tokens of cultural status.[32]

"Equipages of the newest and nicest fashion" were as attractive and desirable to Virginians as horses were. In 1753 Francis Jerdone wrote from Yorktown to London that "you'll hardly Believe it when I tell You there are Sundry Chariots now in the Country which cost 200 guineas, and One that cost 260." They were a mark of gentry culture as much as any other item of personal possession. Wealth was displayed and status proclaimed in the ornamentation of them, and critical judgments were involved. "Your chariot is at last completed," wrote Richard Bennett Lloyd from London to his brother-in-law John Cadwalader in Philadelphia in June 1769. "It is elegant, but in my eye heavy. Were my advise asked in a carriage for America, I would have it as light and free from carv'd work as possible. Such chariots as these are only used from the Palace to the house of Lords."[33] Lloyd, a scion of the Maryland gentry family, questioned his merchant relation's judgment in this important matter and did not scruple to point it out. He could no more let the matter drop as being of little consequence than the Virginia gentry could stop talking—endlessly in Fithian's estimation—of "the Excellence of each others Colts—Concerning their Fathers, Mothers (for so they call the Dams) . . . to the fourth Degree!"[34]

Between the state coach and the humble cart adjacent to it in the inventory was a stylistic gulf, yet the latter vehicle served a fundamentally important purpose for the household. A short surviving account of Thomas Gale's work with the cart reveals that coachman daily turned into carter and interacted with diverse elements of the community, bringing in all kinds of foodstuffs, fodder, fertilizer, wood, coal, and a multitude of supplies from nearby wharves, ferries, and landings. He carried the baggage of visiting dignitaries to and from the ship at Yorktown. He hauled away rubbish and dung and brought in large quantities of gravel for unspecified reasons. The effort to maintain fuel supplies in the winter was enormous—Fithian observed that a cart and three pair of oxen brought in four loads of wood each day to Nomini Hall "and yet these very severe Days we have none to spare." In effect, the cart, the horse(s) that pulled it, and the man who drove it represented a lifeline between the viceregal compound and the outside world.[35]

The spaces located by the inventory as being in the vicinity of the stables contained living quarters as well as prime work areas. The servants and slaves who used the great numbers of artifacts listed in those spaces also lived in the midst of them. Only their supervisor removed himself at night from the scene. Gale and King, for example, worked and slept in a jumble of harness, bridles, saddles, and assorted tack, to judge by the copious lists of equipment in their work and living spaces. Their constant presence was an obvious security measure amid the profusion of valuable items of equipment and livestock. To them the servants' hall was probably an occasional necessity, a neutral environment and pleasant relief from the stables and their activities. Other servants in the complex included John Draper, the smith, who shoed horses and repaired or replaced vehicle hardware or implements when necessary and also specialized in (at least minor) equine disorders. Joshua Kendall, the carpenter, was frequently called on to repair carts or garden tools and supply new items such as a grease box or turkey coop. His work ran the gamut of styles—repairing Botetourt's new library table, "fixing" the governor's bed, refurbishing the chaise, making a large bird cage with four apartments, repairing an old jack, and mending a spade handle. Four of the specialists in this group—Gale, Draper, Kendall, and Wilson the gardener (who was a local man)—anticipated enough of a demand for their services in the community that they launched into business on their own, the first two at least remaining in the vicinity for more than twenty years. Draper, Kendall, and possibly Gale too were also sufficiently versatile to serve periodically as waiters in the main house on special occasions—an aptitude that must have been to their advantage later as tradesmen seeking to ingratiate themselves with affluent patrons.[36]

In this complex the gardener occupied a position comparable in certain ways to the cook on the opposite side of the house. Part of his function followed necessity (produce for the table) while part of it honored fashion. In many wealthy English households the gardener's importance was magnified by the flourishing interest of the gentry in horticulture and the landscape of beauty. Farms were transformed into parks, and nature in the environs of the main house was rearranged in a dazzling array of harmonious and picturesque ways. Botetourt was keenly interested in these matters and evinced it in several ways in Williamsburg, yet as a practical matter he probably concluded that it was unnecessary for him to invest substantial moneys in property he did not own or that would not serve directly as promotion or propaganda (such as the ballroom). Thus his gardener in Williamsburg, though he was assigned his own bedchamber, earned only £20 in comparison to Kidd at £40, Kendall at £30, and Draper at £18.5.0. Gale and King were even lower at £16.1.0 and £14.2.0 respectively. They supplemented their incomes, as did Kendall and Draper, by being paid for performing tasks for the governor that were outside their normal responsibilities, something that the gardener does not seem to have done. One of the few marks of distinction in the gardener's functional area revealed by the inventory was the presence of orange tubs and tree, implying that the gardens may have included the sophisticated feature of an orangery.[37] Wilson (who may have been of Scottish background as gardeners characteristically were in the colonies) later took his Palace experience with him to the College of William and Mary, whose grounds and gardens he maintained for several years.

In many English houses, the presence of the laundry or at least a drying yard near the stable and its complement of male servants frequently gave rise to interaction of another kind—laundry maids had the habit, with great regularity, of getting pregnant. The only reference to a servant or slave to perform the menial but indispensable function of laundry at the Palace is precisely in this context. Marshman's accounts show payment in 1769 for both a midwife and a nurse for the laundry maid, presumably a slave. Hers was not a negligible responsibility, however; Botetourt's inventory of linen was sufficiently extensive (over 820 items were listed in the kitchen storage alone) and in all probability sufficiently valuable (the duke of Beaufort requested that it all be sent back to him) that the washing and ironing of it was a major task.[38]

Through Blandford were channeled the responsibility and the accounts for this group of servants and slaves. Where he maintained his work space is unclear from the record unless he combined it with his private quarters in a garret chamber of the main house. This room did include a mahogany desk and writing equipment and contained furnishings similar to the adjacent room probably used by Marshman and Fuller. It was approximately equal in status. Though he appears to have been a younger man than the butler, Blandford's introduction to the responsibilities of supervision in the colonial context was presumably similar to that of Marshman, although he had not received the indoctrination in military discipline that Marshman's background had afforded him. His father's reputation and experience were such, however, that

The stables and coach house, the live and rolling stock they contained, and the equipment associated with them all represented a vast outlay of money for the governor and needed extensive supervision. At right, a satirical view of a servants' hall, where the occupants ape the airs and preoccupations of the family they serve. Called High Life Below Stairs, *the painting was completed in London in 1763 by John Collet.* H: 28"; W: 41⅝". CWF L35.

Blandford was considered an excellent prospect—indeed, the duke directed the trustees of the estate to retain him (rather than Marshman) for assistance in settling the estate, but by the time his letter was received their appointment of Marshman and Fuller had already been made.[39]

In the conventional system of household service, the responsibilities of the land steward were more diverse than those of the house steward. Agriculture, livestock, gardens, and the specialized trades encompassed a wider range than the skills normally encountered in house and kitchen. It may be questioned how extensive Marshman's knowledge of all these areas was, the more so since he had formerly served as a footman or under butler. To assure his master that the monthly accounts were just and reasonable, Marshman presumably relied a good deal on the assurances of Blandford. And if the latter was, as it appears, young and relatively inexperienced, he in turn must have had to depend greatly on the knowledge and honesty of the tradesmen he supervised. Yet the Palace "estate" was small compared to most English properties requiring a land steward, and Botetourt probably selected his tradesmen precisely for their perceived honesty (with promises of their future independence into the bargain) in order to provide the son of his long and loyal steward at Stoke with a valuable training experience and an excellent opportunity.

Except for the layout of the service dependencies at Tryon's Palace discussed

THE FAMILY 255

above, relatively little is known about the governors' families in Annapolis, New Bern, and Charleston. The extent of Tryon's retinue in North Carolina is not known, though it was probably comparable to the partially documented one in New York. There it consisted of at least ten servants, including at least one black. The inventory cited spaces for a butler (a room and a bedchamber); a housekeeper (a room plus a bedchamber); a steward (bedchamber); housemaids (a chamber with two beds); kitchen maid (bedchamber); and a handsomely furnished bedchamber for Colonel Fanning, the governor's secretary, who himself had two servants. Depositions concerning the fire that destroyed the house in 1773 were taken from ten servants in all, including—in addition to the above named—a lady's maid who slept in the same room as the Tryons' young daughter, a footman, and two "boys." No cook was mentioned, nor any garden or stable hands. What distinguishes Tryon's family from that of Botetourt is the presence of at least five white women and the smaller number of recorded Negroes. Comparisons of the contents of the servants' bedchambers reveal little difference in the quality of furnishings, with the notable exception of Tryon's housekeeper's room, which had a distinctively elegant tone to it, including several pieces of mahogany furniture, a partially gilt looking glass, and several silver tea items. Yet Tryon claimed less than half the quantity of silver and linen that which Botetourt owned.[40]

In Eden's residence five servants slept in the garret. These included (somewhat unusually) the coachman, with expensive saddles and tack being listed in his room, boys, a servant man, a servant woman, and possibly a person in the "Long Garrett" in which were also stored three stoves and related tools, "sundry old picture frames," and an extraordinary "large equal Altitude Instrument and Apparatus" appraised for the huge sum of £333. The secretary had a bedchamber on the same floor as the governor and his wife and a well-furnished office on the ground floor. Next to the office in the inventory was listed the butler's pantry containing furnishings similar to those in the Williamsburg pantry though the quantity of plate is modest compared to that which Botetourt owned. The housekeeper's room served as a bedchamber and also as storage for a small quantity of linen, china, and glass. Near that room were the kitchen and scullery, laundry, dairy, beer cellar, and servants' hall (in which stood chandeliers still in their packing crates, valued at £285).[41]

Lord William Campbell's extensive inventory gives little indication of what servants he retained except for a housekeeper (Mrs. Sidney), a secretary (Captain Innes), and two unspecified servants. Even the steward's room contained no bed but a large amount of china and queensware instead. Conventional work spaces were listed—stables, kitchen, and so on—as plentifully stocked as those in Williamsburg. The quantities of silver, glass, and linen listed are as extensive as those belonging to Botetourt. One major difference between the two inventories is the listing of Campbell's Inverary plantation on the Savannah River that included eighty-eight slaves, presumably acquired through Campbell's marriage into the Izard family of South Carolina. At a total value of £5,510, the declared worth of these forty-one male, thirty-two female, and fifteen boy slaves was 94 percent (only £350 less) of the entire contents of his well-furnished house. Removing the five horses, coach, chariot, and wines from the inventory of the latter increases the ratio of slave to chattel value to 120 percent.[42]

To the small, urban community that surrounded it, and even more to the large, rural society of which it was the symbolic center, the Governor's Palace probably conveyed a distinct, perhaps poignant, English flavor. Nowhere was this more apparent than in the constitution of the family. Twelve hand-picked white men composed an elite work force that contrasted sharply with the predominately black force of even the richest Virginia establishments. It may have been as much a source of envy to some onlookers as the matched team of horses probably was to others. Not that it was a permanent situation; it, too, changed organically in response to the environment. Indeed, Botetourt's experience of watching valuable servants die or be reluctant or unable to adapt to the new locale, of seeing skilled servants attracted by the prospect of becoming their own masters in a society where the competition was less fierce than in England, was typical of the realities of the labor market in the colonies. Still, it was a different family from the kind normally found in affluent Virginia households. One of the best documented of these served at the newly built mansion of Councillor Robert Carter in the 1770s. Through the pages of the diary kept there by the children's tutor the affluent rural family in Virginia can be observed in action and interaction. Fithian, the tutor, came from New Jersey so he was as unfamiliar with the Virginia scene as Botetourt had been five years earlier. His reactions to the work routine and to the white and black work force—and clearly it was the differences that engaged his attention more than the similarities—in the microcosmic Virginia world of the plantation provide at least some measure of the kinds of responses that Botetourt might have had to the novel environment and particularly to its most conspicuously different feature, the slaves.

Like most plantations, the ratio of whites to blacks at Nomini Hall was very low. In addition to the Carters and their nine young children, there were only five whites in the immediate vicinity of the house. Only one of the five stayed in the main house—Sarah Stanhope, the housekeeper. Fithian, on a one-year contract, worked and slept in the nearby schoolroom while two clerks, one presumably retired and another who also acted "in the character of a . . . Steward," lived nearby. A white gardener completed the roster, though he may not have been a full-year employee. Slaves, on the other hand, numbered over five hundred. Undoubtedly many never came near the main house, some were billeted on far distant quarters, and all were under the supervision of white overseers. Yet there were still communities of them within sight of the great house, a reassuring or unsettling sight depending on the prevailing emotional climate among the small white group. Twenty-five male and female slaves at the house figured in Fithian's pages, either by name or trade. Since he referred only vaguely to the garden staff and never mentioned the kitchen staff at all, it is likely that there were up to twice the above number of slaves in the immediate vicinity of the main house. Most of the conventional functionaries were cited—men and maids in waiting and in the house, footmen, coachman, postilion, groom or hostler, carter, cooper, carpenter, and so on. These he and the other whites interacted with on a daily or hourly basis.

Fithian's benefits or perquisites included his own chamber (though he periodically shared it with white boys), black servants to wait on him, and a horse at his disposal. In addition, he was expected at the dinner table where he might converse with the constant stream of white visitors. Sarah Stanhope, by contrast, shared her room with the five girls of the family as well as a black maid—a somewhat confining existence. Since her name never appears in the diary as a participant in dinner table conversations, it is reasonable to assume she was rarely granted even that diversion from the constant (and perhaps unremitting) interaction with the other members of the household.

By nature prim, aloof, and self-conscious, Fithian frequently found that his tendency to censure was at odds with his firmly assumed Christian duty to be charitable, even in the seclusion of his diary. Yet he rarely commented on the individual failings or accomplishments of the blacks in the way he did of most of the whites. Apart from deploring specific incidents of drunkenness, his judgments on the blacks were generic rather than individual. Like many Virginians, he presumably regarded such comments as immaterial since they assumed that blacks were capable of only the coarsest feelings, if they were capable of feeling at all, far from the finely attuned intellectual and emotional states of members of the gentry level. Yet his attention was captured by the interaction he witnessed between white and black, and it provoked his most scathing censure and indignant rebuke. Only two months after his arrival in Virginia a chance comment by a Negro maid prompted Fithian to ask the "inoffensive, agreeable" clerk or steward about the Negroes' food rations. On learning that Carter, who was conceded to be "by far the most humane to his Slaves of any in these parts," assigned only one peck of corn and one pound of meat per person each week, Fithian was deeply shocked. "Good God!" he wrote, "Are these Christians?" His diary entry for that same day continued with details gathered from a neighbor's overseer of fiendish punishments (tantamount to torture) devised for slaves, since "whipping of any kind does them no good, for they will laugh at

The stable yard to the east of the house and dependency as reconstructed 1930–1932.

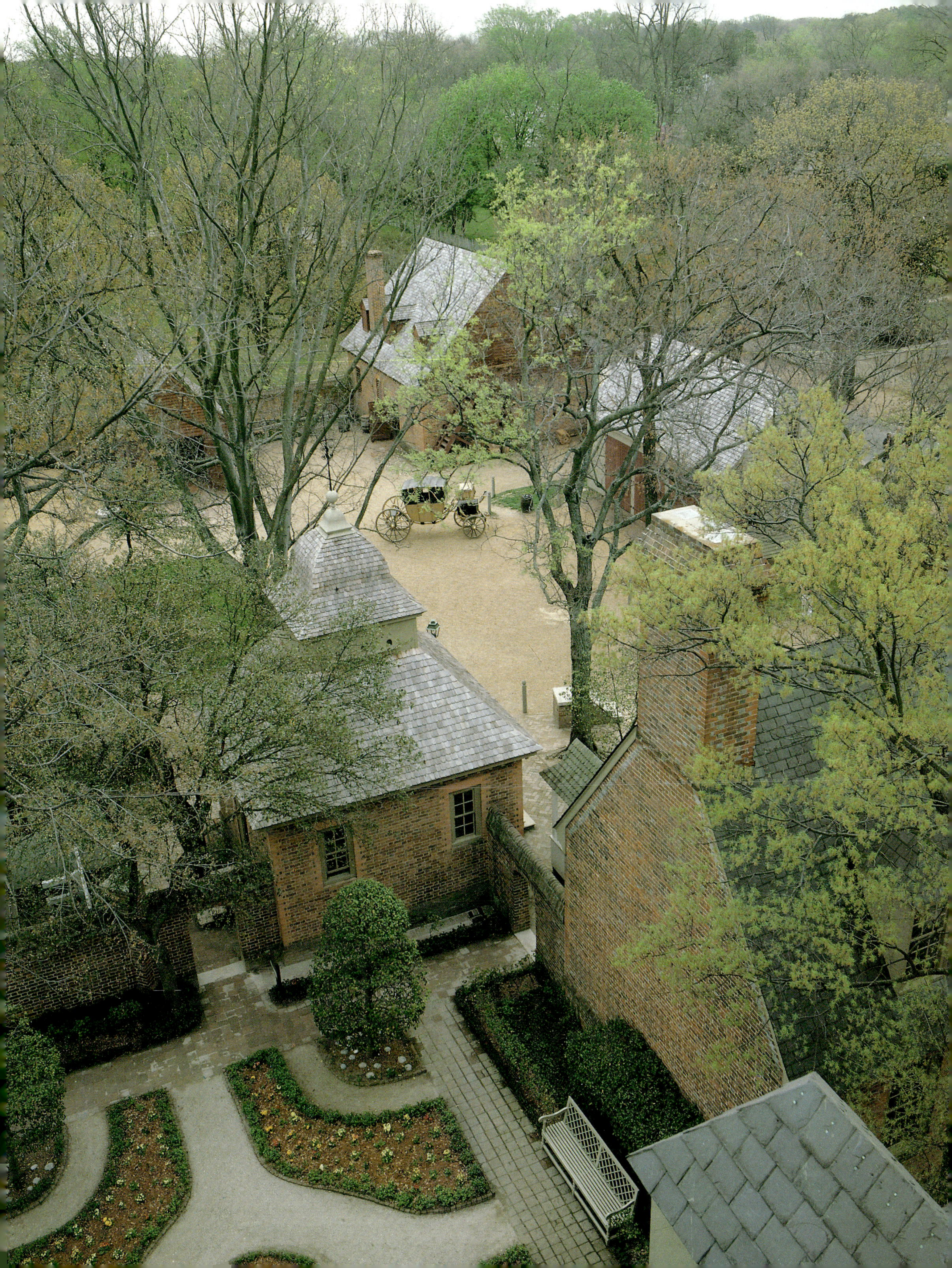

your greatest Severity." At that point in his narrative, indignation failed him and Fithian meekly continued, "I need say nothing [more] seeing there is a righteous God, who will take vengeance on such Inventions."[43]

A few months after this incident Fithian recorded a conversation with Mrs. Carter, whom he admired deeply, on the subject of the Negroes in Virginia. He found that "she esteems their value at no higher rate than I do"—a misanthropic viewpoint. He registered their mutual lament at the waste, inefficiency, and desperate travail of the whole system. How much more dignified and profitable was the English system of land management (portrayed in arcadian tones from a safe distance)! When Carter later boasted that one of his slaves was so accomplished that he would not sell him for five hundred pounds ready cash, Fithian grumbled to himself that "it is more Money than I would give for all [the Negroes] he owns on his Estate." After approximately the same length of experience with slaves that had elapsed at the Palace between the arrival of the governor and his retinue and the first Negro flogging, Fithian confided to paper his basic pessimism about the system and its individuals. Negroes were generally perceived (by whites, of course) as inherently and irredeemably lazy, a characteristic totally at odds with one of the basic tenets of conscientious Protestant society, namely, to use time wisely and productively. Negroes seemed to their masters to be incapable of comprehending the rules that kept orderly society together; they could only be taught and improved by constant punishment. Negroes lacked the ability or sensitivity to understand the advantages of industry, as whites perceived it, and the benefits of continual improvement of individual talents. They were necessary, totally necessary, yet they were perpetually exasperating and independent, untrustworthy, and unpredictable.[44]

The biracial interaction produced pessimism, despair, frustration, and violence. Fithian could observe without censure Carter "severely" flogging his sixteen-year-old son for "not having given seasonable Notice" that he had no shoes and so missing his dancing school at the Turbervilles' house. He could contemplate the dancing master striking young girls for faulty performance even in the presence of their mother with no more comment than an exclamation point. Such discipline produced predictable results, it was correcting and improving and the response in those to whom it was administered could generally be gauged; it was comprehensible. The blacks' response was often incomprehensible and their reactions produced bewilderment and resentment. Many of those who deplored the situation could find no alternative. "Another unhappy effect of many negroes is the necessity of being severe. Numbers make them insolent, and then foul means must do what fair will not," William Byrd confessed to his old friend John Perceval, earl of Egmont, in 1736.[45]

Fithian became skeptical and pessimistic, yet in his diary he deplored the cruelty, the inhumanity, the cynicism. He was aghast to note that a Negro coachman was actually chained to his seat on the coach lest he run away while his master and mistress enjoyed themselves at a ball. He sneered at the Virginia "Lords" for looking on their slaves as "improper subjects for so valuable an institution" as marriage and forbidding it. He despaired that "the ill Treatment which this unhappy part of mankind receives here, would almost justify them in any desparate attempt for gaining that *Civility*, and *Plenty* which tho' denied them, is here, commonly bestowed on Horses!" Yet when rumors of such "desparate attempts" and reactions against oppression surfaced, Fithian lay awake fearfully all night with his bedroom door securely locked.[46]

Fithian took careful note of the interdependence of white and black society in this rural setting. He observed the labor force in the fields and recorded the essential daily tasks performed in all their manifold variety in and around the main house by black men and women, and by implication assessed their indispensable contribution to the gentry life-style of the Carters and their friends. He discovered that it was "common here for people of Fortune to have their young Children suckled by the Negroes!" Frances Carter acknowledged that that had been the case with several of her children. Fithian saw the Carter girls playing and sleeping with a black girl, and the Carter boys playing, dancing, and gambling with black boys. He saw how closely entwined the races were, and could record the interaction with simple, utterly poignant language; for example, when "an old Negro Man" came to plead for his peck of corn with Robert Carter, "the humble posture in which the old Fellow placed himself before he began moved me." Yet everywhere there was disdain; despair that blacks would ever achieve white levels of organization, productivity, and personal regimen; and a resort to harsh discipline, threats, and violence in order to set example, gain control, and bring the blacks out of what was regarded as their natural abyss of sloth and inherent disregard of civilized values. Everywhere the system created ambivalence.[47]

The scarcity of white labor, the inevitability of the slave system, and the overpowering strength of its traditions make sentiments such as those expressed by Francis Fauquier all the more admirable. They were Enlightenment sentiments, but reality was unrelenting. Fauquier's family could not have maintained the household and sustained him in his duties without recourse to slaves. Freeing his slaves would have been difficult at best, since statute required the consent of governor *and* Council in each individual case, and even then "meritorious service" had to be proved. Thus he did all that was feasible in the circumstances and allowed them to choose their masters after his death, requiring that women and children be allowed to stay together but not necessarily with their men.[48]

A generation earlier Gooch had also deplored the propensity of society to hostility and cruel subjection. In the aftermath of a slave "insurrection" of alarming proportions in 1731, the lieutenant governor wrote to the bishop of London of some of the less fortunate consequences of a missionary aspiration to baptize slaves. In his letter he noted that "some Masters . . . use their Negroes no better than their Cattle, and I can see no help for it." But he went on to point out that a bitter existence was not confined to the colonies nor was it the prerogative of a slave-owning society: "Tho' far the greater Number [of slaves], having kind Masters, live much better than our poor labouring Men in England." Though his comment was similar to the self-justifying passage from Robert Beverley's earlier *History of Virginia*, Gooch had little to gain in this context by promoting or rationalizing slavery and he was certainly familiar with both the English and the Virginia situations. Whether his observation was still true in the more benign economic climate of the 1760s is debatable, but the harsh inequality of society was an inescapable reality even in the midst of the Enlightenment.[49]

Slavery was abominable, but in Virginia in the eighteenth century it was unavoidable. It could not be changed or eliminated without enormous adjustments that the great majority were simply not able or prepared to make. Fauquier might abhor it, but he could not do without it. Robert Beverley, educated like Fauquier in England but a scion of an old Virginia family, might declare in 1761: "'Tis something so very contradictory to Humanity, that I am really ashamed of my Country whenever I consider of it; and if ever I bid adieu to Virginia, it will be from that Cause alone." But he could not manage his plantations nor build himself a grand house in the latest fashion on the banks of the Rappahannock without slave labor. Arthur Lee wrote home similarly from Edinburgh: "The extreme aversion I have to slavery and to the abominable objects of it with you, the Blacks."[50] It was easier to be so principled from the English vantage point. When existence depended on slaves, the sentiment was much more likely to be "Indeed, Slaves are devils, and to make them otherwise than slaves will be to set devils free"—written by a not insensitive or uncaring man, Landon Carter. He believed there was "nothing so certain as spoiling your slaves by allowing them but little to do; so sure are they from thence to learn to do nothing at All," thus justifying his harsh disciplinary methods. Slaves were less honest and more imperfect than white men and "not born to" liberty.[51] Thus they must remain shackled to their masters even as their masters were preparing for a bitter fight, perhaps losing all, to resist becoming what they considered slavishly bound to the British imperial will.

Regrettably, the record of Botetourt's assessment of this aspect of Virginia society is silent. In view of the inevitability of slavery to the economic system of the colony, he probably maintained a diplomatic neutrality on this subject. He too needed, owned, and used slaves. Though he was clearly a kind, benevolent master to white members of his family, he approved corporal

The Palace kitchen as reconstructed 1930–1932. The long lists of items for use in the preparation and service of food, the extensive and complex materials and foodstuffs ordered (noted in the Sparrow account book), and the substantial costs involved all indicate how important this center was to the Palace life. The kitchen staff provided far more than mere sustenance, but a cultural service to the governor too, often of considerable ambition.

THE FAMILY 263

punishment for blacks in his household. Whether he was, in the privacy of his own thoughts, as charitable to the unfortunate "objects" of the system as his predecessor, or even more so, can only be surmised.

Early in the eighteenth century and again briefly during the last year of royal occupation, the Governor's Palace bore a certain resemblance to a fortress—a simile that was more in men's minds than it was in bricks and mortar. For most of the third quarter of the eighteenth century the building and the life it housed took on a more open quality. The wall between the street outside and the entrance door was probably removed. Like many Virginia mansions, the Palace was visible from afar. It was deliberately created to be conspicuous, to show all who saw it from a distance that it dominated its setting. The life that was lived in it was equally conspicuous. The governor and the wealthy Virginia gentry were constantly surrounded, in virtually every one of their daily actions, by up to thirty people, black and white, who were performing vital tasks and services and continually relieving their masters of endless routine chores. Privacy was virtually impossible in such circumstances, and even personal life became as much a matter of the life of the group as it was of the individual. What was created in each of these great houses was more of a personal sense of place, community, or "family" than the life of a private individual.

The family was a pyramidal structure designed to assist as far as possible the activities of the figure at its peak and sustain the image of his life and culture. It was an indispensable ingredient in the cultural image of a man of property. Each member of the family played an integral role in a complex framework of relationships. Without the laundry maid, for instance, the personal appearance of the governor and his primary servants would have been flawed, the look of the dinner table spoiled, the effect of guest beds found wanting. Even this lowly servant had in her charge several hundreds pounds' worth of prized possessions that she could carelessly damage or ruin. Ordinary postilion played a key part in the maintenance, operation, and proper effect of one of the governor's most lavish and costly possessions, the state berlin and its matched team of horses. At other times he was called on to relay important messages within the community or, neatly trimmed in livery, to help play out the vital daily ceremony of dinner with its luxurious staging and complex rituals. Highly skilled senior members of the family such as the auditor, the housekeeper, and the chef-de-cuisine had a profound effect on the daily life and cultural image of the head of the household. Because of the extent of their responsibilities and the range of their skills, the relationships between them and their master often became mutually loyal and dependent.

Clearly defined interaction within the family was an essential element of its structure and operation, though it was often colored by the most subtly perceived distinctions of hierarchy. Within the governor's family, small as it was, flexibility was a vital component of the interaction. The coachman was required to drive the most extravagant wheeled vehicle that most people around him had ever beheld, haul dung in a cart, and be a waiter at a ball celebrating majesty, all within the space of a few hours. The gardener was expected to produce staple vegetables for the table but might also be called on to explicate the fine details of landscape architecture shaped by philosophy and classical learning. The butler must clearly comprehend orders and in turn command, delegate, oversee, inventory, and record, coordinating the multitude of details and the ultimate effect of male and female servants, fine wines, exotic table settings, brilliant arrays of silver and cut glass, and exquisite suits laced with gold and silver, as well as deal with native Americans, Negroes, visitors' servants, and beggars. Each member of the family had to be aware of the governor's presence and preferences and remain alert, in his or her individual ways, to the fact that they were serving and sustaining a senior representative of the king.

While the governor's family had a traditional, clearly structured hierarchy, it was an organic unit that adapted quickly and flexibly in response to the new environment. Lord Botetourt's family was exceptional insofar as it represented (or at least aspired to) the pinnacle of taste and experience in the community yet had to adapt to novel conditions and situations. It was extraordinary in that certain of its members (white tradesmen) saw in it a vehicle for greater opportunity, self-improvement, and freedom than was possible for them in the traditional, narrowly confined society of England while others (the blacks) saw their service as the antithesis of freedom and their life as a basic denial of human dignity.

As concepts of hospitality in Virginia changed after the Revolution, so notions of privacy and relationships between black and whites went through a metamorphosis. The "gentry closed themselves off from the outer world" and refashioned the kin family unit. Exploration of inner emotional and psychological worlds was one characteristic result of this turn inward, certainly a retreat from the relentless openness of daily life as it appeared in colonial Virginia. Jefferson is an exemplar of this trend in the generation following the Revolutionary War. Allied to the republican movement, the evangelical movement created new thresholds of toleration and understanding in blacks' perceptions of their own lives and of their relationships with their white masters. Traditional concepts of authority and of the family were seriously disturbed.[52]

Epilogue

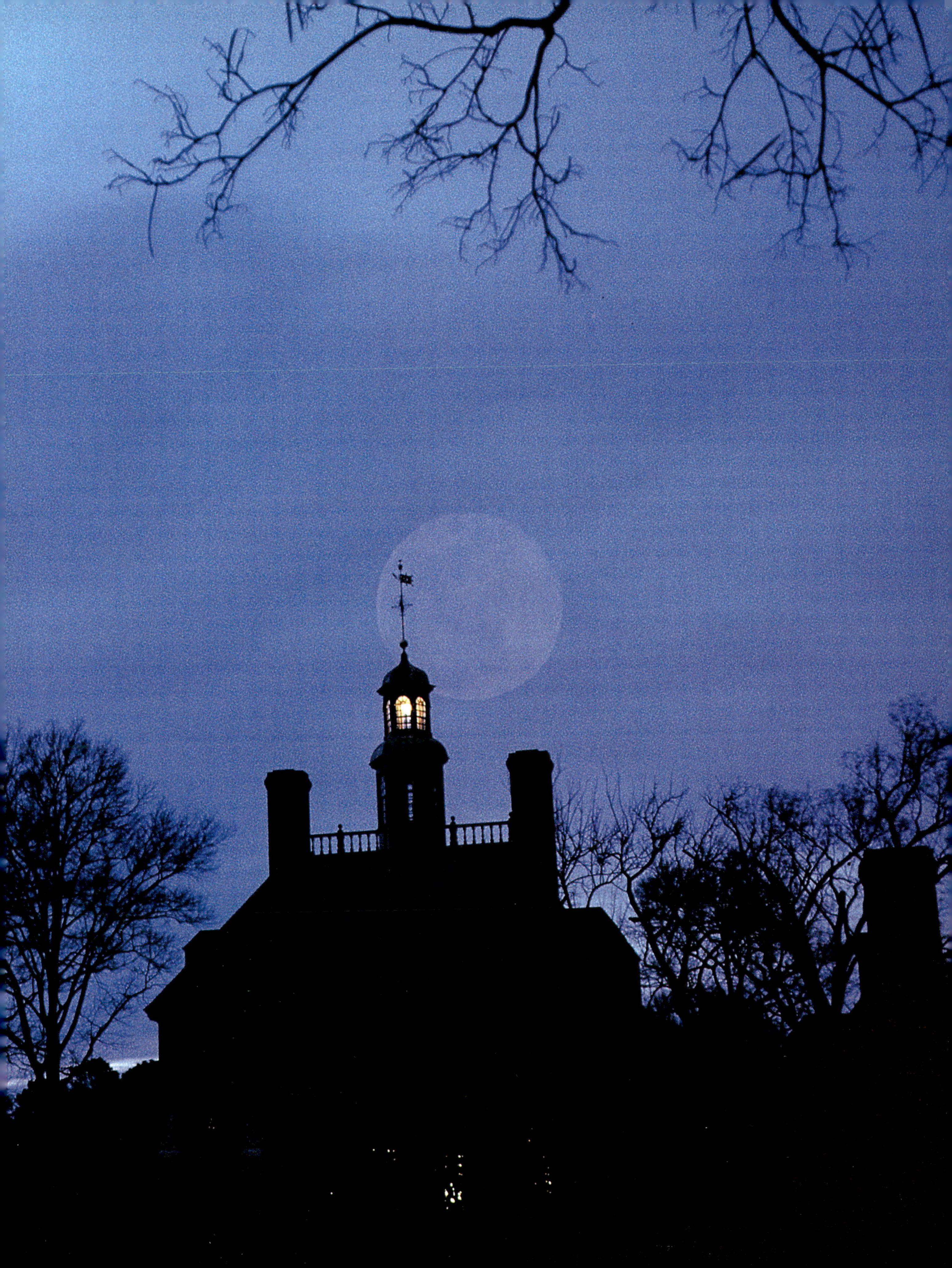

268 EPILOGUE

Epilogue

Marble statue of Lord Botetourt. Following its removal from the Capitol piazza, it stood in the college forecourt for the following one hundred and fifty years as a pleasant reminder of the man who foresaw such excellence for the institution that he so obviously cared for. It now graces the Swem Library. Courtesy, College of William and Mary.

The salutary effects of Lord Botetourt's interaction with Virginians continued to be noted and felt long after the state funeral. In the lengthy interlude between his death and the arrival from New York in September 1771 of the successor to the governor's post, John Murray, earl of Dunmore, colonists had numerous opportunities to recall the special qualities of virtue, diligence, and affability that Botetourt had personified. Even as the late governor's accounts were being called in and his debts settled, a remarkable example of his thoughtfulness and generosity to the colonists appeared. A large cast-iron warming machine or dutch stove that he had ordered from London in the spring of 1770 arrived in Williamsburg in early December in seven packing crates. Made by the same tradesman who had supplied the stoves that Botetourt had installed in the ballroom and supper room of the Palace, the new object was larger, more imposing, and clearly a presentation piece. Word was promptly received from the duke of Beaufort that he would honor his "most worthy and late friends intention" by approving payment for the stove so that it could be placed in the House of Burgesses. It was promptly installed in the legislative chamber, in a conspicuous place "at the upper End" near the Speaker's chair. It stayed in that location until 1780 when it was moved to the new chamber of delegates in Richmond, and has survived until the present day.[1]

Far more than a practical device for producing comfort, the stove was an imposing, highly ornate, and pointedly ceremonial object. Its three tiers of cast plates (the largest size available) were covered with modish decoration in the neoclassical style, the key surfaces containing the arms of the colony of Virginia in high relief and the figure of Justice with scales in her right hand, her left hand being placed on the Magna Charta which was open on the altar of liberty. To those who pondered this novel item, the connection with the stove in the Palace ballroom, a space resonant with royal association, was implicit. Thoughtful observers may also have linked the imagery to that in the large portrait of William Pitt which had arrived in Virginia from London in the preceding months, intended for a group of Westmoreland County gentry.[2] Botetourt's careful selection of the iconography for this ceremonial yet useful object destined for the colonial legislature was a masterful touch. The warming machine's inherent link with the emphatic royalty of the Palace ballroom, its more explicit association with Botetourt's stylish tastes, and its articulate symbols of liberty and justice must have made it, in its conspicuous location, a provocative object of contemplation for many of the elected representatives of the colonial people.

The public auction of Botetourt's belongings was held at the Palace in May 1771 for several days. Surviving accounts unfortunately specify only the purchasers and not the items they acquired, the sole exception being the horses that were bought for £200 by William Byrd III. Yet the list of purchasers is an impressive testimony to the dissemination of many of Botetourt's tangible possessions—and, therefore, an important measure of his tastes and values—through the ranks of Virginia society. The colonial authorities paid more than £300 for goods that were presumably destined to remain at the Palace for the use of succeeding governors. Other major buyers included the secretary of the colony, the treasurer, the Speaker, the attorney general, nine members of the Council, and eight colonels, all prominent members of Virginia gentry society with whom Botetourt had interacted. Individuals purchased as much as £575 worth of goods (William Nelson), or as little as a few shillings' worth. The gentry were not the only purchasers. Merchants, tradesmen, and tavern keepers also participated in the event. More than £3,000 worth of Botetourt's material possessions were thus dispersed, for use and for ornament, as keepsakes and souvenirs. Many of the items presumably continued to remind their new owners of the late governor and his remarkable qualities for several years to come.[3]

The trustees also received word from the duke of Beaufort that he wished to present to the colony the state coach and the state portraits of the king and queen hanging in the Palace ballroom for future governors' use. These conspicuously royal objects the Council accepted as a "genteel Memento of a dear, departed Friend." The duke also proceeded with his intention to erect a monument to his late uncle in the college chapel and corresponded with Robert Carter Nicholas, on behalf of the trustees, concerning details of its placement and measurements. The president and professors of the college "signified . . . their unanimous and warmest approbation," and Nicholas assured the duke that "Virginians will Be much pleased with this and every other Monument, that tends to perpetuate, amongst them, the Remembrance of a Governor they held in such high Estimation."[4]

At the first session of the assembly following the death of Lord Botetourt, held in July 1771, acting governor and president of the Council William Nelson publicly reminded the legislators of the late governor's many merits: "We were

Cast-iron warming machine or stove of grand triple-tier size, made in London in 1770 by Abraham Buzaglo on the commission of Lord Botetourt. It arrived in Williamsburg in the winter of 1770–1771 and was installed in the House of Burgesses in the Capitol. At upper left are the arms of the colony of Virginia. One of the two largest plates is embellished with the symbolic figure of Justice. The ornamentation, with its mix of late rococo and early neoclassical motifs, is highly modish. It was probably the earliest and undoubtedly the most elaborate item in this novel style to be seen in the colony. H: *(to top of third plate) 7′ 4″;* W: *(of lower section) 2′ 11″. On loan from the Commonwealth of Virginia to* CWF.

EPILOGUE 271

the frequent Witnesses of his Excellency's constant and uniform Exertion of every public and private Virtue, and had abundant Reason to be convinced that he made the real Happiness of this Colony an Object of his most ardent Wishes." The burgesses responded to Nelson immediately:

>Our deep Sense of the Loss this Country sustained by the Death of our late excellent and worthy Governor, the Right Honourable Lord *Botetourt*, cannot but excite in us all the Warmth of the most sincere Affection and Gratitude to his Memory, and we heartily lament, with your Honour, upon an Event so unfortunate to this Country.

>When we reflect on his Lordship's unremitted Zeal in promoting the Cause of Religion and Virtue; On that Dignity, tempered with so becoming and proper a Degree of Affability, with which he filled his exalted Station; when we recall to our Remembrance his Excellency's unwearied Diligence and Activity in Business, and his

Wax portrait of Lord Botetourt, modeled by Isaac Gossett in 1772–1773 from an original he had modeled from life in the mid-1760s. Overall height 7". Courtesy, Hill Carter, Shirley Plantation, Charles City County, Virginia.

uniform Exertion of every public and private Virtue, we have the strongest Conviction that he made the real Happiness of this Colony the Object of his most ardent Wishes: We should, therefore, think ourselves wanting in Duty to his Majesty, and in the Regard we owe to our Country, did we not seize this first Opportunity of publicly paying a just Tribute to so high a Character.[5]

Not content with grandiloquent statements, the burgesses then resolved:

That an elegant Statue of his late Excellency the Right Honourable *Norborne*, Baron de *Botetourt* be erected in Marble at the Public Expence, with proper Inscriptions, expressing the grateful Sense this House entertains of his Lordship's prudent and wise Administration, and their great Solicitude to perpetuate, as far as they are able, the Remembrance of those many public and social Virtues which adorned his illustrious Character. That the same be sent for to Great-Britain . . .[6]

News of this unusual display of sentiment on the part of the legislature (and its not insignificant cost) was quickly broadcast throughout the colony in the *Virginia Gazette* and dispatched to England by various correspondents. On only one previous occasion had the assembly gone so far as to propose the commission of a public statue, and that was of George III in 1766 after the repeal of the Stamp Act. Nothing had come of it. Whether the burgesses reminded each other during their discussion of the proposed Botetourt monument that they had quietly dropped the proposal for a statue of the king a few years previously is unknown. A marble statue rather than a slightly less prestigious memorial such as a full-length portrait could have been viewed by the court as an inconsiderate act, at least. In any event, the burgesses appropriated funds for the statue and delegated Nelson as chairman of a committee to procure it.[7]

Nelson turned for help on the critical matter of the choice of sculptor to his old friend John Norton, the London merchant. Norton consulted with the duke, who was flattered that the colonial assembly should have such genuinely high regard for his relative, then made a prudent decision by appointing Richard Hayward, an unexceptionable London sculptor with ties to the new style and to aristocratic patrons of Robert Adam. The duke provided further assistance by supplying the sculptor with a portrait of his late uncle—the only one "that has been taken within the last five and twenty or thirty years"—from which to model the likeness of the head of the statue. This portrait, a "Medal in Wax that is reckon'd tolerably like" made by "the famous" Isaac Gossett, gave Norton an idea for some subtle cultivation of key Virginia friendships. He promptly commissioned four replicas of the wax portrait from Gossett, which he dispatched to Virginia in the spring of 1772 along with Hayward's proposed design of the statue. The gifts of the "exceed'g good likeness[es] of L. Bottetourt" in wax were intended for the president of the Council, the Speaker, the treasurer, and Norton's son, Hatley, then living in Yorktown.[8] These delicate little memorials of the late governor were much admired in Williamsburg and probably reminded viewers of the set of thirteen waxes (almost certainly by the same modeler) that Botetourt had hung in the dining room of the Palace. Nicholas later wrote to Norton asking him to order several more replicas of the wax from Gossett for local "Gentlemen of [his] Acquaintance" who had expressed interest in acquiring one of their own, another instance of the dissemination of Botetourt's taste among the colonists. One of these waxes even hung later at Monticello, being listed in an inventory of the art collections there after 1809, by which time Jefferson was becoming increasingly Anglophobic. It hung between a bronze medal of Benjamin Franklin and a medal of the "infant America protected by Minerva from the lion." That object has since disappeared, but remarkably, in view of the wax's inherent fragility, another example has survived at a Carter family mansion in Virginia.[9]

Treasurer Nicholas and Speaker Randolph carefully examined Hayward's drawing of the proposed statue in Williamsburg in the late spring of 1772. They suggested changes to the wording of the inscriptions to be carved on the pedestal of the figure and commented on the decorative motifs surrounding the inscriptions. In conveying these opinions to Norton, Nicholas noted the impending arrival of the wax portraits which he eagerly anticipated: "I shall take the greatest Pleasure in looking at any thing that has even a Semblance of an Original, whose Memory is exceedingly dear to me; indeed it becomes more so almost every Day."[10] Such a sentimental recollection of the late governor may have been prompted by the difficulties that Virginians were experiencing at that moment with "their new *Scotch* Governor." Lord Dunmore had approached his office with such "Negligence and Disregard of [its] Duties," with such "haughty Airs" that the colonists had deputed "one of their Lawyers to remonstrate against this supercilious Behavior" in the spring of 1772. Dunmore realized his errors of judgment and changed his ways, to "the great Advantage of the important Colony he presides over. Thanks to the true *American* Spirit of Liberty." His behavior must have made Botetourt's diligence seem all the more praiseworthy.[11]

Authorization to proceed with the statue was sent to Norton by both Nicholas and Nelson, and by March 1773 the completed work was packed on board Norton's ship *Virginia*, accompanied by one of Hayward's masons to supervise the unloading and installation. By the following June the mason had completed his assignment "in a most expeditious and faithful Manner," erecting the statue on the piazza of the Capitol and placing round it the iron railings that the London participants in the commission had deemed appropriate. Its cost was substantial—between £750 and £1,000. "The Statue is universally admired," Nicholas wrote to Norton, even though "the likeness is not so striking as that of the Medallion."[12]

Standing in a highly public location, the only full-length marble figure in Williamsburg (probably in the entire colony), and the only memorial figure to a governor ever commissioned in the American colonies, the statue must have attracted much attention. Botetourt was represented in contemporary formal dress with a full cloak, in a formal stance that was, in fact, the mirror image of the king's pose in the state portrait hanging in the ballroom of the Palace, a resemblance that some sensitive observers must have noted and commented on. The five-foot-high pedestal contained the copious inscriptions surrounded by a virtual lexicon of neoclassical decorative motifs similar to those on the nearby warming machine, though finer and more developed. The front panel of the pedestal featured Botetourt's name, title, and coat of arms, while the rear panel displayed figures of Britannia and America, each holding an olive branch over an altar bearing the flame of liberty and the inscription CONCORDIA. One side panel contained the formal inscription:

> DEEPLY IMPRESS'D WITH THE WARMEST SENSE
> OF GRATITUDE FOR HIS EXCELLENCY THE
> RIGHT HONBLE LORD BOTETOURT'S PRUDENT
> AND WISE, ADMINISTRATION, AND THAT THE
> REMEMBRANCE OF THOSE MANY PUBLIC AND
> SOCIAL VIRTUES, WHICH SO EMINENTLY
> ADORN'D HIS ILLUSTRIOUS CHARACTER, MIGHT
> BE TRANSMITTED TO LATEST POSTERITY,
> THE GENERAL ASSEMBLY OF VIRGINIA
> ON THE XX OF JULY ANN; DOM; MDCCLXXI
> RESOLVED WITH ONE UNITED VOICE TO ERECT
> THIS STATUE TO HIS LORDSHIP'S MEMORY
>
> LET WISDOM AND JUSTICE PRESIDE IN ANY COUNTRY;
> THE PEOPLE WILL REJOICE AND MUST BE HAPPY.

The opposite side of the pedestal contained a more spirited and personal, though still grandiloquent, declamation:

> AMERICA, BEHOLD YOUR FRIEND
> WHO LEAVING HIS NATIVE COUNTRY
> DECLINED THOSE ADDITIONAL HONOURS WHICH
> WERE THERE IN STORE FOR HIM THAT
> HE MIGHT HEAL YOUR WOUNDS AND RESTORE
> TRANQUILITY AND HAPPINESS TO THIS
> EXTENSIVE CONTINENT; WITH WHAT ZEAL
> AND ANXIETY HE PURSUED THESE GLORIOUS
> OBJECTS, VIRGINIA, THUS BEARS HER
> GRATEFULL TESTAMONY.[13]

The statue was the object of sufficient popular interest that within weeks of its installation, Williamsburg milliner Margaret Hunter thought it commercially feasible to offer affordable mementos in the form of "Models of Lord Botetourt," which she advertised among a "Genteel" assortment of millinery and other goods. Almost certainly these were plaster miniatures derived from the marble statue, though perhaps they were profiles in a wax or glassy material, for seven months later the same shopkeeper offered "Busts of the late Lord Botetourt" among an assortment of millinery "in the newest taste."[14] A small print clearly derived from the wax was also issued about this time, a charming and affordable souvenir. These items are yet further evidence of the cultural influence of Botetourt on the colonial populace. The marble memorial was venerated to the extent that the state of Virginia paid for a periodic cleaning of it, at least through the middle of the Revolutionary War. It was "remarkable," declared one visitor to Williamsburg during the hostilities, that the statue was "not in the least defaced." In the latter years of the century the statue unfortunately became "défigurée," in the words of La Rochefoucauld-Lian-

Life-size statue of George Washington, modeled by Jean-Antoine Houdon between 1785 and 1788, carved in marble by 1791, and installed in the rotunda of the new state capitol in Richmond in 1796, where it remains. Courtesy, Commonwealth of Virginia. The Botetourt statue, and upper right, detail of the plinth of the statue showing its correct Adamesque ornamentation. Hayward had worked for Sir Nathaniel Curzon and with Robert Adam at Kedleston. Relief from the reverse of the plinth shows Britannia and an Indian queen exchanging olive boughs over the flaming altar of concord. Courtesy, College of William and Mary.

276 EPILOGUE

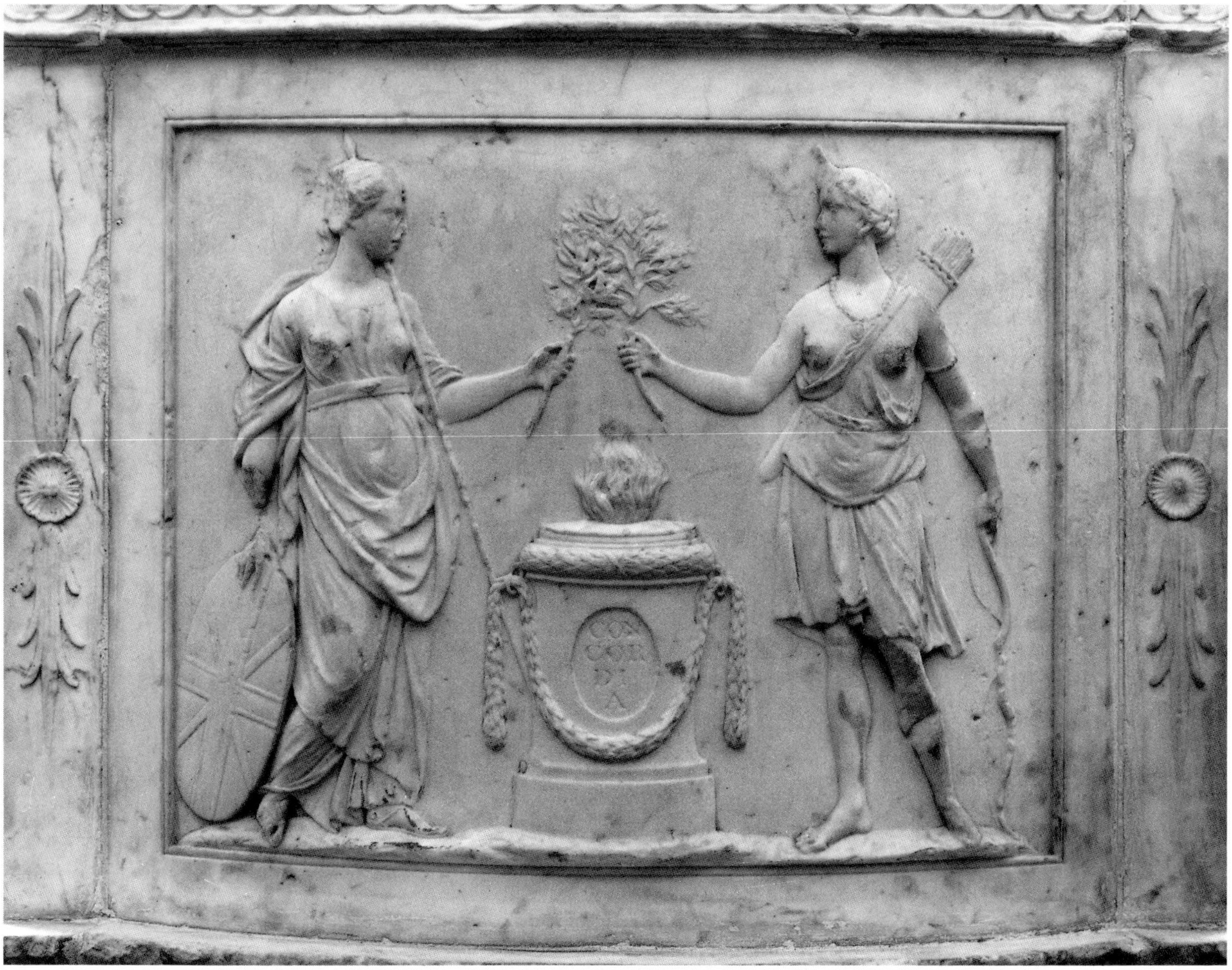
CON
COR
DI
A

court, but it was frequently noted in travelers' accounts of the former colonial capital, even meriting a watercolor sketch by Benjamin Latrobe. It was purchased and moved to the campus of the College of William and Mary in 1800 where it survives, the sole full-length statue of the colonial period to remain from the four known to have been erected in American colonial capitals.[15] Edmund Randolph later described it as "a statue not more admired for its exquisite workmanship than for being a memorial of a statesman more than great, because truly honest." By the end of the eighteenth century, however, it had probably been supplanted in the esteem of most Virginians by another extremely rare full-length marble figure of a beloved leader, a truly great work of art standing in the state capitol in Richmond, the statue of George Washington in contemporary clothing, his military equipment turned into a plowshare, his hand resting on fasces, the symbol of authority and justice, sculpted by Thomas Jefferson's personal selection for this important commission, the French artist, Jean-Antoine Houdon.[16]

Virginians' explicit admiration for Lord Botetourt and the actions that showed that their gratitude for his estimable example was more than conventional deference extended through much of the administration of his successor, Lord Dunmore. The colonists' assessments of Botetourt's many attributes and their responses to his untimely death were in private undoubtedly heartfelt and in public sincere and genuine. In the presence of a new chief executive who seemed by nature to be haughty and disdainful, the colonists did not hesitate to enunciate Botetourt's distinctive qualities. Foremost among them was virtue—public, social, and private. His "unremitted zeal in promoting the Cause of . . . Virtue," his "active and exemplary virtue," his "uniform Exertion of every public and private Virtue" made him truly admirable and praiseworthy. The late governor had personally and professionally set and followed high standards of upright behavior and correct deportment, above the reproach of self-interest or greed. In his life and in his conduct he had exemplified excellence and goodness. He had actively pursued and observed the cardinal qualities of a civilized man, the natural or moral virtues of wisdom, courage, temperance, and justice. An integrity and moral probity had informed his life, making him zealous for the truth in religion and for the good in worldly matters. His active and sincere observance of the established religion was particularly laudable. Goodness had combined in him with wisdom to produce prudence, which in turn had given proportion and direction to his energy and zeal. His inheritance, his responsibilities and public offices, and his virtue had coalesced in a noteworthy dignity, a grace and polish all the more remarkable for his not being haughty and distant but rather approachable and congenial. In his zeal for truth and goodness he had been diligent and in his pursuit of righteousness indefatigable. Through all these affirmations it is obvious that Virginians perceived him as an exemplar, the "compleat" gentleman who had clearly followed Christian precepts based on platonic ideals. "Virtue [is the] grand Fountain of publick Honour and Felicity," the Reverend William Stith had declared in Williamsburg in 1752, and the tone of the public resolutions and inscriptions echoed those sentiments almost a quarter of a century later.[17]

Above all, to those Virginia gentry who had made the key decisions on the wording of the public statements, as well as to those whose private opinions have survived, Botetourt had been a peacemaker: "America, behold your friend!" He had "presided" (not ruled) over Virginians with wisdom and justice and formed an unusual conjunction with them and with the "American spirit of liberty" to create a "dawning happiness." Healing wounds, restoring tranquillity, making the "real" happiness of Virginians his main goal—these beneficent aims or "glorious objects" had produced harmony again within the divisive family. Botetourt's energy, acumen, and fairness had actively revived Virginians' sense of "order," their self-esteem and happiness, which the recent divisions and conflicting opinions within the extended family had grievously damaged.

Throughout the public and private phrases recurred the words "America" and "happiness" alongside the descriptions of Botetourt's many virtues. America, "this extensive continent," was the maturing progeny within the imperial family, subject to delicate balances between established authority and new awareness. To many the progeny was coming of age, was realizing its own distinctive character, was ready to assume its rightful place in the natural hierarchy. They could not understand why the patriarch (the king, advised, of course, by his ministers) failed to comprehend his progeny's natural evolution toward maturity, its expectation of the rights and privileges that were a natural constituent of the family's heritage. Self-conscious of its new maturity the progeny undoubtedly was—it needed strong paternal encouragement that the king had withheld (probably because of malicious advice from his corrupt ministers) but that Botetourt had provided to the extent that colonists could ideally see themselves as an independent entity to stand beside Britannia sharing tokens of peace and reconciliation over the flames and altar of liberty. Indeed, Virginians believed that Botetourt had, in his speech to the assembly in 1769, pledged to do all he could in "establishing the American principle." Without that strong support, confusion or disorder reigned (in the opinion of so thoughtful, if tendentious, a member of the progeny as Landon Carter) because of the youthful instinct on the part of the less than fully mature colonists to squander rather than to husband their resources.[18]

"Happiness" resulted from the recognition by those in authority of this new maturity—this evolutionary step in the natural hierarchy—and their wise and judicious guidance of it through the uncertainties or confusions of youth to an adult sense of "order." Botetourt had provided that guidance and had set a praiseworthy example. "Happiness" implied the ability to make decisions and to act on them, rather than being kept dependent, abjectly like slaves. The late governor had perceived this even if, as an individual, he was not wholly empowered to bring it about, even if his goodness had not been able to overcome the "dirty tyrannic" designs of ministers in England. It was his realization, his wisdom, allied to inherent goodness and natural dignity that had so endeared him to the "people in America."

Botetourt's successor, by contrast, arrived (late) in Williamsburg heralded by the rumor that he was uninterested in his new post and by a reputation as "a Gamester, a Whoremaster and a Drunkard." Lord Dunmore was, furthermore, of Scottish ancestry which, for those Virginians who prided themselves on their English background, was a further condemnation. Even those colonists who refused to be influenced by such insinuations found his disdain of duty, his "negligence and disregard" for the business of his office impossible to accept and remonstrated.[19] Though the governor recanted and had become by late 1774 "as popular as a Scotsman can be amongst weak prejudiced people"—because of his stand on the opening and exploitation of western territory, his exercising the imperial muscle against the Shawnee Indians, and his bringing in for one year his attractive and popular consort—assessments of his governorship by Virginians contrasted sharply with their fulsome praise of Botetourt. "To external accomplishments he [Dunmore] pretended not and his manners and sentiments did not surpass substantial barbarism, a barbarism which was not palliated by a particle of native genius nor regulated by one ingredient of religion. His propensities were coarse and depraved." Thus Edmund Randolph compared Dunmore's signal lack of progress on the path from barbarity to civilized, virtuous man with Botetourt's grace and polish. In the fortuitous conjunction of Botetourt's integrity and sophistication with Virginians' newfound maturity, Randolph (like Landon Carter earlier) sensed the advent of a new golden age, but it had been dashed by Botetourt's premature death and the succession of an unpolished, irreligious barbarian. Instead of monuments, memorials, and souvenirs, Dunmore's administration merited such pungent epitaphs as "Oblivion would be the mildest fate his memory could find in American annals."[20]

Earlier in the century, Virginians had bridled at the proud men's contumely of Nicholson and Spotswood, but even amid all the bickering they had still absorbed the significant cultural contributions those unusual soldier-administrators had to make. The 1770s were a different era. Nobleman or not, Dunmore was perceived as arrogant and impatient, haughtily patronizing rather than affable. Underendowed with the tact and polish that made Botetourt so effective an administrator, Dunmore also seems to have been unable to realize that he was interacting with a group that was highly conscious of its new maturity, its capacity for unity (as evidenced in the responses to the Stamp Act and the Townshend Duties), and its status as "Americans." He was apparently insensitive to the current trend in Virginia to question openly traditional forms of deference. Dunmore evidently chose to overlook the portent at the time of his first ball at the Palace on the anniversary of the king's accession, only a month after his own inauguration, when the proprietor of the Raleigh Tavern (that unofficial house of assembly) announced in the *Virginia Gazette* that the tavern would be open with free liquor for those "who did not choose to attend at the Palace." Too much could have been made of that incident, but Dunmore's subsequent disdain for routine business did nothing to alleviate the rumors or to assuage his critics. A more thoughtful and sensitive man might have pondered on the reports and tangible evidence of his predecessor's abilities and successes and have used them as a guide. But, brusque and impatient as he was, Dunmore either failed to understand their implications or he ignored them. He lacked the "more than ordinary qualifications" to get Virginians to think again about the advantages of submission to the imperial will. Pursuing the goals that he did from 1772 to 1774 inevitably brought him into conflict with the colonists' increasing resentment of authoritarian ministries. Dunmore signally failed to read the growing political antagonism clearly until the situation became militaristic. By that time Virginians had judged him insensitive or indifferent to their concerns and their causes. Diplomacy failed after Dunmore deserted the Governor's Palace for the security of British naval vessels, and relations became irreconcilable when he made good his threat to free the slaves who joined his forces. In the eyes of the Virginia gentry that last act was unforgivable. Almost eighty years after Nicholson had designed and laid out the capital city Dunmore, the last representative of royal government, unceremoniously fled from it with a reputation for duplicity and boorishness and recriminations on most peoples' lips.[21]

Governors played a key role in the transference of political and cultural precepts and practices from the mother country to receptive colonists. Beyond the political influence they wielded through their office, they were a nodal point in the dissemination of English culture through their experience and their example. Even when their personal ambition or too individual an interpretation of their political responsibilities brought them into direct conflict with Virginians, there was still an evident cultural benefit to the colonists who interacted with these English gentlemen. Despite the personal altercations, for instance, between Nicholson, Spotswood, and the numerous Virginians who aspired to be, or prided themselves on being, "English gentlemen" too, there is ample evidence of those governors' enduring cultural influence on the expanding and increasingly affluent colony. But during the administrations of Fauquier and

Botetourt altercation moved to a significantly higher threshold. Ambition and aberration were then perceived by the colonists to be less personal characteristics than systemic ones. Yet even in the hostile atmosphere sparked by these profound political differences, the agents of the (imperial) system, Fauquier and Botetourt, were widely admired, even venerated. Their memories evoked glowing (and lasting) tributes to their personal qualities and prompted striking expressions of gratitude for the cultural contributions they had made to the colony and to individuals within it. The success of these governors' cultural interaction with Virginians elevated them above the political imbroglio and preserved their memories and their reputations from the bitter recriminations that the political divisions caused.

It was the gentry with whom the governors primarily interacted in Virginia, who modeled themselves on the English gentry paradigm, who comprised the "People of Fortune who [were] the pattern of all behaviour" in the colony, in whom most of the local power was concentrated, and who effectively ran the colony. And in the third quarter of the eighteenth century the gentry were in a state of disequilibrium. They were suffering in varying degrees from a crisis of confidence as their values were besieged and affronted on all sides. The great success of the evangelical religions in the colonies provoked in the adherents of the established church something of a siege mentality that was then splintered by internal dissension—the bitter and prolonged troubles of the Parsons' Cause and the arguments over the American episcopacy, particularly notable in Virginia in the decade before the Revolution. Fluctuations in the economy, in tobacco prices, and in crops caused recurrent uncertainty, and the planters' mounting debts with English merchants were a source of constant irritation or anxiety, depending on the prevailing economic mood and how insistently (or churlishly) the merchants pressed for repayment. Further disagreements with the merchants and the ministry over the colonial issuance of paper money exacerbated the economic insecurities, and the Speaker Robinson affair of 1766 produced a catastrophic blow to the Virginia "establishment." If these financial uncertainties were not enough, the increasing demand for luxuries only fueled the troubles. Social competition for luxury and other consumer goods was undeniable, and the goods themselves were seductive if not insidious. Unfortunately, luxuries were associated in the minds of moralists, who did not hesitate to speak out on the matter, with decadence—they were the harbingers of moral decay. "Pride and Luxury always find an Entrance in with Riches" admonished Landon Carter as he envisaged the dire consequences of the enfeebling trend.[22]

Inextricably related to this uneasy topic was the matter of slavery, an economic necessity in Virginia undoubtedly, but a factor in society that historically bred indolence, dependence, weakness, and a disturbingly brutal superiority in masters. Not only were the sheer numbers of slaves physically unsettling, but the institution itself was coming under widespread attack throughout the empire from religious and humanitarian groups. Such massive dependence on enslaved peoples as occurred in Virginia was not equated, without a certain logical hiatus, with those all-important notions of independence that provided many who had attained some degree of financial sufficiency with a notable measure of their self-esteem. To compound the unsettling effects of all of these shifting values and difficult questions, the traditional, hierarchical world of the Virginia planter was crumbling. Deference was openly questioned, if not assaulted, everywhere, within the family as well as without. For the older gentry the erosion of their authority was most clearly visible in the assertive attitudes of the electorate and the changing composition of political representation throughout the colony and was highlighted by the reactions to the Colonel Chiswell affair of 1766. When more coercive imperial policies began to issue from Whitehall after the conclusion of the Seven Years' War, apparently in defiance of the precedents that the colonists believed were established by custom if not by law, the disintegration of the familiar world of the Virginia gentry seemed to be assured.[23]

Into this climate of changing values, into this mood of defensiveness and disarray came Fauquier and Botetourt, who were models of that English gentlemanly role on which the Virginia gentry had endeavored to model themselves. Clearly, and most importantly, above the squabble of personal advancement and enrichment, they were not only friends to liberty, protectors of the constitution, and promoters of the colony's welfare (as James Horrocks wrote of Fauquier in 1763), but they were also men of virtue, enlightenment, and culture. In perceiving the psychological needs of the colonists for reinforcement, in acknowledging their maturity, in proving that they "loved Order and Justice," and in emphasizing, even exemplifying, the nature of the heritage that was the common patrimony of Englishmen and Virginians, they reassured the colonists that it was possible for Englishmen of position and (at least some) influence to uphold their birthrights and not seek to betray them.[24]

At a time when many of the gentry's basic values were shifting, sometimes subtly, sometimes jarringly, it was natural that they should reach for and focus on one of the great certainties of their existence—their past, their heritage. When the burgesses declared to Fauquier at the conclusion of the Seven Years' War that "Our Dependence upon Great Britain, we acknowledge and glory in, as our greatest Happiness and only Security," they had more in mind than the jubilation of victory and the satisfaction of Britain's increased power; they affirmed their belief in the fundamental values of British civilization. They might express the essence of these values as kingship or as the constitution. Until the eve of the Revolution, the king was heralded as the

284 EPILOGUE

The statue of the "great and good" Lord Botetourt. It shows the results of its long exposure to weather and the occasional exuberances of undergraduates. Courtesy, College of William and Mary.

foremost upholder and defender of the rights of the people: "There can be found in no Part of his Majesty's Dominion a warmer and more cordial Attachment to his sacred person and Government than prevails throughout the Continent of America," Robert Carter Nicholas wrote as late as 1774.[25] In regarding the monarch as the fixed and immutable guarantor of the rights of Britons—"the King can do no wrong"—the colonists were expressing their loyalty to the civilization that was their patrimony and, as Landon Carter pointed out in 1760, "Loyalty is the very Genius of the Country." The "pure British Constitution" was another phrase that colonists used to convey their perception of the crucial center of their heritage, "the most valuable Part of our Birthright as Englishmen," Richard Bland had declared at mid-century.[26]

At a time when so many of the colonists' values were shifting, it was reassuring to turn to formal, fundamental principles, to values that had been approved and codified by outstanding minds. These principles included the glorious political traditions of the English gentry, the constitution, and they included the cultural traditions, too. It was reassuring to turn to Georgian rules of taste that had been canonized by the finest minds in pattern books and in approved models and that were visible in the increasingly standardized forms and decorations that the "English system" produced in such quantities. The principles of Georgian proportion that underlay so many of the forms of contemporary architecture, furniture, and silver were based on classical precepts and prototypes that had been rediscovered, analyzed, and codified by some of the most brilliant English talents. These principles were solid, perdurable, and right—some even thought they were divine. It was a phenomenon of colonial culture in the third quarter of the eighteenth century that increasingly it subscribed to and depended on approved forms, on academic models, and on published patterns. This trend is discernible in architecture, both domestic and religious, furniture, and silver, all of the gentry level of quality. To cite one prototypical example, it was natural for the Truro vestry (a typical gentry-centered group), given the propensity of the period for approved form, to note that the altar, the centerpiece and focal point of their newly constructed church in Fairfax County, needed to be reconfigured so that it was absolutely "according to the proportions of Architecture . . . according to the true proportions of the Ionic order." Individual variation was unacceptable; what was important was that form follow established principle and be correct.[27]

To the colonists, Governors Fauquier and Botetourt personified the best elements of the English gentry tradition and culture. They embodied the principles of justice and virtue and epitomized the enviable sense of order and harmony that were among the ideals of the age. They were proper surrogates for the "patriot king," for the "sacred person and Government" of majesty. They were models of the form. Not only were they intelligent and diligent, politically sensitive to the needs of a people situated far from the imperial center who were subject to forces that the imperial authorities did not fully comprehend, but they were also humane, cultivated, civilized gentlemen. Their human impulses were marked by thoughtfulness, refined by virtue, and polished by elegance. They empathized with Virginians, moreover, had "their good at heart," and absorbed elements of their culture as well as liberally bestowing their own. Virginians thus dissociated them and their admirable values from the occasionally disagreeable actions required of them by their office and venerated them in word and deed. At a time of greatly heightened sensibilities, these governors came to symbolize the culture that Virginians did not wish to, or could not, reject.

In these chapters I have tried to show how particular things, or groups of things, in identifiable spaces can be the keys to open up for us worlds of behavior and belief. In the actions and attitudes that these things represent or reflect can be found premeditation, choice, and purpose. The things are not inert, they are powerful symbols of personal, social, and political values and motives. In the particular environment of the governor's residence, in the largest of Britain's American colonies in the decades prior to revolution and independence, these things show vividly how the king—the metaphor for the sovereign state—was the pinnacle of the social system based on the need of the weak to be protected by the powerful. The objects both embodied and glorified that power. As personal emissary of the king, the governor resided in the far distant provincial society, the instrument of the king's wishes and the chief intermediary between him and the people whose rights he protected. The governor embodied the personal and social virtues that the king epitomized and sought to improve and dignify the provincial group by his cultivated example, by his grace, and by his justice. The governor encouraged and facilitated the progress of the people toward civility and refinement, toward maturity. With thoughtful condescension the governor mingled in the provincial society, both imparting and absorbing values, the personal agent of a system of culture that had ancient roots and that was buoyant and alive. The cultural values—the refinement of mind, tastes, and manners—endured.

Appendix 1

AN INVENTORY OF THE PERSONAL ESTATE OF HIS EXCELLENCY LORD BOTETOURT BEGAN TO BE TAKEN THE 24th OF OCTOBER 1770.

Cash found in house £57:2:1½

In the front parlour

- 2 Leather Smoking Chairs
- 2 Card Tables, Mahogany
- 1 Walnut Writg Table
- 1 Couch Mahogony frame covered with checks
- 2 small looking Glass
- Fry Jefferson's Map of Virga
- Bowen's & Mitchell's Map of N. America.
- 1 pr Tongs, Shovel Poker Fender and hearth Broom
- 11 Chelsea China figures. 2 Venitian blinds

Standing furniture

- 34 Scripture Prints
- 2 Shades in Frames
- 2 Brass Branches
- 7 Mahogony Chairs
- 1 Iron Grate.
- Fry & Jefferson's Map in the Closet.—

In the Closet

- 1 old finear'd Beaureau
- 1 Mahogy Card Table
- 1 large black Ink stand
- 1 small Japan'd do
- 1 Green wax Taper & stand
- 1 Venetian blind
- 1 Glass Lanthern
- 16 Medn Passes.

In the Hall & Passage below

- 2 Mahy red damask Elbow chairs covered with checks
- 8 Chairs of the same
- 10 large globe lamps

Standing furniture

Arms & Colours. 2 looking Glasses—6 fine leather Buckets
- 1 step Ladder—1 step Ladder

Dining Room

- 2 leather smokg chairs
- 12 mahy chairs hair bottoms
- 1 large mahy ding table
- 1 smaller do
- 1 walnut writg table
- 1 mahogy plate warmer & 12 bottle stands
- 1 mahogy wine cooler
- 1 mahogy library table containg papers public & private
- 1 mahogy Desk, containg sundry papers private & public, one embroidd pocket book a miniature drawing, 1 Diamd mourng ring & a pair of Gold sleve buttons, pruning knife & a steel pencil. white wax taper & stand.
- 1 black Ink stand
- 13 wax portraits
- 1 Shovel, pair Tongs poker & Fender & hearth broom.
- 1 Mahog fire Screen
- 11 Chelsea china figures
- Henry's Map of Virga
- 1 Oval lookg Glass
- 3 Venitian blinds
- 1 East india fire lock.
- 1 small readg desk 1 large oyl Cloth at Mr Kids

Standing Furniture

- 1 pr brass Sconces.
- 1 Side Board wth Marble Slab

In the Bowfat

- 2 large enamd China bowls
- 2 lessr blue & white do
- 2 pr English china Candlesticks
- 56 pieces ornamental china
- 12 large cut water Glasses
- 12 small do
- 4 large cut glass tumblers
- 3 small do
- 28 cut wine glasses
- 4 strong beer glasses
- 1 Hock glass
- 1 { full round Box & 3 pieces of English Sweet Meats—part of a Box of Barbadoes Sweet Meats—part of a Box rock Sugar—part Box candid Lemon Peel, part of a Box of English Sweet Meats—4 dozen Oranges

Ball Room

- 3 large mahogy dining tables
- 1 large round walnut do
- 12 mahogy chairs hair bottoms
- 1 large dutch stove
- 3 glass lustres with 6 branches each & gauze covers
- 2 large paintings of the King & Queen gauze covers
- 2 Venetian blinds

Standing furniture

- 19 Leather Bottom Mahogony chairs
- 8 long stools
- 8 stockoe Brackets.
- 6 brass Branches.

Supper Room

- 1 large dutch Stove

Standing furniture

- 2 long walnut dining Tables
- 16 Walnut Leather bottom chairs
- A Glass Lustre wth 12 Branches

In the Porch

- 2 large deal Benches

Powder Room

- 1 Boot Jack
- 1 old pine table
- 2 Coppr coal scuttles
- 1 Wig block with Screw Stands
- 1 copper warmg pan
- 6 old japan candlesticks
- 1 Brass do
- 1 stone Cistern with brass cock
- 1 small wire cage
- 4 wooden do
- 2 japan bread baskets
- 4 Tin & wicker plate baskets
- 2 Fowling pieces
- 1 large & 1 small hair Sieve
- 4 round large glasses for candles
(A Parcel of old Glass Tho's Perquisite)

Standing furniture

- 2 Dressers

Little middle Room

- 2 oval mahogy tea boards brass hoops
- 1 Trivet, 1 Hanger, Cheese toaster.
- 1 Oak linnen press
- 1 Scollop'd claw tea table
- 1 Fender poker tongs & Shovel
- 1 hearth brush & pair bellows
- 1 old oak chest of Drawers
- 1 old umbrella
- 19 japanned Waiters
- 1 small wire bird cage
- 1 coppr boiler, 2 large tea kettles
- 2 japd plate baskets
- 5 Maps

Standing furniture

Chimney & 2 brass Sconces—
a Dresser & Monumental Piece to Thos Fairfax
an old Glass Lanthorn
- 1 pr Steps

Closet to the little Room

- 3 dutch lead boilers with heaters
- 1 do do tea kettle
- 4 do coffee pots & lamps
- 1 hand do mill
- 1 do do fix'd
- 2 Coppr coffee pots
- 3 chocolate pots with four mills
- 1 lime squeeser & stand
- 3 Sugar hatchets
- 1 large butter scoop
- 3 toasting forks

2 Sieves
2 Japan'd tea chests & canisters
4 jap^d sug^r tongs
1 large blue & white Tea pot
2 red china tea pots
6 bleu & white breakf^t cups & saucers
12 d^o small
6 d^o Coffee cups
1 d^o sug^r bason
1 d^o slop bason
1 d^o cream pot with top & stand
1 d^o tea jug with top & stand
1 d^o bread & butt^r plate
4 Staffordsh^e coffee pots
4 d^o tea pots
2 d^o q^t mugs
3 d^o p^t mugs
3 d^o cream pails & ladles
10 d^o fruit baskets & 14 dishes
2 d^o lip'd cream pots
7 d^o sug^r basons
2 d^o butt^r basons
29 d^o tea cups & 64 saucers
30 d^o coffee cups
8 d^o wash hand Basons
3 d^o q^t slop basons
7 d^o bowls
1 d^o pickle stand
7 d^o small breakf^t plates
16 d^o large d^o d^o
24 d^o soup plates
68 d^o shallow d^o
1 tin canister painted old
1 d^o funnel
1 wooden lemmon strainer
2 wicker plate baskets
1 Iron cork screw
5 tin canisters plain
1 wooden bowl
5 bottles arrack & 6 barbadoes Spirit

Pantry
1 Ticken couch, Mattrass boulster 3 blankets white quilt & red check covering
1 Library table with a Stool
1 Wash hand bason, bottle & stand
1 Mahog^y Beaureau. 1 small blk walnut Table
1 Chest of tools
1 small drying horse for linnen
1 small washing tub. 1 Fender, poker tongs and shovel. 1 toast^g fork, 1 hearth brush.
4 Meat & 2 Glass trays of Mahog^y
1 wire bird cage with balance weight
1 small copp^r tea kettle
2 Maps. 14 prints. 1 iron chest in closet next the fire & 2 braces of pocket pistols
1 cloath's brush

Standing furniture
1 Gilt looking Glass
3 paintings over the Door Map of New England

4 Leather Bottom Mahogony Chairs.
1 p^r old Money Scales

Pantry continued Closet
Broken pots of pickles
Vials of colour'd sugars
4 ½ Vials of Capilare

Physic closet contains a variety of Medicines, & a case of Instruments in Surgery
2 pair of Apothecaries scales.
2 Wire & 2 wooden cages
1 Shav^g pot, Bason & case of 6 Rasors
1 Stone. 1 Water jug.
1 Lanthern. 1 small tin funnel. Vinegar jug. part of a jug of Lamp, and part of a jug of sweet Oil.
40 bottles of Rum, & 2 of Virg^a Cyder.
4 d^o Burgundy. 24 of Madeira. Thread pins &c in library table draw
7 Setts of card counters in 3 damask silk bags.
6 doz. Mould tallow candles. 5 doz dipp'd d^o
7 d^o & 3 spermaciti d^o 7 large wax d^o
1 d^o & 10 large night lamps wax
5 d^o of small d^o
5 d^o & 7 wax tapers
4 Mahog^y & 1 walnut knife box
3 doz. strong black handle knives & forks little us'd
31 black handle knives & 35 forks pretty much worn.
34 buck handle knives & 35 forks
5 Green handle carving knives & forks &
1 d^o white china handle.
3 Staffordshire Mugs & Bason
3 large japann'd Jacks 1 half pint mug.
1 small dutch oven.
13 japann'd hand waiters
2 japann'd wine Cisterns
1 Lignumvitæ stand with 4 Casters
2 small Cedar tubs. Omit^d

Plate, in the Pantry.
27 Dishes.
60 Plates
1 Turin & Ladle
8 Butt^r boats
1 Bread basket
1 Large tea board
4 Salvers
1 Large waiter
6 small hand d^o
6 Large Salts & Shovels
1 Wash bason
1 Chamber pot
2 Half pint cans
1 large Lamp
1 small d^o
6 small Salts & Spoons
4 carving Spoons

3 Soup Spoons
1 Stand with 3 Casters & 2 Cruets
3 Large Casters
16 Candlesticks. 1 flat Candlestick
2 Taper candlesticks
3 Pr Snuffers with 1 Stand & 1 Pan.
8 French plate Candlesticks
3 d^o Soop Ladles
1 Silver fish Slice
1 d^o Lemon Strainer
1 d^o writing stand Bell & 2 Casters
2 d^o Branches with 4 Nozzles
2 d^o d^o with 2 d^o
2 d^o d^o with 1 d^o
2 Nozzles & pans
6 Gold cups
18 Silver bottle Labells
3 d^o punch Ladles
8 Skewers
1 Wine strainer
30 Tea spoons
2 p^r Sug^r tongs
2 Cream pots
12 Card counters
54 large Knives & 55 forks with 3 prongs
2 black Shagreen Cases contaning each
1 Doz large Knives & 1 doz. forks & 1 doz large table Spoons.
1 Case containing 1 doz Knives & 1 doz Forks with China Handles.
1 small Shagrine Case cont^g 1 doz Desert Gilt Silver handled Knives; 1 doz Silver Forks & 1 doz Spoons
1 d^o cont^g 1 doz Silver handled desert Knives & Forks & 1 doz Spoons.
1 d^o cont^g eleven Silver handled desert Knives—
1 Doz large table Spoons with Lady Hereford's Arms
1 ½ doz large table Spoons engraved with a Unicorn
1 Sheffield ware tea Kitchen
2 p^r ornamental steel Snuffers & stands.
1 d^o steel spring Snuffers
3 d^o common
1 large mettal oval dish.

Glass in Pantry
5 cut glass wine decanters
16 plain qu^t d^o
12 quart water d^o
4 pint d^o
4 long beer glasses
6 flower'd small ones.
3 large cut beer glasses
28 d^o plain d^o
6 flowered wine glass & 13 Hock glasses
1 large tumbler & 10 small ones
3 Canns
6 double flint cut Salts
35 plain wine Glasses
30 flowered d^o
4 glass cruets 2 small flowered d^o

40 cut wash hand glasses & 47 Saucers
8 ground stoppers
3 p^r nut crackers 1 iron cork screw.

Memorandum

Mr Treasurer rec'd in charge
His Lordship's watch Seal & Key
1 Dia^d Hat button
2 Gold & 1 steel seals.
1 Diam^d ring for Lady Winne
2 p^r of gold buttons.
 a Lady's picture in Minature
 a Diam^d stock buckle
 a p^r of Stone Shoe & Knee buckles
 a Silver stock buckle (Marshman has it)
1 red leather case cont^g a p^r of stone Shoe & Knee buckles.
1 Shagreen d^o of paste Shoe buckles
1 d^o of 8 chaced Spoons & sug^r tongs.
1 p^r cut Steel Shoe Buckles; 2 p^r plain Shoe & knee Buckles—2 morocco Pocket Books
3 Cases Surveyor's Instruments, 2 Snuff Boxes
1 small Ivory Box, 1 tooth pick Case
 Sundries packt in a small Mahogony Case—

Passage up Stairs

6 large globe glass Lamps
1 Spider table
12 Mahog^y hair bottom chairs

Standing furniture

3 large Roman Catholick Pictures
1 glass Lanthorn
1 large looking Glass. 1 p^r Steps in the Passage Closet—

Library

1 Shovel, tongs, poker fender, hearth broom
 Map of N. & S. America.
20 Prints
1 blue venetian blind.
1 Wilton carpet
 Books as Pr Catalogue with the 2 Curtains which cover them
1 Japann'd ink stand, 1 green wax taper with japann'd stand.

Study—Standing furniture

1 Looking Glass.
1 check Curtain & Rod
1 Writing Table

Closet off the Passage up stairs

12 doz packs playing Cards.
30 packs of Message Cards
11 Buckling Combs 5 tooth brushes.
 a parcel of tooth picks 6 Tobacco pipes.
19 Doz & 5 Short wax tapers contain'd in 9 papers.
3 doz. long wax candles.
5 d^o & 2 middling wax tapers.
6 d^o large wax lusters
14 d^o smaller size d^o
 A parcel of broken wax candles
11 bunches of green wax tapers
14 d^o white d^o
24 lb of chocolate.
 A Canister of about 4 ½ lb of Hyson Tea
2 large & 1 small canister

Chamber over the Dining Room

1 Oak bedst^d with Chints curtains & valens bed, bolster a p^r of pillows 2 Matrasses 2 blankets & white quilt 1 bed carpet
1 Mahog^y night table.
8 Green bamboo chairs with check'd Cushions
1 Mahog^y cloaths press.
 A green hammer cloth laced with gold
 A p^r of Pistols with furniture housing gold laced.
5 small Swords. & some of his Lordsh's wearing apparel.
1 Mahog^y Desk, empty.
1 painted chimney board.
1 Iron Grate, Shovel, tongs poker, fender & hearth broom.
2 p^r green stuf window Curtains & rods
1 Japann'd Ink stand, white taper & stand.
1 old Mahog^y dress^g table.

Standing furniture

2 looking Glass with black Frames & 2 glass Sconces
2 outer Window Screens
10 Prints in Frames in the Closet
 one looking Glass wth painted Frame

In the Closet

 small look^g Glass Mahog. frame
 small Mahog. table with leaves.
 Wash bason & Mahog. Stand compleat
1 large deal toilet table.

Chamber over the front Parlour

1 Oak bedst^d with a Suit of white callico Curtains & valens, bed, 2 mattrasses, bolster, p^r of pillos & white Virg^a cloth counterpane, & carpet.
4 Green Bamboo chairs with check cushions
1 Cloaths press Mahog^y
1 Mahog. chest of draws
1 small walnut table
1 Chimney board, Grate, Shovel, tongs poker fender & hearth broom
1 Wash Bason with Mahog. stand compleat.
1 Japann'd ink stand. 1 white taper & stand.

Standing furniture

1 looking Glass. 14 Prints

Middle Room

1 Large Chimney Glass gilt carv'd frame & 4 Gilded brackets
3 Suits of Window curtains
1 Desk & book case with glass doors empty.
2 Mahog^y cloaths presses with apparel, 2 Snuff boxes 1 small ivory box & the Seal of the Colony.
8 Crimson damask chairs with red check covers
1 small arm d^o
1 large easy arm chair
1 d^o Mahog. Table.
2 small d^o end d^o
1 Wash Bason Mahog. stand compleat
1 Chim^y board. Grate, fender, shovel, tongs poker and hearth brush.

Standing furniture

2 long looking Glasses with red gilded frames
1 large Glass on the Side of the Room with carved gilt frame
 Glass Lustre with six Branches

His Lordship's Bed chamber

 a Gold Watch, and Walking Cane
1 Mahog. Bedst^d 2 Matrasses, 1 Bolster 2 pillows 2 blankets 1 white quilt & Bedstead in 3^d Store Room
 Chintz & green sattin furniture & 1 bed carpet
1 Mahog. night table with close stool pan & chamber pot
1 Wash bason & Mahog. stand compleat with a dressing Glass.
1 large Walnut chest of draws contain^g his Lod^p's Linnen, Gloves, Stock^{gs} &c
3 Seal[s]kin cases of surveyor's Instruments &c. 1 Shagreen case contain^g 8 chas'd Silver tea spoons & 1 p^r of tongs. 1 d^o a pair of paste buckles 1 red leather case a p^r of stone shoe & knee buckles. 2 Morrocco Asses Skin Pocket books of Memorandums
1 Deal box 1 diam^d stock buckle 1 p^r of stone shoe & knee buckles 1 dia^d Hatt buckle 2 gold Seals 1 Steel d^o
3 Gold loops & 3 gold hat buttons
5 parcels of silver livery hat lace with loops & buttons.
1 p^r of gold buttons.
6 Sets of mourn^g shoe & knee buckles
5 p^r of sleeve buttons, mourn^g
2 p^r of gild'd buckles.
3 gilded stock buckles.
2 Sets of New steel Shoe & Knee buckles. 1 p^r cut steel Shoe Buckles. p^r of old d^o
5 Mourn^g Stock buckles
1 silver stock buckle
3 steel breeches buckles
1 handsome toothpick case.

1 small chest of draws some stocking & caps.
8 yellow bottom chairs & two stools of walnut. Grate, fender, Shovel, poker, tongs & hearth broom.
1 Japan ink stand & taper with stand.
1 Mohg^y dress^g table.

Standing furniture
One Chimney looking Glass
a Shade—
a Stand of Shelves

In the Store Rooms. 1st
10 Loaves treble refined Sugar.
22 d^o double.
27 d^o single—
 3/4 of a Chest of Congo Tea. 21 ½^lb Turkey Coffee 22 ½ w^t India d^o
6 ^lb Cannister of Congo tea
4 Jars of Raisins.
 a broken Case of different Sorts of Spices
 a Box of Corks. a Box of Tar.
1 large Chest; 3 plate Boxes & a leather plate Case
1 old Leather Trunk with Papers said to belong to the late Govr Fauquier.
1 old traveling Trunk. 1 small empty deal Box—
1 old traveling Leather Trunk—
6 empty deal Boxes.
26 p^r plain Negroes Shoes.
32 hair Sifters of different Sorts
11 gauze d^o—
5 tin Funnels. 1 Muffin Toaster—1 toast^g Fork—1 Wine Crane—3 Egg Strainers
2 large & 4 small Graters—1 wooden rolling Pin
3 Soup & 1 doz table Pewter Spoons
3 butter Scoups—7 paint Brushes
6 small & 10 large wooden Spoons
4 tin fish strainers—5 Iron tin'd Ladles—2 tin sauce Pans—32 balls Pack thread—2 plate Baskets—
20 large Lamps with Irons & tin Covers
3 black Japan Cans—2 tin pepper Boxes—4 tin Candle Sticks—
50 ^lb of Starch—3 tin Cullendars—
1 broken paper pearl Barley—2 d^o white mackaroons—2 d^o yellow d^o—1 broken paper Bag of Morells—1 d^o Truffles—
1 d^o Gensing 1 d^o Snake Root—3 Cannisters flour of mustard—2 Powder Machins—1 paper green Grass—
1 broken paper of ston blue—28^lb powder'd blue—6^lb sweet Almonds
6 ^lb d^o in Shells—a large Paper of Sarsaparilla—2 Boxes Bristol Soap
20 Cakes Soap in another Box—
2 ½^lb Bees wax—26^lb common hair Powder—27^lb best d^o—5 Carpet Brooms—

3 Hearth d^o—6 doz cain brooms. 2 d^o whisks—3 iron dust Pans—2 coal d^o & Mops.—16 hair dust brushes—two Bottle Brushes—3 wooden Lemon Strainers—13 plate Brushes—7 hearth Stones—3 quart Bottles Wine—2 pints strong waters not full, 1 small Cruet & 3 phials
2 cloaths Brushes—6 shoe Brushes—
10 dry rubing brush Clamps—8 flat clamp brushes—
1 p^s Holland—3 p^s Sheeting
11 3/4 y^ds coarse Irish Linen—
17 y^ds d^o 12 y^ds d^o—13 ½ y^ds Huccoback
10 Y^ds holland sheeting—2 Y^ds worsted gauze—1 p^s Morees—1 p^s fine Damask Napkining—21 damask breakfast Cloths—2 p^s Oznabrigs
37 y^ds Oznabrigs—76 y^ds & ¼ d^o
4 p^s checkt Handkerchiefs—
7 Checkt Handkerchiefs—
8 ¼ y^ds brown Holland—5 ½ y^ds printed Cotton—1 Woman's Cotton Gown
5 small remnants of white Flannel.
1 p^s crimson Shalloon—1 p^s br. Fustian
18 3/4 y^ds d^o—8 ½ y^ds crimson Shag.
21 ¼ y^ds crimson Cloth & a remnant of Livery Lace—17 y^ds light coll^d d^o
9 y^ds d^o for great Coats—25 ¼ y^ds d^o
16 ¼ d^o 7 y^ds deep green Cloth
8 y^ds light col^d d^o—20 ½ y^ds blue plains
8 ¼ green d^o—2 p^s & 18 3/4 y^ds Russia Drab—1 Bale unopen'd cont^g 3 p^s green & 3 p^s blue plains—
11 Men's Castor Hats—23 p^r coarse thread Hose—23 p^r worsted d^o
25 p^r Yarn d^o—4 Parcels of worsted & 3 of Metal Buttons—1 paper & a piece of Pins—19 pieces of white Tape—
2 p^s green ferriting—6 cut pieces of Ribband of diff^t Sorts—37 hks Mohair of different Sorts—7 Bunches of Cruels
32 hks & a Ball of Silk—12 Bunches Thread—1 doz thread Laces—
16 papers of thread & 2 doz thread waist coat Buttons—2 small brown Linen bags—a dble body Girth—1 horn handled carving Knife & 2 forks—5 p^r spring steel Snuffers—3 pocket Knives
2 p^r Scissars wth Chagrine Cases—2 dble Pen Knives—2 Steel pencils—6 wooden Pencils—a chagrine Case of Raisors &^c
11 Oyster Knives—1 Hone & 1 Raisor Strap
18 empty Knife & Raisor Sheaths—
7 quire Cartridge & a Ream of common brown Paper—a Parcel of Shells—
2 Bow & 12 Arrows—a Pott of bitter almond Powder—4 old Cartouch Boxes
2 Bayonets—1 brass Fender—1 very small mahogony Box—

2^d Store Room—
33 large Beer Glasses. 8 Cruetts—
6 q^t Water Decanters—2 pint d^o—

1 qu^t & 1 p^t wine Decanter—
45 wine Glasses—28 Hock d^o—29 wash hand glasses wth 21 Saucers—2 large glass Shades—4 glass Covers—28 Japan'd tea boards & waiters—2 Japan'd Cheese Trays—2 flat green Candlesticks Snuffers & Extinguishers—9 Japan'd Candle Extinguishers—6 p^r common Snuffers—
3 green taper Candlesticks—one broke—
14 copper paste moulds—1 plate Basket
6 wooden Moulds—1 Dutch Metal Tea Kitchen—2 Tea kettles 1 copper Boiler
3 Dutch metal Coffee Pots—
11 tin Night Candlesticks & 1 tinder Box
1 tin Still—12 pewter Water Plates
3 doz pewter plates—12 blue & white China Tea Cups & 12 Saucers—6 d^o Coffee Cups—1 d^o milk pot—2 Slop Basons & 1 Sugar Dish—10 white d^o coffee Cups & 10 Saucers—2 cream Pales & Ladles—1 Slop Bason & Sugar Dish—2 white stone Tea pots—
Staffordshire Ware
7 Coffee Pots—3 Tea pots—3 Sugar Basons
9 butter Basons—12 Tea Cups & 24 Saucers
39 soup Plates—133 shallow d^o—15 breakfast plates—36 smaller d^o 2 flower Pots—
1 wash Bason & 1 Bowl—17 water Bottles
15 lip Jugs—6 round d^o—6 Lamps—
3 stone close stool Pans—

Standing furniture
1 long Box with a Parcel of broken Sconces—

3^d Store Room
100 feet fly Lattice—100 feet Bird Cage d^o
1 Chimney Board belonging to the dining Room—1 Canvass Portmantua—1 gr[torn] Coat bag—2 Curtain Rods—4 Window Blinds—4 Leather Portmantuas—1 p^r Saddle Bags—2 Leather Straps—3 wooden Curtain Frames—a long Box of Gilt bordering intended for the supper Room. Donn's Map of Bristol—1 Box Bermuda Coral—1 Chinese Temple set with Shell[torn] part of a bag of black Lead—an old Box with a little whiting in it—3 Kegs with small Quantities of Colours—2 spare Branches &^c belonging to the Lustre in the Ball Room—3 doz brass branches unopen'd a Paper of Prussian Blue—2 ½ doz small Pullies—6 brass Branches for Globe Lamps
1 Bunch brass large curtain Rings & 2 Bunches of small—a paper white Studds

a parcel of Nails with brass Heads & small Tacks—a parcel of white Tacks—an empty deal Box—3 Mahogony Waiters

Standing furniture

6 spring Blinds—4 Billiard Tacks—parts of a Bedstead—1 brass Sconce
a Parcel of old Iron

4th Store Room—

60 flint glass Bottles for preserving Insects—2 Remnants of Rush Matting

In the Passage up Stairs

4 large Chests & 2 Trunks—4 wooden Bird Cages—

Standing furniture

4 very old black Leather Chairs

In a Closet

3 blue Moreen Window Curtains belonging to the dining Room—1 blue baise d° for Supper Room—4 pr Blankets—
1st Chest contg a Parcel of Maps & Prints—
2d 2 green Damask Curtains—Oznabrigs intended to paste the Paper on in the Supper Room.
3d 2 Venitian Suits of Gauze Curtains—4 Chex Covers for the Smoking Chairs—a Remnant of Silk & 1 d° blue worsted Line—
4th 4 Remnants of Carpiting—

Garrett Room over his Lordships bed Chamber

2 Mahogany field Bed steads wth red Che[x] Curtains—2 feather Beds—2 Mattrasses
3 Bolsters 1 Pillow—3 Blankets—
2 Quilts—1 Oak Chest of Draws
1 old red Table; Wash Bason—[illeg] Stand & Bottle—1 small Mahogy sta—[illeg]
1 Fender—Donn's map of Bri[stol]

Standing furniture

1 looking Glass with Gilt Frame
Stand of Shelves—

in a Closet

8 long green Cushions for Stools in the Ball Room—
Supper Room Carpet—Dining Room d°
Front Parlour d° Middle Room on second floor d°—4 Remants of old Matting—large Sand bag for supper Room—

Room over the Study

1 old oak Desk—19 old Prints—1 old red Table—1 Bedstead; Mattrass, bolster 2 Blankets—1 red & white flower'd Quilt—1 suit blue & white Linen Curtains—2 old wire Bird Cages—

Garrett Room over Front Parlour

[No entries here.]

Cellars

in the Passage 6 Casks strong & 6 d° small Beers—unopen'd
1 Barrel of Cranberries
1 Hogshead Molasses Beer
2 empty Hhds—2 powdering Tubbs

Standing furniture

Wooden Horses—1 Rope

small beer Cellar

1 empty Carboy; 7 Iron Hoops—1 empty cask—2 Bushel Cask of Split Pease

the Passage

[No entries here.]

Rum Cellar

1 Hhd Rum & abt ⅓.2 brass Cocks. 2 earthen pans—1 stooper—

Stone Cellar

abt 11 doz Hotwell water. 4 doz gallipots english moist sweet Meats—2 potts Virga sweet Meats.—a box & paper of twisted glass & frost—3 entire & 5 broken Potts of sweet meats—part of a pot of pickled mangoes. 1 whole & 1 broken pot of Tamarin
4 entire pots of Walnuts. 2 full Jars of Currants—3 full Boxes of Sperma Caeti Candles—11 Bottles of Capers—3 d° Olives
2 d° anniseed Water 1 d° english Ginn
1 Whole Box mould tallow Candles 1 pr of d° 1 pr dipt d° a Parcel of old Boxes

Cooks Cellar

9 Bottles gooseberries; 3 Bottles dble distill Vinegar—⅓ of a Cask Currants—⅔ of Cask brown Sugar—half Cask Rice—
3 parts of three Pots Lard—

Binn Cellar

N° 1. contains
   17 doz & 4 bottles old Hock—Ben. Kenton
   8 ½ doz d° Mr Fauquier
2. 7 ½ doz: —Madeira—
3. 37 doz & 7 Madeira—
4. 9 doz & 3 Bottles English small Beer
5. 37 ½ doz. strong beer very fine
6. 14 Bottles old Madeira.
7. 9 doz & 4 Bottles of Porter
8. 27 doz & 5 Bottles Claret—
9. 11 doz & 2 Bottles Burgandy
10. 18 ½ doz red Port—
11. 12 doz & 2 Bottles Madeira.

In the Vault

6 doz & 8 Bottles of Claret—
2 doz 1 Bottle white Wine—

16 Bottles Arrack—
4 doz malmsay Madeira—Mr Fauquier
11 doz peach Brandy—2 Bottles Honey
6 Bottles old Claret—3 Bottles Champaine
14 Bottles old Spirits—6 Bottles fine Arrack
11 Bottles french Brandy—3 doz & 4 Bottles old Spirits

Cyder Cellar

1 Barrel peach Brandy—1 Brass Cocke in an old Cask—3 doz & 5 Bottles english Cyder—2 gr. & half Virga Cyder

Strong beer Cellar

3 doz 9 Bottles damaged Ale—
1 Hhd of Rum; abt half a Hhd of Spirits
24 doz & 8 Bottles of strong Beer

Madeira & Cheese Store

6 Pipes of Madeira Wine—
   small Part of a Hogshead of Molasses
   a Case wth about forty Pound of Hops
2 dble Gloster Cheeses—37 single d° a small Box of Corks & Bottle Stopper

Standing Furniture

in the Wine Store
1 Step Ladder & old Chair
3 Horses—2 Large Shelves

The Out-Houses

1 State Coach, & Harness for a pair of Horses
1 Post Chaise, with Harness compleat for four Horses & a Leather Trunk in the Store Room
1 Post Coach with Harness compleat for Six Horses & two draw Boxes (in the Store Room)
1 Green park Chair
1 Setter and Grease Box
1 New Waggon & a Cart, with Harness for Six Horses with Leather Collars & Iron Traces
1 Roller, 1 plough, & 1 pair of Harrows, & 1 Bush Frame, and 1 plough paddle
5 Grey Coach Horses, & 1 Mare
2 Grey Saddle Horses, & 1 Mare, & 1 Bay Filly
4 Cows, 1 Bull, 5 Stears, and 3 Calves
2 Barrow pigs, & 1 Boar at the Attorneys
37 Head of Sheep
19 Weathers
1 Stack of Hay
1 Large Wheel Barrow
23 Bushels of Indian Corn
47 ½ Bushels of Oats
23 Bushels of English Wheat

Standing furniture

1 Handmill—

Negroes
Hannah
Sally & her Child Billy
Doll
Dan
Matt Piper
Cesar
Phillis

Poultry
20 Turkeys
18 Geese
9 Ducks

Garden Implements
2 Weeding Knifes, 2 Asparagus Knifes
4 Wheel Barrows, 4 p^r Garden Shears, 1 Saw
4 Watering pots, 1 Small Hatchet, 3 Baskets
5 Spades, 5 Rakes, 4 Large Drawing Howes
3 Small Howes, 3 Dutch Howes, 1 Tarping Spade, 1 Edging Knife, 1 Dung Fork
1 Small Gravel Rake, 1 Dock Iron
2 Scythes, 22 Large Bell Glasses, 1 Small Bell Glass, 21 Dozen of Earthen Flower pots
1 Wire Sieve, 1 Cap Glass

Standing furniture
12 leaden & six stone flower Potts
1 Rolling Stone—Tubbs & orange Tree & Roller for the Tubbs—

Park Implements
4 Madocks, 1 Grubbing Hoe, 1 Small Sledge, 4 Maddocks pick Axes, 2 Felling Axes, 1 Broad Axe, 1 Small D^o 1 Faggot Bill, 7 Iron Wedges, 2 Mauls with Iron Hoops, 1 Broad Howe, 8 Spades, 1 Cross Cut Sawe, 4 Short Forks, 1 pitching Fork, 3 Scythes, 6 Mawls, a parcel of Wooden Rakes, 1 Line, 1 Logger, 1 Hand Saw, 1 Drawing Knife, 2 Augures, a 14 Round Ladder, a 25 D^o 1 Waggon Rope, 4 Casks with Clover & Rhye Grass Seeds, 2 Calf Muzzles, 1 Thistle paddle, 1 plank of Cherry Tree, 1 Hay Cutting Knife, 7 paddlocks, 6 wheel Barrows, a parcel of Old Lumber 1 Turkey Coop—

Coachman's Room & Closet Adjoyning
—In Deal Case
6 Horse Sheets, 6 Fillet Cloaths, 3 White Rubbers, 6 Rollers, 4 Saddle Cloaths, 2 Inside Brushes, 6 Horse Brushes, 5 Water Brushes, 3 Oyl Brushes, 1 Hard Brush,
1 Brass Brush, 5 Main Combs & Spunges
2 p^r of Stirrup Irons, 2 Spunges, 1 Green Cover for the post Coach

—In Post Coach Trunk
8 Horse Nets, Oyl Cloath Cover to Trunk

—In Large Deal Case
2 Oyl Cloath Portmanteau Cases, 2 Horse Muzzles, 17 Rack Reins, 3 Black Stirrup Leathers, 4 Black Straps, 3 Hempen Halters,
4 Currey Combs, 1 Card & Spunge for ye Horses Mains, 2 p^r of Hobbles, 1 Girt, 6 Horse Collers new, 6 D^o used, 12 Coller Reins, 14 ½ Sheets of Scowring paper, 2 Coach Horse Whips, 1 Phaeton D^o (2 Corn Sieves in ye Stable)
1 Field Mahogany Bedstead, 2 Mattrasses, 1 Bolster, 3 Blankets
1 Red and White Flowered Quilt with Red Check Curtains, 1 Old Oak Table, 1 Walnut Writing Desk, 4 Old Green Bottom Chairs,
1 Swing Looking Glass, 2 Iron Dogs, with Brass Nobs, 1 Poker, 1 p^r Tongs, 1 Hair Broom, 1 Boot Jack—

Groom's Room & Closet Adjoyning
1 Field Mahogany Bedstead, 2 Mattrasses, 1 Bolster, 3 Blankets,
1 Old Red and White Flowered Quilt, with Red check Curtains, 2 Old pine Tables, 2 Chamber pots,
1 Close Stool,
3 Silver Stitched new Saddles, with Saddle Cloaths, 1 plain Saddle & Cloath, 1 New Livery Saddle with Furniture, 2 Old Livery Saddles with Furniture, 1 Old plain Saddle,
6 New Snaffle Bridles, 2 New pelham Bit Bridles, with polished Bits, 1 New D^o with Gold Bosses, and polished Bit, 1 D^o almost New with cased Bit,
1 Snaffle D^o with cased Bit, 1 Furniture Bridle with Gold Bosses and Blue Badson, 4 New White Rubbers, 6 Horse Sheets almost New, 4 New Fillet Cloaths, 4 New Saddle pannels, 4 New Rollers,
2 D^o a little Worn, 5 New Horse Nets, 1 New Red Saddle Cloath with white Binding, 1 White D^o with Green Binding, 3 Old Furniture Saddle Cloaths,
1 New Breast plate to a Saddle, 3 New Heads & Reins to Furniture Bridles, 7 p^r new Stirrup Leathers, 1 p^r D^o used
2 Watering Bridles
1 New Running Martingale, 5 New Cruppers, 3 Old D^o 2 p^r Old Girts, 15 p^r New Single Girts, 6 p^r New Double D^o 3 New Surcingles, 3 Old Saddle pannels,

2 New Mail pillions and Straps, 2 New Horse Collars, Old Horse Collars, 6 New Rack Reins, 6 New Hempen Halters, 1 p^r New Stirrup Irons and Leathers, 1 New Crupper, 2 New powder Flasks, 1 p^r Holsters almost new, 3 New thin Skins, 1 New Furniture pad, 12 Brass Saddle Buttons and Staples, 1 New Currey Comb, 1 p^r of polished Stirrup Irons, 3 p^r Silver Mounted Horse pistols, 4 New Horse Joggs, 1 New Furniture Whip
1 Boot Jack (1 Half Bushel, 1 Iron Sieve, 1 Old Cask in Granary) Laundry
5 Flat Irons, 2 Box Irons, with one Heater to each,
2 Iron Stands, 1 p^r of Tongs, 1 Large Boyling Copper,
1 Long Stool, 2 pine Tables, 1 Linnen Horse, 1 Mangle,
1 Large Iron pot, 1 Brass Skillet, 2 Linnen Baskets,
3 Washing Tubs, 2 pails, 1 piggin, 4 Mangle Cloaths,
2 Ironing Cloaths, 1 Wooden Funnel, 1 Hair Sieve,
3 Rensing Tubs (⅓ part of a Barrel of Lamp Oyl, a small Quantity of Tar in ye Cellar adjoyning to the Laundry)

Dairy
5 Tin pans, 5 Earthen pans, 1 Small Churn, 1 pail
1 piggin, 1 Small Brass Kettle, 1 Tin D^o
1 Large Double Turkey Coop—

Small Room adjoyning to Poultry House
1 Old Mattrass, 2 Old Blankets

Gardiner's Room
1 Small Field Bedstead, Feather Bed, Mattrass, Bolster, pillow, 3 Blankets, 1 Red and White flower'd Quilt, with Green and White Cotton Curtains, 1 Old pine Table, 1 Old Red D^o 2 Old Iron Dogs, Fender, Tongs and Shovel.—

Servant's Hall
2 Old Iron Dogs, 1 poker—2 Old pine Tables, 2 Mahogany Waiters, 2 Black Cans

Out Houses belonging to the Kitchen
Larder
2 Barrells pickled Tripe, 1 Whole Kitt of Salmon,
1 piece of D^o 1 Jar of Virginia Mangoes, 1 Jar of Candid Lemmon, 1 piece of Hogs Lard, 1 piece of Jar of pickled Anchovies, about ⅓ of Firkin of Butter, 2 Neat's Tongues,

1 Cake of Tallow, part of a Carboy of Vinaigre, 6 Ropes of Onions. A parcel of broken Staff^e ware.
1 large wooden Tray. 5 empty Cags

Smoke House.
a Barrel & 2 Tubs of soft soap
133 pieces of Bacon. 4 large powdering tubs

In the Cole house is about 1000 Bushels of Sea Coal by conjecture—

In the Salt house is 6 whole Sacks of Salt & a piece. 9 pieces of Tubs Pots & Kitchen Stuff. an empty fish Barrel.

Charcoal house about 40 bush^{ls} to appearance & 2 Wooden bushel Meas^e and some lumber

Scullery
2 Wash^g tubs. 6 water pails
3 Iron pots. 1 p^r Iron Dogs.
1 p^r of Iron spit racks
6 Spits. 1 Coffee & 1 Chestnut roaster. 1 Iron frying pan. 1 old tin candle box. 1 chop^g board.
1 Stand for candle moulds.
2 Wooden Trays. 1 small stone jug
1 old sieve. 1 Iron Oven peel
1 old wooden Chair. 1 old pick^g pot. 1 old jelly stand. 1 old plate rack. 1 Ax.

Kitchen
1 large meat Jack & Appurtanences.
1 Dutch Oven. 1 Salamander. 1 p^r Bellows
1 Skimer & 1 flesh fork. 2 Gridirons
2 Iron Trivets. 1 poker & Tongs.
1 large boil^g copp^r 1 Box iron & a heater.
1 old wooden chair. 1 large Fire Screen.
1 blue Salt box. 1 Marble Mortar.
5 Stone jarrs empty. 1 large Glass Lanthern
1 half bushel hand basket.
2 Iron meat cleavers. 21 Pewter Dishes & 15 plates. 1 pewter fish Strainer.
12 White stone Scollop & 5 Tea Canisters
2 round coffee canisters. 1 parcel of Hartshorn Shav^{gs} & 1 d^o Ising Glass.
1 small & 1 large Sieve. 1 Case of 18 Lard^g Needles. 16 pewter ice Moulds
16 Earthen sweet meat pots
2 pair steak tongs.
3 Wooden roll^g pins 1 knife & fork.
1 Coffee mill fix'd. 4 doz. cop^r Moulds.
3 pewter Ice moulds. 9 doz. & 9 Tin moulds of different forms. 2 paste brushes. 5 paste markers. 2 small iron stands
1 old 8 day clock. 26 pewter cand^e moulds
8 old hair Sieves. 1 p^r of 2 lb copp^r—scales & weights. 1 old pewter dish.
1 small flower keg. 1 hand Dinner Bell. 1 stone jarr candied orange peel.
1 small Gauze Sieve.

2 Tin cullenders.
21 Cop^r Stew pans & 24 Covers.
4 d^o Soup pots & covers
1 d^o Alamode pot & cover
1 d^o preser^g pot & d^o
1 d^o small fish kettle & cover
5 d^o Sauce pans & d^o
1 d^o dripp^g pan
1 d^o fish Strainer.
1 Bell mettle pestle & morter
2 chop^g knives
2 round cop^r paste pans & 2 oval tin d^o
4 Iron bird Spits
3 d^o Soup ladles 1 Iron bast^g ladle
1 Tin ventilator 1 d^o soup horse
1 d^o Skimmer 3 Funnels.
4 large tin graters 4 tin maples bisket pans. 1 large tin flat candlestick.
21 tin meat covers. 2 large pewter water dishes
3 cop^r chafing dishes

Glass
21 Glass Salvers
1 cut glass pirimid & frame compleat
1 plain d^o with 14 pails
5 flat plates. 3 look^g glass frames.
4 Scollopt plates
21 glass flower stands 4 green d^o
2 round cut glass cream basons covers & dishes
2 d^o oval d^o & 2 d^o
4 Scollopt plates.
3 d^o sweet meat glasses for a change
67 Orgeat glasses.
46 plain flint jelly & Silibub glasses
5 butt^r dishes & covers.
50 cut jelly & Silibub glasses
39 plain square jelly d^o
87 Jelly & silibub d^o of different sorts
16 Tart pans glass. 8 flat sweet meat pans.
3 common sweet meat mid^g glass.
41 pieces of common desert glasses
39 d^o of best cut—d^o d^o
a small quantity of Izing glass.

Linnen
26 Pillow cases
2 p^r very large fine Sheets
17 p^r lesser fine d^o
18 ½ p^r Servants d^o
4 Damask long Dinner table cloths
6 Doz. Napkins to D^o
4 Damask long table Cloths
3 ½ doz. Napkins to d^o
4 long Diaper table cloths
4 Middle Cloths to d^o
5 doz. Napkins to d^o
2 long Damask table cloths
4 doz. Napkins to d^o
1 large Damask table cloth
1 Middle cloth to d^o
1 doz. Napkins to d^o

6 Fine damask table cloths
6 doz. Napkins to d^o
2 Damask table cloths
2 doz Napkins to d^o
30 Dinner table cloths & 5 doz odd Napkins
36 Breakfast cloths
12 Servants table cloths
2 ½ doz fine diaper tea Napkins
35 Damask d^o
3 doz. fine diaper Towels
27 Huckaback d^o
64 Brown Rubbers
5 Round Towels
2 Coarse dresser cloths.

Cook's Bed Chamber
1 Field bedst^d 2 Matrasses 3 blankets 1 Quilt 1 Bolster & pillow, Red check Curtains.
1 Round Mahog^y Table with leaves.
1 d^o d^o Tea d^o
1 Green easy Chair with green cover^g & Cushion
1 Arm chair leather bottom.
6 Mahog^y Chairs Hair bottoms
1 Walnut Desk.
3 p^r red check'd window Curtains.
2 pokers 1 Fender, Tongs Shovel & hearth brush 1 dust pan. hang^g trivet
1 Copp^r Tea kettle
15 Prints. 2 Tea pots 3 cups & Saucers
1 Sug^r dish & 2 bottles of Staffordshire ware
2 black jappann'd Canns.
7 Canisters. 1 Sieve. 1 Basket.
6 Artificial flowers.
1 glass tumbler.

Servant's Hall
67 Staffords. round Dishes
64 d^o oval d^o
23 d^o pudd^g d^o 1 Sallad Dish.
10 soup plates
11 shallow d^o
6 large & 4 small breakfast plates
6 round & 6 oval fish strainers
4 Turins & covers. 5 Sauce boats
4 Egg Cups.

Celler
14 Gross of empty bottles.

Garret over the front Parlour
1 Field bedst^d feather bed, Matrass bolster pillow 1 blanket 1 Quilt red checks Curt^s
1 Mahog^y night table. 1 Mah. Desk.
1 pewter bed pan. 1 claw fire screen
1 small black walnut table
1 Grate, fender poker tongs & Shovel
1 Wash hand bason & stand compleat
1 old red japann'd table.
1 japann'd Ink Stand.

A CATALOGUE OF Yᵉ BOOKS IN LIBRARY

nº of Volumes

[Books on shelf 1]

1 {
- 3 Clarendon's History of the Rebellion
- 2 Postlethwayt's Dictionary
- 2 Johnson's Dictionary
- 7 Statues at Large
- 2 Anderson on Commerce
- 3 Plinius Harduini
- 2 Miller's Gardener's Dictionary
- 1 Virginia Laws
- 1 Laws of Virginia
- 2 Ralegs History of the World
- 1 Virginia Laws—
- 1 Pamphlet Military Devotion
- 1 Byron's Narrative—
- 1 Ode to Shakespear
- 1 Journal of H. Burgesses—
- 1 Seat of the late War—
- 1 Map North America
- 1 Kerkead—
- 1 Ignorant Philosopher—
- A parcel of Pamphlets & old Magazines—
- 1 Atlas—3 Books of Prints & Drawings in paste board
- 1 red Letter Case—
}

[Books on Shelf 2]

2 {
- 1 Conquest of Mexico
- 1 Jacobs Law Dictionary
- 4 Bacon's Works
- 3 Lockes Works
- Acts of George the second begining in the 15 yʳ of His Reign, ending the 30th
- 1 Coopers Dictionary
- 2 Traps Virgil
- 1 Ansons Voyage
- 1 Journal of the House of Burgesses
- 3 Minutes of the Lord from Janʸ 1765 to May 1768
- 1 Universal Dictionary of the marine
- 1 Map of Virginia
}

[Books on Shelf 3]

3 {
- 6 Hanmers Shakespeare
- 1 Carter's Epictetus
- 6 Popes Illiad
- 5 Popes Odyssey. 2 Vols Goldsmith's Roman History—
- 4 Smollets His. of England
- 9 Ciceronis Opera Oliveti
- 3 Robert's His: of Charles the 5th 1ˢᵗ Vol. missing
- 3 Blackstones Commentaries 2ⁿᵈ Dᵒ 1 & 3ᵈ dᵒ lent out & not returned
- 2 L'Esprit des Loix
- 6 Humes His: of England—all missing—E.R. dᵒ
- 1 Observations on the Statutes
- 1 Plays
- 1 Prussian Exercise
}

[Books on Shelf 4]

4 {
- 1 Hainsworths Dictionary
- 1 Dictionare de Boyer
- 1 Caesar Auden dorpii
- 1 Boyers Dictionary
- 1 Littletons dᵒ
- 26 Statutes at Large 24ᵗʰ dᵒ
- 20 Universal History
- 1 Bible & 1 Prayer Book
- 1 Diseases of the Army
- 1 Stat. Will. & M. Coll.—
- 1 Virgᵃ Laws abridg'd
- 1 Johnson's Dictionary—dᵒ
- 2 Knox's historical Journal.
}

[Books on Shelf 5]

5 {
- 1 Stiths His: of Virginia
- 1 Essays on Husbandry
- 1 Cordens His of Canada
- 1 Postlethayt's System
- 1 Pounal on the Colonies
- 4 Sherlocks Sermons
- 8 Oeuvres de Voltaire
- 2 Leland's Demosthenes—
- 9 Popes Works
- 1 Camp Discipline
- 4 Smollet's Continuation
- 4 Atterbury's Sermons
- 2 Douglass's North America
- 2 European Settlements
- 1 Military Essay
- 1 Bailey's Dictionary
- 1 Meiges Dᵒ
- 1 Boyers Dᵒ Abridged
- 6 Tom Jones
- 9 Letter's de Maintenon
- 6 L'Ami de Hommes
- Sherlock's 3ʳᵈ Volume not his Lordship's
- 1 Discourse of Trade
}

[Books on Shelf 6]

6 {
- 6 Treatise on Ventilators
- 1 Telemaque
- 3 L'Esprit de la Lique
- 6 Memoirs de Maintenon
- 1 Belisaire
- 2 Adventures of Jos. Andrews 1 missing only one
- 1 Spinkes Devotion
- 8 Swift's Works
- 2 His: of the 5 Indian Nations
- 0 Select Plays T & 1 T.6
- 9 Dᵒ C 2ᵈ Mr Stark
- 8 Oeuvres de Moliere 1,2,Dᵒ
- 4 Fool of Quality
- 2 Antoninus's Meditations
- 1 Milton's Paradise lost
- Court & City Register for 1768 dᵒ 1769 & 1770
- Virginia Almanack dᵒ
- Flora Virginica
}

Books doubtful to whom they belong

- 3 Books of Journals—sent to Mr Wythe Attorney
- 1 Flora Virginica—said to come from Mr Clayton—
- 3ᵈ Vol of Rapins History—
- 3 Vol's Sherlock's Sermons said to be in the House when my Lord came—
- 1 Book of engross'd Letters—retᵈ to the Office—

WEARING APPAREL

In Chamber over Dining Room

- 1 Blue Cloth Frock wᵗʰ white Lining
- 2 Blue Frocks, & 2 Waistcoats
- 2 Pʳ Leather Breeches, 5 Pʳ Black Silk Dᵒ
- 3 Pʳ Black Velvet Dᵒ 1 Pʳ of white Cloth Dᵒ
- 1 Pʳ White Velvet Dᵒ 1 White Sattin Under Waistcoat
- 1 Crimson Silk Under Waistcoat
- 1 White watered silk Embroidered Waistcoat
- 1 Thickset Frock, 1 Brown Doyley Dᵒ
- 1 Fustian Frock & Waistcoat, 3 White Silk Waistcoats
- 1 Old Brown, & 1 Old Blue Great Coat
- 2 White Cloth Waistcoats, 1 Old Scarlet Dᵒ Gold Laced
- 1 Blue Silk Dᵒ, 2 Blue Great coats, 1 Scarlet Cloak
- 4 Green Bays Wrappers—

In the Middle Room

- 1 Compleat suit of pale Crimson Cut Velvet
- 1 Dᵒ wᵗʰ Gold Buttons, deep coloured Dᵒ
- 1 Dᵒ of White Cloth, and White Silk Waistcoat, laced with Silver,
- 1 Dᵒ Gold Tissue, 1 Dᵒ of a Larger Pattern
- 5 Black, and 1 White Hats
- 1 Suit of Mourning with Weepers
- 1 Mourning Frock and Waistcoat
- 1 Raven Grey Dᵒ—and Dᵒ
- 2 Full Suits of Black Cloth
- 1 Full trimmed Suit of Crimson Cloth
- 1 Dᵒ of Scarlet, 1 Blue Cloth Coat full trimmed
- 1 Brown Rateen Frock, 1 Scarlet Dᵒ Waistcoat,
- 1 Scarlet Rateen Coat and Waistcoat full trimmed,
- 1 Scarlet Gold Laced Frock
- 2 Gold Laced Buff Waistcoats, 1 Pʳ Buff Breeches
- 1 Camblet Sea Cloak, lined with Green Baize
- 1 Bed Gown and Night Cap
- 2 Pʳ of Flannel Drawers, 1 Dᵒ Under Waistcoat,
- 2 Cotton Under Waistcoats, 5 Linnen Dᵒ
- 3 Pʳ Linnen Drawers, 11 Pʳ of Cotton Dᵒ

Arrived since the taking the foregoing Inventory,
- 1 Scarlet Gold Laced Frock,
- 1 blue plain D⁰
- 6 Pʳ of Cotton Drawers,

His Lordship's Bed Chamber
- 56 Ruffled Shirts, 6 plain D⁰
- 51 Cambrick Stocks, 2 Doz Suits of Laced Ruffles,
- 1 Pʳ Mourning Ruffles, 37 Cambrick Handkerchiefs,
- 5 Sword-knots in Ban Boxes, 1 Small Gilt case of Phyals, 3 ½ Yᵈˢ of Cambrick, 5 New and 1 Old pʳ of Kidd Gloves, 1 New Silk Wig Bag, 2 Remnants of Black Crape, 6 Black Silk Cockades,
- 15 Pʳ of Wash Leather & Doe Skin Gloves,
- 1 Pʳ of Yellow Kidd D⁰, 1 Black Silk Stock,
- 1 Black Silk Cravet, 11 Pʳ Cambrick Weepers,
- 1 purple Sprig in a Cockle Shell
- 26 Silk Handkerchiefs, 6 Pʳ New Black Worsted Stockings
- 6 Pʳ of White D⁰ 6 Pʳ Brown Thread D⁰ 1 Pʳ White [D⁰]
- 10 Pʳ of Black Worsted D⁰, 1 Pʳ Black Worsted Gauze [D⁰]
- 20 Pʳ plain White Worsted D⁰, 6 Pʳ Ribbed D⁰
- 9 Pʳ White Worsted Gauze D⁰, 10 Pʳ Brown Thread [D⁰]
- 1 Pʳ of Boot D⁰—28 Pʳ White Silk D⁰
- 18 Pʳ Black Silk D⁰ 30 Pʳ White Cotton D⁰
- 4 Pʳ Leggings, 2 Cravets, 2 Single Caps,
- 23 Cambrick and Linnen Caps, 16 Flannel D⁰
- 3 Pʳ New Shoes, 1 Pʳ pumps D⁰
- 20 Pʳ Shoes worn, 8 Pʳ pumps D⁰
- 5 Pʳ Slippers, 4 Pʳ Boots D⁰, 2 Pʳ lased Spurs
- 5 Wigs worn, 1 New D⁰, 2 Flesh Brushes,
- 1 Whisk, 1 Cloaths Brush, 3 Wig Stands

THINGS TO BE SENT TO ENGLAND

In My Lords Bed chamber
Gold Watch and Walking Cane
Three seal skin Cases of surveyors Instruments
  one Shagreen Case contᵍ Eight Chas'd Silver Tea Spoons and one pair of Tongs, one Pair of Paste buckles
one red Leather Case a pair of Stone Shoe and Knee Buckles, two Morrocco Asses Skin Pocket Books of Memorandums, one Diamond Stock buckle
one Pair of Stone Shoe & Knee Buckles
one Diamond Hatt Buckle, two Gold Seals, one Steel Seal, one Pair of Gold Buttons, two setts of New steel shoe & Knee Buckles, one Pair of cutt steel shoe & Knee Buckles, one Handsome Tooth Pick Case,

In Dining Room
The Public & Private Papers and other Things contain'd in the Library Table and Mahogany Desk, to be put in the Most convenient of the Two & be sent carefully to England the thirteen Wax Portraits, The East India Firelock

In Chamber over Dining Room
The Pistols with furniture & five small Swords

In Middle Room
Two Snuff Boxes one Small Ivory Box

In Store Room
One Piece of Fine Damask Napkining
All the Maps and all the Books
All the Plate in General. & Knives Forks and Spoons—
All the China
All the Table & House Linen
Three Pipes of Madeira to be fill'd & Well Cas'd
None of the Staffordshire Ware to Come.

Botetourt Papers, Virginia State Library and Archives, Richmond.

Appendix 2

INVENTORY OF GOODS AND EFFECTS BELONGING TO THE ESTATE OF THE HONBLE FRANCIS FAUQUIER ESQUIRE DECEASED TAKEN AT WILLIAMSBURG VIRGINIA.

		Currency
4	Hearth Broms	0: 8: 0
20	Scrubing Brushes 3 of which Dry Rubbers	3: 0: 0
4	Hair Brushes	0: 4: 0
4	House Broms	0: 8: 0
16	Hair Ditto	0:16: 0
6	Horse Brushes and 2 Curry Combs	0:12: 0
2	Cloths Brushes	0: 4: 0
5	Mopps	0: 7: 6
6	Bottle Brushes	0: 3: 0
16	Cakes of Old Soap	0:16: 0
1	Paper Bag of Gingsang Harts Horn & Ising Glass	0: 5: 0
68	lbs of Coffee	3: 8: 0
11	Loaves dble refined Sugar	5:10: 0
3	Loaves Single Refined Sugar	1: 5: 0
12	Bottles Spirits	0:10: 0
3	Coal Shovels	0: 5: 0
3	Wooden Punch Strainers & 3 Wooden Spoons	0: 1: 3
4	Boxes Spermaceti Candles 170 lb Loose 3 doz & five Do 8 178 lb a 2/6	22: 5: 0
2	Papers and 1 doz loose white wax Candles 15 Lb a 3/	2: 5: 0
2	Funnells 1 Tinder Box 2 Cake Baskets	0: 6: 0
16	½ lbs Almonds with 2 Stone Jarrs a 1/3	1: 0:7½
1	Copper Coal Skuttle	1: 0: 0
1	Copper Cistern	1:10: 0
1	New Copper Tea Kettle	0:15: 0
3	Old Tea Kettles	0:10: 0
2	Chafing Dishes	0:10: 0
3	Papers Starch 12 lbs a 1/3	0:15: 0
9	Sifters 8 Searches 10/ 1 Night Lanthorn 2/6	0:12: 6
1	Cannister fine Hyson Tea 26/	
3	Ditto of Green Tea a 12/6 }	3: 3: 6
6	large Lanthorn Glasses	6: 0: 0
1	large Glass Pyramid	15: 0: 0
14	Water Glasses	0:12: 0
55	Wine Glasses at 10/ per Dozen	2: 5: 0
22	Tart Pans (Glass)	0:10: 0
5	Champn and 4 Beer Glasses	0:10: 0
15	Decanters	2: 5: 0
8	Crewets	0: 5: 0
2	Mustard Potts	0: 2: 6
2	Blue and Gilt Small Crewets	0: 5: 0
59	Syllabub Glasses	1:10: 0
53	Jelly Glasses	1: 6: 0

16	Unsorted Syllabub Glasses	0: 5: 0
1	Fine Grate with 2 Setts of Shovels &c	4:15: 0
10	White Delph Wash Basons	0: 5: 0
6	Chamber Potts	0: 5: 0
2	Small Pyramids	6: 0: 0
2	pr. old Billows	0: 5: 0
1	Milk Strainer	0: 1: 0
23	Salver Glasses	6: 0: 0
13	Enameled China Dishes	8: 0: 0
31	Enameled Plates	2:10: 0
3	Blue and white China Dishes	0:15: 0
3	doz and 8 Oblong China Dishes	5:10: 0
2	large Round China Dishes	0:15: 0
8	Blue and white Dishes	1: 4: 0
1	large Soup Dish	0: 7: 6
25	Soup Plates	1: 5: 0
8	Half pint Bowls	0: 8: 0
6	Pint Bowls	0:10: 0
20	½ Dozen Blue and White Plates	12: 6: 0
10	Bowls of different Sizes	10: 0: 0
6	Butter Boats	1: 0: 0
6	China Salts	0: 6: 0
2	flowered long Dishes	0:10: 0
16	pieces Ornamental China	8: 0: 0
24	Ditto for Cabinets	3: 0: 0
3	flower Pots	0: 1: 6
2	Turenes with Dishes	3: 0: 0
2	China Jarrs	0:10: 0
28	pieces Ribbed China	5: 0: 0
39	pieces Nankeen China for Tea	5: 0: 0
1	Spider Table	0: 5: 0
10	pieces white China	0:10: 0
34	pieces Coloured China	1: 0: 0
2	Enamelled Sugar Dishes	1: 0: 0
5	Blue and white Sugar Dishes	0: 7: 6
22	Coffee Cups	0:10: 0
25	Saucers	0:15: 0
19	Cups	0:10: 0
6	Brown Tea pots	0:15: 0
1	Brown China Tea pot	1: 0: 0
1	Brown Coffee Pot	0: 5: 0
1	Brown Milk Pot 2 Brown Sugar Dishes	0: 3: 0
18	Hair Bottom Chairs	18: 0: 0
1	Walnut Desk	3: 0: 0
1	Shovel, Tongs, Fender Andiron & Poker	1: 0: 0
1	Japan Tea Board	0:15: 0
1	Bird Case	0:10: 0
1	large Round Tea Table	1: 0: 0
1	Scolloped Ditto Ditto	1: 0: 0
1	Dressing Table	1:10: 0
1	Small Chest of Drawers	2: 0: 0
1	Bed Stead	0:15: 0
1	Dressing Glass	0:15: 0
1	Mahogany Table	0: 7: 6
1	Walnut Desk	4: 0: 0
1	Bed Bedstead & three Blankets Mattress and Furnuture	8: 0: 0
1	Leather Trunk	0: 5: 0
34	Yds Coarse white Linnen 1/6	2:11: 0

36	Towilling in 2 pieces	1: 0: 0
1	Looking Glass	0: 5: 0
9	yds Knife Cloths	0: 3: 0
28	yds Dowlass 1/6	2: 2: 0
1	old Grate &c	0:10: 0
46	yds Printed Cotton 1/6	3: 9: 0
12	yds worsted Chex	1:10: 0
1	Bed Stead	2: 0: 0
4	Window Blinds	2: 0: 0
	Bed Bedstead and 3 Blankets	1:10: 0
1	doz Hatts	3: 0: 0
6	pair yarn Stockings	0: 7: 6
11	Pr. Worsted Ditto	1:10: 0
8	Pr. Womens Ditto	1: 0: 0
1	pr. Blue Shalloon	2:10: 0
5	yds blue Shagg	1:10: 0
20	yds blue plains	2:10: 0
6	yds white Cloth	3:10: 0
6	½ yards blue broad Cloth	3: 0: 0
1	pair new Boots	1: 0: 0
	Some Livery Lace & 3 Shoulder Knots	3: 0: 0
34	Hanks twist	0:10: 0
19	pieces Tape	0:19: 0
7	lbs Oznabrigs Thread	1: 5: 0
4	dozen Laces	0: 4: 0
6	dozen Metal Buttons	0: 7: 6
2	Bags Mohair Buttons	0:15: 0
2	½ pieces Oznabrigs	15: 0: 0
	Camp Equipage	20: 0: 0
2	Chests with some Cabinet Tools	2:10: 0
1	Glass Gilt Frame over the Chimney	8: 0: 0
1	old Tea Chest	0: 2: 6
8	Pictures in Gilt Frame & 2 Small Do in Ditto	30: 0: 0
1	Desk and Book Case with Glass Doors	8: 0: 0
2	Card Tables	8: 0: 0
1	Fire Screen	2:10: 0
1	Grate and Appurtenances	3:10: 0
1	Settee	6: 0: 0
1	Small 1 Large arm Chairs & 8 Chairs	15: 0: 0
4	Gilt Brackets	1: 0: 0
1	pine Dressing Table	0:10: 0
3	pair Damask Window Curtains	15: 0: 0
1	piece of Gauze	2: 0: 0
12	Neck Cloths	3:10: 0
	Sundrys in the Desk	1:10: 0
2	Bedstead with furniture 3[?] Mattresses and three Blankets	0:15: 0
1	Table	0: 7: 6
8	Chairs	2:10: 0
1	Grate	3: 0: 0
1	Arm Chair	1: 0: 0
1	Feild Bedstead with Curtains 1 Bed 3 Blankets }	4: 0: 0
1	Close Stool Bed pan	0: 2: 6
1	Desk	0:15: 0
1	Blue Fringed Housing	0:16: 6
1	Press for Linnen	1: 0: 0
1	Sedan	7: 0: 0

35 Table Cloths a 20/	35: 0: 0
21 Breakfast Table Cloths a 10/	10:10: 0
70 Napkins a 5/	17:10: 0
18 Huckaback Towells	1: 0: 0
24 Glass Napkins	0:15: 0
16 Glass Wipers	0: 8: 0
9 pair fine Holland Sheets a 30/	13:10: 0
6 pair pillow Cases	0:15: 0
6 Counterpanes a 30/	9: 0: 0
1 Sprigged Quilt	1:10: 0
3 old Quilts	1: 0: 0
16 pair Servants Sheets 12/	9:12: 0
3 Single Pillow Cases	0: 1: 6
8 Table Cloths	2: 0: 0
4 Breakfast Table Cloths	0:12: 0
4 Dirsters	0: 5: 0
1 large Wilton Carpet	6: 0: 0
2 Small Ditto and 3 Red Ditto	2:10: 0
1 Pyramid in the french Taste	1:10: 0
1 Bed Bedstead and furniture	25: 0: 0
1 large Chest of Drawers	12: 0: 0
1 Small D° D°	6: 0: 0
8 Chairs and two Stools	5: 0: 0
1 Grate &c	5: 0: 0
1 Close Stool	1: 0: 0
1 old Chest	0: 5: 0
1 Cloathes Press	10: 0: 0
1 Couch	2: 0: 0
1 Backgammon Table Chess Men and Board	4: 0: 0
1 Walnut table	1:10: 0
1 Small old D°	0:10: 0
1 Dressing Box	3: 0: 0
1 Microscope	2: 0: 0
1 Letter Case & Perambulater	2: 0: 0
1 Spy Glass	1:10: 0
1 Saddle and Furniture	20: 0: 0
1 Telliscope	10: 0: 0
1 Bureau	8: 0: 0
1 Gold Watch	40: 0: 0
1 old Watch	10: 0: 0
2 Cases Containing 4 doz Table Knives & forks	30: 0: 0
1 Case 2 doz Desert Ditto	10: 0: 0
5 pair Mens Shoes	3: 0: 0
Some Plate a 10/ per oz sent home	
1 pair Gold Sleeve Buttons	1:10: 0
1 Iron Chest	4: 0: 0
1 Small Collection of Books	20: 0: 0
Ditto of Music and Instruments	10: 0: 0
1 Blunderbus and Short gun	4: 0: 0
1 Liberary and Table Stool	6: 0: 0
1 large Chest Stationary	7:10: 0
1 Ink Pot	0: 2: 6
2 Pewter Ink Stands	0:10: 0
1 Slate	0: 1: 3
1 House Clock	4: 0: 0
1 old Chest of Drawers and Table	0:10: 0
1 parcel of tin Prints and Moulds	1: 0: 0
2 Trays and 7 Stands &c	2: 0: 0
1 large Copper Set	5: 0: 0
1 Iron Pot Set	0:15: 0
2 Iron Ditto	1: 0: 0

1 Copper Fish Kettle	2: 5: 0
1 large Copper Dripping Pan	1:10: 0
1 new Copper Duch Oven with 2 Covers	4: 0: 0
1 Marble Morter	0:15: 0
1 Jack	3: 0: 0
1 dozen Water plates	3: 0: 0
2 Water Dishes	1: 0: 0
1 Warming pan	0:10: 0
5 old Copper Sauce pans 1 old Copper Soup Kettle and Cover 4 Stew pans 1 preserving pan	5: 0: 0
1 Coffee Pot 2 Chocolate D° 3 Chafing Dishes	
1 Copper Pot for Boiling Tea Kettle & Boiler	2: 0: 0
1 parcel of Pewter Moulds	1: 0: 0
4 Potting Potts	0: 2: 0
34 Pewter Plates	1:14: 0
1 parcel of old Pewter	2: 0: 0
Tin Ware	1: 0: 0
3 Spitts	1:10: 0
1 Bell Metal Skillet 1 Gridiron 1 Bell Metal Morter Salamander Poker Shovel Flesh fork	1:10: 0
1 large pair of Steel Yards	1:10: 0
Old Brass and Copper	0:15: 0
Parcel of Pails Piggins Tubs & Plate Rack	1: 0: 0
86 Hams Bacon	
83 Sides D°	
31 Chops D° weighing 1823 lb a 6	45:11: 6
Part of a Hogshead Molasses 124 Gal 1/8	10: 6: 8
10 Pipes of Wine £50	500: 0: 0
76 Gallons Rum a 3/	11: 8: 0
10 D° Peach Brandy a 3/	1:10: 0
3 doz and 10 Bottles old Wine a 40/	7:18: 4
7 doz and 4 Bottles Draft D° a 24/	8:16: 0
5 Bottles of Arrack a 5/	1: 5: 0
210 Pint Bottles of Malmsey Wine a 20/doz	17:10: 0
2 Casks Porter	6: 0: 0
1 Jug Sallad Oyl	2: 0: 0
36 doz Bottles of old Syder a 3 per Bottle	5: 8: 0
3 doz Porter	1: 0: 0
26 Bottles Clarrett a 3/ per Bottle	3:18: 0
3 D° of Champaign 6/	0:18: 0
20 Bottles Tokay	3: 0: 0
112 Bottles a 1/3	7: 0: 0
6 Casks Cyder	6: 0: 0
13 ½ doz old Hock 6/	42: 6: 0
3 Jarrs Browns Sugar and Jarrs	2: 5: 0
1 Jarr Split Pease	0: 5: 0
Part of 2 Firkins of Butter	2: 0: 0
20 Candle Moulds and Stand	1: 0: 0

8 Horses	100: 0: 0
a parcel of Saddles and Cloths	2: 0: 0
12 Sheep	7: 0: 0
2 Stalled Beeves	15: 0: 0
17 Head of Cattle	40: 0: 0
9 Hogs	7:10: 0
1 Post Chaise and Harness	25: 0: 0
1 Shaft Chair and Ditto	20: 0: 0
1 Coach and Harness for 2 Horses	40: 0: 0
1 Cart and D° for 3 Ditto	5: 0: 0
4 Calves	3: 0: 0
6 Flatt Irons	0:10: 0
1 large Copper	6: 0: 0
2 large Pine Tables & 2 Irong. Blankets	1:10: 0
1 Mangle	5: 0: 0
2 Horses for Clothes	1: 0: 0
1 Bed and Furniture	4: 0: 0
3 Old Beds	1:10: 0
2 Setts old Curtains 2 Blankets & Pillows	3: 0: 0
2 Small Mattresses	3:
3 lbs Chocolate 2/6	7: 6
2 Walnut Tables	8:
10 Chairs 40/	20:
2 Small Mahogany Tables	2:
35 Bell Glasses @ 5/	8:15:
325 Earthen Potts 2d	2: 4: 2
a parcel of Tools	2:
8 pieces of Painting @ £5	40:
1 Oval looking Glass	6:
1 Card Table	1:10:
1 Mahogany Table	5:
1 Side Board Table	1:10:
1 Round Table	1:10:
4 Smoking Chairs	6:
Blue Paper	4:
White and Brown Paper	13:
7 Bushels Wheat Sold Chr.Ayscough 4/6	1:11: 6
Negroes	
Tidus	£55: 0 0
Lancaster	£70
Old John	£40
Young John	£60
Tom	£60
Bristol	£55
Suckey & 2 Children Mary & Sall	£140
Nanny and her Child Sukey	65
Sall and her Child Harry	70
Hannah	60
Doll	40
Mary and her Child Jemina	70
	785 0 0
25 Bushels Wheat	@ 4/ 5
Oyl	2
12 Barrels Corn Sold Christopher Ayscough	6

York County, Virginia, Records, Wills and Inventories, XXII, 1771–1783, pp. 83–89, microfilm, CWF.

Appendix 3

SCHEDULE OF LOSSES SUSTAINED BY THE EARL OF DUNMORE, HIS MAJESTY'S LATE GOVERNOR OF THE COLONY OF VIRGINIA. 25 FEBRUARY 1784.

In the Palace at Williamsburg. The Furniture of 25 Rooms compleatly furnished, with all the Beds, Bedding, Looking Glasses, Bureaus, Book Cases valuable Tapestry, Damask Curtains, Carpets, &c. A number of Valuable Pictures by Sir Peter Lely, and a number of costly Prints. A large quantity of very valuable China, Glass, and Household Utensils of every kind. A valuable Library consisting of upwards of 1300 Volumes, 3 Organs, a Harpsicord, a Piano-Forte, and other Musical Instruments.
The greatest and most valuable part of His Lordship's Cloaths, Linnen, and Servants Cloathing. The greatest part of His Lordship's private Arms which were Valuable, with many Articles of value and Curiosity. All the beds, bedding, and furniture of the Servants Rooms, all the furniture of the Kitchen; Laundry, and other Offices. A quantity of Mahogany and other Woods; with tools for four Cabinet Makers, and a Complete set of Blacksmiths Tools. In short everything in and about the Palace, Gardens, Offices, &c　　　　　　　3200:
　42　Pipes and Hogsheads of Wine, the greatest part Madeira at £40　　　　1680:
　12　Gross of Claret, Burgundy, Champagne, Port, Hock, Sherry, Frontiniac, Creme de Noyaux &c. at 32/ pr Doz　　　　　230. 8. 0
　4　Hogsheads of Old Rum, suppose 480 Galls at 5/7　134. 0. 0
　　Common Rum, Molasses &c　　　　　　　　80. 0. 0
　2　Coaches, one quite new　160.
　　A Chariot　　　　　　　40.
　　A Phaeton, and Two One Horse Chaises　　　80.
　　Carts, Waggons, &c. at the Palace　　　　　40.
　　　　　　　　　　　　　320.

Goods imported from England for Family Use　　　　　　600.
154　Head of Cattle in the Park at Williamsburg @ 48/　369.12. 0
150　Sheep @ 8/　　　　　60. 0. 0
13　Coach and Saddle Horses @ £32　　　　　　416. 0. 0
A 3 year old Colt for which £120 had been offered　　　80. 0. 0
　3　Valuable Colts @ £24　72. 0. 0
　12　Indented Servants mostly Tradesmen who had about four years to serve @ £32　　　　　　382. 0. 0
House and Lott of Land in Williamsburg　　　　　80. 0. 0

A.O. 13/28, Public Record Office, London, transcript, CWF.

Appendix 4

PROPOSAL [CA. 1710]

For rendring the new House Convenient as well as Ornamental
　That such necessary places as Stable, Coach house, Cowhouse & Hen-house together with an enclosed Yard for Poultry be made.
　That a Kitchen Garden and Orchard be paled in at leaste
　That a Flower Garden behind the House as well as the Courtyard before it be enclosed with a Brick wall 4 foot high with a Ballustrade of Wood on the Top
　That the Land belonging to the House being about 60 acres may be enclosed with a Ditch & Fence for a Pasture.
　That 3 doz Strong fashionable Chairs & 3 large Tables 3 large looking Glasses & four Chimney Glasses be bought for the furniture of the lower Apartments, as also one Marble Buffette or sideboard wth a Cistern & fountain
　That the great Room in the second Story be furnished with gilt Leather hangings 16 Chairs of the same, two large looking glasses with the Arms of the Colony on them according to the new Mode, two small Tables to stand under the Looking Glasses and two Marable Tables Eight Glass Sconces.
　That there be one large looking Glass more for the largest of the Bed Chambers and four Chimney Glasses for the said Floor
　One great Lanthorn for the Hall
　That all standing Furniture for the Kitchen and Brew house such as a Copper for washing another for brewing Stove Irons and other things that must necessaryly be fixed to the House be bought & furnished at the publick Charge.
[Endorsed:] Mr *Robertson* for the house

H. R. McIlwaine, ed., *Legislative Journals of the Council of Colonial Virginia* (Richmond, Va., 1918–1919), III, p. 1557.

Appendix 5

AN INVENTORY OF THE HOUSEHOLD FURNITURE &c OF HIS EXCELLENCY ROB.t EDEN ESQ.r LEFT ON HIS DEPARTURE IN HIS DWELLING HOUSE AT THE CITY OF ANNAPOLIS TAKEN THE 26th DAY OF JUNE 1776 VIZt.

N.º 1 Store Room   Currency

10	long handled scrubbing Brushes @3/	£ 1.10.0
1	Loaded one	. 5.
4	Clamps	. 6.
2	long handled Hair Brooms @5/	.10.
2	Painted Hearth Brooms @5/	.10.
1	Pier Glass in Mahog.y frame	6. .
1	Box of [illegible], 1 Small Bag of Harts Horn Shavings	2. .
2	Case Bottles of Capers	1. .
9	Loaves of double refined Sugar wt 67l @3/6	11.19.6
40	Bushels fine Salt @10/	20. .
28	Small pictures framed & Glazed @5/	7. .
4	Street Door Lamps @40/	8. .
2	Globe Glass Lanthorns with Brass work for hanging @60/	6. .
4	long Glass Candle shades @25/	5. .
		70. .6

N.º 2 Coachman's Bed Room

1	Feather Bed 1 Bolster & 1 Pillow	5.10.
1	Blanket & 1 Rug	2. .
1	Sacking Bottom Bedstead	2. .
2	New Velvet Jocky Caps	4. .
1	Hunting Saddle with plaited Stirups and Striped Saddle Cloth	5. .
4	d.º....ditto with polished steel Stirrups	20. .
1	Womans Hunting Saddle with furniture	4. .
2	Snaffel plated Bridles	2.10.
1	Curb Steel Bitted Bridle	.15.
1	Portmantua Saddle with pad & straps	2. .
1	Rase Saddle	2. .
11	Fly Netts made of white Twine fringed	5.10.
		55. 5.

N.º 3 Boys Bed Room

1	Feather Bed and 1 Pillow	3. .
1	Plank Bottom'd Bedstead	. 7.6
1	Rug and 1 Blanket	1. .
		4. 7.6

N.º 4 Long Garrett

1	Large polished steel Stove with an open fret work Fender	10.10.
1	Small d.º with plain Fender	6. .
1	Common Stove	1.10.
2	pair large Dog Irons and 2 pair small ditto	7. .
4	Setts fire Shovels Tongs and Pokers @25/	5. .
	Amo.t Carried over £	30. .
		£ 129.13.0
	Amount brought over £	30. .
		£ 129.13.
1	[illegible] Leather Screw	6. .
1	[illegible] Windsor Chairs	2. .
3	old Wilton Carpits	6. .
1	Cloaths Horse & 1 Iron Fender	3.10.
1	Feather Bed & Bolster	4. .
1	old Bedstead	.10.
	Sundry old picture frames	3. .
1	Large equal Altitude Instrument and Apparatus	333. .
		388. .

N.º 5 Servant mans Bed Room

1	Corded Bedstead, flock Mattrass, Bolster, 1 Rug, 1 Windsor Chair	3. .

N.º 6 Servant Woman's Bed Room

1	Large Chest containing the following Articles Viz.t	
2	Stuff damask window Curtains £	7. .
5	y.ds Wilton Carpet	5. .
2	Setts of Tent Bed furniture of Red and White Check	8. .
4	Setts of Check Covers for large Soffas	6. .
3	Red and White Check Window Curtains	4.10.
1	Hammer Cloth for Coach	2. .
16	Large Chair Check Covers	4. .
30	Small ditto	1. .
	Chest	1. . 38.10.
1	Large easy Chair with Stufft backs & Elbows	5. .
1	Mahogany dressing Table	2. .
1	Swinging dressing Glass	1. .
1	ditto...d.º in Walnut frame	.15.
1	Mahogany Nights Stool	.10.
1	.......ditto	.15.
1	Guittar and Case	5. 5.
1	pair fire Shovel Tongs and fender	1.15.
1	Sacking Bottom Bedstead	2. .
		64. 5.

N.º 7 Mrs Eden's Dressing Room

1	Feather Bed and Bolster	6.10.
1	large flock Mattrass	3. .
1	Sacking Bottom'd Bedstead	2.10.
1	Mahogany dressing Table	3. .
1	large .. Ditto Chair	1.15.
		16.15.
	Amo.t carried over £	601.13.
	Amount brought up £	601.13.

N.º 8 His Excellency's Bed Room

1	Mahogany 4 post Bedstead with white Dimothy furniture ornamented Cornice with Vases compleat	25. .
1	Large Feather Bed, bolster and pillows	10. .
1	Hair Mattrass	4. .
1	Small Blanket	.15.
1	Large White Counterpain	3. .
1	Mahogany Night Table	4. .
1	Large Elbow Chair with stuft back and Elbows	5. .
1	French commode Table with rose wood & brass ornaments	15. .
1	Mahogany dressing Table with Glass Compleat	10.10.
1	ditto Book—case	15. .
1	ditto Chair 1 ditto Stool	2.15.
1	pair White Dimothy window Curtains	6. .
		101. 0.0

In the Closet in said Room

18	large Blankets @25/	22.10.0
2	White Cotton Counterpains @60/	6. .
1	Compleat Sett of Red and White Check Bed furniture for a 4 post Bedstead	10. .
2	Setts Japan'd dressing Boxes	7. .
4	Earthen Chamber pots	.10.
3	Wash hand Basons and Bottles	.15.
3	flesh Brushes	. 7.6
2	pair Venician Blinds	3.10.
		50.12.6

N.º 9 Passage adjoining his Excellency's Room

2	Oval pier Glasses in White carved frames	14. .
1	Mahogany Cloaths press	12. .
1	d.º Cooler and Stand	7. .
8	Small Moco pictures framed and Glazed	8. .
		41.10.

EDEN LOSSES 299

N.º 10 Bed Room, head Best Stairs

1	Maho: 4 post Bedstead with Green and White furniture	15. .
1	Feather Bed, 1 Bolster and pillow and one old flock Mattrass	9. .
1	large Blanket	1. 5.
1	large Chintz Counterpain	3. .
2	large Mahogony Chairs	3.10.
1	ditto Stool	1. .
1	d.º dressing Table with Marble Slabs in laid with dove coloured Marble	15. .
1	Dressing Glass in swinging frame	3. .
1	Damask Window Curtain	3.10.
2	Setts Venecian Window Blinds	4.10.
3	Chamber potts & 1 Wash Bottle	.12.6
		59. 7.6
	Amount carried Over £	854. 3.0
	Amount brought over	854. 3.

N.º 11 Billiard Room

1	Compleat Billiard Table with Maces Balls &c	80. .
8	Windsor Chairs	8. .
1	long handled hair Broom	.10.
		88.10.

N.º 12 The Bed Room adjoining the Billiard Room at the head of the Stairs

1	four post Mahogany Bedstead with blue & white Check furniture	15. .
1	Feather Bed and Bolster	8. .
2	large Mahogony Chairs	3. .
1	Dressing Table and Glass in a Swinging frame	8. .
2	Flag Bottomed Chairs	.15.
1	Wash hand Bason and Bottle	. 7.6
		35. 2.6

N.º 13 M.r Smith's Bed Room

1	Four post Mahogany Bedstead	6. .
1	Feather Bed, Bolster, pillow and Hair Mattrass	10. .
1	Pembroke Table	3. .
1	dressing Glass	1.15.
1	Night Stool	1. .
1	Mahogony Chair	1.15.
2	Reams of Writing Paper	6. .
		29.10.0

N.º 14 Nursery

1	Mahogany Desk	8. .
1	d.º Writing Table	10. .
1	d.º Chest of Drawers	6.10.
1	Wash hand Stand	1. 5.
1	Small looking Glass	1.10.
2	Check Window Curtains	3. .
1	large Hair Trunk	1.15.
2	Mahogony Chairs	3.10.
1	ditto Arm Chair	2. 5.
1	Small Hair Trunk	1. .
		38.15.0

N.º 15 Best Stair Case

1	Large square Hall Lanthorn	4. .
1	Bell.....d.º	2. .
3	Windsor Chairs	3. .
1	Large Hair Trunk	4. .
1	Elligant portrait of Charles 1st by Vandike	40. .
1	d.º...d.º of his Excellency by Peale	40. .
1	Painted floor Cloth	5. .
		98. .
	Amo.t carried up £	1144. 0.6
	Amount brought up £	1144. .6

N.º 16 Studdy

2	Handsom Mahogony Book cases	50. .
1	ditto...d.º Desk and ditto	35. .
1	large handsom Soffa with Check cover	10. .
1	Mahogony wash hand stand with sliding Glass &c	6. .
4	d.º Chairs	8. .
2	Small pictures in Gilt frames	10. .
		119. .

N.º 17 Gilt Leather Parlour

10	Mahogony Chairs with hair Bottoms	22.10.0
2	Elbow ... ditto....d.º	6. .
2	Mahogony Card Tables	6. .
1	Pembroke ... d.º	3. .
2	Jappand corner Cupboards	2.10.0
2	Crimson Stuff Damask Window Curtains	6.10.
2	Setts Venecian Window Blinds	4. .
1	Pier Glass in a Carved and Gilt frame	16. .
1	Dutches	12. .
2	China India figures	2. .
1	piece of painting representing Dunkirk	15. .
		95.10.0

N.º 18 Right hand parlour

14	Mahogony Chairs with horsehair Bottoms	28. .
1	large Maho: Dining Table	4.10.
1	Maho: Card Table	3. .
1	Maho: Fire Screen	2.10.
1	pier Glass in a Carved and Gilt frame	16. .
8	Eligant pieces of painting of ruins and water prospects in ditto	70. .
2	Small ditto of Landscips	10.10.
2	Eligant small Battle pieces in Gilt frames	14. .
1	d.º representing Shipping ..... ditto	12. .
		160.10.0

N.º 19 Long Room

16	Maho: Chairs with horsehair Bottoms	32. .
3	large Mahogony Dining Tables	13.10.
1	large Maho: Cloaths Chest	8. .
1	Small round dining Table	3.10.
1	Carved claw and pillar Tea Table	3.10.
1	Maho: wine cooler with brass hoops & Stands	5.10.
1	Maho: Candle Stand	2. .
1	Backgammon Table	2. 5.
1	Eligant Iron Dutch Stove	40. .
1	Handsome Chimney Glass	10. .
1	Elligant piece of painting of ruins on the breast of the Chimney	15. .
	Amo.t carried over £	135. 5.0
		£1519. 0.6
	Amount brought over	135. 5.
		£1519. .6
2	Small circular pieces of painting on ditto	10.10.
4	large handsome pieces of painting waterpieces and Landscips in carved and gilt frames	56. .
2	Eligant pieces of painting representing Stags	20. .
6	d.º representing Rivers landscips &c in carved gilt frames	33. .
		254.15.

N.º 20 Secretary's Office

1	Secretary of Mahogony	16. .
1	Sideboard Table with Marbel Slab vased with dove coulour'd Marble	15. .
1	Eight day Table Clock	10.10.
1	Maho: nest of drqwers with folding Doors	10. .
1	Small couch covered with Green and white Check	5. .
5	Maho: Chairs	8.15.
1	Walnut Table	3. .
1	Pine Table	2. .

300 APPENDIX 5

2	Handsome pictures framed and Glazed, representing the death of General Woolf, and the Marquis of Granby distributing Charity to the Soldier	4. .	
2	Small d.º	2. .	
1	piece of painting Province Arms	6. .	
1	Maho: case with 6 flint Bottles	5. .	
1	large Tin fender	.10.	
1	large Glass Lanthorn	.10.	
1	pair small hand Irons	1.10.	
1	fire Shovel and Tongs	.10.	
1	Hair Trunk	1.10.	
		91.15.0	

N.º 21 Butler's Pantry

6	large french plate Candlesticks	10. .
2	Small ..... ditto	2.10.
4	large China Bowls	7.10.
5	Small ..... ditto	5. .
11	Silver Table Spoons	13.15.0
1	Silver Punch Ladle	1. .
21	Wash hand Glasses, cut	17.17.6
1	doz Small Dram Glasses	.12.6
14	plain Wash hand .. ditto	3.10.
6	Small Glass Water Bottles	1. 5.
1	Quart Tumbler, Cut Glass, 1 Pint d.º	.12.6
5	Punch Glasses with handles, and 3 without handles	. 8.
8	Small Cut Glass Cluits	1. .
7	½ Doz Wine Glasses	3. 9.
11	Quart Decanters with ground Stoppers	4. 2.6
	Amount carried up	£ 62.11.6
		£1865.10.6
	Amount brought up	62.11.6
		£1865.10.6
4	pint Decanters with ground Stoppers	1. .
1	pair Silver Salts	2. .
1	pair Cut glass...d.º	.17.6
5	large Queen's Ware pitchers	1.17.6
2	Wash hand Basons	. 5.
2	Maho: Trays	2.10.
1	Walnut Desk Bedstead	7. .
1	Flock Mattrass and pillows	3. .
2	Maho: Plate Baskets with brass handles	3. .
1	Flag Bottomed Chair	.10.
2	Iron Candlesticks and 1 pair Snuffers	. 7.6
1	Doz and 10 Green handles Knives and forks	5. .
2	large Carving Knives & 2 forks	1. 5.
11	Green handled Desert Knives & 12 forks	1.15.
5	Small Silver handled Knives	1. 5.

2	Maho: Knife Cases lined with Bays	1. .	
2	Wainscot.....ditto	. 7.6	
3	Tin Spitting Boxes	.15.	
6	Japand Tin Lamps	1. 2.6	
4	Leather Decanter stands	.17.6	
1	Japand Bread basket	.10.	
1	Large Stone Jug	. 5.	
2	Tin Knife Trays	.10.	
1	Quart pewter pott	. 4.	
1	Silver Wine Strainer	.12.	
		100. 7.6	

N.º 22 Housekeepers Room

1	four post Bedstead with blue and white Check furniture	8. .
1	Feather Bed and 1 Bolster	6. .
2	Blankets and 1 Quilt	4. 5.
1	Maho: Writing Desk	5.10.
1	ditto Table	2.10.
1	Iron Stove Shovel and poker	2.10.
3	Tea Bords	2. 5.
12	pair fine Sheets	21.12.
2	pair Oznabrig.....d.º	2. .
1	doz Damask Napkins	7.10.
10	Small....ditto	5. .
6	Huckaback...ditto	2. 5.
3	Large New Damask Table Cloths	10.10.
2	large Huckaback.....d.º	7.10.
4	Damask Breakfast Cloths	6. .
2	old Damask Napkins	.15.
9	Small Table Cloths	9. .
4	Pillow Cases	1. .
22	Doylers	3. 6.
8	Old Breakfast Cloths	4. .
	Amount carried up	£ 111. 8.
		£1965.18.0
		Currency
	Amount brought Over	111. 8.
		£1965.18.
4	Large Damask Table Cloths	12. .
4	Jack Towells	1.10.
6	Knife Cloths	.12.
56	yards Oznabrigs @3/	9. 8.
2	large Queen's Ware Dishes	.15.
11	Middle Sized ... d.º	2. 5.
15	Small ... d.º	2. 5.
24	Soop plates	1. 4.
1	Turine	.10.
15	Small plates	.12.6
4	doz plates	2. .
7	Butter Boats & stand	1. 1.
1	Salad Dish and fish Strainer	. 2.
4	Scollop Shells	. 4.
4	pie Dishes	1. .
4	fruit Baskets & Stands	2. .
1	Sett Red & White China	4. .
11	Silver Tea Spoons & 2 p. Tea Tongs	5. .
½	Doz large blue and White China Cups & Saucers	1. .

½	doz Blue and White Coffee ... d.º	.15.	
9	blue and White Tea Cups and saucers	.15.	
5	China Tea pots	.15.	
1	China bowl and 1 Small ditto	. 8.	
1	China Pie Dish	. 7.6	
2	ditto Tart Pans	. 7.6	
13	odd China plates	2. .	
2	large China Dishes	1. 5.	
5	Small ditto	1.17.	
2	Glass Sugar Dishes	.10.	
1	Jappand Coffee pott	.12.6	
1	Silver Coffee pott	5. .	
2	Tin Sugar Cannesters	1. .	
2	Tin Bisquet Moulds	. 7.6	
1	Jelly Glass Stand	.17.6	
3	doz and 4 Jelly Glasses	2. .	
1	Delph Bowel	. 2.6	
2	Black Jacks	. 5.	
1	Hair Sifter	. 2.6	
1	Sugar Chopper	. 2.	
		178. 6.6	

N.º 23 Adjoining Housekeepers Room

1	Maho: Desk	6. .
6	Wood Bottomed Chairs	.18.
1	Walnut Table and 2 Coffee Mills	3. .
7	Earthen Jars, 1 Stone Jug, 3 Earthen Crocks & 2 yellow Basons	2. 3.
2	Glass Jars, 2 Brass Candlesticks & 1 Iron d.º	.10.
		12.11.0
	Amo.t carried up	£2156.15.6
	Amount brought up	2156.15.6

N.º 24 In the Kitchen and Scullary

1	Copper fish Kettle and strainer	2. .
1	ditto Stue pan and cover	1. .
3	Copper Sauce pans two with covers	1. 1.
2	Cofee pots and 1 Chocolate pott	1.10.
6	Chafing Dishes	2. 5.
4	Tea Kettles	2. .
1	Copper Boiling pot and Cover	2. .
1	half Gallon pot	.15.
1	Small Copper Boiler fixed	8. .
1	large ditto not fixed	20. .
1	Skillet and 1 Copper Coal Scuttle	.18.
7	Pewter Water plates	1.15.
16	Pewter plates and 4 Dishes	2. 7.
2	large Iron potts	1.10.
2	pair pot Hooks	.10.
1	Iron Crane and 6 pot racks	3. .
2	Grid Irons and 2 Frying pans	1.10.
6	Trivits and 1 Dripping pan and stand	1.10.

1 Smoak Jack and 3 Iron Spits	15. .	
1 pair large Hand Irons	4. .	
1 Dutch Oven fixed	8. .	
4 Iron scewers, 1 Chopping Knife & 1 Bal^s scewer	.17.6	
4 Cuckold Scewers	1. .	
1 large fire Shovel Tongs and poker	1. 5.	
1 pair Stilliards	2. 5.	
1 Cleaver and 1 Butchers Steel	1. .	
1 Tin Duch Oven and 1 Tin Cullender	.12.6	
1 Tasting ladle and dripping pan and 2 Egg Slicers	.13.	
1 Tin Cover, 1 Wickor Basket Tind	1. .	
3 pint potts and 1 Candle Box	. 8.	
1 Eight Day Clock	10. .	
2 large Brass soop Spoons and a Dinner Bell	1. .	
1 large Table and 2 forms	4. .	
1 Jappand Tea Kitchen	1. .	
1 Fire Screen lined with Tin and 1 plate Rack	2.15.	
4 Washing Tubs, 3 plates, 2 half Bushels & 2 Chopping Blocks	1. 9.6	
	109.16.6	

N.º 25 In the Room over the Kitchen

1 New large Markee Compleat	30. .	
Amount Carried over	£2296.12.0	
	Currency	
Amount brought forward	2296.12.0	

N.º 26 The Landry

1 pair Dog Irons 1 Shovel and Tongs	2. 7.6	
1 large Iron Skillet	. 7.6	
4 Sad. Irons, 2 Box Irons and 2 Stands	1.12.6	
1 large Copper fix'd	15. .	
1 large Iron Kettle d^o	9. .	
7 Washing Tubs	1.10.	
3 Cloaths Horses	1.10.	
1 large pine Table & 1 small ditto	3. .	
3 Stools 3 Coaths Baskets and 1 Corner Cupboard	1. 7.	
	35.14.6	

N.º 27 Servant's Hall

6 Handsome Chandaliers in packing Cases the cost of same in London and charges here	285. .	
1 New fishing Seine with Ropes	25. .	
1 old ..... ditto	7.10.	
1 large Dining Table and 2 Forms	2.10.	
1 X Cut Saw	1. 2.6	
1 Shoulder of Mutton Sail belonging to the flat	5. .	
2 Hair Brooms, 2 Scrubbing Brushes & 2 Mops	1. .	
1 pair Steps	.10.	
1 pair Dog Irons	1. 5.	
1 Carved and Gilded Picture frame	1. .	
	329.17.6	

N.º 28 In the passage leading to the Cellar

4 Iron Bound hogsheads	2. .	
4 Empty Barrels	1. .	
	3. .	

N.º 29 Dairy

9 Earthen Milk pans, 3 Wooden Dishes and 2 Small Churns	1. 7.0	
1 Paste Board and 2 Milk Piggins	.12.6	
2 Powdering Tubs with Covers	1.10.0	
2 Barrels Bisquit and 1 Barrell Corn	2. 5.	
4 Stone Jugs and 7 Empty Casks	.17.6	
	6.12.0	
	2671.16.	

N.º 30 Beer Cellar

1 Barrel Baltimore Beer	1. 5.	
1 d^o Common Vinegar	2.10.	
2 Hh^ds London porter	66. .	
60 Gallons Wine Vinegar	15. .	
90 Gallons West India Rum	33.15.	
195^l Cheese	11. 2.6	
1 Barrell Hickory Nutts and 1 Nest wooden Ware	1.12.6	
1 Empty Hh^d 3 piggins and 1 Tunnell	1. 2.6	
3 pair of leading Lines, 2 Corn Baskets & Cheese Stand	.19.6	
2 Gallons Honey and Jug 2 Tunnels 1 Keg yellow Oaker	2.15.	
	136.12.0	
Amo.^t	£2808. 8.0	

A.O. 13/60, pt. 1, Claims, American Loyalist Series II, Temporary Support, Maryland, pp. 196–207, Public Record Office, London, microfilm, Lib. Cong.

Appendix 6

AN INVENTORY OF THE
FURNITURE WHICH WAS
DESTROY'D IN HIS EXCELLENCY
GOVERNOR TRYON'S HOUSE IN
FORT GEORGE IN NEW YORK THE
29 DECEMBER 1773.

COUNCIL CHAMBER

Their Majestys' Pictures
King William and Queen Ann.
King George the first.
King George the second and Queen.
King George the third and Queen Charlotte.

- 1 Large Polish'd Streel [sic] Grate with furniture compleat.
- 2 Large Mahogany Dining Tables with green broadcloth covers.
- 1 Square Mahogany writing Ditto with Ditto.
- 13 Square Elbow Chairs Stuff't seats and hair covers.
- 3 Large Gilt pier Glasses.
- 2 gilt Sconces.
- 4 Green Marine Window Curtains fring'd & tossels &c.
- 1 Large Scotch Carpet.

CHINTS ROOM

- 1 Large polish'd Steel grate, with furniture compleat.
- 1 Chimney Glass, carv'd & gilt frame with Ornaments.
- 1 Dozen blue damask chairs with stuff'd seats & backs with blue & white calico musslin covers.
- 3 Mahogany Card Tables.
- 1 Painted silk Firescreen with a Mahogany frame, and a green silk cover.
- 3 Blue Damask window curtains.
- 1 Large Wilton Carpet.

DINING ROOM

- 1 Large polish'd Steel grate, with furniture compleat.
- 1 Large chimney glass, carv'd & gilt frame, with ornaments & sconces.
- 3 Oval Glasses, carv'd & gilt frames, with Ditto & Ditto.
- 2 Carved and Gilt Gerandoles.
- 2 Dozen Mahogany Chairs & 2 Elbow ditto stuff't seats and blue marine Covers.
- 3 Mahogany Card Tables.
- 5 Blue marine window Curtains, fring'd and tossels &c.
- 1 Large Wilton Carpet.
  Pictures
  Mary Queen of Scots
  Marquis of Granby
  Mr. Reid

MRS. TRYON'S DRESSING ROOM

- 1 Polish'd steel grate with furniture compleat.
- 1 Palmuletto Cloths press.
- 1 Mahogany Bureau.
- 1 Ditto Drawing Table.
- 1 Book case.
- 1 Square Mahogany Table.
- 1 Oblong Ditto....Ditto....
- 1 Dressing Table with a Toilet &c.
- 1 Dressing Glass.
- 1 Dozen Mahogany Chairs, Tapestry work seats, fine printed cotton covers fringed, 2 Elbow Ditto & 2 Stools.
- 2 Large and 2 Small Gerandoles, carv'd & gilt frames.
- 1 Four leav'd gilt leather screen.
- 4 Fine printed cotton window curtains, Fring'd & Tossels &c.
- 1 Couch with a fine printed cotton cover, fringed and 3 Pillows.
- 1 Large Scotch Carpet, fring'd.

BED CHAMBER

- 1 Polished Steel Grate.
- 1 Mahogany Bedstead Venetian Cornishes, fluted and turned posts, India Chints hangings, lined throughout with Calico Muslin.
- 1 Fine white Calico Bed Quilt, a Chints pillimpon.
- 1 Feather Bed, 1 White holland & 1 large hair Mattresses, 1 Bolster, 2 pillows and Blankets.
- 3 Fine Printed Cotton Window Curtains, lin'd with Irish linnen, Fringed and Tossels &c.
- 2 Rose Wood Chests of Drawers.
- 2 Small nests of Drawers.
- 1 Medicine Chest and 1 Chest of the same size.
- 1 Mahogany Spider-legg'd Table.
- 1 Ditto.... Wash hand stand.
- 3 Ditto.... Chairs, stuff't seats with fine printed Cotton covers fringed.
- 1 Pier Glass, gilt frame, 6 agate cups, 1 paper House. His Excellency's picture in plaster of paris, with Eleven more of the same size.
- 2 Side Bed Carpets.
- 1 Small Box inlaid with Eboney—with silver furniture.

HIS EXCELLENCY'S STUDY

- 1 Bath polished Stove Grate with furniture compleat.
- 1 Large five shelved Mahogany Book Case with folding Doors and Crown glass.
- 1 Wallnut-tree writing Desk.
- 1 Rose wood writing Table with a Drawer.
- 1 Pier Glass, carved & gilt frame.
- 6 Mahogany Chairs, Horse-hair seats.
- 1 Ditto.... Stool.... Ditto.... Ditto....
- 1 Globe, 1 pr. of Silk Colour's, 2 Swords & 1 Hanger.
- 1 Picture over the Chimney.
- 1 Small Carpet.

HIS EXCELLENCY'S DRESSING ROOM

- 1 Bath Polish'd Stove Grate with furniture compleat.
- 1 Mahogany Bureau.
- 1 Ditto Desk & Book Case.
- 1 Ditto Pillar & Claw Table.
- 1 Ditto Tea Vase stand with Chinese Rails.
- 1 Tea Chest with Silver furniture.
- 8 Mahogany Chairs, with hair Seats, and 2 Elbow Ditto.
- 1 Ditto Wash-hand stand, 1 looking glass.
- 1 Turkey Carpet.

THE PASSAGE UPON THE FRONT STAIR CASE

- 2 Large Mahogany square Dining Tables.
- 1 Eight day Clock.
- 1 Large Globe Lantern, with an Iron chain.

HALL

- 1 Glass Lantern each side of the Door.
- 10 Leather Buckets with His Excellency's Crest on.
- 3 Lanterns upon the Front & back Stair Cases.

THE BUTLERS ROOM

- 1 Bath polish'd Stove Grate, with furniture compleat.
- 1 Small Mahogany Writing Table.
- 1 Marble Slab with a frame.
- 2 Coolers, Brass hoops with stands.
- 1 Large Mahogany Tea-board with Chinese Rails.
- 1 Large Japan'd Tea-tray.
- 5 Mahogany Dinner trays.
- 3 Tea Vases, Dutch Metal.
- 1 Japann'd plate warmer.
- 2 Twige Plate Baskets lin'd with Tin.
- 1 Small Moving Desk.
- 1 Square Glass lantern.
- 4 Chairs, horse hair seats.

THE HOUSEKEEPERS ROOM

- 1 Bath polish'd Stove grate with furniture compleat.
- 1 Large Mahogany Dining Table.
- 1 Mahogany Press, with folding Doors, Shelves and Drawers.
- 1 Mahogany pillar & claw Tea table & Square with Chinese Rails.
- 1 Ditto Ditto Ditto with a Square top.
- 1 Mahogany Tea Vase stand with Chinese Rails.

1 Small Pier Glass, Wallnut tree frame with gilt edges.
1 Small beach 2 leaved table.
8 Chairs horse hair seats.
1 Japann'd Tea-tray.
2 Twig plate Baskets.
1 Silver two quart Saucepan with a Cover.
3 Pr. of Silver Tea tongs.
2 Dozen & 8 Silver Tea spoons.
3 French plate Crosses.
1 Old Turkey Carpet.

COL. FANNING'S BED-CHAMBER

1 Large Pr. of steel dogs, with Poker, Shovel & Tongs.
1 Four post Bedstead with printed cotton furniture, Lin'd throughout with Calico.
1 Large Calico Quilt, 1 Feather bed Mattress, Bolster, Pillow & Blankets.
1 Large Mahogany writing Desk.
1 Rose Wood Chest of Drawers.
5 Mahogany Chairs, stuff't & hair covers, 1 Elbow Ditto.
1 Ditto Wash-hand stand.
1 Table.
1 Looking Glass.
1 Turkey Carpet.
1 Pr. of plated Candlesticks.

MISS TRYON'S BEDCHAMBER

1 Bath polish'd Stove grate, with furniture compleat.
1 Tent Bed-stead with fine Linnen hangings.
1 White Calico Bed Quilt, 1 Feather bed, Mattress, Bolster, pillow & Blankets.
1 Tent Bed-stead with check'd furniture.
1 New flowred Calico Bed Quilt.
1 Feather Bed, Mattress, Bolster, pillow & Blankets.
1 Mahogany Chest of Drawers.
1 Large Swing Glass, with Drawers & Silver furniture.
1 Round pillar & claw Table.
1 Writing Table with a Drawer.
4 Chairs Stuff't & horse hair seats.
1 Small Scotch Carpet.

THE HOUSEMAIDS CHAMBER

1 Bath polish'd Stove grate with furniture compleat.
1 Four post Bedstead with Green marine hangings.
1 Flowered Cotton Bed Quilt, Feather Bed, Bolster, Pillow & Blanketts.
1 Looking Glass, 1 Table with a Drawer.
1 Tent Bedstead, with green marine hangings.
1 Linen Bed Quilt, feather bed, Bolster, Pillow & Blanketts.
2 Horse hair and 2 rush bottomed Chairs.

THE KITCHING MAID'S CHAMBER

1 Tent Bedstead, with green Marine hangings.
2 Horsehair & 2 Rush bottom'd Chairs.
1 Table with a Drawer.

THE BUTLER'S BEDCHAMBER

1 Bath polish'd Stove grate, with furniture compleat.
1 Tent Bedstead with Check'd hangings.
1 New Flower'd Calico Bed Quilt, Feather Bed, Mattress, Bolster, Pillow & Blanketts.
1 Looking Glass, 2 Tables.
6 Chairs horsehair Covers.
1 Kettle Drum.

THE STEWARDS BEDCHAMBER

1 Tent Bedstead with check'd hangings.
1 Flowr'd Bed Quilt, feather bed, mattress, Bolster, pillow & blanketts.
1 Tent Bedstead with Green Marine hangings, 1 Quilt, feather Bed, Mattress, Bolster, pillow & Blankets.
2 Hair and 2 Rush bottom'd Chairs.
1 Table with a Drawer.

THE HOUSEKEEPERS BEDCHAMBER

1 Pr. of Steel Andirons, brass tops, with Poker Shovel Tongs and Fender.
1 Four post Bedstead with old Chints hangings lin'd with Calico.
1 Calico BedQuilt, feather bed, bolster, pillow and blankets.
1 Mahogany Chest of Drawers.
1 Ditto Tea chest, Inlaid with Eboney.
1 Swing Dressing Glass with Drawers.
1 Dressing table, and 1 writing Ditto.
4 Large Chests containing 3 white holland Mattresses, 4 Strip'd window curtains, lin'd with Calico, lines & tossels.
1 Muslen hangings, for a Tent-Bed.
5 Musketto Ditto.... for Ditto....
3 Fine White Calico Bed Quilts.
21 Linnen Chair Covers.
Several Yds. of New Sheeting Cloth.
Several Ditto of New Towelling.
Other Articles
1 Bedspread which came from the Hill, Fluted Post Venetian Cornishes.
Very fine cotton hangings, with 3 Window curtains (not in use) of the same, with Tossels &c.
6 Mahogany Chairs Stuff't seats, cover'd with Silk, not in use.
1 Long Tea-table fret work, Chinese rails, Not in use.
1 Half pint Silver sauce pan.
1 Small Wilton Carpet.
4 Chairs horsehair Covers.

IN THE PASSAGE UP TWO PR. OF STAIRS

1 Large Sofa with Cover & 2 Pillows.
1 Ditto.... Dining Table Jamaica Mahogany, with a Green broad Cloth cover.
1 Large Maple Dining Table.

GARRET

1 Russia Duck Markee, lin'd throughout with Printed Cotton & all the articles belonging to it.
12 Muskets with Accoutrements.
Tin Lamps & Frames, for his Majesty's Birth Days illuminations &c.

LINNEN

14 Pr. of fine Irish cloth Sheets.
12 Pr. of Coarse Ditto & Ditto.
22 Fine Irish Pillow cases.
12 Coarse Ditto Ditto.
8 Large India Huckaback Table Cloths.
12 Tea Napkins of Ditto.
2 Fine large Damask Table Cloths.
12 Tea Napkins of Ditto.
3 Birds-eye Diaper Table Cloths.
12 Tea Napkins of Ditto.
4 Large Diaper Table Cloths each cover'd 2 Tables.
7 Diaper Table Cloths.
4 Damask side board Cloths.
6 Fine fringed breakfast cloths.
10 Glass Cloths.
4 Round Towels.
6 Dozen common Towels.
1 Dozen Knife Cloths.
6 Doyley's
4 China Cloths.
4 Kitching Table Cloths.
38 Old Towels of diff't. sorts.

CHINA

1 Full set of Burn't in Oblong India China.
1 Set of Ditto.... Round Ditto....
5 Dozen Plates of Ditto.
4 Tureens, Dishes & Covers of Ditto.
2 Syllabub fluted bowls with covers of Ditto.
4 Oblong Baking Dishes of Ditto.
3 Urns with covers of Ditto.
1 Sett of enamell'd blue & gold.
3 Tureens with covers of Ditto.
4 Dozen Plates of Ditto.
1 Small sett of blue & white China.
2 Dozen of Plates of Ditto.
3 Large gold enammel'd punch bowls.
3 Small Punch Bowls.
6 Small India Jars.
6 Burnt-In China Caudle cups and saucers.
6 Dragon Basons and plates, 6 China potts.
8 Setts of Tea & Coffee China, some enamell'd with gold. One of Dresden, some India & some Common.

A Quantity of Odd China.
1 Sett Desert frames with Italian temples, Vases, China Images, Basket & flowers &c.
1 Large full sett of English China for a Desert.
4 Doz. Plates for Ditto.
1 Desert sett of Queens ware.
2 Dozen Plates of Ditto.

PLATE

4 Cases of Table Knifs Forks & Spoons 1 Doz. of each..............
1 Case of Ditto without spoons
2 Cases of Desert Knifs, Forks & Spoons 1 Doz. of each..............
2 Large Oval Waiters
3 Smaller Wrought Ditto
2 Smaller Ditto
1 Tea Kittle [sic] Vase
1 Tea Kittle & Lamp
2 Coffee Potts
3 Pr. of Pillar Candlesticks.
3 Pr. of diff't. pattern
1 Pr. of flatt handled Ditto
1 New fashion'd stand for Oil & Vinager [sic]
1 Ditto Vase for Sugar
1 Ditto Ditto for Pepper
1 Ditto Ditto for mustard
1 Crevet stand containing Oil, Vinager, pepper, Sugar & mustard
2 Plain pint Muggs
2 Ditto.... half pint Ditto
2 Wrought half pint Ditto
1 Bread Basket
1 Large Cup & Cover
4 Large Salt-cellers with spoons.
8 Smaller Ditto with Ditto
6 Butter boats with Ditto
2 Soup Spoons
2 Gravey Ditto
8 Decanter Ticketts
2 Nursery Spoons
3 Saucepans
1 Pap boat
1 Decanter funnel
1 Punch strainer
2 Ditto Ladles

LIQUORS

2 Pipes of Madeira Wine
1 Puncheon of Jamaica Rum
1 Cask of Ditto contg. 50 gallons
1 Barrel of Peach Brandy
1 Keg of French Ditto
2 Hogsheads of Vinager
2 Barrels of Lispenards Ale

In Bottles

25 Doz. Port Wine
10 Dozen of Madeira
6 Ditto.... Mountain
7 Ditto Arrack
3 Ditto Malmsea Maderia
2 Ditto Minorca Wine

2 ½ Ditto Hock...28 Doz. porter
2 ½ Ditto Fronteniac
4 Ditto Claret
1 Ditto Jamaica Rum

BOOKS

Literature	No. Vol.
Essay on the English Language	1
Bollingbrok's Letters	1
Dialogues of the Dead	1
Pleasures of the Imagination	1
Carractere de Madame de Puissieux	2
Origine of Evil	1
Human Prudence	1
School of Man	1
Wake's principles	1
The Economy of Human Life	1
Reflexion sur l'ellgance de la politesse du stile	1
R. sur ce que peut plair	1
L'art de conaitre les homes	1
Fitzosborn's Letters	1
Philosophical Letters	1
Carters Epictectus	2
Spectators	8
Lettre de Madm. de sivigné [sic]	8
Sentimental Journey	2
Pope's Letters	1
Guardian	2
Dilworth's Assistant	1
Plyni's Letters	2
Sr. Wm. Temples Works	2
Dalrympl's Memoirs	1

History	
Releich's of the world	4
Baronnetage of England	5
Of the late War	2
Revolutions of Rome	2
Ditto of Sweden	1
Grecians by Stanians	2
Of the Romans	1
Seats of War in Europe	1
Of the Emperor Ch' Au' 5	3
Hisie Francoise et galante	1
Antony's Commentary	1
Present State of England	2
Fourfold State	1
Comparative View	1
Camdens Britania	1
Barne's Edward the Third	1
Newton's Chronologie	1
Davila's Histy. of France	1
Lady Mary W. M. Letters	3
Maxime de la society civile	1
Vicar of Wakefield	2
Hutcheson on Beauties	1
Diffee. entre l'homme et la Béte [sic]	1
Essays on writing and genius	1
Seeds posthumes works	1
Quinces Dispensatory	1
Motto's to the Spectators	1
Lettre de Voltair	1

Crudens Concordance	1
Heraldry Display'd	1
Extract from Martinet	1
Lock's Essays	2
Salmons Grammer	1
Swifts Works	6
Doctor Burnet	3
Common accidence	1
Burnet's own time	2
Persian Letters english & French	2
Tolitsons Works	1
Belisaries	1
Frederic & Faramond	1
Histy. of Greenland	2
Moeurs des sauvages	2
Histy. of Spain by Mariana	1
L. C. Bacon's Works	1

Military	
Memoire Millitair	2
Ditto par un Holandois	2
Instruction Millitair	1
Memoire de Coulon	1
Artillery de le Blond [sic]	1
Muller on Fortification	1
Prussion Infantry	1
Ditto.... Cavelry	1
Muller on Attack't & Defence of Places	1
Blands Military Dicipline	1
Heath on Fortresses	1
Military Engineer	2
The Accomplished Officer	1
Memoire de puysegur	2
Ceaser's [sic] commentary	1
Code Millitaire	2
Charleton on Stonehenge	1
Rapin's H. of England	15
Wisharts commentary	1
Histoire de la N. France	6
State of Pennsylvania	1
Of Carolina	1
Collins Peerage	6
Hooks Roman History	3
Robertsons Histy. of Scotland	2
Revolutions de Portugal	1
Grandeur et Decadance des Romains	1
Roman History	3
Smiths Histy. of N. York	1
Herberts Travels	1
Sandy's Ditto	1
History of Animals	1
Abridgmt. of the Histy. of Engd.	3
Kingdom of England	1
Memoire de Turenne	2
Ditto.... de Sully	2
Voyage d l'amerique meridional & loha [sic]	2
Smiths Discours's in America	1
La sale's voiage, journal	1
Hobes's tucibide	1
Kennedy's Chronologie	1
Bolinbrook on History	2

Age of Lewis the 14th	2
Plurality of Worlds	1
European Settlements in America	2
Douglas's America	2
Euchards Gazetteer	1
Decription of Carolina	1
Salmons gazette	1

Navigation
Crosby's Navigation	1
Lydiarts Naval History	1
Voyage to Hudsons Bay	1
Dampiers voyages	1
Discovery of America	1
Sience du Pilotte	1
Naval Instruction	1
Ansons Voyage	1
Traite'de Legions	1
Etat Millitaire	2
Perfait Capitan	1
Bariff's Dicipline	1
Instruction du Marll. Broglio	1
Memoire sur la guerre	1
Memoire de Turenne	2
Ditto de Montecuculy	1
Ordonance du Roy	1
Dictionaire de lingenia	1
Journeaux des seiges	1
Historie de Polybe	6
Ingenieur de Campagne	1
Tactique de l'infantry	1
Grey on Gunnery	1
Kanes Campaign's	1
Fortification de Vauban	1
New Art of War	1

Mathematical
Practical Surveyor	1
Kerts Euclide	1
Ellements of Euclide	1
Table des logarithme	1
Hoppus on Measuring	1

Geography
System of Geography	2

Poetry
Poems on Chess	1
Triumph of fame	1
Alexanders feast	1
Paradice Lost	1
Ester, Judas Machabe	1
Sampson Messiah	1
Oeuvres de moliere	8
Tasso	2
Poems of Underwoods	1
Pope's Odessy	5
Ditto Illiade	6
Ditto Works	8
Shakespears works	7
Miltons Paradice Lost	1
Plyni's Operas	2
Collection of Poems	3

Miscelanies
Tissot on Health	1
Avis aux peuples	1
Ellements of Heraldry	1
Unitas fratrum	1
Italian Grammr	1
Thompson's seasons	1
Time's tellescope	1
Leonidas	1
Apocriph	1
Rules of Chess	1
Burlemaque	
Cambridge Editions of the Bible	2

Classic's
Guthries Cicero	2
Orations of Demosthenes	1
Seneca's Morals	1
Watt's Logic	1
Saluste	1
English Grammer	1
Trapp's Virgil	3
Middletons Cicero	2
Watsons Horace	1
Newtons Philosophy	1
Lucians Works	4

Politicks
Memoire of Torcy	2
Rolts powers of Europe	4
Spirit of Laws...Engh.	2
Ditto...French	2
Vatils Law of Nations	1
Turkish Spy	8
Humes political Histy.	2

Architecture
Hydrolique de Belidor	4
Lemuel	1

Novels & Fables
Marmontels tales	3
Don Quichotte	6
Gay's Fables	1
Profete Nostradamus	1
The Lady's friend	1

Morality
Passion of the Soul	1
Direction for Prayers	1
Religious perfections	2
The Soul of Man	1
Bible de Martinet	1
New Duty of Man	1
Nelson's festivals	1
Pearson on the Creed	1

Sermons
Beverige's Sermons	1
Seeds Ditto	2
Clarks Ditto	8
Wakes Ditto	1
Barrows Ditto	1

Agriculture
Putleins culture of Silk	1
Botanist	1
Bartlets farrery	1
Body of Husbandry	4

Dictionary's
Chamber's Dicty.	2
Posthlewaits Ditto	2
Boyer's Ditto	2
Altiery's Ditto	2
Bayl's Ditto	1
Militaire Ditto	1
Classic Ditto	1
De Bayles	3
Dixionaires des anecdotes	2

Index to all Ditto	1 Ditto
Cay's Abridgt. of the Statues	2 Ditto
Jacob's Law Dictionary	1 Ditto
Hales' Pleas Crown	2 Ditto
Hawkin's Ditto	1 Ditto
Woods Institutes	1 Ditto
Statutes at Large	9 4vo
Reports of Cases in Chancery	3 Ditto
Virginia Laws	1
North Carolina Ditto	1
Les Egarements du cour et de lesprit	1
Le Comte de Warwick	2
The Man of 40 Crowns	1
Esops fables	1
Comte mogol	3
Batchelier de Salamanq	2
Avanture de Thelemaque	2
Ditto de Gil blas	4

Law
Viners Abridgement	24 Folio
New York Ditto	2
Burn's Justice	3 8vo
Chancery practises by Har.	2 Ditto
Dalrymple on feudal property	1 Ditto
Attorney's Practise in King's Bench	2 Ditto
Attorney's Ditto in Common Pleas	2 Ditto

To which is to be included (not mentioned in the foregoing Inventory) The total Consumption of Governor Tryon's Cloaths, Public and Private papers with £200 paper currency, as also the loss Mrs. Tryon Sustained in her Jewels, all her pearls &c wearing apparel and a very valuable Collection of Music. The whole Damage sustained by the Governor & Mrs. Tryon on this melancholy Occasion amounting upon a moderate Estimation to Six Thousand Pounds Sterling.

[In Tryon's Handwriting:] London 28th June 1774 Wm. Tryon

Dartmouth MSS, Box 22, fol. 916, Salt Library, Stafford, England.

Appendix 7

INVENTORY OF THE GOODS & CHATTELS LEFT IN THE HOUSE OF HIS EXCELLENCY THE RIGHT HONBLE LORD WILL.m CAMPBELL CHARLESTOWN SOUTH CAROLINA.

       £ S p

DINING ROOM

1	Settee of Crimson Silk Damask with Linnen Cover	11. 0.	0
10	Chairs of D.o	21. 0.	0
2	Easy Chairs of D.o	6. 6.	0
1	Large Green Worcester Carpet	17. 0.	0
2	Card Tables lined with Green Cloth	5. 5.	0
2	Oval Glasses with Ornamented & Gilt Frames	14.14.	0
1	Fire Grate, Ornamented w.th Brass, Shovel, Tongs, Poker and Fender	6. 6.	0

DRAWING ROOM

1	Large Elegant Lady's Writing Desk of Mahogany	40. 0.	0
2	Round Stands .... of D.o	4. 4.	0
1	D.o Dressing Table ... of D.o	1.11.	6
8	Hair Bottom Chairs .. of D.o	8. 8.	0
1	Yellow Worcester Carpet	20. 0.	0
1	Elegant Harpsichord, double Rows of Keys, Fineerd &c.a	84. 0.	0
1	Grate, Fender, Shovel, Tongs & Poker, Brass Mounted	8. 8.	0
1	Mahogany Tambour Screen	1. 7.	0
1	D.o .... Fire Screen	1. 7.	0
1	Ebony Ink Stand Compleat	1. 4.	0

NORTH EAST BED CHAMBER

1	Mahogany Four Post Bedstead	6. 6.	0
1	D.o ..... Wash Hand Stand w.th Looking Glass &Cet.a	5. 5.	0
1	D.o ..... Bureau Desk	5. 5.	0
1	Stone Wash Hand Bason & Stand	1. 1.	0
1	Mahogany Model of a Rice Machine	6. 6.	0
2	Green Chairs with Rush Bottoms	1. 4.	0

SOUTH EAST BED CHAMBER

1	Mahogany Four Post Bedstead	6. 6.	0
1	Feather Bed	8. 8.	0
1	Mahogany Nest of Drawers Single	4. 4.	0
5	Green Chairs w.th Rush Bottoms	3. 0.	0
1	Cyprus Toilet	0.15.	0
4	India Blinds Painted	2.16.	0
18	Small Baskets, from the Madeiras & Indies	1.16.	0
2	Mahogany Tambour Frames & one Stand	7. 7.	0

LANDING PLACE

1	Small Glass Lanthorn	1.11.	0
1	Long Broom	0. 5.	0
	Carried over	£313.16.	0
		£ S	p
	Brought over	313.16.	0

CAP.t INNES'S CHAMBER

1	Maple 4 Post Bedstead w.th Blue Harriteen Furniture	5. 5.	0
1	Feather Bed	4. 4.	0
1	Matrass	1.11.	6
1	Pillow	0. 5.	0
1	Blanket	0. 8.	0
1	White Cotton Counterpane	1.11.	6
1	Other Maple 4 Post Bedstead w.th Blue Harriteen Furniture	5. 5.	0
1	Matrass	1.11.	6
1	Pillow, 1 Blanket & 1 White Cotton Counterpane	2. 4.	6
1	Square Mahogany Night Table	2. 2.	0
1	...... D.o ..... Night Chair	2. 2.	0
1	...... D.o ..... Writing Desk	5. 5.	0
1	Looking Glass	1.11.	6
1	Large Tellescope	5. 5.	0
1	Green Pavillion	2.14.	0
1	Stone Bottle & Bason	0. 4.	0
1	Very large Cut Glass Decanter in a Plate Basket	8. 8.	0
4	Green Chairs with Rush Bottoms	2. 8.	0
1	Large Map of South Carolina on Rollers	2. 0.	0

NURSERY

1	Green Field Bedstead, Mohair Curtains, Feather Bed Blanket, Bolster & Quilt	12.12.	0
1	Childs Cot w.th Matrass, Pavilion, Pillow & Stand	1. 0.	0
1	Green Pavilion	1.10.	0
1	Small Cyprus Table	0. 7.	0
3	Pair of Sheets	7.17.	6
6	Table Cloths	5. 8.	0
3	Towels	0. 3.	0
4	Rubber Cloths	0. 2.	0
6	Knife D.o	0. 3.	0

SERVANTS BED CHAMBER

2	Four Post Bedsteads, Feather Bed, Bolster & Pillow	18.18.	0
2	Pair of Sheets	2.10.	0
2	Quilts	2. 2.	0
2	Blankets	0.18.	0
1	Pavilion	1. 0.	0
1	Quilting Frame	0.10.	0

M.rs SIDNEY'S ROOM

1	Small Mahogany Nest of Drawers	4. 4.	0

1	Cypruss Table	0. 7.	0
2	Green Chairs	1. 4.	0
6	White D.o	2. 2.	0
1	Four Post Bedstead of Maple w.th Matrass, Bolster, Pillow & 2 Blankets	9. 9.	0
1	Pair Fire Dogs/Iron w.th Brass Knobs/Shovel, Tongs & Poker	3. 3.	0
1	Pistol Tinder Box	0. 3.	0
	Carried over	£443.14.	6
		£ S	p
	Brought over	443.14.	6

CLOSET THE WESTERMOST

1	Violencello & case	14.14.	0
	Harriteen Furniture for 2 Beds Compleat	5. 5.	0
4	Crimson Silk Damask Curtains	12. 0.	0
1	Blue Window Curtain, Harriteen	2. 2.	0
	Remnants of Livery Cloth, Black Hair Shagg, Yellow Cloth, Shalloon, Thicksett &c	14. 0.	0

PARLOUR The Breakfast

1	Hair Couch Mahogany Frame on Castors & 2 Bolsters	7. 7.	0
2	Elbow Chairs w.th Hair Bottoms	6. 6.	0
9	Common D.o ... w.th D.o	9. 9.	0
2	Mahogany Frames for Books	4. 4.	0
1	Large Oval Glass w.th Gold & Carved Frame	36. 0.	0
2	Small Mahogany Breakfast Tables	5. 5.	0
2	Large D.o ..... Oval Dining D.o	8. 0.	0
2	Brass Branches	7. 7.	0
4	Green Harriteen Window Curtains, w.th Hooks, Lines &C.a	8. 8.	0

PARLOUR The Dining

1	Large Mahogany Side Board	6.16.	6
3	D.o ... D.o .... Dining Tables	25. 0.	0
2	...... D.o .... Armed Chairs w.th Hair Bottoms	3. 3.	0
7	...... D.o .... Common D.o ... w.th D.o	7. 7.	0
3	Green Straw Bottomed Chairs	1.16.	0
1	Silver Mounted Butler	8. 8.	0
2	Bottle Stands	0. 3.	0
1	Ornamented Steel Grate, Fender, Poker, Tongs & Shovel	8. 8.	0
1	Green Fire Screen	1.11.	6
4	Blue Moreen Curtains	8. 8.	0
1	Painted Floor Cloth	10. 0.	0
1	Japand Plate Warmer	0.16.	0
4	Glass Shades	1.16.	0
1	Dozen Basket Bottle Stands	1. 4.	0
10	Straw Dish Plates	0. 3.	0
1	Large Green Cloth, to Cover the Tables	3. 3.	0

PASSAGE On The Ground Floor

1	Glass Lanthorn	5. 5. 0
1	Large Eight Day Dial	8. 8. 0

THE LIBRARY

1	Mahogany Writing Desk	12.12. 0
1	Guittar & Case	3. 3. 0
1	Bassoon & Case	5. 5. 0
3	Portraits of L^d & L^y Willm & Mrs Campbell in Oil, by Hone	37.16. 0
1	Mahogany Settee, Hair Bottoms, wth Red Check Cover	7. 7. 0
6	Green Chairs wth Rush Bottoms	3.12. 0
2	Hautboys	2. 2. 0
	Carried over £	757.14. 6
		£ S p
	Brought over	757.14. 6

THE LIBRARY Continued

1	Large Mahogany Library, Glazed & Cet^a 17 feet Long	100. 0. 0
1	Brass Barrel Wind Gun	25. 0. 0
3	Pair Brass Mounted Pistols	12.12. 0
1	Blunderbuss	2. 2. 0
1	Post Chaise Gun	1.11. 6
6	Kegs of Philadelphia Flour	3. 3. 0

BOOKS
Vols

2	Chambers Dictionary	4. 4. 0
2	Supplement to D^o	8. 8. 0
1	Mathematical Manuscript by Ld Willm Campbell	5. 5. 0
6	Popes Shakespear	3. 3. 0
1	Ansons Voyage	1. 1. 0
1	Wrights Travels	1. 1. 0
7	Collins's Peerage	2.12. 6
2	Humes Essays	0.12. 0
2	Duncan Caesar	0.10. 0
2	Dictionarium Rusticum	0.10. 0
1	History of Algiers	0. 4. 0
1	Xenophons History of Greece	0.14. 0
10	Annual Register	3. 0. 0
1	Grand Cyrus/the 2nd Volume/	0. 3. 0
2	Ant^y Parliamentary History	0. 8. 0
1	Centaur not Fabulous	0. 5. 0
1	Statutes of the Admiralty	0.10. 6
	Boyers Dictionary	1. 5. 0
7	Bowers History of the Popes	4. 4. 0
	Cleopatria & Octavia	0. 3. 0
	Cambridges War in India	1. 1. 0
	Exhart of Treaties between Great Britain & other Powers	0.12. 0
	Boyers Dictionary/a Second one/	1. 5. 0
	French Pilot	0.10. 6
	Memoirs of Russia	1. 1. 0
3	Clio & Euterpe/Music/	0.14. 0
4	Sherlocks Sermons	1. 0. 0

	Salmons Geographical Grammer	0. 6. 0
	Chronological Annals of the War	0. 5. 0
	Euclids Elements	0. 5. 6
3	Des Maizeaux's Works of St Euremond	0.15. 0
2	Preceptor	0.12. 0
7	Spectacle de le Nature wth Cuts	3. 3. 0
2	Estimate of the Manner of the Times	0. 7. 0
4	Perigine Pickle	0.12. 0
1	Pilhingtons Memoirs	0. 3. 0
3	The Dean of Colerain	0. 9. 0
	Bailey's Dictionary	0. 6. 0
2	History of Pompedour	0. 6. 0
	Travels of Cyrus	0. 8. 0
	Concies History of Philosophy	0. 3. 0
	Hallifax's Miscellanies	0. 4. 0
6	Tully's Memoirs	0.18. 0
2	Roderic Random	0. 6. 0
8	Hookes Roman History	2.14. 0
	Carried over	£958.12. 0
	Brought over	958.12. 0

BOOKS in the Library Continued
Vols

2	Kalms Travels into Nile	0.12. 0
10	Beaumont & Fletchers Plays	3. 0. 0
2	Melmoths Pliny	0.10. 0
2	Life of Marlborough	0.10. 0
2	History of Europe	0.10. 0
3	Tales of the Genie	0.14. 0
2	Miltons Paradice Lost	0.12. 0
4	Sternes Sermons	0.12. 0
4	Belles Letters	0.12. 0
2	Idler	0. 6. 0
2	Placid Man	0. 6. 0
7	Comp of Voyages	1. 1. 0
9	Pope Works	1. 7. 0
6	Drydens Plays	0.18. 0
3	D^o .... Virgil	0. 9. 0
2	Miltons Works	0. 6. 6
	Comment on Popes Works	0. 5. 0
	Barrets Italian Grammer	0. 4. 0
3	Marmontels Coxdes Moraux in French	0.10. 6
4	The Adventreses	0.12. 0
2	Browns Estimate	0. 7. 0
	Mullers Mathematical Elements	0. 6. 0
	Hudibras	0. 3. 6
	Cardinal Bentivoglio's Letters	0. 3. 0
4	Rambler	0.12. 0
8	Spectator	0.16. 0
10	Rollins Antient History	3. 0. 0
2	Fieldings Letters	0. 6. 0
6	Arabian Nights Entertainments	0.18. 0
4	Don Quixote	0.12. 0
13	Rosseaus Works	1.19. 0
3	History of Sid Biddulph	0. 9. 0
2	History of Catheart & Renton	0. 6. 0
1	D^o .... of Clementina	0. 3. 0

2	European Settlements in America	0.10. 0
2	Female Quixote	0. 6. 0
2	Sentimental Journey	0. 6. 0
2	Rowes Works	0. 6. 0
4	Tristam Shandys Life	0.12. 0
	Lady Catesby's Letters	0. 3. 0
2	Collection of Novels	0. 6. 0
	Boyers Dictionary/Small/	0. 7. 0
8	Plutarchs Lives	1.10. 0
	Italian Grammer	0. 5. 0
	Caleaton Masonry	0. 3. 0
	Boyers Grammer	0. 2. 0
8	Humes History of England	2. 8. 0
7	Smollets D^o	2. 2. 0
35	Voltiers Works	5. 5. 0
20	Swifts D^o	3. 0. 0
3	D^o .... Letters	0. 9. 0
	Prayer Book	0. 3. 0
	New Testament	0. 3. 0
	Novia Scotia Acts of Assembly	0.13. 0
31	Odd Volumes	1.11. 0
36	D^o ..... in Blue Covers	1. 7. 0
60	D^o ... Magazines &c^a	1. 0. 0
	French Coasting Pilot	0. 1. 0
	Carried over £	1,005.15. 0
		£ S p
	Brought over	1,005.15. 0

BOOKS in the Library Continued

	Burneby's Travels	0. 3. 6
	Voyage to the Pacifick Ocean	0.10. 6
3	Robinsons History of Charles the 5th	3. 3. 0
	Piersons Lloyds Sermons	0. 5. 0
28	Music Books in Marbled Covers	36. 0. 0
4	D^o .... in Sheep Skin	2.16. 0
14	D^o .... in Blue Paper Covers	7. 7. 0
1	Plan of New York on Rollers	1.14. 0
2	Print of ye Falls of Niagara	1. 8. 0
	D^o ... of Whitehaven	2. 0. 0
4	Drawings about Halifax	2. 2. 0
6	Small Mahogany Music Stands	3. 3. 0
1	Ebony Ink Stand	1. 4. 0
5	Cakes of Ink	0. 2. 6
16	Packs of Message Cards	0.16. 0
	Box of Wafers	0. 1. 0
5	Prints Views of Halifax	2.12. 6
	Shining Sand/a Parcel/	0. 5. 0
200	Quills	0.12. 0
200	Pens	0.12. 0
8	Pieces of Red Tape	0. 4. 0
1	Paper of Pounce	0. 1. 0
	Black Lead Pencils/a Small Parcel/	0.15. 0
34	Half Quires small Gilt Paper	0.17. 0
3	Quire of Blue Blotting Paper	0. 1. 6
5	Small Blank Books	0. 2. 6
1	Mahogany Box s^d to Contain 1 or 2 German Flutes	7. 0. 0
1	Back Gamon Table	1.11. 6
5	Stable Brushes	0. 8. 9

4	Curry Combs	0. 7. 0	12	Do... Turkey Figs	0. 6. 0	1	Gallon Jug	0. 4. 0
4	Handles for Whips	0. 4. 0	25	Do... Do ... Coffee	6. 5. 0	1	Half Gallon Do	0. 2. 0
3	Lashes for Do	0. 2. 6	112	Do... Currants	2.16. 0		CHINA	
4	Horse Combs with Sponges	0. 4. 0	66	Do... Cheshire Cheese	1.10. 0	1	Large Blue Bowl	0.10. 6
1	Box of Playing Cards	14. 8. 0	41	Do... Double Gloucester Do	0.18. 9	12	Coffee Cups & 8 Saucers	1. 1. 0
	GLASS WARE		2	Quarts of Barberries	0. 6. 0	10	Tea Cups & 7 Saucers	1. 2. 0
3	Five Quart Decanters	1. 7. 0	2	Do ..... Sampher	0. 6. 0	1	Tea Pot wth Silver Chain & Spout	1. 1. 0
1	Half Gallon Do	0. 4. 6	8	Do ..... Capers	1. 4. 0	1	Small Bowl	0. 4. 6
11	Quart Do	1. 7. 6	2	Pints Lemon Pickle	0. 6. 0	12	Coffee Cups	0.15. 0
10	Pint Do	0.15. 0	6	Do ... India Joy	0.18. 0	17	Tea Do	1. 2. 0
3	Quart Do ...... Cut	1.11. 6	12	Do ... Ketchup	0.15. 0	6	Caudle Cups wth Saucers	0.12. 0
4	Pint Retailers	0. 4. 0	2	Quarts Anchovies	0. 8. 0	1	Tea Pot	0.10. 0
25	Small Do	0.18. 9	½	Pound Turmerick	0. 2. 0	3	Bread & Butter Dishes	0. 9. 0
3	Cut Cream Potts	0.15. 0	¼	Do ... Cochineal	0. 8. 0	1	Mahogany Tea Board	1. 1. 0
1	Do ...... without a Cover	0. 4. 6	¼	Do ... Cayon	0. 4. 0	1	Japand ... Do	1. 1. 0
8	Diamond Cut Salts	2. 0. 0	6	Do ..... Powder Blue	0.10. 0	1	Copper Kitchen	1. 5. 0
3	Cut Cruets	0. 9. 0	2	Do ..... Ivory Black	0. 2. 8	2	Bread Toasters	0. 5. 0
3	Plain Glass Salvers	2.12. 6	1	Sett of Shoe Brushes	0. 2. 6	2	Japand Knife Boxes	0. 6. 0
1	Cut Glass Pyramid	0.10. 6	2	Westmoreland Hams	1. 8. 3	1	Do ... Sugar Carriage	0. 6. 0
8	Do ...... Sweetmeat Glasses	0.16. 0	1	Yorkshire Do	0.15. 9	1	Do ... Do .... Larger	0. 8. 0
4	Do ...... Do ...... Stands	0. 8. 0	31	Gallons best Vinegar	3. 2. 0	3	Do ... Waiters Small	0. 6. 0
5	Lemonade Glasses	0. 3. 4		STEWARDS ROOM		1	Sett of Small Ebony Castors Silver Mounted	2. 2. 0
52	Jelly & Syllabub Glasses	2.12. 0	1	Sett of Queens Ware wth Green Borders for a Desert	4.11. 2	2	Japand Bread Basketts	0. 8. 0
2	Butter Glasses Cut with Plateau Covers	1.10. 0	1	Do .... wth Blue Do ..... for Do	4.11. 2	3	Shagreen Cases of Green Handled Knives & Forks	8. 8. 0
3	Three Quart Flummery Glasses	0.15. 0	2	Old China Vases not large	0.14. 0	24	Knives & 24 Forks, loose	4. 6. 6
11	Sweet Wine Glasses	0. 4. 7	1	China Pickle Stand	0. 5. 0	24	Do ... & 24 Do ... Desert	4. 0. 0
80	Wine Glasses of 2 Patterns	1.13. 4	4	Do ... Sauce Boats	0.10. 0	28	Do ... & 28 Do ... Black Handles Tipped wth Silver	8.15. 0
	Carried over £1,120. 8. 9		6	Do ... Quart & Pint Mugs	0.15. 0	28	Do ... & 28 Do ... Do	8.15. 0
	£ S p		2	Do ... Pint Bowls	0. 8. 0	6	Common Knives & Forks	0.10. 6
	Brought 1,120. 8. 9		3	Do ... Tureens wth Dishes & Covers	6. 6. 0	2	Mahogany Knife Boxes	1. 1. 0
	GLASS WARE Continued		48	Do .. Dishes of Sorts	38. 8. 0	1	Do ..... Do	0.10. 6
15	Ale Glasses	0. 7. 6		Carried over £1,216.11. 11		3	Do ..... Trays	2. 5. 0
2	Long Stomach Glasses	0. 2. 0		Brought over 1,216.11. 11		2	Plate Baskets	0. 6. 0
31	Wine & Water Glasses/large/	1. 3. 3		STEWARDS ROOM Continued			Carried over £1,307.19. 11	
3	Goblets	0. 3. 0	5	China Round Dishes	4. 0. 0		Brought over 1,307.19. 11	
1	Sugar Dish & Cover Cut	0.10. 0	7	Do... Patty Pans	0.10. 6		STEWARDS ROOM Continued	
1	Mustard Pot	0. 1. 6	54	Do .. Soup Plates	7. 1. 9	4	Small Mahogany Waiters	0. 6. 0
20	Wash hand Glasses	2. 0. 0	125	Do.. Flat Plates	16. 8. 0	2	Cyprus Presses	8. 8. 0
2	Coolers of Queens Ware	1. 1. 0	12	Do .. Coffee Cups	0.15. 0	1	Small Mahogany Table	1.11. 6
2	Glass Shades	0.18. 0	13	Do .. Tea Cups	0.16. 3	1	Cyprus Table	0. 7. 0
1	Do .... Mounted in Brass & Ceta	1. 4. 0	22	Do .. Saucers	1.10. 0	5	Green Chairs wth Rush Bottoms	3. 0. 0
4	Bottles Double Distild Lavendar Water	1. 0. 0	3	Do ... Round Scallopt Dishes	1. 1. 0	1	Desk Coverd with Green	1. 1. 0
2	Pound Double Scented Hair Powder	0. 4. 0	1	Do ... Sugar Dish & Cover	0. 4. 0	1	Pair of Iron Dogs wth Brass Knobs, Shovel, Tongs & Poker	2.10. 6
3	Bottles, Icpemine, Burgemot & Lavender	0.15. 0	1	Do ... Sallad Dish	0. 4. 0	1	Canister with 2 lbs of Green Tea	2. 0. 0
7	Pound Common Hair Powder	0. 7. 0	2	Do ... Quart Bowls	0. 7. 0	1	Paper Parcel of Morels	1. 1. 0
1	Box of Perfume for Cloaths	0.17. 0	1	Do ... Tea Pot	0.10. 6	1	Do .... of Scotch Barley	0. 2. 0
1	Do .. of Macoirns Cakes	0.16. 0	6	Do ... Half Pint Basons	0. 6. 0	1	Do .... of Artichock Bottoms	0.17. 6
1	Do .. of Vermicilli	0.16. 0	4	Do ... Pint Basons	0. 6. 0	1	Do .... of Truffles	1. 1. 0
1	Speaking Trumpet/Small/	0. 2. 6		QUEENS WARE		12	Pound of Hartshorn Shavings	1. 0. 0
1	Box of Dried Citron	2. 0. 0	9	Dishes of Sorts	2. 0. 0	10	Do ... of Pearl Barley	0. 2. 6
3	Pound White Pepper	0. 7. 6	2	Fish Plates	0. 5. 0	4	Do .... of Lintels	0. 2. 0
2	Do ... Bitter Almonds	0. 2. 0	12	Soup Do	0. 4. 0	12	Do ... of Isinglass	3.18. 0
12	Do... Indian Do	1. 0. 0	48	Flatt Do	0.16. 0	1	Paper Parcel of Cinnamon	1.18. 0
34	Do... Bloom Raisons	0.19. 10	5	Small Do	0. 1. 0	12	Wash Balls	0. 6. 0
10	Do... Pruens	0. 3. 4	4	Saucers for Pickles	0. 1. 0			
			2	Sauce Boats	0. 2. 6			

1 Pound of Black Pepper	0. 2. 0	KITCHEN		
1 Paper of Mace	1.16. 0	15 Copper Stew Pans with Covers	8. 7. 0	
1 Do ... of Nutmegs	1. 8. 6	4 Do .... Sauce Pans	2. 7. 6	
1 Do ... of Ginger	0. 3. 0	2 Do .... Do .... Lined with Silver	10.10. 0	
1 Do ... of Cloves	1. 8. 0	1 Do .... Steam Kettle	1. 1. 0	
1 Do ... of Safron	0.16. 0	1 Do .... Do .... large wth 3 large		
2 Rolls of Pomatum	0. 1. 0	Cocks & Funnel	1.14. 0	
1 Paper of Mushroom Powder	0. 8. 0	1 Do .... Fish Kettle	2.13. 6	
1 Do ... of Anniseed	0. 1. 0	1 Do .... Carp Do	1. 4. 9	
1 Do ... of Pimento	0. 5. 0	1 Do .... Turbor Do	4.10. 0	
1 Do ... of Salt Petre	0. 8. 0	1 Do .... Devil or Boiler	12.12. 0	
1 Do ... of Mustard Seed	0. 1. 4	2 Do .... Oval Pye Pans	0.12. 0	
2 Do ... of Dried Mushrooms	0.14. 0	2 Do .... Round Do .... & large	1. 1. 0	
1 Do ... of Carraway Seeds	0. 0. 6	7 Do .... Do .... small	0.14. 0	
1 Do ... of Coriander Seeds	0. 0. 6	2 Do .... Square	1. 1. 0	
1 Do ... of Black Lead	0. 2. 8	2 Do .... Plates for Pastry	0.18. 0	
1 Do ... of Red Lead	0. 0. 8	1 Do .... Spice Pot	0.12. 0	
5 Cakes of Blacking for Shoes	0. 5. 0	1 Do .... Quart Mug	0. 3. 6	
1 Paper of Sal Prunell	0. 6. 0	1 Do .... Gallon Do	0.12. 6	
1 China Jar wth Sugar Candy		2 Do .... Graters	0.14. 0	
wth Lock & Cover	0.16. 0	2 Do .... Chocolate Pots	0.15. 0	
2 Papers of Emory & Rotten		1 Do .... Coffee Pott	0. 7. 0	
Stone Paper	0. 3. 0	1 Do .... Boiler large	2. 2. 0	

1 Choping Block	0.10. 6			
1 Iron Jack Compleat	9. 9. 0			
1 Salamander	0.15. 0			
1 Clever	0. 4. 6			
1 Dutch Stove	0. 5. 0			
1 Gridiron & Gridiron	0.14. 0			
1 Do ..... Smaller	0.12. 0			
1 Marble Pestle & Mortar /Small/	0.12. 6			
1 Do .... & Do .../Large/	1. 1. 0			
1 Iron Coffee Mill	0.12. 0			
1 Do .. Pepper Do	0.12. 0			
4 Do .. Candlesticks	0.12. 0			
3 Tin Do	0. 6. 0			
1 Do .. Tea Kettle	0. 3. 0			
1 Do .. Lanthorn	0. 2. 6			
1 Iron Grate fixed /wth compleat				
Apparatus/	11. 0. 0			
1 Large Cyprus Table	1. 1. 0			
8 Fixed Stoves	2.12. 0			
1 Plate Rack	0.10. 6			
2 Trammel Irons	0. 5. 0			

LOFT 6

101 Bottles of Madeira 7 Years Old	25. 5. 0	
6 Loaves of Treble Refined Sugar	1.18. 6	
24 Do ... of Single Do	9. 0. 0	
8 Baskets of Lisbon Salt	0. 8. 0	
1 Glass Lamp mounted in Brass	2. 2. 0	
2 Powder Horns, Carved	2. 2. 0	
8 Large Music Stands	1. 4. 0	
3 Coach Trunks	4.14. 6	
1 Body Cloth for a Horse	0.16. 0	
2 Sets of Furniture for Servants Horses	5. 5. 0	
1 Box Containing a Carved Chimney Piece in Wood for a Very Large Room	36. 0. 0	
1 New Plate Basket	0. 4. 0	
3 Carpet Brooms	0. 6. 0	
4 Window Blinds	4. 4. 0	
1 Fishing Rod	1. 1. 0	
6 Rackets	0.15. 0	
6 Cricket Bats	1.10. 0	
2 Do ... Balls	1. 4. 0	
2 Trap Balls	0. 6. 0	

Carried over £1,445. 3. 1

£ S p
Brought over 1,445. 3. 1

LOFT Continued

2 Trap Ball Shoes	0. 4. 0
1 Frame for Small Bowl	0.10. 6
18 Balls for Do	0.18. 0
Remnant of Green Canvas	1. 1. 0
3 Pieces of Red Velvet Paper Hangings	0.14. 0
5 Large House Brushes	0.10. 0
1 New Hair Broom	0. 2. 6
1 Dust Shovel	0. 1. 6
A Parcel of Tin Plates	4. 0. 0

6 Do .... Blamanche Moulds	1. 4. 0
5 Do .... for Cuting Pastry	0. 8. 0
6 Do .... Jelly Moulds small	0.12. 0
17 Do ... Do .... smaller	1.12. 6
10 Do ... Patty Pans Do	0. 4. 6
9 Do .... Oval Do .... Do	0. 4. 0
4 Do .... Scoups & Chiggers	0. 6. 0
3 Brass Larding Pins	0. 2. 0
1 Pewter Pott to Jug Hares	0.18. 0
1 Woodsaw	0. 4. 0
1 Adze	0. 3. 0
1 Tin Cheese Toaster	0. 2. 6
1 Do Stew Dish & Lamp	0. 5. 0
16 Do .... Covers	0. 6. 6
1 Do ..... Candle Box	0. 1. 4
8 Do ..... Stew pans and Covers	1.18. 0
3 Do ..... Saucepans	0. 4. 0
3 Do ..... Fish Kettles	0.18. 0
1 Do ..... Milk Pan	0. 3. 0
1 Do ..... Dutch Oven	0. 4. 0
1 Do ..... Chamber Lamp	0. 1. 0
2 Do ..... Cullenders	0. 3. 6
3 Do ..... Soup Pots	1. 4. 0
1 Do ..... Moulds small /Lot/	0. 6. 0
2 Do ..... Driping Pans	0. 7. 6
3 Do ..... Drudging Boxes	0. 2. 0
8 Ladles, Tin & Copper	0.12. 0

Carried over £1,520.12. 8
£ S p
Brought over 1,520.12. 8

KITCHEN Continued

2 Argyles	0. 4. 0
2 Tin Rasps	0. 2. 0
1 Cradle Spit	1.16. 0
2 Single Do	0.12. 0
3 Bird Spits	0. 3. 0
1 Pair of Steelyards	0. 8. 0
2 Choppers	0. 4. 0

2 Frying Pans Do	0. 5. 0
2 Brass Pails	3. 5. 0
1 Iron Crane in ye Chimney	1. 1. 0
1 Steel	0. 2. 6
3 Pair Flatt Irons	0.12. 6
1 Bellows	0. 5. 0
6 Straw Bottom Chairs	0.18. 6
1 Leaden Sink	3. 3. 0
1 Wire Sieve	0. 1. 6
2 Hair Do	0. 2. 0
2 Scrubing Brushes wth Handles	0. 4. 0
1 Do .... wth Lead	0. 5. 0
3 Hair Brooms	0. 4. 6
1 Sett Shoe Brushes	0. 2. 6
1 Do ... Plate Do	0. 2. 0
1 Quart Pewter Tankard	0. 4. 0
1 Chocolate Mill	0. ?
5 Candlesticks Tin	0. ?
3 Nutmeg Graters	0. 3. 0
3 Egg Slicers	0. 1. 6
1 Pepper Box	0. 0. 6
1 Three Pint Pot	0. 1. 6
2 Quart Black Jacks	0. 2. 0
2 large Tin Pye Pans	0. 6. 0
1 Smaller Do	0. 2. 0
3 Do .... Do	0. 3. 0
6 Oval Patty Pans	0. 4. 0
16 Round Do ...... 3 Sizes	0. 8. 0
2 Larding Pins Brass	0. 1. 4
1 Coffee Roaster	2. 2. 0
1 Lignum Vite Rolling Pin	0. 3. 0
2 Bird Spits	0. 2. 0
1 Chafing Dish	0.10. 0
1 Pion Candlestick	0. ?

Carried over £1,572. 3. 0
£ S p
Brought over 1,572. 3. 0

FRONT CELLAR

12 Bottles of Damsons	1. 4. 0
8 Do ..... of Rose & Orange Flower Water	0. 6. 6

6 Do ..... of Mushrooms	1.16. 0	
1 Do ..... of Onions	0. 2. 10	
6 Do ..... Ketchup, Elder Vinegar &ca &ca &ca	0. 6. 9	
4 Do ..... Cherry Brandy	1.12. 0	
10 Do .... Goosberries	1. 0. 0	
11 Do .... Sweet Oil	1. 7. 6	
3 Do ..... Durham Flower of Mustard	0.12. 0	
12 Pound Castile Soap	0.16. 0	
2 Large Boxes of Wax Candles	25. 4. 0	
2 Do .... of Spermeceti Do	23. 8. 0	
1 Do .... Ullage of English Soap	3.15. 0	
1 Do .... Do ... of Currants	1.18. 6	
12 Small Boxes of Nostrums	3. 0. 0	
1 Paper Parcel of Starch	0. 6. 9	
10 Pots of Anchovies, Mangoes &ca &ca &ca	1.12. 0	

COACH HOUSE & STABLES

1 Chest of Carpenters Tools Compleat	47. 0. 0	
1 Chair Cramp	1. 1. 0	
1 Glue Pot	0.15. 0	
1 Carpenters Bench	1.11. 6	
3 Mahogany Planks	4.14. 6	
1 Grindstone	6. 1. 0	
Sundry Peices of Mahogany Do .... of Do ..... for Fineering	4. 4. 0	
1 Coach	150. 0. 0	
1 Chariot	135. 0. 0	
5 Coach Horses	600. 0. 0	
4 Pair of Harness wth Bridles	30. 0. 0	
5 Saddles	8.15. 0	
1 Side Saddle	4. 4. 0	
3 Curb Bridles	1. 4. 0	
2 Do .... Silver Bits	3. 3. 0	
2 Pair Watering Bridles	2. 0. 0	
1 Stable Lanthorn & Lamp	0. 3. 0	
6 Halters	0. 9. 0	
3 Stable Pails	0. 6. 0	
1 Fork	0. 1. 3	
2 Shovels	0. 6. 6	
6 Curry Combs	0.10. 6	
7 Brushes	0.10. 6	
2 Water Brushes	0. 3. 0	
1 Main Comb	0. 1. 0	
4 Rollers	0.14. 0	
4 Whips	0. 6. 0	
1 Suit of Cloths for a Horse	1. 1. 0	
2 Furnitures wth 1 Pair of Holsters	5.14. 0	
2 False Collars	2.14. 0	

LOFT over ye Coach House

Sundry old Bridles & Bits	1. 1. 0	
1 Body Cloth	0.16. 0	
4 Winches for Carriages	0. 6. 0	
Carried over	£2,650. 6. 7	
	£ S p	
Brought over	2,650. 6. 7	

LOFT over ye Coach House Continued

1 Wire Sieve	0. 2. 0	
1 Rice Machine	20. 0. 0	
1 Corn Mill	2.10. 0	

YARD

1 Alderney Cow	10.10. 0	
1 Black Boar China Breed	5. 0. 0	
2 Cords of Fire Wood	1.14. 0	
4 Washing Tubs	0.12. 0	
1 Step Ladder	0.10. 0	

WINE CELLAR

3 Pipes of London Madeira	150. 0. 0	
1 Do ... of Do	50. 0. 0	
2 Hogsheads of London Porter	10. 0. 0	
1 Do ...... of Small Ale	10. 0. 0	
1 Do ...... of Small Beer	5. 0. 0	
1 Ullage ½ Cash Malmsey Madeira	12.10. 0	
42 Bottles of Frontiniac	6. 6. 0	
69 Do .... of Claret	20.14. 0	
144 Do .... of Rhenish	30. 0. 0	
5 Do ..... of Port Wine	1. 0. 0	
108 Do ... of Porter	19.16. 0	
24 Do .... of Ale	2. 8. 0	
2 Bags of Corks	0.17. 0	

COMMON CELLAR

1 Empty Case for Wine wth 12 Bottles large	2. 0. 0	
1 Water Jar & Brass Cork	4. 0. 0	
1 Jar, Half full of Neats Foot Oil	4. 4. 0	
4 Gross of Empty Bottles	6. 0. 0	

PASSAGE between the Cellars

1 Sett of Coach Wheels	8. 0. 0	
1 Horse Bedstead	0.15. 0	
1 Cypruss Table	0.10. 0	
1 Do .... wth 3 Leaves	1.11. 6	
2 Cloths Horses	1. 1. 0	
A Sett of Maple Dresing Boxes Unfinished	8. 8. 0	
A Large Matrass in the Mens Bed Room	1.11. 6	
A Matrass & 2 Blankets in Mr Seigels Room	2.12. 6	
A White Cotton Counterpane in Do	1.11. 6	
2 Pair of Sheets in Do	6. 6. 0	
2 Pillow Cases in Do	0. 8. 0	
1 Feather Bed & Blanket in Jones the Cooks Room	4. 4. 0	
1 Pair of Sheets in Do	2. 2. 0	
2 Blankets the Negro Boys had wth a Small Matrass	1. 1. 0	
2 Diaper Breakfast Table Cloths	3. 0. 0	
Carried over	£3,069. 1. 7	
	£ S p	
Brought over	3,069. 1. 7	
2 Damask Breakfast Table Cloths	6. 6. 0	
6 Servants Table Cloths	3. 0. 0	
1 Wafer Iron	3. 0. 0	

3 Servants Livery Hatts Laced	3. 3. 0	
1 Grooms Hats Do	2. 2. 0	
3 Suits of Servants Livery	36. 0. 0	
21 Large Damask Table Cloths	132. 6. 0	
12 Breakfast Do	37.16. 0	
32 Damask Napkins	8. 8. 0	
12 Diaper Do	2. 2. 0	
1 New Diaper Table Cloth	1.10. 0	
18 New Huckaback Towels	1.11. 6	
12 Common Do	0.16. 0	
6 Pair of Fine Sheets	31.10. 0	
4 Do ... of Servants Do	8. 8. 0	
6 Do ... of Pillow Cases	3. 3. 0	
12 Yards of Green Lutestring	5. 8. 0	
24 Shifts	25. 4. 0	
18 Pair of Stockings	5. 8. 0	
4 Under Petticoats Dimity	3.12. 0	
2 Flouncd Do ..... Do	3.18. 0	
4 Pair of Pockets Do	2. 0. 0	
1 Pink Striped Sacque	8.16. 0	
1 Winter ..... Do	33. 0. 0	
1 Long Polonese	5.19. 0	
1 Manchester Cotton Gown	5. 5. 0	
1 Borderd Chints	5. 5. 0	
1 Pink Sattin Petticoat	3. 3. 0	
12 Muslin Handkerchiefs	3. 0. 0	
6 Pocket Do	2. 8. 0	
3 Night Caps	0.15. 0	
2 Bed Gowns	2. 2. 0	
1 Pink Lutestring Slip	2.16. 0	
6 Frocks	12.12. 0	
18 Pair of New Cotton Stockens	9. 9. 0	
4 Dimity Petticoats	4. 4. 0	
6 Shifts	6. 6. 0	
2 Pockets	0.10. 0	
2 Pair of Silk Shoes	1. 6. 0	
2 Bed Gowns	4. 4. 0	
1 Japand Tea Board	1.11. 6	
22 Cups & 12 Saucers	2. 4. 6	
Half a Peice of Irish Linnen	2. 5. 0	
Half a Peice of Long Lawn	3. 3. 0	
7 Pound of Best Hyson Tea	6. 6. 0	
3 Washing Gowns	6. 6. 0	
12 Shifts	12.12. 0	
4 Pair of Thread Stockings	1. 4. 0	
4 New Dimity Under Petticoats	4. 4. 0	
2 Upper Do ...... Petticoats	4. 4. 0	
1 Blue Sattin Do	3. 3. 0	
1 White Lutestring Night Gown	3. 3. 0	
1 Blue & White Sattin Do	3. 3. 0	
1 Muslin Apron & Pair of Ruffles	3. 3. 0	
2 Pair of Sattin Shoes	1. 6. 0	
10 Yards of Coarse Stuff intended for Jack Towels	0.10. 0	
1 Suit of Point Lace	53. 0. 0	
1 Do ... of Brussels Do	30. 0. 0	
1 Pair of Common Lace Ruffles	15.15. 0	
1 New Silk Hat	2. 2. 0	
6 Caps Blond Lace	12.12. 0	
3 Fine Chip Hatts	0. 9. 0	
1 French Bonnet	1. 1. 0	
Carried over	£3,680. 0. 1	

	£	S	p
Brought over	3,680.	0.	1
Several Pieces of Old Lace	2.	2.	0
Bows of Ribbon of Different Colours	3.	3.	0

PLATE Chest the First

	£	S	p
2 Mahogany Silver Mounted Cases wth a Dozen Knives a Dozen Forks a Dozen Spoons Each & a Marrow Spoon	38.	0.	0
1 D^o ..... Desert wth Knives & Forks	14.14.	0
1 Silver Cup wth a Cover	27. 2.	6
1 D^o ... Waiter	16. 2.	0
1 D^o ... D^o ... Smaller		
2 D^o ... D^o ... D^o	20. 0.	0
1 D^o ... Stand wth 5 Cruets	13.13.	0
4 D^o ... Sauce Boats	33. 0.	0
8 D^o ... D^o ... Spoons	8.10.	0
2 D^o ... Gilt D^o		
1 D^o ... Coffee Pot	10.10.	0
1 D^o ... Lemon Strainer	2.12.	6
1 D^o ... Basket Small	2.10.	0
1 D^o ... Skewes	1.16.	0
2 D^o ... Table Spoons		
4 D^o ... Desert D^o		
14 D^o .. Tea Spoons & 10 Salt Spoons	9.16.	0
1 D^o ... Pair of Tea Tongs		
3 D^o ... Pair of Candlesticks	45. 0.	0
8 D^o ... Labells or Bottle Tickets	2. 2.	0
1 D^o ... Hand Candlestick wth Extinguisher & Snuffers	5. 5.	0
1 D^o ... Pair of Small Fluted D^o	7. 7.	0
2 D^o ... Mounted Horn Cups		
2 D^o ... D^o .... Larger	5. 0.	0
1 D^o ... Urn	42. 0.	0
4 Pair of Steel Snuffers	1.10.	0

CHEST the Second

1 Silver Bread Baskett	20. 0.	0
1 D^o ... Salver Large	37. 0.	0
1 D^o ... Cross Lamp		
2 D^o ... Pair of Branched Candlesticks	90. 0.	0
4 D^o ... Candlesticks	10. 0.	0
1 D^o ... Pair of Fluted D^o	2.10.	0
1 D^o ... Soup Spoon		
6 D^o ... Table D^o	7. 0.	0
2 D^o ... Salt D^o		
1 D^o ... Hand Flat Candlestick & Snuffers		
2 D^o ... Fluted Candlesticks Small	13. 0.	0
1 D^o ... Cheese Toaster	5. 0.	0
1 D^o ... Fish Slicer	2.10.	0
1 Leather Flask & 2 Basket Flasks	3. 3.	0

CHEST the Third

1 Epergne wth 2 Suits of Glasses	70. 0.	0
1 Case for the Silver Urn	1. 1.	0
2 Plate Chests	12.12.	0
1 Chest for the Epergne	1. 5.	0
A Large Wardrobe of Lord Willm Campbell's Cloaths Lace Ruffles, Swords, Fire Arms &c^a &c^a &c^a	494. 0.	0
Packing Cases, Casks, Cartage & Charges of Shiping of the before mentioned Furniture Horses &c^a	42. 8.	0
Carried over	£4,803. 4.	3

	£	S	p
Brought over	4,803. 4.	3
Insurance of the before mentioned Furniture Horses &C^a &C^a &C^a	95. 4.	4
Policys of Insurance at different Times	3. 0.	0
Freight & Primage of ye Furniture, Horses &^a &^a &^a	350. 0.	0
Interest on £5251.8.7 @ £5 per cent per Ann from ye 1st of Jany 1775 to 26th of April 1777 being 2 Years 3 Months & 26 Days	609.18.	7
Carried over	£5,861. 7.	2
Brought over	5,861. 7.	2

AN INVENTORY of the Negroes Lands &Cet^a of Inverary Plantation on the River Savannah Belonging to His Excellency The Right Honble Lord William Campbell.

NEGROE MEN

1	July ... Driver	150. 0. 0
	Sampson .. Carpenter	150. 0. 0
	John ..... D^o	150. 0. 0
	Joe ...... Cooper	150. 0. 0
5	Adam ..... D^o	150. 0. 0
	Aleck .... D^o	150. 0. 0
	Samuel	100. 0. 0
	Tom	90. 0. 0
	Mingo	90. 0. 0
10	Scipio	70. 0. 0
	Abraham	80. 0. 0
	Bristol	70. 0. 0
	Will	70. 0. 0
	Bob	80. 0. 0
15	Peter	70. 0. 0
	Bob	65. 0. 0
	Robin	65. 0. 0
	Sampson	60. 0. 0
	Gilbert	70. 0. 0
20	George	50. 0. 0
	Jupiter	65. 0. 0
	Jamie	65. 0. 0
	Pompey	65. 0. 0
	Marlborough	70. 0. 0
5	Limus	78. 0. 0
	Sambo	65. 0. 0
	Cain	70. 0. 0
	Sandy	55. 0. 0
	Aaron	52. 0. 0
30	Jacob	35. 0. 0
	Billy	70. 0. 0
	Sharper	80. 0. 0
	Quaco	70. 0. 0
	Captain	60. 0. 0
5	Charles	70. 0. 0
	Cuffie	40. 0. 0
	Joe	60. 0. 0
	Booby	70. 0. 0
	Abraham	70. 0. 0
40	Quamine	60. 0. 0
	Joe	70. 0. 0

WOMEN

1	Amantha	45. 0. 0
	Jeany	40. 0. 0
	Kenny	60. 0. 0
	Peggy	60. 0. 0
5	Sarah	60. 0. 0
	Rinah	40. 0. 0
	Lucy	50. 0. 0
	Margaret	48. 0. 0
	B[?]	60. 0. 0
10	Charlotte	35. 0. 0
	Hannah	65. 0. 0
	Betty	60. 0. 0
	Rose	64. 0. 0
	Nelly	45. 0. 0
15	Daphne	60. 0. 0
	Phillis	65. 0. 0
	Dell	65. 0. 0
	Rinah	62. 0. 0
	Carried over	£10,115. 7. 2
	Brought over	10,115. 7. 2

NEGROE WOMEN Continued

19	Nancy	58. 0. 0
20	Betty	50. 0. 0
	Maria	50. 0. 0
	Jenny	40. 0. 0
	Doll	45. 0. 0
	Betty	40. 0. 0
5	Rose	42. 0. 0
	Tenah	40. 0. 0
	Diana	35. 0. 0
	Nancy	25. 0. 0
	Moll	20. 0. 0
30	Judith	20. 0. 0
	Esther	20. 0. 0
	Rose	20. 0. 0

BOYS

1	Jamie	62. 0. 0
	John	60. 0. 0
	Tony	45. 0. 0
	London	40. 0. 0
5	Dick	30. 0. 0
	Tom	30. 0. 0

	Aleck	35. 0. 0	
	Bob	35. 0. 0	
	Pompey	25. 0. 0	
10	Joe	62. 0. 0	
	Andrew	65. 0. 0	
	Caesar	60. 0. 0	
	Primus	65. 0. 0	
	Job	63. 0. 0	
15	Robin	64. 0. 0	

149	Barrels of Rice @ Mr Graham's Plantation called Mulberry Grove	
25	Do ..... of Do ... Mr Houston	
1	Do ...... of Do ... Mr Mont	
25	Do ..... of Do ... Mr Dupi	
200	Do .... of Do @ £ 2.5.9 per Bll	457.10. 0
215	Do .... of Do @ the Plantation @ £2.5.9 per Bll	491.16. 3
19	Head of Cattle @ £8 per Head	152. 0. 0
9	Horses @ £20 per Horse	180. 0. 0
5	Working Oxen @ £16 per Ox	80. 0. 0
750	Acres of Land all River Swamp	4,185.14. 3
	Barn, Machine & Negroe Houses	428.11. 5
	Overseers House	110. 0. 0

Annual Profit of the Estate of Inverary from the 1st Jany 1775 to the 26th Day April 1777 @ £830 per Ann   1,928. 0. 0

Compound Intst thereon @ £8 per Ct per Ann being the legal Interest of the Provence of South Carolina   111. 0. 0

Quarter Share of the Stock & Cattle of the late Ralph Izard Esqr Father to Lady Willm Campbell amounting to the Sum of £420 wth Compound Intst thereon from the 1st of Jany 1772 to 26th April 1777 @ £8 per Ct per Ann   633. 1. 2

By Cash at Interest per Bonds as per Receipt of Heny Middleton Esqr of Charles Town South Carolina Granted to Collin Campbell Esqr my Attorney   2,061.16. 3

Sallary due from the Provence from the 1st Jany 1775 to the 26th April 1777 @ £600 per Ann   1,393.15. 0

Compound Interest thereon @ £8 per Ct per Ann   80. 4. 9

Carried over £23,654.16. 3

                 £   S   p

Brought over   23,654.16. 3

House Rent from 1st Jany 1775 to 26th April 1777 @ £200 per Ann   464.11. 8

Compound Interest thereon @ £8 per Ct per Ann   26.15. 0

Fees from the Secretary Office from Do to Do @ £1200 per Ann   2,787.10. 0

Compound Interest thereon @ £8 per Ct per Ann   160. 9. 7

£27,094. 2. 6

T. 1/541, Public Record Office, London, microfilm, CWF.

Notes

Prologue
page numbers 12–25

1. Details are given in the Botetourt papers preserved at Badminton House, Gloucestershire, and the Gloucester County Records Office, hereafter called Badminton Papers. Copies of all relevant documents and transcripts of virtually all of them are in the Foundation Library, Colonial Williamsburg Foundation, Williamsburg, Va. The Badminton Papers are incompletely cataloged so in describing them I have referred primarily to the correspondents and to the date as well as to the precise nature of the document. William Nelson to the fifth duke of Beaufort, Oct. 30, 1770, John Randolph to Beaufort, Oct. 15, 1770, Badminton Papers. In contrast to the expeditious manner in which the trustees performed their task, some details of the estate of Botetourt's predecessor, Francis Fauquier, were still unsettled several years later. Robert Carter to Francis Fauquier, July 5, 1783, Robert Carter Letterbook, V, 1782–1784, Carter Papers, MSS Division, Duke University Library, Durham, N. C. Botetourt's background has been comprehensively studied by Bryan Little, "Norborne Berkeley, Gloucestershire Magnate," *Virginia Magazine of History and Biography*, LXIII (1955), pp. 379–409. John Blair, Sr., was president of the Council when Botetourt died. On account of his advanced years, he was persuaded to stand down on Oct. 15 and allow the younger Nelson to become president and therefore acting governor on Botetourt's death. H. R. McIlwaine, Wilmer L. Hall, and Benjamin J. Hillman, eds., *Executive Journals of the Council of Colonial Virginia* (Richmond, Va., 1925–1966), VI, pp. 366–367.
2. J. Randolph to Beaufort, Oct. 15, 1770, Badminton Papers.
3. R. Carter to Beaufort, Oct. 9, 15, 1770, *ibid*.
4. Rind's *Virginia Gazette* (Williamsburg), Oct. 18, 1770; McIlwaine, Hall, and Hillman, eds., *Executive Journals of the Council*, VI, p. 376.
5. The invitation is reprinted in Charles Washington Coleman, "Norborne, Baron de Botetourt, Governor–General of Virginia, 1768–1770," *William and Mary Quarterly*, 1st Ser., V (1896), p. 170.
6. Nelson to Beaufort, Oct. 30, 1770, Richard Starke to Beaufort, Oct. 25, 1770, Badminton Papers.
7. Jack P. Greene, ed., *The Diary of Colonel Landon Carter of Sabine Hall, 1752–1778*, I (Charlottesville, Va., 1965), p. 512.
8. William Aitchison to Charles Steuart, Oct. 17, 1770, MS 5040, 1747–June 1784, Charles Steuart Papers, National Library of Scotland, Edinburgh, microfilm, CWF.
9. Robert Beverley to Samuel Athawes, Oct. 17, 1770, Robert Beverley Letter Book, 1761–1793, Beverley Papers, Library of Congress, transcript, CWF.
10. William Marshman to d'Aussy, Oct. 17, 1770, Marshman to John Marshman, Nov. 8, 1770, Badminton Papers.
11. The obituary in Rind's *Va. Gaz.*, Oct. 18, 1770, reads in full: "On Monday the 15th Instant, about One o'Clock in the Morning departed this Life, universally lamented throughout this Colony, his Excellency the Right Honourable NORBORNE Baron de BOTETOURT, his Majesty's Lieutenant, Governor General and Commander in Chief of the Colony and Dominion of Virginia, and Vice Admiral of the same.

    Truly and justly to express the many great Virtues and amiable Qualities which adorn'd this noble Lord, as well in his public as private Character, would demand the Skill of the ablest Penman. Suffice it then to inform such Parts of the World as were Strangers to his transcendent Merits, that Virginia, in his Fall, sorely laments the Loss of the best of Governours, and the best of Men. Let his distant Relations and Friends be told that we have all anticipated, and shall, to the latest Period, share their Griefs and deep Afflictions; and that we condole with them, with the Warmth of the most tender Affection."
12. Edmund Randolph, *History of Virginia*, ed. Arthur H. Shaffer (Charlottesville, Va., 1970), p. 165; Coleman, "Norborne, Baron de Botetourt," p. 170; Nelson to Beaufort, Oct. 30, 1770, Badminton Papers. Botetourt's death even inspired a "Song to the Memory of the late Ld Bot. by B. W." (probably Benjamin Waller, clerk of the court in Williamsburg) which scans to the tune of "God Save the King"! Manuscript Notebooks, M-116, Webb-Prentis Collection, Alderman Library, University of Virginia, Charlottesville.
13. All the details of the funeral expenses are contained in tradesmen's vouchers submitted to Botetourt's estate. These vouchers were carefully kept by Robert Carter Nicholas, who even refused to send them to England for inspection by the duke's auditor in case of their loss. They are now among the Robert Carter Nicholas Papers at the Lib. Cong.; transcripts are at CWF. Details of the cost of ingredients for the funeral cakes are in the Botetourt Papers. See also Purdie and Dixon's *Va. Gaz.* (Williamsburg), Oct. 18, 1770. For funeral customs, see Clare Gittings, *Death, Burial and the Individual in Early Modern England* (London, 1984), pp. 155–158. Reference courtesy of Patricia A. Gibbs. For the use of chapel vaults in Virginia, see Dell Upton, *Holy Things and Profane: Anglican Parish Churches in Colonial Virginia* (New York, 1986), p. 202.
14. One other dramatic and elaborate ceremony in Williamsburg, the proclamation of the death of William III and the accession of Queen Anne in 1702, approaches the Botetourt funeral in detail. See Jane Carson, *Colonial Virginians at Play* (Williamsburg, Va., 1965), pp. 198–203. Despite the brilliant quality of the reportage, the delineation of hierarchy in that event is not made so particular and clear as the Botetourt funeral.
15. Rhys Isaac, *The Transformation of Virginia, 1740–1790* (Chapel Hill, N. C., 1982), pp. 326–328.
16. Nelson to Beaufort, Oct. 30, 1770, Badminton Papers. "Rules of Precedency" for "the Settlement of the Precedency of MEN and WOMEN in America" only appeared later in Williamsburg, in the *Va. Gaz.* (Purdie and Dixon), May 26, 1774, under the sanction of Joseph Edmonson, the Mowbray Herald.
17. Nelson to Beaufort, Oct. 30, 1770, Beaufort to the trustees, Jan. 2, 1771, Badminton Papers; Christopher Gilbert, *The Life and Work of Thomas Chippendale* (New York, 1978), I, pp. 248–252.
18. The inventory is dated Oct. 24, 1770. Nelson to Beaufort, Oct. 30, 1770, Badminton Papers.
19. Beaufort to Nelson, Jan. 2, 1771, *ibid*. It was not until June 1771 that goods valued at £3,000 were ready to be shipped to the duke. By that time Marshman and Fuller had completed their work and planned to return on the same ship. A delay occurred because of tremendous storms, so Marshman and Fuller transferred to another vessel. The ship carrying Botetourt's goods back to the duke never arrived. Trustees to Beaufort, May 27, June 8, July 25, 1771, Botetourt Papers, Virginia State Library and Archives, Richmond; Beaufort to the trustees, Mar. 6, 1772, Badminton Papers.
20. Both John Randolph and William Nelson raised the question with the duke of offering the residue of Botetourt's estate in the Palace to his successor. Botetourt had purchased over £700 worth of goods in the Palace from *his* predecessor's estate. The fact that Botetourt's possessions were subsequently sold at public auction strongly suggests that Lord Dunmore declined this offer. Final accounts of the estate dated May 5, 1772, entered into the General Court records the same day, Badminton Papers.
21. For condescension and deference, see Isaac, *Transformation of Virginia*, esp. pp. 76–78, 109–110, 131–135, 328–329.

The Inventory
page numbers 26-37

1. The working copy of the inventory and the list of standing furniture are among the Botetourt Papers, Va. State Lib. and Arch.; the fair copy, identical in virtually every respect, is among the Badminton Papers. Peter Pelham's bill is in the Nicholas Papers. For Blandford, see Beaufort to the trustees, Jan. 2, 1771, Badminton Papers. W. Marshman to J. Marshman, Nov. 8, 1770, *ibid.* John M. Hemphill II identified James Cocke, clerk of the Treasury, as an assistant to Nicholas in this task. "Role of Peter Pelham at the Governor's Palace," memorandum, 1988, CWF.
2. William Gooch and Francis Fauquier brought "kin" families with them; Lord Dunmore brought his for only one year.
3. For the physical layout of the Palace, see pp. 38–71 and Marcus Whiffen, *The Public Buildings of Williamsburg: Colonial Capital of Virginia* (Williamsburg, Va., 1958), pp. 53–66.
4. For a comparable secretary's office at Tryon's Palace, New Bern, N. C., see Thomas Tileston Waterman and Frances Benjamin Johnston, *The Early Architecture of North Carolina* (Chapel Hill, N. C., 1947), pp. 32–33, 82–86.
5. Nelson to Beaufort, Oct. 30, 1770, trustees to Beaufort (in Nicholas's handwriting), June 8, 1771, Badminton Papers.
6. Final accounts of the estate, May 5, 1772, *ibid.* From these accounts, from the known values (when acquired) of the portraits and state coach that the duke presented to the colony and the other items such as wallpaper and stoves left at the Palace, plus the amount of insurance placed on goods returned to the duke in England, the sum of approximately £6,000 was arrived at. In the estate of Lord William Campbell, governor of South Carolina, 1773–1776, for instance, the value of the slaves constituted 94% of the worth of the contents of his well-furnished house. See pp. 256–257 and Appendix 7.
7. Local Virginia accounts are found in the Nicholas Papers. Other accounts and financial records are in the Badminton Papers, which include all of Botetourt's Papers.
8. Hunter Dickinson Farish, ed., *Journal & Letters of Philip Vickers Fithian, 1773–1774: A Plantation Tutor of the Old Dominion* (Williamsburg, Va., 1957), pp. 81, 178. Upton, *Holy Things and Profane*, pp. 205–214, discusses sequences in varied Virginia landscapes in the eighteenth century. See also D. W. Meinig, "The Beholding Eye: Ten Versions of the Same Scene," in D. W. Meinig, ed., *The Interpretation of Ordinary Landscapes: Geographical Essays* (New York, 1979), pp. 33–48.
9. For a fuller discussion of this topic, see Cary Carson, "Doing History with Material Culture," in Ian M. G. Quimby, ed., *Material Culture and the Study of American Life*, Winterthur Conference Report 1975 (New York, 1978), pp. 41–64; Thomas J. Schlereth, ed., *Material Culture Studies in America* (Nashville, Tenn., 1982), esp. pp. 1–173; Thomas J. Schlereth, "Material Culture and Cultural Research," in Thomas J. Schlereth, ed., *Material Culture: A Research Guide* (Lawrence, Kans., 1985), pp. 1–34; and Dell Upton, "The Power of Things: Recent Studies in American Vernacular Architecture," *ibid.*, pp. 57–78.
10. The definition of culture is from the *Oxford English Dictionary*. The anthropological definition of culture is taken from James Axtell, "The Ethnohistory of Early America: A Review Essay," *WMQ*, 3rd Ser., XXXV (1978), pp. 110–144, esp. p. 114. See also Kenneth L. Ames, "The Stuff of Everyday Life: American Decorative Arts and Household Furnishings," in Schlereth, ed., *Material Culture: A Research Guide*, pp. 79–112, esp. p. 86.
11. For a discussion of these topics, see Peter Thornton, *Seventeenth-Century Interior Decoration in England, France and Holland* (New Haven, Conn., 1978); John Fowler and John Cornforth, *English Decoration in the 18th Century* (Princeton, N. J., 1974); Mark Girouard, *Life in the English Country House: A Social and Architectural History* (New Haven, Conn., 1978); and Neil McKendrick, John Brewer, and J. H. Plumb, *The Birth of a Consumer Society: The Commercialization of Eighteenth-Century England* (Bloomington, Ind., 1982). Richard L. Bushman discusses this cultural phenomenon in a wide colonial context in a most perceptive essay, "American High-Style and Vernacular Cultures," in Jack P. Greene and J. R. Pole, eds., *Colonial British America: Essays in the New History of the Early Modern Era* (Baltimore, Md., 1984), pp. 345–383. A recent essay discusses much of the literature of the consumer revolution; see T. H. Breen, "An Empire of Goods: The Anglicization of Colonial America, 1690–1776," *Journal of British Studies*, XXV (1986), pp. 467–499.
12. Jack P. Greene, "Society, Ideology, and Politics: An Analysis of the Political Culture of Mid-Eighteenth-Century Virginia," in Richard M. Jellison, ed., *Society, Freedom, and Conscience: The American Revolution in Virginia, Massachusetts, and New York* (New York, 1976), pp. 69–70, 74–75. McKendrick has written of the debate on luxury in "The Cultural Response to a Consumer Society: Coming to Terms with the Idea of Luxury in Eighteenth Century England," paper presented at a colloquium organized by the Institute of Early American History and Culture, Williamsburg, Va., Sept. 1985.
13. Farish, ed., *Journal & Letters of Fithian*, p. 27; Dell Upton, "New Views of the Virginia Landscape," *VMHB*, XCVI (1988), pp. 403–470; Upton, "The Power of Things," in Schlereth, ed., *Material Culture: A Research Guide*, passim; Bushman, "American High-Style and Vernacular Cultures," in Greene and Pole, eds., *Colonial British Society*, pp. 345–346.
14. Hugh Jones, *The Present State of Virginia*, ed. Richard L. Morton (Chapel Hill, N. C., 1956), p. 80; Randolph, *History of Virginia*, ed. Shaffer, p. 176. Greene, "Society, Ideology, and Politics," in Jellison, ed., *Society, Freedom, and Conscience*, constitutes a particularly graceful and informative survey of the Virginia gentry around mid-century. See also John E. Selby, *The Revolution in Virginia, 1775–1783* (Williamsburg, Va., 1988), pp. 23–40.
15. Louis B. Wright, *The First Gentlemen of Virginia: Intellectual Qualities of the Early Colonial Ruling Class* (San Marino, Calif., 1940), p. 2. See also pp. 1–94. For the instructions to children, see p. 232.
16. Robert "King" Carter to William Robertson (?), May 15, 1727, Robert "King" Carter Letterbook, 1727–1728, Alderman Lib.; Carson, *Colonial Virginians at Play*, pp. 207–208.
17. John Clive and Bernard Bailyn, "England's Cultural Provinces: Scotland and America," *WMQ*, 3rd Ser., XI (1954), p. 211, noted in Upton, *Holy Things and Profane*, p. 27.
18. Bushman, "American High-Style and Vernacular Culture," in Greene and Pole, eds., *Colonial British Society*, pp. 346–348; Upton, "New Views," pp. 422–425, 434–439, 444–451. An interesting commentary on the above and also on the "rebellion" against English culture in the "first gentlemen" is Martin H. Quitt, "Immigrant Origins of the Virginia Gentry: A Study of Cultural Transmission and Innovation," *WMQ*, 3rd Ser., XLV (1988), pp. 629–655.
19. Beverley to Athawes, Apr. 15, 1771, Beverley Letter Book; McKendrick, Brewer, and Plumb, *Birth of a Consumer Society*, passim; Breen, "An Empire of Goods," pp. 467–499; T. H. Breen, "'Baubles of Britain': The American and Consumer Revolutions of the Eighteenth Century," *Past and Present*, CXIX (1988), pp. 73–104; Carole Shammas, "Consumer Behavior in Colonial America," *Social Science History*, VI (1982), pp. 67–86; Ann Finer and George Savage, eds., *Selected Letters of Josiah Wedgwood* (London, 1965), p. 28; Bushman, "American High-Style and Vernacular Culture," in Greene and Pole, eds., *Colonial British Society*, pp. 348–365.
20. For more on this topic, see John M. Murrin, "The Great Inversion, or Court versus Country: A Comparison of the Revolution Settlements in England (1688–1721) and

America (1776–1816)," in J. G. A. Pocock, ed., *Three British Revolutions: 1641, 1688, 1776* (Princeton, N. J., 1980), pp. 368–453; Edmund S. Morgan and Helen M. Morgan, *The Stamp Act Crisis, Prologue to Revolution* (Chapel Hill, N. C., 1953), pp. 88–98, 287–294; Randolph, *History of Virginia*, ed. Shaffer, pp. 170–171; "Meade Family History: Autobiography of David Meade," *WMQ*, 1st Ser., XIII (1904), p. 88; and David John Mays, *Edmund Pendleton, 1721–1803: A Biography*, I (Cambridge, Mass., 1952), pp. 250–257.

21. For Gov. William Tryon, see Waterman and Johnston, *Architecture of North Carolina*, pp. 32–33, 82–86; Alonzo Thomas Dill, *Governor Tryon and His Palace* (Chapel Hill, N. C., 1955), passim; and B. D. Bargar, ed., "Governor Tryon's House in Fort George," *New York History*, XXXV (1954), pp. 297–309. Gov. Robert Eden's inventory is in Audit Office 13/60, pt. 1, Claims, American Loyalist Series II, Temporary Support, Maryland, pp. 196–207, Public Record Office, microfilm, Lib. Cong. See also Morris L. Radoff, *Buildings of the State of Maryland at Annapolis* (Annapolis, Md., 1954), pp. 48–54, 81–85.

22. Schlereth, "Material Culture," in Schlereth, ed., *Material Culture: A Research Guide*, p. 14; Upton, "Power of Things," *ibid.*

23. Mark R. Wenger, "Reconstruction of the Governor's Palace in Williamsburg, Virginia," research report, 1980, CWF; Upton, "New Views," pp. 437–438.

The Setting
page numbers 38–71

1. The standard reference on the Governor's Palace is Whiffen, *Public Buildings*. See also Daniel D. Reiff, *Small Georgian Houses in England and Virginia: Origins and Development Through the 1750s* (Cranbury, N. J., 1986), pp. 221–294. For Nicholson's town plan, see John W. Reps, *Tidewater Towns: City Planning in Colonial Virginia and Maryland* (Williamsburg, Va., 1972), pp. 76, 116–118, 123–132, 141–180. The conversion of the front courtyard garden shown on the "Bodleian plate" to a carriage turnaround is based on my reading of the Jefferson sketch, the Frenchman's Map, and other maps of Williamsburg of the 1770–1790 period, none of which shows a wall in front of the Palace. Whiffen, *Public Buildings*, pp. 58–61, 93–94, 175, and endpapers. The archaeological evidence dating from the late 1920s is inconclusive, though suggestive. For "Georgianization," see Henry Glassie, *Folk Housing in Middle Virginia: A Structural Analysis of Historic Artifacts* (Knoxville, Tenn., 1975); and a brief evaluation in Upton, "The Power of Things," in Schlereth, ed., *Material Culture: A Research Guide*, pp. 67–69.

2. Henry Hartwell, James Blair, and Edward Chilton to Board of Trade, 1697, in Warren M. Billings, John E. Selby, and Thad W. Tate, *Colonial Virginia: A History* (White Plains, N. Y., 1986), p. 135; Henry Hartwell, James Blair, and Edward Chilton, *The Present State of Virginia, and the College*, ed. Hunter Dickinson Farish (Williamsburg, Va., 1940), p. 3. See also Reps, *Tidewater Towns*, pp. 141–151.

3. H. R. McIlwaine and John Pendleton Kennedy, eds., *Journals of the House of Burgesses of Virginia, 1702–1712* (Richmond, Va., 1905–1915), pp. 223, 181.

4. William Waller Hening, ed., *The Statutes at Large; Being a Collection of All the Laws of Virginia, from the First Session of the Legislature in the Year 1619*, III (Philadelphia, 1823), p. 285. See also McIlwaine, Hall, and Hillman, eds., *Executive Journals of the Council*, II, pp. 42, 117, 131, 137, 316; McIlwaine and Kennedy, eds., *Journals of Burgesses, 1695–1702*, pp. 137–138, 146, 174–175, 207–209, 238–239, 325; and *ibid., 1702–1712*, pp. 135, 165, 168, 180–181.

5. Robert Beverley, *The History and Present State of Virginia*, ed. Louis B. Wright (Chapel Hill, N. C., 1947), pp. 289–290. In the 1722 edition of his history of Virginia, Beverley stressed that the Palace was "begun in Prest. [president of the Council and acting governor] Jennings' time," thus giving it a local emphasis. In his well-known citation of the source for the so-called Wren Building of the College of William and Mary, Hugh Jones was the first to note that Virginia gentlemen adapted architectural designs. *Present State of Virginia*, ed. Morton, p. 67. The separation of work areas from the main house had a social as well as an aesthetic purpose. See Dell Thayer Upton, "Early Vernacular Architecture in Southeastern Virginia" (Ph.D. diss., Brown University, 1980), pp. 148–172; and Fraser D. Neiman, *The "Manner House" Before Stratford: (Discovering the Clifts Plantation)* (Stratford, Va., 1980), pp. 30–36. The "central passage plan" characteristically became more strictly symmetrical in later Georgian buildings than it is at the Palace. The "Georgian plan" also stressed unity of mass, the preference for external visual symmetry or order over the functional disposition of door and window openings, the primary importance of the architectural envelope over internal organization, the more rigorous adherence to approved classical models in formulating details, and so on. I am grateful to my colleague, Mark R. Wenger, for his comments on these architectural matters.

6. Whiffen, *Public Buildings*, pp. 58–63. My Colonial Williamsburg colleagues, Margaret B. Pritchard and Virginia L. Sites, have produced an excellent study of the "Bodleian plate," the 1740 engraving of the Palace, that is awaiting publication. For an authoritative account of the development of seventeenth-century Virginia architecture, see Upton, "Early Vernacular Architecture"; and Dell Upton, "Vernacular Domestic Architecture in Eighteenth-Century Virginia," *Winterthur Portfolio*, XVII (1982), pp. 95–119. For earlier construction, see Fraser D. Neiman, "Domestic Architecture at the Clifts Plantation: The Social Context of Early Virginia Building," in Dell Upton and John Michael Vlach, eds., *Common Places: Readings in American Vernacular Architecture* (Athens, Ga., 1986), pp. 292–314; Cary Carson, Norman F. Barka, William M. Kelso, Garry Wheeler Stone, and Dell Upton, "Impermanent Architecture in the Southern American Colonies," *Winterthur Portfolio*, XVI (1981), pp. 135–196; Reps, *Tidewater Towns*, pp. 173–174; and James D. Kornwolf, "So Good a Design": The Colonial Campus of the College of William and Mary: Its History, Background, and Legacy* (Williamsburg, Va., 1989). For the Capitol, see Whiffen, *Public Buildings*, pp. 34–50; and Carl R. Lounsbury's studies of Virginia courthouses and the colonial Capitol, both awaiting publication. References courtesy of Mark R. Wenger and Carl R. Lounsbury.

7. Philip Ludwell to William Blathwayt, Mar. 29, 1716, Miscellaneous MSS, Series oo, Individual Items, 1618–1885, Blathwayt Papers, microfilm, CWF; Edmund Jenings to Blathwayt, May 25, 1716, *ibid.*; Beverley, *History and Present State of Virginia*, ed. Wright, pp. 234–235; Jones, *Present State of Virginia*, ed. Morton, p. 70.

8. For further discussion of this topic, see Upton, *Holy Things and Profane*, pp. 3–98; Upton, "New Views," pp. 439–444; and A. G. Roeber, *Faithful Magistrates and Republican Lawyers: Creators of Virginia Legal Culture, 1680–1810* (Chapel Hill, N. C., 1981), pp. 32–41.

9. Whiffen, *Public Buildings*, pp. 60–63. For more details on these topics, see Nancy Halverson Schless, "Dutch Influence on the Governor's Palace, Williamsburg," *Journal of the Society of Architectural Historians*, XXVIII (1969), pp. 254–270. Dutch influence probably appeared more through Anglo-Dutch houses than it did through pattern books. Jones, *Present State of Virginia*, ed. Morton, p. 70; Kornwolf, "So Good a Design," pp. 121–153; Isaac, *Transformation of Virginia*, pp. 34–42. I thank Mark R. Wenger for his insights on the Governor's Palace and its architectural influence in Virginia.

10. Mark R. Wenger, "The Central Passage in Virginia: Evolution of an Eighteenth-Century Living Space," in Camille Wells, ed., *Perspectives in Vernacular Architecture*, II

(Columbia, Mo., 1987), pp. 137–149. I have begged the question of whether or not the central hall and the parlor were originally one room, a question that the archaeological evidence raised. I have presumed, in the absence of more conclusive evidence, that the floor plan shown on the Jefferson sketch was the same as originally planned. See Whiffen, *Public Buildings*, pp. 63–65; and Reiff, *Small Georgian Houses*, pp. 226–231.

11. Upton, "Vernacular Domestic Architecture," p. 102; Wenger, "Central Passage," in Wells, ed., *Perspectives in Vernacular Architecture*, II, pp. 137–138; Isaac, *Transformation of Virginia*, pp. 34–42. For further discussion of progression, see p. 98 and n. 3.

12. McIlwaine and Kennedy, eds., *Journals of Burgesses, 1702–1712*, p. 240; Hening, ed., *Statutes at Large*, III, pp. 482–486. See also Dell Upton, "White and Black Landscapes in Eighteenth-Century Virginia," in Robert Blair St. George, ed., *Material Life in America, 1600–1860* (Boston, 1988), pp. 357–358, 363–366.

13. H. R. McIlwaine, ed., *Legislative Journals of the Council of Colonial Virginia* (Richmond, Va., 1918–1919), III, p. 59.

14. Upton, "Vernacular Domestic Architecture," p. 103; McIlwaine, Hall, and Hillman, eds., *Executive Journals of the Council*, IV, pp. 134–135; McIlwaine, ed., *Legislative Journals of the Council*, III, p. 1557.

15. Whiffen, *Public Buildings*, pp. 55, 57, 63, 92, 94, 140. For Tryon's Palace, see Waterman and Johnston, *Early Architecture of North Carolina*, pp. 32–33, 82–86. Archaeological information was provided by my colleague, Ivor Noël Hume. It is possible that a separate kitchen was constructed at the Palace during the later part of the colonial period, though the evidence is far from conclusive.

16. Hening, ed., *Statutes at Large*, III, pp. 483–484.

17. Whiffen, *Public Buildings*, pp. 140–144.

18. Carter's Grove, James City Co., Va., built in the early 1750s, features a broad hall narrowing down to a passage at the rear, which contains the stairs. Directly above the hall is a room equal in size. Thomas Tileston Waterman, *The Mansions of Virginia, 1706–1776* (New York, 1945), pp. 180–192, and passim. Sabine Hall, Richmond Co., Va., is another grand house with a wide hall or passage and comparable space on the second floor. *Ibid.*, pp. 130–136, and passim. For plainness, see Upton, *Holy Things and Profane*, pp. 213–214; Kornwolf, "So Good a Design," pp. 121–153; and Reiff, *Small Georgian Houses*, pp. 234–237.

19. Mark R. Wenger has in conversation cited the following Virginia mansions or public buildings that bear a resemblance either in elevation or plan to the Palace: The Brafferton and the President's House, College of William and Mary; Berkeley, Charles City Co.; Rosewell, Gloucester Co.; Stratford Hall, Westmoreland Co.; Ampthill, now Richmond, formerly Chesterfield Co.; Cleve, King George Co.; Gunston Hall, Fairfax Co.; Wilton, now Richmond, formerly Henrico Co.; Ambler House, Jamestown, now destroyed; Tuckahoe, Goochland Co.; Westover, Charles City Co.; Mount Airy, Richmond Co.; Kenmore, Fredericksburg. I tend to see more similarity than does Mr. Wenger, to whom I am much indebted for his information. See also Bushman, "American High-Style and Vernacular Cultures," in Greene and Pole, eds., *Colonial British Society*, pp. 358–367.

20. I am profoundly indebted to John M. Hemphill II for information on the official powers and duties of the governor. The information in this paragraph is culled from his research report (with Shomer S. Zwelling), "Royal Governance in Eighteenth-Century Virginia," 1981, CWF. His book-length work (with Jon Kukla) on the political and constitutional history of the colonial governors who resided in the Palace is forthcoming. I am also grateful to Patricia A. Gibbs and Kevin Kelly for information on this subject.

21. Hemphill, "Royal Governance," pp. 27–36.

22. For more details on these subjects, see Morton, *Colonial Virginia*. Vol. II: *Westward Expansion and Prelude to Revolution, 1710–1763* (Chapel Hill, N. C., 1960), passim; and Billings, Selby, and Tate, *Colonial Virginia*, pp. 140–308.

23. My analysis of the functions and locations of the governor's family is based on my reading of the inventory and its related documentation, in the context of English servants' manuals of the time, summarized in J. Jean Hecht, *The Domestic Servant in Eighteenth-Century England*, rev. ed. (London, 1980). Further references and citations are given in pp. 228–265. Patricia A. Gibbs has been very generous with her knowledge of this subject also. See Patricia A. Gibbs, "The Governor's Household and Its Operations," research report, 1981, CWF.

24. John M. Hemphill II compiled valuable notes on the functions of the governor's clerk in "Role of Peter Pelham."

25. For further information, see Morton, *Colonial Virginia*. Vol. I: *The Tidewater Period, 1607–1710*, pp. 334–392; Bruce T. McCully, "From the North Riding to Morocco: The Early Years of Governor Francis Nicholson, 1655–1686," *WMQ*, 3rd Ser., XIX (1962), pp. 534–556; Stephen Saunders Webb, "The Strange Career of Francis Nicholson," *ibid.*, 3rd Ser., XXIII (1966), pp. 513–548; Bruce T. McCully, "Governor Francis Nicholson, Patron *Par Excellence* of Religion and Learning in Colonial America," *ibid.*, 3rd Ser., XXXIX (1982), pp. 310–333; Reps, *Tidewater Towns*, pp. 76, 116–118, 123–132; and Kornwolf, "So Good a Design," pp. 29–74.

26. Jones, *Present State of Virginia*, ed. Morton, pp. 68–69; Reps, *Tidewater Towns*, pp. 141–180; Kornwolf, "So Good a Design," pp. 121–133.

27. Reps, *Tidewater Towns*, pp. 23, 121–128, 141–180; Morton, *Colonial Virginia*, I, p. 371. The quotation is from Mark Girouard, *Cities and People: A Social and Architectural History* (New Haven, Conn., 1985), p. 252.

28. Whiffen, *Public Buildings*, pp. 7–14, 53–57; Reps, *Tidewater Towns*, pp. 154–157, 173–177; McCully, "Governor Francis Nicholson," p. 323.

29. Whiffen, *Public Buildings*, p. 48; McCully, "From the North Riding," pp. 538–539; McCully, "Governor Francis Nicholson," pp. 317–326. For the ceremony, see Carson, *Colonial Virginians at Play*, pp. 198–202. I discuss the ceremony further on pp. 75–78.

30. Whiffen, *Public Buildings*, p. 8.

31. John Custis to Ludwell, Apr. 18, 1717, MSS. 1/LS1/folder 64, sec. 46, Lee Family Papers, Virginia Historical Society, Richmond; Leonidas Dodson, *Alexander Spotswood, Governor of Colonial Virginia, 1710–1722* (Philadelphia, 1932), passim; Morton, *Colonial Virginia*, II, pp. 409–489; Jones, *Present State of Virginia*, ed. Morton, p. 70; Whiffen, *Public Buildings*, pp. 58, 65–68, 88–95; Reps, *Tidewater Towns*, pp. 174–179.

32. The comment on the deer park is from William Gooch to his brother on his arrival in Williamsburg, 1727, transcripts, restricted file, Lt. Gov. William Gooch Letters, CWF. See also Jones, *Present State of Virginia*, ed. Morton, p. 70. Spotswood's book, presented to the College of William and Mary on his death, is in Special Collections, Earl Gregg Swem Library. See also Peter Martin, " 'Promised Fruits of Well-Ordered Towns'—Gardens in Early 18th-Century Williamsburg," *Journal of Garden History*, II (1982), pp. 309–324; Peter E. Martin, "Williamsburg: The Role of the Garden in 'Making a Town,' " in Harry C. Payne, ed., *Studies in Eighteenth-Century Culture*, XII (1983), pp. 187–204; Peter Martin, " 'Long and Assiduous Endeavours': Gardening in Early Eighteenth-Century Virginia," *Eighteenth-Century Life*, VIII (1983), pp. 107–116; James D. Kornwolf, "The Picturesque in the American Garden and Landscape before 1800," *ibid.*, pp. 93–106; and Kornwolf, "So Good a Design," pp. 121–153.

33. Whiffen, *Public Buildings*, pp. 68–70, 77–100. Whether the church as built was the one that Spotswood designed is disputed. See Upton, *Holy Things and Profane*, pp. 34, 81, 15; Graham Hood, *Charles Bridges and William Dering: Two Virginia Painters, 1735–1750*

(Williamsburg, Va., 1978), pp. 29–37; and Dodson, *Alexander Spotswood,* passim.

34. Jones, *Present State of Virginia,* ed. Morton, p. 124; Martin, "Williamsburg: The Role of the Garden," pp. 190–191; Hugh F. Rankin, *The Theater in Colonial America* (Chapel Hill, N. C., 1960), pp. 10–15; Mary C. Beaudry, "Fort Christanna: Frontier Trading Post of the Virginia Indian Company," in Albert E. Ward, ed., *Forgotten Places and Things: Archaeological Perspectives on American History* (Albuquerque, N. M., 1983), pp. 133–140. For the Indian school at the college, Brafferton, in which Spotswood may have had some involvement, see J. E. Morpurgo, *Their Majesties' Royall Colledge: William and Mary in the Seventeenth and Eighteenth Centuries* (Williamsburg, Va., 1976), pp. 33–34, 42–45, 56, 66–67, 83–88; and Kornwolf, "So Good a Design," pp. 139–153.

35. Gooch to his brother, 1727, Gooch Letters.

36. Morton, *Colonial Virginia,* II, pp. 500–598; Hood, *Bridges and Dering,* passim; William L. Joyce, David D. Hall, Richard D. Brown, and John B. Hench, eds., *Printing and Society in Early America* (Worcester, Mass., 1983), pp. 132–173.

37. Whiffen, *Public Buildings,* pp. 104, 123–127; E. G. Swem, ed., *Brothers of the Spade: Correspondence of Peter Collinson, of London, and of John Custis, of Williamsburg, Virginia, 1734–1746* (Barre, Mass., 1957), passim; Wallace B. Gusler, *Furniture of Williamsburg and Eastern Virginia, 1710–1790* (Richmond, Va., 1979), pp. 25–27.

38. William P. Cumming, *The Southeast in Early Maps* (Princeton, N. J., 1958), pp. 47–48, 82, 198–200, 219–221; George Frederick Frick and Raymond Phineas Stearns, *Mark Catesby: The Colonial Audubon* (Urbana, Ill., 1961), passim; Raymond Phineas Stearns, *Science in the British Colonies of America* (Urbana, Ill., 1970), pp. 48–49; Arthur MacGregor, ed., *Tradescant's Rarities: Essays on the Foundation of the Ashmolean Museum, 1683, with a Catalogue of the Surviving Early Collections* (Oxford, 1983).

39. Whiffen, *Public Buildings,* p. 140. See also *ibid.,* pp. 143–144, 174–181; Morton, *Colonial Virginia,* II, pp. 599–713; and Murrin, "The Great Inversion," in Pocock, ed., *Three British Revolutions,* pp. 368–453.

40. Mays, *Pendleton,* I, p. 149. Dispersal of some of Dinwiddie's effects is noted in most unsatisfactory detail in the letterbook of Richard Corbin, deputy receiver general of Virginia, 1758–1768, Richard Corbin Papers, 1746–1825, CWF.

41. George Reese, ed., *The Official Papers of Francis Fauquier, Lieutenant Governor of Virginia, 1758–1768* (Charlottesville, Va., 1980–1983), I, p. xxxix. The Jefferson quote is from Andrew A. Lipscomb and Albert Ellery Bergh, eds., *The Writings of Thomas Jefferson* (Washington, D. C., 1903–1904), XIV, pp. 231–232. See also Dumas Malone, *Jefferson and His Time.* Vol. I: *Jefferson the Virginian* (Boston, 1948), pp. 75–80. I owe much to John M. Hemphill II who shared with me his notes on Fauquier as "English *Philosophe* and Intellectual Godfather to Thomas Jefferson" in 1983. See also Morton, *Colonial Virginia,* II, pp. 714–832.

42. Morton, *Colonial Virginia,* II, pp. 740–741.

43. Bushman, "American High-Style and Vernacular Cultures," in Greene and Pocock, eds., *Colonial British Society,* p. 364; Mays, *Pendleton,* I, p. 173.

44. Bushman, "American High-Style and Vernacular Cultures," in Greene and Pocock, eds., *Colonial British Society,* pp. 360–373, provides an excellent recent summary of this. See also Breen, "An Empire of Goods," p. 485. See also the discussion relevant to Anglican Church architecture in Virginia in this period in Upton, *Holy Things and Profane,* pp. 157–160.

45. Little, "Norborne Berkeley," pp. 407, 409.

Ceremony
page numbers 74–79

1. For a study of kingship and monarchical culture in a sister colony, see Richard L. Bushman, *King and People in Provincial Massachusetts* (Chapel Hill, N. C., 1985), esp. pp. 1–17, for its relevance to this discussion.

2. Ceremony involved the clear articulation of time as well as of space. A brilliant example of this was precisely noted by Philip Fithian at Nomini Hall in the Northern Neck of Virginia in 1774, when he described the "three grand divisions of time at the Church on Sundays, Viz. before Service . . . 2. In the Church at Service . . . 3. After Service is over . . ." Farish, ed., *Journal & Letters of Fithian,* p. 167. For ceremony in Virginia colonial society, see Isaac, *Transformation of Virginia,* pp. 58–87. For ceremony and symbolism in Virginia churches and courthouses, see Upton, *Holy Things and Profane,* pp. 163–173, 199–232; and Roeber, *Faithful Magistrates,* pp. 73–111. Extracts from both these volumes are reprinted in St. George, ed., *Material Life in America,* pp. 357–369 and pp. 419–437 respectively. My colleague, Carl R. Lounsbury, has made the most extensive study to date of Virginia courthouses, their origins, and functions, and is preparing a monograph on this subject.

    While welcoming the usefulness of Upton's concise discussion on symbolism, particularly as it applies to the Anglican churches of Virginia, I have deliberately used the term here in a broader way, as I have tried to use the word "culture" in its several meanings.

3. Carson, *Colonial Virginians at Play,* pp. 196–202.

4. Isaac, *Transformation of Virginia,* pp. 374–422; Jan Lewis, *The Pursuit of Happiness: Family and Values in Jefferson's Virginia* (Cambridge, 1983), pp. 1–38; Bushman, "American High-Style and Vernacular Cultures," in Greene and Pole, eds., *Colonial British Society,* pp. 355–356; John E. Ferling, *The First of Men: A Life of George Washington* (Knoxville, Tenn., 1988), pp. 375–377.

The Hall: The Power of the Crown
page numbers 80–97

1. Thomas Sheraton, *Cabinet Dictionary,* I (London, 1803; reprint ed., New York, 1970), p. 217.

2. McIlwaine and Kennedy, eds., *Journals of Burgesses, 1773–1776,* p. 273. *Of the Tower, and its Curiosities,* a 1753 guide to the Tower of London, described a considerably larger display in the small armory at the Tower as "fit for Service at a Moment's Warning; a Sight that no one ever beheld without Astonishment." P. 36. It is true that the arms were remarkable, and frequently remarked, even if one might question whether Stephen Saunders Webb is going too far in asserting that "it was as a place of arms that the site of Williamsburg took on the political importance that would make it the capital of Virginia." *The Governors-General: The English Army and the Definition of the Empire, 1569–1681* (Chapel Hill, N. C., 1979), p. 374.

3. Louis B. Wright and Marion Tinling, eds., *The Secret Diary of William Byrd of Westover, 1709–1712* (Richmond, Va., 1941), p. 420; R. A. Brock, ed., *The Official Letters of Alexander Spotswood,* II (Richmond, Va., 1885), pp. 65–66. The first tentative reference to Spotswood occupying the "new house" is from the entry for Dec. 18, 1714: "The Committee . . . Accordingly waited on his Honr. at the Palace." McIlwaine, ed., *Legislative Journals of the Council,* I, p. 586. See also *ibid.,* p. 440.

4. Jones, *Present State of Virginia,* ed. Morton, p. 70. McIlwaine, Hall, and Hillman, eds., *Executive Journals of the Council,* III, p. 399: "The musquetts now in the Governors hall being a hundred and Sixty in number and in very good order." The 1750 inventory was taken of the arms belonging to the crown in the Magazine and the Governor's House. Thomas Lee to Secretary of State, July 12, 1750, C.O. 5/1338, fol. 53, P.R.O.; Radoff, *Buildings of Maryland,* pp. 48–54, quotation on p. 49.

5. Wayne Andrews, ed., *A Glance at New York in 1697: The Travel Diary of Dr. Benjamin Bullivant, New York Historical Society Quarterly* (1956), pp. 61–62. Reference courtesy of

Cary Carson. Fletcher's additional placement of Indian weapons in the arrangement in his study is a rare and early instance of an "ethnic" exhibit and suggests the predilections of a collector as well as the instincts of a military official.

6. S. K. Stevens, Donald H. Kent, and Autumn L. Leonard, eds., *The Papers of Henry Bouquet* (Harrisburg, Pa., 1951–1984), I, p. 404. St. George Tucker's handwritten comments on William Wirt's MS are in "William Wirt's Life of Patrick Henry," *WMQ*, 1st Ser., XXII (1913–1914), p. 257.

7. These drawings came originally from the collection of the first Lord Dartmouth, master of the ordnance when the arrangements at Hampton Court and Windsor were being installed by Harris. Courtesy A. V. B. Norman, master of the armouries, Tower of London. See also Sarah Bevan, "Three-Dimensional Decorations: Displays of Arms in English Houses," *Country Life*, Oct. 24, 1985, pp. 1229–1238. *Of The Tower, and its Curiosities*, p. 38, concluded the description of the small armory: "A discerning Eye will discover a thousand Peculiarities in the Disposition of so vast a Variety of Arms, which no Description can reach; and therefore it is fit that every one who has a Taste for the admirable Combinations of Art, should gratify that darling Passion with the Sight of a Curiosity the noblest in its kind the World affords."

8. Whiffen, *Public Buildings*, p. 61. Information on the arms arrangement at Chevening was kindly supplied by Claude Blair and Vesey Norman. See also H. Avray Tipping's series of three articles on Chevening entitled "Chevening: Kent, the Seat of Earl Stanhope" in *Country Life*, Apr. 17, 1920, pp. 512–520, Apr. 24, 1920, pp. 548–556, and May 1, 1920, pp. 586–593. For a painted display of weapons at the Royal Hospital, Chelsea, see Marcus Binney, "The Royal Hospital, Chelsea—II," *ibid.*, Nov. 18, 1982, p. 1583.

9. Stevens, Kent, and Leonard, eds., *Papers of Bouquet*, I, p. 403. The 1774 reference to Dunmore's concern for the Palace arrangement is from McIlwaine and Kennedy, eds., *Journals of Burgesses, 1773–1776*, p. 223. Lt. Gov. Hugh Drysdale had complained of the condition of the arms as early as 1723: "I find great part of them very much out of Repair . . . these Arms were at first given by the Crown for the defence of the Country and are Lodged there to be ready on any Suddain Emergency." *Ibid.*, 1712–1726, p. 380. See also Stevens, Kent, and Leonard, eds., *Papers of Bouquet*, I, pp. 403–404, II, p. 60: "On the Prests reflecting what he had done about Arms, he had all those in the Govrs house pack'd up and put on board of a Vessell, which saild from York for Fredericksbourg the 2d Inst," June 9, 1758. Sir John St. Clair wrote to the Council from Winchester, May 19, 1758, that the second Virginia Regiment was without arms "which he desired they might be supplied with out of the Governor's House, as the Arms there can never be put to better use." McIlwaine, Hall, and Hillman, eds., *Executive Journals of the Council*, VI, pp. 95–96. Fauquier shipped arms, "many of them out of repair," to the frontier in Sept. 1763 and had them replaced with a "thousand stand of good muskets" from James Furniss, comptroller of the ordnance in New York, by Dec. of the same year. Gage Papers, 1763–1775, William L. Clements Library, University of Michigan, Ann Arbor, microfilm, CWF.

10. McIlwaine and Kennedy, eds., *Journals of Burgesses, 1773–1776*, p. 273. Details of the removal of the arms from the Palace to the Magazine, June 24, 1775, are in Charles Campbell, ed., *The Bland Papers: Being a Selection from the Manuscripts of Colonel Theodorick Bland, Jr., of Prince George County, Virginia*, I (Petersburg, Va., 1840), pp. xxiii–xxiv. The colonists felt no compunction about appropriating the arms; as they explained in a letter to Dunmore: "Though these Arms, my Lord, may be considered, in some sort as belonging to his Majesty . . . yet we humbly conceive that they were originally provided, and have been preserved, for the Use of the Country, in cases of Emergency." McIlwaine and Kennedy, eds., *Journals of Burgesses, 1773–1776*, p. 273. Their awareness of the threat the arms could pose shows very clearly in this letter. Because the arms were officially considered the property of the king in 1770, they were not included in the Botetourt inventory. Selby, *Revolution in Virginia*, pp. 1–22, 40–47.

11. Upton, *Holy Things and Profane*, p. 97. The portrait painter Charles Bridges, active in Virginia 1735–1745, painted the royal arms for county courthouses. See Hood, *Bridges and Dering*, p. 10. Charles Willson Peale also painted a battle flag in 1774 for a Williamsburg client, the Independent Company of Williamsburg, in 1774. Charles Coleman Sellers, "Charles Willson Peale with Patron and Populace," *Transactions of the American Philosophical Society*, LIX, Pt. 3 (1969), p. 14. The "Colours" in the hall may well have been the Virginia Regiment colors or flags (including the king's color and the Union flag), probably fashioned after the British military warrant of 1743, which specified design and fabrication of regimental colors. See also Bushman, *King and People*, pp. 1–54.

12. For the Virginia patriarchy, see the extensive discussion in Isaac, *Transformation of Virginia*, pp. 20–21, 41–57.

13. Translation of the Latin inscription courtesy of Professors Ward Jones and John H. Willis, Jr., of the College of William and Mary. See also Dill, *Governor Tryon and His Palace*, pp. 103–127. For the plans of Tryon's Palace, see Waterman and Johnston, *Architecture of North Carolina*, pp. 32–33, 82–86. See also Radoff, *Buildings of Maryland*, pp. 52–53.

14. For the decoration of English houses in the 1770s, see Girouard, *Life in the English Country House*, p. 136. Botetourt's country house, Stoke Park, near Bristol, contained 9 firelocks, 10 bayonets, 2 fowling pieces, 2 hangers (swords), and 5 pistols. Stoke inventory, 1770, Badminton Papers.

15. Alexander Spotswood to the Board of Trade, Nov. 15, 1718, C.O. 5/1318, fol. 348.

16. Sept. 11, 1727, Robert "King" Carter Diary, 1722–1727, Alderman Lib.; Gooch to his brother, Sept. 18, 1727, Gooch Letters; Carson, *Colonial Virginians at Play*, pp. 204–206, 252–254.

17. Isaac Ware, *A Complete Body of Architecture* (London, 1756), p. 335.

18. *The Builders Dictionary, Or Universal Dictionary for Architects* (London, 1774).

19. Two sets of ten chairs were listed in Fauquier's inventory of 1768, one for £18 among a group of furniture corresponding closely to that kept by Botetourt in the upper "Middle Room" (the chairs noted in 1770 as being covered with crimson damask), and one for £20 that cannot be given a specific location. The close similarity in values, however, suggests that the latter are the same ones as the only other set of damask chairs to appear in the Botetourt inventory, in the hall. Chairs of this "backstool" variety are most uncommon in Virginia inventories. Two with a Virginia history are known, both from Westover; they are mentioned, and one is illustrated, in Esther Singleton, *The Furniture of our Forefathers* (New York, 1900), p. 69. Some early chairs at the Capitol were distinguished by "A Mark and Superscription . . . being the Sovereigns Crown and Cypher." They were most uncommon. Reference to these chairs is in Spotswood to the Board of Trade, Nov. 15, 1718, C.O. 5/1318, fol. 348. For references to Windsor chairs, see Wenger, "Central Passage," p. 148. Hall chairs in English country houses were frequently embellished with the arms of the owner, even if they did have wooden seats. Chairs at the Palace embellished in such a way would probably have survived to 1770, however.

20. Gilbert, *Chippendale*, I, pp. 173, 192. In Chippendale's accounts for Nostell Priory, Yorkshire, the set is described as "8 Large Globe Lamps on wrought brass Scrolls and shades to do. Supported with brass Scrolls . . ." In the Botetourt inventory are listed in storage "6 brass Branches for Globe Lamps," as well as "2 large glass Shades," suggesting therefore that the lamps in the hall were in-

NOTES 319

deed similar to the English prototype illustrated. Globe lamps were apparently used in Philadelphia as early as the late 1750s, when they were described by Benjamin Franklin. Leonard W. Labaree, ed., *The Autobiography of Benjamin Franklin* (New Haven, Conn., 1964), pp. 203–204. Fauquier also used such a device on the stairs of the Palace, according to a letter from his son asking for the return of certain effects that were left in the Palace after 1768—"Two carved mahogany stands with one glass globe standing on the stairs." Note in George Wythe's handwriting, photostat, CWF. Fauquier's intimate friend, Councillor Robert Carter, who owned the large house next to the Palace on Palace green, ordered from London in 1762 "Two glass Globes for Candles to light a Stair Case." Robert Carter to John Morton Jordan, Feb. 16, 1762, Robert Carter of Nomini Hall Letter Book, 1761–1764, p. 21, CWF. Despite the earlier references, however, globes were still obviously fashionable by 1770, although references to them in Virginia documents are most uncommon.

21. See Appendixes 6 and 7.
22. Robert Adam and James Adam, *The Works in Architecture of Robert and James Adam* (London, 1773; reprint ed., New York, 1980), p. 3. See also "Wirt's Life of Henry," p. 252. Botetourt had 22 servants and slaves. Nicholas Papers. See pp. 228-265.
23. William Stevens Perry, ed., *Historical Collections Relating to the American Colonial Church*, I (Hartford, Conn., 1870), p. 464.
24. Gooch to his brother, Mar. 1, 1746, Gooch Letters. The observation on Dunmore was printed in the *South-Carolina Gazette* (Charleston), Sept. 10, 1772, quoting a London source of June 19, 1772. Rutherfoord Goodwin, *A Brief & True Report Concerning Williamsburg in Virginia* (Williamsburg, Va., 1941), p. 64. Information on Botetourt's retinue is given fully in pp. 228–265.
25. Isaac, *Transformation of Virginia*, p. 35; Wenger, "Central Passage," pp. 139–141.
26. Farish, ed., *Journal & Letters of Fithian*, pp. 130, 129.
27. For the chair of state, see Thornton, *Seventeenth-Century Decoration*, pp. 59–60, 171–174. I am indebted for information on livery in Virginia to my colleague, Linda Baumgarten, who is preparing an extensive work on clothing in eighteenth-century Virginia. References to individual gentry ownership of livery are too numerous to cite. Ms. Baumgarten has pointed out that the custom was so ingrained that Jefferson took it to the White House and kept servants in livery there.
28. For Spotswood on Nicholson, see Webb, "Strange Career of Nicholson," p. 528. Webb also noted that "the years 1709–10 saw a ninefold increase in the regular army garrisons in the Northern colonies alone." *Ibid.*, p. 544. In 1710 the duke of Marlborough had proclaimed "no one but soldiers should have the government of a plantation." Wright and Tinling, eds., *Secret Diary of Byrd*, p. 159.
29. With a degree of defensiveness perhaps unbecoming to the new republic, but with the same idea presumably in mind, Jefferson as governor approved the cementing of broken glass on top of the walls surrounding the Palace in 1779. Pp. 7, 25, 31, Ledger B, 1776–1791, Humphrey Harwood Account Book, 1776–1794, CWF.
30. See n. 7, p. 319. For the full quote, see p. 9. The definition of "sentiment" is from the 1771 edition of *Encyclopaedia Britannica*.
31. Campbell, ed., *Bland Papers*, I, pp. xxii–xxv. For the transfer from "imperial parliamentary Sovereignty" to "popular sovereignty," see Edmund S. Morgan, *Inventing the People: The Rise of Popular Sovereignty in England and America* (New York, 1988), esp. pp. 239–262; and Selby, *Revolution in Virginia*, pp. 40–47.

The Middle Room Upstairs: The Presence of the Governor
page numbers 98–115

1. The first quotation is from the 1710 proposal. See Appendix 4.
2. *Builders Dictionary*, p. 276.
3. By an unusual coincidence, Botetourt was designing an allée bordered with trees in a provincial town at virtually the same time (1737) as Gooch enriched the Palace vista with catalpa trees. His influence on the development of the new spa town of Cheltenham in Gloucestershire in this period and his design for an allée are noted in Little, "Norborne Berkeley," p. 386. For a comparable ritual progression through exterior spaces and then into the interior spaces of a plantation house, see Upton, *Holy Things and Profane*, pp. 207–209.
4. For a discussion of the development of the English "Great chamber," see Girouard, *Life in the English Country House*, p. 93, and passim.
5. In 1686 William Fitzhugh ordered for his house in Stafford Co., Va., "a Suit of Tapestry hangings for a Room twenty foot long sixteen foot wide, and nine foot high and half a dozen Chairs suitable." Richard Beale Davis, ed., *William Fitzhugh and His Chesapeake World, 1676–1701: The Fitzhugh Letters and Other Documents* (Chapel Hill, N. C., 1963), p. 142. Three years later Fitzhugh described his house as a "very good dwelling house, with 13 Rooms in it, four of the best of them hung." *Ibid.*, p. 175. For gilt leather hangings, see Thornton, *Seventeenth-Century Interior Decoration*, p. 362; and John Waterer, *Spanish Leather* (London, 1971), p. 65. For information on looking glasses, see Percy Macquoid and Ralph Edwards, *Dictionary of English Furniture, from the Middle Ages to the Later Georgian Period*, II, 2nd ed. (London, 1954), pp. 320–325, 326–334, for the "verre églomisé" type; and John Hardy, Sheila Landi, and Charles D. Wright, *A State Bed from Erthig* (London, 1972), p. 4; and Martin Drury, "Early Eighteenth-Century Furniture at Erddig," *Apollo*, CVIII (1978), pp. 46–55 for the carved type. The latter type of looking glasses are especially interesting since Belchier, the maker of the Erthig examples, is known to have sent furniture to Virginia later. John Mercer Ledger, 1725 (1741)–1750, 1725–1732, Bucks County Historical Society, Doylestown, Pa., microfilm, CWF. Reference courtesy of Harold B. Gill, Jr.
6. Radoff, *Buildings of Maryland*, p. 49. Placing the "center of power" at a height above the surroundings was not new, of course. It was expressed in the Virginia landscape by the elevation of many of the plantation houses above their surroundings, a conspicuous feature frequently noted in the colonial period. See, for example, Isaac, *Transformation of Virginia*, p. 35; and Fithian's description of Nomini Hall, visible from a distance of almost six miles, Farish, ed., *Journal & Letters of Fithian*, p. 80.
7. *Builders Dictionary*, p. 33. In 1769 William Eddis visited Annapolis and toured the governor's house recently acquired by Gov. Eden; he described the view "from the saloon" of the house, which may have been the room described in the inventory of 1776 as the "long room," though Eden's changes to the building after he purchased it make this unclear. Radoff, *Buildings of Maryland*, p. 72.
8. Thomas Sheraton, *Cabinet-Maker and Upholsterer's Drawing-Book* (London, 1794), pp. 443–444; Sheraton, *Cabinet Dictionary*, II, p. 218. Readers of the *Va. Gaz.* (Purdie and Dixon), Aug. 25, 1768, could take notice of a report from London that "a grand saloon is now building at Sion House, the seat of his Grace the Duke of Northumberland, which it is supposed, when finished, will be one of the finest rooms in all Europe."
9. Fauquier's inventory is given in full in Appendix 2. For the use of crimson in state rooms, see Fowler and Cornforth, *English Decoration*, pp. 58, 71–72; and John Cornforth and Leo Schmidt, "Holkham Hall, Norfolk—III: The Seat of the Earls of Leicester," *Country Life*, Feb. 7, 1980, pp. 359–362.
10. Because the leather hangings would be attached to the wall and would not be portable, they would not appear in the inventory or in the list of standing furniture. For Eden's Annapolis inventory, see Appendix 5.

11. Sheraton, *Cabinet-Maker and Upholsterer's Drawing-Book*, p. 443. The Dinwiddie reference is in the *Va. Gaz.*, Nov. 17, 1752.
12. Fauquier's account is in a letter to the Lords of Trade, Aug. 1, 1765. Reese, ed., *Official Papers of Fauquier*, III, p. 1266. For Botetourt, see McIlwaine, Hall, and Hillman, eds., *Executive Journals of the Council*, VI, pp. 361–366, quotation on p. 366.
13. A good example of Virginians' possessive interest in the arms is in the St. Clair letter. See p. 86 and n. 9.
14. Tryon's visit was detailed in the *Va. Gaz.* (Rind), June 15, 1769. For Eden's visit, see *ibid.* (Purdie and Dixon), Sept. 6, 1770. For more on Tryon's Palace, see Dill, *Governor Tryon and His Palace*, pp. 103–127.
15. Sir William Draper's presence in Williamsburg in 1770 is documented in the Botetourt Papers. The Williamsburg delegation is described in Botetourt to Hillsborough, Jan. 24, 1770, Dianne J. McGaan, "The Official Letters of Norborne Berkeley, Baron de Botetourt, Governor of Virginia, 1768–1770" (M.A. thesis, College of William and Mary, 1971), p. 193.
16. Sheraton, *Cabinet Dictionary*, II, p. 201. For the transition from saloons to drawing rooms, see Girouard, *Life in the English Country House*, pp. 201–203; and Fowler and Cornforth, *English Decoration*, p. 71.
17. The Fauquier family was most interested in paintings, among them surviving portraits of Francis by Benjamin Wilson (1757), of his brother William by George Knapton (1743), and of Francis's son William by John Smart (a miniature). William, the brother, built a notable collection of old master and contemporary paintings. David Carritt, "Mr Fauquier's Chardins," *Burlington Magazine*, CXVI (1974), pp. 502–509. See also Appendix 2.
18. Sheraton, *Cabinet Dictionary*, II, p. 218. For the "circle," see Girouard, *Life in the English Country House*, pp. 12, 238–239. Note also Fithian's description of the "semi-circle." Farish, ed., *Journal & Letters of Fithian*, p. 34. Botetourt's general level of culture is discussed more fully in pp. 122–167.
19. "A bell-glass lanthorn which hung on the landing between Mr. Fauquier's dressing room and the china closet" is mentioned in a letter from George Wythe to Francis Fauquier, Jr., regarding effects left in the Palace after the lieutenant governor's death. Photostat, CWF. Other Virginia references to dressing rooms are noted in Wenger, "Central Passage," p. 143.
20. George III's levee is described by John Brooke, *King George III* (New York, 1972), p. 296. See also pp. 293–298. Botetourt mentioned a London levee, possibly the king's, to the duke of Grafton in January 1768: "Jan 20th 3/4 past nine morning—I will be at the Levee to day and do promise Your Grace not to utter upon the subject of your letter till I have had the honour to see you." Badminton Papers.
21. The closest reference to such an event at the Governor's Palace is in a letter from Botetourt to Beaufort, Dec. 28, 1769: "I constantly attend . . . morning prayers [at the College] at seven o'clock and never miss evening Service unless when I am kept at home by d[o]ing Companies." Badminton Papers. This can be read to suggest that "companies" occurred either in the mornings, in the form of a levee, or in the evenings, in the form of dinners or other assemblies.
22. Ware, *Body of Architecture*, p. 432.
23. Protests against Dunmore recorded in the *S.-C. Gaz.*, Sept. 10, 1772. For Washington's levees, see Ferling, *First of Men*, p. 376; and John C. Fitzpatrick, ed., *The Writings of George Washington from the Original Manuscript Sources, 1745–1799*, XXX (Washington, D. C., 1939), pp. 319–321, 359–361. For Jefferson's opinion on levees, see Lipscomb and Bergh, eds., *Writings of Jefferson*, X, pp. 260–261.
24. Sheraton, *Cabinet Dictionary*, I, p. 8; Ware, *Body of Architecture*, p. 432.
25. Gooch to his brother, Aug. 7, 1750, Gooch Letters. Note some comparable Virginia instances in Wenger, "Central Passage," p. 139.
26. The church in Wilmington, N. C., is St. James. The picture—an *Ecce Homo*—is of late seventeenth-century date, Spanish in origin, and has a local tradition stretching back to 1748 of being taken from a pirate ship that ran aground in the Cape Fear River. Reference courtesy of Cary Carson. Carved and polychromed wooden figures of cherubim that adorn the Old North Church in Boston have a similar history. Elise Lathrop, *Old New England Churches* (Rutland, Vt., 1938), p. 25. Lathrop records a similar occurrence in a church in Stratford, Conn. *Ibid.*, p. 124. Dr. Edgar P. Richardson, whose help with this matter is gratefully acknowledged, suggested a similar provenance for a Spanish *Last Supper* in St. Barnabas Church, Prince George Co., Md. The Reverend George Cleaveland also provided invaluable help from his vast store of knowledge of Virginia's religious history. For his proposed gallery at Monticello, Jefferson drew up a list of desiderata about 1771 and included among the largely classical subjects a "St. Ignatius at Prayer" inspired by a painting attributed to Murillo, reportedly confiscated from a captured Spanish treasure ship, which Jefferson had seen in the home of the former lieutenant governor of Philadelphia, James Hamilton, about 1766. Seymour Howard, "Thomas Jefferson's Art Gallery for Monticello," *The Art Bulletin*, LIX (1977), pp. 583–600.
27. Dill, *Governor Tryon and His Palace*, pp. 122–123; Waterman and Johnston, *Early Architecture of North Carolina*, pp. 82–86; Bargar, ed., "Governor Tryon's House in Fort George," pp. 297–309; Hugh Buckner Johnston, "The Journal of Ebenezer Hazard in North Carolina, 1777 and 1778," *North Carolina Historical Review*, XXXVI (1959), p. 375.
28. See Appendix 5 for the Eden inventory; and Radoff, *Buildings of Maryland*, pp. 81–85.
29. Details are taken from the Campbell inventory, Appendix 7. The quote is from Sheraton, *Cabinet Dictionary*, II, p. 201. Note that the term "drawing room" *is* used in the inventory, its furnishings resembling more those of a lady's dressing room. It is possible that those who took the inventory were not quite familiar with the more elegant room usages!
30. Tryon's penchant for ceremony is noted in a public letter signed by "Atticus" published in the *Va. Gaz.* (Purdie and Dixon), Nov. 7, 1771: "The arrogant Reception you gave to a respectable Company at an Entertainment of your own making, seated with your Lady by your Side on Elbow Chairs, in the Middle of a Ball Room, bespeak a Littleness of Mind." Botetourt's country house, Stoke Park, contained no room quite so formal, to judge by the inventory of its contents taken in 1768 and again in 1770. An "Octagon Room" contained yellow damask chairs and curtains and a full-length double portrait of Botetourt and his sister. Two tables and a carpet completed the main furnishings. The "Drawing Room" listed next held "caned bottom" couch and chairs complete with blue cushions, blue curtains, carpet, two large dining tables, and ten large and small pictures.
31. John Randolph, deed of trust on his Williamsburg properties, drawn up in Aug. 1775 and recorded in 1777, executed with Peyton Randolph, John Blair, and James Cocke, empowering them to sell his house and personal property for payment of his debts. Tazewell Papers, CWF. Randolph noted a "Saloon" in the schedule of the contents of his house; the saloon contained only a glass lantern, four girandoles, twelve mahogany chairs, and two mahogany tables. The space may have been a large hall on the first or second floor, in the manner of nearby Carter's Grove, the contemporary uses of which are unfortunately not known. Tuckahoe featured a large central hall connecting the two wings that was termed in the 1790s a "Saloon." To judge by its contents, Randolph's saloon could well have served the purpose of "summer dining." See also Wenger, "Central Passage," pp. 142–146, 148.

32. Quoted in Girouard, *Life in the English Country House*, p. 122.
33. Upton, *Holy Things and Profane*, pp. 177–178, 199–232. For a discussion of the influence of the militia on Virginia colonial society, see Isaac, *Transformation of Virginia*, pp. 104–110.

Public Life
page numbers 118–121

1. Upton, *Holy Things and Profane*, p. 165.
2. Michael Zuckerman, "William Byrd's Family," in *Perspectives in American History*, ed. Donald Fleming, XII (1979), pp. 253–311, esp. pp. 292, 299, 305; Michael Zuckerman, "Fate, Flux, and Good Fellowship: An Early Virginia Design for the Dilemma of American Business," in Harold Issadore Sharlin, ed., *Business and Its Environment: Essays for Thomas C. Cochran* (Westport, Conn., 1983), pp. 161–184, esp. p. 171. See also Upton, *Holy Things and Profane*, pp. 165–166.
3. Zuckerman, "Fate, Flux, and Good Fellowship," in Sharlin, ed., *Business and Its Environment*, p. 173.
4. Alexander Spotswood to John Spotswood, Mar. 20, 1710/11, Alexander Spotswood Papers, CWF. For the Gooch references, see n. 63, p. 325.
5. Isaac, *Transformation of Virginia*, pp. 80–87, Daniel B. Smith, *Inside the Great House: Planter Family Life in Eighteenth-Century Chesapeake Society* (Ithaca, N.Y., 1980), pp. 175–230.
6. Isaac, *Transformation of Virginia*, esp. pp. 80–87, 115–142; Upton, *Holy Things and Profane*, pp. 199–232; Wright, *First Gentlemen of Virginia*, pp. 1–37.
7. McKendrick, Brewer, and Plumb, *Birth of a Consumer Society*, passim; Breen, *Tobacco Culture*, pp. 124–159; Breen, " 'Baubles of Britain,' " pp. 73–104; Breen, "An Empire of Goods," pp. 467–499.
8. Breen, " 'Baubles of Britain,' " passim.

The Dining Room and Parlor: Apartments of Conversation
page numbers 122–167

1. Adam, *Works in Architecture*, p. 3.
2. *Ibid.*
3. Girouard, *Life in the English Country House*, pp. 88–94, 120–122, 162. "It is further Ordered that the great Dining room and Parlour thereto adjoining be new painted, the one of pearl colour the other of cream colour." McIlwaine, Hall, and Hillman, eds., *Executive Journals of the Council*, IV, p. 135.
4. Autographed letter from Franklin to Jane Mecom, May 30, 1787, cited in an auction catalog, Sotheby's, New York, N.Y., May 23, 1984, no. 130. For Tryon's rooms, see Appendix 6. The use of the parlor as a room of "common reception" is noted in this chapter. For a reference to visitors after dinner, see p. 126.
5. See Farish, ed., *Journal & Letters of Fithian*, p. 80, for a description of rooms, and *ibid.*, p. 34, for a reference to semicircle. See also p. 42. The only time Fithian recorded this practice was when he was visiting another house with Mrs. Carter and the children. It does not seem to have been customary at Nomini Hall. As noted, Fithian listed two dining rooms on the first floor of Nomini Hall, one for the children and one for company, yet he does not distinguish between the two subsequently in his diary, and the children often joined their parents for dinner and/or supper.
6. Adam, *Works in Architecture*, p. 3; Gooch to his brother, Mar. 6, 1747, Gooch Letters.
7. Adam, *Works in Architecture*, p. 3. See *ibid.*, pl. 16, for a beautifully engraved representation of sideboard, knife boxes, display of plate, and looking glass. See also McIlwaine, Hall, and Hillman, eds., *Executive Journals of the Council*, IV, p. 135.
8. Botetourt's wax portraits are likely to have been a set by Isaac Gossett, who carved the original wax portrait of Botetourt and subsequently the copies for a number of Virginia gentlemen. E. J. Pyke, *A Biographical Dictionary of Wax Modellers* (Oxford, 1973), pp. 56–60. Sets of portraits, including the royal family and learned men such as philosophers, authors, etc., are listed therein. Gossett also probably carved and gilded the frames for the full-length portraits of George III and Charlotte in the ballroom. Oliver Millar, *Later Georgian Pictures in the Collection of Her Majesty the Queen*, I (London, 1969), pp. 93–95.
9. Wright and Tinling, eds., *Secret Diary of Byrd*, p. 431.
10. The phrase "well instructed" is from Farish, ed., *Journal & Letters of Fithian*, p. 34. Gooch mentioned his wife's role at the table in a letter to his brother, Mar. 1, 1746, Gooch Letters. Botetourt owned the remarkable tally of 87 silver plates and dishes and a far larger quantity of Staffordshire plates and dishes of many sizes and shapes. The plate was stored in the pantry, while the Staffordshire ware was actually divided between the closet to the little middle room (under the main staircase) and the servants' hall near the kitchen, the bulk of it in the latter location. The sideboard table was included in the ca. 1710 proposal as "one Marble Buffette or Sideboard with a Cistern and fountain," and described in the later list of standing furniture as "1 Side Board with Marble Slab," almost certainly the same piece. Girouard, *Life in the English Country House*, pp. 203–204, gives a fine description of a formal dinner.
11. The phrase "calling for drink" is from Gooch to his brother, Mar. 6, 1747, Gooch Letters. Thirty-seven glass decanters cut and plain, large and small, for wine and water were listed in the inventory, together with eighteen silver bottle labels or tickets. Botetourt's glasses and pyramids were noted in the inventory in the bowfat in the dining room, the pantry, and near the kitchen (the servants' hall?); the glass for dessert in the latter location is a remarkable assemblage. The silver and the gold cups were normally kept in the pantry when not in use. The "Chinese temple" was listed in the inventory on the third floor. Tryon's china included "1 sett desert frames with Italian temples, vases, China images, basket and flowers etc."
12. Farish, ed., *Journal & Letters of Fithian*, pp. 67, 138.
13. Gooch to his brother, Mar. 6, 1747, Gooch Letters. The Fauquier incident is given in more detail in Perry, ed., *Historical Collections Relating to the American Colonial Church*, I, pp. 463–472. For toasts, see Farish, ed., *Journal & Letters of Fithian*, pp. 57, 59, 64. On the occasion of Botetourt's dissolution of the assembly, May 17, 1769, the burgesses repaired to the Raleigh Tavern and there, over the next two days, passed the Virginia Nonimportation Resolutions, which were concluded with toasts to "The King. The Queen and Royal Family. His Excellency Lord Botetourt, and Prosperity to *Virginia*. A speedy and lasting Union between *Great-Britain* and her Colonies. The constitutional *British* Liberty in *America*, and all true Patriots, the Supporters thereof. Duke of Richmond. Earl of Shelburne. Col. Barre. The late Speaker. The Treasurer of the Colony. The Farmer and Monitor." Julian P. Boyd et al., eds., *The Papers of Thomas Jefferson*, I (Princeton, N.J., 1950), p. 31.
14. For the American effects of Wedgwood's Queensware, see Graham Hood, *Bonnin and Morris of Philadelphia: The First American Porcelain Factory, 1770–1772* (Chapel Hill, N.C., 1972), pp. 19–22, 71–74. For Chelsea porcelain figures, see John C. Austin, *Chelsea Porcelain at Williamsburg* (Williamsburg, Va., 1977), pp. 113–116, 121–129, 130–139.
15. Nelson to Fauquier, Jr., Aug. 16, 1768, Nelson Letter Book.
16. The quote is from Breen, " 'Baubles of Britain,' " p. 91. See also pp. 91–93. The reference to Botetourt's private criticism of the ministry's acts is in "Meade Family History," p. 88. Botetourt was overheard to say (at "Mr. Treasurer Nicholas' house in Williamsburg") that "he should write to Lord Hillsborough (who was then seventy years old) who was then in the American Department of State, and as-

sure him that unless the obnoxious acts of Parliament were repealed, he should desire to be recalled from his government." *Ibid.*, p. 88. The ball at the Capitol was described in the *Va. Gaz.* (Purdie and Dixon), Dec. 14, 1769. Botetourt's purchase of the Virginia cloth counterpane is documented in the Marshman account book, Badminton Papers. Seventy years previously a rich Virginia planter had noted with pleasure how lucky he was that a consignment of silver had arrived just two or three days before the governor came to stay with him and "hansell" (inaugurate) it with honor. Davis, *William Fitzhugh and His Chesapeake World*, pp. 269–273.

17. The quote is from Adam, *Works in Architecture*, p. 3. There were two *Virginia Gazettes* in this period, a *Maryland Gazette*, and a *North Carolina Gazette*. Richard Beale Davis, *Intellectual Life in the Colonial South, 1585–1763*, II (Knoxville, Tenn., 1978), pp. 609–622.

18. Donald Jackson, ed., *The Diaries of George Washington* (Charlottesville, Va., 1976–1978), I–III, passim. Would that he had been more communicative on paper! His laconism reached its peak in an entry during the admittedly arduous second presidency: "Much such a day as yesterday in all respects." Marcus Cunliffe, *George Washington: Man and Monument* (Boston, 1958), p. 180.

19. Jackson, ed., *Diaries of Washington*, III, pp. 56–208, passim.

20. The quote is from Jones, *Present State of Virginia*, ed. Morton, p. 81. The fragmentary diary of Robert Wormeley Carter shows a similar pattern in May and Aug. 1774 after he was elected a burgess. MSS.2, C2462b, Landon Carter Papers, Va. Hist. Soc. See also Zuckerman, "Fate, Flux, and Good Fellowship," in Sharlin, ed., *Business and Its Environment*, pp. 166–169; and Isaac, *Transformation of Virginia*, pp. 70–78.

21. E. C. Branchi, trans., "Memoirs of the Life and Voyages of Doctor Philip Mazzei," *WMQ*, 2nd Ser., IX (1929), p. 166.

22. Parker to Steuart, Aug. 5, 1770, Steuart Papers. For the Beverley wager, see Wright, *First Gentlemen of Virginia*, pp. 90–91. Charles Carter's efforts to cure sturgeon were also mentioned in the award of the medal—it is not clear if it was for both endeavors. Carter certainly sent wine to London. American Correspondence of the Royal Society of Arts, London, 1755–1840, MSS, Library of the Royal Society of Arts, microfilm, CWF.

23. Little, "Norborne Berkeley," pp. 399–405.

24. For Spotswood, see Dodson, *Alexander Spotswood*, passim. Gooch's interests are noted in Gooch to his brother, Mar. 27, 1728, Gooch Letters. Fauquier's involvement in lead mines is noted in Mays, *Pendleton*, I, p. 203. See also Reese, ed., *Official Papers of Fauquier*, I, pp. xxxv–xlviii.

25. Greene, ed., *Diary of Landon Carter*, I, p. 512; "Meade Family History," pp. 87–88; John Page, Jr., to John Norton, May 27, 1769, Frances Norton Mason, ed., *John Norton & Sons, Merchants of London and Virginia* (Richmond, Va., 1937), p. 94.

26. Thomas Norton to Messrs. Norton & Son, Aug. 1, 1770, Mason, ed., *Norton & Sons*, p. 140. The London merchant Samuel Athawes wrote to his friend Edward Ambler of Jamestown, Aug. 17, 1768: "His Lordship has the character here and from what I have seen seems to deserve it of a Good humour'd Sensible and Candid Man and I trust will make himself very acceptable to the Colony." Botetourt impressed the merchant as "perfectly dispos'd . . . to give satisfaction to Individuals and promote the General Welfare and prosperity of the Colony. I shall esteem it a favour if you would lose no time in paying your Congratulatory Compliments to him on his Arrival. Wishing perfect unanimity and Concord may prevail during his administration." MS, Va. Hist. Soc.

27. Farish, ed., *Journal & Letters of Fithian*, pp. 27, 216; *S.-C. Gaz.*, Sept. 10, 1772.

28. Lipscomb and Bergh, eds., *Writings of Jefferson*, I, pp. 1–64, quotations on pp. 3–4.

29. *Ibid.*, XIV, p. 231.

30. *Ibid.*, p. 3. Fauquier's will was signed on Mar. 26, 1767. For the registered copy, see Prob. 11/973, p. 480, Principal Probate Registry, Somerset House. Reese, ed., *Official Papers of Fauquier*, I, pp. xxxv–xlviii, esp. pp. xxv, xli–xlv; Norman Dain, *Disordered Minds: The First Century of Eastern State Hospital in Williamsburg, Virginia, 1766–1866* (Williamsburg, Va., 1971), pp. 6–8.

31. Reese, ed., *Official Papers of Fauquier*, I, pp. xxxv–xxxvii. For Jefferson's prototypical library—the "Skipwith Library"—see Boyd et al., eds., *Papers of Jefferson*, I, pp. 74–81. For William Fauquier, see Louise Lippincott, *Selling Art in Georgian London: The Rise of Arthur Pond* (New Haven, Conn., 1983), passim. See also Little, "Norborne Berkeley," p. 384. For Gibbs, see Terry Friedman, *James Gibbs* (New Haven, Conn., 1984), pp. 172, 273, 300, 325; and Bryan Little, "Trivia: Francis Fauquier and an English Architect," *WMQ*, 3rd Ser., XII (1955), pp. 475–476. See also Fiske Kimball, *Thomas Jefferson, Architect* (Boston, 1916; reprint ed., New York, 1968), pp. vi, 22–23.

32. Randolph, *History of Virginia*, ed. Shaffer, p. 170; Little, "Norborne Berkeley."

33. Little, "Norborne Berkeley," 388, 392; Badminton Papers; Christopher Hussey, *English Country Houses. I: Early Georgian, 1715–1760* (London, 1955), pp. 161–166; Helena Hayward and Pat Kirkham, *William and John Linnell: Eighteenth Century London Furniture Makers*, I (London, 1980), pp. 92, 106–108. The fourth duke of Beaufort was one of the charter subscribers to Thomas Chippendale's great pattern book, *The Gentleman & Cabinet-Maker's Director* (London, 1754). For Robert Adam, see Damie Stillman, *The Decorative Work of Robert Adam* (London, 1966); and Geoffrey Beard, *The Work of Robert Adam* (Edinburgh, 1978).

34. Millar, *Later Georgian Pictures*, pp. 93–95; National Portrait Gallery, *Johann Zoffany* (London, 1976), nos. 24–25; Lionel Cust, *History of the Society of the Dilettanti* (London, 1898). This trip resulted in the publication of *Ionian Antiquities*. See David Lambert and Stewart Harding, "Thomas Wright at Stoke Park," *Garden History: The Journal of the Garden History Society*, XVII (1989), pp. 68–82.

35. Robert C. Alberts, *Benjamin West: A Biography* (Boston, 1978), pp. 73–90. See the notices on West in the *Va. Gaz.* (Purdie and Dixon), Aug. 24, 1769, June 7, 1770.

36. Notices of Peale's portrait of Pitt are in the *Va. Gaz.* (Purdie and Dixon), Apr. 20, 1769; and *ibid.* (Rind), Apr. 21, 1769. For statues of Pitt, see Wayne Craven, *Sculpture in America* (New York, 1968), pp. 47–50; and *Va. Gaz.* (Purdie and Dixon), Nov. 27, 1766. For John Wilton, see Margaret Whinney, *Sculpture in Britain, 1530–1830* (Baltimore, Md., 1964), p. 143. For further details of the Peale portrait of Pitt, see Charles Coleman Sellers, "Portraits and Miniatures by Charles Willson Peale," Amer. Phil. Soc., *Trans.*, XLII, Pt. 1 (1952), pp. 172–173; and Charles Coleman Sellers, "Virginia's Great Allegory of William Pitt," *WMQ*, 3rd Ser., IX (1952), pp. 58–66.

37. Labaree, ed., *Autobiography of Franklin*, p. 80. According to Franklin in his extremely biased retrospection, the promises received from Sir William Keith were never fulfilled.

38. Alberts, *Benjamin West*, pp. 66–143; E. P. Richardson, "West's Voyages to Italy, 1760, and William Allen," *Pennsylvania Magazine of History and Biography*, CII (1978), pp. 3–26; Lillian B. Miller, ed., *The Selected Papers of Charles Willson Peale and His Family*, I (New Haven, Conn., 1983), p. 120.

39. William Sawitzky, *Matthew Pratt, 1734–1805: A Study of His Work* (New York, 1942), pp. 29–30.

40. Hood, *Bridges and Dering*, pp. 3, 4, 1–98. Bridges's special qualities were recognized by his being commissioned to paint the royal arms for several of the new county courthouses that were being built in the economically positive years of the second quarter of the century.

41. Louis Morton, *Robert Carter of Nomini Hall: A Virginia Tobacco Planter of the Eighteenth

Century (Charlottesville, Va., 1964), p. 35. See also pp. 45, 49–50.

42. Lyon G. Tyler, "Virginia's Contribution to Science," *WMQ*, 1st Ser., XXIV (1915), pp. 221–223; "Historical and Genealogical Notes," *ibid.*, IV (1896), pp. 200–201; *Va. Gaz.* (Purdie and Dixon), May 13, 1773. The quote is from Randolph, *History of Virginia*, ed. Shaffer, p. 197.

43. Botetourt to Beaufort, Dec. 28, 1769, Badminton Papers.

44. *Va. Gaz.* (Purdie and Dixon), Nov. 21, 1771; Randolph, *History of Virginia*, ed. Shaffer, p. 196. For Gwatkin and Henley, see Isaac, *Transformation of Virginia*, pp. 184–240.

45. Botetourt to Beaufort, Dec. 28, 1769, Badminton Papers; "The First Collegiate Medals," *WMQ*, 1st Ser., IV (1895), pp. 263–264. The Badminton Papers contain information on payment to Thomas Pingo for the dies for the medal (now owned by the College of William and Mary) and the first strikes. The total cost was a little under £100. Botetourt was also recorded by the *Va. Gaz.* (Purdie), Nov. 2, 1769, to have presented "the Reverend Dr. Witherspoon" with £50 for his "excellent and growing foundation" at Princeton, N. J. For the background of his reforms at the college, see Morpurgo, *Their Majesties' Royall Colledge*, pp. 147–155; and Robert Polk Thomson, "The Reform of the College of William and Mary, 1763–1780," Amer. Phil. Soc., *Proceedings*, CXV (1971), pp. 187–213.

46. Starke to Beaufort, Oct. 25, 1770, Badminton Papers. Whether he was the same Richard as the son of William and Mary Bolling Starke and author of *Justice of the Peace* who was noted in Lyon Gardiner Tyler, *Encyclopedia of Virginia Biography*, s.v. "Starke, Richard," or whether he was a son of that Richard is unclear.

47. Fauquier's will includes the bequest to Halifax. Reese, ed., *Official Papers of Fauquier*, I, pp. xxxv–xlviii; Gooch to his brother, Mar. 6, 1747, Gooch Letters.

48. Gooch to his brother, Mar. 6, 1747, Gooch Letters.

49. Lipscomb and Bergh, eds., *Writings of Jefferson*, XIV, p. 232. Each of the other governors I have included in my group for study owned musical instruments. Eden's household contained at least one guitar. Tryon owned a "very valuable collection of music," but his schedule of losses included only one instrument—a kettle drum in the butler's bedchamber! Lord William Campbell possessed a diverse collection of musical instruments, enough for a chamber ensemble. In addition to an "elegant" double-manual harpsichord, he had a cello, guitar, bassoon, two oboes (hautboys), two German flutes in a mahogany box, plus six small and eight large mahogany music stands. His library contained 49 music books, of which 28 in marbled covers were very expensive.

50. "Letter of Anne Blair to Martha Braxton," *WMQ*, 1st Ser., XVI (1907–1908), pp. 174–180. Botetourt's name appears among the list of subscribers to William Felton's *Eight Concertos for the Organ*, printed in London in 1762. Reference courtesy of Martha Katz–Hyman. Pelham, whose father was an engraver who married the Widow Copley in Boston, gave recitals at Bruton Church for which admission was paid, while John Blair's diary for 1751 records recitals at private houses and at the college. Carson, *Colonial Virginians at Play*, pp. 246–248, 250–251.

51. The accounts of musical evenings at the Palace and at Tazewell Hall are given in the Journal of Augustine Prevost for July 1774, London Library, microfilm, CWF.

52. Farish, ed., *Journal & Letters of Fithian*, pp. 48, 43, 51. Dunmore's musical instruments are cited in his schedule of losses and in Mason, ed., *Norton & Sons*, pp. 329–331. For concerts in Virginia, see Carson, *Colonial Virginians at Play*, pp. 246–252.

53. For the reference to the college garden and further information on Nicholson's and Spotswood's designs, see Martin, " 'Promised Fruits of Well-Ordered Towns' "; Martin, "Williamsburg: The Role of the Garden"; and Martin, " 'Long and Assiduous Endeavours.' " Gooch's interest is mentioned on p. 155 and documented in Edmund Berkeley and Dorothy Smith Berkeley, *The Life and Travels of John Bartram: From Lake Ontario to the River St. John* (Tallahassee, Fla., 1982), pp. 56–57. For Thomas Wright, see Eileen Harris, "Architect of Rococo Landscapes: Thomas Wright," Part III, *Country Life*, Sept. 9, 1971, pp. 612–615. For the quote, see Lambert and Harding, "Thomas Wright," p. 68. For Beverley, see pp. 168–193.

54. The petty cash account book in Marshman's writing (audited monthly by Botetourt) records daily expenses including direct costs of the specimens normally about 1/–, or tips such as to "Col. Lee's Servt. for . . . ," normally half a crown. For the seventeenth-century contacts, see Martin, " 'Promised Fruits of Well-Ordered Towns.' " The Botetourt diary was discovered by my colleague, Patricia A. Gibbs. For this rich subject, see Edmund Berkeley and Dorothy Smith Berkeley, *John Clayton, Pioneer of American Botany* (Chapel Hill, N. C., 1963); Edmund Berkeley and Dorothy Smith Berkeley, *Dr. John Mitchell: The Man Who Made the Map of North America* (Chapel Hill, N. C., 1974); and E. G. Swem, ed., *Brothers of the Spade: Correspondence of Peter Collinson of London, and of John Custis of Williamsburg, Virginia* (Barre, Mass., 1957).

55. Undated, unsigned letter, not in Botetourt's own hand but clearly dictated by him, beginning, "I anchored in Hampton Roads, Tuesday, 25th of October . . . ," Badminton Papers.

56. Perry, ed., *Historical Collections Relating to the American Colonial Church*, I, pp. 463–472; Reese, ed., *Official Papers of Fauquier*, I, pp. xxxix–xl.

57. William Fenton's account book is in the Badminton Papers; Joshua Kendall's account is in the Nicholas Papers.

58. Little, "Norborne Berkeley," p. 406; Botetourt to Eden, June 24, 1770, Maryland State Papers (Sharf Collection), 19999–116/30. Botetourt to Hillsborough, May 23, 1769, was forceful to the point of bluntness. McGaan, "Official Letters," pp. 138–139.

59. Payment to John Henry is recorded in the account books, Badminton Papers. See also Botetourt to Hillsborough, Nov. 24, 1768, McGaan, "Official Letters," pp. 62–64, 266–267. Botetourt's predilection for maps is further indicated by the fact that he brought with him from London "firescreens with maps on both sides." Botetourt Papers.

60. Fauquier to Richard Bland, July 28, 1760, McGregor Collection, 10, 127a, Alderman Lib.; Perry, ed., *Historical Collections Relating to the American Colonial Church*, I, p. 470. The Reverend John Camm wrote, "And it was taken notice of it seems, that I did not put off my hat to Mr. Fauquier and Captain Fauquier when I happened to meet them in the Streets. This compliment I never failed to pay the Governor . . . because custom here gave it to him from everybody." Camm to the bishop of London, Sept. 8, 1768, Fulham Palace Papers 14, no. 188.

61. "Wirt's Life of Henry," pp. 253–256. For more on rank and deference, see Upton, *Holy Things and Profane*, pp. 205–206; and Roeber, *Faithful Magistrates*, pp. 73–80. A portrait traditionally said to be of Nathaniel Walthoe, appointed clerk of the General Assembly in 1744 and later clerk of the Council, hung at Westover, the Byrd family seat, in the eighteenth century and was removed to Brandon, the Harrison seat, in the nineteenth century. It was described in the latter house about 1870 with the comment that "Mr. Waltham [sic] . . . left a diamond ring to the second Col. Byrd, upon condition that he would permit his portrait to hang up in the same room with those of the noblemen, with his hat on." The other portraits referred to were William Byrd II's well-known gallery of portraits of English gentry of his acquaintance. Hood, *Bridges and Dering*, pp. 23–24, 114–118; Breen, *Tobacco Culture*, p. 34; David Meschutt, "William Byrd and His Portrait Collection," *Journal of Early Southern Decorative Arts*, XIV (1988), pp. 18–47. See the great irony of gentlemen

doffing their hats to an Indian queen in Williamsburg in 1702 in Carson, *Colonial Virginians at Play*, p. 202.
62. Perry, ed., *Historical Collections Relating to the American Colonial Church*, I, p. 476. Upton, *Holy Things and Profane*, pp. 195–196, details a similar incident in a public space earlier in the century and notes its symbolic character.
63. Gooch to his brother, Mar. 27, 1728, Dec. 28, June 24, 1727, July 24, 1730, June 9, 1728, Gooch Letters.
64. Farish, ed., *Journal & Letters of Fithian*, p. 83. It is possible that the Scripture prints were the same as, or similar to, those bound into Bibles of the time, such as the 1720 edition of the J. Field Bible of 1660, published in Cambridge, that Lady Gooch left to the College of William and Mary on her death in 1773. Sets of prints such as those by Pieter de Houdt were also published separately in France and Holland in the period.
65. Ware, *Complete Body of Architecture*, p. 408.
66. Adam, *Works in Architecture*, p. 3.
67. A Mediterranean pass issued by the Admiralty was necessary to protect a British ship entering there from the Barbary pirates. It cost £1.15.0. Part of the pass was clipped at the time of sale and returned to the Admiralty to be matched up with the used pass later.
68. See I. N. Phelps Stokes, *The Iconography of Manhattan Island* (New York, 1915–1928), IV, p. 844, for a description of Tryon's fire. Eden, Campbell, and Botetourt used horsehair upholstery in their dining rooms, while carpets and painted canvas floorcloths were also their preference for the floor. See Appendixes 1, 5, and 7. Botetourt's English country house, Stoke Park, also featured horsehair upholstery and blue moreen curtains in the dining room with six pictures, of which three were large or "full length." This practice was not uncommon in Virginia—for example, Landon Carter at Sabine Hall kept fourteen Boydell prints and six small pictures in his dining room; inventory, Feb. 1779, Carter Papers, Univ. of Va.
69. J. Randolph, deed of trust, Tazewell Papers.
70. Peyton Randolph's inventory, taken in 1775, does not include room divisions or designations. However, the first group of furnishings listed obviously corresponds to a dining room which in turn corresponds to the large easternmost room on the first floor. York County, Virginia, Records, Wills and Inventories, XXII, 1771–1783, pp. 337–341, microfilm, CWF. Portraits of Peyton and his wife by John Wollaston, 1755–1757, are now owned by the Va. Hist. Soc. The reference to Jefferson's tract being read in the house is in Randolph, *History of Virginia*, ed. Shaffer, pp. 204–205.
71. Farish, ed., *Journal & Letters of Fithian*, p. 95. The Fielding Lewis inventory of Kenmore, 1781, shows the only desk and bookcase in the house as located in the dining room. "An Appraisement of the Estate of Colo. Fielding Lewis 17th April 1781," with commentary by P. Russell Bastedo, June 1974, transcript, CWF. Benjamin Harrison at Berkeley, 1791, had one of only two desks in the house in his dining room. "Genealogy: Harrison of James River," *VMHB*, XXXIV (1926), p. 88. Rawleigh Downman at Morattico, 1781, had a study in his house but placed a desk and bookcase and a mahogany desk in his dining room. Lancaster County, Virginia, Wills and Deeds, XX, 1770–1783, fols. 200–204, transcript, CWF. Edward Ambler of Jamestown, 1769, located a large mahogany library desk in his dining room. "Appraisement of the Estate of Mr Edwd Ambler Decd" [1769], Alderman Lib., transcript, CWF. Thomas Nelson of Yorktown, 1789, kept a walnut desk in his dining room. York Co. Recs., Wills and Inventories, XXIII, 1783–1811, pp. 181–183, microfilm, CWF.
72. The details of Mt. Airy are in Farish, ed., *Journal & Letters of Fithian*, p. 34. See also Isaac, *Transformation of Virginia*, pp. 75–78.

The Ballroom and Supper Room: Fashionable Gatherings
page numbers 168–193

1. Ware, *Complete Body of Architecture*, p. 295.
2. Ibid. For the addition of the ballroom, see Whiffen, *Public Buildings*, pp. 143–144.
3. Spotswood to the Board of Trade, Nov. 15, 1718, C.O. 5/1318, fol. 348; Gooch to his brother, Feb. 18, 1728, Gooch Letters; Carson, *Colonial Virginians at Play*, pp. 252–254. For more on the paternalistic system, see Isaac, *Transformation of Virginia*, pp. 110–115.
4. *Va. Gaz.*, July 11, 1746.
5. Ibid. (Rind), Dec. 14, 1769. The story spread to the other colonies and to London. Carson, *Colonial Virginians at Play*, p. 217; Louis B. Wright and Marion Tinling, eds., *Quebec to Carolina in 1785–1786: Being the Travel Diary and Observations of Robert Hunter, Jr., a Young Merchant of London* (San Marino, Calif., 1943), p. 231.
6. Isaac, *Transformation of Virginia*, pp. 80–87. Patterns of behavior are well documented in three articles on assembly rooms by Mark Girouard in *Country Life*: "Moonlit Matchmaking: Assembly Rooms of the 18th Century," Aug. 21, 1986, pp. 540–544; "The Most Elegant Recreation," Sept. 11, 1986, pp. 766–768; and "Spreading the Nash Gospel," Oct. 2, 1986, pp. 1057–1059. An excellent illustration of what relief a ball might have spelled from the normal male recreations of the time is provided by Allan Kulikoff, *Tobacco and Slaves: The Development of Southern Cultures in the Chesapeake, 1680–1800* (Chapel Hill, N. C., 1986), pp. 217–231. See also Zuckerman, "Fate, Flux, and Good Fellowship," in Sharlin, ed., *Business and Its Environment*, pp. 167–173. The characteristic Virginia settlement pattern was often noted. Jane Carson, *We Were There: Descriptions of Williamsburg, 1699–1859* (Williamsburg, Va., 1965), passim; T. H. Breen, "Horses and Gentlemen: The Cultural Significance of Gambling among the Gentry of Virginia," *WMQ*, 3rd Ser., XXXIV (1977), pp. 239–257.
7. "Extracts from the County Records," *VMHB*, VIII (1901), pp. 171–172; Carson, *Colonial Virginians at Play*, pp. 198–202, quotation on p. 202.
8. Carson, *Colonial Virginians at Play*, pp. 252–255; Wright and Tinling, eds., *Secret Diary of Byrd*, passim; Jones, *Present State of Virginia*, ed. Morton, p. 70.
9. Gooch to his brother, Dec. 28, 1727, Gooch Letters; Farish, ed., *Journal & Letters of Fithian*, p. 177. Whiffen details the costs of the ballroom wing addition, *Public Buildings*, p. 143.
10. Girouard, *Life in the English Country House*, pp. 182–183, 190–194; Girouard, "Moonlight Matchmaking," pp. 542–543; Carl Bridenbaugh, *Cities in the Wilderness: The First Century of Urban Life in America, 1625–1742*, 2nd ed. (New York, 1955), pp. 438–441.
11. Marcus Whiffen, *The Eighteenth-Century Houses of Williamsburg* (Williamsburg, Va., 1960), pp. 133–135, 190–193; Waterman, *Mansions of Virginia*, pp. 294, 139.
12. The dedicatory quote is from Girouard, "The Most Elegant Recreation," p. 768, and was inscribed for the new assembly rooms in Newcastle, 1774. See Farish, ed., *Journal & Letters of Fithian*, pp. 97, 154, for civic ballrooms. See also Edward A. Chappell, "Reconsidered Splendor: The Palace Addition of 1751," research report, 1985, CWF. The Raleigh Tavern was available with free liquor in 1771 when citizens were supposed to celebrate the anniversary of George III's accession. *Va. Gaz.* (Rind), Oct. 31, 1771; Carson, *Colonial Virginians at Play*, p. 213.
13. *Va. Gaz.*, Nov. 17, 1752.
14. Stephen Hawtrey to his brother Edward, later master of the grammar school at the college, Mar. 26, 1765, Faculty/Alumni file, College Archives, Swem Lib.
15. Mary Spotswood, a descendant of the former lieutenant governor, wrote to her mother in May 1769 or 1770 to describe life in Williamsburg at the time. MSS/SP 687L-19, Va. Hist. Soc.
16. *Va. Gaz.* (Purdie and Dixon), Oct. 27, 1768. Botetourt's lineage was given in the Oct. 6 issue, *ibid*. Little, "Norborne Berkeley," pp. 390–398; "Meade Family History," pp. 87–88. See also Randolph, *History of Virginia*,

ed. Shaffer, p. 171, who stressed that Virginians "were proud in no longer being governed by a deputy."

17. *Va. Gaz.* (Purdie and Dixon), May 26, 1774; Farish, ed., *Journal & Letters of Fithian*, pp. 48, 33–34. Fithian confessed he had "seldom [been] more dash'd" than when his excuse for *not* dancing was exposed. P. 12. Some dancing masters also painted portraits, increasing their familiarity with genteel behavior and their usefulness to gentry society. Hood, *Bridges and Dering*, pp. 99–122. Kulikoff, *Tobacco and Slaves*, pp. 261–312, gives an excellent synthesis on the "Rise of the Chesapeake Gentry." For etiquette, see Carson, *Colonial Virginians at Play*, pp. 254–255; and Wright, *First Gentlemen of Virginia*, p. 83.

18. M. Spotswood to her mother, MSS/SP 687L-19. William Byrd described the opening of a ball at which the governor danced with Mrs. Byrd: "The Governor was very gallant to the ladies and very courteous to the gentlemen." Morton, *Colonial Virginia*, II, p. 484. An important source of information on polite manners was François Nivelon, *The Rudiments of Genteel Behaviour* (London, ca. 1737). See also Kellom Tomlinson, *The Art of Dancing* (London, 1724; reprint ed., New York, 1970), passim.

19. Girouard points out that provincial assemblies developed that sometimes betrayed Nash's ideal, where "No . . . clerk . . . or shopkeeper . . . shall be admitted"; "Spreading the Nash Gospel," p. 1059. Robert Wormeley Carter letter, May 6, 1770, MSS.2, C2462b, L. Carter Papers, Va. Hist. Soc.

20. "Lord Dunmore and His Negro Followers," *Lower Norfolk County Virginia Antiquary*, V (1906), pp. 33–35, n. 2.

21. Girouard, *Life in the English Country House*, p. 193; Girouard, "Moonlight Matchmaking," pp. 542–543; Farish, ed., *Journal & Letters of Fithian*, pp. 56–57.

22. Farish, ed., *Journal & Letters of Fithian*, p. 154. Girouard documents some of the hazards (to mothers, that is) of young girls with attractive, but poor, young men at assemblies; Daniel Defoe wrote in 1724 of the assemblies at Bury St. Edmunds where "the daughters of all the gentry of the three counties come hither to be picked up"; "Moonlight Matchmaking," p. 540.

23. Farish, ed., *Journal & Letters of Fithian*, pp. 154–155.

24. Wright and Tinling, eds., *Quebec to Carolina*, pp. 208, 207.

25. Farish, ed., *Journal & Letters of Fithian*, p. 33. However, there are many quotes to prove that a ball could be disagreeable. Misanthropes abounded: "Conceive to yourself one hundred and fifty to two hundred people met together, dressed in the extremity of the fashion, painted as red as Bacchanals; poisoning the air with perfumes, treading on each other's gowns, making the crowd the blame, not one in ten able to get a chair; protesting that they are engaged to ten other places, and lamenting the fatigue they are obliged to endure, ten or a dozen card tables crowded with dowagers of quality; grave ecclesiastics and yellow admirals and you have an idea of an assembly." Hannah More thus described an assembly held by the Bishop of St. Asaph. Rosamond Bayne-Powell, *Housekeeping in the Eighteenth Century* (London, 1956), pp. 109–110. Reference courtesy of Linda Baumgarten.

26. A. G. Bradley, ed., *The Journal of Nicholas Cresswell, 1774–1777* (New York, 1924), p. 53; Isaac, *Transformation of Virginia*, pp. 84, 80–87; Upton, *Holy Things and Profane*, p. 219.

27. Petty cash account book kept by William Marshman, Badminton Papers.

28. Carson, *Colonial Virginians at Play*, pp. 223–245; Rankin, *Theater in Colonial America*.

29. Beverley to Athawes, Apr. 15, 1771, Beverley Letter Book. Joseph Kidd's charges are noted in the Nicholas Papers.

30. Bank passbooks with Drummond and Co., Badminton Papers; Botetourt to Hillsborough, Nov. 10, 1768, McGaan, "Official Letters," p. 52; Millar, *Later Georgian Pictures*, pp. 93–95.

31. Fauquier had sent his family back to London in 1766. Reese, ed., *Official Papers of Fauquier*, I, p. xxxviii. George Mercer to James Mercer, Aug. 16, 1768, George Mercer, Letters to His Brother, 1768 and 1771, Mercer-Garnett Papers, Va. State Lib. and Arch., photostat, CWF. For a description of the king's rooms at Buckingham House, see Olwen Hedley, *Queen Charlotte* (London, 1975), p. 83.

32. Gooch to his brother, Mar. 27, 1728, Gooch Letters; Botetourt to Hillsborough, May 10, 1769, McGaan, "Official Letters," p. 118.

33. Political talk and activity were, of course, not unknown at a social ball. Girouard gives English parallels in "The Most Elegant Recreation."

34. A generic name for fine linen, oznabrigs served as the first layer on the walls, brown paper being pasted on that and white "cartridge" paper, in elephant folio size sheets, as the final layer in preparation for painting. Three layers were an excellent precaution against cracking and gave a triple-lamination for strength when painted. Two or three coats of paint were necessary to provide an even color, and, when finished, the appearance was as rich, soft, and beautiful as many a lovely textile, and considerably less expensive. For a period description of this technique, see Fowler and Cornforth, *English Decoration*, p. 179. Kidd also charged Botetourt for "pressing and nailing down a large carpet for the ballroom" on Nov. 28, 1769. Nicholas Papers.

35. The Jefferson reference is in the MSS diary and account books for 1769, 42393.15.B.1, Alderman Lib.; Beverley to Athawes, Apr. 15, 1771, Beverley Letter Book. The R. Carter Letterbook, II, 1774–1775, Duke Univ. Lib., cites plain crimson and yellow as well as blue; the earlier R. Carter Letter Book, 1761–1764, is at CWF. Washington had in fact ordered plain paper is early as 1763, probably under the influence of his affluent neighbor, George William Fairfax of Belvoir (orders to Robert Stark, Mar. 1763, archives of Gunston Hall, Va.). Fairfax had seen the papers in England and immediately ordered plain green and yellow in addition to blue. Franklin sent instructions from London in 1765 to his wife in Philadelphia to paper one room blue. Catherine Lynn, *Wallpaper in America: From the Seventeenth Century to World War I* (New York, 1980), p. 125. Fairfax and Franklin were doing what the Virginia governor was also doing—responding to the latest English fashion and transferring it to the colonies.

36. Beverley to Athawes, Apr. 15, 1771, Beverley Letter Book. For a discussion of Virginians' preference for "plain and neat," see Gusler, *Furniture of Williamsburg*, pp. 7–8, 119. One of the most engaging surveys of neoclassicism is Hugh Honour, *Neo-Classicism* (Harmondsworth, Eng., 1968).

37. Mary Stephenson, *Carter's Grove Plantation: A History* (Williamsburg, Va., 1964), p. 61. See also pp. 57–61. The Buzaglo stove is discussed in further detail in the Epilogue.

38. For Peale's portrait of Pitt, see pp. 147–148 and n. 36. For West, see Helmut von Erffa and Allen Staley, *The Paintings of Benjamin West* (New Haven, Conn., 1986), pp. 33–54. For the Buzaglo stove, see the Epilogue. George Hamilton advertised in the *Va. Gaz.* (Purdie and Dixon), July 28, 1774. Conversations with Wallace B. Gusler, who is studying the putative work of Hamilton and other carvers of the period, have been informative and helpful. The Custis silver is discussed in Kathryn C. Buhler, *Mount Vernon Silver* (Mount Vernon, Va., 1957), pp. 24–33.

39. Worthington Chauncey Ford, ed., *Journals of the Continental Congress, 1774–1779*, I (Washington, D. C., 1904), pp. 28–29; Philadelphia Museum of Art, *Philadelphia: Three Centuries of American Art* (Philadelphia, 1976), pp. 128–130. For Jefferson's furniture, see Charles F. Montgomery, *American Furniture: The Federal Period* (New York, 1966), pp. 9, 133. Gusler, *Furniture of Williamsburg*, pp. 97–100, discusses a piece of Williamsburg-made furniture with neoclassical features

40. Radoff, *Buildings of Maryland*, pp. 50–51; Dill, *Governor Tryon and His Palace*, pp. 120–123. The chandeliers may also have been intended for the assembly rooms in Annapolis. Reference courtesy of Michael Trostell.
41. Ware, *Complete Body of Architecture*, pp. 335–337. Waterman, *Mansions of Virginia*, gives basic information on the Virginia plantation houses, including floor plans.
42. When Spotswood and the burgesses were discussing negotiations with the Indians to be conducted in Albany, N. Y., in 1722, the assembly appointed envoys "suitable to the dignity of his Majesty's first and most ancient colony in America," Morton, *Colonial Virginia*, II, pp. 478–479.
43. Isaac, *Transformation of Virginia*, p. 113.
44. For the decline of hospitality in Virginia, see Lewis, *Pursuit of Happiness*, p. 23; and Isaac, *Transformation of Virginia*, pp. 302–303.

Private Life
page numbers 196–201

1. Smith, *Inside the Great House*; Isaac, *Transformation of Virginia*, esp. pp. 303–322; Lewis, *Pursuit of Happiness*. The wider literature of colonial childhood, family development, and emotional expression is well documented in these three works. See also Isaac's review of Smith, *Inside the Great House*, *WMQ*, 3rd Ser., XXXIX (1982), pp. 226–230.
2. Morton, *Colonial Virginia*, II, p. 741; Reese, ed., *Official Papers of Fauquier*, I, p. 418; W. Marshman to J. Marshman, Nov. 8, 1770, Badminton Papers.

The Bedchambers and Study: The Person of the Governor
page numbers 202–227

1. Girouard, *Life in the English Country House*, pp. 128–136, 205–206.
2. Wright and Tinling, eds., *Secret Diary of Byrd*, p. 246.
3. Quoted in Fowler and Cornforth, *English Decoration*, p. 81.
4. The description of the ducal house is from Adam, *Works in Architecture*, p. 3.
5. *Va. Gaz.* (Purdie and Dixon), June 15, 1769. For chatty details about the Tryons' visit, see "Letter of Anne Blair," pp. 174–176. The Gooch letter about the Baltimores' visit is dated July 20, 1733, Gooch Letters.
6. Lady Dunmore's arrival was extensively reported in the *Va. Gaz.*, both the Rind and the Purdie and Dixon editions, Feb. 10, 24, Mar. 3, 10, 1774.
7. The description of the Carter house is in Farish, ed., *Journal & Letters of Fithian*, p. 80.
8. The birth of a daughter to Dunmore was announced in the *Va. Gaz.* (Purdie and Dixon), Dec. 8, 1774. See also McIlwaine, Hall, and Hillman, eds., *Executive Journals of the Council*, IV, p. 115.
9. In Dec. 1700 Nicholson formally opened the new sessions of the assembly from the bedchamber of his small house in Williamsburg since he was too ill to move. Morton, *Colonial Virginia*, I, p. 371; McIlwaine and Kennedy, eds., *Journals of Burgesses, 1742–1749*, pp. 228–229. See also pp. 225–226; and *Va. Gaz.* (Purdie and Dixon), Mar. 3, 1768.
10. Parker to Steuart, Dec. 1770, Steuart Papers. A slightly different version of this event, with R. C. Nicholas instead of Randolph, is in William Meade, *Old Churches, Ministers, and Families of Virginia* (Philadelphia, 1857; rev. ed., Baltimore, Md., 1966), pp. 183–184. Reference courtesy of Betty Leviner. For Dr. John de Sequeyra ("Seccari"), see Harold B. Gill, Jr., *The Apothecary in Colonial Virginia* (Williamsburg, Va., 1972), pp. 60, 95–96. Starke was mentioned in pp. 152–153.
11. W. Marshman to J. Marshman, Nov. 8, 1770, Starke to Beaufort, Oct. 25, 1770, Badminton Papers.
12. Girouard, *Life in the English Country House*, pp. 128–135. The configuration of the back stairs opening, on the first floor, into the main passage is shown clearly in Jefferson's sketch. In building this element in 1929–1932, the Colonial Williamsburg Restoration architects planned the second floor opening to be similarly oriented—immediately outside the doors to the Middle Room. The drawings for Tryon's Palace in New Bern disclose a similar arrangement; the backstairs there are side by side with the main stairs and open on the upper floor immediately adjacent to the main stairs. For local opinions on Botetourt, see pp. 122–167 and n. 25. Dunmore, on the other hand, was rumored to be a "Gamester, a whoremaster, and a drunkard." Parker to Steuart, Apr. 19, 1771, Steuart Papers.
13. *Builders Dictionary*, p. 93.
14. Botetourt to Hillsborough, May 10, 1769, McGaan, "Official Letters," p. 118. Botetourt's letter to his sister is dated May 31, 1770, Badminton Papers.
15. For a recent survey of British state beds, see John Cornforth, "British state beds," *Antiques*, CXXIX (1986), pp. 392–401. See also Thornton, *Seventeenth-Century Interior Decoration*, pp. 149–179.
16. See Appendixes 5 and 6. As far as it is possible, in the confused economy of Revolutionary Maryland, to convert the cost of both beds to sterling, Botetourt's in 1768 cost £20 while Eden's in 1776 cost £22.12.6, a comparable value in view of the differences involved.
17. Stools rarely appear in other Virginia inventories, although it is notable that John Randolph of Tazewell Hall in Williamsburg and Fielding Lewis of Kenmore in Fredericksburg—both houses of pretension and ambition—retained them in the main bedchambers.
18. Fenton account book, Badminton Papers. Christopher Gilbert, in his extensive work on the cabinetmaker Thomas Chippendale, has noted similar discrepancies between various inventory takers' descriptions as blue or green when citing the same piece of furniture. The earliest chairs in this style known at this time are by John Linnell and were made in 1767 for William Drake's house Shardeloes, "The Schedule of Clients of John Linnell," *Furniture History*, V (1969), p. 33. Hayward and Kirkham, *William and John Linnell*, I, p. 101, fig. 58.
19. Farish, ed., *Journal & Letters of Fithian*, pp. 26, 141.
20. For Washington references, see order of May 1, 1759, and invoice from Philip Bell of London, Aug. 1759, Invoices and Ledgers, 1755–1766, courtesy of Mount Vernon Ladies Association of the Union, Mount Vernon, Va.
21. The Kidd reference is in the Nicholas Papers. The Sheraton reference is from the *Cabinet Dictionary*, II, pp. 215–219, s.v., "Furnish." Pepys is quoted in Girouard, *Life in the English Country House*, p. 135. See also pp. 165–170 for a discussion of libraries.
22. Nelson to Beaufort, Oct. 30, 1770, Badminton Papers.
23. The notation on clothes sent from Stoke to Williamsburg is in the inventories of Stoke in 1768 and 1771, Badminton Papers. David Meade commented on the state coach that Botetourt employed with "much greater state than any Governor of Virginia had ever before displayed." "Meade Family History," p. 87.
24. *Ibid.*
25. Jones, *Present State of Virginia*, ed. Morton, p. 71. The Collinson quote is in Breen, "Horses and Gentlemen," p. 246.
26. As quoted in Linda Baumgarten, *Eighteenth-Century Clothing at Williamsburg* (Williamsburg, Va., 1986), p. 11.
27. Small's comments are detailed in pp. 174–176. The Robert Carter quote is in Baumgarten, *Eighteenth-Century Clothing*, p. 69.
28. Greene, ed., *Diary of Landon Carter*, I, p. 18; Gooch to the bishop of Norwich, June 4, 1740, Gooch Letters. For planter indebtedness, see Breen, *Tobacco Culture*, pp. 160–196.
29. J. Randolph to Beaufort, Oct. 15, 1770, inventories of Stoke Park for 1768 and 1770, Badminton Papers.
30. At least one book is known today with Lord Botetourt's name as owner—a handsome copy of Joseph Dalby's *The Virtues of Cinnabar and Musk, Against the Bite of a Mad Dog*, printed by Baskerville and published in Birmingham in 1762—which is in Swem Lib. Botetourt

was a charter subscriber to the work. Botetourt's Williamsburg books finished up on the ocean floor since the vessel carrying them and other items the duke of Beaufort sent for never arrived. For the importance of Bolingbroke's works, see Richard Beale Davis, *A Colonial Southern Bookshelf: Reading in the Eighteenth Century* (Athens, Ga., 1979), pp. 59–61. The quote is from the Jefferson correspondence with his kinsman, Robert Skipwith, regarding a recommended library. See n. 31, p. 323.

31. J. Randolph to Beaufort, Oct. 15, 1770, Badminton Papers. Jefferson the bibliophile is discussed in William Harwood Peden, "Thomas Jefferson: Book Collector" (Ph.D. diss., Univ. of Va., 1942); and William Bainter O'Neal, *Jefferson's Fine Arts Library: His Selections for the University of Virginia Together with His Own Architectural Books* (Charlottesville, Va., 1976). See also Frederick R. Goff, "Jefferson: The Book Collector," *Quarterly Journal of the Library of Congress*, XXIX (1972), pp. 32–47.

32. Carter's library is detailed in Farish, ed., *Journal & Letters of Fithian*, pp. 211–229; and discussed in Morton, *Robert Carter*, pp. 214–216, 250, 272. William Byrd's library is discussed in Edwin Wolf, 2nd, "The Dispersal of the Library of William Byrd of Westover," *Proceedings of the American Antiquarian Society*, LXVIII (1958), pp. 19–106; and Edwin Wolf, 2nd, "More Books from the Library of the Byrds of Westover," *American Antiquarian Society*, LXXXVIII (1978), pp. 51–82. See also Wright, *First Gentlemen of Virginia*, pp. 117–154; and Greene, "Society, Ideology, and Politics," in Jellison, ed., *Society, Freedom, and Conscience*, pp. 73–74.

33. For the college library, see John Melville Jennings, "Notes on the Original Library of the College of William and Mary in Virginia, 1693–1705," *Papers of the Bibliographical Society of America*, XLI (1947), pp. 238–267. The Council library was mentioned several times by Byrd at the beginning of the century and several times in the 1770s by Jefferson; in the latter's account books payments for services were recorded to "Rose the Librarian to the Council," Jefferson account book. Peyton Randolph's library was bequeathed him by his father and is mentioned in the inventory taken after his death in 1775, "Copy of Will of Sir John Randolph," *VMHB*, XXXVI (1928), pp. 376–381; York Co. Recs., Wills and Inventories, XXII, pp. 308–310. Jefferson's mention of having bought this library dates from ca. 1784–1789. Randolph G. Adams, *Three Americanists: Henry Harrisse, Bibliographer; George Brinley, Book Collector; Thomas Jefferson, Librarian* (Philadelphia, 1939), facing p. 39. Little is known about Wythe's library. For what is known, see Mary R. M. Goodwin, "The George Wythe House: Its Furniture & Furnishings," Appendix, pp. xliii–liv, research report, 1958, CWF. In addition to his well-known importance as a teacher and influence on Jefferson, Wythe also proposed opening a private school in Williamsburg in 1787 to teach Latin and Greek, English literature, and arithmetic, for which he would have needed, of course, a diverse library. *Va. Gaz.* (Nicholson), Aug. 2, 1787.

34. The three repositories of the books listed in the preceding two paragraphs are the rare book collection, CWF; special collections, Swem Lib.; and the Va. Hist. Soc. For Parks's and his successors' retail trade, see Joyce, Hall, Brown, and Hench, eds., *Printing and Society in Early America*, pp. 132–173. Jefferson's acquisitions are documented in his MSS account books for Nov.–Dec. 1778.

35. Kenneth A. Lockridge, *The Diary, and Life, of William Byrd II of Virginia, 1674–1744* (Chapel Hill, N. C., 1987); Greene, ed., *Diary of Landon Carter*, I, esp. pp. 1–61.

36. See Hayward and Kirkham, *William and John Linnell*, I, pp. 106–108. Certain of Botetourt's commonplace books among the Badminton Papers, dating from the 1750s, are apparently full of quotations from Prior, Pope, and the classics. Lambert and Harding, "Thomas Wright," p. 77. They need to be studied more systematically.

The Family
page numbers 228–265

1. For Botetourt's will, see p. 12. For Fauquier's will, see Prob. 11/973. It is cited in Reese, ed., *Official Papers of Fauquier*, I, p. xlv.

2. Complete references to the literature are given in Hecht, *The Domestic Servant*, esp. pp. 35–70. For the duties of blacks, see Kulikoff, *Tobacco and Slaves*, pp. 396–415.

3. Nelson to Beaufort, Oct. 30, 1770, Badminton Papers. For Botetourt's encounter with George Mercer, see p. 184 and n. 31.

4. The smallpox epidemic is documented in William Quentin Maxwell, ed., "A True State of the Smallpox in Williamsburg, February 22, 1748," *VMHB*, LXIII (1955), pp. 269–274. The Dunmore reference is in his schedule of losses. See Appendix 3. Fauquier's slaves are listed in his inventory. See Appendix 2. The Burwell slave is documented in Burwell Ledger 2, Burwell Papers, CWF.

5. I would like to thank George Reese and John M. Hemphill II for information on Fauquier's clerks. Pelham is documented in the Robert Carter Letter Books, 1760–1771, p. 22, Va. Hist. Soc., microfilm, CWF; and in the entry for Nov. 18, 1769, William Cabell Diary, Jan. 1769–Feb. 1770, no. 23338 [1], Va. State Lib. and Arch. Fauquier's last clerk, Edward Westmore, became keeper of the Gaol after his master's death, as did Pelham after Botetourt's. The position was obviously a minor grace-and-favor one.

6. Minzies is documented in Loyalist Claims, 1776–1789, A.O. 13/31; and in Mason, ed., *Norton & Sons*, p. 329. Dunmore's private secretary was Capt. Edward Foy, mentioned in Randolph, *History of Virginia*, ed. Shaffer, p. 196. Botetourt's chaplain was Arthur Hamilton, *Va. Gaz.* (Purdie and Dixon), Nov. 3, 1768. "One of" Dunmore's chaplains was Thomas Gwatkin, *ibid.* (Dixon), Feb. 2, 1775.

7. Byrd's comment in his letter to the earl of Orrery, July 5, 1726, has often been cited, notably in Isaac, *Transformation of Virginia*, pp. 39–40. Isaac discusses the distinctions between patriarchy and paternalism *ibid.*, pp. 308–310. See also Zuckerman, "William Byrd's Family," pp. 274–278, 283.

8. The Parke letters are in "Virginia Gleanings in England," *VMHB*, XX (1912), pp. 375, 377. For the Botetourt letter, see n. 10, p. 327.

9. There is some uncertainty about the second servants' hall. The Badminton copy of the inventory, unlike the working copy in the Va. State Lib. and Arch., has the word "contd." written (apparently in another hand) after the second listing for the servants' hall, implying, therefore, that there was only one.

10. For references to Tryon's Palace designs, see n. 13, p. 319.

11. See, for example, the last words of the Botetourt inventory, which are "Ret'd to Office." Appendix 1.

12. For plans of Kingsmill and Carter's Grove, see Waterman, *Mansions of Virginia*, pp. 61–62, 77–81. Information on Nomini Hall is from Farish, ed., *Journal & Letters of Fithian*, pp. 80–82.

13. The Badminton Papers contain a catalog of the family, lists of duties for servants, and seating arrangements for servants at Netheravon, Wilts.; the Stoke accounts detail Botetourt's Gloucestershire servants; and his London accounts give information on some of the servants at his townhouse.

14. The muster list is in the Admiralty Muster Book, pp. 68–69, Adm. 36/7483, P.R.O. Thomas Conway was the duke's auditor and obviously someone on whom Botetourt relied. He is memorialized with a plaster bust that dominates the muniment room at Badminton, the only person represented there.

15. W. Marshman to J. Marshman, Nov. 8, 1770, Badminton Papers. The militia allowance Marshman received in Virginia was approximately £16 sterling.

16. W. Marshman to J. Marshman, Nov. 8, 1770, Beaufort to the trustees, Jan. 2, 1771, *ibid.* That Marshman sold some of the clothes is suggested by the later notoriety of a black musician, Sy Gilliatt, who claimed to be wearing Botetourt's clothes, Samuel Mordecai,

Virginia, Especially Richmond, in By-gone Days; With a Glance at the Present: Being Reminiscences and Last Words of an Old Citizen (Richmond, Va., 1860), pp. 352–353.

17. Botetourt purchased the only library table in Fauquier's inventory for £6 currency. See also pp. 258–259 and n. 57.

18. Kendall's bill is in the Nicholas Papers. The third bedchamber in the garret was listed in the working copy of the Botetourt inventory as "Garrett over the front parlour," after "Mr. Blan" (Mr. Blandford) was crossed out. Fuller's salary and his percentage of tips were the same as Marshman's (£12.5.0 sterling), but his militia allowance was less—approximately £9 sterling a year.

19. Petty cash books kept by Marshman from June 14, 1768, until the last entry the day before Botetourt died, Oct. 14, 1770, "To Canary Seed for the Linnets . . . £0.2.6," Badminton Papers.

20. Jefferson's Accounts Books are a good source of information regarding tips for servants—such as "gave servt. of A.C's 1/3 . . . gave G.W.'s Ben 12/–. . . gave Westover postillions 12/–. . . gave Zachary at Tuckahoe 6/–."

21. Hannah Crew was sold to Botetourt for 25 percent under her appraised value of £60 currency. Lavie may have been the same as "James Levey," who charged the estate for seven days' and nights' attendance on Botetourt (probably during his illness), "shaving him after death," and "writing one half the company"—the latter presumably funeral notices. Nicholas Papers. For the flogging of white indentured servants, see Roeber, "Authority, Law, and Custom," p. 431. Kulikoff, *Tobacco and Slaves*, pp. 295–298, also gives examples of how desperately white servants could fare.

22. Kidd signed on at £40. He does not appear in the Badminton records before Aug. 1768. He may well be the same who served an apprenticeship in Newcastle as an upholsterer, bound in 1759, Inland Revenue Books, 53/163, P.R.O. Reference courtesy of Ronald L. Hurst. Kidd was advertising his own business in Williamsburg in the *Va. Gaz.* by May 4, 1769, though he was paid wages by Botetourt until Nov. 11, 1769. His charges for work at the Palace started Nov. 28, 1769. Dunmore referred to him in a letter to Hillsborough of Apr. 11, 1772, as "a very honest man." In 1775 he became an ensign in the Williamsburg militia and several years later quartermaster for the Brunswick Co. regiment. *Va. Gaz.* (Pinkney), Apr. 6, 1775.

23. The bill for clothing for servants was from Robert Nicolson, Williamsburg tailor, and is in the Nicholas Papers. Footman William Knight died at the Palace the same day as Botetourt, after twenty-seven years of service to him. He was eulogized in a poem, "On the death of a Footman," in the *Va. Gaz.* (Purdie and Dixon), Oct. 18, 1770. The stipend "for washing" amounted to £2.6.9 for a little over fourteen months. Dunmore ordered "strip'd flannel for grooms waistcoats." Mason, ed., *Norton & Sons*, p. 330. Dunmore later advertised in the *Va. Gaz.* (Rind), Mar. 26, 1772, that nineteen turkeys had been stolen from an outhouse at the Palace.

24. Perry, ed., *Historical Collections Relating to the American Colonial Church*, I, p. 476.

25. Nelson to Beaufort, Oct. 30, 1770, Badminton Papers; Nicholas to J. Norton, June 12, 1771, Mason, ed., *Norton & Sons*, p. 160.

26. Will of Fauquier, Prob. 11/973. Ayscough was a seedsman in town from 1759. After Fauquier's death the Ayscoughs ran a tavern in town for some years, *Va. Gaz.* (Purdie and Dixon), Oct. 6, 1768. Ayscough served in the post of "door-keeper to the Council," McIlwaine and Kennedy, eds., *Journals of Burgesses, 1770–1772*, June 27, 1770.

27. Mrs. Wilson was paid a salary of £36, her son £22. Dunmore employed a French chef, Lambert Lefebure, for an indefinite period. This is noted in a letter from the latter's wife, Aug. 1, 1774, 38-514, Alderman Lib.

28. "An account of cash Paid by William Sparrow for his Excellency Lord Botetourt, Governor of Virginia at Williamsburg July 3, 1769," Badminton Papers.

29. Mrs. Scott is documented in an order for supplies, mainly consisting of clothing, in which she sought the recommendations of the merchant's sister, rather than his own advice, in the matter of feminine garb and warned that the stays should be made "easy and full in the Stomick." Mason, ed., *Norton & Sons*, pp. 328–331.

30. "Meade Family History," p. 87.

31. The work done on the state berlin by Catton and Butler in Sept. 1768 covers six pages of an account book, Badminton Papers. William Nelson had been involved with the disposition of Fauquier's coach. William Nelson Letter Book, 1766–1775, Va. State Lib., microfilm, CWF. In his letter to John Norton, July 9, 1768, he wrote, "What's to be done with the Old Coach? To lay its Bones here or to be sent home to be new ground in the Mill? as the old People say they wish for." Mason, ed., *Norton & Sons*, p. 57. It was offered to Botetourt, who politely declined. Nelson later bought Botetourt's post coach for "£50 less than the cost, hardly the worse for wear, perhaps the best bargain of the whole [sale]." In 1781, New Englander Timothy Pickering visited Williamsburg and saw, with Puritan disapprobation, the state coach: "In a building near the palace are to be seen the remains of the richly-ornamented *state coach*, which was brought over with Lord Botetourt, and once used by him to carry him from the palace to the Capitol. 'Tis a clumsy machine, and enormously heavy,—perhaps equal to two common wagons. It is gilded in every part, even the edges of the tires of the wheels. The arms of Virginia are painted on every side. The motto of the arms led me to remark how peculiarly disposed the Virginians have been to adopt ideas of royalty and magnificence . . . The motto is, *En dat Virginia quartam*,—that is, 'Virginia gives a fourth quarter to the world.'" Octavius Pickering, *The Life of Timothy Pickering*, I (Boston, 1867), pp. 297–298. An excellent illustration of the degree of elaborateness that this machine embodied may be seen in the preserved and restored Lord Mayor's coach from London made in 1757, Marcus Binney, "Apotheosis of the Rococo: The Lord Mayor's Coach," *Country Life*, Nov. 16, 1978, pp. 1596–1598.

32. Nelson to Athawes, Dec. 6, 1770, Nelson Letter Book; J. Randolph to Beaufort, Oct. 15, 1770, Badminton Papers; Washington, Ledger A, M-89-2, fol. 357, Invoices and Papers. One visitor from England in 1736 noted, "You perceive a great Air of Opulence amongst the Inhabitants, who have some of them built Houses equal in Magnificence to many of our superb ones at St. James's; as those of Mr. Lightfoot, Nelson, etc. Almost every considerable Man Keeps an Equipage, tho' they have no Concern about the different Colours of their Coach horses, driving frequently black, white, and chestnut, in the same Harness," Breen, *Tobacco Culture*, p. 37.

33. The Jerdone quote is from Roeber, *Faithful Magistrates*, pp. 143–144. The Lloyd quote is from the Cadwalader Papers, Historical Society of Pennsylvania, Philadelphia, noted in Philip D. Zimmerman, "A Methodological Study in the Identification of Some Important Philadelphia Chippendale Furniture," *Winterthur Portfolio*, XIII (1979), p. 208.

34. Farish, ed., *Journal & Letters of Fithian*, p. 177. See also Breen, "Horses and Gentlemen," pp. 256–257; and Isaac, *Transformation of Virginia*, pp. 98–101.

35. "Work done with the cart, no. 5," Feb. 17, 1769–Nov. 9, 1770, by Thomas Gale, Badminton Papers; Farish, ed., *Journal & Letters of Fithian*, p. 61.

36. Gale (hired at £10, increased to £16 including washing, in 1770) was kept on by William Nelson to care for the horses. See n. 31. He was still in the Williamsburg area in 1790. Harwood Ledger C, p. 34. Kendall was hired at £30. The record of his work is preserved in the Kendall account book in the Nicholas Papers. He stayed until his death in Aug. 1777, *Va. Gaz.* (Purdie), Aug. 15, 1777. Draper, hired at £18, became a local blacksmith and farrier until his death in 1789, Williamsburg land tax records, 1789, Va. State Lib. and

Arch. Wilson succeeded Botetourt's first gardener, James Simpson, who was hired at £16, increasing to £20 in Jan. 1769, and who returned to England in Sept. 1769. Wilson, hired at £20, was subsequently employed as the college gardener, "Journal of the President and Masters or Professors of William and Mary College," *WMQ*, 1st Ser., XV (1906), pp. 166, 170.

37. There is certain archaeological evidence to suggest the existence of an orangery at the Palace. There was one at Mount Airy, Waterman, *Mansions of Virginia*, p. 260, and one at the governor's house in Annapolis by 1764 — Governor Sharpe was presented with a thermometer for the building. Reference courtesy of Michael Trostell.

38. Information on English laundry maids courtesy of Mark Girouard.

39. Beaufort to the trustees, Jan. 2, 1771, Badminton Papers. Apart from being specified in Botetourt's will and left an annuity, Silas Blandford, Sr., appears frequently in the Badminton Papers. He took the inventory of Stoke when Botetourt left for Virginia and again at the time of his death.

40. Depositions in Dartmouth MSS, box 19, fol. 784, box 24, fol. 1040, Salt Library, Stafford, Eng.

41. See Appendix 5.

42. See Appendix 7.

43. Farish, ed., *Journal & Letters of Fithian*, pp. 38–39.

44. A sensitive discussion of these issues, and whites' perception of blacks' qualities or lack of them, is in Mechal Sobel, *The World They Made Together: Black and White Values in Eighteenth-Century Virginia* (Princeton, N.J., 1987), esp. pp. 31–67, 127–153.

45. Farish, ed., *Journal & Letters of Fithian*, pp. 33–34, 156. Byrd's letter is cited in Wright, *First Gentlemen of Virginia*, p. 344. See also Sobel, *The World They Made Together*, pp. 194–197.

46. Farish, ed., *Journal & Letters of Fithian*, pp. 84–85, 187; Kulikoff, *Tobacco and Slaves*, pp. 381–420. Kulikoff also notes Washington's observation that it was inevitable for white workers to "get disgusted by living among the Negros," p. 395.

47. Farish, ed., *Journal & Letters of Fithian*, pp. 39, 129; Sobel, *The World They Made Together*, pp. 140–153.

48. Reese, ed., *Official Papers of Fauquier*, I, pp. xliii, xlviii, nn. 24, 25.

49. Gooch to the bishop of London, May 28, 1731, Fulham Palace Papers. See Jones, *Present State of Virginia*, ed. Morton, pp. 10, 74–76, 130, for the Beverley quote which Hugh Jones reiterated twenty years later and Gooch paraphrased ten years after that.

50. Breen, *Tobacco Culture*, p. 132.

51. Greene, ed., *Diary of Landon Carter*, I, pp. 27, 21. See also Jefferson's well-known comment, "The whole commerce between master and slave is a perpetual exercise in the most boisterous passions, the most unremitting despotism on the one part, and degrading submissions, on the other," cited in Kulikoff, *Tobacco and Slaves*, p. 194.

52. Lewis, *Pursuit of Happiness*, p. 210. See also pp. 1–40, 209–230; and Isaac, *Transformation of Virginia*, pp. 302–310.

Epilogue
page numbers 269–286

1. Thomas Conway, auditor to the duke of Beaufort, to the trustees, Jan. 28, 1770, Badminton Papers. The description of the stove is in Fred Shelley, ed., "The Journal of Ebenezer Hazard in Virginia, 1777," *VMHB*, LXII (1954), p. 409. The stove, signed and dated by Abraham Buzaglo, 1770, is on long-term loan to Colonial Williamsburg from the Commonwealth of Virginia. Buzaglo's colorful career is documented in Cecil Roth, "The Amazing Clan of Buzaglo," *Transactions of the Jewish Historical Society*, XXIII (1971), pp. 11–21. See also Christopher Gilbert and Anthony Wells-Cole, *The Fashionable Fire Place, 1660–1840* (Leeds, 1985), pp. 63–65. One other complete stove by this maker, signed and dated 1774, has been recently discovered at Knole, Kent. A single stove plate bearing his signature is also known. It formerly was in the collection of Claude Blair, London. Buzaglo also supplied stoves to the divinity schools at Cambridge University in 1774 — these have since disappeared but his trade card is preserved there. Another stove was installed at Winchester College in 1772, but that has also disappeared. Information courtesy of Claude Blair. The Margaret Chapel in Brock Street, Bath, also had two Buzaglo stoves between ca. 1773 and 1780. Information courtesy of Mark Girouard.

2. For the portrait of Pitt, see pp. 147–148 and n. 36.

3. The list of purchasers and details of amounts paid are included in the final accounts of the estate, dated May 5, 1772, Badminton Papers.

4. Trustees to Beaufort (in Nicholas's handwriting), May 27, 1771, Botetourt Papers, Va. State Lib. and Arch.; McIlwaine, Hall, and Hillman, eds., *Executive Journals of the Council*, VI, p. 398; Whiffen, *Public Buildings*, pp. 122–123, 216–217.

5. McIlwaine and Kennedy, eds., *Journals of Burgesses, 1770–1772*, pp. 119–120, 122–123.

6. *Ibid.*, pp. 138–139.

7. *Va. Gaz.* (Purdie and Dixon), July 25, 1771; Thomas Everard to J. Norton, July 20, 1771, Norton Papers, CWF; Richard Bland to Thomas Adams, Aug. 1, 1771, "Virginia in 1771," *VMHB*, VI (1899), pp. 132–133; *Va. Gaz.* (Purdie and Dixon), Nov. 27, 1766. Fifty-five years earlier the burgesses had actually appropriated funds for a marble tomb to the memory of the short-lived lieutenant governor, Edward Nott, perhaps as a sly dig at his successor, Alexander Spotswood. The monument still survives in Bruton Parish churchyard. Morton, *Colonial Virginia*, II, p. 458.

8. "Correspondence Relating to Lord Botetourt," *Tyler's Quarterly Historical and Genealogical Magazine*, III (1921), pp. 118–119; Mason, ed., *Norton & Sons*, pp. 224–226, 245, 264–268, 313. Sir Nathaniel Curzon ordered a stone cistern in the antique style from Hayward in Rome for Kedleston, one of Adam's chief works of the 1760s. John Hardy and Helena Hayward, "Kedleston Hall, Derbyshire: The Seat of Viscount Scarsdale," Part II, *Country Life*, Feb. 2, 1978, p. 263. See also Whinney, *Sculpture in Britain*, p. 143.

9. Mason, ed., *Norton & Sons*, p. 314. For Jefferson's wax portrait of Botetourt, see Howard, "Jefferson's Art Gallery," pp. 583–600. The surviving wax portrait hangs at Shirley plantation, Charles City Co., Va.

10. Mason, ed., *Norton & Sons*, pp. 244–245.

11. *S.-C. Gaz.*, Sept. 10, 1772, quoting a London source of June 19, 1772; Ivor Noël Hume, *1775: Another Part of the Field* (New York, 1966), pp. 21–22; *Va. Gaz.* (Rind), May 20, 1773.

12. Mason, ed., *Norton & Sons*, pp. 331–332. See also pp. 264–268, 313–314. Nicholas to J. Norton, June 4, 1773, Norton Papers; Craven, *Sculpture in America*, pp. 47–50; "Historical and Genealogical Notes," *Tyler's Quarterly*, I (1919), p. 143. In the early 1780s Benjamin Harrison wrote Jefferson that the statue cost £950 plus expenses.

13. Statuary was noted by Fithian, unfortunately in inadequate detail, at Mount Airy in 1774. Farish, ed., *Journal & Letters of Fithian*, p. 95. See also Martin, "'Promised Fruits of Well-Ordered Towns,'" p. 319; Whiffen, *Public Buildings*, pp. 166–171; and Bradley, ed., *Journal of Cresswell*, p. 207.

14. *Va. Gaz.* (Purdie and Dixon), Oct. 14, 1773, May 12, 1774. The print was a mezzotint by H. Ashby, dated London, 1774. An example is in the collections of CWF.

15. Harwood Ledger B, pp. 7, 31; Bradley, ed., *Journal of Cresswell*, pp. 207–208; *Voyage dans les Etats-Unis d'Amerique. Fait en 1795, et 1797, Par La Rochefoucauld-Liancourt*, IV (Paris, 1797), in Helen Bullock, "The Botetourt Statue," pp. 16–17, research report, 1936, CWF; Henry St. George Tucker to St. George Tucker, Aug. 8, 1801, "Botetourt Statue," *WMQ*, 2nd Ser., X (1930), p. 164. A particularly savage indictment of the vandalism on the statue is found in R. Brookes, M.D.,

Brookes' General Gazetteer Improved: Or, a New and Compendious Geographical Dictionary (Philadelphia and Richmond, 1812), s.v. "Williamsburg": "A marble statue in honour of the virtuous lord Boutetourt, the patron of science and the colony, which is now miserably defaced by the gothic hands of negroes and others."

16. Randolph, *History of Virginia*, ed. Shaffer, p. 173; Craven, *Sculpture in America*, pp. 51–54.
17. Greene, "Society, Ideology, and Politics," in Jellison, ed., *Society, Freedom, and Conscience*, p. 53. Some of the language of the public declarations is formulaic and may be derived from an essay on virtue or a manual on manners. See Arthur M. Schlesinger, *Learning How to Behave: A Historical Study of American Etiquette Books* (New York, 1947); and Christina Dallett Hemphill, "Manners for Americans: Interaction Ritual and the Social Order, 1620–1860" (Ph.D. diss., Brandeis University, 1987). Robert Carter Nicholas may have been instrumental in drafting the inscriptions; some of the sentiments are similar to those he expressed in his "Considerations on the Present State of Virginia Examined," 1774, Earl G. Swem, ed., *Considerations on the Present State of Virginia Examined* (New York, 1919): "List of Qualifications necessary to make a proper Representative, . . . he ought to be a Man of *private* as well *as public Virtue*; One who *really loves his Country*, and would support her true Interest, even though he should be forced to sacrifice *every sinister, selfish Consideration*." P. 77.
18. In discussing Botetourt's qualities, Edmund Randolph later used the phrases "American principle" and "American partisan." Randolph, *History of Virginia*, ed. Shaffer, pp. 172–173. Landon Carter's opinion is from Greene, ed., *Diary of Landon Carter*, I, p. 512. The parent-child analogy was used pointedly by Attorney General John Randolph in his "Considerations on the Present State of Virginia," 1774, in Swem, ed., *Considerations*, pp. 21–24. For a discussion of Virginians on the eve of the Revolution, see Billings, Selby, and Tate, *Colonial Virginia*, pp. 309–374; and Selby, *Revolution in Virginia*, pp. 1–54.
19. Nelson to Athawes, May 16, 1771, Nelson Letterbook; Noël Hume, *1775*, pp. 20–22; Parker to Steuart, Apr. 19, 1771, Steuart Papers; *Va. Gaz.* (Rind), Oct. 31, 1771.
20. Parker to Steuart, Jan. 27, 1775, Steuart Papers; Randolph, *History of Virginia*, ed. Shaffer, pp. 196–197; "Meade Family History," pp. 88–89; Bushman, "American High-Style and Vernacular Culture," in Greene and Pole, eds., *Colonial British America*, pp. 355–367.
21. Billings, Selby, and Tate, *Colonial Virginia*, pp. 337–367; Selby, *Revolution in Virginia*, pp. 1–22, 41–54; Randolph, *History of Virginia*, ed. Shaffer, pp. 196–197; Murrin, "The Great Inversion," in Pocock, ed., *Three British Revolutions*, pp. 397–404; Greene, ed., *Diary of Landon Carter*, I, pp. 56–61, 75–77.
22. Farish, ed., *Journal & Letters of Fithian*, p. 27; Greene, ed., *Diary of Landon Carter*, I, p. 55.
23. The most recent discussion of the unsettled Virginia gentry in the fifteen years preceding the Revolution is in Billings, Selby, and Tate, *Colonial Virginia*, pp. 285–374; and Selby, *Revolution in Virginia*, pp. 23–40. See also Breen, *Tobacco Culture*, pp. 124–203; Roeber, *Faithful Magistrates*, pp. 112–159; Isaac, *Transformation of Virginia*, pp. 115–157; and Jack P. Greene, *Pursuits of Happiness: The Social Development of Early Modern British Colonies and the Formation of American Culture* (Chapel Hill, N. C., 1988), pp. 170–206.
24. The Horrocks quote is noted in Greene, "Society, Ideology, and Politics," in Jellison, ed., *Society, Freedom, and Conscience*, p. 43. Colonists' suspicions of governors and other officials who were more concerned about their own good than the public good are discussed in Bushman, *King and People*, pp. 91–99.
25. Greene, "Society, Ideology, and Politics," in Jellison, ed., *Society, Freedom, and Conscience*, p. 64.
26. Swem, ed., *Considerations*, p. 41; Greene, "Society, Ideology, and Politics," in Jellison, ed., *Society, Freedom, and Conscience*, p. 46; Greene, ed., *Diary of Landon Carter*, I, pp. 55–70, quotation on p. 55.
27. Joseph Burke, *English Art, 1714–1800* (Oxford, 1976), pp. 3–38; Upton, *Holy Things and Profane*, p. 159. See also pp. 132–133, 158–160; and Gusler, *Furniture of Williamsburg*, pp. 2–11.

Acknowledgments

I started to write this book in 1978, having become acquainted with the Botetourt inventory about five years previously. Clearly a crucial document for the furnishings of the Governor's Palace in Williamsburg, the inventory intrigued me with its awesome and evocative detail, its encompassing sense of definitiveness. The more I studied it, the more it divulged about the building and its contents, the more it intimated of life beyond the cryptic lists of objects, suggesting patterns of usage, purpose, and design. At this time Mark Girouard's trail-blazing *Life in the English Country House* appeared and helped me better understand the social uses of the magnificent and often overwhelming spaces in English eighteenth-century houses, and to show me that the usages of the Palace rooms suggested by the inventory were characteristic for this period and this social level. I also became more acquainted with Peter Thornton's seminal work on period interiors. To these scholars I owe a large debt of gratitude. Because of their work and their interest in mine I became even more engrossed in the Botetourt inventory, perhaps even obsessed with it.

The tradesmen's accounts and vouchers that Robert Carter Nicholas so carefully preserved among his papers shed further light on the brilliant particularity of the inventory. After intense study and a difficult, internal colloquy, I settled on the structure of the book which I have had reason to modify only slightly since, although remarkable developments continued to occur. I discovered at Badminton House in Gloucestershire and at the nearby County Record Office an extraordinary cache of documents pertaining to Lord Botetourt, including his preparations for departure to Virginia, activities and daily household events while in Williamsburg, and many more details of the settling of his estate. I met Rhys Isaac and became acquainted with early stages of the brilliant, innovative work he subsequently published as the Pulitzer Prize-winning *The Transformation of Virginia, 1740–1790*. We had independently encountered and used for different purposes the evocative account of the funeral of Lord Botetourt. I have retained my use and interpretation of it here as well as including part of his analysis. I also became more familiar with and stimulated by the work of material culturists, including two who were exploring somewhat different aspects of the same Virginia terrain, Dell Upton and Cary Carson. The courses that each of the above historians was charting through colonial Virginia history intersected at places with the one I was arduously plotting. They were surer and more adept than I, but always generous and supportive. I owe much to their encouragement and example.

As I began to plan this book I received critical encouragement from Norman S. Fiering and Thad W. Tate of the Institute of Early American History and Culture in Williamsburg. Without their support I am sure I would have quailed; having now finished the book, I realize how much I owe them. I have also been the fortunate and most thankful recipient of support in moral and material ways from Carlisle H. Humelsine, Charles R. Longsworth, Robert C. Birney, and Dennis A. O'Toole, my esteemed colleagues at the Colonial Williamsburg Foundation. They literally made it possible for me to write this book, and without their belief in it and me I could not have done it.

My past and present curatorial colleagues at Colonial Williamsburg have contributed much to this book in the way of insights, material, and support. I am most grateful to John C. Austin, Linda R. Baumgarten, John D. Davis, Joan D. Dolmetsch, James M. Gaynor, Margaret S. Gill, Elizabeth P. Gusler, Wallace B. Gusler, Ronald L. Hurst, Brock Jobe, Betty C. Leviner, Sumpter T. Priddy III, Margaret B. Pritchard, and John O. Sands. Colonial Williamsburg historian Harold B. Gill, Jr., supplied concise answers to innumerable questions. Visiting English scholar Christopher Gilbert provided much illumination in lengthy discussions, as did Martin Drury and John Cornforth. The tenth duke and duchess of Beaufort were most cooperative and gracious and made my visits to Badminton much more memorable. Mr. S. Bywater and Mrs. Margaret Richards at Badminton and Mr. D. J. H. Smith at the Gloucester County Record Office were extremely helpful. Readers of all or part of my manuscript at various stages of development also included Robert C. Birney, John Bivins, Jr., Cary Carson, A. Roger Ekirch, Patricia A. Gibbs, John M. Hemphill II, Kenneth A. Lockridge, Paul C. Nagel, Jan Seidler, John E. Selby, Dennis A. O'Toole, and Mark R. Wenger. Each generously gave advice and provided substantial improvement. Whatever clarity graces the text is due to the keenness and expertise of editor Catherine E. Hutchins. That the text made its way into type at all is only because of the lengthy and tireless ministrations of Emily D. Seats, who made the otherwise inscrutable clear and to whom I am enormously grateful. Hans Lorenz and Craig McDougal utilized their great expertise, as they so often do in so modest a manner, in providing the illustrations which Laurie Suber helped me organize, saving me countless hours in her efficient way. Jan Gilliam supplied important assistance in an editorial role. D. Stephen Elliott, Joseph N. Rountree, Donna C. Sheppard, and Amy Zakrzewski each contributed an important element to the production of the book, which Greer Allen designed so gracefully.

To all of the above I owe a debt that I am only too conscious this book repays in part merely.

I did not set out to make this a material culture book any more than I intended to make it a decorative arts book; yet I have included far more information and analysis of objects than most of the present generation of social historians do in their work. I certainly do not claim any expertise in the fields of ethnohistory or anthropology, and my use of the word culture was meant to be more general than specific. I hope my work is of some interest to students of each of the above disciplines. I have also been guided in the writing of this book by a profound instinct that history is allusion, poetry, and myth as well as fact, logic, and deduction.

Gale, Sarah, and Jorin Hood have inspired, challenged, supported, provoked, exhorted, motivated, humbled, and suffered me. Without them I would not even have wanted to finish this work. For the innumerable contributions and the priceless gifts that Gale has proffered I owe thanks beyond counting.

Index

Accounts
   by English staff, 235
   of estate, 315
   by Marshman, 164, 181, 228, 238, 242, 248, 254
   by Marshman, in petty cash book, 139, 182, 246, 324
   by merchants/tradesmen, 28, 156, 250
   by Palace staff, 28, 139, 155, 236, 241, 248
   by Sparrow, 246, 248, 262
   by trustees, 23
Adam, Robert, 93, 122, 126, 128, 129, 164, 273, 276, 330
Adam, Robert and James, 145, 146
Adams, Sir Thomas, 240
Aitchison, William, 15
Ambler, Edward, 323, 325
Ambler House, 167
Amherst, Jeffrey, 67, 70, 201
Annapolis, Md.
   Council chamber in, 82, 88, 100, 112, 190–191
   Governor flees from, 37
   Governor's residence in, 94, 104, 112, 164–165, 191, 206, 214, 224, 256, 320
   Maryland Assembly in, 82
   plan of, 54. See also Assemblies and balls; Eden, Robert
Antechamber, 110, 111
Architecture, 32, 38, 42, 285
   Fauquier's interest in, 144
   Jefferson's interest in, 144–145
   in Virginia, 38, 40, 42, 43, 44, 46, 48, 285, 316. See also Room arrangements
Assemblies and balls, 120–121, 171–172, 176, 178–182, 192, 221, 240, 261
   in Annapolis, 190–191
   in England, 326
   at Hobbes Hole, Va., 180
   at Lee Hall, Va., 179, 181
   in Norfolk, Va., 178
   in North Carolina, 112, 190, 191
   by subscription, 90, 172
   in Williamsburg, 44, 60, 112, 118, 168
   in Williamsburg, at Capitol, 132, 169–170, 171, 172, 218
   in Williamsburg, at Governor's Palace, 132, 135, 168, 172, 173–174, 176, 182, 184, 186, 248, 281, 326. See also Assembly rooms; King's birthday ball
Assembly rooms, 46, 50, 190–192
   in England, 172–173, 179, 184
   in Fredericksburg, Va., 173. See also Assemblies and balls; Ballrooms

Athawes, Samuel, 15, 183, 189, 190, 323
Ayscough, Anne, 246–247, 250, 329

Badminton House, 20, 70, 89, 145, 155, 156, 227, 328
Ballroom, Governor's Palace, 25, 26, 46, 92, 170, 173, 176, 184–186, 187, 193, 252
   function of, 118, 181, 182, 186, 192
   furnishings of, 20, 183–184, 186, 189, 269, 270, 275, 322, 326
   and supper room wing, 36, 38, 46, 48, 63, 75, 90, 91, 98, 168, 172, 173, 181, 186
Ballrooms, 126, 168, 173, 180, 191, 321
   in Marlborough, Md., 173
   at Mount Vernon, 173, 188, 191
   at Nomini Hall, 173, 191, 207, 216
   in Tappahannock, Va., 173
   at Tryon's Palace, 112. See also Assembly rooms; Ballroom, Governor's Palace
Balls. See Assemblies and balls
Baltimore, Lord and Lady, 205
Banister, John, 56
Bartram, John, 220
Bedchambers, 126, 196, 202–203, 204, 206–208, 211, 212. See also Bedchambers, Governor's Palace; His Lordship's Bed Chamber, Governor's Palace; Servants' sleeping arrangements
Bedchambers, Governor's Palace, 27, 108, 203, 204, 206, 214–215, 217, 227. See also Closet, Governor's Palace; His Lordship's Bed Chamber, Governor's Palace
Beds, 65, 203, 211–214, 216, 253, 327
   Eden's, 214
   fabric for, 203, 206, 207, 213, 214, 216
   field, 240, 250
   of state, 75, 212–213
   Tryon's, 214. See also Servants' sleeping arrangements
Behavior, 23, 31, 34, 177, 232
Berkeley, Elizabeth, fourth Duchess of Beaufort, 70, 145, 146, 147, 211
   portrait of, 147
Berkeley, Norborne, Baron de Botetourt, 23, 38, 89, 128, 227, 252, 278
   clothing of, 27, 28, 30, 103, 108, 207, 214, 217–218, 227, 238, 329
   coffin of, 12, 16, 18, 209
   debts of, 12, 13, 28, 269
   diary of, 156
   early career of, 70–71, 109, 120, 138, 145–147
   and entertaining, 132, 135, 176, 186
   estate of, 12–13, 20, 23, 28, 314
   funeral of, 13, 16–20, 79, 314
   and furnishings, 13, 20, 91, 96–97, 106, 113, 114, 130, 132, 159, 192, 214
   furnishings associated with, 123, 126

furnishings of, bought from Fenton, 158, 215, 217
and gardens, 155, 156, 254, 320
goods of, acquired from Fauquier's estate, 53, 91, 158, 329
goods of, auctioned, 23, 270, 314
goods of, shipped to duke, 23, 314, 315
and governmental duties, 12, 16, 19, 31, 33, 36, 104, 105, 138-140, 159, 211, 322–323
on Governor's Palace, 156
illness and death of, 12, 13, 15, 25, 208–209, 210, 269, 270, 314, 329
life-style of, 93, 94, 108, 227
as man of culture, 143, 145–147, 148, 153, 154, 155–156, 222
as model of culture, 33–34, 70, 193, 248, 282, 283, 285–286
papers of, 12, 20, 28, 31, 158, 250
personal life of, 198, 201, 204, 211
portrayals of, 14, 69, 134, 147, 272, 273, 274, 276, 321
opinion of, by government, 13, 176, 270, 272–273
opinion of, by Nelson, 16, 270, 272
opinion of, by Randolph, 16, 145, 152, 278, 331
opinion of, by servants, 15, 152, 201, 210
opinion of, in *Virginia Gazette*, 16, 152, 176, 314
opinion of, by Virginians, 13, 15, 18, 33, 137, 138, 139, 208–209, 269, 270, 274, 275, 278–280, 323
refurnishing of ballroom and supper room by, 171, 183–184, 187
and slavery, 262, 264
social functions of, as governor, 46, 132, 186
and warming machines, 186, 188, 189, 270
and William and Mary College, 152
will of, 12, 13, 16, 228, 246
and wine-making scheme, 13. See also Books; Botetourt inventory; Botetourt medal; Botetourt statue; Coat of arms; College of William and Mary; Patronage; Servants of Botetourt; Slaves; Somerset, Henry, fifth Duke of Beaufort
Berkeley, 167, 325
Beverley, Robert, 15, 35, 155, 183, 187, 188, 262
Beverley, Robert (historian), 42, 137, 262, 316
Black, William, 190–191
Blair, Rev. James, 38, 58, 60, 150
   portrait of, 151
Blair, John (president of the Council), 67, 86, 173, 314, 324
Blair, John, Jr. (clerk of the Council), 12
Bland, Richard, 18, 285
Blandfield, 187

Blandford, Silas, Jr., 26, 236, 240, 248, 250, 254–255
Blandford, Silas, Sr., 238, 246, 254, 255, 330
Blathwayt, William, 40, 42
Board of Trade, 38, 48
Bodleian Plate, 25, 27, 40, 45, 58, 316
Bookpresses, 223, 224, 226
Books
    of Botetourt, 13, 23, 27, 30, 152, 156, 181, 212, 217, 222–223, 224, 225, 226, 327–328
    of Byrd II, 224
    of Campbell, 223, 324
    of Carter, 150, 224
    of Dunmore, 223, 226
    of Fauquier, 224, 226
    of Gooch, 65, 225
    of Jefferson, 224, 226
    of Nicholson, 56, 225
    sold at printing office, 61, 226
    of Spotswood, 58, 224, 226
    of Tryon, 223. *See also* Libraries; Library, Governor's Palace
Boscawen, Mrs., 204
Botetourt. *See* Berkeley, Norborne, Baron de Botetourt
Botetourt inventory, 53, 100, 217, 218, 287–295
    compiling of, 13, 20, 26–28, 217
    evidence of room usage in, 91, 93, 101, 118, 130, 156, 161, 186, 205, 254
    as expression of Botetourt's life, 20, 23, 25, 31, 33, 36, 198, 211
    objects listed in, 98, 108, 156, 210, 212, 213, 214, 222, 225, 238, 322
    re-creates life at Palace, 30, 31, 36, 37, 48, 230, 232
    spaces identified in, 26–28, 45, 46, 202, 253, 328, 329
Botetourt medal, 152, 153, 188, 324
Botetourt statue, 136, 190, 268–269, 273, 274–278, 284, 285, 330–331
Boucher, Jonathan, 220–221
Bowfat, 130, 166, 322
Brackets, 103, 104, 183
Brafferton School, 40, 48, 49, 60. *See also* College of William and Mary
Braxton family, 65
Bridges, Charles, 61, 149–150, 196, 319, 323
Bruton Parish Church, 13, 16, 40, 56, 154, 330
    rebuilding of, 58, 60, 63
Buckingham House, 146, 184
Bucktrout, Benjamin, 16
Builder's Dictionary, 91, 211
Bullivant, Benjamin, 82–83
Bureau, 164
Burgesses, 76, 186, 208, 272, 273, 322. *See also* House of Burgesses
Burlington, Lord, 32
Burwell, Nathaniel, 153, 188–190, 240. *See also* Carter's Grove

Butlers, 51, 52, 111, 130, 164, 198, 265. *See also* Marshman, William
Buzaglo, Abraham, 188, 270, 330. *See also* Stove
Byrd, William, II, 56, 60, 62, 119–120, 150, 224, 226–227, 324, 328
    comments on Palace, 82, 83
    comments on plantation "family," 231–232
    comments on slaves, 260
    at Palace for dinner, 129
    portrait of, 119
    visits Spotswood, 80, 82, 172, 202–203, 326. *See also* Books; Westover
Byrd, William, III, 162, 240, 248, 252, 270

Cabinet, 211. *See also* Libraries
Cadwalader, John, 252
Camm, Rev. John, 94, 160, 324
Campbell, Colen, 56
Campbell, Lord William, 37, 112, 113, 223, 224, 257, 315
    "family," 256–257
    furnishings in residence of, 93, 112, 165, 223, 224, 324
    inventory of, 256–257, 307–313
    residence of, 113, 165. *See also* Books; Slaves
Canaletto, Antonio, 145
Capitol, 42, 75, 76, 90, 137, 225
    building of, 39, 40, 54, 56, 60
    burning and rebuilding of, 61–62
    description of, 55
    entertainment at, 132, 168, 169, 171, 172
    furnishings for, 56, 188, 190, 269, 319
    statue on piazza of, 136, 269, 274. *See also* Council; House of Burgesses; General Court
Cards, 108, 179
    playing of, 128, 172, 174, 178, 179, 203
Carpets, 52, 104, 111, 113, 126, 203, 212, 213, 227, 321, 325, 326
    for funeral, 16, 18
Carriages, 13, 52, 252. *See also* Chariots; Coaches
Carter, Charles, 137, 323
Carter, Frances, 176, 215–216, 260, 261, 322. *See also* Carter, Robert; Fithian, Philip
Carter, Landon, 138, 222, 279, 282, 285, 325
    comment on Botetourt's death, 15
    comment on slaves, 262
    diaries of, 226–227, 232
Carter, Mr., 222, 240
Carter, Robert, 34, 90, 222
Carter, Robert (councillor), 95, 131, 141, 150, 173, 232
    family of, 167, 207, 232, 260, 261, 322
    furnishings of, 187–188, 320
    letters by, to duke, 13
    library of, 216, 224
    and music, 154

    portrait of, 151
    servants of, 181, 257–258
    slaves of, 257, 260. *See also* Books; Carter, Frances; Fithian, Philip; Nomini Hall
Carter's Grove, 188, 190, 191, 231, 233, 317, 321. *See also* Burwell, Nathaniel
Cary, Henry, 40, 42
Case furniture, 103, 156, 158, 211. *See also* Bookpresses; Bureau; Chest of drawers; Clothespresses; Desk and bookcase; Desks
Catesby, Mark, 56, 62, 65, 156
Cellars, Governor's Palace, 27, 30, 39, 52, 131, 232, 236, 238
Ceramics, 23, 52, 130, 181, 238, 256
    Chelsea porcelain, 131–132
    china figures, 113, 128, 130, 131, 132, 248
    Chinese blue and white, 132
    Nanking tea china, 113
    ornamental china, 130, 165, 186
    queensware, 131, 256
    Staffordshire, 130, 248, 322
    transfer-printed ware, 248
Ceremony, 74–79, 98, 114, 168, 169, 170, 172, 193, 318, 321
    upon accession of George II, 90
    and ceremonial spaces, 25, 100, 101, 104, 106, 114
    of the circle, 106, 108, 123, 126
    upon death of William III and accession of Queen Anne, 57, 76, 172, 314
    at dinner, 52
    of funeral, 13, 16, 19, 20, 23
    at Palace, 34, 75, 90, 91
    of toasts, 130, 131, 169, 179, 322
    use of, by governor, 49, 100, 108, 109. *See also* Dining; Governor
Cesar (slave), 244
Chairs, 112, 164, 321, 327
    armchair, 101
    associated with governors, 126
    backstools, 91, 101, 164, 319
    bamboo, 203, 206, 214–215, 227
    damask, 91, 93, 112, 162, 163, 319
    easy, 205, 250
    elbow, 91, 93, 111, 217, 321
    hall, 91, 319
    horsehair, 111, 162, 325
    leather, 92, 98, 100, 162, 183
    mahogany, 113, 321
    in Palace, 110, 130, 161, 186, 213, 214, 215, 227, 250
    of state, 95, 101
    Windsor, 91, 94
Chamber, 99–100, 114, 123. *See also* Bedchambers
Chapel of College of William and Mary, 13, 17, 18, 20, 56, 209, 270
Chariots, 65, 252, 257. *See also* Carriages; Coaches
Charlotte, Queen, 156

336 INDEX

portrait of, 185
Check textiles, 164, 212, 214, 227, 240, 250
Chelsea factory, 131
Cherokee Indians, 67, 104, 173
Chest, 238
Chest of drawers, 207, 213, 214, 217, 240
Chevening House, 84, 86
Chilton, Edward, 38
Chimney boards, 113, 126
Chintz textiles, 164, 203, 213, 216, 227
Chippendale, Thomas, 20, 70, 145, 319, 323
    Gentleman & Cabinet-Maker's Director, 156, 323
Chiswell affair, 283
Christmas boxes, 241–242, 248
Churchill, John, 58
Cistern, 45
Clayton, John, 62, 156
Clerk, for governor, 51, 128, 164, 181, 231. *See also* Pelham, Peter
Clock, 212
Closet, Governor's Palace
    of Botetourt's bedchamber, 27, 45, 202, 204, 207, 210, 226
    of east bedchambers, 27, 202, 204
    of hall, 93
    of little middle room, 27, 52, 130, 322
    of pantry, 27
    of parlor, 26, 51, 92, 111, 161, 164
Clothespresses, 108, 217, 218
Coaches, 52, 181
    of Dinwiddie, 65
    of Fauquier, 329
    of Lord Mayor of London, 251, 329
    post, 329
    state, 20, 75, 218, 250–252, 264, 270, 315, 327, 329. *See also* Carriages; Chariots
Coat of arms
    of Botetourt, 51, 188, 275
    on buckets, 92, 93
    on looking glass frames, 100, 101
    royal, 74, 76, 84, 88, 159, 319, 323
    as symbol, 30, 74, 88
    of the Virginia colony, 45, 92, 98, 100, 101, 250, 251, 269, 270, 329
College of William and Mary, 18, 40, 42, 60, 76, 150, 278
    Botetourt buried at, 19
    Botetourt's interest in, 152
    building of, 54, 58
    forecourt, 48, 49, 61, 269
    gardens of, 154, 254
    Jefferson at, 141
    library of, 56, 224, 225, 226, 325
    professors at, 55, 141, 152, 174, 270
    servants at, 242. *See also* Brafferton School; Chapel of College of William and Mary; President's House; Wren Building
Collinson, Peter, 220
Consumer goods, 68, 121, 132, 282
    importance of, 31, 32, 33, 35, 68

objects as symbols, 216, 286. *See also* Consumerism; Fashion
Consumerism, 32, 35, 65, 67, 68, 70, 121, 132, 222. *See also* Consumer goods; Fashion
Continental Congress, 190, 193
Conway, Thomas, 328
Cooke, John, 247, 248
Cooks, 52, 181, 236, 241, 247–248, 250. *See also* Cooke, John; Lefebure, Lambert; Scott, Mrs.; Sparrow, William; Towse, Thomas
Couches, 95, 106, 161, 165, 210, 216, 228, 238, 245, 321
Council, 20, 49, 50, 55, 63, 76, 123, 174, 176, 198, 261, 270
    chamber, 50, 55, 56, 82, 113
    clerk of, 162
    elects acting governor, 13
    library, 50, 225, 328
    meets at Palace, 75, 104
    members of, 12
Covers
    for carpet, 126
    for chairs, 91, 93, 164, 215
    for fire screen, 164
    of gauze, 188
    for tables, 111, 131
    toilet cloth, 108
Crew, Hannah, 243, 244, 329
Culloden, Battle of, 168, 169
Culture, 31–36, 56, 264, 285
    expression of, 19
    through governor, 25, 49, 153–154, 192, 193, 281, 286
    growth of, in America, 68, 70
    through patronage, 150
Cumberland, Duke of, 169, 250
Curtains
    in Campbell's residence, 112, 165
    in Eden's residence, 104, 112, 164
    in Governor's Palace, 52, 101, 212, 250
    in Stoke Park, 321, 325
    in Tryon's Palace, 111, 164
    in Virginia houses, 113, 216
Custis, John, 58, 61, 62
Custis, John Parke, 190
Cutlery, 130, 132, 238

Damask textiles, 91, 96, 162, 163
    blue, 93, 164
    crimson, 98, 101, 104, 112, 164, 319
    crimson silk, 93, 112
    red, 91, 101
    yellow, 321
Dance, 32, 118, 169, 176–177, 178, 179, 180
    importance of, 120–121, 172
    by Indians, 76
    slave-derived jig, 121, 180–181. *See also* Assemblies and balls; Dancing master
Dancing master, 176–177, 181, 260, 326

Deference, 19, 20, 23, 34, 48, 96, 167, 192, 210, 278, 281, 283
    to governor, 108, 159, 324
    to king, 182, 184–185
    of Negro, 95, 261. *See also* Hierarchy
De la Force, Jean Aimar Piganiol, 58
Desk and bookcase, 325
Desks, 28, 156, 158, 166, 216, 250, 254, 325
D'Estave (applicant for naturalization), 137
Dietszche, Barbara Regina, 156
Dining, 76, 99, 129, 135, 158, 186, 248
    after dinner, 106, 122, 126, 128
    as display, 45, 75, 119, 120, 128, 264
    as mode of exchange, 120, 135–136, 141, 167
    objects for, 32, 124, 130, 131–132, 248
    preparations for, 51–52, 118, 130
    service of, 130. *See also* Dining Room, Governor's Palace; Dining Rooms
Dining Room, Governor's Palace, 25, 26, 43, 46, 130, 154, 161, 167, 169, 186, 240, 243
    early reference to, 45, 126, 128
    function of, 50, 118, 132, 135, 137, 141, 156, 158, 159, 160
    furnishings of, 28, 45, 126, 129–132, 156, 158–159, 162, 274, 322
Dining rooms, 112, 126, 164, 165–167, 207, 322
    function of, 122–123, 126
    furnishings of, 128–129, 165–166, 325. *See also* Dining; Dining Room, Governor's Palace
Dinwiddie, Lt. Gov. Robert, 63, 67, 104, 173
    furnishings of, 65, 318
    portrait of, 66. *See also* Coaches
Ditchley, 145
Draper, John, 250, 253, 254
Draper, William, 105, 240, 329
Drawing rooms, 106, 112, 113, 123, 126, 128, 164, 165, 166, 321
Dress, 132, 220–222, 265
    ceremonial, 76, 172, 174–175
    for funeral, 16, 17
    of servants, 16, 233, 244–245, 329. *See also* Berkeley, Norborne, Baron de Botetourt, clothing; Fashion; Livery
Dressing rooms, 109–110, 204, 205, 321
    at Governor's Palace, 108, 204
    at Tryon's Palace, 205
    in Virginia, 207–208
Drysdale, Lt. Gov. Hugh, 34, 60, 208, 319
Drysdale, Mrs., 198
Duke of Gloucester Street, 12, 40, 55, 67, 149
Dunmore. *See* Murray, John, fourth Earl of Dunmore

Eddis, William, 320
Eden, Gov. Robert, 37, 104, 112, 191, 214, 218, 223, 224, 320, 324

INDEX 337

inventory of estate of, 191, 214, 256, 299–302
visits to Virginia by, 37, 105, 135, 191, 204. *See also* Annapolis, Md.; Servants
Ehret, Georg, 156
English influence
through governor, 31, 33–34, 35–36, 57, 60, 113, 281–282, 283, 285–286, 326
at Governor's Palace, 30, 33, 43, 156, 227, 230
in town plan, 55–56
on Virginians, 34, 35, 68, 70, 115, 180–181, 281, 282. *See also* Consumerism; Fashion
Enlightenment, 141, 143, 145, 152, 188, 193, 261
Evelyn, John, 156
Everard, Thomas, 139, 181, 240

Fairfax, George William, 326
Fairfax, Lord, 61
Family "kin," 196, 198–201, 202, 204, 232, 264, 265, 315
Fanning, Colonel (secretary), 256
Fashion, 35, 68, 70, 118, 121, 132, 227, 252
in dress, 218, 222
in Virginia, 34, 35, 188, 190, 192
Fauquier, Catherine, 106, 184, 204
portrait of, 140
Fauquier, Lt. Gov. Francis, 38, 53, 67, 89, 138, 140, 159, 185, 201, 230, 319
and Camm incident, 94, 160
and entertaining, 120
family portraits of, 321
furnishings of, 129, 320, 321
goods of, sold, 53, 91, 158, 213, 214, 216, 314
illness and death of, 70, 198, 208, 247
influence on Jefferson, 141, 143, 148, 153
inventory of, 101, 106, 108, 213, 224, 319
as man of culture, 143–144, 152, 153, 154
meets with Indians, 104
as model of culture, 67, 70, 141, 150, 193, 282, 283, 285–286
and music, 153–154
opinion of, by others, 283
portrait of, 66, 140
private life of, 204, 315, 326
and Robinson affair, 131, 158
slaves of, purchased from estate, 231, 243, 244
on trade with England, 67, 68
will of, 143, 153, 228, 246–247. *See also* Books; Coaches; Patronage; Servants; Slaves
Fauquier, Francis, Jr., 132
Fauquier, William, 143–144, 145, 321
Fenton, William, 28, 156, 158, 215
Finnie, Alexander, 173
Fire buckets, 91, 92, 93, 94

Fireplace equipment, 113
Fireplace mantel, 189, 190
Fire screens, 28, 126, 164, 324
associated with Botetourt, 123
Fithian, Philip, 173, 176, 253, 257, 258, 322
on balls, 179, 180, 181
on Carter, 232
on dances, 172, 177, 179–180, 326
on dining, 126, 130–131, 167
on horses, 252
on music, 154
on prints, 163
on room usage, 95, 126, 322
on slaves, 258, 260–261
on Sundays, 318
use of library, 216
Fitzhugh, William, 320, 323
Fletcher, Benjamin, 82, 319
Flitcroft, Henry, 145
Floorcloths, 126, 325
Footmen, 74, 91, 94, 155, 181, 241, 256, 258
duties of, 51, 93, 94, 130, 131, 240. *See also* Cesar; King, Samuel; Knight, William; Matt; Rodgers, John
Fort Christanna, 60
Fort St. George, 82–83
Foundling Hospital, London, 67, 143
France, 60, 63, 86, 96, 122
Franklin, Benjamin, 126, 148, 274, 323, 326
Frenchman's Map, 38, 45, 316
Fry-Jefferson Map, 62, 159, 160, 161
Fuller, Thomas, 240, 244, 245, 254, 329
after Botetourt's death, 13, 15, 26, 255, 314. *See also* Salary

Gale, Thomas, 245, 250, 253, 254, 329
Gaol, 51
Gardeners, 241, 243, 246, 253–254, 257, 265. *See also* Simpson, James; Wilson, James
Gardens, Governor's Palace, 30, 38, 53, 232, 238, 254, 316
layout of, by Spotswood, 46, 58, 60, 154–155
observations on, 42, 60, 156
orangery in, 254, 330. *See also* Gardeners
Garret, Governor's Palace, 27, 45, 53, 205, 240, 254, 329
General Court, 12, 13, 19, 23, 49, 55, 75, 186
Gentleman & Cabinet-Maker's Director. See Chippendale, Thomas
George III, 70, 104, 109, 146, 147, 176, 273
accession of, celebrated, 90, 325
Georgian, 38, 40, 43, 46, 48, 49, 285, 316
Germain family, 145
Gibbs, James, 70, 144–145
portrait of, 146
Gilliatt, Sy, 328–329
Glassware, 52, 165–166, 181, 244, 256, 265, 322

decanters, 130, 132, 228, 238, 322
drinking glasses, 130, 132, 228, 238, 248, 322
epergne, 165–166
pyramids, 130, 131, 186, 248, 322
wash-hand glasses, 132
Gooch, Lady Rebecca, 130, 131, 153
Gooch, Lt. Gov. William, 60–62, 94, 138, 139–140, 153, 161, 226
author of pamphlet, 226
on dance, 172
and entertaining, 90, 120, 128, 130, 131, 153, 160–161, 169, 205
illness of, 169, 208
involvement of, with Palace, 45, 155, 320
letter from, to brother, 150
in London, 110–111
as patron of Bridges, 149–150
private life of, 198, 204, 222, 231, 315
on slaves, 261–262. *See also* Books; Patronage
Gossett, Isaac, 15, 272, 273, 274, 322
Governor, 19, 23, 138, 193, 204, 224, 265
and ceremony, 75, 98, 110, 114, 120, 130, 137, 169, 177, 182
duties of, in colony, 48–51
as model to colonists, 35–36, 48, 70, 121, 135, 153, 192–193, 281, 283, 286
and patronage, 148, 149, 153, 181
wife of, 50, 128, 198. *See also* Berkeley, Norborne, Baron de Botetourt; Campbell, Lord William; Ceremony; Culture; Dinwiddie, Lt. Gov. Robert; Drysdale, Lt. Gov. Hugh; Eden, Gov. Robert; English influence; Fauquier, Lt. Gov. Francis; Gooch, Lt. Gov. William; Murray, John, fourth Earl of Dunmore; Nicholson, Lt. Gov. Francis; Nott, Lt. Gov. Edward; Salary; Spotswood, Lt. Gov. Alexander; Tryon, Gov. William
Governor's Council. *See* Council
Governor's Palace
additions and repairs to, 126, 168, 172, 173, 184
architectural antecedent of, 113
birth at, 196, 198, 208
building of, 38–40, 42, 44, 48, 58, 63, 316
comments on, 40, 42, 60, 71
compound, 26, 30, 31, 33, 42, 43, 45, 46, 58, 232, 238, 264
condition of, 63
deaths at, 12, 196, 208
"doing Companies" at, 109, 321
English society at, 30, 33
floor plan of, 24
funeral at, 13, 18
government at, 50, 75, 104, 105, 174, 208
influence of, 46, 48, 49, 60, 115, 192, 257
Jefferson's occupation of, 320

338 INDEX

music at, 154
official business at, 111, 135
servants at, 13, 30, 231, 247, 257
setting of, 96, 156
1710 proposal for furnishing of, 44, 45, 46, 98–99, 100, 298
symbols in, 74–75, 78, 92, 114
visits to, 37, 50, 105, 132, 135, 204. *See also* Ballroom, Governor's Palace; Bedchambers, Governor's Palace; Botetourt inventory; Cellars, Governor's Palace; Closet, Governor's Palace; Dining Room, Governor's Palace; Garden, Governor's Palace; Garret, Governor's Palace; Governor; Hall, Governor's Palace; His Lordship's Bed Chamber, Governor's Palace; Kitchen, Governor's Palace; Library, Governor's Palace; Little Middle Room, Governor's Palace; Middle Room upstairs, Governor's Palace; Outbuildings, Governor's Palace; Pantry, Governor's Palace; Parlor, Governor's Palace; Passage downstairs, Governor's Palace; Passage upstairs, Governor's Palace; Powder Room, Governor's Palace; Room arrangements; Stables, Governor's Palace; Standing Furniture, Governor's Palace; Supper Room, Governor's Palace
Grand Tour, 145, 146
Great Room, Governor's Palace. *See* Middle Room upstairs, Governor's Palace
Greenhow, John, 67
Gwatkin, Rev. Thomas, 152

Halifax, Earl of, 153
Hall, Governor's Palace, 25, 26, 45, 46, 74, 80, 98, 105, 115, 160, 317
function of, 43–44, 75, 89–91, 93–94, 97, 169
furnishings of, 88, 91–93, 163
weapons in, 80–89, 318. *See also* Closet, Governor's Palace; Weapons
Hallam, Lewis, 174
Halls, 43, 80, 82, 88–89, 90, 93, 94–96, 98, 99, 163. *See also* Hall, Governor's Palace
Hamilton, George, 190
Hamilton, James, 148, 149
Hampton Court, 84, 86
Handel, George Frideric, 144
Harris, John, 84, 86
Hartwell, Henry, 38
Hayward, Richard, 136, 273, 274, 276, 330
Heathcote family, 20
Henley, Rev. Samuel, 152
Henry, John, 159, 160
Hierarchy
of America, 279
in architecture, 43, 48, 100, 320

in ceremony, 17, 19, 74, 114, 115, 186, 314
in dance, 121, 177
elite, 42, 115, 120, 196, 282
in England and colonies, 35, 164, 187
expression of, through goods, 121, 252
expression of, through symbols, 88, 100, 115
of household, 230
of paintings, 32
of servants, 51–53, 93, 235, 244, 246, 247, 265
in society, 17, 19, 23, 34, 68, 176–177, 181, 192, 283, 286
Hillsborough, Earl of, 71, 184, 186, 211, 322, 329
His Lordship's Bed Chamber, Governor's Palace, 25, 27, 45, 202, 204, 210, 226
function of, 211, 217
furnishings of, 205, 207, 211–212, 213–214, 215, 217. *See also* Closet, Governor's Palace
Hogarth, William, 141, 143
Horrocks, James, 181, 240, 283
Horsehair upholstery, 111, 162, 325
Horses
for funeral, 16
owned by Botetourt, 13, 23, 30, 52, 251, 252, 257, 264, 329
sale of, 20, 252, 270
in Virginia, 329
Hospitality, 118, 119, 120, 160, 165, 192, 265. *See also* Sociability
Houdon, Jean-Antoine, 276, 278
House of Burgesses, 49, 55, 56, 169, 330
clerk of, 12, 153
stove for, 189, 269, 270. *See also* Burgesses
Hudson, Thomas, 145
Hunter, Margaret, 275–276

Indians, 60, 86, 104, 115, 174, 201, 240, 242, 265, 327
participate in ceremonies, 76, 172, 173
school for, 60
visit Palace, 50, 75, 80, 104, 105, 174. *See also* Brafferton School; Cherokee Indians; Fort Christanna; Little Carpenter, Chief; Oconostota (Indian chief); Pamunkey Indians; Salloue (Indian chief); Shawnee Indians
Innes, Captain (secretary), 256
Isaac, Rhys, 120, 199, 200

James (slave), 231
Jamestown, Va., 40, 54
Jefferson, Thomas, 136, 144–145, 150, 155, 167, 187, 188, 190, 192, 265, 274, 278, 320, 321, 330
author of "A Summary View of the Rights of British America," 166
as governor, 61, 224, 320

influenced by Fauquier, 141, 143, 148, 153–154, 193
and learning, 224, 328
and levees, 110
opinion by, of Fauquier, 67
portrait of, 140
sketches Palace, 40. *See also* Books; Monticello
Jefferson sketch, 25, 38, 40, 41, 93, 233, 316, 317, 327
Jenings, Edmund, 42, 316
Jerdone, Francis, 252
Johnson, Dr. Samuel, 109
Jones, Hugh, 34, 42, 55, 60, 82, 83, 172, 220, 316

Keith, Sir William, 148, 323
Kendall, Joshua, 16, 17, 158–159, 250, 253, 254, 329
Kenmore, 167, 190, 325, 327
Kent, William, 70, 145, 155
Kidd, Joseph, 16, 183–184, 216, 217, 244, 247, 254, 326, 329
King, Samuel, 244, 245, 250, 253, 254
King's birthday ball, 170, 181
dress for, 222
given by Dinwiddie, 173–174
at Palace, 34–35, 90, 121, 160, 169, 172, 178, 184
Kingsmill, 233
King William School, 54
Kitchen, Governor's Palace, 26, 28, 46, 181, 232, 238, 262, 317
cost of running, 248
funeral preparations in, 17
plan to build, 39, 40
work in, 52, 130, 131
Knight, William, 244, 245, 247, 329

La Rochefoucauld-Liancourt, Duc de, 276, 278
Latrobe, Benjamin, 278
Lavie (James Levey), 244, 329
Leather hangings, 98, 100, 104, 112, 129, 164, 320
Leather upholstery, 92, 100, 162, 183
Lee, Arthur, 262
Lee, Richard Henry, 190
Lefebure, Lambert, 250, 329
Levee, 75, 108–110, 321
Lewis, Jan, 199–200
Libraries, 211, 223, 224, 225–226, 328
closet, 211, 217
furnishings of, 217, 224
at Nomini Hall, 207, 215–216
weapons in, 83. *See also* College of William and Mary; Council; Library, Governor's Palace
Library, Governor's Palace, 27, 30, 45, 202, 204, 205, 210, 226, 227
function of, 211
furnishings of, 212, 215, 216, 217. *See also* Books

INDEX 339

Lighting, 91–92, 94, 238
    branches, 113, 165, 183
    chandelier, 101, 183, 184, 186, 188, 191, 256
    girandoles, 321
    globe lamps, 90, 91, 93, 110, 319–320
    lanterns, 84, 110, 321
    sconces, 98, 100, 111
Linen, 13, 23, 52, 131, 254, 256, 326
    closet for, 131
Linnell, William and John, 145, 227, 327
Liquor, 20, 52, 131, 238, 240
    beer, 52, 130, 240
    Bumbo, 181, 182
    at entertainments, 34, 76, 169, 325
    at funeral, 17
    in inventory, 13, 30
    returned to duke, 23. *See also* Wine
Little Carpenter, Chief, 104
Little Middle Room, Governor's Palace, 27, 52, 130, 161, 243. *See also* Closet, Governor's Palace
Livery, 94, 95–96, 164, 320
    for Botetourt's servants, 51, 91, 244–245
    as symbol, 74, 93
Lloyd, Richard Bennett, 252
Locke, John, 156
London, Bishop of, 262
London, George, 154
Looking glasses, 101, 129, 166, 256, 320
    chimney, 45, 101, 103, 113
    dressing, 205
    in Palace, 45, 84, 91, 93, 98, 101, 103, 104, 110, 129, 227
    pier, 100, 101, 111, 112, 113, 164
    swing, 214, 215
Lords of Trade, 39, 67
Ludwell, Philip, 40
Luxury, 32, 68, 282

Macaronis, 222
Managers (of funeral), 13, 16, 19
Maps, 23, 28, 92, 129, 164, 216, 217, 240, 324. *See also* Fry-Jefferson Map; Henry, John; Popple, Henry
Marshman, William, 236, 238, 245, 247, 254, 255, 328
    after Botetourt's death, 13, 15, 26, 246, 314
    day book of, 240, 243, 244
    duties of, 52, 236, 238, 240–244
    letter by, regarding Botetourt, 15, 201, 210, 238
    opinion of, by Botetourt, 209
    workspace, 210, 228, 238. *See also* Accounts; Salary
Matrix, 101, 104
Matt (slave), 244
Mazzei, Dr. Philip, 136–137
Meade, David, 218, 220, 222, 250, 327
Mediterranean pass, 50, 51, 164, 325
Mercer, George, 184
Middle Plantation, 54

Middle Room upstairs, Governor's Palace, 25, 27, 44–45, 75, 82, 128, 129, 169, 174, 202
    function of, 50, 104–106, 108, 110, 113, 115, 210
    furnishings of, 45, 93, 98, 100–104, 108, 217, 218, 319
    as symbol, 74, 78, 100, 108, 110, 112–113, 114
Minzies, James, 231
Monticello, 187, 191, 274, 321
Morattico, 167, 325
Moreen textiles, 111, 165, 325
Mount Airy, 166
Mount Vernon, 135, 148, 190, 191
    ballroom at, 173, 188
Murray, Charlotte, Lady Dunmore, 136, 178, 205, 208
Murray, John, fourth Earl of Dunmore, 54, 152, 211, 269, 278, 329
    at ball, 178, 281
    birth of daughter of, 196, 198, 208
    declines to buy Botetourt's estate, 23, 314
    and entertaining, 135, 136–137
    flight of, from Williamsburg, 80, 88, 97, 281
    furnishings associated with, 126, 154, 186, 212, 216
    and music, 154
    opinion of, by others, 152, 274, 280
    portrait of, 133
    private life of, 198, 205, 208, 315
    schedule of losses of, 232, 298
    and Virginians, 79, 93, 94, 96, 110, 132, 140, 274, 280–281
    and weapons at Palace, 86, 88, 97, 319. *See also* Books; Servants; Slaves
Music, 76, 118, 153–154, 181, 324
Musical instruments, 76, 154, 165, 181, 224, 324
Muster list, 236, 238, 247

Nash, Beau, 177–178, 326
Native Americans. *See* Indians
Natural history, 143, 154, 155–156
Nelson, Thomas, 325
Nelson, William, 30, 188–190, 240, 273, 329
    as acting governor, 13, 270, 272, 314
    and Botetourt statue, 273, 274
    goods bought by, from Botetourt estate, 252, 270
    letter from, to duke, 16, 20, 217, 230, 231, 252
    letter from, to Fauquier, Jr., 132
    as trustee, 12, 246
Nelson House, 167
Newcastle, Duke of, 153
Nicholas, Robert Carter, 209, 240, 270, 273, 274, 285, 322, 331
    compiles inventory, 26, 30
    as trustee, 12, 13, 26, 246, 270, 314
Nicholson, Lt. Gov. Francis, 62, 118–119, 280, 281, 327

    career of, 54, 56–57
    and ceremony, 76, 172
    designs by, for Palace, 39, 42, 56, 154
    in Maryland, 54
    opinion of, by others, 57, 96
    and town plan, 38, 39, 54–56, 58, 281. *See also* Books; Patronage
Nomini Hall, 130–131, 177, 215, 224, 232, 253, 257, 318, 322
    layout of, 235
    spaces in, 95, 126, 173, 191, 207, 322
    wallpaper for, 187
Nonimportation Agreements, 121, 132, 137, 171, 322
Norton, Hatley, 273
Norton, John, 273, 274, 329
Norwich, Bishop of, 131, 150, 153
Nott, Lt. Gov. Edward, 39, 57, 330

Oconostota (Indian chief), 104
Outbuildings, Governor's Palace, 26, 27–28, 46, 52–53, 232. *See also* Kitchen, Governor's Palace; Stables, Governor's Palace

Page, John, Jr., 138, 141, 150, 152
    portrait of, 151
Page, Mann, II, 65
Paintings, 106, 112, 113, 129, 164, 166, 224
    of horses, 166
    of landscapes, 164, 165. *See also* Pictures; Portraits; Prints
Palace Street, 18, 40, 43, 45, 58, 173
    Gooch's modifications of, 155, 320
Pamunkey Indians, 242
Pantry, Governor's Palace, 27, 28, 130, 164, 210, 250
    function of, 45, 52, 228, 238
    furnishings of, 52, 158, 162, 210, 228, 238, 242, 322. *See also* Closet, Governor's Palace
Parke, Daniel, 156, 232
Parker, James, 137
Parks, William, 61, 65, 226
Parlor, Governor's Palace, 25, 26, 45, 46, 126, 178–179, 243, 317
    function of, 92–93, 108, 111, 118, 128, 161, 163–164, 165
    furnishings of, 92, 106, 111, 128, 159, 161–162. *See also* Closet, Governor's Palace
Parlors, 99–100, 112, 123, 126, 163, 164–165
Passage downstairs, Governor's Palace, 26, 43, 45, 46, 74, 82, 91
    furnishings of, 91, 93
Passages, 94–96
Passage upstairs, Governor's Palace, 45, 74, 82, 110, 111, 202, 210, 211
    furnishings of, 84, 110–111, 162, 215
Patronage, 42, 137, 148–149, 153
    of Botetourt, 145, 152, 227
    of Fauquier, 67, 231

340 INDEX

of Gooch, 149–150, 153
of Nicholson, 56, 62
of Spotswood, 60
of Virginians, 62, 150
Peale, Charles Willson, 147, 148, 190, 319
  portrait of, 149
Pelham, Peter
  as gaoler, 328
  as governor's clerk, 13, 26, 154, 181, 231
  inventory transcribed by, 20
  as musician, 154, 181, 324
Penn, Governor, 136
Pepys, Samuel, 217
Perceval, John, Earl of Egmont, 260
Physic closet, 238
Pictures, 165, 166, 217, 321, 325
  Roman Catholic, 84, 110, 111, 162. *See also* Paintings; Portraits; Prints
Pingo, Thomas, 324
Pitt, William, 147–148, 190, 269
  portrait of, 146
Plate warmer, 130
Popple, Henry, 62, 65
Portraits
  Dutch, 114
  of English gentry, 162, 324
  of the king and queen, 20, 111, 146, 170, 184, 186, 188, 270, 275, 315, 322
  of the monarch, 56
  of royalty, 106, 111, 129, 183, 184
  wax, 129, 274, 322. *See also* Paintings; Pictures; Prints
Powder Magazine, 58, 60, 62, 82, 86, 88, 97
Powder Room, Governor's Palace, 27, 205, 244
Pratt, Matthew, 148, 149, 221
Pratt, Roger, 114
Precedency, 75, 121
  rules of, 19, 176, 314
President's House, 40, 48, 49, 61. *See also* College of William and Mary
Prints, 92, 206, 216, 217, 223, 250, 325
  of Botetourt for sale, 276
  by Boydell, 325
  by Catesby, 62
  hanging of, 217
  of the king and queen, 113, 165
  scripture, 106, 111, 162, 163, 325. *See also* Paintings; Pictures; Portraits
Privacy, 45, 196, 198, 204, 215, 264, 265
Public Hospital, 143, 153

Raleigh Tavern, 281, 322, 325
Ramsay, Allan, 146, 184
Randolph, Edmund, 16, 34, 145, 152, 278, 280, 331
Randolph, John (attorney general), 31, 135, 173, 240, 270
  family of, 154
  furnishings of, at Tazewell Hall, 113–114, 165–166, 321, 327
  letter by, to duke, 12–13, 222, 224, 252, 314

  servants of, rented out, 248. *See also* Tazewell Hall
Randolph, Sir John, 61, 150, 166, 226
Randolph, Peter, 65
Randolph, Peyton, 135, 166, 173, 208, 240, 270, 273, 274
  inventory of estate, 325
  library of, 226, 328
Rippon (naval vessel), 236
Robertson, William, 34
Robinson, Rev. William, 131, 158, 246
Robinson affair, 282
Rodgers, John, 244
Room arrangement/usage
  in England, 99, 101, 106, 114, 123, 196, 204, 206
  in Palace 37, 38, 43, 45, 100, 110, 118, 173, 202, 205, 210
  in plantation houses, 233, 235
  in Tryon's Palace, 111–112, 205, 206
  in Virginia, 43, 46, 89, 94–95, 165, 204, 206, 317. *See also* individual rooms
Routs, 168, 170
Royal Society, 56, 67, 143, 152
Russell, Mrs., 198, 202–203
Rysbrack, John Michael, 145

Sabine Hall, 15, 191, 232, 317, 325
St. Clair, Sir John, 86
St. John, Lady, 56
Salary
  of Fuller, 240, 244, 329
  of governor, 17, 28, 184, 248
  of Marshman, 238, 244, 247, 329
  of servants, 17, 158, 181, 242, 247, 252, 254, 329, 330
  of Sparrow, 238, 247, 248
Salisbury, Bishop of, 153
Salloue (Indian chief), 104
Saloons, 101, 106, 112, 173, 191, 320, 321
Sanitation equipment, 209, 211
  chamber pot, 205, 215
  close stool pan, 205
Scott, Mrs. (cook), 250, 329
Scott, Peter, 61
Seal of the colony, 74, 98, 101, 103, 104
Servants, 50, 198, 228, 230, 255, 264–265
  attitudes toward, 232, 246
  of Campbell, 256
  discipline of, 244
  of Dunmore, 52, 231, 250, 328, 329
  duty of, to "family," 231–232
  of Eden, 240, 256
  from England, 230
  of Fauquier, 94, 231, 246–247
  hired/rented, 181, 230, 241–242, 248
  at Governor's Palace, 231, 257
  as members of "family," 50–53, 236, 244, 248, 250, 264–265
  at Nomini Hall, 257, 258
  of Tryon, 240, 256
  "for waiting," 241. *See also* Butlers; Cooks; Footmen; Gardeners; Salary;

Servants of Botetourt; Servants' sleeping arrangements; Slaves
Servants of Botetourt, 25, 30, 48, 93, 110, 254, 257, 265, 320
  brought to Virginia, 236, 238
  fate of, in Virginia, 158, 230, 236, 244, 247, 253, 254, 257, 329, 330
  during illness of Botetourt, 208, 210, 232
  involvement of, in funeral, 16, 18, 19, 228
  at Stoke Gifford, 235, 328. *See also* Blandford, Silas, Jr.; Blandford, Silas, Sr.; Cooke, John; Draper, John; Fuller, Thomas; Gale, Thomas; Kendall, Joshua; Kidd, Joseph; King, Samuel; Knight, William; Marshman, William; Pelham, Peter; Rodgers, John; Simpson, James; Sparrow, William; Towse, Thomas; Wilson, James; Wilson, Mrs.
Servants' hall, 254
  at Badminton, 89
  in Eden's residence, 191, 256
  in Governor's Palace, 28, 130, 164, 232, 248, 250, 253, 322, 328
  in Tryon's Palace, 164
Servants' sleeping arrangements
  in Eden's residence, 256
  in England, 238
  furnishings for, 238, 240, 245, 250, 254, 256
  in Governor's Palace main building, 27, 45, 55, 205, 206, 210, 238, 240, 254
  in Governor's Palace outbuildings, 28, 55, 248, 250, 253
  in Tryon's Palace, 256
Settee, 93, 106, 112, 113, 186
Seven Years' War, 67, 68, 96, 184, 283
Sharpe, Horatio, 148
Shawnee Indians, 86, 280
Sheraton, Thomas, 9, 97, 101, 106, 108, 110, 113, 217
Shirley, 191, 274
Sideboard, 45, 129, 130, 322
Sidney, Mrs. (housekeeper), 256
Silver, 23, 52, 65, 181, 210, 228, 238, 242, 256, 265, 323
  American-made, 190
  coffin furniture, 12, 16, 18, 209
  cups (gold), 130, 322
  epergne, 65
  hollowware, 186
  plates, 186, 322
  salvers, 130
  service, 190
  table, 65
  teawares, 193, 256
Simpson, James, 250, 330
Skipwith, Robert, 224
Slavery, 201, 231, 261, 262, 282–283. *See also* Slaves
Slaves, 17, 181, 228, 229, 240, 242, 253, 254, 257, 262, 264, 265

INDEX 341

attitude toward, 232, 246, 258, 260, 261, 262, 330
of Botetourt, 13, 20, 27, 28, 30, 229, 231, 236, 243–244, 246, 250, 254, 320
buildings for, 30, 235
of Campbell, 257, 315
dance of, 121, 180–181
discipline of, 244, 258, 260, 263–264
of Dunmore, 231
Dunmore's threat concerning, 281
of Fauquier, 94, 143, 160, 228, 231, 246–247, 261
furnishings for, 30, 245
hired, 229, 230, 231, 244
interaction with whites, 34, 261, 264, 265
at Nomini Hall, 257–258, 260–261
payment to, 243
and place in "family," 50, 53, 198, 228, 230, 231–232, 246, 261, 264, 265
sleeping arrangements for, 53, 245–246
trial of, 49
of Tryon, 256. *See also* Cesar; Crew, Hannah; Matt; James; Susan
Small, William, 141, 143, 152, 174, 176, 184, 221–222
portrait of, 143
Smith, Daniel Blake, 199, 200
Smith, Francis and William, 145
Sociability, 108, 118, 119, 120, 171–172, 177, 192, 193. *See also* Hospitality
Society for the Advancement of Useful Knowledge, 150, 152
Society for the Encouragement of Arts, Manufactures & Commerce, 67, 137
Society for the Propagation of the Gospel in Foreign Parts, 56
Society of the Dilettanti, 143, 145, 146, 147
Sofa, 106
Somerset, Lady Henrietta, 156
Somerset, Henry, fifth Duke of Beaufort, 23, 30, 209, 218, 232, 238, 270, 273, 314, 315
goods in Virginia shipped to, 20, 23, 217, 254, 314, 328
house of, improvements to, 145
letter by, to Virginians, 20, 23, 255, 269, 270
letter to, from Botetourt, 109, 321
letter to, from Carter, 13
letter to, from Nelson, 16, 20, 217, 230
letter to, from Randolph, 12, 222, 252
letter to, from Starke, 152–153, 210, 225
minority of, 70, 145
portrait of, 22
steward of, 15
South Sea Company, 67, 138
Sparrow, William, 238, 246, 247, 248. *See also* Salary
Spotswood, Lt. Gov. Alexander, 38, 54, 57–58, 60, 62, 96, 168, 203, 327
and burgesses, 58, 173, 198, 330
comment about Nicholson, 96
comment about Williamsburg, 120

commissioned portraits, 150
cultural influence of, 58, 60, 280, 281
and entertaining, 90, 169, 172, 326
furnishings of, 80, 82, 98
involvement of, with Bruton Parish Church, 63, 317
involvement of, with building of Governor's Palace, 42, 44, 58, 80, 224, 226
involvement of, with Governor's Palace gardens, 46, 154, 155
and iron foundries, 138
opinion of, by others, 58, 60
portrait of, 59
private life of, 196, 198
and town plan, 58, 60. *See also* Books; Patronage
Spotswood, Mary, 177
Stables, Governor's Palace, 26, 27, 39, 40, 46, 53, 232, 238, 250, 254
Stamp Act, 36, 67, 68, 70, 148, 273, 281
Standing furniture, Governor's Palace, 23, 26, 36, 92, 202, 208, 270, 322
in ballroom, 183
in middle room, 101
in parlor, 92, 162
in supper room, 186
Stanhope, James, 86
Stanhope, Sarah, 257, 258
Starke, Richard, 152–153, 178, 208, 209, 210, 222, 225, 324
Stepladders, 91, 93
Steuart, Charles, 15
Stith, William 279
Stoke Gifford, 235, 236, 238, 255, 330
Stoke Park, 147, 155, 156, 222, 319, 321, 325
Stools, 183, 213, 214, 215, 327
Stoves, 184, 188, 269–270, 275, 315
Buzaglo, 189, 190, 330
Dutch, 183, 186, 269
in Eden's residence, 191, 256
in England, 330
Stuart and Revett, 146–147
Study. *See* Library, Governor's Palace
Style
classical, 70, 145, 147, 148, 285
"neat," 188, 216
neoclassical, 159, 188, 189, 190, 193, 269, 270, 275
rococo, 159, 188, 270. *See also* Georgian
Supper Room, Governor's Palace, 25, 26, 46, 171, 173, 178, 185, 186
function of, 118
furnishings of, 186, 189, 269. *See also* Ballroom, Governor's Palace
Susan (slave), 243–244

Tables, 98, 104, 110, 240
breakfast, 165
card, 106, 112, 113, 128, 161, 164, 165, 179
dining, 111, 129–130, 165, 186, 321

dressing, 108, 203, 205, 207, 211
library, 28, 30, 156, 158–159, 228, 238, 253, 329
mahogany, 112, 250, 321
marble, 98, 100, 322
night, 203, 205, 209, 214
pier, 100, 101, 104
silver, 65
tea, 65, 113, 250
writing, 158, 164, 165, 211
Tayloe, John, 15, 166
Tayloe family, 65
Tazewell, Mr., 240
Tazewell Hall, 113, 154, 165, 173, 191, 327
Tea, 75, 79, 104, 126, 128, 203
equipment for, 112, 113, 131, 250
Textiles. *See* Check textiles; Chintz textiles; Damask textiles; Moreen textiles; Virginia cloth
Theater, 60, 174, 181
Thomson, Charles, 190, 193
Tobacco Inspection Act, 226
Tower of London, 82, 83, 84, 86, 96, 318, 319
Townshend Duties, 67, 70, 132, 138, 159, 281
Towse, Thomas, 247
Tradescant, John, 62
Trumbull, John, 141, 142
Truro vestry, 285
Trustees, 20, 246, 255, 270, 314
appointed, 12
compile inventory, 28, 31, 217
plan auction, 23
plan funeral, 13, 19
Tryon, Gov. William, 37, 58, 93, 111, 218, 256, 322, 324
and ceremony, 79, 113, 321
New York residence, 37, 94, 111, 164, 206, 223, 256
plans of, for palace, 88, 94
schedule of losses of, 303–306, 324
visits by, to Williamsburg, 37, 105, 204–205. *See also* Books; Servants; Slaves; Tryon's Palace
Tryon's Palace, 58, 113
bedchamber in, 205, 206
Council chamber in, 111–112, 191, 223
drawing room/dining room in, 126, 164
furnishings for, 93, 94, 111
hall in, 88–89, 105
layout of, 46–47, 232–233, 234, 255, 327
library in, 223
Tuckahoe, 191, 321
Tucker, St. George, 83
Twopenny Act, 67, 158

Vails, 242–243, 245, 329
Venetian blind, 212
Virginia cloth, 132, 206
Virginia Gazette, 16, 19, 247, 273, 281
on Botetourt, 152, 176, 324
Botetourt's obituary in, 314

celebration described in, 169–170
funeral described in, 18
paintings mentioned in, 147, 148
Rules of Precedency published in, 176
on Tryon, 321
Virginia plantations, 30, 38, 60, 95, 155, 233, 264, 320
Virginia society
    familial relationships in, 198, 199–200, 264, 265
    gentry of, unsettled, 282–283, 285–286
    interest in business, 135, 136, 140
    polite society in, 60, 70, 120, 176–177, 180
    symbols of power/order in, 42, 74, 105, 114, 115. *See also* Hospitality; Sociability
Vobe, Mrs. Jane, 149

Waddill, William, 12, 16
Wallcoverings
    gilt border for paper, 183, 184, 186
    hanging technique for, 326
    paper, 101, 112, 183–184, 186, 187–188, 326
    tapestries, 128, 320. *See also* Leather hangings
Waller, Benjamin, 314
Walpole, Horace, 71, 159, 212
Walthoe, Nathaniel, 162, 324
    portrait of, 162, 324
Ware, Isaac, 90, 91, 94, 101, 109–110, 163, 168, 170, 185, 204
Warming machine. *See* Stoves
Warmley Company, 138
Washington, George, 148–149, 155, 190, 192, 216, 252, 326
    in Maryland, 135
    in Pennsylvania, 136
    portrait of, 133

as president, 110
statue of, 276, 278
visits Williamsburg, 132, 135, 136. *See also* Mount Vernon
Washstand, 214, 215, 240
    basin for, 108
Weapons
    in Annapolis, 82, 88
    at Badminton, 89
    at Chevening, 84, 86
    comments on, 82, 83, 86, 319
    display of, dismantled, 80, 86, 88, 97, 319
    display of, by Spotswood, 58, 60, 80, 82, 96
    in Governor's Palace, 60, 83, 86, 89, 97, 100, 318, 319
    of Indians, 83, 319
    in London, 83–84, 96, 318, 319
    in New York, 82–83
    pistols, 238
    in Powder Magazine, 318
    at Stoke Park, 319
    swords, 218
    as symbols, 30, 74, 80, 82, 86, 88, 96, 97, 114
Webb, Daniel, 143
Webb, George, 65
Wedgwood, Josiah, 35, 131
West, Benjamin, 147, 148, 149, 190
Westmore, Edward, 328
Westover, 60, 95, 162, 224, 319, 324
    portraits at, 162, 324
Wetherburn, Henry, 173
William and Mary, College of. *See* College of William and Mary
Williamsburg, Va.
    building in, 173
    ceremony in, 75–76, 90, 121, 172
    development of, 38, 40, 45, 54–56, 58, 60
    drawing made in, 27, 40

furniture made in, 216
as "garden city," 60
government at, 12, 192
Independent Company of, 319
influence of, 36
map of, 39, 44, 55
paintings exhibited in 148, 149
petition from citizens of, 105
portraits shipped to, 146
Society for the Advancement of Useful Knowledge established in, 150, 152
statue in, 274, 275
theater in, 181
tradesmen in, 12, 16, 61, 70, 145, 190, 226, 244, 275
vineyard near, 137
visits to, 135, 136, 149, 165, 191, 276, 329. *See also* Assemblies and balls
Wilson, Benjamin, 143
Wilson, James, 247, 250, 253, 254, 330
Wilson, Mrs. (cook), 247, 329
Wilton, Joseph, 148, 190
Windsor Castle, 83, 84, 86
Wine, 52, 130, 131, 236, 238, 240, 257, 265
    cooler, 28, 130
    making of, 137
Withdrawing rooms, 123, 202, 203, 204
Witherspoon, Rev. Dr., 324
Wren, Christopher, 54
Wren Building, 40, 54, 60, 150, 316. *See also* College of William and Mary
Wright, Thomas, 155
Writing equipment, 13, 159, 163, 164, 211, 254
Wynn, Sir Watkin Williams, 146
Wythe, George, 12, 141, 143, 226, 240, 328
    portrait of, 142

Yorktown, Va., 244, 252, 253

Zoffany, Johann, 146